T0190165

Communications
in Computer and Information Science   1777

Rationale

The CCIS series is devoted to the publication of proceedings of computer science conferences. Its aim is to efficiently disseminate original research results in informatics in printed and electronic form. While the focus is on publication of peer-reviewed full papers presenting mature work, inclusion of reviewed short papers reporting on work in progress is welcome, too. Besides globally relevant meetings with internationally representative program committees guaranteeing a strict peer-reviewing and paper selection process, conferences run by societies or of high regional or national relevance are also considered for publication.

Topics

The topical scope of CCIS spans the entire spectrum of informatics ranging from foundational topics in the theory of computing to information and communications science and technology and a broad variety of interdisciplinary application fields.

Information for Volume Editors and Authors

Publication in CCIS is free of charge. No royalties are paid, however, we offer registered conference participants temporary free access to the online version of the conference proceedings on SpringerLink (http://link.springer.com) by means of an http referrer from the conference website and/or a number of complimentary printed copies, as specified in the official acceptance email of the event.

CCIS proceedings can be published in time for distribution at conferences or as post-proceedings, and delivered in the form of printed books and/or electronically as USBs and/or e-content licenses for accessing proceedings at SpringerLink. Furthermore, CCIS proceedings are included in the CCIS electronic book series hosted in the SpringerLink digital library at http://link.springer.com/bookseries/7899. Conferences publishing in CCIS are allowed to use Online Conference Service (OCS) for managing the whole proceedings lifecycle (from submission and reviewing to preparing for publication) free of charge.

Publication process

The language of publication is exclusively English. Authors publishing in CCIS have to sign the Springer CCIS copyright transfer form, however, they are free to use their material published in CCIS for substantially changed, more elaborate subsequent publications elsewhere. For the preparation of the camera-ready papers/files, authors have to strictly adhere to the Springer CCIS Authors' Instructions and are strongly encouraged to use the CCIS LaTeX style files or templates.

Abstracting/Indexing

CCIS is abstracted/indexed in DBLP, Google Scholar, EI-Compendex, Mathematical Reviews, SCImago, Scopus. CCIS volumes are also submitted for the inclusion in ISI Proceedings.

How to start

To start the evaluation of your proposal for inclusion in the CCIS series, please send an e-mail to ccis@springer.com.

Deep Gupta · Kishor Bhurchandi ·
Subrahmanyam Murala ·
Balasubramanian Raman · Sanjeev Kumar
Editors

Computer Vision and Image Processing

7th International Conference, CVIP 2022
Nagpur, India, November 4–6, 2022
Revised Selected Papers, Part II

 Springer

Editors
Deep Gupta
Visvesvaraya National Institute
of Technology Nagpur
Nagpur, India

Kishor Bhurchandi
Visvesvaraya National Institute
of Technology Nagpur
Nagpur, India

Subrahmanyam Murala
Indian Institute of Technology Ropar
Rupnagar, India

Balasubramanian Raman
Indian Institute of Technology Roorkee
Roorkee, India

Sanjeev Kumar
Indian Institute of Technology Roorkee
Roorkee, India

ISSN 1865-0929   ISSN 1865-0937 (electronic)
Communications in Computer and Information Science
ISBN 978-3-031-31416-2   ISBN 978-3-031-31417-9 (eBook)
https://doi.org/10.1007/978-3-031-31417-9

This Springer imprint is published by the registered company Springer Nature Switzerland AG
The registered company address is: Gewerbestrasse 11, 6330 Cham, Switzerland

Preface

The 7th International Conference on Computer Vision and Image Processing (CVIP 2022) was organized by Visvesvaraya National Institute of Technology Nagpur, Maharashtra, INDIA. CVIP is a premier conference focused on image/video processing and computer vision. Previous editions of CVIP were held at IIT Ropar (2021), IIIT Allahabad (CVIP 2020), MNIT Jaipur (CVIP 2019), IIIT Jabalpur (CVIP 2018), and IIT Roorkee (CVIP 2017 and CVIP 2016). The conference witnessed extraordinary success with publications in multiple domains of computer vision and image processing.

The Team composed of Kishor Bhurchandi (VNIT Nagpur), Pritee Khanna (IIIT DMJ), Prashant Patil (Deakin University, Australia), Gaurav Bhatnagar (IIT Jodhpur), Satish Kumar Singh (IIIT Allahabad) and Shiv Ram Dubey (IIIT Allahabad) organized CVIP 2022 and coordinated the event so efficiently. Moreover, the publicity for the submissions of research articles at CVIP' 2022 by Herkeerat Kaur (IIT Jammu), Nidhi Goel (IGDTUW, Delhi), Sneha Singh (CWRU, USA) and R. B. Keskar (VNIT Nagpur) made CVIP 2022 altogether a great success, with an overwhelming submission of 307 research papers. Also, the efficient teamwork by volunteers of VNIT Nagpur helped to overcome the different challenges during the event.

CVIP 2022 received 307 regular paper submissions that went through a rigorous review process by approx. 300 reviewers from various renowned national and international institutes and universities. The technical program chairs, Vishal R. Satpute (VNIT Nagpur), Santosh Kumar Vipparthi (IIT Ropar), Deepak Mishra (IIST Trivandrum), Ananda S. Chowdhury (Jadavpur University), Debashis Sen (IIT Kharagpur), Rama Krishna Sai Gorthi (IIT Tirupati), Saugta Sinha (VNIT Nagpur), Puneet Goyal (IIT Ropar), Emanuela Marasco (George Mason University, USA), Shital S. Chiddarwar (VNIT Nagpur) and Snigdha Bhagat (Blackrock Gurugram), coordinated the overall review process which resulted in the acceptance of 121 research articles. Out of them, 113 papers were scheduled for oral presentation in 22 technical sessions around the research areas of Medical Image Analysis, Image/Video Processing for Autonomous Vehicles, Activity Detection/Recognition, Human-Computer Interaction, Segmentation and Shape Representation, Motion and Tracking, Image/Video Scene Understanding, Image/Video Retrieval, Remote Sensing, Hyperspectral Image Processing, Face, Iris, Emotion, Sign Language and Gesture Recognition, etc.

Keynote Talks: CVIP 2022 was scheduled with four keynote talk sessions for each day. CVIP 2022 commenced with a keynote talk on "Digital pathology for detection of cancer from breast FNAC and oral histopathology images" by Ajoy Kumar Ray (IIT Kharagpur) followed by keynote talks by Petia Ivanova Radeva (University of Barcelona, Spain), Fabio Dell'Acqua (University of Pavia, Italy) and Ayellet Tal (Technion, Israel). On the second day, Daniel P. Lopresti (Lehigh University, USA) presented his talk on "Research reproducibility research: Opportunities and challenges". The keynote talks by Bharat Biswal (New Jersey Institute of Technology, USA), Ramesh Jain (University of California, Irvine, USA), and Prabir Kumar Biswas (Indian Institute of Technology, Kharagpur) also gave an informative discussion on image processing and computer vision. The last day of the conference began with an informative keynote talk on "Advances in adversarial robustness and domain adaptation of deep models" by R. Venkatesh Babu, (Indian Institute of Science, Bangalore), and the keynote talks by Jayanta Mukhopadhyay (Indian Institute of Technology, Kharagpur), Vikram M. Gadre (Indian Institute of Technology, Bombay), and Sumantra Dutta Ray (Indian Institute of Technology, Delhi) enlightened the audience with an informative discussion on image processing.

Awards: CVIP 2022 presented high-quality research works with innovative ideas. All the session chairs were invited to vote for five different categories of awards. Five different awards were announced: IAPR Best Paper Award, IAPR Best Student Paper, CVIP 2022 Best Paper Award, CVIP 2022 Best Student Paper Award, Sir M. Visvesvaraya Best Student Paper Award.

Also, CVIP 2022 awarded to Santanu Chaudhury, IIT Jodhpur a CVIP Lifetime Achievement Award for his remarkable research in the field of Image Processing and Computer Vision. The awards were announced in the valedictory ceremony by Conference Chair, Deep Gupta (VNIT Nagpur).

The next edition of CVIP will be organized by IIT Jammu, India.

November 2022

Deep Gupta
Kishor Bhurchandi
Balasubramanian Raman
Sanjeev Kumar
Subrahmanyam Murala

Organization

Patron

Bidyut Baran Chaudhuri   ISI Kolkata, India

General Chairs

Pramod M. Padole (Director)   VNIT Nagpur, India
Petia Radeva   University of Barcelona, Spain
Tom Gedeon   Curtin University, Australia

General Co-chairs

Balasubramanian Raman   IIT Roorkee, India
Avinash Keskar   VNIT Nagpur, India

Conference Chairs

Deep Gupta   VNIT Nagpur, India
Subrahmanyam Murala   IIT Ropar, India
Partha Pratim Roy   IIT Roorkee, India
Sanjeev Kumar   IIT Roorkee, India

Conference Convenors

Kishor Bhurchandi   VNIT Nagpur, India
Pritee Khanna   IIITDM Jabalpur, India
Gaurav Bhatnagar   IIT Jodhpur, India
Satish Kumar Singh   IIIT Allahabad, India
Shiv Ram Dubey   IIIT Allahabad, India

Technical Program Chairs

Vishal R. Satpute	VNIT Nagpur, India
Santosh Kumar Vipparthi	IIT Ropar, India
Deepak Mishra	IIST Trivandrum, India
Ananda S. Chowdhury	Jadavpur University, India
Debashis Sen	IIT Kharagpur, India
Rama Krishna Sai Gorthi	IIT Tirupati, India
Snigdha Bhagat	Blackrock Gurugram, India
Saugata Sinha	VNIT Nagpur, India
Abhinav Dhall	IIT Ropar, India
Puneet Goyal	IIT Ropar, India
Emanuela Marasco	George Mason University, USA
Shital S. Chiddarwar	VNIT Nagpur, India

Website Chairs

Ankit Bhurane	VNIT Nagpur, India
Poonam Sharma	VNIT Nagpur, India

Publicity Chairs

Harkeerat Kaur	IIT Jammu, India
Sneha Singh	CWRU, USA
Nidhi Goel	IGDTUW, India
R. B. Keskar	VNIT Nagpur, India
M. H. Kolekar	IIT Patna, India

Publication Chairs

Poonam Sharma	VNIT Nagpur, India
Prashant W. Patil	Deakin University, Australia
Sachin Chaudhary	PEC, India

Local Organizing Committee

Ashwin Kothari	VNIT Nagpur, India
Vipin Kamble	VNIT Nagpur, India
Joydeep Sen Gupta	VNIT Nagpur, India
Pradnya Ghare	VNIT Nagpur, India
K. Surender	VNIT Nagpur, India
Neeraj Rao	VNIT Nagpur, India
Prabhat Sharma	VNIT Nagpur, India
Punitkumar Bhavsar	VNIT Nagpur, India
Anamika Singh	VNIT Nagpur, India
Praveen Pawar	VNIT Nagpur, India
Amit Agrawal	VNIT Nagpur, India
Himanshu Padole	VNIT Nagpur, India
Arvind Kumar	VNIT Nagpur, India
Vivek Raghuwanshi	VNIT Nagpur, India

International Advisory Committee

Daniel P. Lopresti	Lehigh University, USA
Sebastiano Battiat	Università di Catania, Italy
Bharat Biswal	NJIT, USA
Jonathan Wu	University of Windsor, Canada
Pallavi Tiwari	CWRU Cleveland, USA
Gaurav Sharma	University of Rochester, USA
Nalini K. Ratha	State University of New York at Buffalo, USA
Satish Viswanath	CWRU Cleveland, USA
Paula Brito	University of Porto, Portugal
Ankit Chaudhary	University of Missouri, USA
Henry Leung	University of Calgary, Canada
Rangaraj M. Rangayyan	University of Calgary, Canada
Anup Basu	University of Alberta, Canada
Kiran Raja	NTNU, Norway
B. S. Manjunath	University of California, Santa Barbara, USA
Mohan S. Kankanhalli	NUS, Singapore
Sule Yildirim Yayilgan	NTNU, Norway
Emanuela Marasco	George Mason University, USA
Ali Reza Alaei	Southern Cross University, Australia
Thinagaran Perumal	Universiti Putra Malaysia, Malaysia
Xiaoyi Jiang	University of Münster, Germany
Sudeep Sarkar	University of South Florida, USA

Vishal M. Patel	Johns Hopkins University, USA
Richard Hartley	Australian National University, Australia
Luc Van Gool	ETH Zurich, Switzerland
Junsong Yuan	State University of New York at Buffalo, USA
Petra Perner	FutureLab Artificial Intelligence, Germany
Rajkumar Buyya	University of Melbourne, Australia
Elisa Barney Smith	Boise State University, USA

National Advisory Committee

Ajoy Kumar Ray	IIT Kharagpur, India
Uday B. Desai	IIT Hyderabad, India
Venkatesh Babu	IISc Bangalore, India
Vikram M. Gadre	IIT Bombay, India
Prabir Kumar Biswas	IIT Kharagpur, India
S. N. Singh	IIT Kanpur, India
A. G. Ramakrishnan	IISc Bangalore, India
Phaneendra K. Yalavarthy	IISc Bangalore, India
Prasanna Chaporkar	IIT Bombay, India
Ram Bilas Pachori	IIT Indore, India
Sibi Raj B. Pillai	IIT Bombay, India
Jayanta Mukhopadhyay	IIT Kharagpur, India
R. S. Anand	IIT Roorkee, India
Sanjay Kumar Singh	IIT BHU, India
Umapada Pal	ISI Kolkata, India
Abhay S. Gandhi	VNIT Nagpur, India
Aparajita Ojha	IIITDM Jabalpur, India
Sushmita Mitra	ISI Kolkata, India
Kishor Kulat	VNIT Nagpur, India

CVIP Reviewers

Alireza Alaei	Southern Cross University, Australia
A. Prabhakar Rao	VNIT Nagpur, India
Amitesh Singh Rajput	Birla Institute of Technology and Science, Pilani
Ananda S. Chowdhury	Jadavpur University, India
Anil Balaji Gonde	SGGS Nanded, India
Anish Kumar Vishwakarma	VNIT Nagpur, India
Anjali Gautam	IIIT Allahabad, India
Ankit Ashokrao Bhurane	VNIT Nagpur, India

Gaurav Gupta   Wenzhou-Kean University, China
Gautam Bhattacharya   UIT, BU, India
Gopa Bhaumik   NIT Sikkim, India
Gorthi Rama Krishna Sai   IIT Tirupati, India
  Subrahmanyam
Guoqiang Zhong   Ocean University of China, China
Gurinder Singh   IIT Ropar, India
Hadia Showkat Kawoosa   IIT Ropar, India
Harkeerat Kaur   IIT Jammu, India
Himanshu Agarwal   Information Technology Noida, India
Himanshu P. Padole   VNIT Nagpur, India
Indra Deep Mastan   LNMIT Jaipur, India
Irshad Ahmad Ansari   IIITDM Jabalpur, India
Jagadeesh Kakarla   IIITDM, India
Jagannath Sethi   Jadavpur University, India
Jagat Sesh Challa   BITS Pilani, India
Jagdeep Kaur   NIT Jalandhar, India
Jasdeep Singh   IIT Ropar, India
Jayashree Vivekanand Khanapuri   K. J. Somaiya Institute of Engineering &
                                        Information Technology, India

Jaydeb Bhaumik   Jadavpur University, India
Jayendra Kumar   NIT Jamshedpur, India
Jeevan J.   Exafluence Inc., USA
Jignesh S. Bhatt   IIIT Vadodara, India
Jitendra A. Maddarkar   NDS Infoserv
Joohi Chauhan   Indian Institute of Technology Ropar, India
Juan E. Tapia   Hochschule Darmstadt, Germany
Junsong Yuan   State University of New York at Buffalo, USA
K. M. Bhurchandi   VNIT Nagpur, India
Kalidas Yeturu   Indian Institute of Technology Tirupati, India
Kapil Rana   IIT Ropar, India
Karthick Seshadri   National Institute of Technology, Andhra Pradesh,
                                        India
Kaushik Roy   West Bengal State University, India
Kaustuv Nag   IIIT Guwahati, India
Kiran Raja   NTNU
Kishor K. Bhoyar   YCCE Nagpur, India
Krishan Kumar   NIT Kurukshetra, India
Krishna P. Miyapuram   Indian Institute of Technology, Gandhinagar, India
Krishna Pratap Singh   IIIT Allahabad, India
Krishna Siva Prasad Mudigonda   VIT-AP University, India
Kuldeep Biradar   SGGSIET

Kuldeep Singh	MNIT Jaipur, India
Kushall Pal Singh	MNIT Jaipur, India
Lalatendu Behera	NIT Jalandhar, India
Madhurima Bandyopadhyay	Continental Automotive Components (India) Pvt. Ltd., India
Maheshkumar H. Kolekar	IIT Patna, India
Malaya Kumar Nath	NIT Puducherry, India
Mandhatya Singh	IIT Ropar, India
Manesh B. Kokare	SGGSIE&T Nanded, India
Manisha Das	VNIT Nagpur, India
Manisha Sawant	VNIT Nagpur, India
Mayur R. Parae	IIIT, Nagpur, India
Milind Mushrif	YCCE, Nagpur, India
Mohamed Akram Ulla Shariff	Samsung R&D Institute India-Bangalore, India
Mohammad Farukh Hashmi	National Institute of Technology Warangal, India
Mohammed Javed	IIIT Allahabad, India
Mohan Kankanhalli	National University of Singapore, Singapore
Monu Verma	MNIT Jaipur, India
Mrinal Kanti Bhowmik	Tripura University, India
Muhammad Suhaib Kanroo	IIT Ropar, India
Naga Srinivasarao Batta Kota	NIT Warangal, India
Nagashettappa Biradar	Bheemanna Khandre Institute of Technology, Bhalki, India
Nancy Mehta	Indian Institute of Technology Ropar, India
Narendra D. Londhe	National Institute of Technology Raipur, India
Naveen Cheggoju	IIIT Una, India
Neetu Sood	Dr BR Ambedkar National Institute of Technology, Jalandhar, India
Neha Nawandar	VNIT Nagpur, India
Nidhi Goel	IGDTUW, India
Nidhi Lal	VNIT Nagpur, India
Nikhil Dhengre	VNIT Nagpur, India
Nikita S. Rathi	Accenture, India
Nirmala Murali	IIST, India
Nishant Jain	Jaypee University of Information Technology, India
N. V. Subba Reddy	Manipal University, India
Palak H.	Delhi Technological University, India
Pallavi K. Parlewar	RCOEM, India
Pankaj Pratap Singh	Central Institute of Technology (CIT) Kokrajhar, India
Paresh Kamble	VNIT Nagpur, India

Partha Pratim Sarangi	Seemanta Engineering College, India
Partha Pakray	NIT Silchar, India
Parul Sahare	IIIT, Nagpur, India
Parveen Kumar	National Institute of Technology Uttarakhand, India
Petia Radeva	University of Barcelona, Spain
Piyush Kumar	National Institute of Technology Patna, India
Poonam Sharma	VNIT Nagpur, India
Praful Hambarde	Indian Institute of Technology Ropar, India
Prafulla Saxena	MNIT Jaipur, India
Pranav Kumar Singh	Central Institute of Technology Kokrajhar, India
Prashant Patil	IIT Ropar, India
Pratistha Mathur	Manipal University Jaipur, India
Pratyusha Rakshit	Jadavpur University, India
Preeti Rai	GGITS, India
Prem S. Yadav	MNIT Jaipur, India
Prerana Mukherjee	Jawaharlal Nehru University, India
Pritee Khanna	IIITDM Jabalpur, India
Pritpal Singh	National Taipei University of Technology, Taiwan, India
Puneet Goyal	IIT Ropar, India
Puneet Gupta	IIT Indore, India
Punitkumar Bhavsar	VNIT Nagpur, India
Raghunath S. Holambe	RJIT, India
Rameswar Panda	MIT-IBM Watson AI Lab, USA
Ratnapal K. Mane	VNIT Nagpur, India
Richa R. Khandelwal	RCOEM, India
Rohini Suhas Ochawar	RCOEM, India
Rubell Marion Lincy George	Indian Institute of Information Technology Kottayam, India
Rubin Bose S.	Madras Institute of Technology, India
Rukhmini Bandyopadhyay	University of Texas MD Anderson Cancer Centre, India
Rusha Patra	IIIT Guwahati, India
S. N. Tazi	RTU, India
Sahana M. Prabhu	RBEI, India
Sahu Abhimanyu	Seemanta Engineering College, India
P. S. SaiKrishna	Indian Institute of Technology Tirupati, India
Sanjay Talbar	SGGSIET, India
Sanjeev Kumar	IIT Roorkee, India
Sanjit N.	IIIT Una, India
Sanjit Maitra	Indian Statistical Institute, India

Sanjiv Vedu Bonde	SGGSIET, Nanded, India
Sanjoy Pratihar	IIIT Kalyani, India
Sanjoy K. Saha	Jadavpur University, India
Santosh Singh Rathore	ABV-IIITM Gwalio, India
Sathiesh Kumar V.	Madras Institute of Technology, India
Satya Prakash Sahu	NIT Raipur, India
Satya Narayan	Government Engineering College Ajmer, India
Satyasai Jagannath Nanda	Malaviya National Institute of Technology Jaipur, India
Satyendra Singh Yadav	NIT, Meghalaya, India
Saugata Sinha	VNIT Nagpur, India
Sevakram Tanaji Kumbhare	Jadavpur University, Kolkata, India
Shanmuganathan Raman	Indian Institute of Technology Gandhinagar, India
Shashi Shekhar Jha	IIT Ropar, India
Shashi Poddar	CSIR- Central Scientific Instruments Organisation, India
Shelly Sachdeva	NIT Delhi, India
Shipla Metkar	COEP Technological University, Pune, India
Shital Chiddarwar	VNIT Nagpur, India
Shitala Prasad	Institute for Infocomm Research, India
Shiv Ram Dubey	Indian Institute of Information Technology, Allahabad, India
Shivakumara Palaiahnakote	University of Malaya, Malaysia
Shruti Jain	Jaypee University of Information Technology, Solan, India
Shruti S. Phutke	Indian Institute of Technology Ropar, India
Sivaiah Bellamkonda	Indian Institute of Information Technology Kottayam, India
Smita Agrawal	TIET, Patiala, India
Snehasis Mukherjee	Shiv Nadar University, India
Snigdha Bhagat	Indian Institute of Technology Delhi, India
Somenath Das	Indian Institute of Science Bangalore, India
Soumen Bag	IIT Dhanbad, India
Soumyadip Sengupta	University of North Carolina at Chapel Hill, USA
Sree Rama Vamsidhar S.	Indian Institute of Technology Tirupati, India
Srimanta Mandal	DA-IICT, Gandhinagar, India
Subrahmanyam Murala	IIT Ropar, India
Sudeep Sarkar	University of South Florida, Tampa, USA
Suman Kumar Maji	IIT Patna, India
Sumantra Dutta Roy	Indian Institute of Technology Delhi, India
Suresh C. Raikwar	Thapar Institute of Engineering and Technology, India

Sushanta Kumar Sahu	Jadavpur University, India
Suvidha Tripathi	LENS Corp., India
Swarup Roy	Sikkim University, India
Syed Taqi Ali	VNIT Nagpur, India
T. Veerakumar	NIT Goa, India
Tannistha Pal	NIT Agartala, India
Tapabrata Chakraborty	University of Oxford
Tapas Si	Bankura Unnayani Institute of Engineering, India
Tasneem Ahmed	Integral University, India
Uday V. Kulkarni	SGGSIET, India
Umarani Jayaraman	IIITDM Kancheepuram, India
Umesh Chandra Pati	National Institute of Technology, Rourkela, India
Vibha Vyas	COEP Technological University, India
Vibhor Kant	IIT BHU, India
Vidya More	COEP Technological University, India
Vijay N. Gangapure	Government Polytechnic, Kolhapur, India
Vijaya Thool	SGGSIET, Nanded, India
Vincenzo Piuri	Università degli Studi di Milano, Italy
Vinti Agarwal	BITS Pilani, India
Vipin Milind Kamble	VNIT, Nagpur, India
Vipin P. Yadav	MIT Academy of Engineering, India
Vishal Ramesh Satpute	VNIT Nagpur, India
Vishnu Srinivasa Murthy Yarlagadda	Vellore Institute of Technology, India
Vishwas Rathi	Indian Institute of Technology Ropar, India
Vivek Tiwari	IIIT Naya Raipur, India
Watanabe Osamu	Takushoku University, Japan
Xiaoyi Jiang	University of Münster, Germany
Yadunath Pathak	VNIT Nagpur, India
Yogesh Sariya	NIT Agartala, India
Yogita	NIT Meghalaya, India

Contents – Part II

Contents – Part I

An Efficient Residual Convolutional Neural Network with Attention Mechanism for Smoke Detection in Outdoor Environment

Shubhangi Chaturvedi$^{(\boxtimes)}$ (ID), Pritee Khanna (ID), and Aparajita Ojha (ID)

PDPM Indian Institute of Information Technology, Design and Manufacturing,
Jabalpur 482005, India
shubhangi@iiitdmj.ac.in

Abstract. Fire hazards have increased in recent years and detecting fire at an early stage is of utmost importance. An upward smoke movement can help identify location of a fire incident. Therefore smoke detection using vision based machine learning techniques have been quite useful. Recent techniques deploy deep learning models for smoke detection in an outdoor environment. Despite advancements in the field, smoke detection in challenging environments is still a concern in real time applications. Further, deep learning models have large memory footprint that hinders their usage in IoT based smoke detection systems. In this paper, a convolutional neural network with attention mechanism and residual learning is proposed for smoke detection using images of outdoor scenes. The model is lightweight with only 1.23 million parameters, reasonably lower than the existing deep learning models. The model achieves a detection rate of 99.13%, and an accuracy of 99.20% on a publicly available dataset. Its performance is also compared with eight existing deep learning smoke detection models that shows its superiority over other models. Features extracted through the model are clustered using t-SNE visualization technique to demonstrate the model's efficacy in distinguishing features of smoke and non-smoke images.

Keywords: Smoke classification · Deep learning · Convolutional neural network · attention mechanism · residual learning

1 Introduction

In recent years, fire accidents have increased with an alarming rate resulting in severe environmental damage and loss of life. Over the last two decades, forest fire and CO_2 emissions have been increasing with the highest emission recorded in the year 2020 [1]. Air pollution is caused due to smoke and gas emissions leading to health related problems such as respiratory difficulties, heart diseases, burning eyes etc. As reported by the World Health Organization (WHO), around 6.2 million people were affected between 1998–2017 due to wildfires and volcanic eruptions. Smoke causes irrevocable harm due to chemicals and particles generated by incomplete burning of carbon-containing materials. The smoke consists of carbon monoxide, carbon dioxide, and particulate matter that is dangerous for human health.

Fire accidents can be identified in their initial stages by detecting early smoke using vision based systems. Because smoke moves upwards and becomes visible even from a distance before the fire, its detection can be useful in controlling fire. But, smoke detection itself is a challenging task using vision based techniques due to various reasons. Varying shape of smoke, its texture, color, motion, background complexity, weather conditions are some of the important challenges in designing an efficient smoke detection system using images and videos. Weather conditions such as foggy, rainy environments and low illumination pose a lot of challenges in smoke detection.

In most of the indoor environments, smoke detectors use sensors that sense gases and combustion products. In a large outdoor environment, as smoke rises gradually, delay may occur in reaching the detector, due to direction of wind. Therefore, essentially these sensors are effective only in a limited range, but the outdoor environment requires a wide range detection capability to cover the entire area [2]. With advancements in digital technologies and vision based machine learning techniques, smoke detection in outdoor environments has been extensively studied in recent years.

Early smoke detection methods were based on image processing and traditional machine learning with handcrafted features [3–5]. With advancements in deep learning (DL) and computer vision, convolutional neural network (CNN) architectures are prevailing in various image classification tasks [2,6–11]. CNNs have shown promising results in many domains including smoke detection due to their powerful feature extraction capabilities [12].

DL-based methods show impressive performance when they are trained on large datasets. However, there are not many publicly available datasets which hinders the development of DL models for real time applications. Transfer learning can help in overcoming the problem and many smoke detection models have been introduced that leverage the transfer learning approach with Deep CNNs. But such architecture have large memory footprint which limits their usage for real time applications deployed on Internet-of-Thing (IoT) infrastructure. In view of this, recent focus has been on the development of lightweight CNN models that can perform well. Some of the recent works on smoke detection using lightweight models have reported impressive performance on datasets with normal and foggy environmental conditions [2,9,10]. However, the challenge remains with false alarm rates especially when the environmental conditions are tough.

In the present paper, a lightweight smoke detection model is proposed that is based on residual CNN with an attention mechanism. While residual blocks accelerate the model's convergence, attention mechanism enhances the feature extraction capability of the model. The proposed model works well with improved accuracy and detection rate as compared with eight recent CNN based methods. The main contributions of the present work can be summarized as follows.

1. An attention based residual convolutional neural network is proposed for smoke detection in images.
2. The proposed model demonstrates high accuracy and detection rate in the outdoor environment as compared to eight existing models.
3. The model has only 1.23 million parameters that makes it suitable for IoT based applications.

The remaining part of the paper is organised as follows. Section 2 discusses some of the important related works on smoke detection. Section 3 presents the proposed DL model for smoke detection. Results of the experiments on performance evaluation and comparison with other methods are discussed in Sect. 4 and concluding remarks are presented in Sect. 5.

2   Related Work

Yin et al. [6] proposed a 14 layer CNN with batch normalization layers called 'deep normalisation and convolutional neural network (DNCNN)' for smoke detection in an outdoor environment. To reduce overfitting due to insufficient data, data augmentation techniques were used. The authors achieved a high detection rate (DR) and low false alarm rate (FAR). In a comparative study by Filonenko et al. [13], various state-of-the-art CNN models were analyzed to find out their suitability for smoke classification. It was found that Xception [14] was the best choice for identification of smoke in scenarios having similarity with training samples. The authors also concluded that inception-based networks [15–17] performed well in comparison to older networks when the training data had a variety of scenarios.

A 12 layer CNN similar to VGG16 [18] was proposed by Namozov and Im Cho [7] for classification of smoke and non-smoke images. In their work, data augmentation was performed using a Generative Adversarial Network (GAN) that helped avoid overfitting issues. The authors experimented with three activation functions and observed that adaptive piecewise linear units were performing better than others. The authors demonstrated that deep CNNs could achieve high classification accuracy even with limited data. Their model showed high accuracy and detection rate with reduced FAR.

Yin and Wei [19] proposed a two stage deep CNN based smoke classification model. Color, growth area, and edge energy were estimated in the first stage. In the second stage, the output from the first stage was passed onto a CNN for feature extraction and classification. Their method was able to achieve high detection accuracy and low FAR. A dual channel network was proposed by Liu et al. [8] in which one channel used residual learning CNN to extract low-level features, whereas the other CNN channel extracted dark channel features. To obtain final prediction, outputs of both the paths were fused together. The authors in [8] prepared a dataset using images from the VSD [20] and adding some challenging images such as clouds, fog, haze, etc. The method was shown to perform well on real-world datasets. The number of model parameters was 158 million that made the model huge in terms of memory requirement. Tao et al. [21] also proposed a CNN architecture based on AlexNet [22]. The model was trained and tested on VSD [20] dataset and showed a good detection rate. Since AlexNet [22] has a large number of parameters, such models are not so well suited for IoT based applications. In a work by Yin et al. [23] deep GAN was used to generate realistic images. To perform feature extraction and classification a combination of CNN and deep convolutional GAN was used by them. The authors used the VIBE algorithm to collect smoke and non-smoke images from dynamic scenes.

Khan et al. [2] also proposed a CNN architecture to classify smoke in normal and foggy environments. The model classified images into four categories: smoke, non-smoke, smoke with fog, and non-smoke with fog. They performed fine-tuning of the pretrained VGG16 [18] and changed the last fully connected layer to 4 output classes. Through their model, they effectively handled challenging scenario of smoke detection in foggy and cloudy environment. Despite providing outstanding classification results, VGG16 [18] has large number of parameters. Muhammad et al. [9] has also proposed a deep CNN model for smoke detection in challenging environment. The authors have fine-tuned MobilenetV2 [24] to build the classification model for smoke detection in images with similar categories as described in [2].

In another work, He et al. [10] have used a network based on VGG16 [18] and attention mechanism to detect smoke in clear and hazy conditions. Their model is able to extract small smoke patches in images. Khan et al. [11] have also proposed a smoke classification and segmentation model in clear and hazy environments. The authors have fine-tuned EfficientNet [25] for classification and used DeepLabv3+ [26] for smoke segmentation. Although their model performs well in most of the cases, in wildfire video dataset testing it could not detect smoke in some cases while trying to differentiate between 'smoke' and 'smoke with fog'. Li et al. [27] have proposed a CNN model for real-time smoke detection along with the regularization loss function to reduce overfitting problems.

Various architectures have different number of parameters needed to train the model. The CNN model proposed by Yin et al. [6] has 20 million parameters, while that proposed by Li et al. [27] has 1.73 million parameters. The smoke detection model by Tao et al. [21] has around 46 million parameters. Higher number of parameters generally indicate that the model's performance will be better. However, many architectures have been proposed in recent years with small memory requirement that have shown excellent performance in different classification tasks [9,11,27]. However, the challenge remains in selecting a suitable lightweight model for IoT applications, as reducing the number of parameters may affect the model's smoke detection performance. In this paper, a smoke detection model is proposed that consists of only 1.23 million parameters. The model performs better than the previously mentioned models and shows better accuracy and detection rates.

3   Proposed Model

In this section, an attention based CNN model is presented for smoke detection that uses residual learning with a feature fine tuning mechanism. Figure 1 shows

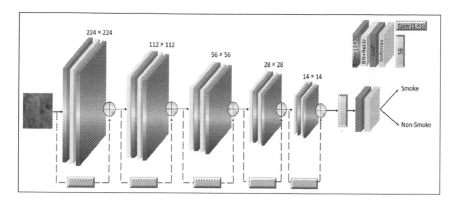

Fig. 1. Proposed model based on residual learning and attention mechanism

the architecture of the proposed model and Table 1 gives its architectural details. The model has 10 CNN layers with 3×3 filters. Total number of parameters in the model are 1.23 million including the 1×1 convolution layers used in the shortcut connections. The model takes an RGB image of size 224×224 as the input. Before passing through the model, all the images are preprocessed using the contrast limited adaptive histogram equalization (CLAHE) method. CLAHE is an image processing technique that is a variant of adaptive histogram equalization (AHE). It is used to improve the contrast of an image by adjusting the over amplification of the contrast. This is helpful in improving the local contrast and in increasing the definition of the edges in an image.

The proposed model consists of 5 residual blocks. The use of residual blocks provides ease of training and reduces overfitting. In every residual connection, while the input vector is passed through the shortcut connection to combine with the output of a later layer, it is projected to match the output dimension of a future layer using a 1×1 Conv layer followed by a Batch Normalization (BN) layer as shown in the figure. The first residual block contains 2 convolution (Conv) layers with 16 filters of size 3×3. Between the first and the second Conv layers, a BN layer and the ReLU activation layer is used. The input projection and the output of the block are then added. The remaining four residual blocks are identical in structure and only vary in the number of filters used as $32, 64, 128, 256$. In these residual blocks, two modules each consisting of BN, ReLU, and a Conv layer with 3×3 filters are present. The output of the fifth residual block is passed through a squeeze and excitation block (SE). In many applications some channels are more meaningful than others, the attention mechanism gives higher weightage to these channels in the SE block. The attention module basically learns to reweigh different channels and to pay attention to salient feature maps for the given task. The output of the SE block is given as the input to a global average pooling (GAP) layer. GAP is used to find the average of feature maps with the reduction in the dimensions of the output layer. Due to reduction of number of parameters, chances of overfitting are also reduced with the use of GAP. After this, the Softmax layer is used at the end to classify the input and obtain the final result.

The model was trained with a learning rate of 0.0001 for 30 epochs with a batch size of 16. Adam optimizer and categorical cross entropy loss function were used for training the network. Different variants to build the proposed model were trained on a DGXA100 system with a 40 GB GPU and 512 GB of RAM. Tensorflow with Keras 2.4.3 IO was used to implement the architectures.

Table 1. Architecture details of the proposed model

Block	Layer (filter size)	No. of filters	Stride
Block 1	Conv$(3,3)$	16	1
	Conv$(3,3)$	16	1
Block 2	Conv$(3,3)$	32	2
	Conv$(3,3)$	32	1
Block 3	Conv$(3,3)$	64	2
	Conv$(3,3)$	64	1
Block 4	Conv$(3,3)$	128	2
	Conv$(3,3)$	128	1
Block 5	Conv$(3,3)$	256	2
	Conv$(3,3)$	256	1

Fig. 2. Sample images of (a) Non-smoke and (b) Smoke from each set of Yuan [20] dataset.

4   Results and Discussion

This section discusses the experimental results on the performance evaluation of the proposed model on Yuan [20] dataset. It contains 4 sets divided in two classes 'smoke' and 'non-smoke'. The performance of the model is evaluated on accuracy, precision, detection rate, f1-score and FAR. Architecture of the proposed model is selected on the basis of an ablation study.

Table 2. Dataset description

Datasets	Smoke images	Non-smoke images	Total number of images	Combination 1	Combination 2
Set 1	552	831	1383	Testing	Testing
Set 2	688	817	1505	Testing	Testing
Set 3	2201	8511	10712	Training	Validation
Set 4	2254	8363	10617	Validation	Training

4.1 Dataset

The dataset used in this paper is known as Video Smoke Dataset (VSD) released by Yuan [20]. The dataset contains smoke and non-smoke images in four sets: Set 1 contains 552 smoke 831 non-smoke, Set 2 has 688 smoke 817 non-smoke, Set 3 has 2201 smoke 8511 non-smoke, and Set 4 has 2254 smoke and 8363 non-smoke images. Table 2 lists the number of images in each set of the dataset and various combinations suggested by the authors for training, validation, and testing. Figure 2 shows sample images of non-smoke and smoke classes from each set of the VSD dataset. In combination 1 (Comb 1), Set 3 is used for training and Set 4 for validation, whereas Set 1 and 2 for testing the model. In combination 2 (Comb 2), Set 4 is used for training and Set 3 for validation, whereas Set 1, Set 2 are used for testing the performance.

4.2 Evaluation Measures

The evaluation measures used to evaluate the model's performance are accuracy (ACC), precision (P), detection rate (DR), F1-Score and FAR. These are defined in terms of true positive (TP), false positive (FP), false negative (FN), and true negative (TN) scores. TP is defined as the number of smoke class images correctly classified as smoke class. FP is the number of images belonging to non-smoke class but predicted as containing smoke. FN is defined as number of images predicted as non-smoke images but actually belong to smoke class. TN is the number of non-smoke images correctly predicted as non-smoke images.

Accuracy (ACC), precision (P), detection rate (DR), F1-score and FAR are defined in terms of TP, FP, TN and FN as follows.

$$ACC = \frac{TP + TN}{TP + FP + FN + TN} \tag{1}$$

$$P = \frac{TP}{TP + FP} \tag{2}$$

$$DR = \frac{TP}{TP + FN} \tag{3}$$

$$F1 - Score = 2 \times \left(\frac{P \times DR}{P + DR} \right) \qquad (4)$$

$$FAR = \frac{FP}{FP + TN} \qquad (5)$$

4.3   Ablation Study

To obtain a suitable model for the given task, eight experiments were performed. The first network was the 'plain residual' network without any attention mechanism. Five residual blocks were connected in sequence, followed by GAP and a softmax classifier. The second model contained the spatial attention (SA) block connected after second residual block. The third model used a combination of SA (connected after second residual) and SE blocks(connected after fifth residual). The fourth model was the one shown in Fig. 1. Initially, experiments were performed on these networks without using CLAHE preprocessing method. Table 3 shows that without applying CLAHE on input smoke, the models were giving good results, but there was a scope of improvement. Thus, for all the above mentioned networks, images were preprocessed using CLAHE and were passed onto the network. It can be seen that the models were able to improve their results. The best result was noticed with the SE based network using preprocessed images. Experiments were also performed by using two combinations of training, validation, and testing sets as detailed in Sect. 4.1.

Table 3. Ablation results on Yuan [20] dataset

	Method	Comb	Set1					Set2				
			ACC	P	DR	F1-Score	FAR	ACC	P	DR	F1-Score	FAR
Without CLAHE	Plain Residual	1	95.01	94.52	95.27	94.89	4.72	93.88	93.79	93.92	93.85	6.07
		2	94.79	94.33	94.96	94.64	5.03	96.54	96.61	96.42	96.51	3.57
	Residual with SA	1	95.87	95.74	95.65	95.69	4.34	96.47	96.41	96.50	96.45	3.49
		2	95.66	95.27	95.78	95.52	4.21	96.94	96.94	96.89	96.91	3.10
	Residual with SA and SE	1	95.52	95.10	95.66	95.37	4.33	97.60	97.53	97.67	97.59	2.32
		2	95.08	95.08	95.45	95.26	4.55	98.00	97.93	98.07	97.99	1.92
	Residual with SE	1	94.21	93.77	94.27	94.02	5.72	93.02	92.93	93.03	92.98	6.96
		2	92.33	91.78	92.46	92.11	7.53	92.15	92.07	92.14	92.10	7.85
With CLAHE	Plain Residual	1	97.46	97.73	97.01	97.36	2.98	97.54	97.66	97.40	97.52	2.59
		2	97.61	97.74	97.28	97.51	2.71	97.40	97.53	97.26	97.39	2.73
	Residual with SA	1	95.01	96.05	95.01	95.52	6.19	95.28	95.96	94.85	95.40	5.14
		2	98.26	98.24	98.13	98.18	1.87	99.13	99.18	99.07	99.12	0.92
	Residual with SA and SE	1	98.69	98.79	98.49	98.63	1.51	98.73	98.79	98.66	98.72	1.33
		2	98.12	97.86	98.25	98.05	1.75	**99.53**	**99.53**	**99.53**	**99.53**	**0.46**
	Residual with SE	1	**99.20**	**99.31**	**99.03**	**99.16**	**0.96**	99.20	99.26	99.13	99.19	0.86
		2	98.48	98.52	98.31	98.41	1.68	98.60	98.65	98.54	98.59	1.45

Table 4. Performance evaluation and comparison with existing works

Method	Technique	Set 1			Set 2		
		ACC (%)	DR (%)	FAR (%)	ACC (%)	DR (%)	FAR (%)
Khan et al. [2]	Network similar to VGG16 [18]	95.16	94.75	3.24	97.08	96.95	1.59
Yin et al. [6]	14 layer convolution and batch normalization	97.83	95.28	0.48	98.08	96.36	0.48
Muhammad et al. [9]	Network similar to MobileNetV2 [24]	98.34	98.28	1.44	98.80	98.79	1.22
Khan et al. [11]	Network similar to EfficientNet [25]	86.48	83.27	0.84	85.32	84.12	1.95
Yin and Wei [19]	Network similar to AlexNet	97.83	95.27	0.48	98.04	96.28	0.42
Tao et al. [21]	Network similar to AlexNet	95.80	96.02	3.97	97.20	97.25	2.74
Yin et al. [23]	DCGAN and CNN	97.65	95.72	**0.32**	98.02	96.65	**0.24**
Li et al. [27]	CNN and authors proposed loss function	98.70	98.55	1.20	-	-	-
Proposed method	Residual with SE Comb 1	**99.20**	**99.03**	0.96	**99.20**	**99.13**	0.86
	Residual with SE Comb 2	98.48	98.31	1.68	98.60	98.54	1 45

Table 5. Number of parameters in millions (M) Gega (G) FLOPs

Method	Number of Parameters (M)	GFLOPs
Khan et al. [2]	134.2	31.0
Yin et al. [6]	20	-
Muhammad et al. [9]	2.2	0.613
Khan et al. [11]	4.0	0.794
Yin and Wei [19]	-	-
Tao et al. [21]	46	2.01
Yin et al. [23]	-	-
Li et al. [27]	1.73	-
Proposed Method	1.23	1.73

4.4   Performance Evaluation

Table 3 shows the results obtained after rigorous experiments on Yuan [20] dataset. Table 5 describes the number of parameters and FLOPs required by the models. The quantitative results show that for both the combinations, the residual network with SE block with preprocessed images achieves the best results. An ACC of 99.2%, DR of 99.03% and an FAR of 0.96% is obtained on Set1 and an ACC of 99.20%, DR of 99.13% and FAR of 0.86% is attained on Set2 for the combination 1. For the combination 2 of sets, an ACC of 98.48% DR of 98.31% FAR of 1.68% is achieved by the model on Set1; and ACC of 98.60%, DR of 98.54% and FAR of 1.45% on Set2.

Figure 3 shows various activation map results obtained from the last Conv layer of the proposed model. In the figure, the first column shows the input image, the second column shows the heatmaps, and the third column indicates the class activation maps (CAM). The first three rows (a, b, and c) show the smoke activation maps, whereas the last three rows (d, e, and f) show non-smoke class activation maps. It may be noted that the activations are clearly visible in the smoke regions. In the non-smoke images, activations are observed on the

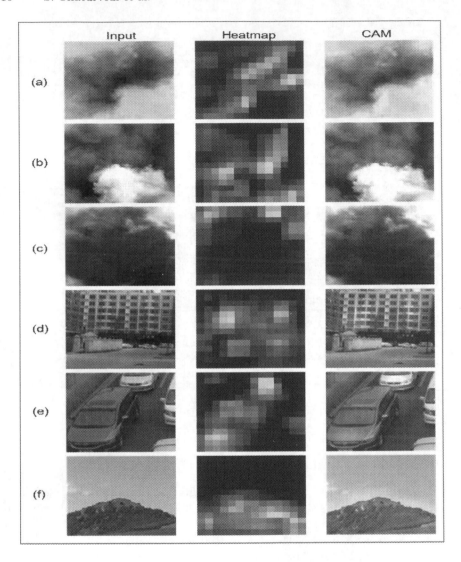

Fig. 3. Activation maps generated by the proposed model for some input images.

objects present in the image instead of the background. Thus the activation maps reflect the discriminative feature extraction capability of the proposed model.

To further illustrate the distinctive feature learning capability of the proposed model, t-SNE plots of the feature maps are also presented [28]. Figure 4 shows the t-SNE on the proposed model with results on Set 1 and Set 2 based on two combinations of datasets. To illustrate the feature distribution, output of the global average pooling layer is considered. It may be observed that the quality of features clusters is good and very few features are misclassified. While intra-class distance is less, inter-class distance is reasonably large.

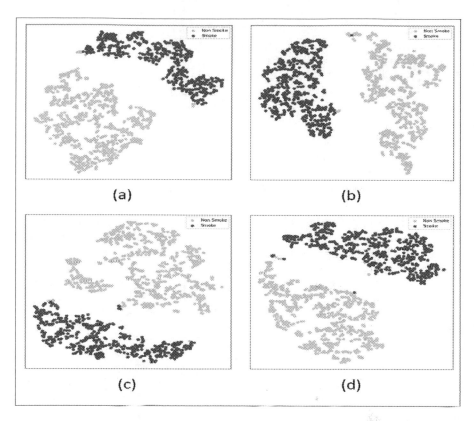

Fig. 4. t-SNE plots of extracted features of input images from (a) Comb 1 and testing Set1 (b) Comb 1 and testing Set2 (c) Comb 2 and testing Set1 (d) Comb 2 and testing Set2.

Table 4 shows the comparative performance of the proposed model and eight state-of-the-art methods on the sets under combination 1. Comparison is performed with methods suggested by - Yin et al. [6], Yin and Wei [19], Yin et al. [23], Li et al. [27], Tao et al. [21], Khan et al. [2], Muhammad et al. [9], Khan et al. [11]. Yin et al. [6] have developed a 14 layer CNN model for smoke classification. The significance of data augmentation on their model was also investigated. The method has achieved 97.83% ACC, 95.28% DR and 0.48% FAR on Set1. On Set2 98.08% ACC, 96.36% DR and 0.48% FAR is achieved by their model. A two-stage deep CNN based classification model has been proposed by Yin and Wei [19]. An ACC of 98.04% and a FAR of 0.42% is achieved by their method on Set2. A model with the combination of generative adversarial networks and CNN proposed by Yin et al. [23] has achieved 97.65% ACC, 95.72% DR, 0.32% FAR on Set1 and 98.02% ACC, 96.65% DR, 0.24% FAR on Set2. A real-time smoke detection model proposed by Li et al. [27] has obtained 98.70% ACC, 98.55% DR. A network similar to AlexNet proposed by Tao et al. [21] has achieved 95.80% ACC, 96.02% DR, 3.97% FAR on Set1 and an ACC of 97.20%, DR of

97.25%, FAR of 2.74% on Set2. Khan et al. [2] has developed a model based on the pretrained VGG16 [18] that has achieved an ACC of 95.16%, DR of 94.75% and an FAR of 3.24% on Set1 and an ACC of 97.08%, DR of 96.95% and an FAR of 1.59% on Set2. Muhammad et al. [9] has also proposed a model based on fine-tuned MobileNetV2 [24] that is shown to attain 98.34% ACC, 98.28% DR and 1.44% FAR on Set1 and 98.80% ACC, 98.79% DR and 1.22% FAR on Set2. A fine-tuned EfficientNet [25] network has been suggsted by Khan et al. [11] that shows 86.48% ACC, 83.27% DR and 0.84% FAR on Set1 and 85.32% ACC, 84.12% DR and 1.95% FAR on Set2.

It may be observed that the proposed smoke detection model has shown the best performance on the test set under the combination 1 with 99.20% ACC, 99.03% DR and 0.96% FAR for Set1 and 99.20% ACC, 99.13% DR, 0.86% FAR for Set2. The reason for the enhancement of results may be attributed to the attention mechanisms used in the present model. The use of the histogram equalisation method as a preprocessing step, which increases the global contrast of images improves the input quality and the residual learning mechanism accelerate the learning and minimizes overfitting. All these modules put together have contributed to improved performance of the model.

5   Conclusion

Smoke detection is important for mitigating fire hazards. For image based smoke classification various methods have been proposed in recent years that use CNNs. The present paper presents an attention based residual CNN for smoke classification in images. The experimental results demonstrate that the proposed model performs well on two different combinations of training and validation sets formed by considering image samples from VSD dataset. Performance of the proposed model is compared with eight state-of-the-art models and it is observed that the model is able to achieve better ACC and DR. Efficiency of distinctive feature extraction capability for smoke and non-smoke classes is also analyzed through t-SNE plots of the feature maps and the activation maps. In summary, the proposed smoke classification model shows impressive performance. In future, it is planned to further reduce the number of trainable parameters while keeping the efficiency level high. Second important problem is FAR that is planned for future research.

References

1. Brazil, B.N.: Forest fires around the world are the biggest in scale and co2 emissions in 18 years (2020). www.bbc.com/portuguese/geral-54202546
2. Khan, S., Muhammad, K., Mumtaz, S., Baik, S.W., de Albuquerque, V.H.C.: Energy-efficient deep CNN for smoke detection in foggy IoT environment. IEEE Internet of Things J. **6**(6), 9237–9245 (2019)
3. Cui, Y., Dong, H., Zhou, E.: An early fire detection method based on smoke texture analysis and discrimination. In: 2008 Congress on Image and Signal Processing, vol. 3, pp. 95–99. IEEE (2008)

4. Yuan, F.: Video-based smoke detection with histogram sequence of LBP and LBPV pyramids. Fire Saf. J. **46**(3), 132–139 (2011)
5. Yuan, F., Shi, J., Xia, X., Yang, Y., Fang, Y., Wang, R.: Sub oriented histograms of local binary patterns for smoke detection and texture classification. KSII Trans. Internet Inf. Syst. (TIIS) **10**(4), 1807–1823 (2016)
6. Yin, Z., Wan, B., Yuan, F., Xia, X., Shi, J.: A deep normalization and convolutional neural network for image smoke detection. IEEE Access **5**, 18429–18438 (2017)
7. Abdulaziz Namozov and Young Im Cho: An efficient deep learning algorithm for fire and smoke detection with limited data. Adv. Electr. Comput. Eng. **18**(4), 121–128 (2018)
8. Liu, Y., Qin, W., Liu, K., Zhang, F., Xiao, Z.: A dual convolution network using dark channel prior for image smoke classification. IEEE Access **7**, 60697–60706 (2019)
9. Muhammad, K., Khan, S., Palade, V., Mehmood, I., De Albuquerque, V.H.C.: Edge intelligence-assisted smoke detection in foggy surveillance environments. IEEE Trans. Ind. Inform. **16**(2), 1067–1075 (2019)
10. He, L., Gong, X., Zhang, S., Wang, L., Li, F.: Efficient attention based deep fusion CNN for smoke detection in fog environment. Neurocomputing **434**, 224–238 (2021)
11. Khan, S., et al.: DeepSmoke: deep learning model for smoke detection and segmentation in outdoor environments. Expert Syst. Appl. **182**, 115125 (2021)
12. Chaturvedi, S., Khanna, P., Ojha, A.: A survey on vision-based outdoor smoke detection techniques for environmental safety. ISPRS J. Photogram. Remote Sens. **185**, 158–187 (2022)
13. Filonenko, A., Kurnianggoro, L., Jo, K.-H.: Comparative study of modern convolutional neural networks for smoke detection on image data. In: 2017 10th International Conference on Human System Interactions (HSI), pp. 64–68. IEEE (2017)
14. Chollet, F.: Xception: deep learning with depthwise separable convolutions. In: Proceedings of the IEEE Conference on Computer Vision and Pattern Recognition, pp. 1251–1258 (2017)
15. Szegedy, C., et al.: Going deeper with convolutions. In: Proceedings of the IEEE Conference on Computer Vision and Pattern Recognition, pp. 1–9 (2015)
16. Szegedy, C., Vanhoucke, V., Ioffe, S., Shlens, J., Wojna, Z.: Rethinking the inception architecture for computer vision. In: Proceedings of the IEEE Conference on Computer Vision and Pattern Recognition, pp. 2818–2826 (2016)
17. Szegedy, C., Ioffe, S., Vanhoucke, V., Alemi, A.A.: Inception-v4, inception-resnet and the impact of residual connections on learning. In 31st AAAI Conference on Artificial Intelligence (2017)
18. Simonyan, K., Zisserman, A.: Very deep convolutional networks for large-scale image recognition. arXiv preprint arXiv:1409.1556 (2014)
19. Yin, H., Wei, Y.: An improved algorithm based on convolutional neural network for smoke detection. In: 2019 IEEE International Conferences on Ubiquitous Computing & Communications (IUCC) and Data Science and Computational Intelligence (DSCI) and Smart Computing, Networking and Services (SmartCNS), pp. 207–211. IEEE (2019)
20. Yuan, F.: Video smoke detection. http://staff.ustc.edu.cn/yfn/vsd.html. Accessed 17 May 2022
21. Tao, C., Zhang, J., Wang, P.: Smoke detection based on deep convolutional neural networks. In: 2016 International Conference on Industrial Informatics-Computing Technology, Intelligent Technology, Industrial Information Integration (ICIICII), pp. 150–153. IEEE (2016)

22. Krizhevsky, A., Sutskever, I., Hinton, G.E.: ImageNet classification with deep convolutional neural networks. Commun. ACM **60**(6), 84–90 (2017)
23. Yin, H., Wei, Y., Liu, H., Liu, S., Liu, C., Gao, Y.: Deep convolutional generative adversarial network and convolutional neural network for smoke detection. Complexity, 2020 (2020)
24. Sandler, M., Howard, A., Zhu, M., Zhmoginov, A., Chen, L.-C.: MobileNetv 2: inverted residuals and linear bottlenecks. In: Proceedings of the IEEE Conference on Computer Vision and Pattern Recognition, pp. 4510–4520 (2018)
25. Tan, M., Le, Q.: EfficientNet: rethinking model scaling for convolutional neural networks. In: International Conference on Machine Learning, pp. 6105–6114. PMLR (2019)
26. Chen, L.-C., Zhu, Y., Papandreou, G., Schroff, F., Adam, H.P: Encoder-decoder with atrous separable convolution for semantic image segmentation. In: Proceedings of the European Conference on Computer Vision (ECCV), pp. 801–818 (2018)
27. Li, C., Yang, B., Ding, H., Shi, H., Jiang, X., Sun, J.: Real-time video-based smoke detection with high accuracy and efficiency. Fire Safety J. **117**, 103184 (2020)
28. Van der Maaten, L., Hinton, G.: Visualizing data using t-SNE. J. Mach. Learn. Res. 9(11), (2008)

Expeditious Object Pose Estimation for Autonomous Robotic Grasping

Sri Aditya Deevi$^{(\boxtimes)}$ and Deepak Mishra

Indian Institute of Space Science and Technology, Thiruvananthapuram, India
dsriaditya999@gmail.com, deepak.mishra@iist.ac.in

Abstract. The ability of a robot to sense and "perceive" its surroundings to interact and influence various objects of interest by grasping them, using vision-based sensors is the main principle behind vision based Autonomous Robotic Grasping. To realise this task of autonomous object grasping, one of the critical sub-tasks is the 6D Pose Estimation of a known object of interest from sensory data in a given environment. The sensory data can include RGB images and data from depth sensors, but determining the object's pose using only a single RGB image is cost-effective and highly desirable in many applications. In this work, we develop a series of convolutional neural network-based pose estimation models without post-refinement stages, designed to achieve high accuracy on relevant metrics for efficiently estimating the 6D pose of an object, using only a single RGB image. The designed models are incorporated into an end-to-end pose estimation pipeline based on Unity and ROS Noetic, where a UR3 Robotic Arm is deployed in a simulated pick-and-place task. The pose estimation performance of the different models is compared and analysed in both *same-environment* and *cross-environment* cases utilising synthetic RGB data collected from cluttered and simple simulation scenes constructed in Unity Environment. In addition, the developed models achieved high *Average Distance* (ADD) metric scores greater than 93% for most of the real-life objects tested in the LINEMOD dataset and can be integrated seamlessly with any robotic arm for estimating 6D pose from only RGB data, making our method effective, efficient and generic.

Keywords: 6D Pose Estimation · Autonomous Robotic Grasping · Deep Learning · Convolutional Neural Networks (CNNs)

1 Introduction

Autonomous Robotic Grasping is the ability of an "intelligent" robot to perceive its immediate environment and *grasp* the objects under consideration. This fundamental ability to grasp object can prove to be invaluable in various applications across a variety of domains. For example, industrial robots can be used for assisting human professionals in performing versatile and repetitive processing tasks such as pick-and-place, assembly and packaging whereas domestic robots can provide support to elderly or disabled people for their day to day grasping tasks.

D. Gupta et al. (Eds.): CVIP 2022, CCIS 1777, pp. 15–30, 2023.
https://doi.org/10.1007/978-3-031-31417-9_2

6D Object Pose Estimation is a critical aspect that helps the robot to get aware of the target object to enable successful grasping. Based on the overall methodology, the object pose estimation approaches can be classified into: Correspondence-based [2,13], Template-based [12,16] and Voting-based [8,10] methods. Note that, each of these methods can be classified further depending upon whether depth information along with RGB data (RGB-D) is used or not.

In this work, a series of convolutional neural network-based pose estimation models without post-refinement stages are designed to efficiently and effectively estimate the 6D pose of an object, using only a single RGB image. The developed models were also benchmarked on various real-life objects present in the LINEMOD dataset. This paper is organized into the following sections: Sect. 2 is a basic overview that helps in establishing a high-level understanding of the entire pose-estimation pipeline. Various details related to pose estimation models designed are provided as a part of Sect. 3. Section 4 specifies the training and testing configuration utilized for evaluating these pose estimation models. Section 5 includes various quantitative and graphical results along with inferences for the collected Unity Synthetic dataset and on a popular object pose estimation dataset LINEMOD. Section 6 concludes the paper by reviewing some avenues of further research.

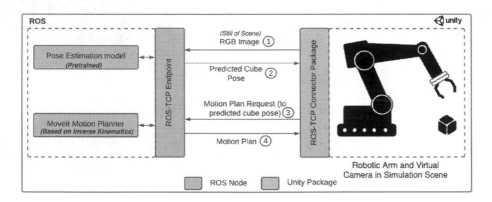

Fig. 1. Bird's Eye View of Pose Estimation Pipeline for object Pick and Place. The numbers ①, ②, ③ and ④ indicate the chronological sequence of events that take place during test phase. Ideally, the object of interest is picked up from the initial location after estimating its pose and placed in its target position, after planning the trajectory for the motion.

2   Overview of the Pose Estimation Pipeline

To create an end-to-end pose estimation pipeline for performing a pick and place task Unity Editor for Robotic Simulation is utilized. A high level flow diagram describing the necessary sequence of events that take place for the picking the object and placing it at the target location is shown in Fig. 1.

2.1   Phases of the Approach

The whole approach can be broadly divided into two main phases:

- *Train Phase* – In this phase, the pose estimation model is *trained* to predict the pose of the object of interest. This phase includes various subtasks including setting up the robotic arm and virtual camera in the simulation scene, configuring domain randomizers (see Sect. 2.2), data collection and training the model.
- *Test Phase* – In this phase, the pose estimation model is deployed and integrated into the simulated pick and place task. This phase uses the pretrained model from the Train Phase to predict the object pose which would be given to the MoveIt Motion Planning service for trajectory generation. Then using Unity *Articulation Bodies*, the arm moves according to the calculated trajectory to pick and place the object on a target mat.

2.2   Synthetic Data Collection

One of the important subtasks in the Train Phase is to collect data from the simulation scenario for training, validation and testing the models. Data includes RGB images (Here, resolution $= 650 \times 400$ px) from the Virtual Camera (equipped with Unity's Perception Computer Vision Package) and *capture* files containing the ground truth annotation information. Note that, along with ground truth annotation pose labels, data regarding the sensor (in this case, a virtual camera) such as camera intrinsic matrix, the pose shift of the sensor w.r.t World frame, and sensor ID are also recorded.

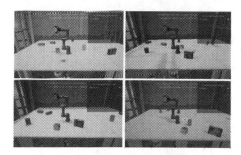

Fig. 2. A collection of images depicting the superimposed effect of all domain randomizers applied to the simulation scenario (specifically, here *Cluttered Scene* is considered). The object under consideration (*cube*) is highlighted (green 3D bounding box) (Color figure online)

Domain Randomization [12] a simple technique for bridging the simulation-reality gap for synthetic data, where instead of collecting data and training a model on a single simulated environment, we randomize the simulator to expose the model to a wide range of environments at training time. In this work, this idea is used extensively (See Fig. 2), and the different custom types of randomizers are configured for randomizing pose of different objects and camera (w.r.t World Frame) in the scene and also for randomizing the colour, intensity and direction of light.

3   Pose Estimation Models

Deep Learning based models are mainly utilized in this work, for single-object (of interest), single-instance 6D pose estimation to enable tasks such as pick and place. The design of the models was carried out iteratively keeping in mind, the following desired qualities:

– *Efficiency* – Use of only RGB image and no depth information
– *Speed* – Use of no post hoc refinement stages for pose prediction
– *Accuracy* – Good performance on relevant metrics such as Average Distance (ADD) of 3D model points

Each model acts as a baseline for demonstrating the performance improvement of the next model, which is designed to address the shortcomings of the previous model.

3.1   Model-1: UnityVGG16

The overall architecture of Model-1 *UnityVGG16* is shown in Fig. 3.

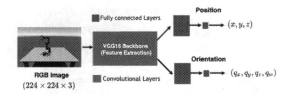

Fig. 3. Model Architecture of *UnityVGG16*. It is a template-based (implicit) approach that directly regresses the pose information from the RGB image.

The image features are extracted by the VGG16 [9] backbone. The network consists two heads made up of fully-connected layers, for regressing the 3D position (x, y, z) and orientation quaternion (q_x, q_y, q_z, q_w) of the object of interest, by the utilizing the extracted features.

3.2   Model-2: Pose6DSSD

In order to improve the performance of pose estimation, the second model designed is *Pose6DSSD*[1]. The complete architecture of the model is illustrated in Fig. 4. Some of the ideas for designing the model were taken from [11].

As it is a correspondence based approach, we first the regress the 2D image coordinates of certain keypoints, which in this approach, are the 8 corners and the centroid of the 3D bounding box around the object of interest. The main feature extraction backbone consists of 27 convolutional layers with residual skip links, and has been adapted from ResNet34 architecture [3]. There are no fully connected layers used as opposed to Model-1 *UnityVGG16*, to limit the number of parameters.

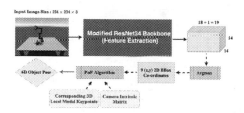

Fig. 4. Model Architecture of *Pose6DSSD*. It is a correspondence-based approach, which involves estimation of the 2D keypoints followed by extraction of pose information using the Perspective and Point (PnP) [6] algorithm.

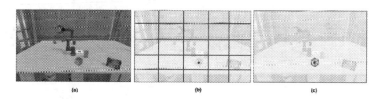

Fig. 5. (a) An example input RGB image. (b) The image is divided into $S \times S$ regions denoted by the square grid. (c) Each cell predicts 2D locations of the corners of the projected 3D bounding box in the image.

3.2.1   Interpreting Feature Extraction Output

For a single image input, the output of the main feature extraction backbone is 3D tensor of dimensions $S \times S \times (2K + 1)$. The input image is partitioned into a 2D regular grid (see Fig. 5) with $S \times S$ cells. In this work, $S = 14$ is considered.

For each grid, $2K + 1$ values are predicted where K is the number of keypoints being considered. We consider a 3D bounding box based approach where $K = 9$ (8 corners + 1 centroid). The remaining one value predicts the confidence value of the grid cell, i.e. how confident the model is that in a given grid cell the object of interest is present. Note that, the model predicts the normalized offset values from the bottom-left grid point of each grid cell, similar to [11].

---

[1] Stands for 6D Pose **S**ingle **S**tage **D**etector

3.2.2   Modelling the Ground Truth Confidence

As proposed in [11], the ground truth confidence values for training the model is modelled with an exponentially decreasing profile. The intuition behind this is the idea that the confidence value is low when there is no object in grid cell, it is high when the object is present in the grid cell.

After feature extraction, the grid cell output with the maximum confidence value is selected as the final candidate. These 2D image coordinate predictions along with the corresponding 3D model points expressed in the local model frame and camera intrinsic matrix, form the input to the PnP block, whose output is the final predicted 6D pose for the object of interest present in the input image.

3.3   Model-3: DOSSE-6D

We can observe that the previous model used a traditional correspondence based (using DL), so it is not an end-to-end approach, as we cannot directly utilize the output 6D pose information for training the model. We rely on indirect supervision (see Sect. 4) for training the model. The third model $DOSSE$-$6D$[4] is an improvement of the previous model in this aspect. Three versions of this model have been developed, each of them having small differences, compared to the other. More details are provided in Supplementary Material. The architecture of $DOSSE$-$6D$_$v2$ is illustrated in Fig. 6.

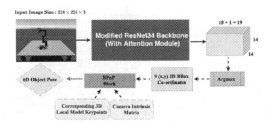

Fig. 6. High Level Model Architecture of $DOSSE$-$6D$_$v2$. It is a correspondence-based approach, which involves estimation of the 2D keypoints followed by extraction of pose information using the BPnP module. Input is an RGB image of resolution 448×448 px.

$DOSSE$-$6D$ is also a correspondence based approach similar to the Pose6DSSD, but with the following modifications:

– PnP Block is replaced by BPnP (Backpropagatable PnP) [2] module to make the model end-to-end trainable.
– The versions 2 and 3 of the $DOSSE$-$6D$ utilize attention modules in their architectures for adaptive feature refinement of intermediate feature maps.

---

[4] Stands for **D**eep **O**bject **S**ingle **S**hot **E**stimator of **6D** object pose

3.3.1   BPnP Module

The BPnP block, as proposed in [2], is a module that backpropagates gradients through a PnP "layer" to guide parameter updates of a neural network. Based on the concept of implicit differentiation, it helps to combine DL network and geometric vision to form an end-to-end trainable pipeline. As suggested in [2], we define a stationary constraint function such that the output pose is local minimum for PnP solver. Then using the Implicit Function Theorem (IFT) and chain rule we can compute the necessary gradients for backpropagation. Using this (instead of Fully connected layers as in Model-1) we can optimise feature based loss and learn geometric constraints in an end-to-end manner. More mathematical details are provided in Supplementary Material.

3.3.2   Attention Module

The main idea behind the use of attention module is to force the model to focus on important features and suppress unnecessary ones, thereby improving its hidden representations. Incorporation of Attention module was done by the considering the best empirical practices in [15] and [14], found by extensive experimentation. Each attention module basically consists of two sub-modules namely:

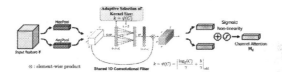

Fig. 7. Channel Attention Sub-Module Architecture. The intuition behind using both the type of features is that Max-pooled features encode the degree of the most salient part in the feature map, whereas Average-pooled features encode global statistics softly.

- *Channel Attention* – The intuition behind channel attention sub-module is to improve the feature maps by cross-channel interaction. One way that can be done is by selectively weighting each feature channel adaptively. We use Efficient Channel Attention (ECA) block, proposed in [14], which uses a 1D convolution, hence limiting the number of parameters. As shown in Fig. 7, in this work, both the Maxpool and Average pool features (pooling performed along the spatial dimensions, to get a 1D vector of length equal to number of channels) are passed through a shared 1D convolutional layer.
- *Spatial Attention* – This submodule computes a spatial attention map is obtained which can be used to improve features utilizing the inter-spatial relationship of features. As shown in Fig. 9, we are using both the Max-pool and Average pool features. Both these feature maps are stacked together and 2D convolution is performed followed by passing the output through a sigmoid non-linearity to restrict the range of values to $[0, 1]$.

For relative placement of submodules, as discussed in [15], a series configuration with channel attention sub-module preceeding the spatial attention submodule is considered. Since, we are using a ResNet adapted backbone in all versions of *DOSSE-6D*, the complete attention module is placed at the end of each ResBlock (consists of two convolutional layers before the skip connnections).

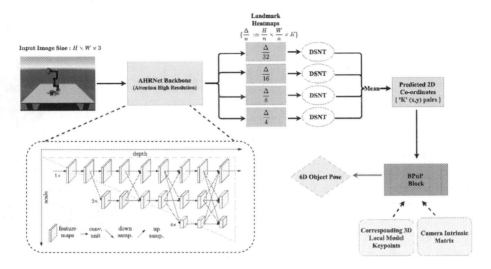

Fig. 8. High-Level Block Diagram of *AHR-DOSSE-6D*. It is a correspondence-based approach, which involves estimation of the 2D landmark heatmaps with keypoints, followed by extraction of pose information using the BPnP module.

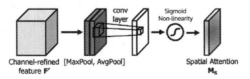

Fig. 9. Spatial Attention Sub-Module Architecture. This sub-module helps the model to basically decide "where" to focus in a feature map.

3.4   Model-4: AHR-DOSSE-6D

The last model designed is $AHR\text{-}DOSSE\text{-}6D^2$, whose high level architecture is illustrated in Fig. 8. It is a correspondence-based approach, which involves estimation of the 2D landmark heatmaps with keypoints, followed by extraction of pose information.

---

[2] **A**ttention **H**igh **R**esolution **D**eep **O**bject **S**ingle **S**hot **E**stimator of **6D** object pose.

Some of the important elements of this model are as follows:

- Single Stage end-to-end trainable model (due to the use of BPnP module discussed in Section II.C) without any post-refinement stages.
- Use of attention module consisting of both spatial and channel attention sub-modules (See Sect. 3.3.2).
- Maintenance of high resolution feature representations throughout the *AHR-Net* feature extraction backbone.
- Use of more geometrical details of the object under consideration by considering Farthest Point Sampling (FPS) [8] instead of 3D bounding box corners.
- Modelled confidence approach as described in Section II.B is replaced with heatmap estimation. The landmark heatmaps are used to obtain the 2D coordinates in normalized form, using the Differential Spatial to Numerical Transform (DSNT) block.
- Provision to use increased image resolution without increase in number of parameters.

1. *AHRNet Backbone:* The complete architecture of *AHRNet* backbone is provided in Supplementary Material. The main idea is the use of repeated multi-scale fusions to improve quality of hidden representations. Note that, as shown in Fig. 8, along depth axis feature map size remains same and along scale axis, typical feature map size reduction happens similar to a typical CNN.
2. *DSNT Block:* The Differentiable Spatial to Numerical Transform (DSNT) [7] block, in simple words, is used for converting the landmark heatmaps produced by the AHR-Net Backbone to normalized 2D coordinates of the corresponding keypoints. It is basically a spatial "soft"-argmax over each feature channel. Some of its desirable properties are that it is fully differentiable thereby helping in end-to-end design, adds no trainable parameters, exhibits good spatial generalization and it also performs well even with low heatmap resolutions.

4 Training Configuration and Model Evaluation

In this section, different attributes of the training configuration utilized such as experimental setup, loss functions and optimizer details are described.

4.1 Experimental Setup

Two simulation scenes were considered namely, *Simple Scene* and *Cluttered Scene* for collecting domain randomized, labelled data (see Fig. 10). Note that, *Cluttered Scene* is a more challenging version of the simple scene. For both the scenarios, data split used for all models is { *Training | Validation | Test* } : {30000 | 3000 | 3000} RGB images. For testing the performance of the model for estimating object pose, we consider the following both Same-Environment and Cross-Environment cases. Same-Environment cases test the model performance

with respect to the generalizability of 6D pose predictions in a *known* environment, by training and testing the model in the same scene. Cross-Environment
cases test the model's robustness and its ability to generalize over both the
environment and the 6D pose predictions.

(a)   (b)

Fig. 10. Stills from Simulation scenes. (a) Simple Scene - Coloured face cube (obj. of
interest) kept on the table where UR3 Robotic Arm is mounted. (b) Cluttered Scene -
typical room environment with various objects placed at random positions (3D models
of the distractor objects are taken from the YCB model set [1]

4.2   Loss Functions

In this subsection, more details about the loss functions utilized for training the
corresponding pose estimation models discussed in Section III will be given. For
Model-1: UnityVGG16, the loss function considered is:

$$\mathcal{L}_1 = \mathcal{L}_{trans} + \mathcal{L}_{orient},$$

where $\mathcal{L}_{trans}$ and $\mathcal{L}_{orient}$ are the Mean Squared Errors (MSE) between the predicted & ground truth translational vectors and the vectors representing the
predicted & ground truth quaternions. The loss function utilized for *Model-2:
Pose6DSSD* is:

$$\mathcal{L}_2 = \lambda_{reproj}\mathcal{L}_{reproj} + \lambda_{conf}\mathcal{L}_{conf},$$

where $\mathcal{L}_{reproj}$ is the MSE between the predicted and true projected 2D image
point (normalized) coordinates and $\mathcal{L}_{conf}$ is the MSE between the predicted and
ground truth confidence values. As proposed in [11], λ_{conf} is region-selective
(more importance given to grid cells with object of interest) whereas $\lambda_{reproj} = 1$
everywhere. The mixture loss function considered for *Model-3: DOSSE-6D* is
given by:

$$\mathcal{L}_3 = \overbrace{\lambda_{reproj}\mathcal{L}_{reproj} + \lambda_{conf}\mathcal{L}_{conf}}^{\text{Indirect Supervision}} + \overbrace{\lambda_{add}\mathcal{L}_{add}}^{\text{Direct Supervision}}$$

where the definitions of L_{reproj} and $\mathcal{L}_{conf}$ are same as earlier. $\mathcal{L}_{add}$ is the average
squared distance of 3D model points $\mathbf{x} \in \mathcal{M}$, between predicted and ground truth
configurations of the object.

$$\mathcal{L}_{add} = \frac{1}{m}\sum_{\mathbf{x}\in\mathcal{M}} \|(\mathbf{Rx} + \mathbf{T}) - (\tilde{\mathbf{R}}\mathbf{x} + \tilde{\mathbf{T}})\|^2$$

where $\mathbf{R}, \tilde{\mathbf{R}}$ are Ground Truth and Predicted Rotation Matrices and $\mathbf{T}, \tilde{\mathbf{T}}$ Ground Truth and Predicted Translational Vectors respectively.

For *Model-4: AHR-DOSSE-6D*, the loss function is given by:

$$\mathcal{L}_4 = \overbrace{\lambda_{reproj}\mathcal{L}_{reproj} + \lambda_{heat}\mathcal{L}_{heat}}^{\text{Indirect Supervision}} + \overbrace{\lambda_{add}\mathcal{L}_{add}}^{\text{Direct Supervision}}$$

where the definitions of L_{reproj} and L_{add} remain the same. $\mathcal{L}_{heat}$ (representing multi-scale supervision) is basically the MSE between predicted and ground truth heat maps:

$$\mathcal{L}_{\text{heat}} = \frac{1}{S}\sum_{s=1}^{S}\frac{1}{K}\sum_{k=1}^{K}\left\|\mathbf{H}_k^{s,pred} - \mathbf{H}_k^{s,\text{true}}\right\|_F^2$$

where

- The heatmap corresponding to the ith keypoint and of scale (dimension) $\frac{\delta}{z}$ is:

$$\{\mathbf{H}_i^{j,pred}, \mathbf{H}_i^{j,true} \in \mathbb{R}^{\frac{\delta}{z}} \mid \frac{\delta}{z} := \left(\frac{H}{z} \times \frac{W}{z}\right), z = 4 \cdot 2^{j-1}\} \quad ; \quad i = 1, 2, \dots, K \text{ and } j = 1, 2, \dots, S$$

- $\|\cdot\|_F$ represents the Frobenius Norm of matrices. S represents the number of "scales" of heatmaps generated. In this work, $S = 4$ is considered.

4.3 Optimizer and Evaluation Details

For training all the pose estimation models, the *ADAM* optimizer is considered and checkpointing of the models is done at the epoch at which the model achieves best validation performance. The different evaluation metrics used for testing the object pose estimation performance of the different models are the popularly used Average Distance (ADD) of model points, Reprojection Error, Translational MSE and Quaternion Error (angular distance between ground truth and predicted quaternions).

5 Results

5.1 Unity Simulation Scenarios

Table 1 provides results for the test performance of the pose estimation models on the Unity Synthetic data. For all the results presented, the object of interest is a coloured face *cube* object of side Length (a) 10 cm (Figs. 11 and 12).

Table 1. Table displaying the average ADD metric values (in cm). The model architectures and other details are described in previous sections. *v3* of *DOSSE-6D* uses low input image resolution whereas *v1* uses no attention module.

S.No.	Approach	Expt. Config.			
		Train-Clutter +Test-Clutter	Train-Clutter +Test-Simple	Train-Simple +Test-Simple	Train-Simple + Test-Clutter
1	UnityVGG16	1.6801	16.5287	2.0248	53.7345
2	Pose6DSSD	1.3976	9.0066	1.0054	39.0549
3	DOSSE-6D_v1	1.2150	3.9213	0.9789	58.1505
4	DOSSE-6D_v2	0.8836	10.5477	0.7604	41.8551
5	DOSSE-6D_v3	0.9540	30.3129	1.0083	48.6070
6	AHR-DOSSE-6D	0.4192	22.6130	0.4685	92.2395

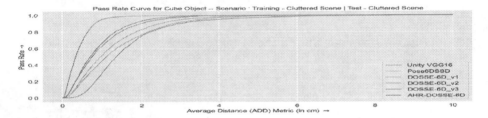

Fig. 11. ADD metric, plotted versus of pass rates (in %), for various models in Expt. Config.: Train-Clutter + Test-Clutter

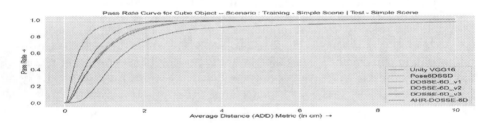

Fig. 12. ADD metric, plotted versus of pass rates (in %), for various models in Expt. Config.: Train-Simple + Test-Simple

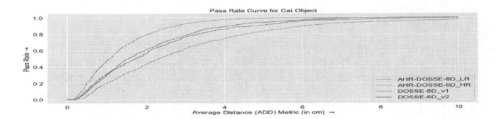

Fig. 13. ADD metric, plotted versus of pass rates (in %), for various models considered for the LINEMOD "cat" object.

5.2   LINEMOD Dataset

Table 2 provides the results for the ADD metric, in terms of pass rates (in %), for various models and objects in LINEMOD [4] dataset. For each model, 10% of the diameter (d) of object threshold for pass rate. Note that, input RGB image sizes of *DOSSE-6D_v1*, *AHR-DOSSE-6D_LR* is 224 × 224 and *DOSSE-6D_v2*, *AHR-DOSSE-6D_HR* is 448 × 448 (Figs. 13 and 14).

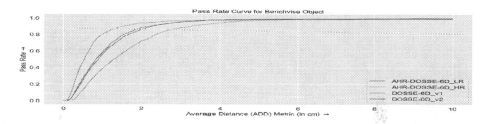

Fig. 14. ADD metric, plotted versus of pass rates (in %), for various models considered for the LINEMOD "benchvise" object.

Some of the inferences extracted from the results of these test experiments are summarized below:

– We can observe that from results for the *Same Environment Cases*, the *AHR-DOSSE-6D* model performs the *best* as compared to the other models. The improvement in performance can be attributed to different elements in its design. Also, *AHR-DOSSE-6D_HR* seems to give a relatively superior performance on all LINEMOD objects tested.
– In general, the performance of *DOSSE-6D* (all versions) models is higher than that of *Pose6DSSD* and *UnityVGG16* model due to the use of *Direct Supervision*.
– It can be seen that the all the models perform poorly as compared to the *Same Environment Cases* as expected, due to the fact that it is a much difficult problem. Here, essentially the "transfer" of pose prediction performance across environments is being tested.
– As expected the generalization capability of the models trained in *Cluttered Scene* is higher, i.e. these models are more robust to changes in environment, due to presence of background distractor objects.
– It is clear by observing the performance of the model pairs *DOSSE-6D_v1* & *DOSSE-6D_v2* and *AHR-DOSSE-6D_LR* & *AHR-DOSSE-6D_HR*, the models which take high input resolution image as input generally tend to perform much better than their counterparts.

– Transfer Learning is utilized in models *UnityVGG16*, *Pose6DSSD*, *DOSSE-6D_v1*. Specifically, all these models consisted of a ResNet34 based feature extraction backbone, whose weights were initialized by pretraining on the ImageNet dataset for classification (a different task). Interestingly, it can be observed such pretraining is highly beneficial for improving generalization ability of the model across environments and leads to improvement in the *Cross Environment* performance of the models.

Table 2. Table displaying the ADD metric pass rates (in %). The rows highlighted in grey colour are some of the popular existing methods that provide results for *single stage, single object, single instance* object pose estimation using RGB images only.

S.No.	Object / Approach	Cat (d = 15.50 cm)	Benchvise (d = 28.69 cm)	Lamp (d = 28.52 cm)	Can (d = 20.20 cm)	Iron (d = 30.32 cm)
1.	SSD-6D [5]	0.51	0.18	8.20	1.35	8.86
2.	Tekin et al. [11]	41.82	81.80	71.11	68.80	74.97
3.	DOSSE-6D_v1	33.45	86.77	74.94	60.19	60.22
4.	DOSSE-6D_v2	50.23	94.53	85.55	78.01	82.45
5.	AHR-DOSSE-6D_LR	45.89	94.30	94.36	84.14	88.10
6.	AHR-DOSSE-6D_HR	68.31	96.69	97.86	95.02	93.63

6   Conclusion

This work is aimed at developing robust, efficient and effective object 6D pose estimation techniques. A complete end to end pose estimation pipeline where a UR3 robotic arm is deployed in a simulated pick and place task is demonstrated. The majority of this work has been focused at developing improved CNN based models for estimating pose from a single RGB image, utilizing neither depth information nor post hoc refinement stages. A series of such pose estimation models are designed, compared and analyzed. In order to test the efficacy of the approaches, they are trained and tested on synthetic data from simple and cluttered scenes, in a same-environment and cross-environment setting. The developed models were also tested on various objects from the LINEMOD benchmark dataset and the results indicated superior performance of the models. An interesting extension of this work is developing an improved pose estimation approach for Multi-object, Multi-instance prediction. One way of doing this is the inclusion of Part Affinity Fields (PAFs) prediction component into the AHR-DOSSE-6D model. Incorporation of additional collision avoidance modules to develop a more robust "safety-critical" approach to minimize the collisions, while executing the planned robotic arm trajectory is also worth exploring.

Supplementary information

Code and supplementary material is available upon request.

References

1. Calli, B., Walsman, A., Singh, A., Srinivasa, S., Abbeel, P., Dollar, A.M.: Benchmarking in manipulation research: Using the yale-cmu-berkeley object and model set. IEEE Robot. Automation Mag. **22**(3), 36–52 (2015). https://doi.org/10.1109/MRA.2015.2448951
2. Chen, B., Parra, A., Cao, J., Li, N., Chin, T.J.: End-to-end learnable geometric vision by backpropagating pnp optimization. In: Proceedings of the IEEE/CVF Conference on Computer Vision and Pattern Recognition, pp. 8100–8109 (2020)
3. He, K., Zhang, X., Ren, S., Sun, J.: Deep residual learning for image recognition. In: Proceedings of the IEEE Conference on Computer Vision and Pattern Recognition, pp. 770–778 (2016)
4. Hinterstoisser, S., Lepetit, V., Ilic, S., Holzer, S., Bradski, G., Konolige, K., Navab, N.: Model based training, detection and pose estimation of texture-less 3D objects in heavily cluttered scenes. In: Lee, K.M., Matsushita, Y., Rehg, J.M., Hu, Z. (eds.) ACCV 2012. LNCS, vol. 7724, pp. 548–562. Springer, Heidelberg (2013). https://doi.org/10.1007/978-3-642-37331-2_42
5. Kehl, W., Manhardt, F., Tombari, F., Ilic, S., Navab, N.: Ssd-6d: Making rgb-based 3d detection and 6d pose estimation great again. In: Proceedings of the IEEE International Conference on Computer Vision, pp. 1521–1529 (2017)
6. Lepetit, V., Moreno-Noguer, F., Fua, P.: Epnp: an accurate o (n) solution to the pnp problem. Int. J. Comput. Vision **81**(2), 155 (2009)
7. Nibali, A., He, Z., Morgan, S., Prendergast, L.: Numerical coordinate regression with convolutional neural networks. arXiv preprint arXiv:1801.07372 (2018)
8. Peng, S., Zhou, X., Liu, Y., Lin, H., Huang, Q., Bao, H.: Pvnet: pixel-wise voting network for 6dof object pose estimation. IEEE Trans. Pattern Anal. Mach. Intell. (2020)
9. Simonyan, K., Zisserman, A.: Very deep convolutional networks for large-scale image recognition. arXiv preprint arXiv:1409.1556 (2014)
10. Tejani, A., Tang, D., Kouskouridas, R., Kim, T.-K.: Latent-class hough forests for 3D object detection and pose estimation. In: Fleet, D., Pajdla, T., Schiele, B., Tuytelaars, T. (eds.) ECCV 2014. LNCS, vol. 8694, pp. 462–477. Springer, Cham (2014). https://doi.org/10.1007/978-3-319-10599-4_30
11. Tekin, B., Sinha, S.N., Fua, P.: Real-time seamless single shot 6d object pose prediction. In: Proceedings of the IEEE Conference on Computer Vision and Pattern Recognition, pp. 292–301 (2018)
12. Tobin, J., Fong, R., Ray, A., Schneider, J., Zaremba, W., Abbeel, P.: Domain randomization for transferring deep neural networks from simulation to the real world. In: 2017 IEEE/RSJ International Conference on Intelligent Robots and Systems (IROS), pp. 23–30. IEEE (2017)
13. Tremblay, J., To, T., Sundaralingam, B., Xiang, Y., Fox, D., Birchfield, S.: Deep object pose estimation for semantic robotic grasping of household objects. arXiv preprint arXiv:1809.10790 (2018)
14. Wang, Q., Wu, B., Zhu, P., Li, P., Zuo, W., Hu, Q.: Eca-net: efficient channel attention for deep convolutional neural networks. In: 2020 IEEE/CVF Conference on Computer Vision and Pattern Recognition (CVPR), pp. 11531–11539 (2020)

15. Woo, S., Park, J., Lee, J.-Y., Kweon, I.S.: CBAM: convolutional block attention module. In: Ferrari, V., Hebert, M., Sminchisescu, C., Weiss, Y. (eds.) ECCV 2018. LNCS, vol. 11211, pp. 3–19. Springer, Cham (2018). https://doi.org/10.1007/978-3-030-01234-2_1

16. Xiang, Y., Schmidt, T., Narayanan, V., Fox, D.: Posecnn: A convolutional neural network for 6d object pose estimation in cluttered scenes. arXiv preprint arXiv:1711.00199 (2017)

SRTGAN: Triplet Loss Based Generative Adversarial Network for Real-World Super-Resolution

Dhruv Patel[1]([✉]), Abhinav Jain[1], Simran Bawkar[1], Manav Khorasiya[1], Kalpesh Prajapati[1], Kishor Upla[1], Kiran Raja[2], Raghavendra Ramachandra[2], and Christoph Busch[2]

[1] Sardar Vallabhbhai National Institute of Technology (SVNIT), Surat, India
dhruv.r.patel14@gmail.com, abhinav98jain@gmail.com,
sim017bawkar@gmail.com, manavkhorasiya@gmail.com, kalpesh.jp89@gmail.com,
kishorupla@gmail.com
[2] Norwegian University of Science and Technology (NTNU), Gjøvik, Norway
{kiran.raja,raghavendra.ramachandra,christoph.busch}@ntnu.no

Abstract. Many applications such as forensics, surveillance, satellite imaging, medical imaging, etc., demand High-Resolution (HR) images. However, obtaining an HR image is not always possible due to the limitations of optical sensors and their costs. An alternative solution called Single Image Super-Resolution (SISR) is a software-driven approach that aims to take a Low-Resolution (LR) image and obtain the HR image. Most supervised SISR solutions use ground truth HR image as a target and do not include the information provided in the LR image, which could be valuable. In this work, we introduce Triplet Loss-based Generative Adversarial Network hereafter referred as *SRTGAN* for Image Super-Resolution problem on real-world degradation. We introduce a new triplet-based adversarial loss function that exploits the information provided in the LR image by using it as a negative sample. Allowing the patch-based discriminator with access to both HR and LR images optimizes to better differentiate between HR and LR images; hence, improving the adversary. Further, we propose to fuse the adversarial loss, content loss, perceptual loss, and quality loss to obtain Super-Resolution (SR) image with high perceptual fidelity. We validate the superior performance of the proposed method over the other existing methods on the RealSR dataset in terms of quantitative and qualitative metrics.

1 Introduction

Single Image Super-Resolution (SISR) refers to reconstructing a High Resolution (HR) image from an input Low Resolution (LR) image. It has broad applications in various fields, including satellite imaging, medical imaging, forensics, security, robotics, where LR images are abundant. It is an inherently ill-posed problem

---

D. Patel and A. Jain—Equal contribution.

D. Gupta et al. (Eds.): CVIP 2022, CCIS 1777, pp. 31–46, 2023.
https://doi.org/10.1007/978-3-031-31417-9_3

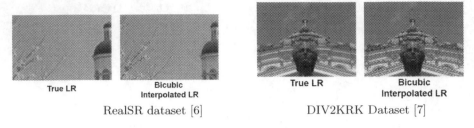

RealSR dataset [6]   DIV2KRK Dataset [7]

Fig. 1. True LR and corresponding bicubic downsampled LR image from ground truth HR of the RealSR dataset [6] and DIV2KRK dataset [7]

since obtaining the SR image from an LR image might correspond to any patch of the ground truth HR image, which is intractable. The most employed solutions are the supervised super-resolution methods due to the availability of ground truth information and the development of many novel methods.

Reconstructing the HR image from LR input includes image deblurring, denoising, and super-resolution operations which makes the SISR a highly complex task. Due to recent technological advances, such as computational power and availability of data, there has been substantial development in various CNN architectures and loss functions to improve SISR methods [1–5]. These models have been primarily tested on the synthetic datasets. Here, the LR images are downsampled from the ground truth HR images by using known degradation model such as bicubic downsampling. For instance, Fig. 1 shows that the characteristics like blur and that details of true and bicubic downsampled LR images do not correspond exactly for both RealSR [6] and DIV2KRK dataset [7]. Such differences can be attributed to underlying sensor noise and unknown real-world degradation. Hence, the models perform well on those synthetically degraded images, they generalize poorly on the real-world dataset [8]. Further, most of the works have shown that adding more CNN layers does increase the performance of the model by some extent. However, they are unable to capture the high-frequency information such as texture in the images as they rely on the pixel-wise losses and hence suffer from poor perceptual quality [9–12].

To address the issues mentioned above, the research community has also proposed using Generative Adversarial Networks (GANs) for SISR task. The first GAN-based framework called SRGAN [13], introduced the concept of perceptual loss, calculated from high-level feature maps, and tried to solve the problem of poor perceptual fidelity as mentioned before. Subsequently, numerous GAN-based methods were introduced that have shown improvements in the super-resolution results [13–15]. GANs are also used for generating perceptually better images [13,14,16]. Motivated by such works, we propose SR using Triplet loss-based GAN (SRTGAN) - a triplet loss-based patch GAN comprising a generator trained in a multi-loss setting with a patch-based discriminator.

Our proposed method - SRTGAN gains superior Peak Signal-to-Noise Ratio (PSNR) and competing Structural Similarity Index (SSIM) [17] values on the RealSR dataset (real-world degradation) [6], which still cannot be considered a valid metric as they fail to capture the perceptual features. Hence, we also evaluate our performance on the perceptual measure, i.e. Learned Perceptual Image Patch Similarity (LPIPS) [18] score. Our SRTGAN outperforms the other state-of-the-art methods in the quantitative evaluation of LPIPS and visual performance on the RealSR dataset. It also provides superior LPIPS results on the DIV2KRK dataset [7] (synthetic degradation). All our experiments on both RealSR and DIV2KRK datasets are done for an upscaling factor of ×4. Even though DIV2KRK happens to be a synthetic dataset, it has a highly complex and unknown degradation model. Hence, our proposed method has been trained and validated on these datasets proving the generalizability on the real-world data.

Our key contributions in this work can therefore be listed as:

- We propose a new triplet-based adversarial loss function that exploits the information provided in the LR image by using it as a negative sample as well as the HR image which is used as a positive sample.
- A patchGAN-based discriminator network is utilized that assists the defined triplet loss function to train the generator network.
- The proposed SR method is trained on a linear combination of losses, namely the content, multi-layer perceptual, triplet-based adversarial, and quality assessment. Such fusion of different loss functions leads to superior quantitative and subjective quality of SR results as illustrated in the results.
- Additionally, different experiments have been conducted in the ablation study to judge the potential of our proposed approach. The superiority of the proposed method over other novel SR works has been demonstrated from the undertaken quantitative and qualitative studies.

The structure of the paper is designed in the following manner. Section 2 consists of the related work in the field. Section 3 includes the proposed framework, the network architecture, and loss formulation for training the Generator and Discriminator networks. The experimental validation is presented in Sect. 4, followed by the limitation and conclusion in Sects. 5 and 6 respectively.

2   Related Works

A Convolutional Neural Network (CNN) based SR approach (referred as SRCNN) was proposed by Dong et al. [2], where only three layers of convolution were used to correct finer details in an upsampled LR image. Similarly, FSRCNN [4] and VDSR [19] were inspired by SRCNN with suitable modifications to further improve the performance. VDSR [19] is the first model that uses a deep CNN and introduces the use of residual design that helps in the faster convergence with improvement in SR performance. Such residual connection also helps to avoid the vanishing gradient problem, which is the most common problem with deeper networks. Inspired by VDSR [19], several works [5, 13, 20–22] have been reported with the use of a residual connection to train deeper models. Apart from a residual network, an alternative approach using dense connections has been used to improve SR images in many recent networks [3, 23, 24]. The concept of attention was also used in several efforts [20, 25] to focus on important features and allow sparse learning for the SR problem. Similarly, adversarial training [26] has been shown to obtain better perceptual

SR results. Ledig et al. introduced adversarial learning for super-resolution termed as SRGAN [13], which shows perceptual enhancement in the SR images even with low fidelity metrics such as PSNR and SSIM. Recent works such as SRFeat [16] and ESRGAN [14], which were inspired by SRGAN, have also reported improvements in the perceptual quality in obtaining SR images. A variant of GAN, TripletGAN [27] demonstrated that a triplet loss setting will theoretically help the generator to converge to the given distribution. Inspired by TripletGAN, PGAN [28] has been proposed, which uses triplet loss to super-resolve medical images in a multistage manner.

The limitation of the majority of the work mentioned above is the use of artificially degraded training data, such as bicubic downsampling. The CNNs typically fail to generalise well on the real-world data, because real-world degradation is considerably different than bicubic downsampling (see Fig. 1). The supervised approaches need real LR-HR pairs in order to generalise to real-world data, which is challenging. For recovering real-world HR images, Cai et al. [6] introduced the RealSR dataset and a baseline network called Laplacian Pyramid-based Kernel Prediction Network (LP-KPN). Thereafter, several research works for SR have been conducted on the RealSR dataset, considering factors from real data into account [29–35].

Further, Cheng et al. suggested a residual network based on an encoder-decoder architecture for the real SR problem [30]. A coarse-to-fine approach was used by them, where lost information was gradually recovered and the effects of noise were reduced. By adopting an autoencoder-based loss function, a fractal residual network was proposed by Kwak et al. [35] to super-resolve real-world LR images. At the outset of network architecture, an inverse pixel shuffle was also proposed by them to minimise the training parameters. Du et al. [33] suggested an Orientation-Aware Deep Neural Network (OA-DNN) for recovering of images with high fidelity. It is made up of many Orientation Attention Modules (OAMs) which are designed for extracting orientation-aware features in different directions. Additionally, Xu and Li have presented SCAN, a spatial colour attention-based network for real SR [34]. Here, the attention module simultaneously exploits spectral and spatial dependencies present in colour images. In this direction, we provide a novel framework based on triplet loss in the manuscript inspired by [27] to enhance the perceptual quality of SR images on the realSR dataset.

Although there have been previous attempts to incorporate the triplet loss optimization for super-resolution such as PGAN [28], which progressively super-resolve the images in a multistage manner, it has to be noted that they are specifically targeted to medical images, and in addition, the LR images used are obtained through a known degradation (such as bicubic sampling) and blurring (Gaussian filtering). Thus, it fails to address real-world degradation. Using the triplet loss, the proposed patch-based discriminator can better distinguish between generated and high-resolution images, thereby improving the perceptual fidelity. To the best of our knowledge, the utilization of triplet loss to the real-world SISR problem has not been explored before. We, therefore, propose the new approach as explained in the upcoming section.

3   Proposed Method

Figure 2 shows the detailed training framework of our proposed method. The proposed supervised SR method expects the LR and its corresponding ground truth HR image as the input. It performs super-resolution on the LR image using the generator network, which is trained in a multi-loss setting using a fusion of losses namely content, perceptual, adversarial, and quality assessment. As depicted in Fig. 2, the content Loss is calculated as L_1 loss (pixel-based difference) between the generated(SR) and ground truth(HR) images. It assists the generator in preserving the content of ground truth HR. As the generator network is trained in an adversarial setting with the discriminator, we use a triplet-based GAN loss, which also boosts the stability of the learning. Apart from the GAN loss, we incorporate multi-layer perceptual loss, which is calculated as L_2 loss between the features of HR and SR, obtained from a pre-trained VGG network as suggested in SRGAN [13]. Moreover, we also use a quality assessment loss based on Mean Opinion Score (MOS) for improving the perceptual quality of generated images [22]. The validation of each setting in the framework is demonstrated in the ablation section later.

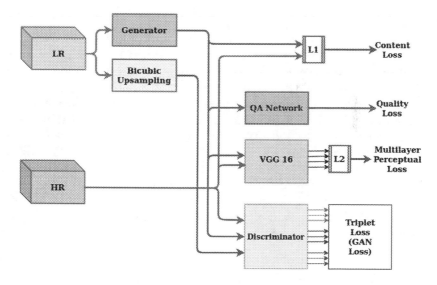

Fig. 2. The training framework of our proposed method - SRTGAN.

Generator Network (G): The design of generator network is shown in Fig. 3, which was published in [36]. The architecture can be divided into Feature Extraction (Low-level Information Extraction (LLIE), High-level Information Extraction (HLIE)) and Reconstruction (SR reconstruction (SRRec)) modules based on their functionality. The LLIE module is initially fed with LR input (I_{LR}) for extracting the low-level details (*i.e.*, I_l). It consists of a convolutional layer with kernel size 3 and 32 channels. This can be expressed mathematically as,

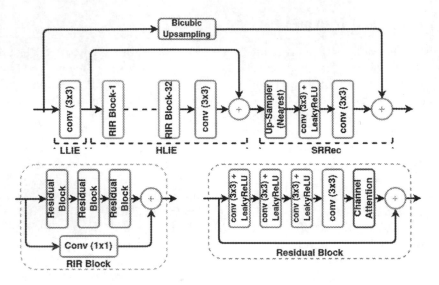

Fig. 3. Generator network [36].

$$I_l = f_{LLIE}(I_{LR}). \tag{1}$$

The edges and fine structural details present in the LR image are extracted by the HLIE module using the low-level information I_l. HLIE module comprises of 32 Residual-In-Residual (RIR) blocks, one 3×3 convolutional layer, and have one long skip connection. The long skip connection here stabilizes the network training [13,14,22,36]. Each RIR block is created using three residual blocks and a skip connection with a 1×1 convolutional layer. The Residual Block comprises of four 3×3 convolutional layers with a serially attached Channel Attention (CA) module. Using the statistical average of each channel, each channel is independently re-scaled via the CA module [20]. As depicted in Fig. 3, skip connections are also used in residual blocks, which aids in stabilizing the training of deeper networks and resolving the vanishing gradient problem. The output from HLIE module can be expressed as,

$$I_h = f_{HLIE}(I_l). \tag{2}$$

Now, feature maps with high-level information (i.e. I_h) are passed to the SR Reconstruction (SRRec) module, which comprises of 1 up-sampling block and 2 convolutional layers. This helps in mapping I_h to the required number of channels needed for output image (I_{SR}). This can be stated as follows:

$$I_{SR} = f_{REC}(I_h), \tag{3}$$

where the reconstruction function of the SRRec module is f_{REC}. The nearest neighbour is used to perform a $2\times$ upsampling with a 3×3 convolutional layer and 32 feature maps in each up-sampling block. Finally, a convolutional layer is used to map 32 channels into 3 channels of SR image in the generator network.

Discriminator (D) Network: We further use a PatchGAN [37] based discriminator network to distinguish foreground and background on a patch with scale of 70×70 pixels. The proposed architecture is shown in Fig. 4. It is designed by adhering to the recommendations made in the work of PatchGAN [37]. It consists of five convolutional layers with strided convolutions. After each convolution, the number of channels doubles, excluding the last output layer which has a single channel. The network uses a fixed stride of two except for the second last and last layer where the stride is set to 1. It is noted that a fixed kernel size of 4 is used for all layers throughout the discriminator network. Further, each convolutional layer except the output layer uses leaky ReLU activation and padding of size one. All intermediate convolutional layers except the first and last layer use Batch Normalisation.

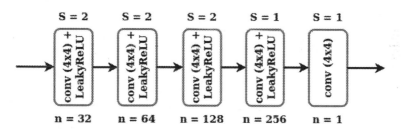

Fig. 4. Discriminator Network. Here, n stands for the number of channels, while S represents stride.

Quality Assessment (QA) Network: Inspired by [36], a novel quality-based score obtained from QA Network is employed which serves as a loss function in training. The design of QA network is shown in Fig. 5, which is inspired by the VGG. The addition of the QA loss in the overall optimization enhances the image quality based on human perception as the QA network is trained to mimic how humans rank images based on their quality. Instead of using a single path to feed input to the network, two paths have been employed in this case. To proceed forward, both of these features are subtracted. Each VGG block has two convolutional layers, the second of which uses a stride of 2 to reduce the spatial dimensions. The network uses Global Average Pooling (GAP) layer instead of flattening layer to minimize the trainable parameters. At fully connected layers, a drop-out technique is used to overcome the issue of over-fitting. The KADID-10K [38] dataset, consisting of $10,050$ images, was used to train the QA network. The dataset has been divided in 70%–10%–20% ratio for train-validate-test purposes respectively during the training process.

3.1 Loss Functions

As depicted in Fig. 2, the generator is trained using a fusion of content loss (pixel-wise L_1 loss), GAN loss (triplet-based), QA loss, and perceptual loss. Mathematically, we can describe the loss of generator by the following formula:

$$L^{gen} = \lambda_1 L_{content} + \lambda_2 L_{QA} + \lambda_3 L_{GAN}^G + \lambda_4 L_{perceptual}. \tag{4}$$

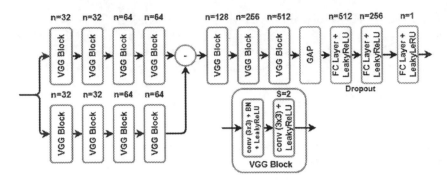

Fig. 5. The architecture of QA network [36].

The values of λ_1, λ_2, λ_3 and λ_4 are set empirically to 5, 2×10^{-7}, 1×10^{-1} and 5×10^{-1}, respectively.

The Discriminator network is trained using triplet-based GAN loss. This can be expressed as,

$$L^{disc} = \lambda_3 L_{GAN}^D \tag{5}$$

where λ_3 is emperically set to 1×10^{-1}.

Both L_{GAN}^G and L_{GAN}^D are defined in Eqs. 9 and 10 respectively.

The content loss in Eqs. 4 has been used to preserve the content of the ground truth, which is an L_1 loss between ground truth HR (i.e., I_{HR}) and generated image SR (i.e., I_{SR}), and same can be expressed as,

$$L_{content} = \sum^N \|G(I_{LR}) - I_{HR}\|_1, \tag{6}$$

where N denotes the batch size in training, and G represents the function of generator. $\sum^N [\cdot]$ denotes an average operation across all images in the mini-batch. The perceptual loss $L_{perceptual}$ is used here for improving the perceptual similarity of the generated image with respect to its ground truth, which can be expressed as,

$$L_{perceptual} = \sum^N \left[\sum_{i=1}^4 MSE(F_{HR}^i, F_{SR}^i) \right]. \tag{7}$$

Here, $MSE(a, b)$ represents Mean Square Error (MSE) between a and b, F^i: Normalised features taken from $layers[i]$ and $layers = [relu_{12}, relu_{22}, relu_{33}, relu_{43}]$. Here, $layers$ is the list of four layers of VGG-16 used for the calculation of perceptual loss [10]. Such loss is calculated as the MSE between the normalized feature representations of generated image (F_{SR}) and ground truth HR (F_{HR}) obtained from a pre-trained VGG-16 network. It is not dependent on low-level per-pixel information that leads to blurry results. Instead, it depends on the difference in high-level feature representations which helps to generate images of high perceptual quality. In addition, the idea of using multi-layer feature representations adds to its robustness. To further improve the quality of SR

Fig. 6. Comparison of background patch in LR and HR images.

images based on human perception, a Quality Assessment (QA) loss is also introduced. It rates the SR image on a scale of 1–5, with a higher value indicating better quality. This predicted value is used to calculate the QA loss i.e., L_{QA}, which is expressed as [36],

$$L_{QA} = \sum_{N} \left(5 - Q(I_{SR})\right), \tag{8}$$

where $Q(I_{SR})$ represents the quality score of SR image from the QA network.

The GAN loss used here is a triplet-based loss function to a patch-based discriminator.

An image can be simplified consisting of 2 parts, Background and Foreground; according to human perceptions, we rate images to be higher quality based on the foreground, which is the focus of the image. On the other hand, the background between LR and HR images is hard to differentiate as shown in Fig. 6. A background patch with a vanilla GAN would be similar to the discriminator perceptually, hence forcing the output for the same to be real/fake could lead to a high erroneous loss and cause instability and noise in training. However, in the case of foreground patches, the idea of vanilla GAN will work well. To solve this problem, we introduce the use of triplet loss: instead of forcing the discriminator output for HR and SR to be opposite labels, we calculate the loss using the relative output produced by the discriminator for HR, LR, and SR images. We formulate this as triplet loss optimization comprising of 3 variables - positive, negative and anchor. The distance between the anchor and the positive is minimised by the cost function, while the distance between the anchor and the negative is maximised. For the generator, the anchor is defined as the generated SR image (I_{SR}), the positive as the ground-truth HR image (I_{HR}), and the negative as the up-sampled LR input ($n(I_{LR})$), where n is the bicubic upsampling factor. The positive and negative are interchanged for training the discriminator. Thus, the triplet-based GAN losses for generator and discriminator can be defined as,

$$L_{GAN}^{G} = \sum_{N} \left[MSE(D(I_{SR}), D(I_{HR})) - MSE(D(I_{SR}), D(n(I_{LR}))) + 1\right] \tag{9}$$

$$L_{GAN}^{D} = \sum_{N} \left[MSE(D(I_{SR}), D(n(I_{LR}))) - MSE(D(I_{SR}), D(I_{HR})) + 1\right] \tag{10}$$

Here, $MSE(a, b)$ represents mean square error between a and b; n denotes upsampling factor. This triplet based GAN loss teaches the Generator to gen-

Fig. 7. Comparison of the results obtained through our proposed method-*SRTGAN* (with QA network and Triplet loss) Vs without incorporating QA Network or Triplet Loss on (A)-RealSR dataset [6] and (B)-DIV2KRK dataset [7]

erate sharp and high-resolution images by trying to converge SR embeddings $D(I_{SR})$ and HR embeddings $D(I_{HR})$ and diverge SR embeddings with LR embeddings $D(n(I_{LR}))$, which are obtained from the Discriminator. Simultaneously, it also trains the patch-based Discriminator to distinguish the generated SR image from the ground-truth HR. The background patch as discussed before is similar for LR and HR images. Applying this triplet-based GAN loss patchwise, improves the adversary as it allows the discriminator to better distinguish the main subject(foreground) of SR and HR images, which helps in generating images with better perceptual fidelity.

4   Experimental Results

4.1   Training Details

Using our proposed framework, we conduct supervised training on the RealSR dataset [6]. In this dataset, the focal length of a digital camera has been adjusted to collect LR-HR pairs of the same scene. To incrementally align the image pairs at various resolutions, an image registration method is developed. Our proposed network has been trained on 400 such images from the RealSR dataset and additionally it has been validated on 100 LR-HR image pairs provided in the same dataset. Finally, DIV2KRK [7] and test set of RealSR dataset [6] are employed for testing purposes. The LR images are subjected to several augmentations during the training phase, including horizontal flipping, rotation of $0°$ or $90°$, and cropping operations. The total trainable parameters of generator and discriminator networks are $3.7M$ and $2.7M$, respectively.

Additionally, we also employ QA network-based loss to enhance the quality of generated images. This method has been referenced from the work of [36]. Our proposed triplet loss optimization improves the visual appearance of the SR images to make them more realistic.

4.2 Ablation Study

We demonstrate the experimental support for incorporating the triplet loss and QA network in this section. Quantitative and Qualitative assessment conducted on the RealSR dataset [6], are shown in Table 1 and Fig. 7, respectively. Our method yields superior SR outcomes on both synthetic and real-world data (RealSR dataset). The proposed method with QA network and Triplet Loss performs better (see Table 1) when compared to the performance obtained using the framework without those modules. This is quantitatively evaluated on various distortion metrics like PSNR and SSIM and perceptual measures, such as LPIPS. The SR images produced using our proposed approach with QA network and Triplet Loss are also perceptually better when compared to without adding these modules, which is shown in Fig. 7. It has been observed that our method without QA Network generates blurry output and variation in the natural color of the image. Our framework when optimized using vanilla GAN loss(instead of triplet loss), closely resembles the colour as anticipated in the real world, but fails to sharpen the edges, causing blurring. The proposed method's advantage may be observed in its ability to produce SR images with an adequate level of sharpening around the edges and preserving the color-coding of the original image. Here, by observing Fig. 7, one may quickly determine the perceptual improvement from our proposed strategy.

Table 1. Quantitative evaluation of SRTGAN (with QA Network and Triplet Loss) Vs without incorporating these modules on the RealSR dataset [6].

Method	PSNR ↑	SSIM [17]↑	LPIPS [18]↓
w/o Triplet Loss (Vanilla GAN Loss)	25.879	0.72199	0.37095
w/o QA Network	16.126	0.39542	0.51217
Proposed	**26.47283**	**0.754585**	**0.283878**

Table 2. Quantitative evaluation of SRTGAN with other state-of-the-art SR methods on RealSR and DIV2KRK dataset

Method	PSNR ↑	SSIM [17] ↑	LPIPS [18] ↓	PSNR ↑	SSIM [17] ↑	LPIPS [18] ↓
	DIV2KRK [7] Dataset			RealSR [6] Dataset		
Bicubic	23.89	0.6478	0.5645	25.74	0.7413	0.4666
ZSSR [39]	24.05	0.6550	0.5257	25.83	0.7434	0.3503
KernelGAN [7]	24.76	0.6799	0.4980	24.09	0.7243	0.2981
DBPI [40]	24.92	0.7035	0.4039	22.36	0.6562	0.3106
DAN [41]	**26.07**	**0.7305**	0.4045	26.20	**0.7598**	0.4095
IKC [42]	25.41	0.7255	0.3977	25.60	0.7488	0.3188
SRResCGAN [15]	24.00	0.6497	0.5054	25.84	0.7459	0.3746
Proposed	24.17	0.6956	**0.3341**	**26.47**	0.7546	**0.2838**

4.3   Quantitative Analysis

The PSNR and SSIM values, which are the accepted measurements for the SR problem, are often estimated for comparison of the results between different approaches. These metrics, however, do not entirely justify the quality based on human perception. Therefore, we also estimate a full-reference perceptual quality assessment score known as LPIPS [18]. A low LPIPS score indicates a better visual quality.

The comparison of all three metrics on the DIV2KRK [7] and RealSR datasets [6] is presented in Table 2. On both datasets, SRTGAN outperforms other novel

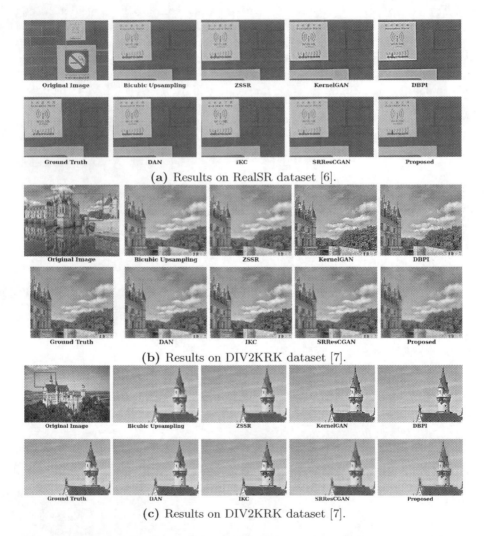

(a) Results on RealSR dataset [6].

(b) Results on DIV2KRK dataset [7].

(c) Results on DIV2KRK dataset [7].

Fig. 8. Qualitative evaluation of SRTGAN with other state-of-the-art methods on RealSR and DIV2KRK dataset

approaches on LPIPS metric, demonstrating the proposed method's superiority in terms of perceptual quality. Our proposed approach also performs superior to other methods on PSNR metric, whereas performs competitively in terms of SSIM, on the RealSR dataset [6]. SRTGAN also performs quite competitively in terms of PSNR and SSIM on the synthetic dataset - DIV2KRK [7]. The perceptual metric, LPIPS obtained using our proposed approach is significantly better for both datasets (see Table 2).

4.4 Qualitative Analysis

In this section, we show the efficacy of SRTGAN through visual inspection. We qualitatively evaluate the SR performance on one image of RealSR dataset (Fig. 8a) [6] and two sample images of DIV2KRK dataset (Fig. 8b and 8c) [7]. In addition, we also make comparison with other novel works such as KernelGAN [7], ZSSR [39], DBPI [40], DAN [41], IKC [42], and SRResCGAN [15]. These SR results demonstrate that SRTGAN significantly reduces the amount of noise in the SR image and improves image clarity in comparison to other novel methods. In addition, SRTGAN can produce colours similar to the ground truth, while competing methods like IKC and KernelGAN over-boosts the colours in the generated images.

Our proposed method - SRTGAN produces SR images of better quality and with fewer noise artifacts than existing state-of-the-art methods. The quantitative assessment of several quality metrics (see Table 2) and the perceptual quality acquired on various datasets (see Fig. 6c, 7 and 8c) support this conclusion.

5   Limitations

The proposed work obtains better results on real-world data; however, we note certain limitations as well. The network is stable only when fine-tuned for all the losses. As we can observe in Fig. 7, the removal of the QA loss leads to undesirable outputs. Thus, fine-tuning of each loss is an expensive process. Another limitation for using the current model is that the generator and discriminator are trained in a supervised manner and hence it requires true HR-LR image pairs which can be difficult to obtain as this will need the same image to be clicked by cameras of two different resolutions. However, our work can be easily extended to unsupervised approach, as the core idea of generative modeling is to treat such unsupervised problems in a supervised manner.

6   Conclusion

We have proposed an approach to the SISR problem based on TripletGAN that fuses the novel triplet loss and no-reference quality loss along with the other conventional losses. We further modify the design of discriminator to be a patch-based discriminator for improving image quality at the scale of local image patches. The triplet loss uses both high-resolution and low-resolution images and hence, it captures the essential information required in the SR image. Applying patch-wise triplet loss improves the adversary as it allows the discriminator to better distinguish the main subject(foreground) of SR and HR images, which helps in generating images with better perceptual fidelity. Through experiments, we have demonstrated that SRTGAN can super-resolve images by a factor of ×4 with improved perceptual quality than other competing methods.

References

1. Tai, Y., Yang, J., Liu, X.: Image super-resolution via deep recursive residual network. In: IEEE CVPR, vol. 1, no. 4 (2017)
2. Dong, C., Loy, C.C., He, K., Tang, X.: Image super-resolution using deep convolutional networks. IEEE TPAMI **38**(2), 295–307 (2016)
3. Tong, T., Li, G., Liu, X., Gao, Q.: Image super-resolution using dense skip connections. In: Proceedings of the IEEE ICCV, pp. 4799–4807 (2017)
4. Dong, C., Loy, C.C., Tang, X.: Accelerating the super-resolution convolutional neural network. In: ECCV, pp. 391–407, October 2016
5. Lim, B., Son, S., Kim, H., Nah, S., Lee, K.M.: Enhanced deep residual networks for single image super-resolutaion. In: IEEE CVPR Workshops, pp. 1132–1140 (2017)
6. Cai, J., Zeng, H., Yong, H., Cao, Z., Zhang, L.: Toward real-world single image super-resolution: a new benchmark and a new model. In: ICCV, pp. 3086–3095, October 2019
7. Bell-Kligler, S., Shocher, A., Irani, M.: Blind super-resolution kernel estimation using an internal-gan. In: NeurIPS, pp. 284–293 (2019)
8. Efrat, N., Glasner, D., Apartsin, A., Nadler, B., Levin, A.: Accurate blur models vs. image priors in single image super-resolution. In: ICCV, pp. 2832–2839 (2013)
9. Mathieu, M., Couprie, C., LeCun, Y.: Deep multi-scale video prediction beyond mean square error. In: 4th International Conference - ICLR 2016, January 2016
10. Johnson, J., Alahi, A., Fei-Fei, L.: Perceptual losses for real-time style transfer and super-resolution. In: Leibe, B., Matas, J., Sebe, N., Welling, M. (eds.) ECCV 2016. LNCS, vol. 9906, pp. 694–711. Springer, Cham (2016). https://doi.org/10.1007/978-3-319-46475-6_43
11. Dosovitskiy, A., Brox, T.: Generating images with perceptual similarity metrics based on deep networks. In: NeurIPS, ser. NIPS'16, pp. 658–666 (2016)
12. Bruna, J., Sprechmann, P., LeCun, Y.: Super-resolution with deep convolutional sufficient statistics, CoRR, vol. abs/1511.05666 (2016)
13. Ledig, C., Theis, L., Huszár, F., et al.: Photo-realistic single image super-resolution using a generative adversarial network. In: IEEE CVPR, pp. 4681–4690 (2017)
14. Ledig, C., Theis, L., Huszár, F., et al.: Photo-realistic single image super-resolution using a generative adversarial network. In: IEEE CVPR, pp. 4681–4690 (2017)
15. Muhammad Umer, R., Luca Foresti, G., Micheloni, C.: Deep generative adversarial residual convolutional networks for real-world super-resolution. In: IEEE CVPR Workshops, pp. 438–439 (2020)
16. Park, S.-J., Son, H., Cho, S., Hong, K.-S., Lee, S.: SRFeat: single image super-resolution with feature discrimination. In: Ferrari, V., Hebert, M., Sminchisescu, C., Weiss, Y. (eds.) ECCV 2018. LNCS, vol. 11220, pp. 455–471. Springer, Cham (2018). https://doi.org/10.1007/978-3-030-01270-0_27

17. Wang, Z., Bovik, A., Sheikh, H., Simoncelli, E.: Image quality assessment: from error visibility to structural similarity. IEEE TIP **13**(4), 600–612 (2004)
18. R. Zhang, P. Isola, A. A. Efros, E. Shechtman, and O. Wang, "The unreasonable effectiveness of deep features as a perceptual metric," in CVPR, 2018, pp. 586–595
19. Kim, J., Lee, J.K., Lee, K.M.: Accurate image super-resolution using very deep convolutional networks. In: 2016 IEEE CVPR, pp. 1646–1654, June 2016
20. Zhang, Y., Li, K., Li, K., Wang, L., Zhong, B., Fu, Y.: Image super-resolution using very deep residual channel attention networks. In: ECCV, pp. 286–301 (2018)
21. Li, Y., Agustsson, E., Gu, S., Timofte, R., Van Gool, L.: CARN: convolutional anchored regression network for fast and accurate single image super-resolution. In: Leal-Taixé, L., Roth, S. (eds.) ECCV 2018. LNCS, vol. 11133, pp. 166–181. Springer, Cham (2019). https://doi.org/10.1007/978-3-030-11021-5_11
22. Prajapati, K., et al.: Unsupervised single image super-resolution network (usisresnet) for real-world data using generative adversarial network. In: CVPR Workshops, June 2020
23. Zhang, Y., Tian, Y., Kong, Y., Zhong, B., Fu, Y.: Residual dense network for image super-resolution. In: IEEE CVPR, pp. 2472–2481 (2018)
24. Haris, M., Shakhnarovich, G., Ukita, N.: Deep back-projection networks for super-resolution. In: IEEE CVPR, pp. 1664–1673 (2018)
25. Zhao, H., Kong, X., He, J., Qiao, Yu., Dong, C.: Efficient image super-resolution using pixel attention. In: Bartoli, A., Fusiello, A. (eds.) ECCV 2020. LNCS, vol. 12537, pp. 56–72. Springer, Cham (2020). https://doi.org/10.1007/978-3-030-67070-2_3
26. Goodfellow, I., Pouget-Abadie, J., Mirza, M., et al.: Generative adversarial nets. In: Advances in NeurIPS 27, pp. 2672–2680 (2014)
27. Cao, G., Yang, Y., Lei, J., Jin, C., Liu, Y., Song, M.: Tripletgan: training generative model with triplet loss, CoRR, vol. abs/1711.05084 (2017). http://arxiv.org/abs/1711.05084
28. Mahapatra, D., Bozorgtabar, B.: Progressive generative adversarial networks for medical image super resolution, CoRR, vol. abs/1902.02144 (2019). http://arxiv.org/abs/1902.02144
29. Shi, Y., Zhong, H., Yang, Z., Yang, X., Lin, L.: Ddet: dual-path dynamic enhancement network for real-world image super-resolution. IEEE Signal Process. Lett. **27**, 481–485 (2020)
30. Cheng, G., Matsune, A., Li, Q., Zhu, L., Zang, H., Zhan, S.: Encoder-decoder residual network for real super-resolution. In: CVPR Workshops, June 2019
31. Feng, R., Gu, J., Qiao, Y., Dong, C.: Suppressing model overfitting for image super-resolution networks. In: CVPR Workshops, June 2019
32. Gao, S., Zhuang, X.: Multi-scale deep neural networks for real image super-resolution. In: The IEEE CVPR Workshops, June 2019
33. Du, C., Zewei, H., Anshun, S., et al.: Orientation-aware deep neural network for real image super-resolution. In: The IEEE CVPR Workshops, June 2019
34. Xu, X., Li, X.: Scan: spatial color attention networks for real single image super-resolution. In: The IEEE CVPR Workshops, June 2019
35. Kwak, J., Son, D.: Fractal residual network and solutions for real super-resolution. In: The IEEE CVPR Workshops, June 2019
36. Prajapati, K., Chudasama, V., Patel, H., Upla, K., Raja, K., Raghavendra, R., Busch, C.: Unsupervised real-world super-resolution using variational auto-encoder and generative adversarial. Network **02**, 703–718 (2021)
37. Isola, P., Zhu, J.-Y., Zhou, T., Efros, A.A.: Image-to-image translation with conditional adversarial networks. In: IEEE CVPR 2017, pp. 5967–5976 (2017)

38. Lin, H., Hosu, V., Saupe, D.: Kadid-10k: a large-scale artificially distorted iqa database. In: Eleventh International Conference on QoMEX 2019, pp. 1–3 (2019)
39. Shocher, A., Cohen, N., Irani, M.: Zero-shot super-resolution using deep internal learning. In: IEEE/CVF Conference on CVPR 2018, pp. 3118–3126 (2018)
40. Kim, J., Jung, C., Kim, C.: Dual back-projection-based internal learning for blind super-resolution. In: IEEE Signal Process Lett, vol. 27, pp. 1190–1194 (2020)
41. Luo, Z., Huang, Y., Li, L., Wang, S., Tan, T.: Unfolding the alternating optimization for blind super resolution. In: Advances in NeurIPS, vol. 33 (2020)
42. Gu, J., Lu, H., Zuo, W., Dong, C.: Blind super-resolution with iterative kernel correction. In: IEEE CVPR, June 2019, pp. 1604–1613

Machine Learning Based Webcasting Analytics for Indian Elections - Reflections on Deployment

Aditi Saxena and Sharad Sinha[(✉)]

Indian Institute of Technology Goa, Ponda 403401, India
{aditi.saxena.18001,sharad}@iitgoa.ac.in

Abstract. India is the largest democracy in the world. Elections play an irreplaceable role in reverberating the voice of its citizens in the governing institutions of this country. To safeguard the power vested in the people, it is essential that the voting process is safe, fair and transparent. This can be very well ensured by effective surveillance of polling activities and analysis of the real-time data that can be gathered from the polling stations. The scattered and widespread locations of the polling stations also requires proper synchronization and organization of the data collection and analysis processes. This paper presents a machine learning-based web analytics system specifically designed to monitor polling stations during the Goa State Assembly elections in 2022. The system accepts as input the CCTV video feeds generated by Internet Protocol (IP) cameras from several polling centres and processes it optimally to produce and transmit analytical information in real-time to the command and control centre. We also highlight the practical challenges faced in deploying this system and their resolution. The successful implementation of this system for the Goa Assembly Elections 2022, first of its kind in India, demonstrates the effectiveness and reliability of this approach.

Keywords: Video Surveillance · Machine Learning · Computer Vision

1 Introduction

Computer Vision is concerned with extracting information from digital images and videos. Great strides have been achieved in posing and solving complex computer vision problems like object detection, motion tracking, action recognition and human pose estimation. However, this list is not exhaustive. These computer vision tasks can find many applications in digital governance. We discuss one such instance of digital governance, where real-time monitoring of polling stations using machine learning-based analytics on real-time streaming video feeds from two hundred cameras, was carried out.

Over the past years, neural network-based machine learning algorithms have been proposed for several tasks, including the computer vision tasks listed above. Among the most prominent factors that contributed to the massive boost in

D. Gupta et al. (Eds.): CVIP 2022, CCIS 1777, pp. 47–57, 2023.
https://doi.org/10.1007/978-3-031-31417-9_4

such approaches is the existence of large, high-quality, publicly available labelled datasets, along with the availability of parallel GPU computing, which enabled the transition from CPU-based to GPU-based training, thus allowing significant acceleration in the training of machine learning and deep learning models [1].

Convolutional and Deep Neural Networks (CNN/DNN) have been highly successful in computer vision tasks like object detection, vision-based robotics and autonomous vehicles. Every layer of a CNN transforms the input image or data to an output image based on neuron activation functions. A series of such transformations results in a mapping of the input data to a 1D feature vector [1]. Some of the most well-known image processing neural networks like You Only Look Once (YOLO) [2], Region-based Convolutional Neural Network (R-CNN) [3], and Single Shot MultiBox Detector (SSD) [4] have Convolutional Neural Networks at their core.

When it comes to interpreting video sequences, object tracking plays an essential role. Tagging an object and tracing its path across frames of a video is indeed a challenging task. In recent times, kernel-based approaches or encoder-decoder networks have been proposed. The most well-performing algorithms include DeepSORT [5], FairMOT [6] and TransMOT [7].

Because of its variety of applications, locating people in images and video frames has been a prominent field of active research in computer vision. In images, such detection can be helpful in subsequent identification, classification and search. While in video sequences, detection followed by object tracking can help in monitoring crowds in public places and thus in effective crowd management. Human detection also finds its application in a range of other applications like autonomous vehicles, human activity recognition and many more [8].

The elections in a democratic country like India pose one such problem statement for the computer vision domain. Live streaming of activities at a polling station on the day of elections is mandated to ensure transparency, safety and security during the elections. Live streaming generates a vast amount of data, which can be utilized to draw valuable insights and facilitate smoother electoral process management. For the system presented in this paper, we aimed at two principal tasks. First, we had to accurately detect and track people in the CCTV video feeds of polling stations to record crowd statistics. Secondly, we had to ensure that the processing and transmitting the processed data happened in real-time to make the system practical for monitoring purposes from a command and control center.

The significant contributions of this proposed and field-tested system are as follows:

- Drawing valuable insights without human error from the real-time surveillance data of hundred scattered polling stations for real-time monitoring from a command and control centre.
- Combining state-of-the-art machine learning models for human detection and tracking to ensure a high prediction accuracy.
- Incorporating parallelism and multithreading to make the system scalable to handle several hundred video feeds simultaneously.

– Identification and solutions to real-time challenges due to data transmission affected by network issues through Real Time Streaming Protocol (RTSP), REST APIs and interval based frame processing.

The paper is organized as follows. We discuss the work previously done in the field of video surveillance using machine learning in Sect. 2, our proposed methodology in Sect. 3 with its implementation details in Sect. 4 and the outcome of its deployment during the state assembly elections of Goa in 2022 in Sect. 4. We specifically discuss the practical challenges of deployment and how we addressed them in Subsect. 4.2.

2   Related Work

People detection and tracking has been a sought after mechanism to monitor crowded public places. The advent of machine and deep learning in computer vision has also propelled the research in applications of this mechanism.

Dahlan et al. [9] have applied video analytics using deep learning for real-time social distance monitoring in a railway station, prompted by the recent COVID-19 pandemic. They build their architecture using YOLOv4 [2] and DeepSORT [5] models and achieve an accuracy of 96.5% on people tracking with actual implementation in Bandung railway station.

Shee Thoo et al. [24] produce a robust real-time CCTV monitoring system to aid security guards, using only input CCTV video footage, an object detection machine learning model and a tracking algorithm. They investigate which object tracking algorithm is best for the task benchmarked on a labelled test dataset and present an elaborate study of metrics.

Ahmed et al. [10] propose a real-time person-tracking system for intelligent video surveillance based on the latest SiamMask network. This approach uses video from an overhead perspective and performs segmentation of people in the frame, in contrast to our approach, which works for a general CCTV angle and uses object detection.

Zhou [11] puts forth a systematic research framework of a video surveillance system, including people detection, tracking and person re-identification using deep learning algorithms. The paper extensively discusses the recent deep learning-based algorithms and presents a comparative study.

Lei et al. [25] proposes a pedestrian detection mechanism in Intelligent Video Monitoring System using a faster and lighter YOLO-Y algorithm. They achieve enhanced accuracy. However, occlusions and redundant counting pose a challenge in absence of object tracking.

Many algorithms for human detection and tracking also use varied input forms. Portmann et al. [12] use aerial thermal views, Liciotti et al. [26] do the same using an RGB-D camera in a top-view configuration, and Munoz-Salinas et al. [13] use stereo vision and colour using Kalman Filters. These applications are primarily dominant in the field of robotics which involves sensor data.

3   Proposed Methodology

This section proposes a machine learning-based solution for the chosen problem of tracking the number of people at polling stations. The solution has been split into six broad components, which, when pieced together, give us the resultant application. We detail each component individually and how they are linked with each other to construct the end-to-end architecture of the deployed system. The major modules of the systems are as follows.

- A cloud server based, real-time, video processing application
- Receive IP camera video streams using the Real-Time Streaming Protocol (RTSP) [14]
- Detect and count the number of people in the room using the YOLOv5 object detection algorithm
- Track the people to avoid redundancy using the DeepSORT algorithm
- Process multiple streams in parallel using Multithreading
- Transmit the processed data values using REST API to a command and control centre

3.1   Real Time Streaming Protocol (RTSP)

The Real-time Streaming Protocol (RTSP) [14] establishes and controls single or several time-synchronized streams of continuous media, such as audio and video that may be transmitted through internet protocol-enabled devices. The streams controlled by RTSP may use RTP [15] or any other transport mechanism. The protocol is similar in syntax and operation to HTTP [16] so that extension mechanisms to HTTP can, in most cases, also be added to RTSP. We use RTSP as the medium to receive our input streams in the cloud-based processing server. The application reads the RTSP links of all the target cameras from a text file and reads the frames using OpenCV. It then forwards the frames to a machine learning model for necessary analysis.

3.2   You Look Only Once (YOLO)

YOLO, an acronym for 'You only look once', is a class of object detection algorithms that divides images into a grid system. Each cell in the grid is responsible for detecting objects within itself. YOLO is one of the most famous object detection algorithms due to its speed and accuracy and has various versions like YOLOv3, YOLOv4 [17] etc. In our developed system, we use YOLOv5 (v6.0/6.1). YOLOv5 (v6.0/6.1) consists of CSP-Darknet53 as the backbone, which extracts essential features from the given input image. SPPF and New CSP-PAN form the neck, which generates feature pyramids that help models to generalize well on object scaling and YOLOv3 Head as the head of the mode, which performs the final detection task. Interested readers are referred to [18] to understand the architectural details of YOLOv5 (Fig. 1).

A sample output of YOLOv5 object detection on an image of the outside of a polling booth can be seen in Fig. 2. As we can see, the algorithms can accurately detect and count the people visible in the frame.

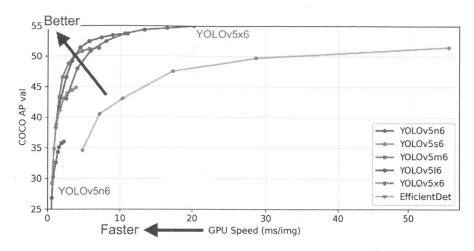

Fig. 1. Performance Metrics of YOLOv5 Source: https://github.com/ultralytics/yolov5

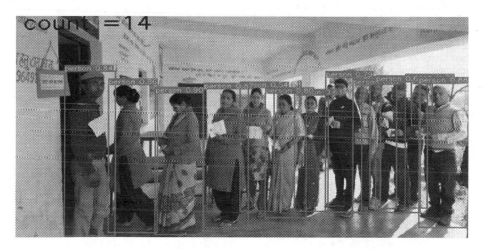

Fig. 2. Sample detection output using YOLOv5 on an image of a polling station

3.3   DeepSORT Tracking Framework

DeepSORT (Simple Online and Realtime Tracking) is a kernel-based state-of-the-art multi-object tracking framework. The algorithm accepts as input the bounding boxes from the object detection YOLOv5 algorithm. Next, it employs Kalman Filters [22] for the path estimation and Hungarian assignment [21] for target association and labelling of the detections. Finally, it tracks the objects during their lifecycle, i.e. the time between them entering and moving out of the video frame [5]. Object tracking is essential for our system to combat the occlusion of people by objects across video frames. Kalman filters ensure that a person is not added to the count multiple times if he disappears out of the view for some time without moving out of the frame view. Readers may refer to [19] for a discussion on the architecture of DeepSORT. Having processed the video through this stage, we get the headcount of people at each timestamp.

3.4 Multithreading for Enhancing Execution Speed

Multithreading is a program execution model that allows multiple threads to be created within a process. These threads execute independently but concurrently share process resources. On the cloud-based server, having initialized the weights and parameters of the YOLOv5 and DeepSORT algorithms in the scope of the process, each video stream is processed using the same parameters on a separate thread. Each thread is also responsible for transmitting the resultant data values from its respective video stream using REST API.

3.5 REST APIs for Analytics Data Transfer

REST (Representational State Transfer) APIs are web APIs which follow the REST constraints, which define how applications can connect and communicate with each other. REST APIs communicate over HTTP requests. After all the stages are complete in the processing server, the data values generated, namely the headcount of people in a frame, the timestamp of the frame and the camera ID, are relayed to the visualization server using the POST request. This method ensures fast and reliable data transfer.

The complete architecture of the deployed system is shown in Fig. 3.

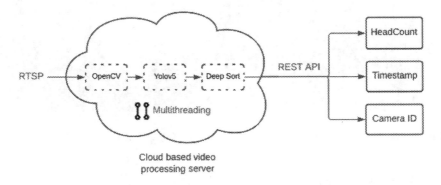

Fig. 3. System architecture of the developed cloud-based application

4   Deployment and Results

In this section, we will highlight the deployment details of the system. As a proof of concept, the proposed system was deployed in the Goa Assembly Election 2022. The system was designed to handle 200 video feeds, coming from 100 polling stations scattered across Goa, in parallel and process them in real time.

4.1   System Architecture

The input to the system was provided by 200 IP cameras in 100 polling stations spread across the state of Goa. The application was deployed on 10 EC2 GPU instances with Tesla T4 GPU and CUDA [23] version 11.6 provided by Amazon Web Services (AWS), with each GPU handling 20 streams using multithreading and CUDA. A stable internet connection in these polling stations was ensured, and the Real-Time Streaming Protocol (RTSP) was used for transmitting video feed from each IP camera to the server. The frames were then processed using YOLOv5 and DeepSORT algorithms to yield the headcount of the number of people visible at a specific timestamp. The processed information was then sent to the visualization server using the REST API POST request. Figure 4 shows a detailed view of the complete end-to-end architecture.

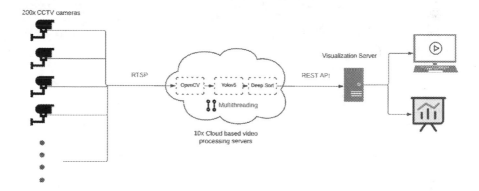

Fig. 4. Complete end to end architecture of the application

The visualization server displayed the result on an integrated portal in the format shown in Fig. 5 using OpenCV image processing. Figure 5 shows images from test video feeds, not the actual polling day video feeds. The actual polling day video feeds cannot be shown for confidentiality reasons. The bounding boxes around individuals, usually seen in object detection-related images, were not drawn in the designed system to reduce the transmission bandwidth from the visualization server. The data on the visualization server was accessed through a browser-based visualization software deployed in the command and control centre by a third party.

Fig. 5. A screenshot of the visualization portal with the resultant headcount on test video feeds

Load statistics of all the servers are shown in Table 1. As can be seen, the system is not utilizing all the GPU resources to their maximum capacity. More threads and video streams can be added per server. Each server can handle 20–22 streams parallel without reducing the accuracy and speed of processing. Rigorous load testing was not done due to the tight development period.

Table 1. Load statistics of the GPU servers

S.no.	No. of Threads	GPU Memory Usage (out of 15360 MiB)	GPU Utilization
1	22	5317 MiB	15%
2	22	5417 MiB	10%
3	23	5325 MiB	19%
4	22	4744 MiB	3%
5	22	5393 MiB	34%
6	22	4766 MiB	27%
7	22	5166 MiB	8%
8	22	4837 MiB	22%
9	20	4846 MiB	36%
10	22	5190 MiB	36%

4.2 Practical Challenges

Real-Time Processing and Frame Freeze: For monitoring and surveillance, the processed output must be updated in real-time [20]. However, if all the video frames go through the entire processing pipeline, the output FPS (Frames Per Second) is way lower than the input FPS. During deployment, we faced the same issue, where the output values (number of people i.e. headcount) were updated after a long interval though the headcount had changed based on the machine learning model. To deal with this issue, we modified the system to process every 15th frame at 30 FPS input. This led to the proposed system having to process just two frames per second instead of 30 without affecting the accuracy of the result since it is practically impossible for people to move that fast in a frame.

Unstable Internet and Reconnection: In a real-world scenario, it is very probable for the internet/network connection to falter midway while the cameras are transmitting the video frames via RTSP or to send corrupt blank frames. In this situation, the cameras get disconnected from the system even after the internet/network connection has been restored. This is a significant issue as it adversely affects real-time monitoring. To resolve this issue, we added checks to the network connection code using OpenCV to attempt reconnection to the camera every 15 s in case of receiving a blank frame or finding a disconnection.

Accuracy and Camera Resolution: The resolution of the frames affects the accuracy of the detection which in turn affects the headcount. Hence, after several trials and errors, we set the resolution to 1920×1080 full HD, which met our accuracy requirements.

5 Conclusion and Future Work

In this paper, we discussed a web-based machine learning-based video analytics system deployed to monitor polling stations. The implementation details of our developed system, the results and load statistics of its deployment and its different optimization approaches based on real-world challenges have also been presented. The successful implementation of the system for 200 cameras in 100 polling stations during the Goa Assembly Elections 2022 proves its effectiveness and reliability to be deployed on a large scale with sufficient real-time accuracy. With minor additions, the system can be used in elections in every part of our country and contribute to their smooth conduct. A good understanding of the underlying machine learning models forming part of the architecture and application-based modification can be helpful in further boosting the performance and flexibility of the system.

The architecture performs human detection and tracking in real-time using machine learning. With modifications, it can be applied to various settings apart from elections. Other features like social distancing can also be incorporated into the existing system. The output statistics can also be used to manage the crowd within the target institutions effectively. Rigorous load testing can also be carried out to study the tradeoff between cost and system performance.

Acknowledgement. The authors acknowledge the support provided by the Election Commission of India (ECI) and the officers from the Office of Chief Electoral Officer (CEO), Goa, especially Shri Kunal, IAS, CEO Goa and Praveen Volvotkar, Nodal Officer (IT) and Joint Director, Department of Information Technology, Goa in piloting the proposed system.

References

1. Voulodimos, A., Doulamis, N., Doulamis, A., Protopapadakis, E.: Deep learning for computer vision: a brief review. Computational Intelligence and Neuroscience 2018 (2018)
2. Redmon, J., Divvala, S., Girshick, R., Farhadi, A.: You only look once: unified, real-time object detection. In: Proceedings of the IEEE Conference on Computer Vision and Pattern Recognition, pp. 779–788, IEEE (2016)
3. Girshick, R., Donahue, J., Darrell, T., Malik, J.: Rich feature hierarchies for accurate object detection and semantic segmentation. In: Proceedings of the IEEE Conference on Computer Vision and Pattern Recognition, pp. 580–587. IEEE (2014)
4. Liu, W., Anguelov, D., Erhan, D., Szegedy, C., Reed, S., Fu, C.-Y., Berg, A.C.: SSD: single shot MultiBox detector. In: Leibe, B., Matas, J., Sebe, N., Welling, M. (eds.) ECCV 2016. LNCS, vol. 9905, pp. 21–37. Springer, Cham (2016). https://doi.org/10.1007/978-3-319-46448-0_2
5. Wojke, N., Bewley, A., Paulus, D.: Simple online and real-time tracking with a deep association metric. In: IEEE International Conference on Image Processing (ICIP), pp. 3645–3649. IEEE (2017)
6. Zhang, Y., Wang, C., Wang, X., Zeng, W., Liu, W.: FairMOT: on the fairness of detection and re-identification in multiple object tracking. Int. J. Comput. Vision **129**(11), 3069–3087 (2021). https://doi.org/10.1007/s11263-021-01513-4
7. Chu, P., Wang, J., You, Q., Ling, H., Liu, Z.: Transmot: spatial-temporal graph transformer for multiple object tracking. arXiv preprint arXiv:2104.00194 (2021)
8. Nguyen, D.T., Wanqing, L., Ogunbona, P.O.: Human detection from images and videos: a survey. Pattern Recogn. **51**, 148–175 (2016)
9. Dahlan, I.A., Putra, M.B.G., Supangkat, S.H., Hidayat, F., Lubis, F.F., Hamami, F.: Real-time passenger social distance monitoring with video analytics using deep learning in railway station. Indonesian J. Electr. Eng. Comput. Sci. **26**(2), 773–784 (2022)
10. Ahmed, I., Jeon, G.: A real-time person tracking system based on SiamMask network for intelligent video surveillance. J. Real-Time Image Proc. **18**(5), 1803–1814 (2021). https://doi.org/10.1007/s11554-021-01144-5
11. Zhou, Y.: Deep learning based people detection, tracking and re-identification in intelligent video surveillance system. In: International Conference on Computing and Data Science (CDS), pp. 443–447. IEEE (2020)
12. Portmann, J., Lynen, S., Chli, M., Siegwart, R.: People detection and tracking from aerial thermal views. In: IEEE International Conference on Robotics and Automation (ICRA), pp. 1794–1800. IEEE (2014)
13. Muñoz-Salinas, R., Aguirre, E., García-Silvente, M.: People detection and tracking using stereo vision and color. Image Vis. Comput. **25**(6), 995–1007 (2007)

14. Schulzrinne, H., Rao, A., Lanphier, R.: RFC2326: Real time streaming protocol (RTSP). RFC Editor, USA (1998)
15. Schulzrinne, H., Casner, S., Frederick, R., Jacobson, V.: RFC3550: RTP: a transport protocol for real-time applications. RFC Editor, USA (2003)
16. Berners-Lee, T., Fielding, R., Frystyk, H.: RFC1945: Hypertext Transfer Protocol - HTTP/1.0. RFC Editor, USA (1996)
17. Bochkovskiy, A., Chien-Yao, W., Hong-Yuan Mark, L.: Yolov4: optimal speed and accuracy of object detection. arXiv preprint arXiv:2004.10934 (2020)
18. YOLOv5 Github. https://github.com/ultralytics/yolov5. Accessed 13 July 2022
19. Parico, A.I.B., Ahmad, T.: Real Time Pear Fruit Detection and Counting Using YOLOv4 Models and Deep SORT. Sensors **21**(14) (2021). https://doi.org/10.3390/s21144803
20. Held, D., Thrun, S., Savarese, S.: Learning to track at 100 FPS with deep regression networks. In: Leibe, B., Matas, J., Sebe, N., Welling, M. (eds.) ECCV 2016. LNCS, vol. 9905, pp. 749–765. Springer, Cham (2016). https://doi.org/10.1007/978-3-319-46448-0_45
21. Kuhn, H.W.: The Hungarian method for the assignment problem. Naval Res. Logistics Quarterly **2**, 83–97 (1955). https://doi.org/10.1002/nav.3800020109
22. Welch, G., Bishop, G.: An introduction to the Kalman filter. SIGGRAPH 2001, Course 8, Los Angeles (2001)
23. Kirk, D.: NVIDIA CUDA software and GPU parallel computing architecture. In: Proceedings of the 6th International Symposium on Memory Management, pp. 103–104, ACM (1997)
24. Shee Thoo, S.J.H.: Visual recognition using artificial intelligence (person detection and tracking using artificial intelligence). Final Year Project (FYP), Nanyang Technological University, Singapore (2022)
25. Lei, Y.A.N.G., Shao-yun, W.A.N.G., Li-ran, L.I.U., Yong-fu, G.O.N.G.: A pedestrian detection method in intelligent video monitoring system. Comput. Modernization **11**, 69 (2019)
26. Liciotti, D., Paolanti, M., Frontoni, E., Zingaretti, P.: People detection and tracking from an RGB-D camera in top-view configuration: review of challenges and applications. In: Battiato, S., Farinella, G.M., Leo, M., Gallo, G. (eds.) ICIAP 2017. LNCS, vol. 10590, pp. 207–218. Springer, Cham (2017). https://doi.org/10.1007/978-3-319-70742-6_20

Real-Time Plant Species Recognition Using Non-averaged DenseNet-169 Deep Learning Paradigm

V. Sathiesh Kumar[1]($\boxtimes$) [iD] and S. Anubha Pearline[2] [iD]

[1] Department of Electronics Engineering, MIT Campus, Anna University, Chennai, India
sathieshkumar@annauniv.edu
[2] Department of Computer Science Engineering, SRM Institute of Science and Technology, Chennai, India
anubhapearl@gmail.com

Abstract. Real-time plant species recognition under unconstrained environment (viewpoint variation, changing background, scale variation, illumination changes etc.) is a challenging and time-consuming process. In this paper, a non-averaged DenseNet-169 (NADenseNet-169) CNN architecture is proposed and demonstrated to perform real-time plant species recognition. The architecture is evaluated on two datasets namely, Flavia (Standard) and Leaf-12 (custom created). The hyperparameters (optimizers, learning rate) are optimized to achieve higher performance metrics with lower computation time. From the experimental investigation, it is observed that Adam optimizer with a learning rate of 0.0001 (Batch size of 32) resulted in obtaining higher performance metrics. In case of Flavia dataset, an accuracy of 98.58% is obtained with a computational time of 3.53 s. For Leaf-12 dataset, an accuracy of 99% is obtained with a computational time of 4.45 s. The model trained on Leaf-12 dataset performed better in identifying the plant species under unconstrained environment.

Keywords: Plant species recognition · Deep learning architectures · Transfer Learning · DenseNet architecture

1 Introduction

Real-time plant species recognition through computer vision is challenging, considering the large diversity in plant species [1]. Also, the recognition accuracy is significantly affected by many factors such as camera viewpoint variation or changes in object orientation, scale changes, illumination variation, structure of leaf (simple or compound leaf), color variation due to aging or seasonal changes, arrangement of leaf in the stem and cluttered background. Conventional methods involve complex processes such as preprocessing of the input data, segmentation or region selection, feature extraction and classification. This method results in

D. Gupta et al. (Eds.): CVIP 2022, CCIS 1777, pp. 58–72, 2023.
https://doi.org/10.1007/978-3-031-31417-9_5

achieving moderate prediction accuracy with higher computation time. Introduction of deep learning method in plant species recognition, resulted in obtaining the state-of-the-art performance metrics. The training time required by the deep learning model is on the higher side when compared with the conventional method. But, the required computation time on test data by the deep learning model is lesser. Hence, utilizing the trained deep learning model in real-time scenario helps in recognizing the plant species efficiently and at a faster rate.

In recent years, pre-trained deep learning models are heavily used to recognize the plant species [2–10]. It minimizes the requirement of utilizing the high-end computing resources for implementing the deep learning-based algorithms. Among several deep learning architectures [11], the DenseNet architecture has gained wider attention due to its strong gradient flow, more diversified features, parameter and computational efficiency. It is used in different applications such as monocular depth estimation [12], remote hyperspectral sensing [13], spotting the keywords [14], Alzheimer's disease identification [15], classifying the lung diseases [16], classification of Cervical cells [17] and Cardiac phase detection [18].

In this paper, the non-averaged DenseNet-169 Convolutional Neural Network (NADenseNet-169) model is proposed and demonstrated to perform real-time plant species recognition in unconstrained environment. Also, the optimization of model hyperparameters are carried out to obtain higher performance metrics.

2 Related Works

Literatures related to the two approaches (Conventional method and Deep learning method) in the context of plant species recognition is described in the following subsections.

2.1 Conventional Methods

In this method, the input dataset images are preprocessed (resizing, contrast enhancement, histogram equalization, noise removal, blurring, sharpening etc.) and segmented (to obtain the region of interest). From the selected region, the features are extracted using image descriptors or feature descriptors. Some of the vital features extracted from the input image are shape, texture and colour features. Later, the extracted features are used in the training cum test process of the plant species recognition system.

Kheirkhah et al. [2] introduced an approach to perform the plant species recognition that involved the GIST technique. The texture feature is extracted using the GIST technique. PCA method is used as a dimensionality reduction technique. The selected features are classified using Patternnet Neural Network, k-Nearest Neighbor (k-NN), and Support Vector Machine (SVM). Wang et al. [3] presented a Maximum Gap Local Line Pattern method to perform feature extraction. Support vector machine is used to classify the extracted features. Zhang et al. [4] integrated the Sparse Representation (SR) method with the Singular Value Decomposition (SVD) technique to carry out classification of plant species.

Anubha et al. [5] studied the performance of plant species recognition system using the conventional and deep learning approaches. In conventional method, Local Binary Pattern (LBP), Haralick textures, Hu moments and Color channel statistics methods are used to extract the features from the input data. For deep learning methods, the pre-trained models (VGG-16, VGG-19, Inception-V3, Inception ResNet-V2) are used in the process of feature extraction. Machine learning classifiers (Linear Discriminant Analysis, Logistic Regression, k-Nearest Neighbor, Classification and Regression Tree, Bagging Classifier and Random Forest) are used in both approaches to recognize the plant species. The authors reported that the implementation of plant species recognition using deep learning method resulted in obtaining higher performance metrics compared to conventional methods.

2.2 Deep Learning Methods

Wang et al. [3] demonstrated a plant species recognition system by constructing a Siamese Network involving two parallel Inception Convolutional Neural Networks. It is based on few-shot learning technique. Hu et al. [19] demonstrated a Multi-Scale Fusion Convolutional Neural Network in relation to plant species recognition. In this network, the multi-scaled images are fed as an input to the convolution layers. Then, the output feature maps from the convolution layers are merged.

Tan et al. [16] proposed a D-Leaf CNN model to accomplish plant species recognition. The model is used as a feature extractor. Then, the features are classified using different classifiers (SVM, Artificial Neural Network (ANN), k-NN, Naïve-Bayes (NB) and CNN). Lee et al. [6] proposed a multi-organ classification using Hybrid Generic Organ Convolutional Neural Network (HGO-CNN) and Plant-StructNet architectures. Zhu et al. [20] treated the task of plant species recognition as an object detection problem. The authors utilized the Faster Region-CNN Inception-V2 model to detect and classify the plant species. Inception-V2 model is used as a feature extractor. He et al. [21] proposed a bi-channel model to perform plant species recognition. It consists of two pre-trained CNNs, namely, VGG-16 and SqueezeNet architectures.

Younis et al. [22] suggested the usage of modified ResNet architecture to classify the herbarium specimens. Ghazi et al. [8] performed a fusion of pre-trained GoogleNet and VGG architectures. It is done to improve the performance of the plant species recognition system. Barre et al. [9] introduced a LeafNet CNN architecture to do the task of plant recognition. Atabay [10] demonstrated the usage of custom CNN model with Exponential Linear Unit (ELU) as the activation function.

Based on the literature survey, it is observed that a significant number of works on plant species recognition has been reported. Two major approaches are followed. They are conventional method and deep learning method. Conventional methods are not able to achieve high accuracy in prediction with lower computation time (on test data). Whereas, the pre-trained deep learning models are able to attain higher performance metrics with lower computation time (test data). It is also observed that the models reported in literatures tend to perform well on standard datasets, but it is not suitable to perform real-time plant species recognition. This is mainly attributed to the dataset used in the training process. Most of the dataset does not include the images with different challenges (Scale variation, Illumination changes, Variation in camera viewpoint, Changes in object orientation, Structure of leaf - Simple leaf and Compound leaf, leaf arrangement in stem, Leaf color changes due to aging and seasonal variation, cluttered backgrounds). Hence, it becomes necessary to develop a real-time plant species recognition model with high efficiency in prediction and lower computation time.

In this paper, the real-time plant species recognition is performed using a modified version of pre-trained DenseNet-169 CNN model. To support real-time plant species recognition, a new dataset named Leaf-12 is created. The dataset includes leaf images with different scenarios such as scale variation, illumination changes, object orientation variation, different camera view point, color variation due to aging or seasonal condition, structure of leaf - simple leaf and compound leaf, arrangement of leaf in the stem and varying background. Also, the optimization of model hyperparameters are carried out to improve the performance of the recognition system.

3 Methodology

Plant species recognition is carried out using a Non-Averaged DenseNet-169 (NADenseNet-169) CNN model. The model is evaluated using two datasets namely, Flavia [23] and custom created Leaf-12.

3.1 Datasets

Flavia is a standard dataset consisting of 32 plant species as shown in Fig. 1. It is an imbalanced dataset with a number of images ranging from 50 to 77 images/class. The under-sampling technique is exploited for balancing the dataset (an equal number of images per class). Hence, 50 images/class is selected in the training cum test process of the NADenseNet-169 model.

Leaf-12 is a real-time custom created dataset containing twelve Indian plant species as shown in Fig. 2. The dataset images are captured under varying lighting condition, object orientation, camera viewpoint, scale variation, different structure of leaf- simple leaf and compound leaf, arrangement of leaf with stem, and different color background. The leaf-12 dataset contains 320 images per class.

3.2 Preprocessing of Dataset Images

The leaf images from the datasets (Flavia, Leaf-12) are resized to 300×300 pixels by maintaining the aspect ratio. Further, using the nearest interpolation method the images are resized to 100×100 pixels. Also, the pixel values in the images are normalized.

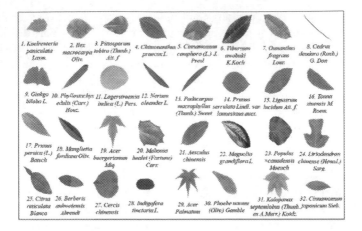

Fig. 1. Sample images in Flavia dataset with its botanical names.

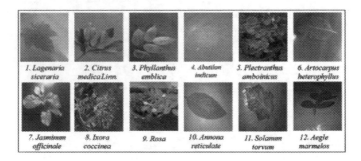

Fig. 2. Sample images in custom created Leaf-12 dataset with its botanical names.

3.3   NADenseNet-169 CNN Model

The block diagram representation of NADenseNet-169 CNN model is shown in Fig. 3. The proposed Non-Averaged DenseNet-169 (NADenseNet-169) architecture is the modified version of the DenseNet-169 model. Traditional DenseNet-169 model is altered by removing the Global Average Pooling (GAP) layer. In traditional DenseNet-169 model, the GAP layer comes in front of final fully connected layer (FCL). GAP uses an average of feature maps obtained from the previous convolution layer. It results in loss of information. Then, the information obtained after the GAP layer is being propagated to FCL. FCL is used in the process of classification. In the modified version of DenseNet-169 (NADenseNet-169), the GAP layer is completely eliminated. So, the features extracted from the earlier layers in DenseNet-169 CNN model is directly propagated to FCL, for the purpose of classification. It resulted in achieving higher performance metrics with lower computation time. This model also eliminates the vanishing gradient problem [11]. It also incorporates the advantages of ResNet, ResNeXt, Fractal-Net, and Highway network. The proposed NADenseNet-169 CNN has 1×1 convolutions similar to Network-in-Network architecture, Inception-V3, and Inception ResNet-V2. The number of parameters used by the proposed NADenseNet-169 CNN (12,963,744 trainable parameters) is lesser than ResNet architecture (24,583,200 trainable parameters).

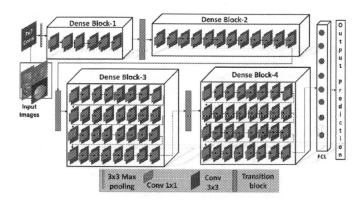

Fig. 3. Plant species recognition using NADenseNet-169 CNN model.

The preprocessed images from the dataset (Flavia and custom created Leaf-12) are fed into NADenseNet-169 model. The model consists of 7×7 convolution layer, 3×3 max-pooling layer, 4 dense blocks, 3 transition layers and a fully connected layer. The features are extracted through the combination of convolution layer, dense blocks and transition layers. The macro-level features are extracted by using the convolution layer with a kernel matrix of size 7×7 and a stride value of 2. The micro-level features are extracted using the dense blocks. Each dense block possesses multiple convolution layers. Four dense block with increasing layers (6, 12, 32, 32) on progression is inbuilt into the architecture. The dense block contains 1×1 convolution followed by 3×3 convolution. 1×1 convolutions are used to reduce the number of input feature maps before it is processed by 3×3 kernels. The feature information in one layer is propagated to all the subsequent layers. It increases the number of input channel in the subsequent layers. In between the dense blocks, the transition layer is embedded into the architecture. Transition layer consists of 1×1 convolution layer and average pooling layer (size $= 2 \times 2$, stride value of 2). This layer is used in the process of dimensionality reduction. The final classification is performed by a fully connected layer (FCL).

3.4   Training Algorithm

The pre-trained weights of ImageNet is employed as initial weights. The hyper-parameter setting employed are 50 epochs, learning rate ($\eta = 0.0001$), Adam optimizer, and a batch size of 32. Adam optimizer [24] is an adaptive optimizer which updates the new weights (θ_{t+1}) based on the learning rate, η and bias-corrected moments $(\hat{m}_t, \hat{v}_t)$. The optimized learning rate (0.0001) is determined for NADenseNet-169 architecture. The accuracy in predicting the plant species is highly affected when the learning rate is set with a value of 0.001 and 0.00001. The Fully Connected Layer (FCL) with a softmax activation function is used. The categorical cross-entropy loss function is used in the model [25]. The algorithm to train a fine-tuned NADenseNet-169 CNN model is specified in algorithm 1.

Algorithm 1: Fine-tuned NADenseNet-169 model to perform plant species recognition

Input: Images, I_N; ImageNet weights, IW; ImageNet biases, IB; Epochs, ep=50; Batch Size, BS=32; η=0.0001

Output: Predicted label, y_i

Step 1: Read N number of I_N trainingimages

Step 2: Resize I_N images to 100x100x3

Step 3: Pass I_N through the Dense blocks, Transition blocks,and FCL

Step 4: Train the CNN using Adam optimizer

for j=1 to ep:

Update weights, IW and biases, IB

End

Step 5: Test the images to predict the label y_i

3.5   Hardware Setup and Software Tools

The utilized hardware setup to train the NADenseNet-169 model on Flavia and Leaf-12 datasets are detailed below. It includes a Windows-10 64-bit OS running on a Intel Core i7-790 CPU combined with NVIDIA Titan X GPU with 3584 CUDA cores. The programming is carried out in Python 3.5 along with Keras (Tensorflow as backend), Scikit-learn, H5py, Numpy, OS, Matplotlib, and Seaborn packages.

4   Results and Discussion

Two datasets namely, Flavia (Standard) and Leaf-12 (custom developed) are used to determine the performance of the NADenseNet-169 model. The images in the dataset are randomly chosen in the ratio of 70:30 to get separated into train-test datasets. The proposed NADenseNet-169 model performance is examined using the metrics [8] such as top-1 accuracy, top-5 accuracy, precision, recall and F1-score. The performance metrics obtained by using the NADenseNet-169 model are discussed in Subsect. 4.1. Comparison between the NADenseNet-169 model with and without Global Average Pooling (GAP) layer is described in Subsect. 4.2.

4.1   Performance Measure of NADenseNet-169 Model

The performance metrics pertaining to different deep learning architectures namely, VGG-16, VGG-19, Inception-V3, ResNet50, Inception ResNet-V2, Xception, MobileNet, DenseNet-121, DenseNet-201 and the proposed NADenseNet-169 are described in this section. The above specified models are evaluated in relation to plant species recognition.

Flavia Dataset

Table 1 lists the performance metrics obtained by utilizing the different deep learning models on Flavia dataset. From the table data, it is observed that the proposed NADenseNet-169 model resulted in obtaining higher performance metrics (Top-1 accuracy = 98.58%, Top-5 accuracy = 99.84%, Precision = 0.99, Recall = 0.99, F1-Score = 0.99) when compared with other advanced deep learning models (VGG-16, VGG-19, Inception-V3, ResNet-50, Inception ResNet-V2, Xception, MobileNet, DenseNet-121, DenseNet-201). This improvement in performance metrics is mainly attributed to the characteristics of NADenseNet-169 model such as dense connection, feature reuse property and non-averaging of final feature maps.

The DenseNet (121 and 201) models resulted in a comparable accuracy to the NADenseNet-169 model, but other performance metrics (precision, recall, F1-score) are relatively lower than NADenseNet-169 model. The removal of global average pooling (GAP) layer from the conventional DenseNet-169 model, resulted in the improvement of performance metrics (as detailed in Sect. 4.3). By utilizing the GAP layer, the final feature map gets averaged out. Fully Connected Layer (FCL) is used to classify the input data. Also, the computation time of DenseNet-201 model (4.37 s, mainly related to the extra layer - GAP

Table 1. Performance Metrics obtained by using different deep learning architectures on Flavia Dataset.

CNN Models	Top-1(%)	Top-5(%)	Precision	Recall	F1-Score	Time(s)
VGG-16	96.88	99.38	0.97	0.97	0.97	0.46
VGG-19	97.29	99.38	0.98	0.97	0.97	0.54
Inception-V3	97.50	99.17	0.98	0.97	0.97	1.75
ResNet-50	98.12	99.79	0.98	0.98	0.98	1.43
Inception ResNet-V2	98.17	99.79	0.98	0.98	0.98	4.60
Xception	98.17	99.79	0.98	0.98	0.98	1.03
MobileNet	97.29	99.58	0.97	0.97	0.97	0.70
DenseNet-121	98.12	99.79	0.98	0.98	0.98	2.43
DenseNet-201	98.38	99.79	0.98	0.98	0.98	4.37
Proposed NADenseNet-169	**98.58**	**99.84**	**0.99**	**0.99**	**0.99**	**3.53**

layer) is high when compared to NADenseNet-169 model (3.53 s). The computation time of the model is mainly related to the number of tunable parameters and layers. The list of parameters in each model is specified in Table 2. The deep learning architectures such as DenseNet-201, DenseNet-121, ResNet-50, Inception ResNet-V2 and Xception produced accuracies greater than 98%. The proposed NADenseNet-169 resulted in high values for both Top-1 and Top-5 accuracies compared to other deep learning architectures.

Table 2. Model's trainable parameters

Model	Number of layers	Number of Trainable parameters
VGG-16	16	14,862,176
VGG-19	19	20,171,872
Inception-V3	48	21,833,920
ResNet-50	50	24,583,220
Inception ResNet-V2	164	54,294,636
Xception	71	21,396,808
MobileNet	28	3,501,920
DenseNet-121	121	7,248,800
DenseNet-201	201	18,300,300
Proposed NADenseNet-169	**169**	**12,963,744**

The larger F1-score value of 0.99 indicates that the number of misprediction is significantly reduced on employing the proposed NADenseNet-169 model in real-time plant species recognition. The performance of the proposed NADenseNet-169 model is compared with other existing literatures (Flavia dataset). This is represented as a bar graph in Fig. 4. The proposed NADenseNet-169 layer outperforms conventional method as well as deep learning method. From the Fig. 4 data, it is observed that the proposed NADenseNet-169 model is highly suitable to be used in the plant species recognition system as compared with other conventional and deep learning methods.

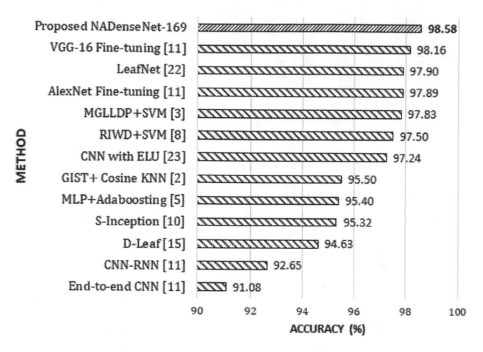

Fig. 4. Comparison of plant species prediction accuracy obtained by using the proposed NADenseNet-169 model with other methods.

Leaf-12 Dataset

The performance metrics obtained by implementing different deep learning archi-tectures on Leaf-12 dataset are listed in Table 3. It is observed that the proposed pre-trained NADenseNet-169 model resulted in achieving higher performance metrics (Top-1 accuracy = 99%, Top-5 accuracy = 100%, Precision = 0.99, Recall = 0.99 and F1-score = 0.99) as compared with other advanced deep learn-ing models (VGG-16, VGG-19, Inception-V3, ResNet-50, Inception ResNet-V2, Xception, MobileNet, DenseNet-121, DenseNet-201). This improvement in per-formance metrics is mainly attributed to the characteristics of NADenseNet-169 model such as dense connection, property of feature reuse and non-averaging of final feature maps. Similar trend is also visualized while training the model on Flavia dataset.

The DenseNet (121 and 201) models resulted in a comparable accuracy to the NADenseNet-169 model, but the other performance metrics (precision, recall, F1-score) are relatively lower than NADenseNet-169 model. The removal of global average pooling (GAP) layer from the conventional DenseNet-169 model resulted in the improvement of performance metrics. The computational time of DenseNet-201 model (5.73 s, mainly related to the extra layer - GAP layer) is high when com-pared to NADenseNet-169 model (4.45 s). The higher values of performance met-rics (Precision, Recall, F1-Score, Top-1 and Top-5 accuracies) indicates that the proposed model is well suited for real-time plant species recognition.

Table 3. Different models performance metrics obtained by utilizing Leaf-12 dataset.

CNN Models	Top-1 (%)	Top-5 (%)	Precision	Recall	F1-Score	Time(s)
VGG-16	98.44	100	0.98	0.98	0.98	0.96
VGG-19	98.09	99.91	0.98	0.98	0.98	1.17
Inception-V3	97.92	99.83	0.98	0.98	0.98	2.44
ResNet-50	98.78	100	0.99	0.99	0.99	2.10
Inception ResNet-V2	98.87	99.83	0.99	0.99	0.99	5.62
Xception	98.26	100	0.98	0.98	0.98	1.57
MobileNet	98.52	99.91	0.99	0.99	0.99	0.82
DenseNet-121	98.26	100	0.98	0.98	0.98	3.17
DenseNet-201	98.26	100	0.98	0.98	0.98	5.73
Proposed NADenseNet-169	**99**	**100**	**0.99**	**0.99**	**0.99**	**4.45**

The performance metrics obtained by the model on custom created Leaf-12 dataset is in correlation with the values obtained on using the standard Flavia dataset. Since the proposed model (NADenseNet-169) performance metrics is on a higher scale, it becomes highly suitable to be used in the plant species recognition system. The Leaf-12 dataset has more variety (illumination changes, scale variation, camera viewpoint variation, changes in object orientation, structure of leaf - simple leaf and compound leaf, arrangement of leaf in the stem, cluttered background) incorporated into it. Hence, the model trained on the images of Leaf-12 dataset is highly adaptable to be used in real-time scenarios.

4.2   NADenseNet-169 Architecture with GAP Layer

The performance metrics are also computed for NADenseNet-169 architecture with Global Average Pooling (GAP) layer. A GAP layer of size 7×7 is considered. The obtained performance metrics of NADenseNet-169 model are compared with DenseNet-169 architecture (NADenseNet-169 with GAP layer) and shown in Fig. 5. It is observed that the addition of the GAP layer to the model resulted in lowering of performance metrics with increased computation (Flavia: 3.62 s, Leaf-12: 4.60 s) time. This trend is visualized irrespective of the two datasets (Flavia, Leaf-12) considered in the studies.

4.3   Real-Time Prediction of Plant Species

The non-averaged DenseNet-169 CNN (NADenseNet-169) model is proposed and demonstrated to perform real-time plant species recognition under unconstrained environment such as variation in viewpoint, cluttered background, scale changes, illumination variation etc. The model is trained on custom created Leaf-12 dataset.

The real-time images shown in Fig. 6 and Fig. 7. From Table 3 data, it is observed that the other deep learning models such as VGG-16, VGG-19, Inception-V3, ResNet-50, Xception, MobileNet, DenseNet-121 resulted in comparable

Performance Metrics	Flavia		Leaf-12	
	With GAP	Without GAP	With GAP	Without GAP
Top-1 Accuracy (%)	98	**98.58**	97.31	**99**
Top-5 Accuracy (%)	99.24	**99.84**	99.91	**100**
Precision	0.98	**0.99**	0.98	**0.99**
Recall	0.98	**0.98**	0.97	**0.99**
F1-Score	0.98	**0.98**	0.97	**0.99**
Computation Time(s)	3.62	**3.53**	4.60	**4.45**

Fig. 5. Comparison of performance metrics obtained by using the pre-trained DenseNet-169 model with and without GAP layer.

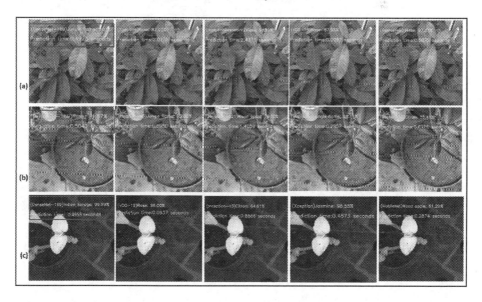

Fig. 6. Real-time leaf prediction using NADenseNet-169 model and other deep learning models. Correct predictions are highlighted in red box. (a) Jungle Flame, (b) Rose and (c) Indian Borage. (Color figure online)

accuracy with lower computation time in-relation to the proposed NADenseNet-169 model. But, these models resulted in a large number of misprediction, when it is tested on real-time images with variable environments. This is visualized in Fig. 6.

The plant species in home garden is used to acquire the real-time leaf images. The proposed model is tested with different settings such as illumination variation, rotation, camera viewpoint and scale changes. These real-time images are

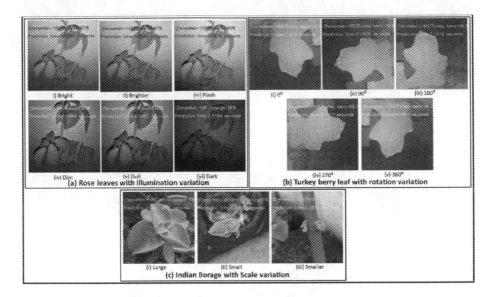

Fig. 7. Prediction of plant species using NADenseNet-169 model with unconstrained settings such as (a) Illumination, (b) Rotation and (c) Scale variations.

used in the process of plant species recognition by different architectures (VGG-16, VGG-19, Inception-V3, ResNet50, Inception ResNet-V2, Xception, MobileNet, DenseNet-121, DenseNet-201 and proposed NADenseNet-169). Figure 7 shows a few examples of prediction of Jungle flame, Rose and Indian Borage plant species by the proposed NADenseNet-169 model and other deep learning architectures (mispredictions shown in the figure). From Fig. 6, it is observed that the NADenseNet-169 model efficiently predicts the plant species compared to other architectures.

Figure 7 shows the prediction results obtained by using the proposed NADenseNet-169 CNN model for images captured under varying illumination condition (Fig. 7(a)), orientation variation (Fig. 7(b)) and scale variation (Fig. 7(c)). It is observed that the proposed NADenseNet-169 CNN model identifies the plant species efficiently in unconstrained environment.

On a summary, it is identified that the NADenseNet-169 model trained on Leaf-12 dataset is highly suitable to perform real-time plant species recognition. As a future work, the proposed model will be tested by considering large number of plant species. Architecture level modification will also be carried out to minimize the computation time.

5   Conclusion

Non-Averaged DenseNet-169 CNN model is proposed and demonstrated to perform plant species recognition. From the experimental investigation, it is observed that the NADenseNet-169 model performed better (Flavia dataset:

accuracy = 98.58%, computation time = 3.53 s; Leaf-12 dataset: accuracy = 99%, computation time = 4.45 s) compared to traditional image processing method and other deep learning approaches. The above-specified metrics are obtained with the optimized hyperparameters (Adam optimizer, learning rate = 0.0001, Batch size = 32). Also, the performance of the architecture gets weakened (lower accuracy and higher computation time) by inserting a Global Average Pooling (GAP) layer with a size of 7×7 into the architecture. The NADenseNet-169 model attains higher accuracy with comparable computation time, while testing it on the non-augmented datasets. The number of misprediction on real-time images is significantly reduced by utilizing NADenseNet-169 model. Hence, the proposed NADenseNet-169 model trained on Leaf-12 dataset becomes highly suitable to be utilized in the real-time plant species recognition system.

Acknowledgements. The authors would like to thank NVIDIA for providing Titan X GPU under the University Research Grant Programme.

References

1. Wäldchen, J., Mäder, P.: Plant species identification using computer vision techniques: a systematic literature review. Arch. Comput. Methods Eng. **25**, 507–543 (2018)
2. MostajerKheirkhah, F., Asghari, H.: Plant leaf classification using GIST texture features. IET Comput. Vis. **13**(4), 369–375 (2019)
3. Wang, X., Du, W., Guo, F., Hu, S.: Leaf recognition based on elliptical half gabor and maximum gap local line direction pattern. IEEE Access **8**, 39175–39183 (2020)
4. Zhang, S., Zhang, C., Wang, Z., Kong, W.: Combining sparse representation and singular value decomposition for plant recognition. Appl. Soft Comput. J. **67**, 164–171 (2018)
5. Anubha Pearline, S., Sathiesh Kumar, V., Harini, S.: A study on plant recognition using conventional image processing and deep learning approaches. J. Intell. Fuzzy Syst. **36**(3), 1997–2004 (2019)
6. Lee, S.H., Chan, C.S., Remagnino, P.: Multi-Organ Plant Classification Based on Convolutional and Recurrent Neural Networks. IEEE Trans. Image Process. **27**(9), 4287–4301 (2018)
7. Raj, A.P.S.S., Vajravelu, S.K.: DDLA: dual deep learning architecture for classification of plant species. IET Image Process. **13**(12), 2176–2182 (2019)
8. Mehdipour Ghazi, M., Yanikoglu, B., Aptoula, E.: Plant identification using deep neural networks via optimization of transfer learning parameters. Neurocomputing **235**, 228–235 (2017)
9. Barré, P., Stöver, B.C., Müller, K.F., Steinhage, V.: LeafNet: a computer vision system for automatic plant species identification. Ecol. Inform. **40**, 50–56 (2017)
10. Atabay, H.A.: A convolutional neural network with a new architecture applied on leaf classification. IIOAB J. **7**(5), 226–331 (2016)
11. Khan, S., Rahmani, H., Shah, S.A.A., Bennamoun, M.: A guide to convolutional neural networks for computer vision. Synthesis Lectures Comput. Vis. **8**(1), 1–207 (2018)
12. Liu, J., Zhang, Y., Cui, J., Feng, Y., Pang, L.: Fully convolutional multi-scale dense networks for monocular depth estimation. IET Comput. Vision **13**(5), 515–522 (2019)

13. Zhang, C., Li, G., Du, S.: Multi-scale dense networks for hyperspectral remote sensing image classification. IEEE Trans. Geosci. Remote Sens. **57**(11), 9201–9222 (2019)
14. Zeng, M., Xiao, N.: Effective combination of DenseNet and BiLSTM for keyword spotting. IEEE Access **7**, 10767–10775 (2019)
15. Cui, R., Liu, M.: Hippocampus analysis by combination of 3-D DenseNet and shapes for Alzheimer's disease diagnosis. IEEE J. Biomed. Heal. Informatics **23**(5), 2099–2107 (2019)
16. Tan, T., et al.: Optimize transfer learning for lung diseases in bronchoscopy using a new concept: sequential fine-tuning. IEEE J. Transl. Eng. Heal. Med. **6**, 1–8 (2018)
17. Lin, H., Hu, Y., Chen, S., Yao, J., Zhang, L.: Fine-grained classification of cervical cells using morphological and appearance based convolutional neural networks. IEEE Access **7**, 71541–71549 (2019)
18. Dezaki, F.T., et al.: Cardiac phase detection in echocardiograms with densely gated recurrent neural networks and global extrema loss. IEEE Trans. Med. Imaging **38**(8), 1821–1832 (2018)
19. Hu, J., Chen, Z., Yang, M., Zhang, R., Cui, Y.: A multiscale fusion convolutional neural network for plant leaf recognition. IEEE Signal Process. Lett. **25**(6), 853–857 (2018)
20. Zhu, X., Zhu, M., Ren, H.: Method of plant leaf recognition based on improved deep convolutional neural network. Cogn. Syst. Res. **52**, 223–233 (2018)
21. He, G., Xia, Z., Zhang, Q., Zhang, H., Fan, J.: Plant species identification by bi-channel deep convolutional networks. J. Phys: Conf. Ser. **1004**, 012015–6 (2018)
22. Younis, S., Weiland, C., Hoehndorf, R., Dressler, S., Hickler, T., Seeger, B., Schmidt, M.: Taxon and trait recognition from digitized herbarium specimens using deep convolutional neural networks. Bot. Lett. **165**(3), 377–383 (2018)
23. Wu, S.G., Bao, F.S., Xu, E.Y., Wang, Y.X., Chang, Y.F., Xiang, Q.L.: A leaf recognition algorithm for plant classification using probabilistic neural network. In: ISSPIT 2007–2007 IEEE International Symposium on Signal Processing and Information Technology, pp. 11–16 (2007)
24. Ruder, S.: An overview of gradient descent optimization algorithms (2016). arXiv preprint arXiv:1609.04747 (2016)
25. Rusiecki, A.: Trimmed categorical cross-entropy for deep learning with label noise. Electron. Lett. **55**(6), 319–320 (2019)

Self Similarity Matrix Based CNN Filter Pruning

S. Rakshith$^{(\boxtimes)}$ ⓘ, Jayesh Rajkumar Vachhani$^{(\boxtimes)}$ ⓘ, Sourabh Vasant Gothe ⓘ, and Rishabh Khurana$^{(\boxtimes)}$ ⓘ

Samsung R & D Institute, Bangalore, India
{rakshith1.s,jay.vachhani,sourab.gothe,k.rishabh}@samsung.com

Abstract. Abstract. In recent years, most of the deep learning solutions are targeted to be deployed in mobile devices. This makes the need for development of lightweight models all the more imminent. Another solution is to optimize and prune regular deep learning models. In this paper, we tackle the problem of CNN model pruning with the help of Self-Similarity Matrix (SSM) computed from the 2D CNN filters. We propose two novel algorithms to rank and prune redundant filters which contribute similar activation maps to the output. One of the key features of our method is that there is no need of finetuning after training the model. Both the training and pruning process is completed simultaneously. We benchmark our method on two of the most popular CNN models - ResNet and VGG and record their performance on the CIFAR-10 dataset.

Keywords: Filter Pruning · Self-similarity matrix · Convolutional Neural Networks · ResNet · VGG · CIFAR-10

1 Introduction

State of the art neural networks that are intended to push the envelope in terms of accuracy and performance, have almost unlimited compute and space at their disposal. However, developers that are creating deep learning applications to be deployed on mobile devices do not have this luxury. With the rising use of AR, facial recognition and voice assistants, it has become more accessible to use ML solutions on mobile devices. There are multiple techniques which are employed to reduce the model footprint and accelerate its speed. These include matrix factorization [2, 15], knowledge distillation [1, 7] and model quantization [8–10, 17]. There are two types of quantization techniques for reducing the model size - post training quantization and quantization-aware training. Quantization reduces the precision of the model parameters thereby reducing the model size and inference time.

One other way of tackling this issue is through network pruning. The process of pruning is accomplished by removing unimportant/redundant weights from a neural network thereby reducing its size. Pruning is a process which is beneficial for all deep learning models especially CNNs which have notoriously high

D. Gupta et al. (Eds.): CVIP 2022, CCIS 1777, pp. 73–83, 2023.
https://doi.org/10.1007/978-3-031-31417-9_6

computational constraints. We hypothesise that similar filters produce similar activations and contribute redundant information to the output layer, because of which such filters can be eliminated from the network. With the rise of mobile inference and machine learning capabilities, pruning becomes more relevant than ever before. Lightweight algorithms are the need of the hour, as more and more applications find use with neural networks.

There are numerous ways of selecting the weights to be pruned. In this paper, we aim to remove redundant weights from convolutional layers based on the similarity measure between filters of the same layer. In statistics and related fields, a similarity metric is a real-valued function that quantifies the similarity between two objects. By removing the similar filters, we can reduce the model size and computational overhead with negligible decrease in performance. In this paper, we devise new methods in computing and ranking redundancy among filters based on their mutual similarity values.

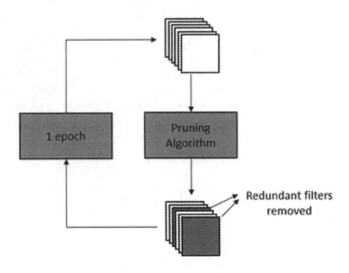

Fig. 1. Pruning operation in 2D CNNs.

We choose to use the "Self Similarity Matrix" to capture the similarity measure. There are two steps in the process of shortlisting the most redundant filters for each layer. Firstly we compute the self similarity matrix (2D matrix) using an appropriate distance metric (L2, cosine, cityblock). Using the information captured in this matrix, we design two algorithms to identify pairs of similar filters and prune one of them. We wish to prove that with such a simple technique we are able to prune CNN models significantly, without much drop in accuracy.

Also our method is designed in such a way that we can prune the models while it is being trained without a need for finetuning. This saves valuable time and computational resources. We demonstrate our results on two state of the models ResNet and VGG on the CIFAR-10 dataset. By using the concept of SSM, we are treating the CNN filters as a sequence of multidimensional vectors. We propose two approaches - greedy approach and area based approach. Both have its own benefits and trade-offs.

Figure 1 highlights the process used for CNN filter pruning. Based on certain criteria according to the pruning algorithm, we identify rendundant filters and then prune them. After this another epoch of the training process is completed to update the weights of the remaining filters. After this the process is repeated iteratively until satisfactory performance is achieved. The details about each of the pruning algorithms are elaborated in the Proposed Method section.

2 Related Works

CNN pruning is one such field where there exists plenty of prior literature study. Many different techniques have been employed to rank and prune filters based on a criterion. In [20], the authors apply a novel spectral cluster method on filters and create efficient groups which are then used to choose redundant filters. The approach in [12] is to prune filters based on the rank of their feature maps. Filters corresponding to lower rank feature maps are pruned as they are believed to contain less information. The authors in [3] utilize the concept of geometric median to choose filters which are most similar to the remaining filters. For practical usecases, they use an approximate version of identifying the geometric median among the filters. In [4], in addition to the norm based criterion, the authors also use the geometric information among the filters.

[16] and [11] are both pruning methods based on the similarity matrix. In [16], the authors finetune the model post training, to obtain the final results. They show results for the accoustic scene classification on a very light weight network. In [11] however, they employ two methods, "diversity-aware" and "similarityaware" to prune filters. There also many other novel approaches such as, [19] where authors mention a novel criterion for pruning inspired from neural network interpretability. In [18], they apply the pruning operation to filters of both convolutional as well as depthwise separable convolutional layers. In [5], The authors utilize a reinforcement learning algorithm to make the pruning process completely automated. In [6], pruning is based on a two-step process - Lasso regression and least square reconstruction. [13] utilizes a label-free generative adversarial learning to learn the pruned network with the sparse soft mask in an end to end manner and in [14] the authors propose a variational Bayesian scheme for channelwise pruning of convolutional neural networks.

3   Proposed Method

In this section we elaborate on the entire procedure for pruning which is applied while the model is trained. One of the advantages of our approach is that we achieve good performance even without fine tuning of the model after pruning. This saves a lot of computational resources and time. We first begin by providing a brief introduction to the "Self-similarity matrix".

3.1   Self-similarity Matrix

For two multidimensional vectors x and y, we can define a similarity function s: F×F → R to return a similarity score. The value s(x, y) is low if the vectors x and y are similar and large otherwise. For a given feature sequence $X = (x_1, x_2, ..., x_N)$, we can compute the N-square 'Self-Similarity Matrix', $S \in R^{NXN}$ defined by,

$$S(n, m) = s(x_n, x_m) \tag{1}$$

Highly similar filters provide almost similar contribution to the output activation distribution. By removing one of the filters we can reduce model size with negligible decrease in performance. Here we devise new methods in computing and ranking filters based on their mutual similarity values. Self-similarity matrix is a graphical representation of similarity among a set of n-dimensional vectors. The basic idea can be seen in Fig. 2, where we first identify sets of similar filters based on the values in the SSM. We then rank these filters and then prune them in the descending order of redundancy.

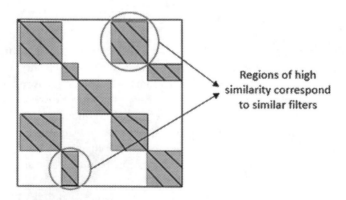

Fig. 2. Self similarity matrix for CNN layer filters.

In Fig. 3, we depict the overall pipeline of the pruning process. For each epoch of training, we iteratively prune the filters of each convolutional layer of the model. For a given convolutional layer, we flatten the corresponding set of 2D filters to create a list of multidimensional vectors. From these vectors we compute the SSM according to Eq. 1. Using this SSM as input, we can devise various methods for ranking and listing the redundant filters. We also input a constant "pruning ratio", which governs the number of filters to be pruned. After this we get a list of filters which need to be pruned from the convolutional layer.

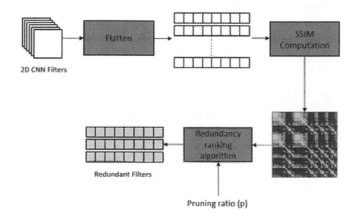

Fig. 3. Highlevel description of the self similarity based pruning algorithm.

3.2   Greedy Method

In this method, we start by calculating the SSM for the filters of each of the convolutional layers. From the SSM, we select the filters to be pruned in a "greedy" approach. For the row of elements corresponding to each filter fi, we identify the filter fj corresponding to the smallest similarity value. We then add (fi, fj) along with the similarity value sij in a dictionary. This process is repeated for each row of the SSM. After this, we sort the elements based on the similarity values and start pruning one filter from the pair of filters. This can be visualized as a local method which considers the one-to-one similarity among only a pair of filters. The pseudo code is specified in Algorithm 1.

3.3   Area Based Method

This is a more global method which considers the similarity of one filter with all the other filters and then ranks it based on that. Here we are treating the similarity values as a 1D curve and the area under this curve can be used as a global measure of similarity. The lower value of area corresponds to a filter which is more similar to the remaining filters. We choose to prune the most similar filters first. These are the filters which can be replaced without significant loss in performance.

Algorithm 1. Greedy Algorithm

$S \leftarrow SelfSimilarityMatrix(N X N)$
$i \leftarrow 0$
$min\_arr \leftarrow []$
while $i \leq N$ **do**
    $min\_arr[i] \leftarrow minimum(S[i,:])$
    $i \leftarrow i + 1$
end while
$min\_indices \leftarrow argsort(min\_arr)$ **return** $min\_indices$

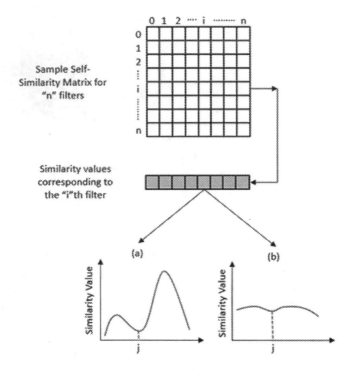

Fig. 4. Comparison between area-based and greedy pruning algorithms.

In Fig. 4, we have considered a sample SSM for a set of "n" filters. We also depict two possible plots corresponding to the "i" th filter. Even though the most similar filter corresponding to the "i" th filter is the "j" th filter in both the cases, we hypothesize that overall the plot in (b) is more similar to the rest of the filters. Based on the plot in (a) it is evident that even though "i" th and "j" th filters are very similar, the remaining filters are quite different from the "i" th filter, this would make pruning of the "i" th filter lose some accuracy of the model. To quantify this, we propose to calculate the area under the curve of the similarity values for each of the filter and then prune the filter whose plot corresponds to the lowest area. By doing this, we are capturing a more "global similarity" of each filter and making sure we are losing only the minimum amount of information by pruning the corresponding filter. The pseudocode is specified in Algorithm 2.

Algorithm 2. Area Algorithm

$S \leftarrow SelfSimilarityMatrix(NXN)$
$i \leftarrow 0$
$min\_arr \leftarrow []$
while $i \leq N$ **do**
    $area[i] \leftarrow trapezoidal\_area(S[i,:])$
    $i \leftarrow i + 1$
end while
$min\_indices \leftarrow argsort(area)$ **return** $min\_indices$

---

4   Observation and Results

In this section, we benchmark our pruning algorithms on two popular image classification networks namely, ResNet and VGG on the CIFAR-10 dataset. By benchmarking on such large CNN models, we can highlight the efficacy and usefulness of our method. We also compare the results with the method used in [16]. Currently we have pruned parameters from convolutional layers only, as they are the highest contributors for the FLOPs in the network. Therefore, all the results of pruned parameters are with respect to those corresponding to the convolutional layers. In Table 1 and Table 4, we list the original model performance details without pruning. For all the other results mentioned, we use a pruning ratio of 10% each epoch for all the convolutional layers. We have used the ResNet-18 variant for the results with respect to the ResNet model.

4.1   ResNet Pruning

Table 2 lists the accuracy drop of the ResNet model on the CIFAR-10 dataset after pruning for different methods. Table 3 shows the reduction in the convolutional layer parameters due to pruning. From Table 2, we see that even though there is a relative decrease (3%) in accuracy for the area based method, there is close to 5x decrease in convolutional parameters compared to the CVSSP

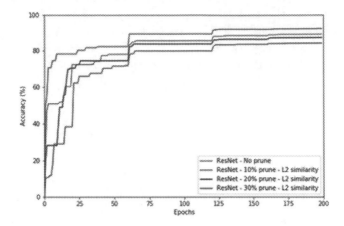

Fig. 5. Accuracy variation for the ResNet model with different pruning ratios.

Table 1. ResNet details

Total convolutional parameters	2,30,832
No prune accuracy (%)	92.78

method. This shows the efficacy of considering the global similarity value of each convolutional filter. In case of the greedy method, both the drop in accuracy and convolutional parameters is high for 10% pruning ratio. This can be adjusted accordingly to obtain requisite performance. In Fig. 5, we have depicted the variation of accuracy as the ResNet model as it is trained for different pruning ratios. This figure clearly depicts the trade-off between the model size and accuracy.

Table 2. ResNet drop in % accuracy after pruning on CIFAR-10 dataset (lower is better)

Pruning method	L2 distance	Cosine	Cityblock	KL Divergence
CVSSP [16]	0.43	0.35	0.81	0.49
Greedy Method	3.81	14.37	4.02	0.14
Area method	0.51	3.61	0.32	3.85

adjusted accordingly to obtain requisite performance. In Fig. 5, we have depicted the variation of accuracy as the ResNet model as it is trained for different pruning ratios. This figure clearly depicts the trade-off between the model size and accuracy.

Table 3. ResNet reduction in % convolution layer parameters after pruning on CIFAR-10 dataset (higher is better).

Pruning method	L2 distance	Cosine	Cityblock	KL Divergence
CVSSP [16]	11.02	7.17	11.02	2.26
Greedy Method	33.32	64.46	34.45	1.89
Area method	10.3	34.12	10.68	34.48

4.2 VGG Pruning

Table 5 lists the performance of the VGG model on the CIFAR-10 dataset after pruning. Table 6 highlights the reduction in convolutional parameters in the VGG model due to pruning. From Table 5 and Table 6, it is evident that both the area based method and the CVSSP method provide similar results for VGG. This maybe due to the fact that the VGG model is almost 64x larger than the ResNet 18 model, and the advantage of the "global similarity" in the area method might be nullified for such a large scale increase in model size. We can also observe that all the distance metrics are not performing equally, especially KL-Divergence and cosine distance, exhibit poor performance.

Table 4. VGG details

Total convolutional parameters	1,47,10,464
No prune accuracy (%)	93.4

Table 5. VGG drop in % accuracy after pruning on CIFAR-10 dataset (lower is better)

Pruning method	L2 distance	Cosine	Cityblock	KL Divergence
CVSSP [16]	0.2	9.2	0.4	10.2
Greedy Method	9	80.1	9.7	−0.2
Area method	0.38	9.2	0.4	10.2

Table 6. VGG reduction in % convolution layer parameters after pruning on CIFAR-10 dataset (higher is better)

Pruning method	L2 distance	Cosine	Cityblock	KL Divergence
CVSSP [16]	19.91	48.85	19.19	48.88
Greedy Method	50.89	76.01	48.84	0.23
Area method	19.91	42.19	19.91	48.88

5   Conclusion

In this paper, we have introduced two self similarity matrix based methods to identify and prune redundant filters from a CNN model. We highlight the trade-offs for both the methods and also benchmark their performance on two state of the art CNN networks namely ResNet and VGG on the CIFAR-10 dataset. The greedy method for filter pruning depends on the local similarity among pairs of filters whereas the area based methods considers the global similarity among all the filters of a convolutional layer. The area based method offers better performance for relatively smaller models such as the ResNet 18, but performs similarly to that of the greedy method on larger models such as the VGG. As a future work, we wish to extend this approach beyond convolutional layers and make it applicable for all layers. We want to work towards making the pruning ratio as a hyperparameter which can be adjusted based on the model and dataset to provide a more customized pruning performance [16].

References

1. Cho, J.H., Hariharan, B.: On the efficacy of knowledge distillation. In: Proceedings of the IEEE/CVF International Conference on Computer Vision, pp. 4794–4802 (2019)
2. Dziugaite, G.K., Roy, D.M.: Neural network matrix factorization. arXiv preprint arXiv:1511.06443 (2015)
3. He, Y., Liu, P., Wang, Z., Hu, Z., Yang, Y.: Filter pruning via geometric median for deep convolutional neural networks acceleration. In: Proceedings of the IEEE/CVF Conference on Computer Vision and Pattern Recognition, pp. 4340–4349 (2019)
4. He, Y., Liu, P., Zhu, L., Yang, Y.: Filter pruning by switching to neighboring cnns with good attributes. IEEE Trans. Neural Networks Learn. Syst. (2022)
5. He, Y., Lin, J., Liu, Z., Wang, H., Li, L.-J., Han, S.: AMC: AutoML for model compression and acceleration on mobile devices. In: Ferrari, V., Hebert, M., Sminchisescu, C., Weiss, Y. (eds.) ECCV 2018. LNCS, vol. 11211, pp. 815–832. Springer, Cham (2018). https://doi.org/10.1007/978-3-030-01234-2_48
6. He, Y., Zhang, X., Sun, J.: Channel pruning for accelerating very deep neural networks. In: Proceedings of the IEEE International Conference on Computer Vision, pp. 1389–1397 (2017)
7. Hinton, G., Vinyals, O., Dean, J., et al.: Distilling the knowledge in a neural network. arXiv preprint arXiv:1503.02531 2(7) (2015)
8. Hubara, I., Courbariaux, M., Soudry, D., El-Yaniv, R., Bengio, Y.: Quantized neural networks: training neural networks with low precision weights and activations. J. Mach. Learn. Res. 18(1), 6869–6898 (2017)
9. Idelbayev, Y., Carreira-Perpinán, M.A.: A flexible, extensible software framework for model compression based on the lc algorithm. arXiv preprint arXiv:2005.07786 (2020)
10. Jacob, B., et al.: Quantization and training of neural networks for efficient integer-arithmetic-only inference. In: Proceedings of the IEEE Conference on Computer Vision and Pattern Recognition, pp. 2704–2713 (2018)
11. Li, H., Ma, C., Xu, W., Liu, X.: Feature statistics guided efficient filter pruning. arXiv preprint arXiv:2005.12193 (2020)

12. Lin, M., et al.: Hrank: filter pruning using high-rank feature map. In: Proceedings of the IEEE/CVF Conference on Computer Vision and Pattern Recognition, pp. 1529–1538 (2020)
13. Lin, S., et al.: Towards optimal structured cnn pruning via generative adversarial learning. In: Proceedings of the IEEE/CVF Conference on Computer Vision and Pattern Recognition, pp. 2790–2799 (2019)
14. Ma, J.: Pruning threshold search algorithm combined with pdarts. In: 4th International Conference on Information Science, Electrical, and Automation Engineering (ISEAE 2022), vol. 12257, pp. 382–387. SPIE (2022)
15. Ponti, E.M., Vulić, I., Cotterell, R., Parovic, M., Reichart, R., Korhonen, A.: Parameter space factorization for zero-shot learning across tasks and languages. arXiv preprint arXiv:2001.11453 (2020)
16. Singh, A., Plumbley, M.D.: A passive similarity based cnn filter pruning for efficient acoustic scene classification. arXiv preprint arXiv:2203.15751 (2022)
17. Tailor, S.A., Fernandez-Marques, J., Lane, N.D.: Degree-quant: quantization-aware training for graph neural networks. arXiv preprint arXiv:2008.05000 (2020)
18. Wang, Z., et al.: Model pruning based on quantified similarity of feature maps. arXiv preprint arXiv:2105.06052 (2021)
19. Yeom, S.K., Seegerer, P., Lapuschkin, S., Binder, A., Wiedemann, S., Müller, K.R., Samek, W.: Pruning by explaining: a novel criterion for deep neural network pruning. Pattern Recogn. **115**, 107899 (2021)
20. Zhuo, H., Qian, X., Fu, Y., Yang, H., Xue, X.: Scsp: spectral clustering filter pruning with soft self-adaption manners. arXiv preprint arXiv:1806.05320 (2018)

Class Agnostic, On-Device and Privacy Preserving Repetition Counting of Actions from Videos Using Similarity Bottleneck

Rishabh Khurana$^{(\boxtimes)}$ ⓘ, Jayesh Rajkumar Vachhani$^{(\boxtimes)}$ ⓘ, S Rakshith$^{(\boxtimes)}$ ⓘ, and Sourabh Vasant Gothe ⓘ

Samsung R&D Institute, Bangalore 560037, India
{k.rishabh,jay.vachhani,rakshith1.s,sourab.gothe}@samsung.com

Abstract. We present a practical, privacy-preserving on-device method to get the repetition count of an action in a given video stream. Our approach relies on calculating the pairwise similarity between each sampled frame of the video, using the per frame features extracted by the feature extraction module and a suitable distance metric in the temporal self-similarity(TSM) calculation module. We pass this calculated TSM matrix to the count prediction module to arrive at the repetition count of the action in the given video. The count prediction module is deliberately designed to not pay any attention to the extracted per frame features which are video specific. This self-similarity bottleneck enables the model to be class agnostic and allows generalization to actions not observed during training. We utilize the largest available dataset for repetition counting, Countix, for training and evaluation. We also propose a way for effectively augmenting the training data in Countix. Our experiments show SOTA comparable accuracies with significantly smaller model footprints.

Keywords: Repetition Counting · Temporal Self-Similarity · Videos

1   Introduction

Repetitive actions are a common occurence in day-to-day life. From a flying bird flapping it's wings, to the reps of an exercise while working out, the ability to detect, understand and count repetitions of an action in a video stream can have multiple applications in a multitude of fields related to computer vision and robotics. This also gives a computer/robotic agent the capability to track progress of an action whose approximate repetition count to completion is known in advance.

Earlier, research in this area had largely been limited, possibly due to lack of good quality and extensive datasets. The QUVA [2] dataset contains just 100 videos, and the UCFRep [3], a subset of UCF101, contains only 526. This changed with the release of Countix [8], a subset of Kinetics [17] dataset with 8757 videos containing repetitive actions manually annotated with counts. However, this

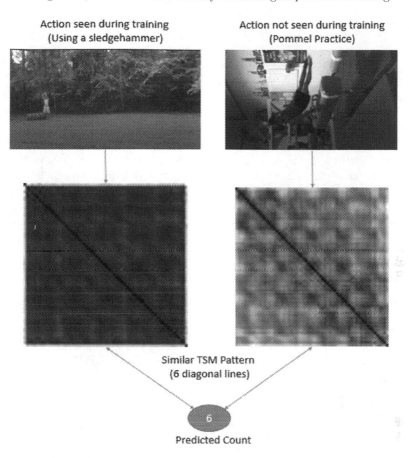

Fig. 1. Temporal Self-Similarity (TSM) matrix visualizations generated from features extracted by our architecture and the predicted count for two action classes, one seen during training and one not seen during training. Darker regions indicate more similarity. Since our count prediction module depends solely on the intermediate TSM bottleneck and not video specific frame features, it can work in a class-agnostic fashion.

dataset, which is also the focus of this research, suffers from certain drawbacks, mainly the uneven distribution of videos for various counts, as shown in Fig. 3. This can make the models trained on Countix biased towards certain counts.

User and data privacy has become an important concern in this day and age, where data is the new gold. It is estimated that the big four (Google, Amazon, Microsoft and Facebook) store at least 1,200 petabytes of data between them [18]. With the spread of education and increase in regulations like GDPR with regards to data privacy, users are becoming increasingly wary of using products and services that collect their personal data. This is specially relevant for the task at hand, where the user might not want his or her videos (of doing an excercise, for example) to be sent to a remote server for processing.

Our goal in this work is to achieve a reasonable accuracy for counting repetitions of an action in a video stream, in a class-agnostic manner, with a model that is lightweight and deployable on-device, thus preserving user data and privacy.

In order to achieve this, we had to make certain assumptions, which although might not always be true, are reasonable enough: 1) Different repetition instances of the same action will have only minor variations, giving rise to certain patterns in the temporal self-similarity matrix. 2) Different repeating actions, even those not seen during training, will yield similar temporal self-similarity patterns in accordance with the number of repetition instances. 3) Temporal self-similarity between sampled frames has enough information to get the final repetition count for the whole video. Our approach using these assumptions is shown in Fig. 1.

To this end, we make the following contributions: 1) An efficient, lightweight, on-device and privacy preserving architecture to count the number of repetitions of an action in a given video stream. 2) A way to augment the Countix training set to remove the inherent bias towards certain counts.

2   Related Work

Video Count/Periodicity Estimation. There has been some research in estimating the count or segmenting periodic action repetitions in videos. Many methods [1,2] utilize handcrafted features or parameters which might not scale and generalize well. Other methods [3,4] are dependent on some kind of classification(action, repetition patterns) which again might not generalize well to unseen actions or patterns in the wild. Another method [5] focuses solely on longer length videos with >15 count, which might not be useful in all applications. Sight and Sound [4] tries to use both visual and audio features in the video to estimate the count. Repnet [8] is the most similar to our approach, but they model the task as a classification problem. Both of these methods have huge model footprints with model sizes going upto a few hundred MBs, making on-device deployment unfeasible. Our method is dependent on learnt features and a learnt regression module, is class-agnostic, and has a considerably lesser footprint(∼30MB), making privacy preserving on-device deployment possible.

Video Feature Extraction. Spatio-temporal 3D convolutional networks like C3D [6], I3D [7] have dominated video feature extraction for the most part. More recently, variations and extensions of vision transformers [9] have also become popular. However both these approaches are resource heavy. Due to resource constraints on device, we utilize MobileNetV2 [10], a 2D image feature extractor preatrained on ImageNet, followed by an efficient (2+1)D [11] convolution for the intermixing of temporal features.

Temporal Self-similarity. TSMs have been used for a wide variety of tasks, like periodic motion detection and analysis [12], view-invariant action recognition [11,13] and generic event boundary detection [16]. TSM is a natural choice for our task, due to their ability to accurately encode periodic information in an inexpensive way. We use TSM as an intermediate representation for information bottleneck, similar to Repnet [8].

Synthetic Training Data and Data Augmentation. It is well known that synthetic data and augmentation can greatly improve the generalization and regularization of deep learning models [14,15]. [1] utilize purely synthetic data

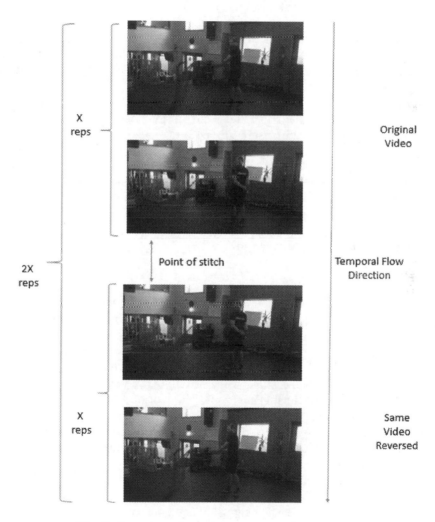

Fig. 2. Overview of our data augmentation strategy

of moving patches for repetition counting. Unlike them, we augment our training data by combining real-world videos from the Countix dataset.

3   Method

In this section, we present the details of our method. We model the problem of calculating the number of repetitions of an action in a given video as a regression problem. Given a video $V = [f_1, f_2, .., f_n]$ consisting of n frames, our task is to predict a number c, which is the count of repetitions of the action in the video.

As a first step, we augment the training data in Countix using our data augmentation method, details of which are provided in section below. To train and test our model, we linearly sample 64 equidistant frames from a given video and resize each frame to the size 112×112. For videos with n < 64, some of the intermediate frames are repeated.

We then pass each of the frame (2D image with 3 RGB channels), through a 2D feature extractor followed by (2+1)D convolutions in the spatial and temporal dimension respectively, to ensure mixing and sharing of information across frames. 64xD dimension feature matrix thus obtained is used to calculate a 64×64 temporal self-similarity matrix S, where S(i, j) is a value that represents how similar the frames i, j are to each other. It's this single channel similarity matrix that acts as the bottleneck and is passed to the count prediction module, which outputs a repetition count for the given video, solely on the basis of this similarity matrix, paying no attention to the input frames or their features for better generalization to unseen classes.

3.1   Data Augmentation

As can be seen from Fig. 3, the countix training set is highly imbalanced towards certain number of repetition counts. To reduce this imbalance, we applied a data augmentation strategy which can be generalized as follows.

We repeat a video with repetition count C_o, N times to get an augmented video with repetition count $C_a (= NC_o)$, by alternatingly using the original and reversed version of the same video while stitching. Reversed video is used to make sure there are no sudden changes and the motion of the action is smooth at the point of stitching. As an example, by repeating a video with $C_o = 1$, $N = 3$ times, we can get an augmented video with repetition count $C_a = 3$, with the order of stitching as Original Video + Same Video Reversed + Original Video to maintain smooth motion of the action at the points of stitching.

Figure 2 provides an overview of our data augmentation method. We tried multiple combinations of C_o and N. Figure 4 shows the distribution of number of videos for each count after augmentation using one such combination with C_o ranging from 1 to 6 and $N = 2$.

3.2   Architecture

Our architecture is composed of 3 main modules. Figure 5 provides the overview of our architecture, and the details of each of the modules are presented below.

Feature Extraction Module. We use MobileNetV2 pre-trained on ImageNet as the per frame feature extractor. We utilize an intermediate layer of MobileNet, which converts our $64 \times 3 \times 112 \times 112$ input to $64 \times 1280 \times 4 \times 4$ features. We then apply $(2+1)$D convolutions for information exchange in the temporal dimension, followed by max pooling and a fully connected layer to get the final 64×512 per frame feature matrix E.

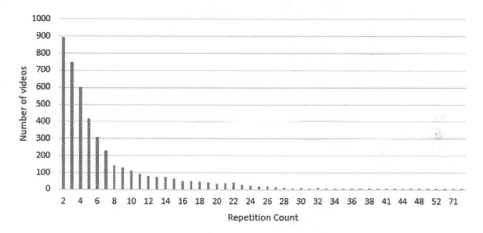

Fig. 3. Distribution of number of videos in the countix training set for each count label before augmentation.

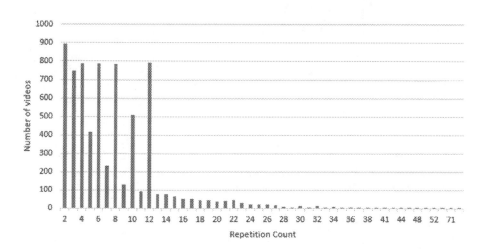

Fig. 4. Distribution of number of videos in the training set for each count label after augmentation.

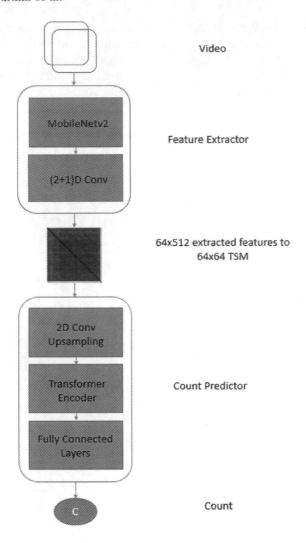

Fig. 5. Overview of our architecture

TSM Calculation Module. The 64 feature vectors of dimension 512 each generated above are then compared with each other using euclidean distance. Equation 1 gives the formulation of the similarity matrix.

$$S(i,j) = ||E(i) - E(j)|| \tag{1}$$

Here i, j are frame indices from 0 to 63 and E(i), E(j) represent the 512 dimension feature vector for frame number i and j respectively.

Count Prediction Module. Our count prediction module upsamples the 64×64 temporal self-similarity matrix (TSM) bottleneck using a combination of 2D convolutions and fully connected layers to get a 64×512 feature representation, which is passed through a lightweight transformer encoder layer to learn rich representations in the TSM. We pass this output through a series of fully connected layers, last of which contains a single neuron, whose ReLU activation is used as the predicted count.

4   Experiments

In this section, we provide details of the architecture variations, the training and evaluation setup, and the results of our experimentation.

4.1   Architecture Variations

We evaluated the following variations of our architecture.

Feature Extraction Module. We experiment with both 2D(ResNet-18 and MobileNetV2) and 3D(X3D) feature extractors. 2D feature extractors are followed by either a 3D convolution or an efficient (2+1)D convolution to enable the intermixing of features in the temporal dimension.

TSM Calculation Module. We use two types of similarity functions in our experiments, euclidean distance and cosine similarity.

Count Prediction Module. The count prediction module has two variations: Dual, which predicts the period and periodicity as a classification problem, similar to [8], and Single, which is our method of directly predicting count as a regression problem.

4.2   Training and Evaluation

Training Loss. For the "Single" variation of the count prediction module, we use the mean absolute error (MAE) between the predicted count and actual count as our loss function during training, as shown in Eq. 2

$$\sum_{i=1}^{N} |c_i - l_i| \qquad (2)$$

where c_i is the predicted count, l_i is the actual count, and N is the number of videos.

For the "Dual" variation of the count prediction module, we use a combination of binary cross entropy and categorical cross entropy, similar to Repnet [8].

Fig. 6. Similarity matrix visualization for count = 4

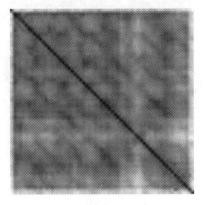

Fig. 7. Similarity matrix visualization for count = 11

Evaluation Metric. We use off by one accuracy (OBO), as shown in Eq. 3 as the evaluation metric for all our experiments. This considers a predicted count which is ± 1 from the label count as being correctly predicted.

$$\frac{1}{N}\sum_{i=1}^{N}[|c_i - l_i| \leq 1] \tag{3}$$

4.3   Results

Visualizations of the 64×64 similarity matrix, based on which count is predicted by our model, is shown in Fig. 6 and Fig. 7. Darker regions indicate more similarity than lighter regions. The main diagonal represents similarity of each frame with itself, and thus should be ignored. We can observe a number of dark diagonals (other than the main diagonal), which seem to closely correlate with the count of repetitions in the video.

Table 1. Comparison of the different variations of our architecture

Feature Extractor	Similarity Function	Count Predictor	OBO Acc (%)	Size (MB)
ResNet-18, 3D Conv	Euclidean	Dual	55	92
MobileNetV2, 3D Conv	Euclidean	Dual	52	45
X3D	Euclidean	Dual	30	30
MobileNetV2, (2+1)D Conv	Cosine	Single	47	30
MobileNetV2, (2+1)D Conv	Euclidean	Single	53	30

The results of the different variations of our architecture are shown in Table 1. We choose MobileNetV2 and (2+1)D Conv in the feature extractor, euclidean distance in the similarity calculation module and "Single" variation in the count predictor as our final architecture. The "Single" variation was significantly faster to train and converge, possibly due to a much simpler loss space. Although ResNet-18 gives us a marginally higher accuracy, the resulting model size is almost 3 times our chosen architecture, which is not desirable for on-device deployment. X3D did not yield a good result, likely due to the built-in temporal context interfering with the framewise similarity calculation.

Table 2 shows the comparison of our chosen architecture with other repetition counting architectures. Repnet [8] has the best accuracy but a significantly larger model footprint than our chosen architecture. Sight and sound [4] is a multimodal architecture that uses both visual and audio features to get the count. Our architecture achieves a good balance of accuracy and model footprint.

Table 2. Comparison with other repetition counting architectures

Model	OBO Acc (%)	Size (MB)
Repnet	69	321
Sight and sound	51	322
Ours	53	30

5   Conclusion

We have shown a way to augment any repetition counting dataset using Countix as an example and provide an efficient, lightweight, on-device and privacy preserving architecture to count the number of repetitions of an action in a given

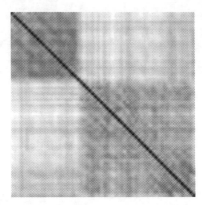

Fig. 8. Similarity matrix visualization for a failure case. The video had a change of orientation from portrait to landscape, which is correctly captured as two dark boxes. Although each box has faint diagonal lines corresponding to count, the model is not able to predict the correct count.

video stream with a reasonably good accuracy. Our method finds applications in various privacy-critical applications of computer vision and robotics, like counting number of reps of an excercise a user has performed, using the video feed from their phone. In combination with a lightweight action classifier, our method can be used to get the action as well as the repetition count of the action in a given video, on-device. The temporal similarity matrix calculated from our learnt features can also be used for a number of other downstream tasks, like temporal action segmentation and boundary detection.

Our method does not come without certain drawbacks. 1) As shown in Fig. 8, the model is not robust to large mid-video orientation and angle changes. 2) Since we sample only 64 frames from the video, some repetitions of a high-speed action might be missed. Although we can mitigate this by sampling more frames, the approach then quickly becomes unfeasible for on-device deployment. 3) Certain actions are composed of a collection of sub-actions. A pull-up for example, contains 2 sub-actions, an upward and a downward motion in a single repetition. In this case, the model sometimes predicts 2x the actual number of repetitions.

As future work, we will be working on addressing these shortcomings and to extend the method to more complicated actions and usecases.

References

1. Levy, O., Wolf, L.: Live repetition counting. In: Proceedings of the IEEE International Conference on Computer Vision, pp. 3020–3028 (2015)
2. Runia, T.F.H., Snoek, C.G.M., Smeulders, A.W.M.: Real-world repetition estimation by div, grad and curl. In: Proceedings of the IEEE Conference on Computer Vision and Pattern Recognition, pp. 9009–9017 (2018)

3. Zhang, H., Xu, X., Han, G., He, S.: Context-aware and scale-insensitive temporal repetition counting. In: Proceedings of the IEEE/CVF Conference on Computer Vision and Pattern Recognition, pp. 670–678 (2020)
4. Zhang, Y., Shao, L., Snoek, C.G.M.: Repetitive activity counting by sight and sound. In: Proceedings of the IEEE/CVF Conference on Computer Vision and Pattern Recognition, pp. 14070–14079 (2021)
5. Hu, H., Dong, A., Zhao, Y., Lian, D., Li, Z., Gao, S.: TransRAC: encoding multi-scale temporal correlation with transformers for repetitive action counting. In: Proceedings of the IEEE/CVF Conference on Computer Vision and Pattern Recognition, pp. 19013–19022 (2022)
6. Tran, D., Bourdev, L., Fergus, R., Torresani, L., Paluri, M.: Learning spatiotemporal features with 3d convolutional networks. In: Proceedings of the IEEE International Conference on Computer Vision, pp. 4489–4497 (2015)
7. Carreira, J., Zisserman, A.: Quo vadis, action recognition? a new model and the kinetics dataset. In: proceedings of the IEEE Conference on Computer Vision and Pattern Recognition, pp. 6299–6308 (2017)
8. Dwibedi, D., Aytar, Y., Tompson, J., Sermanet, P., Zisserman, A.: Counting out time: class agnostic video repetition counting in the wild. In: Proceedings of the IEEE/CVF Conference on Computer Vision and Pattern Recognition, pp. 10387–10396 (2020)
9. Dosovitskiy, A., et al.: An image is worth 16×16 words: Transformers for image recognition at scale. arXiv preprint arXiv:2010.11929 (2020)
10. Howard, A.G., et al.: Mobilenets: efficient convolutional neural networks for mobile vision applications. arXiv preprint arXiv:1704.04861 (2017)
11. Tran, D., Wang, H., Torresani, L., Ray, J., LeCun, Y., Paluri, M.: A closer look at spatiotemporal convolutions for action recognition. In: Proceedings of the IEEE conference on Computer Vision and Pattern Recognition, pp. 6450–6459 (2018)
12. Cutler, R., Davis, L.S.: Robust real-time periodic motion detection, analysis, and applications. IEEE Trans. Pattern Anal. Mach. Intell. **22**(8), 781–796 (2000)
13. Körner, M., Denzler, J.: Temporal self-similarity for appearance-based action recognition in multi-view setups. In: Wilson, R., Hancock, E., Bors, A., Smith, W. (eds.) CAIP 2013. LNCS, vol. 8047, pp. 163–171. Springer, Heidelberg (2013). https://doi.org/10.1007/978-3-642-40261-6_19
14. Dwibedi, D., Misra, I., Hebert, M.: Cut, paste and learn: surprisingly easy synthesis for instance detection. In: Proceedings of the IEEE International Conference on Computer Vision, pp. 1301–1310 (2017)
15. Tremblay, J., et al.: Training deep networks with synthetic data: Bridging the reality gap by domain randomization. In: Proceedings of the IEEE Conference on Computer Vision and Pattern Recognition Workshops, pp. 969–977 (2018)
16. Kang, H., Kim, J., Kim, K., Kim, T., Kim, S.J.: Winning the CVPR'2021 Kinetics-GEBD challenge: contrastive learning approach. arXiv preprint arXiv:2106.11549 (2021)
17. Kay, W., et al.: The kinetics human action video dataset. arXiv preprint arXiv:1705.06950 (2017)
18. Science Focus. https://www.sciencefocus.com/future-technology/how-much-data-is-on-the-internet/. Accessed 13 July 2022

Vehicle ReID: Learning Robust Feature Using Vision Transformer and Gradient Accumulation for Vehicle Re-identification

Rishi Kishore[1], Nazia Aslam[1]([✉])[iD], and Maheshkumar H. Kolekar[2]

[1] Video Surveillance Lab, Department of Electrical Engineering,
Indian Institute of Technology Patna, Daulatpur, Bihar, India
rishikishore77@gmail.com, n.aslam921@gmail.com
[2] Department of Electrical Engineering, Indian Institute of Technology Patna,
Daulatpur, Bihar, India
mahesh@iitp.ac.in

Abstract. Vehicle re-identification involves searching for images of identical vehicles across different cameras. For intelligent traffic control, re-identification of vehicles is very important. Convolutional Neural Networks (CNN) have succeeded in re-identification, but CNN-based methods process only one neighbourhood at a time and information is lost during pooling operation. To mitigate this shortcoming of CNN, We have proposed a novel vehicle re-identification framework (Vehicle ReID) based on vision transformer with gradient accumulation. The training images are split into different overlapped patches, and each patch is flattened into a 1D vector. Positional, camera and view embeddings are added to the patch embeddings and given as input to the vision transformer to generate a global feature. After that, this global feature is fed to three branches: ID, colour and type classification. For ID branch, triplet and cross-entropy losses are used. For colour branch and type branch, only cross-entropy loss is used. Gradient accumulation is employed at the training time to accumulate the gradient during each iteration in an epoch, and the neural network weights get updated only when the number of iterations reaches a predefined step size. This allows the model to work like being trained with a greater batch size without upgrading GPUs. To validate the effectiveness of the proposed framework, mean average precision (mAP), Rank-1, and Rank-5 hit rate have been computed on the VeRi dataset.

Keywords: Re-identification · Vision transformer · Gradient accumulation

D. Gupta et al. (Eds.): CVIP 2022, CCIS 1777, pp. 96–107, 2023.
https://doi.org/10.1007/978-3-031-31417-9_8

1   Introduction

Vehicle are an inevitable part of our lives. Re-identification of vehicles is a significant topic if we compare to other vehicle related tasks like detection, tracking and classification. Having a query image of a vehicle, the task of vehicle re-identification is to identify the same vehicles among non overlapping cameras. This is pictorially shown in Fig. 1. Re-identification using license plates [3] is not an easy task due to the different lighting conditions, and viewpoint variations. Hence re-identification using appearance features is the feasible method. Vehicle re-identification is mostly dominated by Convolutional Neural Networks (CNN) based methods [4,16,23,27]. The effective receptive field of CNN is Gaussian distributed [21]. So the focus will be on small discriminative region. Also due to the downsampling operation (pooling and strided convolution), the resolution of the feature map is reduced [12]. Hence it finds difficulty in distinguishing different vehicles having similar appearance.

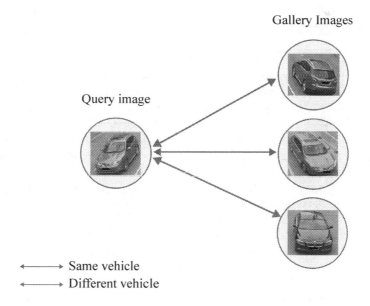

Fig. 1. Vehicle in query image re-identified from gallery image.

Vision transformers have emerged as a saviour for these drawbacks. Vision Transformer is the application of transformer on images by splitting them into patches. When pretrained on large datasets and transferred to fewer datapoints, vision transformers achieves excellent results. Vision Transformer solves the drawbacks of CNN by using multi head attention modules. It also doesn't have any downsampling operation [6].

Using only the vehicle ID label solely cannot give good results. The key to vehicle re-identification is to use features which are invariant to the viewpoint like color and type. Color and type along with the vehicle ID can improve the accuracy of re-identification. Therefore, inspired by [6], we have designed a novel vision transformer based vehicle re-identification framework (Vehicle ReID) that is capable of learning robust features. Also, gradient accumulation is added during training phase that allows the model to take larger batch sizes that is needed while training the transformers. Since Color and type features are invariant to the viewpoint, these features are also included with the ID feature to improve the performance.

In-short the summary and contribution of our work are as follows:

1. To re-identify the vehicles, we have designed a novel vehicle re-identification framework (Vehicle ReID) based on vision transformer.
2. Gradient accumulation is added during the training process to deal with the small batch size problems.
3. We have found a better mAP, Rank-1 and Rank-5 accuracy over other state-of-the-arts methods on VeRi dataset.

2   Related Work

Early methods of vehicle re-identification involved usage of magnetic sensors [10] and inductive loops [11] to obtain signatures of vehicles. Performance of these models were very low. Images contain more information about vehicles. Initial image processing methods of vehicle re-identification involved using hand crafted features like histogram of color and oriented gradients [9]. This was also having poor performance. Nowadays, with the growth of deep learning, popular methods in vehicle ReId involves using CNN backbone (e.g. ResNet) and designing a suitable loss function.

Liu et al. [2] proposed a neural network that employs siamese neural network with contrastive loss for training. They also introduced the VeRi dataset. In [5], Liu et al. proposed a Deep Relative Distance Learning (DRDL) method. It employs a two-branch deep convolutional network to project raw vehicle images into an Euclidean space where distance can be directly used to measure the similarity of arbitrary two vehicles. In [4], Tang et al. estimated 36 keypoint coordinates of the vehicle using CNN based on HR Net. It is fed to another network based on Densenet 121 for multi task learning where loss is calculated for color, type and id features obtained. Triplet loss calculated for id feature and cross entropy loss for color and type features.

Group group loss was proposed in [14]. Vehicles of same id were grouped together and separated from other groups in a feature space and loss is calculated for group of images and not individual images. They also employed a global regional feature to distinguish different but identical vehicles by exploiting regional features like decorations on windshield. In [15], Zhou et al. employed CNN and LSTM to learn viewpoint-invariant multi-view feature representation of a vehicle from one input view for the ReID problem. In [13], Li et al. employed viewpoint aware triplet loss to nullify the effects of intra-class variance and inter-class similarity. Intra-view triplet loss and inter-view triplet loss was introduced.

In [8], Xiong et al. employed CNN to obtain color, type, make and re id features. A similarity matrix is made between the features of upstream and downstream vehicles. Based on the velocity of vehicle, a time window is calculated so that the features of upstream vehicle are compared with those vehicles in downstream that are in the time window.

Transformer model was introduced to deal with sequential data [7]. In [6], Dosovitskiy et al. used Vision Transformer (ViT) for classification. Image is divided into patches and applied to transformer. In [1], He et al. used vision transformer for object re-identification. Global feature is obtained from the transformer output which has rich information from all the patches. It employed a jigsaw patch module to obtain local features from the transformer output which has information from selected patches of image.

3 Methodology

3.1 Overview

Our proposed vehicle ReID method utilize the idea of image classification using transformers, but with some major improvements. The block diagram of the proposed system is shown in Fig. 2. The framework has two stages, i.e. feature extraction and supervised learning.

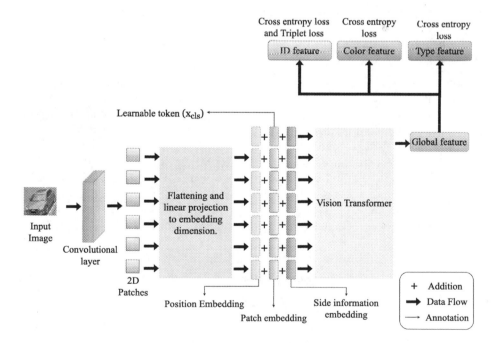

Fig. 2. Vision Transformer

For an input image $x \in \mathbb{R}^{h \times w \times c}$, where h, w and c are the height, width and number of channels, we split it into N overlapped patches. Each of the N patches are flattened as 1D vector and is denoted by $\{x_p(k)|k = 1, 2, .., N\}$. An extra learnable token embedding x_{cls} having same dimension as the patches is prepended to the flattened patches of every image. The final state of this token at the output of vision transformer is used as the aggregate feature or global feature representation f of the image. This is because when passing through the vision transformer, its value denotes how much attention is given to each of the patch embeddings of the input image. To add spatial information in the patches, we have employed a learnable position embedding to each patches.

The input to transformer is given as,

$$W_0 = [x_{cls}; \Phi(x_p(1)), \Phi(x_p(2)), ..., \Phi(x_p(N))] + \mathcal{E}_{pos} \qquad (1)$$

where $\mathcal{E}_{pos} \in \mathbb{R}^{(N+1) \times D}$ is the position embedding. Φ is a transformation which projects the patches to vector having dimension D. To learn feature representations, L transformer layers are used.

The patches are formed in an overlapping fashion. This ensures that the information in the boundary of patches is not lost. For this we take stride size less than the patch size. If we denote the patch size as p, stride size as s, then for an image having dimension $h \times w$, the number of patches N is given as:

$$N = N_h \times N_w = \lfloor 1 + \frac{h - p}{s} \rfloor \times \lfloor 1 + \frac{w - p}{s} \rfloor \qquad (2)$$

where, N_h and N_w are the number of patches across height and width respectively. $\lfloor . \rfloor$ is the floor function.

3.2   Vision Transformer

Vision transformer is the backbone of our model. The input image $x \in \mathbb{R}^{h \times w \times c}$ is split into N overlapping patches and each patch is flattened as 1D vector of dimension D. A learnable classification token x_{cls} having the same dimension of a patch embedding is also prepended to the input. This is fed to the vision transformer. i.e., if $W_0 \in \mathbb{R}^{(N+1) \times D}$ is the input to the vision transformer, then $W_0(0) = x_{cls}$. Vision transformer consist of alternate layers of multi-head self attention (MSA) units and multi layer perceptron (MLP) blocks. Before every block, layer normalization is applied and after every block, residual connection is applied. This is shown pictorially in Fig 3. The MLP has two layers with GELU activation function. Assume we have L layers of transformer blocks. By Eq. 1,

$$W_0 = [x_{cls}; \Phi(x_p(1)), \Phi(x_p(2)), ...\Phi(x_p(N))] + \mathcal{E}_{pos}$$

$$W'_L = MSA(LN(W_{L-1})) + W_{L-1} \qquad (3)$$

$$W_L = MLP(LN(W'_L)) + W'_L \qquad (4)$$

where W_0 is the input to vision transformer and $W_L \in \mathbb{R}^{(N+1) \times D}$ is the output of the Lth transformer layer. We extract only the transformed x_{cls} token $W_L(0)$ which is the global feature. $W_L(0)$ is fed to three branches to obtain ID, color and type feature.

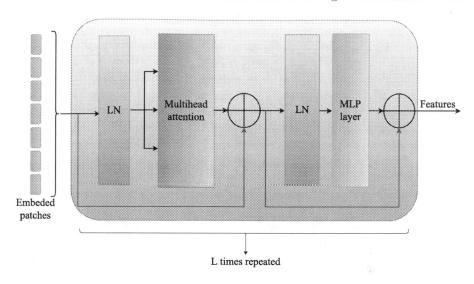

L times repeated

Fig. 3. Vision Transformer

3.3 Gradient Accumulation

Sometimes, due to the limitations of GPUs, we will not be able to train the model with a large batch size. Gradient accumulation solves this issue by splitting the global batch used for training into smaller mini batches and running them sequentially. We run a configured number of steps without updating the model variables, but at the same time accumulating the gradients of those steps. These accumulated gradients are used to compute the updates for weights and biases. As we are not updating the variables at all steps, the mini batches use the same model parameters to calculate the gradients. This ensures that same gradients are calculated as if we use the global batch size.

If we need to do gradient accumulation over N steps, we accumulate gradients of $N - 1$ steps without updating the variables. At N^{th} step, we use the accumulated gradients of past $N - 1$ combined with the gradient of N_{th} step to compute and assign variable update. The total accumulated gradient in N steps is given by,

$$Gradient\ accumulated = \sum_{i=1}^{N} grad_i \qquad (5)$$

where $grad_i$ is the gradient computed for the ith mini batch. We use this gradient as the parameter for optimizer. For SGD optimizer, the variable updates will become as:

$$V_t = V_{t-1} - lr \times (\sum_{i=1}^{N} grad_i) \qquad (6)$$

where V_t is the value of a trainable variable at t^{th} update and lr is the learning rate. In our proposed method, the global batch size is 64 which employs gradient accumulation in 2 steps i.e., minibatch size of 32.

3.4   Side Information Embedding

There can be failure in distinguishing the same vehicle from different perspectives due to viewpoint variations. Hence a learnable side information embedding is employed to include non-visual information like camera and viewpoint. If there are N_C cameras, the side information embedding is given as $\mathcal{E}_C \in \mathbb{R}^{N_C \times D}$. If the camera id is u, then its camera embedding is $\mathcal{E}_C[u]$. The camera embedding are same for all patches of the image unlike position embedding.

Similarly, we can add view embedding to all patches as $\mathcal{E}_V[v]$ where $\mathcal{E}_V \in \mathbb{R}^{N_V \times D}$ and N_V represents the number of viewpoint IDs.

To include both camera and view information, we can encode them together as, $\mathcal{E}_{(C,V)} \in \mathbb{R}^{(N_C \times N_V) \times D}$. The side information embedding is added to the input patch before passing to the vision transformer.

$$W_0' = W_0 + \lambda * \mathcal{E}_{(C,V)}[u * N_V + v] \tag{7}$$

where W_0' is the modified input to transformer after adding position embedding and λ is a hyper parameter.

3.5   Optimization Objective

The global feature output is fed to three different branches to calculate ID loss, type loss and color loss. For ID loss, we combine triplet loss with cross entropy loss.

$$L_{ID} = L_{htri}(a, p, n) + L_{xent}(y_{ID}, \hat{y}_{ID}) \tag{8}$$

where $L_{htri}(a, p, n)$ is the hard triplet loss with soft margin and a, p, n being the anchor, positive and negative samples respectively.

$$L_{htri}(a, p, n) = log[1 + exp(||f(a) - f(p)||_2^2 - ||f(a) - f(n)||_2^2)] \tag{9}$$

where $f(a)$, $f(p)$ and $f(n)$ are the global features of anchor image, positive image and negative image respectively.

L_{xent} is the cross entropy loss which is calculated for ID, color and type feature.

$$L_{xent}(y, \hat{y}) = -\frac{1}{N} \sum_{i=1}^{N} y_i log(\hat{y}_i) \tag{10}$$

where y is ground truth and $\hat{y}$ is the estimated value and N is the number of vehicle IDs.

The loss in color and type is given as,

$$L_{color} = L_{xent}(y_{color}, \hat{y}_{color}) \tag{11}$$

$$L_{type} = L_{xent}(y_{type}, \hat{y}_{type}) \tag{12}$$

The total loss to optimize the weights of the model is the weighted summation of ID loss, color loss and type loss, and given by the following equation:

$$L_{total} = L_{ID} + \lambda_{color} L_{color} + \lambda_{type} L_{type} \tag{13}$$

We set the regularizing parameters λ_{color} and λ_{type} to lower than 1. This is because sometimes the vehicles having same color and/or type may not have the same identity.

4 Experiments

4.1 Dataset

We have trained our model on VeRi dataset [2]. The dataset consist of multiple images of vehicles from 20 cameras and 8 different views. The dataset contains approximately 50,000 images of 776 vehicles. Each vehicle in the dataset is captured by atleast two cameras from different viewpoints, lighting and background. The dataset is divided into training set which has 37,781 images of 576 vehicles, testing set containing 11,579 images of 200 vehicles and a query set containing 1678 images of 200 vehicles. Statistics of dataset used is summarised in Table 1. The dataset contains labels for vehicle id, camera, viewpoint, color and type of vehicle.

Table 1. Statistics of the datasets used

Dataset	totalID	train ID	test ID	query ID	train images	query images	test images
VeRi	776	576	200	200	37,781	1,678	11,579

4.2 Evaluation Metric

We rank the images in gallery according to the similarity of its global feature with query image. For evaluation, we measure the mean average precision (mAP) and rank-K hit rate. To find mAP, we calculate the mean of the average precision of all queries, which is the area under Precision-Recall curve.

$$Average\ Precision\ (AP) = \frac{\sum_{k=1}^{n} P(k) \times rel(k)}{Number\ of\ matching\ images\ in\ gallery} \tag{14}$$

where n is the number of gallery images, $P(k)$ is the precision at k^{th} position of result and $rel(k)$ is a function which takes value 1 if the result at k^{th} position is matched correctly and 0 otherwise.

Mean average precision is given as,

$$mAP = \frac{\sum_{q=1}^{Q} AP(q)}{Q} \tag{15}$$

where Q is the number of query image and $AP(q)$ is the average precision of kth query image.

Rank-K hit rate means the probability of finding at least 1 true positive within top K positions of the re-identified vehicles. We also obtain the cumulative matching characteristics (CMC) by plotting between rank-K hit rate and K.

4.3   Implementation Details

We resize all images to 256×256. Data augmentation is done by padding, random horizontal flipping, random erasing and random cropping. We have taken a batch size of 64 with gradient accumulation of 2 steps. The mini batch has 4 images per id i.e., images of 8 different vehicles are present in a mini batch. The optimizer used is stochastic gradient descent (SGD) optimizer with learning rate of 0.01 and momentum of 0.9. The model is trained for 50 epochs.

The patch embedding of the input image is done using a convolutional layer. Input image of $3 \times 256 \times 256$ is convolved with filters of 16×16 dimension and stride size of 12 and the resulting features are flattened and projected to get the patch embeddings which are 1D vectors having dimension of 768.

For the vision transformer, initial weights are trained on Imagenet 21K and fine tuned on imagenet 1K. For positional embedding, pretrained weights of Imagenet cannot be used because the dimension of images used in pretraining is different from that of images used by us. So a bilinear 2D interpolation is done.

4.4   Results and Discussion

Our model is tested on VeRi dataset achieved very good results. The mean average precision (mAP) comes out to be 75%. We also obtained a Rank-1 hit rate of 95.4% and Rank-5 hit rate of 98.2%. The cumulative matching characteristics (CMC) curve is shown in Fig. 4. The results of our model compared with other models are summarised in Table 2. Our model clearly outperforms some state of the art vehicle ReID methods when tested on VeRi dataset.

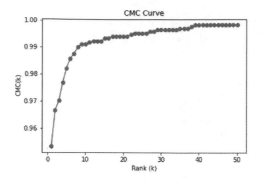

Fig. 4. CMC curve when tested on VeRi dataset

Table 2. Comparison of state of the art vehicle Re ID methods on VeRi dataset.

Method	mAP(%)	Rank-1(%)	Rank-5%
FACT [17]	20.0	59.7	75.3
XVGAN [18]	24.7	60.2	77.0
OIFFE [20]	48.0	65.9	87.7
PROVID [2]	48.47	76.76	91.40
VAMI [19]	50.1	77.0	90.0
FDA-Net [25]	55.5	84.3	92.4
AAVER [26]	61.2	89.0	94.7
RAM [26]	61.5	88.6	94.0
VA Net [22]	66.34	89.78	95.99
SPAN [24]	68.9	94.0	97.6
PAMTRIS [4]	71.88	92.86	96.97
FDA-Net [25]	55.5	84.3	92.4
AAVER [26]	61.2	89.0	94.7
RAM [26]	61.5	88.6	94.0
Our Method	**75**	**95.4**	**98.2**

5   Conclusion

In this paper, we propose a novel Vision Transformer based vehicle re-identification framework. Appearance features like color and type of the vehicle is used along with the vehicle ID for precisely re-identifying the vehicle. For boosting the performance, gradient accumulation is also employed during training. The results of our proposed method outperforms some of the state of the art vehicle re-identification methods by a good margin. The results also show that transformers are more effective than CNN based re identification methods and should be extended to other image classification tasks. In future we aim to extend our work by including different challenging datasets. We will also include day-night scenario and weather conditions to check the efficiency of the model.

References

1. He, S., Luo, H., Wang, P., Wang, F., Li, H., Jiang, W.: Transreid: transformer-based object re-identification. In: Proceedings of the IEEE/CVF International Conference on Computer Vision, pp. 15013–15022 (2021)
2. Liu, X., Liu, W., Mei, T., Ma, H.: Provid: progressive and multimodal vehicle reidentification for large-scale urban surveillance. IEEE Trans. Multimed. **20**(3), 645–658 (2017). https://doi.org/10.10007/1234567890
3. Wen, Y., Lu, Y., Yan, J., Zhou, Z., von Deneen, K.M., Shi, P.: An algorithm for license plate recognition applied to intelligent transportation system. IEEE Trans. Intell. Transp. Syst. **12**(3), 830–845 (2011). https://doi.org/10.1109/TITS.2011.2114346
4. Tang, Z., et al.: Pamtri: pose-aware multi-task learning for vehicle re-identification using highly randomized synthetic data. In: Proceedings of the IEEE/CVF International Conference on Computer Vision, pp. 211–220 (2019)
5. Liu, H., Tian, Y., Wang, Y., Pang, L., Huang, T.: Deep relative distance learning: tell the difference between similar vehicles. In: IEEE Conference on Computer Vision and Pattern Recognition (CVPR) 2016, pp. 2167–2175 (2016). https://doi.org/10.1109/CVPR.2016.238
6. Dosovitskiy, A., et al.: An image is worth 16x16 words: Transformers for image recognition at scale. arXiv preprint arXiv:2010.11929 (2020)
7. Vaswani, A., et al.: Attention is all you need. Advances in neural information processing systems 30 (2017)
8. Xiong, Z., Li, M., Ma, Y., Xinkai, W.: Vehicle re-identification with image processing and car-following model using multiple surveillance cameras from urban arterials. IEEE Trans. Intell. Transp. Syst. **22**(12), 7619–7630 (2020)
9. Zapletal, D., Herout, A.: Vehicle re-identification for automatic video traffic surveillance. In: Proceedings of the IEEE Conference on Computer Vision and Pattern Recognition Workshops, pp. 25–31 (2016)
10. Sanchez, R.O., Flores, C., Horowitz, R., Rajagopal, R., Varaiya, P.: Arterial travel time estimation based on vehicle re-identification using magnetic sensors: performance analysis. In: 2011 14th International IEEE Conference on Intelligent Transportation Systems (ITSC), pp. 997–1002 (2011). https://doi.org/10.1109/ITSC.2011.6083003
11. Sun, C.C., Ritchie, S.G., Joyce Tsai, K., Jayakrishnan, R.: Use of vehicle signature analysis and lexicographic optimization for vehicle reidentification on freeways. Transp. Res. Part C-emerging Technol. **7**, 167–185 (1999)
12. Luo, H., Gu, Y., Liao, X., Lai, S., Jiang, W.: Bag of tricks and a strong baseline for deep person re-identification. In: IEEE/CVF Conference on Computer Vision and Pattern Recognition Workshops (CVPRW) 2019, pp. 1487–1495 (2019). https://doi.org/10.1109/CVPRW.2019.00190
13. Li, Y., Liu, K., Jin, Y., Wang, T., Lin, W.: VARID: viewpoint-aware re-identification of vehicle based on triplet loss. IEEE Trans. Intell. Transp. Syst. (2020)
14. Liu, X., Zhang, S., Wang, X., Hong, R., Tian, Q.: Group-group loss-based global-regional feature learning for vehicle re-identification. IEEE Trans. Image Process. **29**, 2638–2652 (2020). https://doi.org/10.1109/TIP.2019.2950796

15. Zhou, Y., Liu, L., Shao, L.: Vehicle re-identification by deep hidden multi-view inference. IEEE Trans. Image Process. **27**(7), 3275–3287 (2018). https://doi.org/10.1109/TIP.2018.2819820

16. Aslam, N., Rai, P.K., Kolekar, M.H.: A3N: attention-based adversarial autoencoder network for detecting anomalies in video sequence. J. Visual Commun. Image Representation **87**, 103598 (2022)

17. Liu, X., Liu, W., Mei, T., Ma, H.: A deep learning-based approach to progressive vehicle re-identification for urban surveillance. In: Leibe, B., Matas, J., Sebe, N., Welling, M. (eds.) ECCV 2016. LNCS, vol. 9906, pp. 869–884. Springer, Cham (2016). https://doi.org/10.1007/978-3-319-46475-6_53

18. Zhou, Y., Shao, L.: Cross-view GAN based vehicle generation for re-identification. In: BMVC, vol. 1, pp. 1–12 (September 2017)

19. Zhouy, Y., Shao, L.: Viewpoint-aware attentive multi-view inference for vehicle re-identification. In: IEEE/CVF Conference on Computer Vision and Pattern Recognition 2018, pp. 6489–6498 (2018). https://doi.org/10.1109/CVPR.2018.00679

20. Wang, Z., et al.: Orientation invariant feature embedding and spatial temporal regularization for vehicle re-identification. In: IEEE International Conference on Computer Vision (ICCV) 2017, pp. 379–387 (2017). https://doi.org/10.1109/ICCV.2017.49

21. Luo, W., Li, Y., Urtasun, R., Zemel, R.: Understanding the effective receptive field in deep convolutional neural networks. Advances in neural information processing systems 29 (2016)

22. Chu, R., Sun, Y., Li, Y., Liu, Z., Zhang, C., Wei, Y.: Vehicle re-identification with viewpoint-aware metric learning. In: IEEE/CVF International Conference on Computer Vision (ICCV) 2019, pp. 8281–8290 (2019). https://doi.org/10.1109/ICCV.2019.00837

23. Aslam, N., Kolekar, M.H.: Unsupervised anomalous event detection in videos using spatio-temporal inter-fused autoencoder. Multimedia Tools and Applications, pp. 1–26 (2022)

24. Chen, T. S., Liu, C.-T., Wu, C.-W., Chien, S.-Y.: Orientation-aware vehicle re-identification with semantics-guided part attention network. In: Vedaldi, A., Bischof, H., Brox, T., Frahm, J.-M. (eds.) ECCV 2020. LNCS, vol. 12347, pp. 330–346. Springer, Cham (2020). https://doi.org/10.1007/978-3-030-58536-5_20

25. Lou, Y., Bai, Y., Liu, J., Wang, S., Duan, L.: VERI-wild: a large dataset and a new method for vehicle re-identification in the wild. In: IEEE/CVF Conference on Computer Vision and Pattern Recognition (CVPR) 2019, pp. 3230–3238 (2019). https://doi.org/10.1109/CVPR.2019.00335

26. Khorramshahi, P., Kumar, A., Peri, N., Rambhatla, S.S., Chen, J.-C., Chellappa, R.: A dual-path model with adaptive attention for vehicle re-identification. In: IEEE/CVF International Conference on Computer Vision (ICCV) 2019, pp. 6131–6140 (2019). https://doi.org/10.1109/ICCV.2019.00623

27. Liu, X., Zhang, S., Huang, Q., Gao, W.: RAM: a region-aware deep model for vehicle re-identification. In: IEEE International Conference on Multimedia and Expo (ICME) 2018, pp. 1–6 (2018). https://doi.org/10.1109/ICME.2018.8486589

Attention Residual Capsule Network for Dermoscopy Image Classification

Anabik Pal[1,2,3], Sounak Ray[3,4], Sameer Antani[2], and Utpal Garain[3,5(✉)]

[1] Department of Computer Science and Engineering, SRM University,
Amaravati, AP, India
[2] National Library of Medicine, National Institutes of Health, Maryland, USA
[3] CVPR Unit, Indian Statistical Institute, Kolkata, India
utpal@isical.ac.in
[4] Department of Computer Science, Columbia University, New York City, USA
[5] Centre for AIML, Indian Statistical Institute, Kolkata, India

Abstract. Automated analysis of dermoscopic images for detecting malignant lesions can improve diagnostic performance and reduce premature deaths. While several automated classification algorithms using deep convolutional neural network (DCNN) models have been proposed, the need for performance improvement remains. The key limitations of developing a robust DCNN model for the dermoscopic image classification are (a) sub-sampling or pooling layer in traditional DCNN has theoretical drawbacks in capturing object-part relationship, (b) increasing the network depth can improve the performance but is prone to suffer from the vanishing gradient problem, and (c) due to imbalanced dataset, the trained DCNN tends to be biased towards the majority classes. To overcome these limitations, we propose a novel deep Attention Residual Capsule Network (ARCN) for dermoscopic image classification to diagnose skin diseases. The proposed model combines the concept of residual learning, self-attention mechanism, and capsule network. The residual learning is employed to address the vanishing gradient problem, the self-attention mechanism is employed to prioritize important features without using any extra learnable parameters, capsule network is employed to cope up with information loss due to the sub-sampling (max-pooling) layer. To deal with the classifier's bias toward the majority classes, a novel Mini-Batch-wise weight-balancing Focal Loss strategy is proposed. HAM10000, a benchmark dataset of dermoscopic images is used to train the deep model and evaluate the performance. The ARCN-18 (modification of ResNet-18) network trained with the proposed loss produces an accuracy of 0.8206 for the considered test set.

Keywords: Capsule networks · Residual learning · Attention learning · Skin lesion classification · Skin disease recognition

D. Gupta et al. (Eds.): CVIP 2022, CCIS 1777, pp. 108–121, 2023.
https://doi.org/10.1007/978-3-031-31417-9_9

1   Introduction

A recent epidemiological study estimated that globally, 325000 new melanoma cases and 57000 deaths due to melanoma occurred in 2020. If 2020 rates remain stable, the global burden from melanoma is estimated to increase to 510000 new cases and 96000 deaths by 2040 [1]. Early diagnosis of this disease helps in patient care and reduces premature death. In clinical practice, a dermatoscope is used to diagnose the disease. The device is used to view affected skin regions under magnification as well as eliminate the surface reflection of the skin. However, significant variability (75%–84%) has been reported in the diagnostic accuracy of trained and experienced dermatologists [10,20]. Advanced computer-aided automated diagnosis systems have the potential to help reduce this variability while simultaneously improving diagnostic accuracy and reducing mortality.

The diagnosis of skin disease from dermoscopic images has been posed as an image classification problem. The development of a robust feature descriptor to represent the skin lesions is challenging due to the presence of various image artifacts (like hairs, veins, air bubbles, etc.), variation in skin color, and diverse ambient conditions of the captured images [2]. These make it difficult to develop robust image classification algorithms using classical approaches. However, over the last four years, there have been several approaches proposed using Deep Convolutional Neural Networks (DCNN) that have resulted in robust skin image classification algorithms [4,5,11,18,22]. This is primarily due to their ability to learn better discriminative features directly from input images in presence of image artifacts and variability in skin color tone.

However, DCNN also has several limitations. First, DCNN models are data-hungry. A large number of representative sample images from every class are required to develop a robust classifier. To alleviate this limitation, several approaches opt to use for fine-tuning the DCNN model trained on ImageNet [14]. Second, a very deep neural network is prone to suffer from the well-known vanishing gradient problem. A residual learning or residual connection approach is used in deep neural networks to cope with this [8]. This has two types of blocks: (a) identity block, and (b) convolutional block. The identity block performs feature enhancement by identity mappings. This is done by adding the input to the block to the output through an identity skip connection. On the other hand, in the convolutional block, there is a selective feedforward of information that contains a stack of few convolutional layers and batch normalization layers. Finally, the prediction model produced from a trained DCNN tends to be biased towards the majority classes. This problem is termed as a class-imbalance problem. Due to class imbalance, a classification model is prone to diagnose an image as the most frequent disease and thus ignore rare cases. To cope with the class imbalance problem, different loss weighting mechanisms have been studied [13].

In this paper, we present a novel deep Attention Residual Capsule Network (ARCN) model for dermoscopic image classification. The proposed model combines the residual learning [8,12], self-attention mechanism [7,9,23], and deep capsule network [15–17,21]. Residual learning is important to address the vanishing gradient problem in training a deep neural network. The attention mechanism is devised because it can produce a robust model giving special attention to the important spatial regions on the input images [9]. We use a self-attention module [23] in our network as it does not require any extra learnable weights for prioritizing important regions. We propose to use capsule networks as they are more robust towards encoding spatial relationships between features in the higher and lower layer than traditional Deep Convolutional Neural Networks (DCNN). In short, capsule networks are devised to alleviate information loss due to pooling layers in traditional DCNN. We hypothesize that the intelligent feature encoding mechanism in the capsule network will capture the skin lesion characteristics in a better way. To deal with dataset imbalance, we develop a novel Mini-Batch-wise weight-balancing Focal Loss function to train the deep networks.

To summarize, the contribution of the paper is as follows:

1. Propose a new DCNN architecture for dermoscopic image classification.
2. Propose a new loss function to deal with the classifier's bias towards the majority classes due to the class imbalance dataset.
3. Compare the performance of several trained DCNN models obtained by cross-crossing competing relevant baseline networks and available classifier's bias removal strategies.

The rest of this paper is organized as follows: Sect. 2 describes the proposed network. The experimental protocol is given in Sect. 3. Section 4 presents and discusses experimental results. Finally, Sect. 5 concludes the paper.

2 Methodology

This section is divided into two parts. Firstly, the proposed architecture is discussed and the latter part discusses the network training.

2.1 Attention Residual Capsule Network (ARCN)

In this paper, a novel Attention Residual Capsule Network (ARCN) is proposed for dermoscopic image classification. ARCN unites residual learning, capsule networks, and an attention mechanism. Attention Convolutional Capsule Block (ACCB) and Attention Identity Capsule Block (AICB) are key components of this network. The important components of ARCN are discussed before discussing the network.

ConvCaps Layer. ConvCaps layer is used in ACCB Blocks and AICB Blocks of the proposed network. This layer replaces the convolutional layer with the convolutional capsule layer which performs the 3D-convolution-based localized routing [16]. The role of the novel intelligent routing is to get optimized performance in terms of execution time and learnable parameters.

Dynamic Routing in ConvCaps Layer. Dynamic routing used in the Con-vCaps layer is a multi-step procedure. Suppose, h^l, w^l, n^l, c^l denote height, width, number of capsules, and the dimension of the capsule for layer l. Then for dynamic routing, firstly, the input tensor (ψ^l) of shape (h^l, w^l, n^l, c^l) received from layer l will be reshaped into a 3D-single channel tensor of shape $(h^l, w^l, n^l \times c^l, 1)$. Then ψ^l is convolved with $(c^{l+1} \times n^{l+1})$ number of 3D con-volution kernels. The kernels in the layer l form the weight matrix. The output of the convolutional operations forms the intermediate votes $\mathbf{V}$, which are to be routed to the higher layers. Maintaining the size of the kernel and keeping the stride as (s_h, s_w, n_l), allow us to get a vote for a single capsule from layer l. The intermediate vote, having shape $(h^{l+1}, w^{l+1}, c^l, c^{l+1} \times n^{l+1})$ is then reshaped to $(h^{l+1}, w^{l+1}, n^{l+1}, c^{l+1}, c^l)$ for making it suitable for dynamic routing.

The logits $\mathbf{B}_s$ $(\mathbf{B}_s \in \mathbb{R}^{(h^{l+1}, w^{l+1}, c^{l+1})})$ to be refined iteratively during routing are initialized to 0 for all capsules s $(s \in c^l)$ of layer l. The corresponding coupling coefficients are calculated using the softmax function on the logits $\mathbf{B}_s$. The logits $\mathbf{B}_s$ are updated using routing-by-agreement where the agreement factor is computed using the dot product between the vote received from input layer l and the output of the next layer's capsules. The output of the next layer is then squashed by Eq. 1 so that their value lies between $[0, 1]$ without changing its direction.

$$\text{Squash}(s_j) = \frac{||s_j||^2}{1 + ||s_j||^2} \frac{s_j}{||s_j||} \tag{1}$$

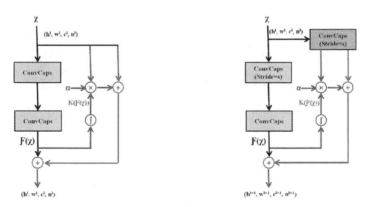

(a) Attention Identity Capsule Block (AICB).

(b) Attention Convolutional Capsule Block (ACCB).

Fig. 1. Build blocks of Attention Residual Capsule Network. (Color figure online)

Attention Identity Capsule Block. Attention Identity Capsule Block (AICB) is a novel extension of identity block available in the skip connection of a Residual Network (ResNet) [8]. AICB replaces the convolutional layer with the ConvCaps layer and adds an attention learning mechanism to improve the learning of the network. The block diagram of AICB used in our network is shown in Fig. 1a. According to Fig. 1a, an AICB has the following three computational paths- (a) direct filter processing path (shown in black color) containing multiple ConvCaps layers, (b) attention weight learning path (shown in purple color), and (c) short-cut path (shown in blue color). The outputs from all three paths are added to produce the final output feature map. The dimension of the input tensor is not changed when it passes through the AICBs.

Attention Convolutional Capsule Block. Attention Convolutional Capsule Block (ACCB) is an improvement of ConvBlock used in the skip connection of a Residual Network (ResNet) [8]. ACCB block replaces all convolutional layers (both in direct path and short-cut path) with ConvCaps layer and adds attention learning mechanism to improve the learning of the network. The block diagram of the proposed ACCB is shown in Fig. 1b. According to Fig. 1b, like AICB, ACCB has the following three computational paths- (a) direct filter processing path (shown in black color) containing multiple ConvCaps layers, (b) attention weight learning path (shown in purple color), and (c) short-cut path (shown in blue color) contains a ConvCaps layer. The outputs from all three paths are added to produce the final output of this block. In comparison with the AICB, the spatial dimension of the input tensor is changed when the tensor is passed through the ACCBs, and in the blue path one ConvCaps layer is placed.

Attention Learning. Attention learning is incorporated into AICB and ACCB blocks used in our network. As the higher layers of a deep model have better semantic abstraction ability than lower layers so the attention ability of higher layers is stronger than lower layers. Hence, in this paper, the semantically more abstract features generated by higher layers are used to generate the attention mask of lower layers. Thus self-attention learning which does not use any extra parameters is achieved.

The attention masks (K) is generated by applying the following normalization function on the output ($F(X)$) obtained from the black path of AICB or ACCB:

$$K(F(X)) = \frac{e^{F(X)_{i,j,k}}}{\sum_{x \in h, y \in w, z \in c} e^{F(X)_{x,y,z}}}, \tag{2}$$

where i $\in$ h, j $\in$ w, k $\in$ c are the spatial positions and the number of capsules respectively. The attention masks (K) is then multiplied with the input tensor to generate the attention-aware feature map. This attention-aware feature map is then multiplied by a learned weighting factor (α), to determine the relative importance of the attention-aware features for the other feature maps.

FlatCaps. The FlatCaps layer is equivalent to reshape layer used in traditional DCNN models. The task of this layer is to remove the spatial relationship of the features available between adjacent capsules. Mathematically, the FlatCaps layer converts a (h, w, c, n) shaped input tensor into a $(h \times w \times c, n)$ shaped output tensor.

DenseCaps. DenseCaps are similar to the final fully connected classification layers in DCNNs. The only difference is that it performs dense routing. This layer converts an input tensor of dimension (a^l, n^l) into (a^{l+1}, n^{l+1}) output tensor.

Network Architecture. The architectural detail of the proposed ARCN is given in the fourth column of Table 1. The number of routing iterations of a ConvCaps layer inside the AICB or ACCB is empirically decided. According to our experience, we receive optimized performance when all ConvCaps layers except the Green colored ConvCaps layer of the last two ACCB use only 1 routing iterations. The Green colored ConvCaps layer of the last two ACCBs uses 3 routing iterations.

The competing networks are kept in the first three columns of Table 1. To understand the competing architectures in detail the readers have to note the following: (i) replacing ConvCaps with Convolutional layer converts ACCB into ACB and AICB into AIB (ii) removal of attention learning (purple path) and replacing ConvCaps with Convolution layer converts AICB into IB. (iii) removal of attention learning (purple path) converts AICB into ICB. (iv) removal of attention learning (purple path) and replacing ConvCaps with Convolution layer converts ACCB module into CB. (v) removal of attention learning (purple path), converts AICB into ICB.

Table 1. Network architectures of ResNet18, ARL18, RCN18, and ARCN18. The number of parameters in each network is shown in the last row. fs: filter size, s: stride, MP= max-pooling, CB: Convolutional Block, IB: Identity Block, ACB: Attention Convolutional Block, AIB: Attention Identity Block, CCB: Convolutional Capsule Block, ICB: Identity Capsule Block, ACCB: Attention Convolutional Capsule Block, AICB: Attention Identity Capsule Block, GAP: Global Average Pooling layer, FC: Fully Connected Softmax classification layer.

ResNet18	ARL18	RCN18	ARCN18
Conv (fs=7×7, s=2) MP (fs=3×3, s=2)	Conv (fs=7×7, s=2) MP (fs=3×3, s=2)	Conv (fs=7×7, s=4)	Conv (fs=7×7, s=4)
CB (s=1) IB	ACB (s=1) AIB	CCB (s=1) ICB	ACCB (s=1) AICB
CB (s=2) IB	ACB (s=2) AIB	CCB (s=2) ICB	ACCB (s=2) AICB
CB (s=2) IB	ACB (s=2) AIB	CCB (s=2) ICB	ACCB (s=2) AICB
CB (s=2) IB	ACB (s=2) AIB	CCB (s=2) ICB	ACCB (s=2) AICB
GAP	GAP	FlatCaps	FlatCaps
FC	FC	DenseCaps	DenseCaps
11.669 million	11.669 million	14.012 million	14.012 million

2.2 Network Training with Imbalanced Data

Literature shows that several techniques have been devised to cope with the bias of a deep model towards majority classes when it is trained with imbalanced data samples. In this regard, Up-sampling minority classes, under-sampling majority classes, loss computation with class weighting, using focal loss, etc. are commonly used approaches. In this paper, we use the following strategies:

Upsampling (UP): Offline data augmentation is done using random rotation ($\pm 20°$), random cropping, random flipping, and color enhancement. This up-sampling strategy generates an increased training set of 16000 images (MEL-2500, NV-5000, BCC-2000, AKIEC-1500, BKL-2000, DF-1500, and VASC-1500).

Mini-Batch Balanced Data Sampling (MBDS): In this novel down-sampling strategy, for every epoch only a fraction of samples from the majority classes are selected and mini-batches are constructed by taking an equal number of images from every class.

Epoch Balanced Focal Loss (EBFL): This is a novel loss re-weighing technique inspired from [13]. Mathematically, Let C denote the number of classes, n_i denote the number of samples in class i, p_j denotes the probability output of softmax layer that the j-th sample belongs to class i, N denotes the total size of the training set, α_i denotes the class-weight factor of class i and $\gamma \in [0, 5)$ is a hyperparameter then the proposed Epoch Balanced Focal Loss (EBFL) is given as:

$$\text{EBFL} = \sum_{i=1}^{C} \frac{1}{n_i} \sum_{j=1}^{n_i} -\alpha_i (1 - p_j)^\gamma (\log p_j)$$

$$\text{where } \alpha_i = \frac{N}{C * n_i}$$

(3)

Mini-Batch Balanced Focal Loss (MBFL): This is another variants of Focal Loss when in Eq. 3, n_i denotes the number of images from i-th class in a mini-batch.

3   Experimental Protocol

3.1   Dataset

For experimental evaluation, we used HAM10000, a publicly available large-size (10015) dermoscopic image dataset [19]. This dataset consists of images from seven skin diseases: Melanoma (MEL), Melanocytic nevus (NV), Basal Cell Carcinoma (BCC), Actinic keratosis (AKIEC), Benign keratosis (BKL), Dermatofibroma (DF), and Vascular lesion (VASC). One representative image sample from every class is shown in Fig. 2. We split the dataset into following three disjoint sets: training set (7012 images), validation set (2005 images), and test set (MEL:111, NV:671, BCC:51, AKIEC:33, BKL:110, DF:10, VASC:12, total:998 images). All three partition follows the same class distribution. The validation set is used for hyper-parameter tuning and experimental evaluation is carried out based on the test set.

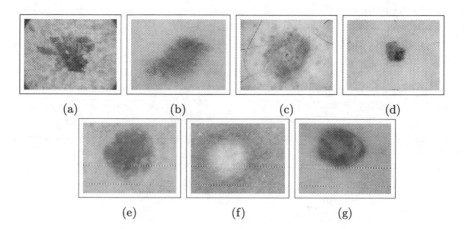

Fig. 2. Images of different skin lesions from HAM10000. (a) Melanoma, (b) Melanocytic nevus, (c) Basal cell carcinoma, (d) Actinic keratosis, (e) Benign keratosis, (f) Dermatofibroma, and (g) Vascular.

3.2   Evaluation Metrics

The main problem while designing a metric for a problem with imbalanced data distribution is that a simple accuracy metric could be very misleading. A simple accuracy metric would give us the illusion that the model is performing well even if it classifies all the images of the over-represented class correctly, which could be critical in the case of diagnosis. So to evaluate our models we use additional three metrics, namely, mean-recall (R_m), mean-precision (P_m) and mean F1-score $(F1_m)$ metrics. If TP denoted the number of true positives, FN denotes the number of false negatives, FP denotes the false positive X_i denotes metric X for i-th class and C denotes the number of classes, then the mathematical definition of R_m, P_m and $F1_m$ can be obtained from the following equations:

$$R_m = \frac{1}{C}\sum_{i=1}^{C} R_i \quad (4) \qquad P_m = \frac{1}{C}\sum_{i=1}^{C} P_i \quad (5) \qquad F1_m = \frac{1}{C}\sum_{i=1}^{C} F1_i \quad (6)$$

where,

$$R = \frac{TP}{TP+FN} \quad (7) \qquad P = \frac{TP}{TP+FP} \quad (8) \qquad F1 = \frac{2 \times P \times R}{P+R} \quad (9)$$

3.3   Implementation Details

In this paper, we investigate how the present skin image classification task will be benefited when capsule network and attention learning are incorporated with the residual network. Due to resource limitations, we consider ResNet-18 as the backbone network. The architectural design for all competing methods is presented in Table 1. All networks take 224×224 size images as input. The networks are initialized with pre-trained Image-Net weight matrices except for the last classification layer. In contrast to the Image-Net 1000-class classification problem, we are training the model for a 7-class classification task. The last layer's weights are initialized with the Xavier Initialization method proposed in [6]. The mini-batch Stochastic Gradient Descent (SGD) algorithm is used to train the networks. The training hyper-parameters are decided from an empirical study. At first, we fine-tuned the final layer with a learning rate of 0.01 for 20 epochs, and then the whole network was trained with a learning rate of 0.001. In the full fine-tuning phase, we reduce the learning rate by a factor of the half when the validation loss did not improve for 20 epochs The epoch number was set to 100. The Keras [3] deep learning toolkit is used for implementing the networks. An Intel® Core™ i7-4770 processor-based workstation with GTX 1080 GPU is used for performing all the experiments.

4   Result and Discussion

The deep networks described in Sect. 2.1 are trained for the present classification problem. The networks are initialized with pre-trained weights (obtained from the ImageNet) and Xavier Initialization is employed for the computational blocks for which pre-trained weights are not available (e.g. weights of 3D-convolution in RCN). After weight initialization, only those layers where the weights are initialized with Xavier's method are fine-tuned. After weight initialization full fine-tuning is performed with the competing learning strategies for all four networks. Note that for comparison same weight initialization technique is employed for all competing training strategies. In the following paragraphs, the quantitative performance of the networks trained with normal Fine-tuning, Upsampling (UP), Mini-Batch Balanced Data Sampling (MBDS), Epoch Balanced Focal Loss (EBFL), Mini-Batch Balanced Focal Loss (MBFL) is explained. Finally, some sample images from the test set along with the class label predictions obtained from considered networks trained with the best learning strategy are given.

Performance of the trained classifiers trained with the **fine-tuning** method for four different architectures are given in Table 2. According to Table 2, the proposed ARCN network is producing the best Accuracy, Mean Precision, and Mean F_Score and achieves a noticeable performance gap over the other competing networks. We receive the best Mean Recall from the RCN network, however, the Mean Recall is comparable with the ARCN.

Performance of the trained classifiers trained with the **offline data augmentation method (Up-sampling method)** for four different architectures

Table 2. Quantitative performance evaluation for Finetuned models. MR: Mean Recall, MP: Mean Precision, MF: Mean F_Score.

Network	Accuracy	MR	MP	MF
ResNet-18	0.8006	0.65 ± 0.136	0.66 ± 0.131	0.66 ± 0.131
ARL-18	0.8016	0.62 ± 0.143	0.67 ± 0.103	0.65 ± 0.122
RCN-18	0.8096	**0.70 ± 0.100**	0.63 ± 0.144	0.66 ± 0.117
ARCN-18	**0.8337**	0.69 ± 0.110	**0.68 ± 0.119**	**0.69 ± 0.109**

is given in Table 3. According to Table 3, the proposed ARCN network is producing the best Accuracy, Mean Precision, and Mean F_Score and achieves a noticeable performance gap over the other competing networks. We receive the best Mean Recall from the RCN network, however, the Mean Recall is comparable with ARCN. In comparison with the traditional fine-tuning method, we find that the bias reduction with upsampling strategy improves only the Mean Recall and all other metrics are not improving.

Table 3. Quantitative performance evaluation for Upsampling training strategy. MR: Mean Recall, MP: Mean Precision, MF: Mean F_Score.

Network	Accuracy	MR	MP	MF
ResNet-18	0.7766	0.70 ± 0.088	0.58 ± 0.162	0.63 ± 0.116
ARL-18	0.7725	0.72 ± 0.085	0.56 ± 0.197	0.57 ± 0.158
RCN-18	0.7675	**0.74 ± 0.069**	0.61 ± 0.274	0.63 ± 0.212
ARCN-18	**0.8096**	0.73 ± 0.087	**0.65 ± 0.177**	**0.68 ± 0.126**

Performance of the classifier trained with the **Mini-Batch Balanced Data Sampling (MBDS)** strategy for four different architectures are given in Table 4. According to Table 4, the proposed ARCN network is producing the best Accuracy and Mean Recall in compromising Mean Precision and Mean F_Score. The overall performance of this training strategy is poor than the previous approaches. The present research reveals that unbiased model development with down-sampling is not suitable for the present research.

Performance of the classifier trained with the **Epoch Balanced Focal Loss (EBFL)** for four different architectures is given in Table 5. According to Table 5, the proposed ARCN network is producing the best Accuracy, Mean Recall, and Mean Precision. In comparison with traditional fine-tuning of ARCN, this loss minimization improves the Mean Recall, however, all other metrics are decreased. The probable reason is that this loss function aims to improve the Mean Recall in a batch.

Performance of the classifier trained with the **Mini-Batch Balanced Focal Loss (MBFL)** for four different architectures is given in Table 6. According to

Table 4. Quantitative performance evaluation for MBDS training strategy. MR: Mean Recall, MP: Mean Precision, MF: Mean F_Score.

Network	Accuracy	MR	MP	MF
ResNet-18	0.7345	0.68 ± 0.049	0.52 ± 0.21	0.57 ± 0.148
ARL-18	0.7325	0.67 ± 0.074	0.53 ± 0.218	**0.62 ± 0.136**
RCN-18	0.7405	0.70 ± 0.068	**0.60 ± 0.225**	0.62 ± 0.146
ARCN-18	**0.7625**	**0.71 ± 0.086**	0.57 ± 0.256	0.60 ± 0.179

Table 5. Quantitative performance evaluation for EBFL training strategy. MR: Mean Recall, MP: Mean Precision, MF: Mean F_Score.

Network	Accuracy	MR	MP	MF
ResNet-18	0.6804	0.69 ± 0.060	0.53 ± 0.212	0.59 ± 0.116
ARL-18	0.7335	0.71 ± 0.068	0.51 ± 0.219	0.57 ± 0.145
RCN-18	0.7465	0.72 ± 0.088	0.55 ± 0.193	**0.61 ± 0.132**
ARCN-18	**0.7966**	**0.72 ± 0.074**	**0.56 ± 0.277**	0.59 ± 0.214

Table 6, the proposed ARCN network is producing the best Accuracy, and Mean F_Score. We find that Mean Recall obtained from RCN is noticeably higher than all other networks, however, it compromises the other three metrics a lot. The best Mean Precision is achieved from ARL which is quite comparable with ARCN. Hence, we consider ARCN based model as our best model.

Table 6. Quantitative performance evaluation for MBFL training strategy. MR: Mean Recall, MP: Mean Precision, MF: Mean F_Score.

Network	Accuracy	MR	MP	MF
ResNet-18	0.7966	0.70 ± 0.095	0.67 ± 0.145	0.68 ± 0.118
ARL-18	0.8016	0.71 ± 0.125	**0.70 ± 0.119**	0.70 ± 0.101
RCN-18	0.7665	**0.76 ± 0.067**	0.59 ± 0.171	0.66 ± 0.101
ARCN-18	**0.8206**	0.74 ± 0.088	0.69 ± 0.108	**0.71 ± 0.094**

In comparison with other unbiased model development strategies and traditional fine-tuning strategies (results available in Table 2, Table 3, Table 4 and Table 5), the MBFL-based training improves the classification performance and produces the best Mean Recall, Mean Precision, and Mean F_Score. Hence, we consider this as the best training strategy. The visual representation of the prediction outcomes obtained from the competing networks trained with the best training strategy (i.e. Mini-batch Balanced Focal Loss) is shown in Fig. 3. In Fig. 3, all diseases are encoded by the following numeric class values: 0 for

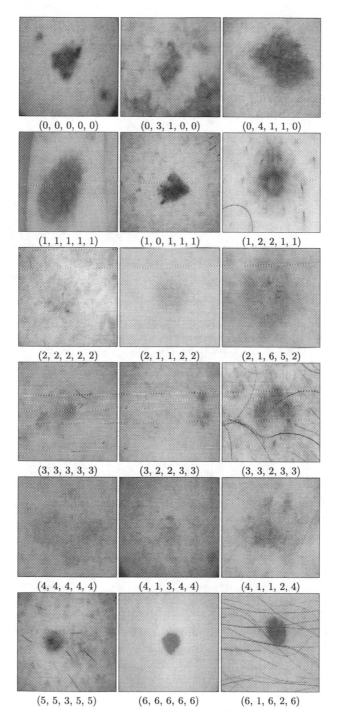

Fig. 3. Images and their ground-truth class label and predicted class labels obtained from ResNet18, ARL18, RCN18, and ARCN18 models respectively when trained with Mini-batch Balanced Focal Loss (MBFL) minimization.

Melanoma, 1 for Melanocytic Nevus, 2 for Basal Cell Carcinoma, 3 for Actinic keratosis, 4 for Benign keratosis, 5 for Dermatofibroma, and 6 for Vascular lesions.

5   Conclusion

This paper presents a novel deep model called the Attention Residual Capsule Network (ARCN) which integrates the advantages of residual learning and attention learning with the capsule network. The capsule network was introduced to boost the object classification tasks but the present research shows that it can also improve the skin lesion classification performance. This work makes a pioneering attempt to develop a capsule network-based deep model containing multiple routing layers. Further, the performance of the proposed model is good for a practical system that can be developed and deployed in under-resourced settings even with modestly powered computational resources. The application of ARCN for building robust image classifiers for other application domains is the next future challenge of this research.

Acknowledgment. Dr. Pal's work is partially supported by the intramural research program of the National Library of Medicine and the National Institutes of Health, USA. Dr. Antani's work is supported by the intramural research program of the National Library of Medicine and the National Institutes of Health, USA. Dr. Garain's work is supported by Science and Engineering Research Board (SERB), Dept. of Science and Technology (DST), Govt. of India through Grant File No. SPR/2020/000495.

References

1. Arnold, M., et al.: Global Burden of Cutaneous Melanoma in 2020 and Projections to 2040. JAMA Dermatol. **158**(5), 495–503 (2022). https://doi.org/10.1001/jamadermatol.2022.0160
2. Barata, C., Celebi, M.E., Marques, J.S.: Improving dermoscopy image classification using color constancy. IEEE J. Biomed. Health Inform. **19**(3), 1146–1152 (2015)
3. Chollet, F., et al.: Keras (2015). https://keras.io
4. Esteva, A., et al.: Corrigendum: dermatologist-level classification of skin cancer with deep neural networks. Nature **546**, 686–686 (2017)
5. Ge, Z., Demyanov, S., Chakravorty, R., Bowling, A., Garnavi, R.: Skin disease recognition using deep saliency features and multimodal learning of dermoscopy and clinical images. In: Descoteaux, M., Maier-Hein, L., Franz, A., Jannin, P., Collins, D.L., Duchesne, S. (eds.) MICCAI 2017. LNCS, vol. 10435, pp. 250–258. Springer, Cham (2017). https://doi.org/10.1007/978-3-319-66179-7_29
6. Glorot, X., Bengio, Y.: Understanding the difficulty of training deep feedforward neural networks. In: AISTATS (2010)
7. Hassanin, M., Anwar, S., Radwan, I., Khan, F.S., Mian, A.: Visual attention methods in deep learning: an in-depth survey. arXiv preprint arXiv:2204.07756 (2022)
8. He, K., Zhang, X., Ren, S., Sun, J.: Deep residual learning for image recognition. In: 2016 IEEE Conference on Computer Vision and Pattern Recognition (CVPR), pp. 770–778 (2015)

9. Jaderberg, M., Simonyan, K., Zisserman, A., Kavukcuoglu, K.: Spatial transformer networks. arXiv abs/1506.02025 (2015)
10. Kittler, H., H., P., K., W., M., B.: Diagnostic accuracy of dermoscopy. Lancet Oncol. **3**(3), 159–165 (2002)
11. Lafraxo, S., Ansari, M.E., Charfi, S.: Melanet: an effective deep learning framework for melanoma detection using dermoscopic images. Multimedia Tools Appl. **81**(11), 16021–16045 (2022)
12. Li, H., Zeng, N., Wu, P., Clawson, K.: Cov-net: a computer-aided diagnosis method for recognizing COVID-19 from chest x-ray images via machine vision. Expert Syst. Appl. 118029 (2022)
13. Lin, T.Y., Goyal, P., Girshick, R.B., He, K., Dollár, P.: Focal loss for dense object detection. In: 2017 IEEE International Conference on Computer Vision (ICCV), pp. 2999–3007 (2017)
14. Pal, A., Chaturvedi, A., Garain, U., Chandra, A., Chatterjee, R.: Severity grading of psoriatic plaques using deep CNN based multi-task learning. In: 23rd International Conference on Pattern Recognition (ICPR 2016), December 2016
15. Pal, A., et al.: Micaps: multi-instance capsule network for machine inspection of Munro's microabscess. Comput. Biol. Med. **140**, 105071 (2022)
16. Rajasegaran, J., Jayasundara, V., Jayasekara, S., Jayasekara, H., Seneviratne, S., Rodrigo, R.: DeepCaps: going deeper with capsule networks. arXiv abs/1904.09546 (2019)
17. Sabour, S., Frosst, N., Hinton, G.E.: Dynamic routing between capsules. arXiv abs/1710.09829 (2017)
18. Salma, W., Eltrass, A.S.: Automated deep learning approach for classification of malignant melanoma and benign skin lesions. Multimedia Tools Appl. 1–18 (2022)
19. Tschandl, P., Rosendahl, C., Kittler, H.: The ham10000 dataset, a large collection of multi-source dermatoscopic images of common pigmented skin lesions. Sci. Data **5** (2018). https://doi.org/10.1038/sdata.2018.161
20. Vestergaard, M.E., Macaskill, P., Holt, P.E., Menzies, S.W.: Dermoscopy compared with naked eye examination for the diagnosis of primary melanoma: a meta-analysis of studies performed in a clinical setting. Br. J. Dermatol. **159**, 669–676 (2008)
21. Xi, E., Bing, S., Jin, Y.: Capsule network performance on complex data. arXiv e-prints arXiv:1712.03480, December 2017
22. Yu, L., Chen, H., Dou, Q., Qin, J., Heng, P.A.: Automated melanoma recognition in dermoscopy images via very deep residual networks. IEEE Trans. Med. Imaging **36**(4), 994–1004 (2017)
23. Zhang, J., Xie, Y., Xia, Y., Shen, C.: Attention residual learning for skin lesion classification. IEEE Trans. Med. Imaging, 1 (2019)

SAMNet: Semantic Aware Multimodal Network for Emoji Drawing Classification

Sourabh Vasant Gothe⬤, Rishabh Khurana(✉)⬤,
Jayesh Rajkumar Vachhani(✉)⬤, S. Rakshith(✉)⬤, and Pranay Kashyap(✉)⬤

Samsung R & D Institute, Bangalore 560037, India
{sourab.gothe,k.rishabh,jay.vachhani,rakshith1.s,
pranay.kashyap}@samsung.com

Abstract. In the current era, the mode of communication through mobile devices is becoming more personalized with the evolution of touch-based input methods. While writing on touch-responsive devices, searching for emojis to capture the true intent is cumbersome. To solve this problem, the existing solutions consider either the text or only stroke-based drawings to predict the appropriate emojis. We do not leverage the full context by considering only a single input. While the user is digitally writing, it is challenging for the model to identify whether the intention is to write text or draw an emoji. Moreover, the model's memory footprint and latency play an essential role in providing a seamless writing experience to the user. In this paper, we investigate the effectiveness of combining text and drawing as input to the model. We present SAMNet, a multimodal deep neural network that jointly learns the text and image features. Here image features are extracted from the stroke-based drawing and text from the previously written context. We also demonstrate the optimal way to fuse features from both modalities. The paper focuses on improving user experience and providing low latency on edge devices. We trained our model with a carefully crafted dataset of 63 emoji classes and evaluated the performance. We achieve a worst-case On-Device inference time of 60 ms and 76.74% top-3 prediction accuracy with a model size of 3.5 MB. We evaluated the results with the closest matching application-DigitalInk and found that SAMNet provided a 13.95% improvement in the top-3 prediction accuracy.

Keywords: Multimodal · Emoji Drawing · Touch-responsive devices

1 Introduction

Strong growth in the usage of mobile, touch-enabled devices(tablets) and their advancement has allowed users to accomplish multiple things in their handwriting with a stylus or fingers. For example, writing down notes, content creation, or basic communication[1], as shown in Fig. 1. In most scenarios, expressions

---

[1] Image Courtesy: https://youtu.be/62AiE3a0Tmo.

D. Gupta et al. (Eds.): CVIP 2022, CCIS 1777, pp. 122–135, 2023.
https://doi.org/10.1007/978-3-031-31417-9_10

and emotions are crucial in conveying a message accurately. To understand the benefits of providing the user with context based Emojis, we conducted a user trial for 100 Android users for one month. We monitored stats related to their emoji usage. Among these 100 users, we observed that each user spends close to 187 s/week (average) in the 'emoji layout' of the keyboard. In the emoji layout, a user can select an emoji, search for an emoji or browse through the list of emojis. If the device understands the user's intent and predicts the desired emoji based on it, this can boost the user's productivity.

Fig. 1. Examples of state of the art communication methods on touch-enabled devices. Our proposed model focuses to improve the user experience in such applications

Google ML Kit released 'DigitalInk', a recognition API[2] that can recognize emojis, shapes, and handwritten text on digital surfaces. DigitalInk takes a sequence of touch points (x,y) as input and predicts the emoji, but it does not consider the text context. On the other hand, models like DeepMoji [3] use only text as input for emoji prediction. They will not be able to utilize the complete context of the input.

Recently there has been an increasing trend of building deep neural networks which use 'multiple' modalities [14]. This proves to be a simple and effective way of improving the model performance by combining insights from different types of inputs. This paper describes a multimodal neural architecture that takes both hand-drawn image and the text context for predicting an emoji. We highlight the performance improvement achieved by adding text context as a secondary input. This paper focuses on improving the user experience in digital handwriting [13] by utilizing all the available context. The input (text+drawing) to the application is received from the user's handwriting on a touch-enabled device.

---

[2] https://developers.google.com/ml-kit/vision/digital-ink-recognition.

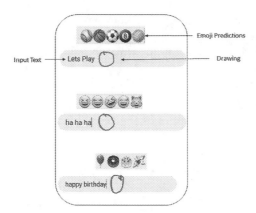

Fig. 2. Proposed method aims to intelligently suggest emojis based on both the text as well as drawing

We use a state-of-the-art handwriting recognizer (HWR) [8] to identify the language script and decode the corresponding text string. The non-text drawing strokes are converted into an image. Therefore, for emoji prediction, we use the proposed multimodal architecture.

The importance of such a solution is shown in Fig. 2. Here we list three instances where a user's drawing is identical ('circle'), but the input text is different. We aim to understand the intent behind the user's message and the accompanying drawing and suggest the most appropriate emoji. This will benefit the user in many real-life scenarios. There is no existing on-device application that uses both text and image to make such intelligent emoji predictions. Any application that uses only a single input cannot provide accurate context-based suggestions.

One of the main challenges in implementing multimodal neural networks is the lack of labeled datasets. Even for this task, there is no readily available dataset. Therefore, we create our own dataset comprising of text and images for 63 emoji classes. We explain the detailed procedure for curating data in Sect. 3.1. We further illustrate the proposed architecture followed by experiments and results.

2   Related Works

Predicting emojis based on text is a popular research work in the NLP domain. The state-of-the-art (SOTA) benchmarks [10] show that BERT-based [2] models largely outperformed the other existing [3] architectures. But BERT-based models are not suitable for devices where memory and response time are constrained. Recently there has been research going on to reduce the memory footprint of BERT [7,15], but still, even the smallest model has around 14M+ parameters.

There have been many attempts to use various modalities and the rich information they provide [4]. There is sufficient proof to show that multimodal architectures improve the SOTA accuracy as compared to conventional single input models for many applications. Zahavy et al. [17] tried to solve a multi-label multi-class classification problem. Here they show the robustness of multimodal networks for e-commerce products by giving examples where either the image or the caption alone is ambiguous but by relying on the other input; the classification can be done. Later Kruk et al. [9] explained classifying the intent of Instagram posts by utilizing both the image and its caption. They also depict various examples to highlight the importance of both parts to understand the post's meaning accurately.

Yang et al. [16] use image and text data from Facebook posts for hate speech classification. They use pre-trained encoders for extracting the image and text features. The final few layers of the combined model are trained through transfer learning. This paper explores multiple network architectures and fusion methods for image and text features. Even with a simple concatenation of image and text features, they exhibit a considerable improvement in classification accuracy. Audebert et al. [1] used multimodal deep networks for image and text-based document classification. More sophisticated fusion methods also provide additional improvements based on the dataset and model used.

Ha et al. [5] present sketch-rnn, a recurrent neural network (RNN) that can construct stroke-based drawings of common objects, which includes various doodles. It is trained on the largest doodles dataset, which includes 50 million drawings from 345 different categories, compiled by Quick draw![3] players. The drawings were recorded as time-stamped vectors labeled with metadata, including the subject matter and the player's country. Google's DigitalInk tries to solve the same problem of drawing to emoji prediction by using recurrent models that utilize the stroke's touch-points but not the text context.

This paper presents an efficient multimodal architecture to predict emojis based on hand-written text and drawings on touch-enabled devices.

3   Proposed Method

In this section, we first discuss the dataset collection, followed by the details regarding the neural network architecture.

3.1   Data

There are more than 1500 emojis that can be used for effective communication. But practically, very few emojis are popular and widely used. We developed a sample Android application where a user can draw the displayed emoji with their finger/stylus on the touch display. This emoji is randomly selected from the available list. We distributed the application to 100 users and collected various stats, including average strokes required for an emoji, total touch points, etc. We devised a list of popular emojis based on a user trial conducted over a month.

We used the following criteria to shortlist the final list of 63 emojis,

---

[3] https://quickdraw.withgoogle.com/.

Emoji	Min Strokes	Max Strokes	Avg Strokes	Max Touchpoints	Is popular
☺	3	5	4	110	1
♥	1	3	1.56452	99	1
✓	1	2	1.04274	44	1
○	3	6	4.09524	173	1
100	3	6	4.54206	73	1
🔥	1	23	4.16191	130	1
👀	2	9	4.31132	136	1
♦	1	4	1.58947	174	1
☁	1	11	4.7579	499	1
♥	2	5	3.45455	309	1

Fig. 3. Top - 10 emojis selected based on the explained criteria, among total of 63 emojis

a. The emoji should be easy to draw, i.e. average number of strokes required should be less than five.
b. The emoji should be present in the 'most popularly used emojis' list.
c. All variants of an emoji are considered as one. For example, there are multiple color variations of the heart emoji, and all of them will be clubbed together as one emoji.

First 10 emojis selected based on this criteria are shown in Fig. 3. As no direct data is available for this specific task, all the drawing data is collected from the user trial conducted among 100 Android device users. Screenshots of the data collection application can be seen in Fig. 4.

Collection of Drawing Data: We re-used the same data collection app (Fig. 4) that was used for obtaining the stats and collected the drawing data for the 63 finalized emojis. Specifically, we collected the touch-point and timestamp (x, y, t) data for each drawing stroke. Along with this, we provided an additional "Add Drawing" button, and the users were instructed to use this in the following scenarios,

a. After an intermediate drawing, the user feels that the current emoji should be predicted after this stroke. (Ex: Anticipating Sun Emoji after drawing the circle and a single ray)
b. After completely drawing the emoji

Moreover, the training and test set drawings are not drawn by the same group of people, which help us to keep a variation in the train and test data. Using this method, we collected around 1500 drawing samples per emoji for all 63 classes.

Collection of Text Data: We crawled the data from Twitter to get the text corpus and performed the following pre-processing steps to obtain the cleaned training data,

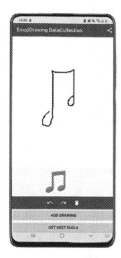

Fig. 4. Data collection app used to collect stats of all the emojis drawings and training samples for the final set of 63 emojis

  i. Tweets are segregated by 'English' language using the language info provided within Twitter data.
 ii. Tweets are converted to lowercase, and white spaces are normalized.
iii. Non-ASCII symbols are replaced with their equivalent ASCII symbol.
 iv. Gender modifier, skin tone modifier, variation selectors, and zero width joiners are removed so that the corresponding emojis are considered equivalent.
  v. Tweets are broken down such that text before any emoji and the corresponding emoji becomes a valid training example.
 vi. Training examples are filtered based on the sentence's length, total emojis, and the number of distinct emojis.

We prepared 10000 text samples per emoji from the cleaned corpus.

Augmentation. With the collected strokes from the users, we re-constructed the emoji drawings as images of 50X50 dimensions by re-scaling all the touch points. While transforming the series of strokes into images, we used the info collected from the "Add Drawing" button to create the image with intermediate strokes along with the complete drawing. This enables the model to predict the emojis even with incomplete drawings and reduces user efforts in drawing the complete emoji.

Further, we applied standard image augmentation techniques such as rotation (20%), horizontal flip, and zoom on the re-scaled image. For every image sample, we mapped the text from that particular emoji class chosen randomly till we obtained the maximum number of training samples per class which is 15000 samples. We split this combined data in the ratio of 90:10% as train and validation data set and use it to train our models.

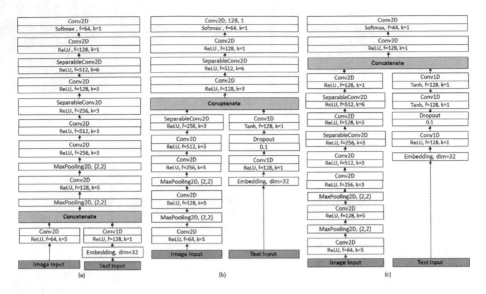

Fig. 5. Multimodal Architectures. (a) Early Concatenation model, (b) Mid Concatenation model, (c) Late Concatenation model

3.2 SAMNet Architecture

The process of fusing the image and text features is very crucial. This is because images and texts have entirely different data distributions and feature representations. Therefore, we propose to extract as much high-level information as possible from both modalities, and only then do we wish to fuse it into a common feature space. We carried out multiple experiments with different model configurations to understand the optimal location for concatenation and feature vector dimension. Finally, we settled on the proposed architecture 'SAMNet' (Semantic Aware Multimodal Network).

Figure 5 depicts the various architectures considered for experimentation. The figure shows that there are two separate pipelines for each of the inputs before they are concatenated into a single multidimensional space.

Image Pipeline: We use a regular Convolutional Neural Network architecture with MaxPool layers to extract the features from the input image. We also substitute some of the Convolutional layers with a "Depth Separable" Convolution layer used in the MobileNet architecture [6]. These layers reduce the model size and inference time and are suitable for resource constraint devices. We use $I_p(i, \theta_p)$ to indicate the image pipeline, where i is the image input, I_p is the model parameterized by θ_p, and p indicates the total number of Conv2D layers used.

Text Pipeline: We process the text at the character level for mainly two reasons. First, word level model would require a high vocabulary size to cover the most popular words, increasing the model size. Second, the character level model takes care of out-of-vocabulary words and typographical errors in the input text. We used the character vocabulary of size 70, which comprises lowercase and uppercase alphabets, punctuation, numbers, and white space. We set a maximum input size for the model as 32 characters. We first obtain a 32-dimensional embedding from the input text and pass through a series of 1D Convolutional, Maxpool, and Dropout layers. We use $T_q(t, \theta_q)$ to indicate the text pipeline, where t is the text input and T_q is the model parameterized by θ_q, and q indicates the total number of Conv1D layers along with the Embedding layer.

Since we are using a static concatenation scheme for fusing features from image and text inputs, we chose a character Embedding+CNN based architecture over an LSTM architecture.

To find the optimal location of concatenation, we experimented with the overall architecture and the network parameters involved. The results are available in the Experiments section. We observed that it is best to extract as much information as possible from each of the modalities before fusing them. After the fusion, we use a 2D Convolutional layer with a Softmax activation function for the final classification. We prefer a Convolutional layer for classification as opposed to a Dense layer because of the massive reduction in the number of parameters. Such reduction in model size is crucial for On-Device solutions.

Complex fusion methods can be an overkill for simpler tasks with smaller datasets, as shown in [11]. Here they prove that simple concatenation of features provides excellent accuracy.

Fusion Methods: A generic representation of fusing features from two modalities can be shown as below,

$$y = H_r\left([I_p, T_q], \theta_r\right) \tag{1}$$

where H_r is the model parameterized by θ_r that takes concatenated features from the image and text pipeline to predict the target class y. Here, r indicates the number of Conv2D layers in the model post concatenation.

1. Early Fusion: In this type of fusion, low-level features from multiple modalities are fused and trained to learn the correlation between modalities. We set $p = 1, q = 2$, and $r = 8$ for the early fusion model.
2. Mid Fusion: This type of fusion allows early layers to learn high-level features from each modality. We set $p = 5, q = 3$, and $r = 4$ for mid fusion model.
3. Late Fusion: This type of fusion allows both pipelines to almost behave as uni-modal architectures that output the decision values. These intermediate features are further fused to obtain the final output. We set $p = 8, q = 4$, and $r = 2$ for the late fusion model.

Further, in the late fusion method, based on the complexity of the input and depending on the use-case of the problem, the feature extractor model can increase or decrease the number of parameters (Fig. 6). For emoji drawing, we applied two such variants, where we tune the complexity of models by varying the number of layers,

1. Text Dominant: Here, the text pipeline T_q has relatively more Conv1D layers than Conv2D layers in the image pipeline I_p ($p = 8, q = 12$). This model intends to capture high-level features from complex text context.
2. Equal Weightage: This model allows I_p and T_q to have equal number of corresponding layers ($p = q = 8$).
3. Image Dominant: This model allows I_p to have more layers than T_q so that the image pipeline can get the high-level features out of complex image input ($p = 12, q = 4$).

The optimal values for p, q, and r of each model are determined by various experiments to obtain maximum validation accuracy.

Text-Emoji Conflict Resolution: It is challenging to distinguish the user's intent on the current drawing; it can be an alphabet or a start of an emoji drawing. To tackle this ambiguity, we introduced an auxiliary 64th class in the model to predict if the current drawing is an alphabet or two-character word (Ex: "OK") along with 63 emoji classes. The training data for the 64th class is obtained from the iam-database [12] by extracting single and double-character words. Furthermore, we commit the drawing as emoji only if the model emits a particular class with more than 80% probability. This helps us resolve the conflict between text and emoji effectively.

Multimodal models work pretty well for tasks involving smaller datasets. Our architecture performs well even when only one of the inputs is available. The two types of inputs to the model improve the accuracy by working in a complementary fashion. This is in no way a prerequisite for achieving a good inference performance, as shown in Sect. 4. We have included such data while training where one of the modalities is blocked. This makes the model robust enough to handle real-life cases where only one input is available to the model.

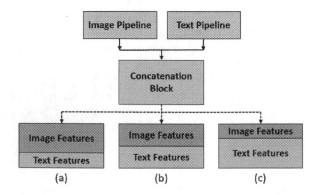

Fig. 6. Variants of Late Concatenation Architecture. (a) Image feature dominated model, (b) Equal weightage model, (c) Text feature dominated model

4   Experiments and Results

To understand how the models perceive the data, we manually curated a test set that contains four types of data and observed the behavior,

1. Only Text, which contains samples like 'happy birthday', 'good morning' etc., for which the emoji can be predicted without the explicit drawing.
2. Only Image, which contains the drawings that reveal the identity with minimal strokes to the model. For example drawing of '✓ '(check mark), 'X' (cancel/NO) etc.
3. Related Text and Image, here both the modalities complement each other to arrive at one emoji class. For example, 'good night' and drawing of 'Moon', 'It is raining' and drawing of 'clouds' etc.
4. Unrelated Text and Image, where the context of both inputs are either opposite, sarcastic or random. For example, 'love it!' and 'fire' emoji.

We first compare the performances of the three types of multimodal architectures described. Then we evaluate ML-Kit's DigitalInk API on that test set.

We prepared the test set such that drawings are unseen by the models, and text data is curated such that it includes empty text, short text, and long text, which are also unseen by the models. The short text comprises a maximum of 4–5 words, while the long text has less than ten words. All the results that are shown in this section are evaluated on this test data.

During the evaluation process, we assume that the complete text input is provided, and the user is yet to start drawing the emoji. In this setting, we calculate three metrics,

1. **Drawing Completion Accuracy:** Every stroke drawn by the user will be converted as an image incrementally and fed to the model with text context. If our model provides the intended emoji before completing the drawing in Top-N predictions, it will be marked as Top-N completion accuracy.

Table 1. Completion Accuracy of multimodal architectures

Architecture	Top-1	Top-2	Top-3	DSR
Early Concatenation	40.702	50.826	57.231	0.423
Mid Concatenation	40.082	49.173	55.165	0.417
Late Concatenation	41.735	50.826	**57.644**	**0.425**

Table 2. Prediction Accuracy of multimodal architectures

Architecture	Top-1	Top-2	Top-3	Size
Early Concatenation	57.364	68.217	73.643	3.7MB
Mid Concatenation	55.813	64.341	72.093	3.5MB
Late Concatenation	57.364	67.441	**74.4186**	**2.8 MB**

2. **Drawing-Stroke Saved Ratio (DSR):** Emoji prediction is a use case where understanding the user intent is very important. We have defined this metric to quantify the minimum time required for a successful prediction. This captures the amount of effort saved by our model by predicting in the early stage. The higher the value of this metric, the more convenient and better it is for the user. To calculate this metric, evaluation is conducted in a similar set-up as completion accuracy. We cumulatively noted the total number of strokes required and the number of strokes actually drawn by the user when the emoji is successfully predicted. If the model fails to predict the correct emoji, the number of strokes drawn will be equal to the number of strokes required.

$$\text{DSR} = \frac{\text{No. of strokes required} - \text{No. of strokes drawn}}{\text{No. of strokes required}} \qquad (2)$$

3. **Prediction Accuracy :** The image of a complete emoji drawing is passed to the model along with text context. So the model has complete context for both the modalities. If the model provides the intended emoji in Top-N predictions, it will be marked as Top-N accuracy.

4.1 Architecture Evaluation

As shown in Fig. 5 we conducted the experiment with three types of multimodal architectures. Namely, early concatenation, middle concatenation, and late concatenation architecture. We trained all three architectures with the same training data and validation data for 35 epochs.

From Table 1 and Table 2 we can observe that the late concatenation model predicts better than other models when evaluated on-device.

We further experimented and applied three modifications to late concatenation architecture based on feature domination with each modality. In Fig. 6 we can see the distribution of features post concatenation block for each variant.

By scrutinizing Table 3 and Table 4 we observe the following,

Observation 1: In a completion scenario where text context is fully available, and the image is incrementally updated stroke by stroke, the Text feature-dominated model performs better because it gives more priority to the text context than the image input.

Table 3. Completion Accuracy on variants of late concatenation

Architecture weightage	Top-1	Top-2	Top-3	DSR
Image feature dominated model	40.289	51.446	58.677	0.440
Equal weightage model	41.735	50.826	57.644	0.425
Text feature dominated model	39.669	51.859	**59.090**	**0.454**

Table 4. Prediction Accuracy variants of late concatenation

Architecture weightage	Top-1	Top-2	Top-3	Model Size
Image feature dominated model	56.589	69.767	**76.744**	**3.0 MB**
Equal weightage model	41.735	50.826	57.644	2.8 MB
Text feature dominated model	57.364	68.992	75.193	3.5 MB

Observation 2: In the prediction case, along with the text, a completely drawn image is also available. Here Image feature-dominated model performs better since it has complete image context to extract and process.

Based on the results of the architecture evaluation, we choose late concatenation architecture as the SAMNet architecture. Further, among the variants of the late concatenation model, the text feature-dominated model is suitable for our case. Since it improves user experience by predicting the emoji as soon as possible, even with an incomplete drawing input (Table 3). We use the same model for comparing with ML-Kit's DigitalInk API.

4.2 DigitalInk Evaluation

DigitalInk[4] is a recognition API exposed by Google's ML-Kit for recognizing hand-written text, shapes, and emojis. We used Digitalink in order to measure the performance of SAMNet and not for comparison since:

1. Our model takes both text and image as input to predict the corresponding emoji, while the Digitalink considers only image content for predicting emojis, autodraw, and shapes.
2. Both models were trained with different number of classes and training data.

Table 5. Completion accuracy comparison with DigitalInk

Model	Top-1	Top-2	Top-3	DSR
SAMNet (image only input)	**39.256**	**51.446**	**59.09**	**0.442**
DigitalInk	26.033	32.64	36.77	0.398

During the evaluation, as there are multiple variants of a single emoji, we grouped them all together, and if DigitalInk predicts any one of them, it is considered a hit. As shown in Table 5 and Table 6, our proposed model performed well even with only one modality, i.e., without text input. The top-10 prediction accuracy of DigitalInk API is 74.41, which is less than the top-3 accuracy of our model. This shows the robustness of our SAMNet architecture.

---

[4] https://developers.google.com/ml-kit/vision/digital-ink-recognition/android.

Table 6. Prediction accuracy comparison with DigitalInk

Model	Top-1	Top-2	Top-3
SAMNet (image only input)	**55.813**	**68.217**	**75.968**
DigitalInk	51.93	60.46	62.01

We performed all the evaluations explained above on an Android device with Octa-Core (2.3 GHz Quad-core + 1.7 GHz Quad-core) processor and 6 GB RAM. We achieved an inference time of less than 60 ms for all the architectures shown.

5   Conclusion

We investigated different types of multimodal architectures and showed an optimal way of concatenation, and proposed a novel architecture to predict the emoji from text and drawing input. To the best of our knowledge, this is the first real-time multimodal approach for drawing to emoji classification reported on ARM platforms. We experiment and show that the late concatenation method works better than other architectures explained. We achieve 76.74% top-3 prediction accuracy and 59% top-3 completion accuracy on a carefully prepared unseen test set. This model can be easily deployed on the edge devices for seamless performance, as it has a quick response time ($\leq$60 ms) and low memory footprint($\leq$3.5 MB). We also show the results with DigitalInk, which is the most related application to ours.

References

1. Audebert, N., Herold, C., Slimani, K., Vidal, C.: Multimodal deep networks for text and image-based document classification. In: Cellier, P., Driessens, K. (eds.) ECML PKDD 2019. CCIS, vol. 1167, pp. 427–443. Springer, Cham (2020). https://doi.org/10.1007/978-3-030-43823-4_35
2. Devlin, J., Chang, M.W., Lee, K., Toutanova, K.: BERT: pre-training of deep bidirectional transformers for language understanding. arXiv preprint arXiv:1810.04805 (2018)
3. Felbo, B., Mislove, A., Søgaard, A., Rahwan, I., Lehmann, S.: Using millions of emoji occurrences to learn any-domain representations for detecting sentiment, emotion and sarcasm. arXiv preprint arXiv:1708.00524 (2017)
4. Gupta, A., et al.: Context-aware emoji prediction using deep learning. In: Dev, A., Agrawal, S.S., Sharma, A. (eds.) AIST 2021. CCIS, vol. 1546, pp. 244–254. Springer, Cham (2022). https://doi.org/10.1007/978-3-030-95711-7_22
5. Ha, D., Eck, D.: A neural representation of sketch drawings. arXiv preprint arXiv:1704.03477 (2017)
6. Howard, A.G., et al.: MobileNets: efficient convolutional neural networks for mobile vision applications. arXiv preprint arXiv:1704.04861 (2017)
7. Jiao, X., et al.: TinyBERT: distilling BERT for natural language understanding. arXiv preprint arXiv:1909.10351 (2019)

8. Keysers, D., Deselaers, T., Rowley, H.A., Wang, L.L., Carbune, V.: Multi-language online handwriting recognition. IEEE Trans. Pattern Anal. Mach. Intell. **39**(6), 1180–1194 (2016)

9. Kruk, J., Lubin, J., Sikka, K., Lin, X., Jurafsky, D., Divakaran, A.: Integrating text and image: determining multimodal document intent in Instagram posts. arXiv preprint arXiv:1904.09073 (2019)

10. Ma, W., Liu, R., Wang, L., Vosoughi, S.: Emoji prediction: extensions and benchmarking. arXiv preprint arXiv:2007.07389 (2020)

11. Mao, J., Xu, J., Jing, Y., Yuille, A.: Training and evaluating multimodal word embeddings with large-scale web annotated images. arXiv preprint arXiv:1611.08321 (2016)

12. Marti, U.V., Bunke, H.: The IAM-database: an English sentence database for offline handwriting recognition. Int. J. Doc. Anal. Recogn. **5**(1), 39–46 (2002)

13. Prattichizzo, D., Meli, L., Malvezzi, M.: Digital handwriting with a finger or a stylus: a biomechanical comparison. IEEE Trans. Haptics **8**(4), 356–370 (2015)

14. Summaira, J., Li, X., Shoib, A.M., Li, S., Abdul, J.: Recent advances and trends in multimodal deep learning: a review. arXiv preprint arXiv:2105.11087 (2021)

15. Sun, Z., Yu, H., Song, X., Liu, R., Yang, Y., Zhou, D.: MobileBERT: a compact task-agnostic BERT for resource-limited devices. arXiv preprint arXiv:2004.02984 (2020)

16. Yang, F., et al.: Exploring deep multimodal fusion of text and photo for hate speech classification. In: Proceedings of the Third Workshop on Abusive Language Online, pp. 11–18 (2019)

17. Zahavy, T., Magnani, A., Krishnan, A., Mannor, S.: Is a picture worth a thousand words? A deep multi-modal fusion architecture for product classification in e-commerce. arXiv preprint arXiv:1611.09534 (2016)

Segmentation of Smoke Plumes Using Fast Local Laplacian Filtering

Vedant Anand Koranne[1]([✉]), Emmett J. Ientilucci[2], Abhishek Dey[3], Aloke Datta[4], and Susmita Ghosh[5]

[1] Rochester Institute of Technology, Electrical Engineering, Rochester, NY, USA
`vk5443@rit.edu`
[2] Rochester Institute of Technology, Center for Imaging Science, Rochester, NY, USA
`emmett@cis.rit.edu`
[3] Bethune College, University of Calcutta, Kolkata, India
[4] The LNM Institute of Information Technology, Jaipur, India
[5] Jadavpur University, Kolkata, India

Abstract. In this paper, we address the problem of smoke plume segmentation from background clutter. Smoke plumes can be generated from fires, explosions, etc. In the mining industry, plumes from blasts need to be characterized in terms of their volume and concentration, for example. Plume segmentation is required in order to start such an analysis.

We present a new image processing approach based on a fast local Laplacian filtering (FLLF) technique. In addition, we discuss how we designed and executed our own field experiments to acquire actual test data of smoke plumes from RGB video cameras. Lastly, we show how the FLLF technique can be used to generate thousands of training samples with applications in machine learning.

Results show that the FLLF technique outperforms state-of-the-art approaches (*i.e.*, SFFCM and an approach by Wang *et al.*) when tested using metrics such as Accuracy, the Jaccard Index, F1-score, False Alarms and Misses. We also show that the FLLF technique is more computationally efficient.

Keywords: Image segmentation · Smoke plume · Local Laplacian Filter · Binary Masks · Color Space · Transfer learning · Deep learning · UNet

1 Introduction and Background

Smoke plumes can originate from a myriad of sources including forest fires, camp fires, explosions, and mining blasts, for example. Segmentation of such plumes

The authors gratefully acknowledge the IEEE Geoscience and Remote Senging Society (GRSS) for sanctioning a project under "ProjNET" where the Western New York, USA, GRSS Chapter has teamed up with the Kolkata, India, GRSS Chapter.

can have applications in determining the location of a plume (from a forest fire image, for example) or even volume and concentration estimation. Isolating a plume from its background, in an image or video sequence, while determining its size and volume, as a function of time, is of great value for gaining insight to the rate of expansion and the origin of the smoke plume. An entity such as the Occupational Safety and Health Administration (OSHA) in the United States is interested in such information.

Smoke plume analysis is a large field of study in which research typically revolves around the actual detection and segmentation of such plumes. In general, this type of analysis falls under the category of *semantic segmentation*, which itself is a vast field. Today, convolutional neural networks (CNNs) have been found to be the most widely used deep learning (DL) model for the purpose of image segmentation. As an example, Long *et al.* [2] proposes a methodology that utilizes a fully convolutional network (FCN) which is an extended version of CNN for the purpose of semantic segmentation. Furthermore, segmentation has been applied, specifically, to the smoke plume problem. Feiniu *et al.* [5] proposed a smoke plume segmentation technique for video data. The method utilized the FCN to obtain binary segmented masks of blurry smoke plume images. Due to lack of data, they proposed a methodology for the generation of *synthetic smoke images*. Lei, *et al.* [1] proposed a clustering based segmentation approach. Their work focused on reducing the computation time of fuzzy C-means clustering and producing segmented images using a superpixel based method. The superpixel-based fast fuzzy c-means (SFFCM) algorithm can be noise sensitive thereby impacting results. Wang *et al.* [4] proposed an image segmentation approach based on a histogram and a region growing algorithm. Wang's approach is a two step method. Firstly, they measure the roughness (*i.e.*, a measure of inaccuracy as defined in [4]) based on approximation boundaries. The histogram of the image is considered as the lower approximation and the Histon histogram is considered as the upper approximation for the measurement of roughness. This roughness measurement is used to compute the roughness histogram followed by thresholding to obtain a segmented image. This process is followed by the region growing approach to improve the segmented result. In [4], Wang *et al.* have also assumed that $R \approx G \approx B$ and hence performed a roughness measurement only on the R channel in order to reduce computation time. This method is limited to white, grayish white or black colored smoke plumes and fails to segment other colored smoke plumes. Additionally, this method is computationally slow due to multiple iterations and a longer execution time.

Generally, most of the computer vision or machine learning approaches related to smoke segmentation lack adequate smoke-plume training samples or labeled data. Therefore, we set out to create our own experiments and data collections to obtain such data sets (described in Sect. 2). These data sets were used to help in the development of our approach. As a consequence, the segmented plume imagery can also be used as training data for developing machine learning based models, though not the specific focus of this paper. The latter topic of applying machine learning approaches to the plume segmentation problem is the subject of on-going research.

The primary goal for us is to devise an accurate, fast and efficient method to segment the smoke plume from background information. We propose a new fast local Laplacian filter (FLLF) technique to perform such segmentation. The FLLF will help us in obtaining an abundance of segmented data and then, this segmented data set may be used as labeled data for a deep learning (DL) model. Thus, our paper focuses on three issues. 1) Our unique smoke plume video data collection, followed by 2) segmentation through our proposed mask generation algorithm (FLLF), with results, and finally, 3) illustrating how generated FLLF masks can be used in a basic UNet DL framework.

Section 2 illustrates the experiments performed for collecting the data. Section 3 presents our FLLF algorithm. Section 4 shows the detailed analysis of qualitative and quantitative results. Section 4.1 comprises the definitions for the metrics which have been used for the quantitative analysis. This is followed by Sects. 4.2 and 4.3 which illustrate results obtained by implementing the proposed algorithm and UNet deep learning model, respectively. Section 5 provides concluding remarks and insight into future endeavors.

2   Smoke Plume Data Collection

The Digital Imaging and Remote Sensing (DIRS) lab, at the Rochester Institute of Technology (RIT), has extensive experience in the area of data collections. For this paper, we utilized RIT's 177-acre test site (called the Tait Preserve) to design and execute smoke plume releases. The data from these experiments was used for the research presented in this paper. In the fall of 2021, we purchased 15 smoke grenades, some white smoke and some orange smoke, as seen in Fig 1. We then mounted eight Canon digital SLR video cameras (see Fig. 1) on the top of wood polls that were 3.1 m high (see Fig. 2). These eight polls formed a circle with a radius of 25 m. Each camera was angled down 12°C so as to look at the center of the circle. At the center of the circle, on the ground, was an EG18 High Output white or orange, wire pull, smoke grenade (see Fig. 2). We turned all our cameras on at 30 fps, fired a strobe light such that all cameras could see it, for camera syncing purposes, and released the smoke grenade (see Fig. 3). The purpose of using eight cameras around the smoke cloud was to test out 3D plume reconstruction techniques, which is the topic of on-going research. These grenades generated smoke, on average, for 90 s. We then repeated the process numerous times. Our video data resolution was 1920×1080 pixels. For future reference in this paper, the data from these cameras is called Cam1, Cam2, Cam3, etc.

3   Proposed Methodology

In this paper, we have proposed an image processing approach for segmentation of smoke plumes. The proposed method includes color space conversion, edge-aware fast local Laplacian filtering, contrast modification, scene understanding

Fig. 1. (left) digital SLR video camera mounted on wood poll and (right) example smoke grenades.

Fig. 2. (left) Placement of smoke centered in a 25 m-radius circle and (right) image showing one of the cameras along with a white smoke release.

Fig. 3. Full smoke plume data collect experiment. Shown is the placement of eight digital SLR video cameras with emerging orange smoke plume in middle of a 25 m-radius circle. (Color figure online)

for difference image computation, and morphological operations. In our algorithm, we assume that the background image is available for each of the smoke plume images to be segmented. That is, the video camera is already capturing data *before* the plume starts. This scenario is observed in strip mining blasts, for example, where workers must document the blast and resulting plume using video cameras.

As an extension to this fast local Laplacian approach, we have also proposed a more general method for smoke plume segmentation in a machine learning environment. In the first step, the FLLF technique is used to generate an abundance of labeled samples which can then be further used in a deep neural network. Thus, plume segmentation would commence via a UNet or similar deep learning technique. Full investigation of this latter idea is the subject of on-going research.

3.1 Segmentation Using the Fast Local Laplacian Filter (FLLF) Technique

In this section, the proposed FLLF algorithm is explained. The general block diagram of the FLLF technique is shown in Fig. 4. As mentioned, this approach is implemented with an assumption that the background image is available for each of the images to be segmented. Firstly, both images (the smoke plume image and its corresponding background image) are converted from RGB color space to YCbCr color space. The Y-channel provides the information regarding the brightness whereas the Cb-channel and the Cr-channel provide the color difference information. This approach can then be divided into two subsections as follows:

(a) Over-Segmentation of the Smoke Plume Image to Include Fine Details. This section utilizes only the spliced Y-channel of the smoke plume image. The extracted Y-channel smoke plume image undergoes tone mapping or contrast modification to enhance the fine details. This contrast-modified image undergoes binarization based on global threshold. To compensate for misses, holes, and false alarms we perform morphological operations namely opening, closing and hole-filling. The resulting image is the over-segmented binary smoke plume image.

(b) Eliminate False Alarms. This is implemented using the fast local Laplacian filter and the absolute difference image generated by the smoke plume image and the background image. To generate the absolute difference image, the smoke plume image and the background image undergoes a Gaussian filter followed by the fast local Laplacian filter. The Gaussian filter is utilized in order to reduce the noise content from the images as the local Laplacian filter is very sensitive to noise and the results might be affected. Also, the local Laplacian filter is edge-preserving and a smoothing filter. The absolute difference image is then passed through the median filter so that the salt and pepper noise generated due to spatial differences (*i.e.,* slight registration errors) in the smoke plume image and the background image can be reduced. Binarization is performed based on one standard deviation (max). This quantity was chosen based on the examination of 100's of images. Morphological operations are performed on the resultant binary image to fill in holes and reduce misses.

Finally, to obtain the segmented binary mask of the smoke plume, logical ANDing is performed on binary images obtained from steps (a) and (b), as seen in Fig. 4.

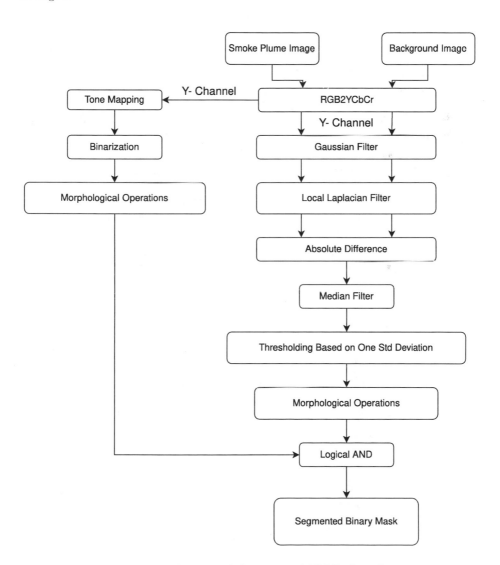

Fig. 4. Block diagram of the proposed FLLF algorithm.

3.2 Deep Learning-Based Smoke/Plume Segmentation with FLLF Training Samples

As previously stated, this article concentrates on both smoke plume acquisition and segmentation of smoke plumes using an image processing technique (*i.e.*, the FLLF technique). However, there is no reason why the FLLF technique can't be used to generate training samples as input to a DL algorithm. Thus, to validate the FLLF technique as a plume *mask generation* algorithm, a basic UNet was also implemented and tested.

CNNs are the most widely used deep learning tools for classification and segmentation. In this paper, an extended version of a CNN, specifically a modified UNet, was utilized. The UNet architecture was originally introduced by Ronneberger *et al.*, [3] for biomedical image segmentation applications. This architecture is comprised of two main blocks. An encoder and followed by a decoder. The encoder block is made up of a combination of convolutional layers and max-pooling which results in the extraction of features. Whereas the decoder block utilizes up-convolution to permit localization. This architecture comprises the fully connected layer network [3].

We used the idea of transfer learning to segment a smoke plume using the UNet deep learning model. As shown in Fig. 5, the input of our overall model consisted of 6988 smoke plume images with their corresponding truth masks. These masks are generated by implementation of our proposed FLLF technique, discussed in Sect. 3.1. These image-mask pairs undergo a train-test split with a ratio of 9:1. The input images are resized to 256×256 and then fed into the input layer of the UNet. The UNet model utilizes pre-trained weights (*i.e.*, ImageNet) along with InceptionV3 as its backbone thereby exploiting transfer learning. The output of the UNet model is fed to the output layer which finally predicts the segmented image.

4 Analysis of Results

This section discusses the results obtained by implementing the FLLF technique as illustrated in Fig. 4. The results are also compared with the SFFCM algorithm [1] and Wang's roughness based and region growing algorithm [4]. *Execution Time, Jaccard Index (IOU), F1-score, Accuracy, Misses* and *False Alarms* are considered as performance measuring indices for the comparison.

4.1 Quantitative Metrics of Evaluation

We have used the true positive pixels (TPP), true negative pixels (TNP), false positive pixels (FPP) and false negative pixels (FNP) for the performance evaluation. For accuracy, we have computed the percentage of total number of pixels of the generated mask which exactly matches with the ground truth mask. That is,

$$Accuracy = \frac{TPP + TNP}{TPP + TNP + FPP + FNP} \tag{1}$$

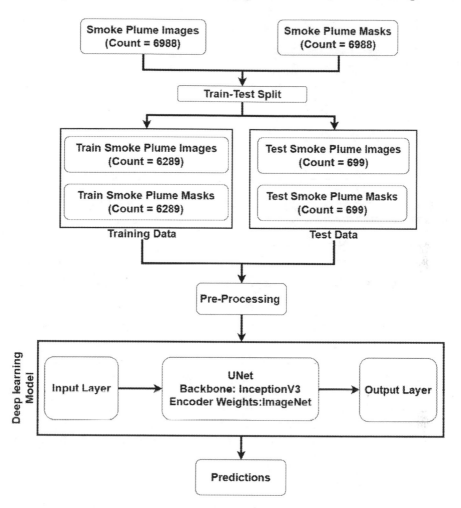

Fig. 5. Flowchart for UNet-based smoke plume segmentation.

The Jaccard Index, also known as intersection over union (IOU), is calculated and used to verify if the accuracy values are valid. In general, it compares members for two sets to see which members are shared and which are distinct. One can think of it as a measure of similarity for two sets of data and has a range from 0 to 1. The closer to 1 the index is, the more similar the data sets. For our usage, the Jaccard Index does not consider using the TNP's. This is to make sure that the accuracy metric is not generating false values based on just TNP's. Thus, the Jaccard Index is computed as

$$\text{Jaccard Index (IOU)} = \frac{TPP}{TPP + FPP + FNP} \tag{2}$$

The F1-score is based on precision and gives a much better understanding about the obtained results. Optimized values for the F1-score should also be equal to 1.

$$F1 - \text{score} = \frac{TPP}{TPP + \frac{FPP+FNP}{2}} \tag{3}$$

False alarms are computed to obtain a quantitative measure on over-segmentation. That is,

$$\text{False Alarms} = \frac{FPP}{TPP + TNP + FPP + FNP} \tag{4}$$

Misses are critical when considering the generation of masks and can be expressed as,

$$\text{Misses} = \frac{FNP}{TPP + TNP + FPP + FNP} \tag{5}$$

4.2   Smoke Segmentation Results Using the FLLF Technique

The true masks of Fig. 6 were hand-crafted binary images. These true masks were the basis for both our qualitative (*i.e.,* visual) and quantitative (*i.e.,* metrics) analysis. In Fig. 6(a) and 6(b), Wang's algorithm outperforms the SFFCM approach in terms or false alarms but misses out on segmenting the smoke plume blended with the sky. We have noticed that this is a challenge for the image processing based mask generation algorithms. However, our proposed algorithm overcomes this challenge and outperforms both the SFFCM and Wang's algorithm. Furthermore, our ultimate goal is to capture video data on drones, *looking obliquely down* not horizontally. Thus, we anticipate collecting fewer images with a skyline present in the future. From the resultant images in Fig. 6(c), it is seen that the SFFCM algorithm generates a high amount of false alarms as compared to Wang's algorithm and our proposed FLLF method. In Fig. 6(d) and 6(e), our proposed method carves out almost the exact smoke region as compared with the other two methods.

The comparative quantitative analysis of our method with SFFCM and Wang's method in terms of execution time, Jaccard index (IOU), F1-score, accuracy (A), false alarms (FA) and misses (M) for all these frames (as shown in Fig. 6) are depicted in Table 1, Table 2 and Table 3. In general, for all the test cases, we can see that our FLLF proposed algorithm outperforms the other tested algorithms.

To run any DL model, an *abundance of labeled data* is needed. As pointed out in Sects. 3 and 4.2, we have used the above mentioned FLLF technique to generate segmented masks on our field-collected data. These segmented masks can also be use as labeled data for a DL algorithmic approach. Results of using this labeled plume data in a basic UNet architecture is illustrated in the next section.

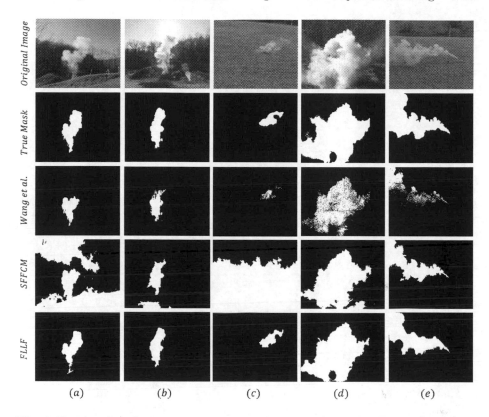

Fig. 6. Results of smoke segmentation using our proposed FLLF technique (row 5) are compared with Wang's method (row 3) and SFFCM (row 4) using five example images. Shown is smoke from (a) Smoke 55 (one of our test data sets), (b) Smoke 19 (another one of our test data sets), (c) RIT Tait collect Cam1 frame 60, (d) an explosion blast and (e) RIT Tait collect Cam3 frame 5564.

Table 1. Quantitative Results in terms of Execution Time (in seconds).

Frame	Wang et al.	SFFCM	Our Method (FLLF)
Smoke55	78.6	11.71	7.92
Smoke19	88.62	10.77	6.18
Tait Collect Cam1 Frame 60	1216	10.81	5.97
Explosive Blast	1514.68	30.74	13.30
Tait Collect Cam3 Frame 5564	434.53	9.59	7.08

Table 2. Quantitative results in terms of Accuracy (A), F1-score and Jaccard Index (IOU).

Frame	Wang et.al A[%], F1-Score, IOU	SFFCM A[%], F1-Score, IOU	Our Method (FLLF) A[%], F1-Score, IOU
Smoke55	96.99, 0.7427, 0.5907	57.88, 0.1683, 0.1021	98.39, 0.8814, 0.7879
Smoke19	97.98, 0.8053, 0.6741	96.19, 0.6237, 0.5579	99.14, 0.927, 0.8639
Tait Collect Cam1 Frame 60	97.9, 0.4884, 0.3231	35.06, 0.0287, 0.0376	99.18, 0.8692, 0.7687
Explosive Blast	84.84, 0.7691, 0.6248	90.24, 0.6563, 0.7749	94.38, 0.9255, 0.8613
Tait Collect Cam3 Frame 5564	85.03, 0.4843, 0.3195	92.61, 0.3802, 0.6669	94.07, 0.8484, 0.7368

Table 3. Quantitative Results in terms of Accuracy (A), False Alarms (FA), and Misses (M).

Frame	Wang et al. A, FA, M [%]	SFFCM A, FA, M [%]	Our Method (FLLF) A, FA, M [%]
Smoke55	96.99, 39.61, 2.95	57.88, 0.061, 2.51	98.39, 0.2, 1.34
Smoke19	97.98, 0.019, 2	96.19, 2.43, 1.38	99.14, 0.54, 0.7
Tait Collect Cam1 Frame 60	97.9, 0.003, 2.1	35.06, 64.37, 0.57	99.18, 0.4, 0.37
Explosive Blast	84.84, 0.01, 15.16	90.24, 2.95, 6.81	94.38, 0.1, 5.51
Tait Collect Cam3 Frame 5564	85.03, 0, 14.97	92.61, 0.1, 7.2	94.07, 0.54, 5.39

4.3   Results Using UNet-Based Image Segmentation with the FLLF Technique

Figure 7 shows the qualitative results of smoke plume segmentation using a pre-trained UNet DL model (trained according to Fig. 5) on our test images. Here we consider the True Smoke mask as that generated using our proposed FLLF algorithm. In Fig. 7(a) the pre-trained UNet yields over-segmented results with higher false alarms and no misses. Figure 7(b) shows an image with no smoke. The UNet was able to recognize this scenario except for some false alarms. In Fig. 7(c) and Fig. 7(d), the UNet misses the very thin part of the smoke. In general, these results indicate that the DL model may provide good results if it is trained with good quality masks. However, none of the results, at this time, were as good as using the FLLF algorithm alone. The idea of using the FLLF technique to create an abundance of training samples for a variety of DL architectures (not just UNet) is the subject of current on-going research.

5   Conclusions

In this paper, we worked on three aspects for smoke plume segmentation. A large-scale smoke data collection experiment, so as to collect ample test data, a new image processing plume segmentation technique (*i.e.*, FLLF), and the idea of using the FLLF technique on our collected plume data to generate large quantities of training samples for further designing novel machine learning-based approaches.

Based on the results, compared to similar approaches, the FLLF technique was more computationally efficient, yielded better coverage of the smoke plume and had reduced misses and false alarms. One of the advantages of this method is that no training samples are required to execute the algorithm.

Overall, the objective of this paper was to show that we can successfully collect smoke data and perform efficient segmentation of smoke plumes using an image processing technique. In this process, we also ended up generating training data, which can be used as input for the DL world. Knowing this process works (and can be re-created) leads to a path forward for improvement and future work.

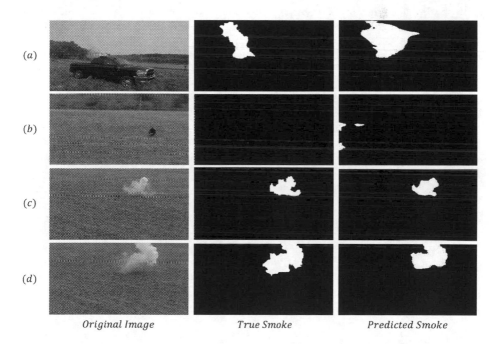

Fig. 7. Segmentation results using a pre-trained (i.e., ImageNet) UNet DL model with additional training data from the FLLF algorithm.

6   Future Work

We continue to perform research in this area of smoke plume segmentation. Our findings using the FLLF technique were sound. However, we feel that factoring in the *temporal* component in video data should only improve results. Clearly the FLLF technique can help in generating thousands of smoke plume masks to be used in DL approaches. We need to fully examine the impact of accurate truth masks (*i.e.,* labels) verses DL output versus various DL approaches. Our proposed FLLF-based segmentation technique needs at least one plume-free frame to perform segmentation (for stand-alone segmentation or to generate training samples) while a well designed DL model does not need such a plume-free image but needs sufficient training data. Lastly, we plan on collecting RGB video data of smoke plumes from drone platforms for further exploration including examining the impacts due to image registration cause by drone motion.

References

1. Lei, T., Jia, X., Zhang, Y., Liu, S., Meng, H., Nandi, A.K.: Superpixel-based fast fuzzy c-means clustering for color image segmentation. IEEE Trans. Fuzzy Syst. **27**(9), 1753–1766 (2019). https://doi.org/10.1109/TFUZZ.2018.2889018
2. Long, J., Shelhamer, E., Darrell, T.: Fully convolutional networks for semantic segmentation. In: 2015 IEEE Conference on Computer Vision and Pattern Recognition (CVPR), pp. 3431–3440 (2015). https://doi.org/10.1109/CVPR.2015.7298965
3. Ronneberger, O., Fischer, P., Brox, T.: U-net: convolutional networks for biomedical image segmentation. In: Navab, N., Hornegger, J., Wells, W.M., Frangi, A.F. (eds.) MICCAI 2015. LNCS, vol. 9351, pp. 234–241. Springer, Cham (2015). https://doi.org/10.1007/978-3-319-24574-4_28
4. Wang H., C.Y.: A smoke image segmentation algorithm based on rough set and region growing. J. Forest Sci. **65**(8), 321–329 (2019). https://doi.org/10.17221/34/2019-JFS
5. Yuan, F., Zhang, L., Xia, X., Wan, B., Huang, Q., Li, X.: Deep smoke segmentation. Neurocomputing **357**, 248–260 (2019). https://doi.org/10.1016/j.neucom.2019.05.011, https://www.sciencedirect.com/science/article/pii/S0925231219306435

Rain Streak Removal via Spatio-Channel Based Spectral Graph CNN for Image Deraining

Thatikonda Ragini[(✉)] and Kodali Prakash

Department of Electronics and Communication Engineering, National Institute of Technology, Warangal, Telangana 506004, India
tr712105@student.nitw.ac.in, kprakash@nitw.ac.in

Abstract. Removing rain streaks from the captured single rainy images plays a dominant role in high-level Computer Vision (CV) applications. Since, many existing deraining methods ignores long range contextual information and utilize only local spatial information. To address this issue, a Spatio-channel based Spectral Graph Convolutional Neural Network (SCSGCNet) for image deraining was proposed and two new modules were introduced to extract representations along spatial and channel wise dimensions. Therefore, we integrate deep Convolutional neural network (CNN) with spatial based spectral graph convolutional neural network (SSGCNN) and channel based spectral graph convolutional network (CSGCNN) modules into a single end-to-end network. Therefore, our network was able to model feature representations from local, global spatial patterns and channel correlations. Experimental results on five synthetic and real-world datasets shows that the proposed network achieves state-of-the-art (SOTA) results.

Keywords: Deep Learning · Image Deraining · Image Processing · Spatio-channel based Convolutional Neural Network (SCCNet)

1 Introduction

Computer Vision (CV) systems such as object detection [1, 2], object recognition [3], object tracking [4], object segmentation [5], scene understanding [6] etc., performance was degraded significantly when images were captured on rainy days as they often contain rain streaks and block other background objects. Therefore, removing rain streaks effectively from single images is an important research domain in computer vision.

Over the past decade, several approaches were developed to remove rain streaks from both videos and single images. However, to solve these two issues current SOTA methods design algorithms either manually using model-driven methods or learn automatically deraining function based on data-driven methods. Since single image deraining is more challenging than compared to video as there is no temporal information available for rain streaks detection. Moreover the success of single image deraining can also be employed directly in video deraining task. Therefore, in this work we focus only to remove rain streaks from single images.

D. Gupta et al. (Eds.): CVIP 2022, CCIS 1777, pp. 149–160, 2023.
https://doi.org/10.1007/978-3-031-31417-9_12

Commonly single image deraining methods were classified into two types: traditional model-driven and modern data-driven. The traditional model-driven methods describe the physical characteristics of rain streaks using handcrafted image features. Many model-driven based deraining methods employs various "priors to separate rain streaks" from single images [7–12]. A single image rain removal network was proposed and they adopted image decomposition method based on morphological component analysis [7]. Initially the applied image was divided into two parts as low and high frequency regions using a bilateral filter. They again decompose high frequency region into two sub-parts as "rain and non-rain" components by applying dictionary learning and sparse coding methods. In [8] an adaptive rain streak network was proposed to remove rain streaks from single images. As rain streaks were elongated in vertical direction and are in elliptical shape, they first detected rain streak regions and then applied nonlocal mean filtering on the selected neighboring pixels and their weights adaptively.

A rain streak network [9] was proposed to improve the overall visibility either by removing the rain streaks completely from the background or over-smoothing the background by using two patch-based priors based on "gaussian mixture models" (GMM's). Wang Y et al. [10] designed an efficient three-layer hierarchical network and adopted all the advantages of image decomposition and dictionary learning techniques for removing both rain streaks and snow from the single-color images. They decomposed input color image into two complementary regions by feeding it to a combined rain/snow detector + guided filter block.

A novel joint Bi-layer optimization network was proposed by Zhu et al. [11] to remove rain streaks. A joint optimization was applied alternatively for removing non-streak rain and rain-streak details using three image priors. Gu S et al. [12] proposed a novel network for removing rain streaks from single rainy images by applying "joint convolutional analysis and synthesis sparse" representation methods.

The modern data-driven based methods describe the physical characteristics of rain streaks automatically using deep convolutional neural networks (CNN's). Many existing state-of-the-art models employed CNN's as their backbones for removing rain streaks both in video and single images. However modern CNNs capture only spatial local information and ignores long-range interrelationships among image pixels. Fu Y et al. [13] designed a deep detailed deraining network to reduce the mapping directly from input to output and which makes learning process easy and simple. During the network training the model focus more on the structure of rain i.e., high frequency region and remove background interference using a prior image knowledge method. Recent survey on the existing SOTA networks for removing rain streaks using both model-driven and data-driven based methods were discussed in [14]. A novel "density-aware multi-stream densely connected CNN (DID-MDN)" [15] was developed for jointly estimating rain density and rain streak removal. This network automatically estimates rain-density information and removes the rain streaks efficiently using the estimated rain-density label.

A deep neural network for image deraining task was proposed by combining deep CNN and recurrent neural networks [16]. As contextual information plays a vital role for rain-streaks removal, they adopted dilated convolution. As heavy rain is an accumulation of multiple rain streak layers, based on transparency and intensity of rain streaks they deployed squeeze and excitation module. They introduced a recurrent neural network to remove rain streaks in later stages as multiple rain streak layers overlap. In [17] a rain model was proposed which jointly performs rain detection and removes heavy rain-streaks by contextual deep neural network. This multi-task deraining network learns three tasks, they are binary-rain streak map, rain-streak layers and clear background. To exploit the regional contextual information, they introduced contextual dilated network to make the proposed network invariant to rain streaks. They also adopted recurrent strategy that can progressively removes rain streaks and could handle overlapping rain streaks. Different from traditional deep CNNs, a semi-supervised transfer learning-based network [18] was proposed to remove rain streaks from rainy images. Their network was adaptively trained on sample of synthesized/non-synthesized rainy images together with real rainy images and transfer the network to adopt real rain pattern domain instead of synthetic rain pattern.

In [19] spatial attentive single image deraining network (SPANet) was developed to remove rain-streaks. They proposed a semi-automatic method which incorporates both temporal priors and humans in the loop to generate a high quality de-rained image. A simple and better progressive deraining network was proposed by Ren D et al. [20] by considering three factors such as input-output, network structure and loss functions. To take the advantage of recursive computation a Progressive ResNet (PRN) was introduced. To exploit the dependencies among deep features across multiple stages a recurrent layer was employed which makes the network as "Progressive Recurrent Network (PReNet)".

A model-driven deep neural network structure [21] was proposed for removing rain streaks from single rainy images. For representing rain, they adopted dictionary learning mechanism and utilize gradient descent method for recursive network design and they refer the network as "rain convolutional dictionary network (RCDNet)". Fu X et al. [22] designed a successive graph convolutional based neural network (SGCNet) for removing rain streaks in single images. In order to explore rich feature representations, they introduced recurrent operations while performing deraining process. SGCNet achieved SOTA results both on real and synthetic rain datasets. Den S et al. [23] proposed "detailed recovery deep neural network via context aggregation network" for image deraining. They proposed a unified framework for both removing rain streaks and detail recovery from single rainy images. They designed two parallel sub-networks to handle rain-streaks removal and recover lost-details caused during the deraining process using a rain residual network. To reconstruct the lost details, they introduced "structure detail context aggregation block (SDCAB)" repair network which reduces the image degradation. Lin Xiao et al. [26] proposed a DECAN deraining network to remove rain streaks from single images. A comprehensive loss function was introduced in their network to remove rain streaks and retain background of a derained image.

To address above limitations, in single de-raining task, we adopted "Spectral Graph convolutional neural networks (SGCNet)" [24] to extract and propagate feature contextual information and its complement. To explore both global spatial patterns and channel correlations among the extracted features we designed spatial and channel spectral CNN modules and to extract local spatial patterns, a dilated convolution module [25] was introduced in the proposed network. However, rain streaks have similar geometry and object structures are long in space, so we adopted and integrate dilated convolution, spatial network and channel network modules in single end-end framework. Therefore, these three modules generate better deraining-specific feature representations and which in turn boosts the proposed network performance.

Our contributions are listed as follows:

- We introduced two spectral graph convolutional networks in successive manner in the proposed work for single image deraining and which allows to explore contextual information.
- Proposed an integrated module which can efficiently computes local spatial, global and channel correlation features for deraining specific task.
- SCSGCNet is easy, simple and end-to-end trainable network for other low-level CV tasks. Experimental results show that the proposed network favorably outperforms over the existing SOTA networks on multiple synthetic and real-world rain datasets.

The outline of the proposed network was discussed. Section 2, covers the detailed proposed methodology. Section 3 covers experimental setup, various baseline methods used and widely used rain datasets. Section 4 covers results and discussion of the proposed network, visual deraining results and finally concludes the paper.

2 Proposed Methodology

The proposed network for single image deraining is shown in Fig. 1. SCSGCNet consists of multiple integrated modules and each integrated module mainly has three blocks, one spatial based spectral graph convolutional neural network (SSGCNN), one channel based spectral graph convolutional neural network (CSGCNN) and one dilated convolutional neural network (DCNN). This integrated module is inserted into a proposed network architecture which has symmetric skip-connections, so that it can pass extracted features from shallow to deeper layers and also avoids vanishing gradient problem. In the proposed network we used 10 integrated modules which would improve the deraining performance. As shown in Fig. 1, the proposed architecture adopts spectral based graph convolutional neural network (SGCNN) and has symmetric skip-connected structure and generates a de-rained image **D** after feeding the network with rainy image **R**. The proposed network has three components namely, two feature extraction layers, multiple integrated modules and one reconstruction layer. To extract shallow features from the input rainy image a 3×3 convolution operation was applied in the feature extraction layers. Therefore, these shallow features were propagated from shallow to deeper layers by using symmetric skip-connections to improve deraining performance by preserving raw information. At last the de-rained image was reconstructed using a reconstruction block as

$$D = R + S = R + f(R) \tag{1}$$

To make learning process easy we directly take the output of SCCNet f(R) is the residual **S**.

For the specific rain streaks removal in the proposed network, three new blocks were introduced and integrated them for learning new feature representations along

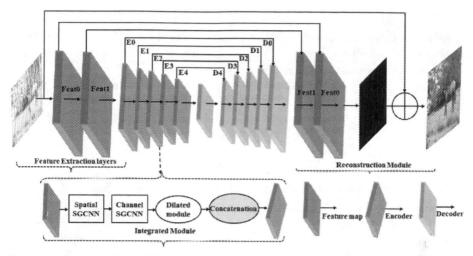

Fig. 1. Spatio-channel based Spectral Graph Convolutional Neural Network (SCSGCNet) Architecture.

multiple dimensions. The integrated module consists of three blocks they are spatial based SGCNN, channel based SGCNN and dilated convolutional network blocks. The goal of spatial based SGCNN module is to capture spatial patterns while the remaining blocks focus on modeling global contextual patterns and channel correlated information. In this way, the proposed network effectively explores the contextual information from multiple dimensions during the deraining process. A gradually improved receptive fields was achieved by employing a standard 3×3 kernel size on stacked vanilla convolutional layers. Since larger receptive fields are much required as both object structures and rain streaks are spatially long, and to utilize them we introduce dilated convolutional neural network [25] in the proposed network. To reduce network parameters, preserve image resolution and increase the contextual information area, are achieved by applying dilated convolutions in the network architecture. However, the contextual information obtained from the dilated convolution block is only from local spatial regions. Therefore, to explore contextual information along both spatial and channel dimensions we introduce spatial based GCNN and channel based GCNN modules in sequential manner.

To model global spatial patterns of contextual information a spatial based GCNN was inserted in the integrated module. This module builds a relation between one pixel and with the surrounding neighbor pixels in extracted feature map. The spatial graph convolution is defined as

$$F^S = BAF_{in} \tag{2}$$

where F_{in} is the input feature map $\in R^{HWxN}$, height, width and number of channels in input feature map, weight matrix B, adjacency matrix A and spatial based spectral graph convolution F^S.

To reduce input feature map channels from N to N/2, we used three 1×1 convolutional layers. This spatial based SGCNN block consider all pixels and allows the SCS-GCNet model to produce coherent predictions, and which benefits to extract contextual information about spatially long rain streaks.

To obtain spatially global correlation among channels from the extracted feature map we designed channel based SGCNN block. In general, to aggregate the contextual information among multiple channels we adopt 1×1 convolution layers $\kappa(\cdot)$ and $\zeta(\cdot)$ on the feature map. The channel graph convolution is defined as

$$F^c = \text{softmax}(\kappa(F_{in})T \zeta(F_{in})) \tag{3}$$

Therefore, by deploying channel based SGCNN block in the proposed network, it allows the model to capture correlations among channels of the input feature map. Specifically for removing rain streaks from rainy images we integrate these three modules spatial SGCNN, channel SGCNN and dilated CNN blocks. Initially spatial SGCNN block extracts the global spatial contextual information from the previous modules. To obtain complementary contextual information to spatial information we deployed channel SGCNN block to explore channel correlations in the input feature map. In order to extract multi-scale local and global patterns of contextual information we applied dilated CNN module (DCM) on the feature map representations. Therefore, the new feature map is defined as

$$F_u = F_{in} + F^s\big((F^c)(\text{DCM})(F_{in})\big), \tag{4}$$

Therefore, all the three blocks were integrated and formed an integrated module and used symmetric skip-connections to avoid vanishing gradient problem and propagates feature map information from neighboring nodes in a layer so which in turn improves the proposed network de-raining performance.

2.1 Loss Function

During the network training we used mean square error loss function (MSE). Because of l_2 penalty, MSE generates more over-smoothed results. To overcome this drawback and maintain an optimal balance between rain removal and detail preservation we adopted mean absolute error (MAE).

$$L = \frac{1}{N} \sum_{j=1}^{N} \|D_j - D_{j,gt}\| \tag{5}$$

where N denotes total training images, D and D_{gt} represents output de-rained image and its corresponding ground truth image respectively.

3 Experiments

3.1 Implementation Details

The proposed network training was implemented on TensorFlow 2.3.0 framework and trained for 300 epochs on rain datasets [9, 13, 15, 17] and adopted ADAM optimizer.

We set initial learning rate as 0.0001; batch size as 16 and employed ReLU activation function in dilated convolution block. To improve the performance of the SCSGCNet various data augmentation techniques such as random crop, horizontal flip, vertical flip and rotation were applied during the network training. We used single Tesla V100 GPU, i7 processor, 16 GB RAM configuration during the proposed model training.

3.2 Baseline Methods

We made a comparative analysis of SCSGCNet deraining network with other eleven existing state-of-the-art (SOTA) baseline networks like GMM [9], DDN [13], DID-MDN [15], RESCAN [16], JORDER-E [17], SIRR [18], SPANet [19], PRENet [20], RCDNet [21], SGCNet [22] and DECANet [26].

3.3 Datasets

The proposed network carried out training on five standard synthetic deraining datasets which includes Rain100L [17], Rain100H [17], Rain12 [9], Rain1200 [15] and Rain14000 [13] as shown in Table 1. These datasets were generated by applying various synthetic strategies. To show the qualitative analysis of the proposed network, we evaluated PSNR and SSIM metrics. As human vision system is sensitive to YCbCr color space, therefore we computed peak signal-to-noise (PSNR) and structural similarity (SSIM) values based on Y (Luminance) channel. As ground truths are not available for real-world rainy images [17], we tested the performance of the proposed network in terms of qualitatively only.

Table 1. Summary of datasets used in the proposed network

S.N. O	Datasets	Train/Test Images
1	Rain100L [17]	200/100
2	Rain100H [17]	1800/100
3	Rain12 [9]	12/0
4	Rain1200 [15]	0/1200
5	Rain14000 [13]	11200/2800

4 Results and Discussions

To show the performance of proposed network, we made comparative quantitative analysis with the existing SOTA networks on five synthetic deraining datasets. The quantitative results of PSNR and SSIM were evaluated on multiple synthetic rain datasets as shown in Table 2. It is clear from table, that our network achieves SOTA results on synthetic rain datasets. The qualitative performance results of SCSGCNet network are shown in Fig. 2.

Table 2. Comparative analysis of the proposed network with existing SOTA networks on five synthetic datasets.

Networks	Datasets				
	RAIN100L	RAIN100H	RAIN12	RAIN1200	RAIN14000
	PSNR|SSIM	PSNR|SSIM	PSNR|SSIM	PSNR|SSIM	PSNR|SSIM
GMM [9]	28.7|0.86	14.5|0.42	32.1|0.91	27.5|0.85	25.5|0.83
DDN [13]	34.7|0.96	26.0|0.80	35.7|0.95	30.1|0.90	31.0|0.91
DID-MDN [15]	35.4|0.96	26.6|0.82	36.2|0.95	31.5|0.91	31.3|0.92
RESCAN [16]	36.0|0.97	26.7|0.83	36.5|0.95	31.9|0.93	33.4|0.94
JORDER-E [17]	37.2|0.97	29.3|0.89	36.7|0.96	32.1|0.93	34.0|0.94
SIRR [18]	34.7|0.97	26.5|0.82	35.7|0.95	30.0|0.91	30.5|0.91
SPANet [19]	35.6|0.96	26.3|0.87	35.9|0.96	29.8|0.91	33.0|0.95
PRENet [20]	37.8|0.98	29.0|0.90	36.6|0.96	32.6|0.94	33.2|0.95
RCDNet [21]	39.2|0.99	30.2|0.91	37.7|0.96	33.0|0.95	34.1|0.95
SGCNet [22]	37.6|0.98	29.1|0.90	36.5|0.96	32.1|0.92	33.5|0.93
DECANet [26]	39.2|0.98	**30.2|0.92**	-|-	32.6|0.92	33.0|0.93
Proposed	**40.4|0.99**	29.8|0.90	**38.4|0.97**	**33.2|0.95**	**34.3|0.96**

To show the robustness of SCSGCNet, we conducted experiments on real-world dataset [15], contains collected rainy images from internet without ground truth. Figure 3 shows the real-world scenarios how the proposed network deals in removing rain streaks and performed comparatively better than existing SOTA models.

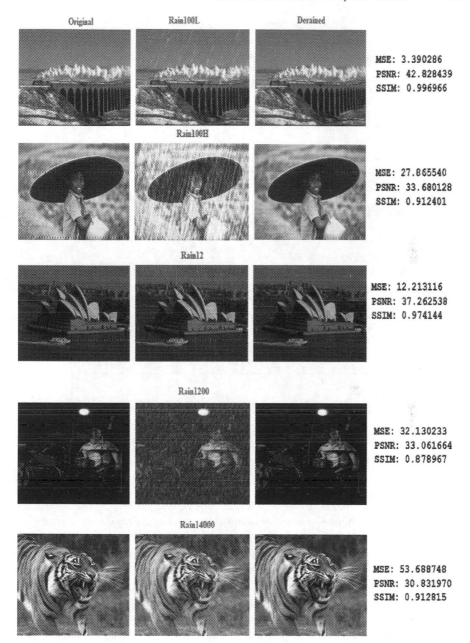

Fig. 2. Visual deraining results of the proposed network on five synthetic deraining datasets.

Fig. 3. Visual deraining results of the proposed network on real rainy images [15] dataset.

5   Conclusion

To explore the contextual information relationships for removing rain streaks in single rainy images, we introduced a new deraining network. For capturing contextual information along spatial and channel wise dimensions, two spectral based GCNN modules were introduced in this network. These two modules were further combined with dilated CNN module and formed an integrated module to extract rich feature representations. This integrated module can efficiently compute local, global spatial patterns and channel correlation features for specific deraining task. Therefore, our SCSGCNet was able to preserve object structures while removing long rain streaks, however it fails to achieve higher PSNR and SSIM while removing heavy rain streaks from single images.

References

1. Mordan, T., Thome, N., Henaff, G., Cord, M.: End-to-end learning of latent deformable part-based representations for object detection. Int. J. Comput. Vision **127**(11), 1659–1679 (2019)

2. Murthy, C.B., Hashmi, M.F., Bokde, N.D., Geem, Z.W.: Investigations of object detection in images/videos using various deep learning techniques and embedded platforms-a comprehensive review. Appl. Sci. **10**(9), 3280 (2020)
3. Zhang, H., Patel, V.M.: Sparse representation-based open set recognition. IEEE Trans. Pattern Anal. Mach. Intell. **39**(8), 1690–1696 (2016)
4. Zhang, T., Ghanem, B., Liu, S., Ahuja, N.: Robust visual tracking via structured multi-task sparse learning. Int. J. Comput. Vision **101**(2), 367–383 (2013)
5. Wojna, Z., Ferrari, V., Guadarrama, S., Silberman, N., Chen, L.C., Fathi, A.: The devil is in the decoder: classification, regression and gans. Int. J. Comput. Vision **127**(11–12), 1694–1706 (2019)
6. Sakaridis, C., Dai, D., Van Gool, L.: Semantic foggy scene understanding with synthetic data. Int. J. Comput. Vision **126**(9), 973–999 (2018)
7. Kang, L., Lin, C., Fu, Y.: Automatic single-image-based rain streaks removal via image decomposition. IEEE Trans. Image Process. **21**(4), 1742–1755 (2012)
8. Kim, J., Lee, C., Sim, J., Kim, C.: Single-imagederaining using an adaptive nonlocal means filter. In: IEEE International Conference on Image Processing, pp. 914–917 (2013)
9. Li, Y., Tan, R.T., Guo, X., Lu, J., Brown, M.S.: Rain streak removal using layer priors. In: CVPR, pp. 2736–2744 (2016)
10. Wang, Y., Liu, S., Chen, C., Zeng, B.: A hierarchical approach for rain or snow removing in a single-color image. IEEE Trans. Image Process. **26**(8), 3936–3950 (2017)
11. Zhu, L., Fu, C.-W., Lischinski, D., Heng, P.-A.: Joint bi-layer optimization for single-image rain streak removal. In: ICCV, pp. 2526–2534 (2017)
12. Gu, S., Meng, D., Zuo, W., Zhang, L.: Joint convolutional analysis and synthesis sparse representation for single image layer separation. In: ICCV, pp. 1708–1716 (2017)
13. Fu, X., Huang, J., Zeng, D., Huang, Y., Ding, X., Paisley, J.: Removing rain from single images via a deep detail network. In: CVPR, pp. 3855–3863 (2017)
14. Yang, W., Tan, R.T., Wang, S., Fang, Y., Liu, J.: Single image deraining: from model-based to data-driven and beyond. IEEE Trans. Pattern Anal. Mach. Intell. **43**(11), 4059–4077 (2021)
15. Zhang, H., Patel, V.M.: Density-aware single image de-raining using a multi-stream dense network. In: CVPR, pp. 695–704 (2018)
16. Li, X., Wu, J., Lin, Z., Liu, H., Zha, H.: Recurrent squeeze-and-excitation context aggregation net for single image deraining. In: Ferrari, V., Hebert, M., Sminchisescu, C., Weiss, Y. (eds.) ECCV 2018. LNCS, vol. 11211, pp. 262–277. Springer, Cham (2018). https://doi.org/10.1007/978-3-030-01234-2_16
17. Yang, W., Tan, R.T., Feng, J., Liu, J., Yan, S., Guo, Z.: Joint rain detection and removal from a single image with contextualized deep networks. IEEE Trans. Pattern Anal. Mach. Intell. **42**(6), 1377–1393 (2019)
18. Wei, W., Meng, D., Zhao, Q., Wu, C., Xu, Z.: Semi-supervised transfer learning for image rain removal. In: CVPR, pp. 3877–3886 (2019)
19. Wang, T., Yang, X., Xu, K., Chen, S., Zhang, Q., Lau, R.W.: Spatial attentive single-imagederaining with a high-quality real rain dataset. In: CVPR, pp. 12270–12279 (2019)
20. Ren, D., Zuo, W., Hu, Q., Zhu, P., Meng, D.: Progressive image deraining networks: a better and simpler baseline. In: CVPR, pp. 3937–3946 (2019)
21. Wang, H., Xie, Q., Zhao, Q., Meng, D.: A model driven deep neural network for single image rain removal. In: CVPR, pp. 3103–3112 (2020)
22. Fu, X., Qi, Q., Zha, Z.-J., Ding, X., Feng, W., Paisley, J.: Successive graph convolutional network for image de-raining. Int. J. Comput. Vision **129**(5), 1691–1711 (2021)
23. Deng, S., et al.: Detail-recovery Image deraining via context aggregation networks. In: CVPR, pp. 14560–14569 (2020)
24. Bruna, J., Zaremba, W., Szlam, A., LeCun, Y.: Spectral networks and locally connected networks on graphs. arXiv preprintarXiv:1312.6203 (2013)

25. Yu, F., Koltun, V.: Multi-scale context aggregation by dilated convolutions. In: ICLR (2016)
26. Lin, X., Huang, Q., Huang, W., Tan, X., Fang, M., Ma, L.: Single image deraining via detail-guided efficient channel attention network. Comput. Graph. **97**, 117–125 (2021)

Integration of GAN and Adaptive Exposure Correction for Shadow Removal

Krunal Mehta, Manish Khare$^{(\boxtimes)}$, and Avik Hati

Dhirubhai Ambani Institute of Information and Communication Technology,
Gandhinagar, Gujarat, India
{202011051,manish_khare}@daiict.ac.in

Abstract. Shadow removal from images and videos is an essential task
in computer vision that concentrates on detecting the shadow generated
by the obstructed light source, and obtains realistic shadow-free results.
In this paper, we present a method based on generative adversarial networks (GANs) for shadow removal by supervised learning. Specifically, we
train two generators and two discriminators to learn the mapping between
shadow and shadow-free image domains. We employ generative adversarial constraints with cycle consistency and content constraints to learn the
mapping efficiently. We also propose an adaptive exposure correction module to handle the over-exposure problem in the shadow area of the result.
We additionally present a method for improving the quality of benchmark datasets and eventually achieving better shadow removal results. We
also show ablation studies to analyze the importance of the ground-truth
data with the adaptive exposure correction module in the proposed framework and explore the impact of using different learning strategies in the
presented method. We validate the approach on the available large-scale
benchmark Image Shadow Triplets dataset (ISTD), and show quantitative
and visual improvements in the state-of-the-art results.

Keywords: Shadow removal · Shadow detection · GANs · Adaptive
exposure correction · Benchmark dataset adjustment

1 Introduction

Shadow detection and removal is a fundamental and challenging task in computer vision and computer graphics. In an image, a shadow is a direct result of
occluding a light source. The accuracy of several computer vision tasks, such as
object segmentation [20], object recognition [2], and object tracking [13], can be
influenced by the shadow since shadows have similar characteristics as objects,
so they can get misclassified as part of an object.

In computer vision, the problem involving shadow detection and removal
has received much attention. Early works related to this task [5,6,21,26,28,29]
used physical models of features like intensity, color, gradient, and texture. However, these hand-crafted feature-based methods suffer in understanding the high-
level features and related semantic content. In recent years, deep learning-based

© The Author(s), under exclusive license to Springer Nature Switzerland AG 2023
D. Gupta et al. (Eds.): CVIP 2022, CCIS 1777, pp. 161–175, 2023.
https://doi.org/10.1007/978-3-031-31417-9_13

approaches for analyzing the mapping relation have made significant progress in this field. Khan *et al.* [11,12] used convolutional neural networks (CNN) for shadow detection and Bayesian model for shadow removal. The model of Qu *et al.* [19] is based on an end-to-end multi-context embedding framework to extract essential characteristics from multiple aspects and accumulate them to determine the shadow matte. Fan *et al.* [4] employed a deep CNN structure containing an encoder-decoder and a refinement model for extracting features with local detail correction and learning the shadow matte. Bansal *et al.* [3] developed a deep learning model to extract features and directly detect the shadow mask. Hu *et al.* [7] presented a direction-aware spatial context (DSC) module, utilized with CNNs, to detect and remove the shadow.

The generative adversarial network (GAN) [1] and its extensions, presented in recent years, are dominant strategies for dealing with diverse image-to-image translation challenges. Conditional GANs (CGANs) [15] are significant GAN extensions that incorporate conditioning information into the generator and the discriminator. Nguyen *et al.* [17] demonstrated the first method of shadow detection with adversarial learning and constructed a CGAN-based architecture to output a shadow mask that can realistically correspond to the ground-truth mask. A shadow image with an adjustable sensitivity factor is used as the conditioning information to the generator and the discriminator. Wang *et al.* [27] presented a supervised model based on two Stacked-CGANs to tackle shadow detection and removal problems simultaneously in an end-to-end manner. Nagae *et al.* [16] developed a model based on the method in [27], with minor changes in the shadow removal CGAN, that estimates the illumination ratio and uses that estimation to produce the output. Although these approaches [7,27] effectively remove the shadow, they tend to generate artifacts and inconsistent colors in the non-shadow area. Hu *et al.* [8] presented a Mask-ShadowGAN framework that enforces cycle consistency by the guidance of masks and learns a bidirectional mapping between the shadow and shadow-free domains. Tan *et al.* [24] developed a target-consistency GAN (TCGAN) for shadow removal that aims to learn a unidirectional mapping to translate shadow images into shadow-free images. These methods [8,24] remove the shadow by maintaining a non-shadow region with cycle and target consistency but suffer from overexposure problems and random artifacts. Also, they require unpaired shadow and shadow-free datasets with the same statistical distribution for better learning.

In this paper, we propose a novel method based on GANs with cycle constraints, and introduce an adaptive exposure correction module for handling the overexposure problem. Figure 1 shows a shadow removal result of the proposed method compared with Mask-ShadowGAN [8], which suffers from over-exposure, particularly in the shadow area. However, our approach handles that problem and generates a result close to the ground-truth. The key contributions of this work are as follows.

- We present a framework that removes the shadow using *generative adversarial* constraints along with *cycle consistency* and *content* constraints.

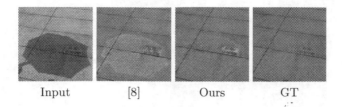

Input   [8]   Ours   GT

Fig. 1. Shadow removal results comparing the Mask-ShadowGAN [8] method with the proposed method.

- We introduce an adaptive exposure correction module for handling the over-exposure problem.
- We introduce a method for enhancing the quality of benchmark datasets and subsequently improving the shadow removal results.

The rest of the paper is organized as follows. Section 2 describes the proposed framework. Section 3 presents experimental results along with the ablation study, and we conclude the work in Sect. 4.

2   Proposed Method

The overall scheme of the proposed method is depicted in Fig. 2. The method is based on CycleGAN [30], in which each adversarial generator learns a mapping to another domain, and the corresponding discriminator guides the learning procedure. Apart from the adversarial and cycle constraints, we also employ content and identity constraints as guidance for better learning. Compared to the baseline Mask-ShadowGAN [8], which required unpaired data with an equal statistical distribution of shadow and shadow-free domains, our method utilizes available shadow, shadow-free, and shadow mask images to learn better mapping for shadow removal.

2.1   Generator and Discriminator Learning

The proposed method learns from both the shadow domain $\mathbb{D}_x$ and the shadow-free domain $\mathbb{D}_y$. While learning from domain $\mathbb{D}_x$, the generator network G_f takes a real shadow image $I_s \in \mathbb{D}_x$ as input, and generates a shadow-free image $\hat{I}_{f*}$. The discriminator network D_f is used to differentiate whether the produced shadow-free image $\hat{I}_{f*}$ is a real shadow-free image or not. To achieve the cycle-consistency, another generator G_s is used to reconstruct the shadow image $\hat{I}_s$ from the generated shadow-free image $\hat{I}_{f*}$ using a ground-truth shadow mask M_{gt*} for the image I_s as a guide.

In the process of learning from the shadow-free domain $\mathbb{D}_y$, the generator network G_s takes a real shadow-free image $I_f \in \mathbb{D}_y$ as input and a ground-truth shadow mask M_{gt} for the image I_f as a guide, and generates a shadow image $\hat{I}_{s*}$.

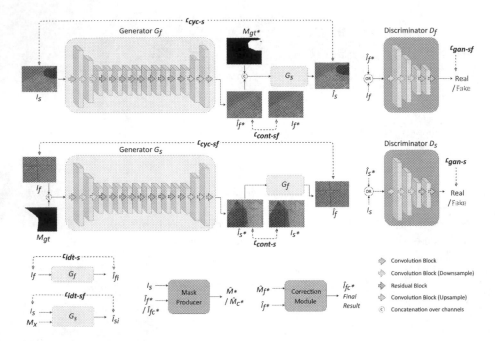

Fig. 2. Illustration of the architecture of the proposed method.

The discriminator network D_s determines if the created shadow image $\hat{I}_{s*}$ is a real shadow image or not. To formulate the cycle-consistency loop, the generator G_f reconstructs the shadow-free image $\hat{I}_f$ from the generated shadow image $\hat{I}_{s*}$.

To summarize, the discriminator network D_s takes either real sample I_s or fake sample $\hat{I}_{s*}$ as input and discriminates whether the input is from $\mathbb{D}_s$ or not. Similarly, discriminator D_f takes either real sample I_f or fake sample $\hat{I}_{f*}$ as input and discriminates whether the input is from $\mathbb{D}_f$ or not. We shall discuss the corresponding loss functions in Sect. 2.3.

2.2   Adaptive Exposure Correction Module

Given a shadow image, the generator network G_f is trained to produce a shadow-free image. But in the absence of any constraints, sometimes the generated shadow-free images are much brighter in the shadow area. To handle this over-exposure problem in the resulting shadow-free images, we propose to use an adaptive exposure correction module that takes the generated shadow-free image $\hat{I}_{f*}$ and an intermediate shadow-free mask $\hat{M}_*$ as inputs, and produces the final shadow-free result $\hat{I}_{fc*}$. The shadow mask $\hat{M}_*$ for the input shadow image I_s is obtained as $\mathbb{B}(\hat{I}_{f*} - I_s, t)$, where the binarization operation $\mathbb{B}$ is performed on the difference between $\hat{I}_{f*}$ and the real input shadow image I_s, and t is a threshold obtained by Otsu's algorithm [18]. $\mathbb{B}$ sets the value as zero or one, where zero indicates non-shadow region (difference $\leq t$) and one indicates the shadow region (difference $> t$). In the adaptive exposure correction module, we extract the shadow and non-shadow areas using $\hat{M}_*$ and apply gamma correction (power-law transformations) in the shadow area. First, we transform the extracted shadow area to the HSV color space, then perform gamma correction on the value channel and convert it back to RGB color space. Finally, we combine the gamma-corrected shadow area with the non-shadow area to generate $\hat{I}_{fc*}$ which is the final shadow-free image with exposure correction. To estimate the gamma value, we calculate the mean difference between the shadow and non-shadow areas and map that to the gamma value range 0 to 2. Ideally, for a non-overexposed image, the gamma value will be 1, and no correction will be done. Then the final shadow mask $\hat{M}_{c*}$ is obtained as $\mathbb{B}(\hat{I}_{fc*} - I_s, t)$.

2.3   Objectives and Loss Functions

Adversarial Losses: The primary principle behind adversarial learning is that the discriminator will differentiate between real and generated results for both domains, encouraging the corresponding generator to deliver a better output concerning image qualities. The shadow-free adversarial loss and the shadow adversarial loss are given as:

$$\mathcal{L}_{gan\text{-}sf(G)} = MSE(P, D_f(\hat{I}_{f*})), \mathcal{L}_{gan\text{-}s(G)} = MSE(P, D_s(\hat{I}_{s*})) \qquad (1)$$

$$\begin{aligned} \mathcal{L}_{gan\text{-}sf(D)} &= MSE(P, D_f(I_f)) + MSE(Q, D_f(\hat{I}_{f*})), \\ \mathcal{L}_{gan\text{-}s(D)} &= MSE(P, D_s(I_s)) + MSE(Q, D_s(\hat{I}_{s*})) \end{aligned} \qquad (2)$$

where $\hat{I}_{f*}$ (generated as $(G_f(I_s))$) and $\hat{I}_{s*}$ (generated as $(G_s(I_f, M_{gt}))$) are the generated shadow-free and shadow images, respectively, with I_s and I_f being the input shadow and shadow-free images, respectively, and $P = 1$, $Q = 0$.

Cycle Consistency Losses: Cycle consistency L_1 losses defined in Eq. (3) and Eq. (4) are applied to encourage the reconstructed images to be comparable to the original input images and to effectively improve the bidirectional mapping in the G_f and G_s networks.

$$\mathcal{L}_{cyc\text{-}s} = \|\hat{I}_s - I_s\|_1 \qquad (3)$$

$$\mathcal{L}_{cyc\text{-}sf} = \|\hat{I}_f - I_f\|_1 \qquad (4)$$

Here, $\hat{I}_s$ (generated as $G_s(G_f(I_s), M_{gt*})$) and $\hat{I}_f$ (generated as $G_f(G_s(I_f, M_{gt}))$) are the reconstructed shadow and shadow-free images, respectively.

Identity Losses: The identity L_1 losses defined in Eq. (5) and Eq. (6) motivate generators G_s and G_f not to change the input image (a shadow image and a shadow-free image, respectively), and maintain color consistency.

$$\mathcal{L}_{idt\text{-}s} = \|\hat{I}_{si} - I_s\|_1 \qquad (5)$$

$$\mathcal{L}_{idt\text{-}sf} = \|\hat{I}_{fi} - I_f\|_1 \qquad (6)$$

where $\hat{I}_{si}$ is the generated image using G_s from I_s and null mask M_x, and $\hat{I}_{fi}$ is the generated image using G_f from I_f.

Content Losses: The L_1 constraint on content losses defined in Eq. (7) and Eq. (8) encourages generators to produce images that are closer to the ground-truth images.

$$\mathcal{L}_{cont\text{-}s} = \|\hat{I}_{s*} - I_{s*}\|_1 \qquad (7)$$

$$\mathcal{L}_{cont\text{-}sf} = \|\hat{I}_{f*} - I_{f*}\|_1 \qquad (8)$$

Here, I_{s*} and I_{f*} are the ground-truth shadow and shadow-free images, respectively, and $\hat{I}_{f*}$ (generated as $(G_f(I_s))$) and $\hat{I}_{s*}$ (generated as $(G_s(I_f, M_{gt}))$) are the generated shadow-free and shadow images, respectively.

Loss Function for Generators: The total generator loss for the proposed method is obtained as a weighted sum of the adversarial losses, cycle consistency losses, identity losses, and content losses, given as:

$$\mathcal{L}_G = \lambda_1(\mathcal{L}_{gan\text{-}s(G)} + \mathcal{L}_{gan\text{-}sf(G)}) + \lambda_2(\mathcal{L}_{cyc\text{-}s} + \mathcal{L}_{cyc\text{-}sf}) \\ + \lambda_3(\mathcal{L}_{idt\text{-}s} + \mathcal{L}_{idt\text{-}sf}) + \lambda_4(\mathcal{L}_{cont\text{-}s} + \mathcal{L}_{cont\text{-}sf}) \qquad (9)$$

where $\lambda_1, \lambda_2, \lambda_3, \lambda_4$ are appropriately chosen weights.

Loss Function for Discriminators: The discriminator loss for the shadow-free discriminator D_f and shadow discriminator D_s in the proposed method are given in Eq. (10) and Eq. (11), respectively.

$$\mathcal{L}_{D_f} = \lambda_5(\mathcal{L}_{gan\text{-}sf(D)}) \qquad (10)$$

$$\mathcal{L}_{D_s} = \lambda_5(\mathcal{L}_{gan\text{-}s(D)}) \qquad (11)$$

Here, λ_5 is the appropriately chosen weight.

2.4   Network Architecture and Training Strategy

We use the model of Johnson *et al.* [10] as the generator network, which consists of 3 convolutional layers, 9 residual blocks, and 2 deconvolution layers. After each convolution and deconvolution operation, the network employs instance normalization and the ReLU (rectified linear unit) activation function. For the discriminator network, we use PatchGAN [9], which focuses on classifying image patches as real or fake. Here, 4 convolutional layers are used with instance normalization and leaky ReLU activation function (slope = 0.2). Adam optimization [14] with a learning rate of 0.0002, with first and second order momentum as 0.5 and 0.999, is adopted during training. A zero-mean Gaussian distribution with a standard deviation of 0.02 initializes the network parameters. For data augmentation during training, images are resized to 286×286 and randomly cropped to 256×256. The network is trained for 200 epochs keeping the mini-batch size as 1 with the PyTorch module and NVIDIA GeForce-RTX2080-Ti GPU.

2.5   Benchmark Dataset Adjustment

Ideally, in the benchmark dataset for the shadow removal task, the non-shadow area of the shadow and the corresponding shadow-free image should be the same. However, there is a significant difference in the color consistency, brightness, and contrast, since both shadow and shadow-free images were captured at different times of the day. On the whole testing dataset of ISTD [27], the root mean square error (RMSE) in the LAB color space between the shadow and shadow-free images in the non-shadow area is 6.83, which should ideally be close to 0. Figure 3 shows the sample triplets from the ISTD dataset, where the difference in the non-shadow area is clearly visible. Supervised models are trained to produce an output close to the ground-truth shadow-free image, and accordingly, the loss function is defined, and models are trained. However, methods yield color, brightness, and contrast inconsistent outputs compared to the non-shadow area of the shadow image. Hence, it is essential to adjust those ground-truth shadow-free images to achieve better results.

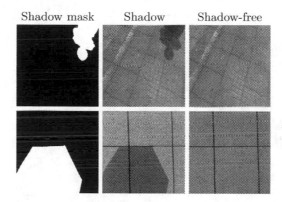

Fig. 3. ISTD triplets, showing issue in the non-shadow area.

To achieve this, we process each image individually to adjust the ground-truth shadow-free images using the regression technique. Following are the steps we used for this correction task.

- The non-shadow area of shadow and shadow-free images were extracted using the shadow mask.
- A regressor makes use of that extracted non-shadow area and learns to transform the non-shadow pixel values of shadow-free image into the corresponding pixel values of the shadow image.
- Finally, the trained regressor takes the shadow-free image as input and generates an adjusted shadow-free image.

We conducted various experiments by using three well-known regressors, Linear Regressor (LR), Decision-Tree Regressor (DTR), and K-Nearest-Neighbor

Regressor (KNNR). Further, we considered both RGB and LAB color spaces. Also, we executed experiments by using single-output regression, where regression is performed on three individual color channels, and by using multi-output regression, where regression is performed on three combined color channels. Finally, we used the optimal decision-tree multi-output regressor in RGB color space for the benchmark dataset adjustment. Following steps describe the algorithm of the decision-tree regressor.

- Given a training vector x and a label vector y, the decision tree divides the feature space in a recursive fashion, such that the samples with similar labels are grouped together.
- Let the data at node n be denoted by D_n having m_n samples. For each candidate split $\delta = (i, t_n)$, where i is feature and t_n is threshold, partition the data into $D_n^{left}(\delta)$ and $D_n^{right}(\delta)$ subsets according to following equations.

$$D_n^{left}(\delta) = \{(x, y)|x_i \leq t_n\} \tag{12}$$

$$D_n^{right}(\delta) = \{(x, y)|x_i > t_n\} \tag{13}$$

- The quality of a candidate split of node n is then measured using an impurity function G and loss function H according to Eq. (14) and Eq. (15), respectively. Here, $\bar{y}_n$ is the mean value, and the mean squared error is used as the loss function.

$$H(D_n) = \frac{1}{m_n} \sum_{y \in D_n} (y - \bar{y}_n)^2, \bar{y}_n = \frac{1}{m_n} \sum_{y \in D_n} y \tag{14}$$

$$G(D_n, \delta) = \frac{m_n^{left}}{m_n} H(D_n^{left}(\delta)) + \frac{m_n^{right}}{m_n} H(D_n^{right}(\delta)) \tag{15}$$

- Parameters that minimize the impurity are selected for splitting, as follows:

$$\delta^* = \arg \min_\delta G(D_n, \delta) \tag{16}$$

- The algorithm is recursed for subsets $D_n^{left}(\delta^*)$ and $D_n^{right}(\delta^*)$ until $m_n = 1$.

3   Experimental Results

Database Description: To analyze the performance of the proposed framework, we experimented with the dataset containing image shadow triplets termed as ISTD [27] and trained models accordingly. ISTD contains 1870 triplets of shadow, shadow mask, and shadow-free image with 1330 image triplets in the training split and 540 in the testing split.

Evaluation Parameters: We followed [17, 25, 27] and used balance error rate (BER) for a quantitative comparison for shadow detection. Balance error rate is calculated as:

$$\text{BER} = 1 - \frac{1}{2}\left(\frac{TP}{TP + FN} + \frac{TN}{TN + FP}\right) \tag{17}$$

where

- True Positive (TP) denotes the number of pixels that the predictive model has labeled as a shadow, and actually, it is a shadow.
- False Positive (FP) denotes the number of pixels that the predictive model has labeled as a shadow, and actually, it is a non-shadow.
- True Negative (TN) denotes the number of pixels that the predictive model has labeled as a non-shadow, and actually, it is a non-shadow.
- False Negative (FN) denotes the number of pixels that the predictive model has labeled as a non-shadow, and actually, it is a shadow.

For the quantitative assessment of shadow removal, we followed recent procedures [7, 8, 24, 27] and used root mean square error (RMSE) in the LAB color space computed between the ground-truth and produced shadow-free images. We resized all images to 286×286 for a fair comparison. Additionally, we calculated the RMSE value in the four scenarios: RMSE value by comparing the resulting shadow-free image $\hat{I}_{fc*}$ with the ground-truth shadow-free image I_{f*} (i) for all pixels (represented with 'O'), (ii) for pixels in the shadow region (represented with 'S'), (iii) for pixels in the non-shadow region (represented with SF), and (iv) by comparing $\hat{I}_{fc*}$ with input shadow image I_s for pixels in the non-shadow region (represented with SF-I). In the experiments, the hyper-parameters $\lambda_1, \lambda_2, \lambda_3, \lambda_4, \lambda_5$ are set as $1, 10, 5, 5, 0.5$, respectively. In the tables, best and second-best results are highlighted in bold and blue, respectively.

Evaluation on Removal: We compare the shadow removal performance of the proposed method with the methods in [5–8, 24, 27, 28] on the test dataset of ISTD. The results are shown in Table 1. Our method achieves the best performance in the O and SF scenarios, and the second-best performance in S and SF-I scenarios. TCGAN [24] achieves the best result in SF-I, but it has poor performance in S. Similarly, DSC [7] achieves the best result in S but performs poorly in SF and SF-I. Our approach achieves comparable results in all aspects and yields the best overall value O, compared to other methods. Figure 4 shows visual performance compared to methods ST-CGAN [27] and Mask-ShadowGAN [8]. While ST-CGAN [27] suffers from color-inconstancy and artifacts, and Mask-ShadowGAN [8] has over-exposure, our approach handles those issues and produces better output.

Evaluation on Detection: We evaluate the shadow detection performance with the recent methods [8, 14, 17, 27] on the ISTD test dataset. The quantitative results are shown in Table 2. The proposed method outperforms the baseline Mask-ShadowGAN [8] and methods CGAN [17], StackedCNN [25]. Methods SCGAN [17] and ST-CGAN [27] achieve better results since these methods

Table 1. Quantitative results of removal with RMSE on ISTD test dataset.

Method	Publication	O	S	SF	SF-I
Original	-	10.97	32.67	6.83	0
Yang [28]	IEEE TIP, 2012	15.63	19.82	14.83	–
Gong [5]	BMVC, 2014	9.3	18.95	7.46	–
Guo [6]	IEEE TPAMI, 2013	8.53	14.98	7.29	–
ST-CGAN [27]	IEEE CVPR, 2018	7.47	10.33	6.93	7.45
Mask-ShadowGAN [8]	IEEE, ICCV, 2019	6.99	11.41	6.17	6.75
TCGAN [24]	ARXIV, 2020	6.85	11.49	5.91	**6.29**
DSC [7]	IEEE TPAMI, 2020	6.67	**9.22**	6.39	6.61
Ours	–	**6.54**	10.03	**5.88**	6.49

Input	[27]	[8]	Ours(-c)	Ours

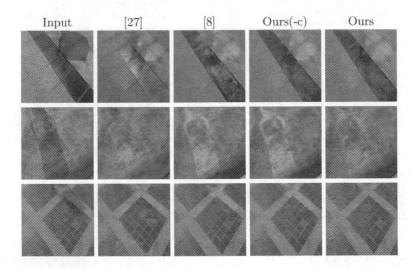

Fig. 4. Visual comparison of shadow removal results of ISTD test dataset.

specifically train their networks for the detection task. As our goal is shadow removal, we do not train any separate network for detection; instead, we extract the shadow mask from the final shadow-free image and input image as discussed in Sect. 2.2. Figure 5 shows the visual performance compared to state-of-the-art Mask-ShadowGAN [8]. Our approach produces a shadow mask result close to the ground-truth shadow mask.

Benchmark Dataset Adjustment: To adjust ground-truth shadow-free images, we experimented with Linear Regressor (LR), Decision-Tree Regressor (DTR), and K-Nearest-Neighbor Regressor (KNNR) in RGB and LAB color spaces. While performing regression in the LAB color space, both shadow and shadow-free images are transformed to the LAB space from the RGB space, and after performing regression and correction, they are again transformed back to the RGB space. Also, we have performed experiments by using a regression

Table 2. Quantitative results of detection with BER(%) on ISTD test dataset.

Method	BER	Method	BER
StackedCNN [25]	8.6	ST-CGAN [27]	**3.85**
CGAN [17]	9.64	Mask-ShadowGAN [8]	7.66
SCGAN [17]	4.7	Ours	6.48

Input	GT	[8]	Ours

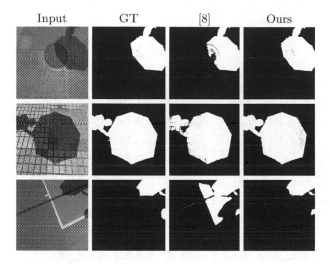

Fig. 5. Visual comparison of shadow detection results on ISTD test dataset.

for each individual color channel (there will be three one-input to one-output regressor) and by using a regression for combined color-channel (multi-output regressor) (there will be one 3-input to 3-output regressor). For implementation, we used regression methods from the scikit-learn python library [22]. The results of the experiments are shown in Table 3.

Table 3. Quantitative results of ISTD test dataset adjustment task with RMSE.

	Original	Individual Channel					
		RGB LR	LAB LR	RGB DTR	LAB DTR	RGB KNNR	LAB KNNR
O	10.97	8.78	8.39	8.41	7.61	11.80	8.04
S	32.67	40.67	39.54	39.63	39.26	41.55	39.23
SF	6.83	2.81	2.55	2.56	1.68	6.23	2.20

	Original	Combined Channel					
		RGB LR	LAB LR	RGB DTR	LAB DTR	RGB KNNR	LAB KNNR
O	10.97	8.67	8.23	**7.56**	7.57	7.95	7.92
S	32.67	40.76	39.37	39.06	39.05	39.03	**38.98**
SF	6.83	2.66	2.39	**1.66**	1.67	2.12	2.11

Experimentally, we observed that the decision-tree combined channel regressor in RGB color space has a lower RMSE value in O and SF scenarios. So finally, we used that method and created a new adjusted ISTD training and testing dataset. Figure 6 shows the visual output of this database adjustment task by using the selected method.

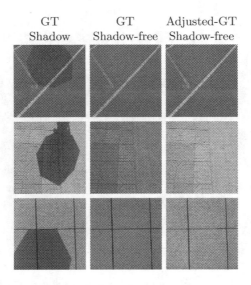

Fig. 6. Visual results of ISTD dataset adjustment task.

Evaluation on Removal with Adjusted Benchmark ISTD Dataset: We compare the shadow removal performance of the proposed method with the methods [8,27], trained and tested on the adjusted dataset of ISTD. Since the official code for the ST-CGAN method [27] is not available, we use the community code [23] for evaluation purpose. The results are shown in Table 4. The proposed method achieves the best performance in O, S, and SF scenarios compared to state-of-the-art methods.

Table 4. Quantitative shadow removal results with RMSE, trained and tested on adjusted ISTD dataset.

Method	O	S	SF	SF-I
Original	7.56	39.06	1.66	0
ST-CGAN [23,27]	8.79	11.35	8.31	4.28
Mask-ShadowGAN [8]	4.47	10.13	3.41	**3.18**
Ours	**4.36**	**9.52**	**3.40**	3.19

Ablation Study: We have done an ablation study on the presented framework by removing the exposure correction module (represented by -c) along with not using ground-truth shadow and shadow-free images (represented by -gt) and not using ground-truth masks (represented by -gtm). While performing an experiment with -gt, we ignored content losses, and for the -gtm experiment, initially, we generated masks by ground-truth shadow and shadow-free images according to Sect. 2.2. Removal and detection results for all the experiments are shown in Table 5. Visual performance for (-c) is shown in Fig. 4. Our approach achieves the best overall performance for removal and detection, and shows the importance of ground-truth data and correction module to achieve the best result.

Table 5. Ablation study.

Aspect	Removal				Detection
Method	**O**	**S**	**SF**	**SF-I**	**BER**
Ours	**6.54**	**10.03**	5.88	6.49	**6.48**
Ours(-gt)	6.98	11.07	6.22	6.54	8.37
Ours(-gtm)	6.85	10.11	6.23	6.93	6.64
Ours(-c)	6.57	10.62	**5.82**	**6.43**	6.76
Ours(-gt -c)	7.03	11.68	6.15	6.47	8.41
Ours(-gtm -c)	6.93	10.63	6.24	6.94	6.76

4   Conclusion

We proposed a method based on GAN to solve the shadow removal task in images. We used different constraints to effectively learn the bidirectional relationship between shadow and shadow-free domains under the paired setting. We also presented a novel process to handle the over-exposure problem after the training. As a result, the proposed method with an exposure correction module achieves the best or comparable performance compared to existing state-of-the-art methods, both quantitatively and visually. We explored the issue in benchmark datasets and introduced a technique for adjusting those benchmark datasets to additionally improve the shadow removal results. We also conducted various experiments to analyze the importance of ground-truth data and exposure correction module in generating better quality output.

Acknowledgements. This work was supported by the Science and Engineering Research Board (SERB), Department of Science and Technology (DST), New Delhi, India, under Grant No. CRG/2020/001982.

References

1. Goodfellow, I., et al.: Generative adversarial nets. In: Advances in Neural Information Processing Systems, vol. 27, pp. 2672–2680 (2014)
2. Russakovsky, O., et al.: Imagenet large scale visual recognition challenge. Int. J. Comput. Vision (IJCV) **115**(3), 211–252 (2015)
3. Bansal, N., Akashdeep, Aggarwal, N.: Deep learning based shadow detection in images. In: Krishna, C., Dutta, M., Kumar, R. (eds.) Proceedings of 2nd International Conference on Communication, Computing and Networking. LNNS, pp. 375–382. Springer, Singapore (2019). https://doi.org/10.1007/978-981-13-1217-5_37
4. Fan, H., Han, M., Li, J.: Image shadow removal using end-to-end deep convolutional neural networks. Appl. Sci. (2019)
5. Gong, H., Cosker, D.: Interactive shadow removal and ground truth for variable scene categories. In: Proceedings of the British Machine Vision Conference (2014)
6. Guo, R., Dai, Q., Hoiem, D.: Paired regions for shadow detection and removal. IEEE Trans. Pattern Anal. Mach. Intell. **35**(12), 2956–2967 (2013)
7. Hu, X., Fu, C., Zhu, L., Qin, J., Heng, P.: Direction-aware spatial context features for shadow detection and removal. IEEE Trans. Pattern Anal. Mach. Intell. **42**(11), 2795–2808 (2020)
8. Hu, X., Jiang, Y., Fu, C., Heng, P.: Mask-ShadowGAN: learning to remove shadows from unpaired data. In: IEEE International Conference on Computer Vision (ICCV), pp. 2472–2481 (2019)
9. Isola, P., Zhu, J., Zhou, T., Efros, A.A.: Image-to-image translation with conditional adversarial networks. In: IEEE Conference on Computer Vision and Pattern Recognition (CVPR), pp. 1125–1134 (2017)
10. Johnson, J., Alahi, A., Fei-Fei, L.: Perceptual losses for real-time style transfer and super-resolution. In: Leibe, B., Matas, J., Sebe, N., Welling, M. (eds.) ECCV 2016. LNCS, vol. 9906, pp. 694–711. Springer, Cham (2016). https://doi.org/10.1007/978-3-319-46475-6_43
11. Khan, S.H., Bennamoun, M., Sohel, F., Togneri, R.: Automatic feature learning for robust shadow detection. In: IEEE Conference on Computer Vision and Pattern Recognition (CVPR), pp. 1939–1946 (2014)
12. Khan, S.H., Bennamoun, M., Sohel, F., Togneri, R.: Automatic shadow detection and removal from a single image. IEEE Trans. Pattern Anal. Mach. Intell. **38**(3), 431–446 (2016)
13. Khare, M., Srivastava, R.K., Khare, A.: Object tracking using combination of Daubechies complex wavelet transform and Zernike moment. Multimedia Tools Appl. **76**(1), 1247–1290 (2017)
14. Kingma, D.P., Ba, J.: Adam: a method for stochastic optimization. arXiv:1412.6980 (2014)
15. Mirza, M., Osindero, S.: Conditional generative adversarial nets. arXiv:1411.1784 (2014)
16. Nagae, T., Abiko, R., Yamaguchi, T., Ikehara, M.: Shadow detection and removal using GAN. In: Proceedings of 28th European Signal Processing Conference (EUSIPCO), pp. 630–634 (2021)
17. Nguyen, V., Vicente, T.F.Y., Zhao, M., Hoai, M., Samaras, D.: Shadow detection with conditional generative adversarial networks. In: IEEE International Conference on Computer Vision (ICCV), pp. 4510–4518 (2017)
18. Otsu, N.: A threshold selection method from gray-level histograms. IEEE Trans. Syst. Man Cybern. **9**(1), 62–66 (1979)

19. Qu, L., Tian, J., He, S., Tang, Y., Lau, R.W.: DeshadowNet: a multi-context embedding deep network for shadow removal. In: IEEE Conference on Computer Vision and Pattern Recognition (CVPR), pp. 4067–4075 (2017)
20. Redmon, J., Divvala, S., Girshick, R., Farhadi, A.: You only look once: unified, real-time object detection. In: IEEE Conference on Computer vision and Pattern Recognition (CVPR), pp. 779–788 (2016)
21. Sanin, A., Sanderson, C., Lovell, B.C.: Shadow detection: a survey and comparative evaluation of recent methods. Pattern Recogn. **45**(4), 1684–1695 (2012)
22. Scikit-learn: https://scikit-learn.org/stable/
23. ST-CGAN: https://github.com/IsHYuhi/ST-CGAN_Stacked_Conditional_Gen-erative_Adversarial_Networks
24. Tan, C., Feng, X.: Unsupervised shadow removal using target consistency generative adversarial network. arXiv:2010.01291 (2020)
25. Vicente, T.F.Y., Hou, L., Yu, C.-P., Hoai, M., Samaras, D.: Large-scale training of shadow detectors with noisily-annotated shadow examples. In: Leibe, B., Matas, J., Sebe, N., Welling, M. (eds.) ECCV 2016. LNCS, vol. 9910, pp. 816–832. Springer, Cham (2016). https://doi.org/10.1007/978-3-319-46466-4_49
26. Wang, B., Chen, C.L.P.: An effective background estimation method for shadows removal of document images. In: IEEE International Conference on Image Processing (ICIP), pp. 3611–3615 (2019)
27. Wang, J., Li, X., Yang, J.: Stacked conditional generative adversarial networks for jointly learning shadow detection and shadow removal. In: IEEE Conference on Computer Vision and Pattern Recognition (CVPR), pp. 1788–1797 (2018)
28. Yang, Q., Tan, K., Ahuja, N.: Shadow removal using bilateral filtering. IEEE Trans. Image Process. **21**(10), 4361–4368 (2012)
29. Yao, K., Dong, J.: Removing shadows from a single real-world color image. In: IEEE International Conference on Image Processing (ICIP), pp. 3129–3132 (2009)
30. Zhu, J., Park, T., Isola, P., Efros, A.A.: Unpaired image-to-image translation using cycle-consistent adversarial networks. In: IEEE International Conference on Computer Vision (ICCV), pp. 2223–2232 (2017)

Non-invasive Haemoglobin Estimation Using Different Colour and Texture Features of Palm

Abhishek Kesarwani[✉], Sunanda Das, Mamata Dalui,
and Dakshina Ranjan Kisku

Department of Computer Science and Engineering, National Institute of Technology,
Durgapur, India
{ak.18cs1102,sd.19cs1111}@phd.nitdgp.ac.in
{mamata.dalui,drkisku}@cse.nitdgp.ac.in

Abstract. Anaemia, caused due to lack of blood haemoglobin levels, is one of the most common diseases which affects billions of people across the world. According to WHO statistics, India is one of the developing countries with highest prevalence of anaemia. Conventional invasive methods are cost-prohibitive and difficult to administer globally which essentially demands non-invasive, accurate, and low-cost approaches for screening of anaemia. The current work targets to combine cutting edge computational approaches with the age-old practice of rough estimation of blood haemoglobin levels by observing pallor in the palm to develop a non-invasive reliable anaemia detection system. The proposed system works with the principle of inducing pallor changes in palm with suitable pressure application and release, measuring the rate of change of colour and performing time-domain analysis thereof to correlate with blood haemoglobin concentration. The entire event of colour changes in palm induced through a customized device, is videophotographed using smartphone camera sensor and is processed and analysed through a set of image processing and analysis techniques. Different handcrafted colour and texture feature extraction techniques are applied on some of the dominant frames considering different colour models on the video samples. The set of features selected through feature selection techniques are provided as input to multi-layer perceptron (MLP) networks comprising of different activation functions and optimizers. The proposed system ensures an accurate estimation of blood haemoglobin level with an average RMSE of 0.597 as determined based on palm pallor video samples of 41 participants.

Keywords: Anaemia · Palm pallor video · Colour models · Feature extraction · Feature selection · Multi-layer perceptron Network

1 Introduction

Anaemia is a condition in which the number of red blood cells decreases and the oxygen-carrying capacity of blood becomes insufficient to meet the physiological needs [24]. In 2013, 27% of the world population (about 1.9 billion people) were

D. Gupta et al. (Eds.): CVIP 2022, CCIS 1777, pp. 176–189, 2023.
https://doi.org/10.1007/978-3-031-31417-9_14

found to be anaemic of which 93% population belongs to low/moderate-income countries [15]. Prevalence of anaemia is quite higher in children and women in developing countries, e.g. in India according to National Family Health Survey (NFHS)-2019 data, approximately 53% of women and 53.4% of children are suffering from anaemia. Anaemia is usually detected through laboratory-based clinical estimation wherein the venous blood sample needs to be collected from an individual. However, invasive procedures pose their own set of challenges.

Huge resource requirements and other practical hindrances make invasive tests for screening of anaemia a difficult task, which effectively demands non-invasive solution(s). The common age-old practices include observing pallor in eye, nail and tongue for a rough estimation of anaemia, especially in rural areas due to the lack of infrastructure and economic issues. Keeping in mind the severity of the disease and associated difficulties concerning the majority of population, it becomes a task of paramount importance to design a robust and accurate procedure for non-invasive anaemia detection system. Therefore, the proposed work suggests a procedure that combines the age-old non-invasive techniques for a rough estimation of blood haemoglobin level with cutting-edge Artificial Intelligence (AI) techniques for accurate estimation of blood haemoglobin level, thereby, alleviating the problems of invasive procedures. Such a low-cost reliable anaemia detector may be more beneficial, especially, in rural areas where there is lack of infrastructure and lack of awareness among the common people.

The non-invasive anaemia kit is a better option for self-diagnosis. Hence, some of the relevant non-invasive approaches have been reported here. Santra et al. [25] have proposed a machine vision-based portable, non-invasive system for measuring haemoglobin levels from the redness of the skin of palm by capturing palm video with the help of a blood pressure arm cuff considering 20 human samples (5 female, and rest male). Mangaras Yanu Florestiyanto et al. [7] have proposed a methodoly to detect whether a person is anaemic or non-anaemic by capturing the digital image of nail and palm from which mean values and standard deviation of red, green, and blue channels are determined and are processed using Naive Bayes classifier. Yunendah Nur Fuadah et al. [9] classify the anaemic and non-anaemic samples by analysing the image of eye conjunctiva. The different features extracted by evaluating mean, variance, skewness, and entropy on different colour spaces are used in the kNN classifier. Mannino et al. [19] have evaluated haemoglobin levels by capturing the nail bed images through smartphone camera and applying multi linear regression model. However, it requires manual selection of region of interest (ROI) for each finger. Tamir et al. [28] have analysed the digital image of the anterior conjunctival eye with the help of a smartphone camera. The study reveals that the green and red colour spectrum components play a vital role in classifying whether a person is anaeamic or non-anaemic with an accuracy of 78.9%. The existing non-invasive solutions for the detection of anaemia, as reported in the literature, are not so accurate and cost-effective. Hence, the objective in this paper is to develop a low-cost reliable non-invasive anaemia detection system.

The proposed system uses different colour space representations upon selected frames. Then different colour and texture features are extracted and the most relevant features are selected. Those features are used for training along with clinical values. The regression-based neural networks with different combinations of non-linear activation functions and optimizers are used to estimate haemoglobin levels. The contribution of the proposed system is summarised as follows:

- Design and development of non-invasive, reliable and user-friendly system for estimation of blood haemoglobin level by analysing dynamic physiological palm pallor evidence
- For better analysis, different colour and texture features are extracted upon different colour models (i.e., RGB, HSV, YCrCb, LAB and LUV)
- Feature selection through mutual information and neural network are done. These features are concatenated and fed into MLP network with different combination of activation functions and optimizers for accurate evaluation.

The paper organisation is as follows. Section 2 presents the detailed description of the proposed haemoglobin evaluation system, followed by the evaluation of the proposed system made in Sect. 3. The last section concludes the proposed work and briefly discusses future works.

2   Proposed Work

This section describes the overall system of the proposed non-invasive anaemia detection technique that makes use of palm pallor. Figure 1 shows the overview of the proposed system which consists of a number of subsystems as described in the successive subsections.

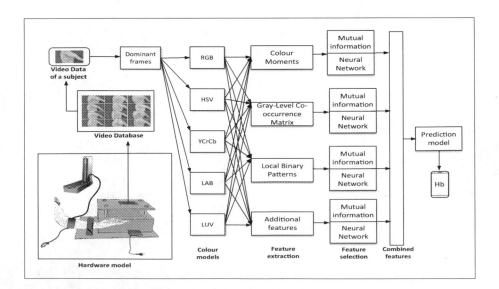

Fig. 1. Overview of proposed methodology.

2.1   Data Acquisition

As there is no benchmark dataset is available on non-invasively acquired physiological evidences, hence the proposed model uses local dataset that has been acquired in different timestamps. To acquire the palm evidence from the video of palm for measuring the haemoglobin concentration, a hardware model has been developed indigenously. The hardware model consists of some components that assist in acquiring the palm evidence with minimal human effort. The hardware prototype helps to capture the evidence by applying uniform pressure in the specified position on palm for approximately 100 s and afterward releasing the pressure. Uniform pressure is applied on the entire palm with the blood pressure arm cuff to decolourise the palm by obliterating the entire venous drainage and a major part of arterial supply to deoxygenate the stagnant blood there. In order for the palm to get oxygenated and thereafter stabilised, the blood flow is allowed suddenly to spread the oxygen to suffocated palm tissues. The timestamps of various stages of palm compression and release can be directly obtained from the video photography of the palm. During data collection, the palm is fixed beneath the camera focus at a permissible distance, velcro strips are used, and the pressure is applied below the left-hand elbow of each participant with the help of a blood pressure measuring pressure cuff. The video is captured with smartphone-based Redmi K20 pro camera sensor with a resolution of 1920 × 1080 dpi (dots per inch). The blood samples contributed by 17 and 21 participants, are collected from Parulia Health Center, Durgapur and ESI Hospital, Durgapur, respectively. A total of 41 samples are collected. The written consent from all the participants have been obtained prior to the study.

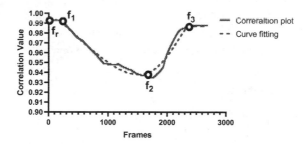

Fig. 2. Extracting dominant frames from correlation approximation.

2.2   Dominant Frame Extraction from Palm Video

To extract the dominant frames from the video of palm, the correlation between first frame (f_r) as a reference frame and all other frames is determined by using $c(H^R, H_j^C)$ as shown in Eq. (1). The correlation values are then plotted with respect to the frames and curve approximation of correlation is determined to extract the dominant frames through gradient as shown in Fig. 2. Three dominant frames such as frame f_1, frame f_2 and frame f_3 are extracted from every video data. The pressure is applied and colour fading starts at frame f_1, maximum fading occurs at frame f_2 and normal colour resumes after releasing the pressure at frame f_3. Total ten frames, including the first frame which contains initial information of the subject, along with one predecessor and one successor frame of each of the three dominant frames, are considered. The predecessor and one successor frames are considered to ensure the effectiveness of dominant frames.

$$c(H^R, H_j^C) = \sum_{j=1}^{f} \frac{\sum_{I=0}^{255}(H^R(I) - \overline{H^R})(H_j^C(I) - \overline{H_j^C})}{\sqrt{\sum_{I=0}^{255}(H^R(I) - \overline{H^R})^2 \sum_{I=0}^{255}(H_j^C(I) - \overline{H_j^C})^2}} \tag{1}$$

where, H^R is the histogram of reference frame, H_j^C is the histogram of jth input frame, f is the total number of extracted frame, $\overline{H_k} = \frac{1}{N}\sum_{I=0}^{255} H_k(I)$ and $N =$ Total number of histogram bins.

2.3   Colour Space Representations

To examine the blood haemoglobin concentration, the colour space representation of skin on the palm can play a crucial role in influencing the prediction by processing the evidence in different colour space domains. The colour space representations refer to a range of colour specific to display unit standards. To make evaluations more meaningful and identify intuitive colours, a combination of different colour space representations reflects the palm skin colour in a more effective way. The proposed system uses different colour space representations such as RGB [22], HSV [8], YCrCb [27], CIE LAB [5,14] and CIE LUV [21] for feature extraction explaining the properties of palm image in different colour domains. Three or more channels constitute a colour space.

2.4   Feature Extraction

Feature extraction exploits different colour space representations that are applied among dominant frames. To extract distinctive and a more diverse set of consolidated features, four different feature extraction techniques, viz colour moments, gray-level co-occurrence matrix, local binary pattern, and additional features relevant to surface intensity, are employed. As these feature extraction techniques found much more relevant to colour space and structural representation, they will be more relatable for analysing the colour information in palm in order to predict blood haemoglobin level through non-invasive way.

Colour Moments. Colour moments are measured and used as colour features to differentiate colour images. The colour moments determine colour similarity or dissimilarity between images. The colour moments make an assumption that the colour in images can be well understood by the probability distribution. An image colour distribution can have three moments based on probability distribution [26] such as, i.e., Mean (first-order), Standard deviation (second-order) and Skewness (third-order). As three or more channels constitute a colour space, moments have to be calculated for each channel. Hence, an image with a specific colour space is distinguished by nine moments from three different colour channels.

Gray-Level Co-occurrence Matrix (GLCM). The GLCM is a second-order statistical method used for analysing the texture of image pattern. It accumulates the occurrence distribution of pixels by determining specific values for frequently occurred pair of pixels in a specified spatial relationship with some distance d in the direction θ. The statistical measures of texture are extracted from GLCM which provides the spatial relationships of pixels in an image. However, this does not provide information about the shape [10]. The main property of GLCM is that there exists equal number of rows and columns as that of the quantization levels of image. Feature extraction considers $d = 1$, $\theta = [0, \pi/4, \pi/2, 3\pi/4]$ and 8-bit pixel representation. From GLCM, different texture and colour properties are explored such as contrast, dissimilarity, correlation and homogeneity. These properties are evaluated with the help of probabilistic value, $P_{i,j}$ as $\frac{V_{i,j}}{\sum_{i,j=0}^{N-1} V_{i,j}}$, where, i is the row and j is the column number, V is the pixel value in the cell (i,j) on the GLCM matrix and N is the number of rows or columns in GLCM matrix. The four texture and colour properties considered here is defined below

-

- Contrast measures the local variations in the gray-level co-occurrence matrix and returns an amount of the intensity contrast and is represented as $\sum_{i,j} P_{i,j}(i-j)^2$.
- Dissimilarity is a measure of distance between pair of pixels in the region of interest denoted as $\sum_{i,j} P_{i,j}|i-j|$.
- Correlation measures the dependency of gray levels among neighbouring pixels linearly and evaluated by $\sum_{i,j} P_{i,j}\left[\frac{(i-\mu_i)(j-\mu_j)}{\sqrt{\sigma_i^2 \sigma_j^2}}\right]$.
- Homogeneity measures the closeness of the distribution of elements in the Co-occurrence matrix and its diagonal which reflects local changes in image texture and evaluated as $\sum_{i,j} \frac{P_{i,j}}{1+(i-j)^2}$

These four properties of GLCM have to be calculated for each channel in different colour spaces. Hence, an image with a specific colour space is distinguished by 12 GLCM properties from three different channels.

Local Binary Pattern (LBP). To enhance the representation capability of image patterns, LBP plays an important role in describing the pattern locally by extracting structural information [12]. It is one of the most popular handcrafted local feature descriptors which is used in many computer vision applications. The basic model of LBP is generated by thresholding the 3×3 neighbourhood of each pixel value with the centre pixel's value of the same neighbourhood. Let C be the gray level of centre pixel around which the neighbourhood is defined in spatial domain. If the gray level value of neighbourhood pixel is found to be greater than C, then the pixel value is set to binary 1; otherwise, it is set to binary 0. The results are combined to obtain the 8-bit pattern. Then the 8-bit pattern is converted into decimal value in order to obtain the LBP feature. Similar to a single-pixel LBP, features are obtained for all pixels in the image. In the proposed system, the feature extraction with LBP is performed by considering different channels with eight neighbouring pixels (P) and a circular neighbourhood radius (R) as 2. For each channel, 10 LBP features are extracted by considering the division of the histogram into ten bins.

Additional Features To make the consolidated feature set more enrich some additional features like smoothness, uniformity and entropy are evaluated [29]. Smoothness of image is defined as $1 - \frac{1}{1+\sigma_i^2}$, where σ is standard deviation. When smoothness is found to be zero, then the surface intensity is flat or homogeny region, and when it approaches to one, then the surface of the region is rough or it has variations in intensity or contrast is high. Unlike smoothness, uniformity measure checks whether all the pixels in an area have the same intensity value or not. It is defined as $\sum_{i,j} P(i,j)^2$, where, $P(i,j)$ is the probability of values occurring in adjacent pixels in the original image. Lastly, entropy is calculated in order to measure the level of randomness of intensity values. Maximum entropy implies that the pixels in the image show fair random distribution, and minimal entropy implies that all the pixels have a similar distribution. In the proposed system, these measures are taken into account for different colour channels considering a feature in different colour spaces.

2.5   Feature Selection

To address the curse of dimensionality issues, feature selection can be a solution to reduce the dimension of feature set and retain the most relevant features. To predict the haemoglobin level closed to gold standard, a consolidated and diverse feature set is obtained by combining statical, local, and complementary features. Although the feature set is found to be enriched, however, it suffers from the curse of dimensionality problem for the proposed model. To obtain a sizeable feature set, a greedy approach called mutual information (entropy) gain is applied. Mutual information measures the amount of information between two random variables, and it could be zero if and only if the variables are independent [3], as shown in Eq. (2). It resembles the decision tree classifier. Further, mutual information measures the dependency of the dependent variable in terms of independent variables like univariate statical tests based on which the features are selected. The higher the score, the effectiveness of the feature is more. In the proposed system, the mutual information is applied to each feature set obtained from the individual feature extraction technique, and the first 40 features are selected from each feature set.

$$I(x;y) = \sum_{i=1}^{N} \sum_{j=1}^{N} p(x(i), y(j)) \cdot \log(\frac{p(x(i), y(j))}{p(x(i)) \cdot p(y(j))})$$ (2)

where, $I(x;y)$ denotes mutual information, x is dependent features, y is independent feature (0 for anaemic and 1 for non-anaemic) and $p(x,y)$ denotes joint mass probability distribution between the feature sets and target value.

Unlike feature selection based on mutual information, a fully connected neural network is used to select the features based on feature modulation propagated across the layers [31]. In this feature selection approach, a multi-layer perceptron (MLP) with two hidden layers, gradient descent [23] optimizer and sigmoid activation function [13] are used. The first hidden layer contains two-thirds of the input nodes, and the second layer contains 40 nodes whose probabilistic values are considered to be extracted features which are chosen through cross-validation. The output layer contains one node, which consists of the independent variable. Although the output layer doesn't contribute to feature selection, however, to achieve backpropagation learning and minimise the mean square error, it is needed to retain the same output layer in the network. After learning is completed and convergence is achieved, the outcome of the second hidden layer is considered to be a reduced set of features.

As the mutual information gives dominant features and the neural network gives probabilistic features, the combination of complementary and reduced feature sets obtained from two different feature selection techniques would enrich the consolidated feature vector for haemoglobin level prediction.

2.6   Prediction Model

The prediction of haemoglobin level is performed with the help of a regression model making use of a neural network. The feature set of different distributions is given as input to the input layer where each neuron denotes a feature. The inputs are propagated across the hidden layers where aggregations and activations take place with the initial weight vector. While generating the output in the output layer, the error function is defined by considering the target output and observed output. Then in the neuron of the output layer, the weight is updated by obtaining the gradient from the error function. To continue the learning process across the hidden layers, the updated weight of the output neuron is propagated back to the hidden layers, where the weight of the neuron in the hidden layers is updated. The learning process will continue unless the optimal convergence is achieved and error gets minimised. To train the model for the prediction of haemoglobin level, a set of activation functions and a set of four optimizers are used with different learning rates. In this prediction model of MLP, three hidden layers are used with 200 neurons in the first hidden layer, 100 neurons in the second hidden layer, and 50 neurons in the third hidden layer. The output layer contains a single neuron. Different neural network properties with such mapping configuration are exploited to achieve better accuracy with collected data samples. The proposed network uses three different non-linear activation functions, viz. Sigmoid [13], Hyperbolic Tangent Function (Tanh) [17] and Rectified Linear Unit (ReLu) [1] to introduce various non-linearity properties into the output of a neuron. And, to minimise the error (cost function) four different optimization technique such as, Gradient descent [23], Adam [16], Momentum [20], and RMSProp [30] are used in the neural network.

3   Evaluation

To predict the haemoglobin level from video data of palm pallor, feature extraction from dominant frames and their neighbouring frames is performed with the help of feature extraction techniques as described in Sect. 2. The evaluation makes use of five different colour spaces from which 3000 features are extracted for ten frames. Among 3000 features, 450 features are obtained from colour moments, 600 features are obtained from GLCM, 1500 obtained from LBP, and 450 features are obtained by considering smoothness, uniformity, and entropy properties. Then mutual information and neural network-based feature selection techniques produce a reduced set of 320 features determined from four feature extraction techniques. To overcome the issues of high influence features and bias, normalisation is performed. In the proposed model, the min-max normalisation

Table 1. MLP-based regression with different parameters

Activation function	Optimizer	Learning rate	Iterations	Average RMSE
Sigmoid	**Gradient Descent**	0.07	200000	0.612
		0.08	200000	0.609
		0.09	**200000**	**0.597**
		0.07	20000	0.631
		0.08	20000	0.628
		0.09	20000	0.613
		0.1	100000	0.619
		0.9	20000	0.632
	Adam	0.001	5000	0.681
	Momentum	0.009	15000	0.665
	RMSProp	0.001	12000	0.762
Tanh	Gradient Descent	0.09	18000	0.986
	Adam	0.001	5000	1.25
	Momentum	0.009	15000	1.35
	RMSProp	0.001	12000	1.085
Relu	Gradient Descent	0.01	25000	1.153
	Adam	0.001	5000	1.52
	Momentum	0.009	15000	1.215
	RMSProp	0.001	12000	0.928

is applied to bind the feature values between 0 and 1. These normalised feature values are then provided as input to the MLP networks, which acts as regression as well as prediction model. Through a number of validations it has been found that 320 number of features exhibit robust performance while selecting features from a set of feature selectors. The experimental results are shown in Table 1 with the number of activation functions and optimizers. The MLP network contains 320 neurons in the input layer, three hidden layers having 200 neurons, 100 neurons and, 50 neurons, respectively and one neuron in the output layer which provide haemoglobin value. The experiment is performed with three different non-linear activation functions, viz. Sigmoid [13], Hyperbolic Tangent Function (Tanh) [17] and Rectified Linear Unit (ReLu) [1], and four different optimization technique such as, Gradient descent [23], Adam [16], Momentum [20], and RMSProp [30]. Further, to perform the experiment with a diverse set of learning rates and convergence criteria with varying number of iterations, the efficacy of the proposed model has been substantiated. However, while using the Sigmoid activation function in combination with the Gradient descent optimizer, average RMSE is found to be minimum for different learning rates compared to other combinations of activation functions and optimizers. For the MLP-based regression model, while using ReLu as an activation function, the Sigmoid activation function is used on the output layer. As ReLu ranges from 0 to ∞, it bounds negative weights to 0 and above, whereas Sigmoid produces a weight vector where each element is a probability (ranging from 0 to 1). The activation function Tanh can be applied on both hidden layers and the output layer as it ranges from −1 to 1.

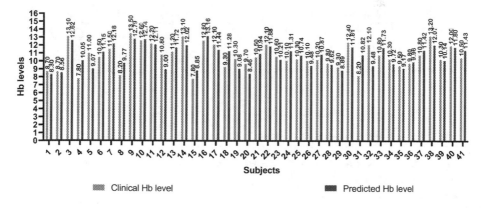

Fig. 3. Clinical vs predicted haemoglobin levels.

The optimal outcome is obtained from the MLP with the Sigmoid activation function and gradient descent optimizer with a learning rate of 0.09 and 200000 iterations. To estimate the haemoglobin level leave-one-out procedure is used among 41 samples. It takes one sample as a test sample and 40 other samples as training samples. The average root means squared error considers a risk of a proposed system. The proposed framework with the above combination of parameters, ensures an average RMSE of 0.597. The bar chart representation between clinical and predicted haemoglobin levels is shown in Fig. 3. Further, this bar chart shows how close the predicted haemoglobin levels are found with respect to the gold standard values.

The objective of the proposed system is to estimate haemoglobin level of individuals and to reduce the misclassification of anaemic and non-anemic classes. The classes According to WHO scale, in pregnant female whose $Hb < 11\,g/dL$, non-pregnant female whose $Hb < 12\,g/dL$ and in males whose $Hb < 13\,g/dL$ are considered as anaemic. In the dataset, 31 subjects are found to be anaemic, among which predicted value of only one subject is showing as non-anaemic and others as anaemic. The sensitivity and specificity of the proposed system are found to be 0.97 and 0.44, respectively. The study shows that the proposed anaemia detection system tends to correctly classify the anaemic subjects as anaemic in more numbers and non-anaemic subjects as non-anaemic in fewer numbers. The classification accuracy is found to be 85.36%. If the proposed system considers the haemoglobin level less than $11.5\,g/dL$ as anaemic for all types of subjects over different ranges as in [11], then the sensitivity, specificity and accuracy of the proposed system are determined to be 0.89, 0.85, and 87.80%, respectively. Tables 2 and 3 exhibits the confusion matrix considering the WHO scale and a threshold of $11.5\,g/dL$ for anaemic/non-anaemic classification, respectively.

Table 2. Confusion Matrix considering the WHO scale for classification

Actual Condition	Predicted Condition		Sensitivity (TP/TP+FN)	Specificity (TN/TN+FP)
	Anaemic	Non-Anaemic		
Anaemic	31 (TP)	1 (FN)	0.97	0.44
Non-Anaemic	5 (FP)	4 (TN)		

Table 3. Confusion Matrix considering a threshold of $11.5\,g/dL$ for classification

Actual Condition	Predicted Condition		Sensitivity (TP/TP+FN)	Specificity (TN/TN+FP)
	Anaemic	Non-Anaemic		
Anaemic	25 (TP)	3 (FN)	0.89	0.85
Non-Anaemic	2 (FP)	11 (TN)		

Comparison with Different Existing Methods

This section discusses a comparison of the proposed system with existing methods. Although, the proposed system uses different evidences for estimating the haemoglobin levels of individuals as compare to existing methods. The comparison with the existing system exhibits a credible study about the performance of the anaemia detection systems. Moreover, the comparison presents how the various performance metrics are used to evaluate the systems more accurately while considering different experimental setups. As the proposed system uses palm pallor evidence for estimating the haemoglobin level having robust features with different colour spaces, the same evidence is observed in work [25]. However, the work [25] uses salient patch for each frame and median of histogram values among red(R), green(G) and blue(B) intensities are determined as sets of features and a quadratic regression model is applied without using different colour models. Due to this structure, the system often fluctuates the performance with fewer data samples having median value of R, G and B channels as a feature. In comparison to this system, the proposed system exhibits a good performance with an average RMSE value of 0.597. The comparison considers various anaemia detection systems with different performance metrics described in Table 4. Similar to proposed system, the performance of different existing methods observed in [2, 4, 6, 7, 9, 18, 19, 25, 28, 32] without estimating similar set of metrics. The proposed system has the ability to estimate haemoglobin level more accurately as compare to existing methods because of less error (RMSE and mean), and more correlation.

Table 4. Comparison with different existing methodology

Papers	Evidence	Sample Size	Age	Hb Range	Gender Ratio(M:F)	RMSE	Sensitivity	Specificity	Accuracy	Correlation	Mean Error
Hema App [32]	Non-invasive(Finger tip)	31	6 to 77 (mean = 31)	8.3-15.8	15:16	-	85.70%	76.50%	-	0.69	1.26
Masimo Pronto [4]	Non-invasive(Finger tip)	18	—	7.5-14	-	-	69.30%	88.20%	-	-	1.28
Masimo Co-oximetry [18]	Non-invasive(Finger tip)	20	20 to 27(mean = 24)	7.5-13.8	11:09	0.94					
G. M. Ahsan [2]	Non-invasive(Finger tip)	84							48.80%	0.56	-
Mannino [19]	Non invasive(Nail bed)	337	1 to 60	5.9-16.8		-	92%	76%			0.97
A. Tamir [28]	Non-invasive(Eye Conjunctiva)	19		6.9-16	1:12	-	-	-	78.90%	-	-
Y. N. Fundah [9]	Non-invasive(Eye Conjunctiva)	80			0:80	-	-	-	71.25%	-	-
S. Das [6]	Non-invasive(Nail Pallor)	50	19 to 62	7.7-14.1	11:39	0.56	-	-			
M. Y. Florestiyanto [7]	Non-invasive(Nail and Palm Pallor)	20			7:13	-	-	-	90%	-	-
Bikash Santra [25]	Non-invasive(Palm Pallor)	20	23 to 50	9.6-13.7	15:05	1.144	-	-		0.563	-
Proposed	Non-invasive(Palm Pallor)	41	18 to 79(mean = 40.22)	7.8-13.5	11:30	0.597	96.8% / 89.3%	44.4% / 84.6%	85.36% / 87.80%	0.72	0.84

4   Conclusion and Future Scope

This paper presents a non-invasive anaemia detection system by capturing the palm video through a smartphone camera and a customized hardware device. The haemoglobin level is evaluated by analysing the palm pallor by extracting dominant frames from the recorded video samples. The experimental results from the proposed framework demonstrate that the colour and texture features are having high correlation with blood haemoglobin level and hence, are useful for estimating the haemoglobin level with high accuracy. Such a low-cost, low-overhead non-invasive approach can even perform accurately in resource-poor environment. It analyses the videos of palm pallor and yields the result with the detected class, whether the subject is anaemic or not, along with the obtained haemoglobin level, which is very close to the clinical result. Further, some automatic feature extraction methods (deep learning based approach) are explored and also increase the size of the dataset.

Acknowledgment. This work was supported by Ministry of Electronics and Information Technology, Government of India under Sanction number:4(3)/2018-ITEA. We sincerely thank to PTMO, Parulia Health Centre Durgapur, and Superintendent of ESI hospital Durgapur, for their help and cooperation in the data collection process during the clinical study.

References

1. Agarap, A.F.: Deep learning using rectified linear units. arXiv preprint arXiv:1803.08375 (2018)
2. Ahsan, et al.: A novel real-time non-invasive hemoglobin level detection using video images from smartphone camera. In: 2017 IEEE 41st Annual Computer Software and Applications Conference (COMPSAC), vol. 1, pp. 967–972. IEEE (2017)
3. Beraha, M., Metelli, A.M., Papini, M., Tirinzoni, A., Restelli, M.: Feature selection via mutual information: new theoretical insights. In: 2019 International Joint Conference on Neural Networks (IJCNN), pp. 1–9. IEEE (2019)
4. Bruells, C.S., et al.: Accuracy of the Masimo pronto-7® system in patients with left ventricular assist device. J. Cardiothorac. Surg. **8**(1), 1–6 (2013)
5. Chen, Y., Hao, P., Dang, A.: Optimal transform in perceptually uniform color space and its application in image coding. In: Campilho, A., Kamel, M. (eds.) ICIAR 2004. LNCS, vol. 3211, pp. 269–276. Springer, Heidelberg (2004). https://doi.org/10.1007/978-3-540-30125-7_34
6. Das, S., Kesarwani, A., Kisku, D.R., Dalui, M.: Non-invasive haemoglobin prediction using nail color features: an approach of dimensionality reduction. In: Huang, DS., Jo, KH., Jing, J., Premaratne, P., Bevilacqua, V., Hussain, A. (eds.) ICIC 2022. LNCS, vol. 13393, pp. 811–824. Springer, Cham (2022). https://doi.org/10.1007/978-3-031-13870-6_66
7. Florestiyanto, M.Y., Peksi, N.J.: Non-invasive anemia screening using nails and palms photos. In: Proceeding of LPPM UPN "Veteran" Yogyakarta Conference Series 2020-Engineering and Science Series, vol. 1, pp. 311–318 (2020)
8. Ford, A., Roberts, A.: Colour Space Conversions, pp. 1–31. Westminster University, London (1998)
9. Fuadah, Y.N., Sa'idah, S., Wijayanto, I., Patmasari, R., Magdalena, R.: Non invasive anemia detection in pregnant women based on digital image processing and k-nearest neighbor. In: 2020 3rd International Conference on Biomedical Engineering (IBIOMED), pp. 60–64. IEEE (2020)
10. Gadelmawla, E.: A vision system for surface roughness characterization using the gray level co-occurrence matrix. NDT & e Int. **37**(7), 577–588 (2004)
11. Ghosal, S., Das, D., Udutalapally, V., Talukder, A.K., Misra, S.: shemo: Smartphone spectroscopy for blood hemoglobin level monitoring in smart anemia-care. IEEE Sens. J. **21**(6), 8520–8529 (2020)
12. Guo, Z., Zhang, L., Zhang, D.: A completed modeling of local binary pattern operator for texture classification. IEEE Trans. Image Process. **19**(6), 1657–1663 (2010)
13. Han, J., Moraga, C.: The influence of the sigmoid function parameters on the speed of backpropagation learning. In: Mira, J., Sandoval, F. (eds.) IWANN 1995. LNCS, vol. 930, pp. 195–201. Springer, Heidelberg (1995). https://doi.org/10.1007/3-540-59497-3_175
14. Jiang, L., et al.: Skin color measurements before and after two weeks of sun exposure. Vision. Res. **192**, 107976 (2022)

15. Kassebaum, N.J., Collaborators, G.A., et al.: The global burden of anemia. Hematol. Oncol. Clin. North Am. **30**(2), 247–308 (2016)
16. Kingma, D.P., Ba, J.: Adam: a method for stochastic optimization. arXiv preprint arXiv:1412.6980 (2014)
17. LeCun, Y., Bengio, Y., Hinton, G.: Deep learning. Nature **521**(7553), 436–444 (2015)
18. Macknet, M.R., Allard, M., Applegate, R.L., Rook, J., et al.: The accuracy of noninvasive and continuous total hemoglobin measurement by pulse co-oximetry in human subjects undergoing hemodilution. Anesthesia Analgesia **111**(6), 1424–1426 (2010)
19. Mannino, R.G., et al.: Smartphone app for non-invasive detection of anemia using only patient-sourced photos. Nat. Commun. **9**(1), 1–10 (2018)
20. Polyak, B.T.: Some methods of speeding up the convergence of iteration methods. USSR Comput. Math. Math. Phys. **4**(5), 1–17 (1964)
21. Rahimzadeganasl, A., Sertel, E.: Automatic building detection based on CIE luv color space using very high resolution pleiades images. In: 2017 25th Signal Processing and Communications Applications Conference (SIU), pp. 1–4. IEEE (2017)
22. Reinhard, E., Adhikhmin, M., Gooch, B., Shirley, P.: Color transfer between images. IEEE Comput. Graph. Appl. **21**(5), 34–41 (2001)
23. Ruder, S.: An overview of gradient descent optimization algorithms. arXiv preprint arXiv:1609.04747 (2016)
24. Sadiq, S., et al.: Classification of β-thalassemia carriers from red blood cell indices using ensemble classifier. IEEE Access **9**, 45528–45538 (2021)
25. Santra, B., Mukherjee, D.P., Chakrabarti, D.: A non-invasive approach for estimation of hemoglobin analyzing blood flow in palm. In: 2017 IEEE 14th International Symposium on Biomedical Imaging (ISBI 2017), pp. 1100–1103. IEEE (2017)
26. Stricker, M.A., Orengo, M.: Similarity of color images. In: Storage and retrieval for image and video databases III, vol. 2420, pp. 381–392. SPiE (1995)
27. Sun, Y., Ren, Z., Zheng, W.: Research on face recognition algorithm based on image processing. Comput. Intell. Neurosci. **2022** (2022)
28. Tamir, A., Jahan, C.S., et al.: Detection of anemia from image of the anterior conjunctiva of the eye by image processing and thresholding. In: 2017 IEEE Region 10 Humanitarian Technology Conference (R10-HTC), pp. 697–701. IEEE (2017)
29. Thawari, P., Janwe, N.: CBIR based on color and texture. Int. J. Inf. Technol. Knowl. Manag. **4**(1), 129–132 (2011)
30. Tieleman, T., Hinton, G.: Lecture 6.5-rmsprop, coursera: neural networks for machine learning. Technical report 6, University of Toronto (2012)
31. Verikas, A., Bacauskiene, M.: Feature selection with neural networks. Pattern Recogn. Lett. **23**(11), 1323–1335 (2002)
32. Wang, E.J., Li, W., Hawkins, D., Gernsheimer, T., Norby-Slycord, C., Patel, S.N.: HemaApp: noninvasive blood screening of hemoglobin using smartphone cameras. In: Proceedings of the 2016 ACM International Joint Conference on Pervasive and Ubiquitous Computing, pp. 593–604 (2016)

Detection of Coal Quarry and Coal Dump Regions Using the Presence of Mine Water Bodies from Landsat 8 OLI/TIRS Images

Jit Mukherjee[1]([⊠])(iD), Jayanta Mukherjee[2], and Debashish Chakravarty[3]

[1] Dept. Computer Science and Engineering, Birla Institute of Technology Mesra,
Ranchi, India
jit.mukherjee@bitmesra.ac.in
[2] Dept. Computer Science and Engineering, Indian Institute of Technology
Kharagpur, Kharagpur, India
[3] Dept. Mining Engineering, Indian Institute of Technology Kharagpur,
Kharagpur, India

Abstract. Surface mining has major environmental, social, and economical adversities, which makes it an active area of research in remote sensing. Surface coal mining has additional adversities of coal seam fires. Thus, the detection, classification, and monitoring of such regions have various research challenges. The surface coal mining land classes cover smaller areas compared to mid-resolution satellite images making them challenging to detect. Coal quarry and coal dump regions are such kinds of smaller land classes. They can be detected as a single land class as discussed in the literature. However, these land classes are observed to be difficult to detect separately as they follow near similar spectral characteristics. Hence, this paper proposes a novel technique to separate these regions using the presence of water bodies. Coal dump regions do not have water bodies, whereas some coal quarry regions may have water bodies. Such quarry regions are detected at first and further, they are used to train an unsupervised single class support vector machine (SVM). This model is used to detect the coal dump regions by detecting the outliers. The proposed technique provides average precision and recall for coal quarry, and coal dump regions as $[84.88\%, 61.44\%]$, and $[70.91\%, 52.79\%]$, respectively over the seasons.

Keywords: Coal Mine Index · Surface Coal Mining · Coal Dump Region · Coal Quarry Region · Morphology Opening · Mine Water Body · Single Class SVM · Bare Soil Index

1 Introduction

Surface mining is a widely used excavation technique, even though it has different adversities in the environment, ecology, and society. It directly impacts the eco-environment, vegetation cover, water pollution, etc. [4,8]. Large scale surface mining has long term effects in soil fertility, lowering of ground water table,

© The Author(s), under exclusive license to Springer Nature Switzerland AG 2023
D. Gupta et al. (Eds.): CVIP 2022, CCIS 1777, pp. 190–204, 2023.
https://doi.org/10.1007/978-3-031-31417-9_15

regional biodiversity, and chances of desertification [4,8]. Furthermore, coal seam fires in surface coal mining regions emit poisonous gases and have intensive effects on air pollution, acid rain, and many other social and environmental hazards [26]. The problems faced by surface coal mining regions have scopes for better understanding and interpretation with the help of advanced remote sensing techniques. It has several challenging problems in different remote sensing applications, like classification, land cover detection and monitoring [3,22,23], mine wastewater detection and management [13,16,21], monitoring coal seam fires [9,15], mining safety, etc. Earlier, surface mine regions were detected from satellite images by supervised and semi supervised methods using machine learning techniques [4,7,10,22]. With the help of field studies, support vector machine (SVM) is used to identify coal mine regions in [4]. In [7], land covers in coal mine regions are mapped by two separate techniques, object and spectral-based. In object-based technique, satellite images were segmented using visual inspection to detect coal mine regions. Further, spectral responses of very near infrared, SWIR, and thermal infrared bands were studied to classify coal mine regions. An SVM classifier has been applied to detect various land classes in surface coal mine areas to quantify the success of reclamation measures in Jharia Coal Fields (JCF) [10]. Different classification techniques have been applied to detect temporal changes in mine waste areas of Tunisia [12]. Detection and monitoring of coal mine areas in such methods have been computed by supervised and semi supervised clustering algorithms. Most of these works do not consider finer land covers and their distinctive characteristics. A few of the works detect finer land classes, such as the detection of mine water bodies [21], and reclamation regions [19], etc. Mine water bodies are detected by analysing the surrounding areas in [16]. In [18], a novel index has been proposed to detect coal quarry regions and coal dump regions together by defining a spectral ratio, namely the coal mine index (CMI). Further, CMI has been used in the literature to detect mine water bodies [17], reclamation regions [19], and coal overburden dump [20]. The performance of CMI is automated by a hierarchical clustering in [14]. It is found to be a challenging task to further separate coal quarry and coal dump regions using CMI or any other indexes [14,18]. One of the major challenges in this work is to detect these finer land classes in a surface coal mine by finding their distinctive characteristics over the season.

1.1 Objectives

Coal quarry and coal dump regions have a high abundance of raw minerals, which distinguishes them from other land covers. The objective of this paper is to quantify such distinguishing features of these two land classes using multispectral images without any labelled dataset. Therefore, a novel method has been proposed, where first, coal quarry and coal dump regions are detected as a single land class using the coal mine index. Mine water bodies are located near the vicinity of surface coal mine regions. A few of these mine water bodies can be found inside a coal quarry regions. Whereas, a coal dump does not have such water bodies. This characterization has been used here to detect the coal quarry regions. However, coal quarry regions, which do not have any nearby mine water body region, can not be detected by this technique. An anomaly detection technique using a single class *SVM* has been employed to detect such coal quarry region. Further, coal dump regions are detected using the outliers of the single class *SVM* model.

2 Background Techniques

Established techniques, which are used in this work, are briefly discussed in this section.

2.1 Coal Mine Index (*CMI*)

Coal mine index is defined as $\psi(\lambda_{SWIR-I}, \lambda_{SWIR-II})$, i.e. $\frac{\lambda_{SWIR-I} - \lambda_{SWIR-II}}{\lambda_{SWIR-I} + \lambda_{SWIR-II}}$, where *SWIR-I*, and *SWIR-II* denote *Short Wave Infra-red one* and *Short Wave Infra-red two* bands, respectively. It extends the concept of clay mineral ratio [5]. Coal quarry and coal dump regions are detected as a single class by *CMI* given a threshold (φ). *CMI* values, which are lower than φ, have higher probability of being a coal mine region. The range of φ is found to be $[0, 0.06]$ as discussed in [18].

2.2 Modified Normalized Difference Water Index

There are several indexes to detect water bodies using different spectrum, such as Normalized Difference Water Index (*NDWI*, $\psi(\lambda_{NIR}, \lambda_{SWIR-I})$, $\phi(\lambda_{Green}, \lambda_{NIR})$), Automated Water Extraction Index, etc. In this work, modified normalized difference water index (*MNDWI*) has been used as it enhances the open water feature [28]. *MNDWI* is proposed as a spectral index of *Green* and *Short Wave Infra-red one* bands, i.e. $\psi(\lambda_{Green}, \lambda_{SWIR-I})$ [28]. Higher values of *MNDWI* and *NDWI* preserve water body features.

2.3 Bare Soil Index (*BI*)

Bare soil index *(BI)* of a region is computed as $\psi((\lambda_{SWIR-I} + \lambda_{Red}), (\lambda_{NIR} + \lambda_{Blue}))$ [2]. Here, $\lambda_{SWIR-I}, \lambda_{Red}, \lambda_{NIR}, \lambda_{Blue}$ are reflectance values of *Short Wave Infra-Red one*, *Red*, *Near Infra-Red*, and *Blue* bands, respectively. Higher values of this index detect bareness of a region.

2.4 Morphological Opening

Morphological opening is derived by the dilation of the erosion of a set X by a structuring element Y, i.e. $X \circ Y = (X \ominus Y) \oplus Y$. Here, $\ominus$, and $\oplus$ are defined as erosion, and dilation, respectively. Erosion and dilation are fundamental morphological operation, which uses a structural element for probing and reducing the shapes, and probing and expanding the shapes, respectively in an image.

Opening is erosion followed by a dilation using similar structuring element. It has been extensively used in image processing to remove smaller objects. In this work, opening has been used over *CMI* image to remove noises and isolated areas. Furthermore, a coal quarry region can be attached to a coal dump region, which affects the accuracy of the proposed technique. Morphological opening has been employed to separate such areas.

2.5   Single Class SVM

Support Vector Machine (*SVM*) is a supervised model, which is used to categorise data by linear or non-linear classifiers. Single class or one class support vector machine is an unsupervised training algorithm, where the model is trained on one type of data [25]. The model learns the boundary of those data points. Further, it can classify any new data whether it resides within the boundary or it is an outlier. Single class *SVM* has been used in various image processing applications, such as, fraud detection, anomaly detection, novelty detection, etc [11,25].

3   Methodology

CMI detects coal quarry and coal dump regions as a single class. The proposed technique uses the outcome of *CMI* to detect coal quarry and coal dump regions separately. A surface coal quarry region may or may not has a mine swamp region. However, a coal dump region does not contain a mine water body region. Further, it is assumed that because of the land cover uses, the bare soil properties of these regions could be different. In this work, these two ideas are utilized to detect coal quarry and coal dump regions. The flow diagram of the proposed technique is shown in the Fig. 1. The proposed technique has seven steps. The flow of the proposed technique is as follows. As shown in the Fig. 1, first, coal quarry and coal mine regions are detected as a single class using *CMI*. Water bodies are detected using *MNDWI*. Further, a morphological opening is used over the outcome of *CMI*. Next, a connected component analysis is applied to check whether any connected component intersects with water bodies. Assuming at least one quarry region has mine water bodies, the regions having mine water bodies are used to train a single class *SVM* with bare soil index values. Further, mine quarry and mine dump regions are detected using anomaly detection with the single class *SVM* model. Last, a thresholding operation over *CMI* values is used to improve the accuracy of coal dump regions.

3.1   Detection of Quarry Regions with Water Bodies

First, coal quarry and coal dump regions are detected together using *CMI*. Let the region be denoted as *R*. As discussed, a few surface coal quarry regions have water bodies. Hence, water bodies are detected using *MNDWI*. As *MNDWI* enhances open water features, it has been used in this technique rather than

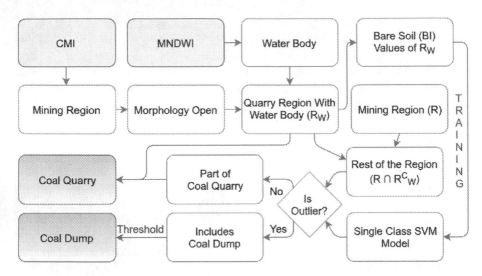

Fig. 1. Flow Diagram of the Proposed Method for Detecting Coal Quarry and Dump Regions

NDWI [28]. The intersection between detected water bodies by *MNDWI* and *CMI* can detect some coal quarry regions. However, a dump region can be attached to a quarry region. Hence, the intersection may detect quarry regions along with dump regions. Thus, the outcome of *CMI* is further refined using morphological opening. Here, the structuring element is chosen as 3×3 kernel empirically. This procedure separates the attached coal quarry and coal dump regions and removes additional noises and isolated areas. Next, connected component analysis is applied over this morphologically opened *CMI* image. In connected component analysis, each component is treated individually. Each component is further checked, whether it has any water body. All the components having water bodies are detected as coal quarry regions. Let the region be denoted as R_w.

3.2   Detection of Coal Quarry and Dump Using Single Class *SVM*

The presence of water bodies detects some of the coal quarry regions. The regions, which are detected by *CMI* but not marked by the presence of water bodies, i.e. $R \cap R_w^C$, are further studied. Let the region be denoted as R_n. Raw minerals are stored at coal dump regions, whereas, coal quarry regions have exposed raw minerals and bare soils. Thus, it is assumed that coal quarry and coal dump regions have different bare soil properties. Bare soil values of R_w are further used to train a single class *SVM*. Bare soil index values of R_n are analysed using the single class *SVM* model to check whether they are outliers or not. Let R_n be consists of two regions such as R_i and R_o. Let the regions, which are detected as non outlier by the *SVM* model be denoted as R_i. R_o denotes the regions, which are detected as outliers. Both the regions detected as non-outlier by the *SVM* model and detected by the presence of water bodies, i.e. $R_w \cup R_i$, is denoted as the detected final coal quarry region. Detected outlier region, i.e. R_o, is denoted to have coal dump regions and few other regions, which are neither part of coal quarry nor part of coal dump regions. Hence, these regions and coal dump regions are separated using a threshold over CMI values. It is observed that most of such regions have higher CMI values than coal dump regions.

In this work, CMI, $MNDWI$, and BI values are used. Thus, the proposed technique is applicable to any satellite modality having $Blue$, $Green$, Red, NIR, $SWIR$-I and $SWIR$-II bands.

4 Data and Study Area

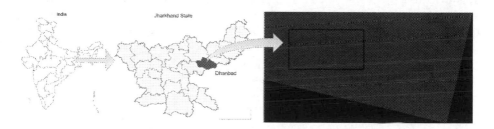

Fig. 2. Region of Interest: Jharia Coal Field in Jharkhand, India

Landsat 8 $L1$ data has been used here for experimentation. Landsat 8 data is collected from United States Geological Survey ($USGS$) earthexplorer website (Path: 140, Row: 43) of 2017. As multi-spectral images are inapplicable with the presence of clouds, an additional criteria of $< 10\%$ cloud cover is also considered. Top of atmosphere (TOA) reflectance is computed from $L1$ data products of Landsat 8 [27]. Jharia Coal Fields (JCF) (latitude: $23°38'N$ – $23°50'N$, longitude: $86°07'E$ – $86°30'E$) is considered here as the region of interest. It is situated in the Dhanbad district of the state of Jharkhand in India as shown in Fig. 2. The right most image of Fig. 2 shows a false color representation of the JCF region. The JCF has vast geographical features, such as mining regions, fresh water bodies, rivers, croplands, grasslands, barren lands, etc. High resolution Google earth images of the JCF are used here for validation. Ground truths of coal quarry and coal dump regions are marked through visual inspection and expert's opinion from high resolution Google Earth images.

5 Results

Landsat 8 $L1$ data products are used in this work for experimentation over the JCF region. The area of interest is cropped using $QGIS$ for further processing. CMI values are computed from these images of area of interest as shown in Fig. 3 (B). Figure 3 (A) shows a sample Google earth image of the same region. Coal dump and coal quarry regions are detected as a single class from CMI values as shown in Fig. 3 (C). Water bodies are detected using $MNDWI$ as shown in Fig. 3 (D). Higher values of $MNDWI$ preserve water bodies. In this work, $MNDWI$ has been used as it enhances the open water features [28]. These outcomes are further used in this work to detect the regions in R, which have water bodies. Mine water bodies are located near the vicinity of a coal quarry region or inside a coal quarry. Extracted coals are stored in a coal dump region. It does not have a mine water body region. Hence, occurrences of mine water bodies can separate a few coal quarry regions from coal dump regions. This idea is further explored in this work. A coal dump region may be attached to a coal quarry region. Hence, if all the regions in R are analysed using the presence of water bodies, some of such coal dump regions get misclassified as coal quarry regions. Hence, a morphological opening has been used as shown in Fig. 3 (E). It can be observed that many smaller isolated regions, mostly noises are removed by this process. Further, nearby coal dump regions get separated from coal quarry regions. Hence, coal quarries can be treated individually. Thereafter, a connected component analysis is applied over this resultant image to study each component independently. All the connected components, which have water bodies, are preserved as shown in Fig. 3 (F). It can be observed from Fig. 3 (E) and (F) that various detected regions in Fig. 3 (E) are discarded in Fig. 3 (F). These detected regions are highly likely to be coal quarry regions. Thus, these regions are considered as the true positive coal quarry region to train a single class SVM classifier. Here, BI index is considered as the feature space and a linear classifier has been used to train the SVM model. Regions, which are detected by CMI but not by R_w, i.e. $R \cap R_w^C$, are further studied with this single class SVM model. $R \cap R_w^C$ region is shown in Fig. 3 (G). The single class SVM is widely used for anomaly and outlier detection. Here, single class SVM has been used here to detect outliers in $R \cap R_w^C$. Hence, bare soil values of all the pixels in $R \cap R_w^C$ are checked. The regions, which are detected as outliers, i.e. R_o, are assumed to contain coal dump regions as shown in Fig. 3 (H). It can be observed that coal dump regions get detected with a few other scattered regions as shown in Fig. 3 (H). As coal dump regions store raw coals, CMI values are assumed to be lower. Hence, coal dump regions are further detected using a threshold of CMI values. Regions having lower values of CMI are preserved as shown in Fig. 3 (I). It is considered as the detected coal dump regions. Further, the regions, which are detected as non-outliers by the single class SVM, i.e. R_i, are considered as part of coal quarry regions. These regions along with the regions having water bodies, i.e. $R_w \cup R_i$, are considered as the detected coal quarry regions as shown in Fig. 3 (J). The proposed technique does not require labelled dataset and multi-modal analysis. It detects coal quarry and coal dump regions using multi-spectral images exclusively. The proposed technique primarily depends on the performance of CMI. Hence, the performance of the proposed technique can be further improved by enhancing the the performance of CMI.

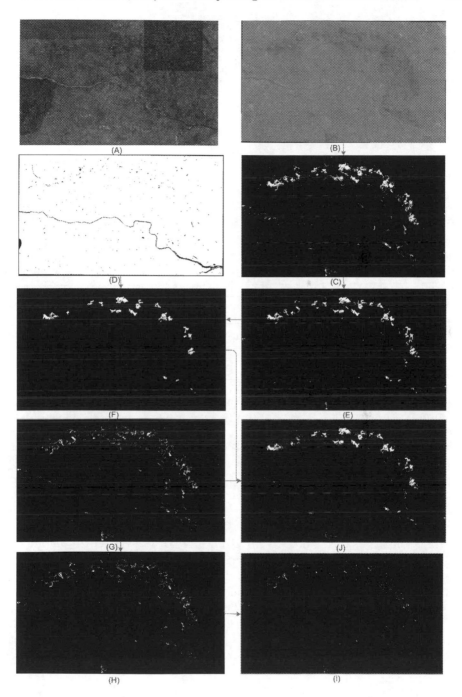

Fig. 3. Results in December 2017. A: Ground Truth GoogleEarth Image B: Coal Mine Index (CMI), C: Threshold Image of B, D: Water Bodies Detected by $MNDWI$, E: Morphological Opening of C, F: Connected Components having Water Bodies, G: $R \cap R_w^C$, H: Outlier of Single Class SVM, I: Final Dump Region, J: Final Quarry Region.

5.1   Spectral Validation

Table 1. Hypothesis Testing: Student t-test Results of $NDVI$, $NDWI$, and BI over the Null Hypothesis $\mu_{quarry} = \mu_{dump}$

	Nov			Dec			Jan			Feb			March			May		
	t_0	df	P Value	t_0	df	P Value	t_0	df	P Value	t_0	df	P Value	t_0	df	P Value	t_0	df	P Value
NDVI	-0.26	199.5	0.78	0.68	190.5	0.49	3.92	194.1	0.0001	4.66	195.4	<0.00001	2.81	163.4	0.005	2.08	173.4	0.047
NDWI	-1.24	198.9	0.21	-1.86	197.8	0.06	-5.98	199.7	<0.00001	-6.13	199.6	<0.00001	-3.75	187.9	0.0002	-4	190.5	0.00009
BI	5.98	167.8	<0.00001	6.24	144.2	<0.00001	6.58	155.1	<0.00001	7.23	151	<0.00001	10.5	185.4	<0.00001	11.6	196.6	<0.00001

In this work, it has been assumed that coal quarry and coal dump regions have different bare soil features. Using high resolution Google Earth images, various coal quarry and coal dump regions are marked as ground truth by vigorous visual inspection and expert's opinion based on prior knowledge acquired by site visits and their correlation with the remotely sensed images. To validate our claim, a hypothesis testing has been performed over the null hypothesis of $\mu_{Quarry} = \mu_{Dump}$ with these ground truth coal quarry and coal dump regions. Vegetation, water bodies, and bare soils are the most prominent land classes observed in the JCF. Therefore, a comparative analysis of $NDVI$, $NDWI$ and BI has been considered in this study. Here, μ_{Quarry}, and μ_{Dump} are denoted as mean values of different indexes of ground truth quarry, and dump regions respectively. Here, alternative hypothesis has been taken as $\mu_{Quarry} \neq \mu_{Dump}$. It is considered that $S_{Quarry} \neq S_{Dump}$, where S_{Quarry}, and S_{Dump} are variances of ground truth coal quarry, and dump regions, respectively. It has been found that the null hypothesis $\mu_{Quarry} = \mu_{Dump}$ cannot be rejected for November and December in the case of $NDVI$, and $NDWI$ as shown in Table 1, whereas, the null hypothesis can be rejected by the alternative hypothesis of $\mu_{Quarry} \neq \mu_{Dump}$ for every season using BI. Therefore, there is a significant difference in bare soil index responses to separate coal quarry and coal dump regions. It has been observed that the null hypothesis can be rejected by the alternative hypothesis $\mu_{Quarry} > \mu_{Dump}$ for BI.

Additionally, box plots of $NDVI$, $NDWI$, and BI are studied to validate our claim as shown in Fig. 4. It can be observed from Fig. 4 that there are significant overlaps of the box plots of quarry and dump regions over the seasons in cases of $NDVI$ and $NDWI$. On the other hand, the overlaps of quarry and dump box plots are less for the bare soil index. This observation also corroborates with the fact that coals are excavated from coal quarry regions, whereas only the extracted coals are dumped in coal dump regions. In coal quarry regions, coal benches are exposed along with bare soils. Hence, bare soil index values over quarry regions are observed to be higher than coal dump regions.

5.2   Performance Analysis

Further, the results are compared with high resolution ground truth Google Earth images. Figure 5 shows the outcome of the proposed technique with ground

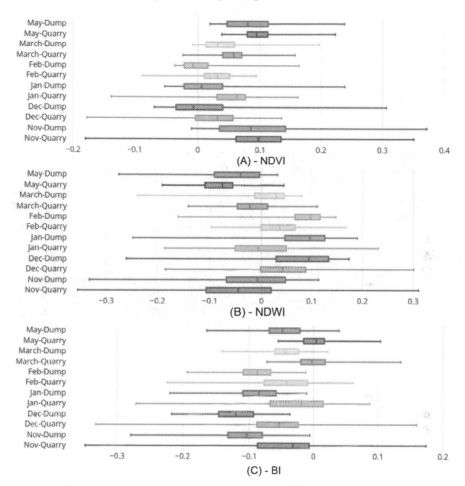

Fig. 4. Box Plot of Coal Mine Quarry and Dump regions by A - NDVI, B - NDWI, and C - BI.

truth coal quarry and coal dump regions. Figure 5 (A), and (B) show marked ground truth coal quarry and coal dump regions, respectively. Coal quarry and coal dump regions are detected as a single class by *CMI* as shown in Fig. 5 (C). Figure 5 (D) shows the outcome of morphological opening over Fig. 5 (C). It can be observed that many of the outliers are removed. Furthermore, the attached coal dump region is isolated from the quarry region. Figure 5 (E) shows the connected components of the detected regions by *CMI*, which have water bodies. It can be observed that very few regions, which are not part of the coal quarry region, get detected here. Thus, it provides higher precision values as shown in Table 2. Bare soil values of such regions are used to train single class *SVM*. It can be observed from Fig. 5, there are some portions of coal quarry regions, which are added using single class *SVM* as shown in Fig. 5 (H). The outliers found from the single class *SVM* are shown in Fig. 5 (F). It can be observed from Fig. 5 (F) that coal dump regions are detected along with a few other misclassified regions. As an example, the pit walls of coal quarries and misclassified regions by *CMI* are falsely detected as coal dump regions. Hence, the *CMI* values of these regions are examined and most of the other regions are separated from coal dump regions as shown in Fig. 5 (H).

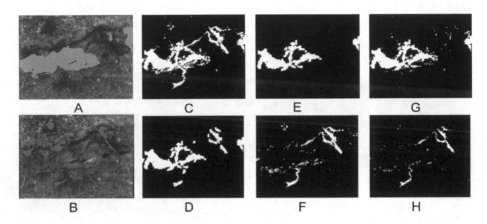

Fig. 5. Results With Ground Truth. A: Ground Truth Quarry Region in Green Color, B: Ground Truth Dump Region in Red Color, C: Outcome of *CMI*, D: Outcome of Morphology Opening, E: Detected Quarry by Presence of Water Body, G: Detected Quarry after Single Class *SVM* (Final Outcome), F: Detected Dump after Single Class *SVM* H: Detected Dump after Thresholding using *CMI* (Final Outcome), C-H: Detected Region in White Color. Results in December 2017 (Color figure online)

Precision and recall[1] of the proposed methods are computed using the ground truth coal quarry and coal dump regions. For coal quarry regions, precision and recall are computed with the presence of water bodies (R_w) and with $R_w \cup R_i$, i.e. final outcome. Similarly, two accuracy computations by precision and recall are performed for coal dump regions such as with the detected outlier (R_o) and with the final outcome after thresholding. The presence of a water body detects coal quarry regions with average precision, and recall of 92.79%, and 22.17%, respectively as shown in Table 2. As coal dump regions can not have water body regions, this process has higher precision. Whereas, there might be some quarry regions, where there is no mine water body. This process does not detect such quarry regions. Thus it has low recall values. Because of higher precision values, bare soil values of these regions are used to train the support vector machine. Bare soil values of the rest of the regions are applied to an outlier detection approach as discussed earlier and it produces the final resultant

---

[1] Precision, and Recall are defined as $t_p/(t_p+f_p)$, and $t_p/(t_p+f_n)$, where t_p, f_p, and f_n, are true positive, false positive, and false negative, respectively. F_1 score is computed as $2 \times (Precision \times Recall)/(Precision + Recall)$.

quarry regions. The final coal quarry region has precision, recall, and F_1 score of 84.88%, 61.44%, and 71.28%, respectively. It can be observed that the precision has decreased from the presence of the water body technique, whereas the recall values have increased significantly. The detected outliers are considered to contain coal dump regions. This provides precision, recall, and F_1 score of 61.4%, 58.21%, and 59.76%, respectively for coal dump regions. It can be observed that the precision of coal dump regions is low as there are few other regions. These regions have few portions, which are neither part of the coal quarry nor part of the coal dump. Further, a threshold over the CMI values of these regions is applied to separate noises from coal dump regions. It has precision, recall, and F_1 score of 70.91%, 52.79%, and 60.52%, respectively (Table 2). It can be observed that recall values of coal dump regions have decreased, while the precision values are significantly improved. Being a very small land class, the detection of coal dump regions needs further experimentation to improve accuracy. It is considered as a future work. In the literature, supervised or semi-supervised techniques are used to detect land cover classes in surface mine regions. A supervised SVM technique has been used for different land classes in surface coal mine regions [10] over a small faction of the JCF region. Supervised maximum likelihood classification has been employed in [3] to detect coal dump regions with an accuracy of 95%. These works use manual supervision, knowledge of filed validation, and supervised modeling to detect such regions. [1] detects surface coal mine regions using unsupervised modeling and multimodal analysis, however finer land classes are not considered. Surface coal mine regions are detected using a object-oriented decision tree with a kappa co-efficient of 0.8 in [29]. However, it considers the extracting areas, stripped areas, and dumping areas together as a single class. [30] provides a multi-modal analysis consisting of a digital elevation model, $RapidEye$, and $SPOT7$ multispectral data to detect mining areas with an overall accuracy of 90.44%. However, quarry and dump regions are not treated separately [30]. In [24], land use land cover ($LULC$) alternation has been quantified over coal mining regions using a support vector machine. It uses a supervised classification technique and does not consider finer land classes of coal mine regions. Further, very few works have explored the detection of such finer land classes of coal quarry and coal dump regions. Whereas in this work, an unsupervised learning algorithm has been used and finer land classes such as coal quarry and coal dump regions are detected using Landsat 8 multi-spectral images exclusively. Further, the distinguishing spectral characteristics of these land classes are also discussed. As the performance depends on CMI, the technique is applicable to bigger regions compared to the size of such finer land classes with similar accuracy. The technique can be fully automated by automating the outcome of water body detection [6] and surface coal mine detection [14]. It needs further experimentation and it is considered as a future work. Further experimentation with other mining regions and surface reflectance values are also considered as a few of the future directions of this work.

Table 2. Precision and Recall of the Proposed Technique

		Metric	Nov	Dec	Jan	Feb	March	May
Quarry	Presence of Water	Precision	97.13	92.69	93.42	92.09	91.92	89.53
		Recall	10.74	28.45	33.04	41.71	4.58	14.52
	Final	Precision	84.66	88.07	89.66	84.45	84.71	77.73
		Recall	43.48	64.22	67.98	71.35	57.07	55.36
Dump	SVM	Precision	54.30	68.47	61.98	60.93	54.26	55.40
		Recall	64.18	58.68	54.62	55.85	57.80	58.16
	Final	Precision	72.66	78.07	79.66	71.22	64.40	59.47
		Recall	53.48	54.22	47.98	53.86	53.23	53.98

6   Conclusion and Future Aspect

Though coal quarry and coal dump regions have a distinguishing factor of high mineral abundance, it is challenging to separate these two land classes from other land covers. The proposed work presents a novel technique to detect coal quarry and coal dump regions using the presence of water bodies. Initially, coal quarries and coal dumps are detected as a single land class using *CMI*, and water bodies are detected by *MNDWI*. Coal quarry regions may have water bodies but coal dump regions do not have them. This idea is further used to detect such quarry regions, which have water bodies. As coal dump regions may be near the vicinity of coal quarry regions, these dump regions may also get detected along such quarry regions. Hence, a morphological opening is applied and it also removes isolated regions. These detected quarry regions are further used to train a single class *SVM* model using bare soil values. It has also been observed that *BI* can significantly separate coal quarry and dump regions, and it can be used as a distinguishing feature. Finally, an outlier detection technique has been applied using this model to mark the rest of the regions as quarry or dump regions. To improve the precision of dump regions, further, a *CMI* based thresholding is also applied. The proposed technique provides average precision and recall for coal quarry and coal dump regions as [84.88%, 61.44%], and [70.91%, 52.79%], respectively over the seasons. This technique is dependent on the performance of the *CMI* and the overall accuracy can be increased by improving the performance of the *CMI*. Further experimentation in this regard has been considered as a future work. The method can further be used for the detection, classification, and monitoring of various land classes in surface mining regions. It can have multi-level applications in the mining industry, monitoring, resource management, etc.

References

1. Aswatha, S.M., Saini, V., Mukherjee, J., Biswas, P.K., Aikat, S., Misra, A.: Unsupervised detection of surface mine sites using sentinel multi-spectral imagery and dual-polarimetric SAR data. In: Proceedings of the 11th Indian Conference on Computer Vision, Graph. Image Process., pp. 1–8 (2018)
2. Chen, W., Liu, L., Zhang, C., Wang, J., Wang, J., Pan, Y.: Monitoring the seasonal bare soil areas in beijing using multitemporal tm images. In: Geoscience and Remote Sensing Symposium, 2004. Proceedings. 2004 IEEE International. 5, pp. 3379–3382. IEEE (2004)
3. Demirel, N., Düzgün, Ş, Emil, M.K.: Landuse change detection in a surface coal mine area using multi-temporal high-resolution satellite images. Int. J. Min. Reclam. Enviro. **25**(4), 342–349 (2011)
4. Demirel, N., Emil, M.K., Duzgun, H.S.: Surface coal mine area monitoring using multi-temporal high-resolution satellite imagery. Int. J. Coal Geol. **86**(1), 3–11 (2011)
5. Drury, S.A.: Image interpretation in geology. No. 551.0285 D796 1993, Chapman and Hall, London (1993)
6. Feyisa, G.L., Meilby, H., Fensholt, R., Proud, S.R.: Automated water extraction index: A new technique for surface water mapping using Landsat imagery. Remote Sens. Environ. **140**, 23–35 (2014)
7. Gao, Y., Kerle, N., Mas, J.F.: Object-based image analysis for coal fire-related land cover mapping in coal mining areas. Geocarto Int. **24**(1), 25–36 (2009)
8. Han, Y., Li, M., Li, D.: Vegetation index analysis of multi-source remote sensing data in coal mine wasteland. NZ. J. Agric. Res. **50**(5), 1243–1248 (2007)
9. Huo, H., Ni, Z., Gao, C., Zhao, E., Zhang, Y., Lian, Y., Zhang, H., Zhang, S., Jiang, X., Song, X., Zhou, P., Cui, T.: A study of coal fire propagation with remotely sensed thermal infrared data. Remote Sens. **7**(3), 3088–3113 (2015)
10. Karan, S.K., Samadder, S.R., Maiti, S.K.: Assessment of the capability of remote sensing and GIS techniques for monitoring reclamation success in coal mine degraded lands. J. Environ. Manage. **182**, 272–283 (2016)
11. Manevitz, L.M., Yousef, M.: One-class SVMS for document classification. J. Mach. Learn. Res., 139–154 (2001)
12. Mezned, N., Dkhala, B., Abdeljaouad, S.: Multitemporal and multisensory Landsat ETM+ and OLI 8 data for mine waste change detection in northern Tunisia. J. Spat. Sci. **63**(1), 135–153 (2018)
13. Mien, T.: Mine waste water management and treatment in coal mines in Vietnam. Geosyst. Eng. **15**(1), 66–70 (2012)
14. Mukherjee, J., Mukhopadhyay, J., Chakravarty, D., Aikat, S.: Automated seasonal detection of coal surface mine regions from Landsat 8 OLI images. In: IGARSS 2019 IEEE International Geoscience and Remote Sensing Symposium, pp. 2435–2438 (2019). https://doi.org/10.1109/IGARSS.2019.8898789
15. Mukherjee, J.: A study on automated detection of surface and sub-surface coal seam fires using isolation forest from Landsat 8 OLI/TIRS images. In: IGARSS 2022–2022 IEEE International Geoscience and Remote Sensing Symposium, pp. 5512–5515 (2022)
16. Mukherjee, J., Mukherjee, J., Chakravarty, D.: Automated seasonal separation of mine and non mine water bodies from Landsat 8 OLI/TIRS using clay mineral and iron oxide ratio. IEEE J. Sel. Topics in Appl. Earth Observ. Remote Sens. 12(7), 2550–2556 (2019)

17. Mukherjee, J., Mukherjee, J., Chakravarty, D.: Automated Detection of Mine Water Bodies Using Landsat 8 OLI/TIRS in Jharia. In: Babu, R.V., Prasanna, M., Namboodiri, V.P. (eds.) NCVPRIPG 2019. CCIS, vol. 1249, pp. 480–489. Springer, Singapore (2020). https://doi.org/10.1007/978-981-15-8697-2_45
18. Mukherjee, J., Mukherjee, J., Chakravarty, D., Aikat, S.: A novel index to detect opencast coal mine areas from Landsat 8 OLI/TIRS. IEEE J. Sel. Topics in Appl. Earth Observ. Remote Sens. 12(3), 891–897 (2019)
19. Mukherjee, J., Mukherjee, J., Chakravarty, D., Aikat, S.: Unsupervised Detection of Active, New, and Closed Coal Mines with Reclamation Activity from Landsat 8 OLI/TIRS Images. In: Deka, B., Maji, P., Mitra, S., Bhattacharyya, D.K., Bora, P.K., Pal, S.K. (eds.) PReMI 2019. LNCS, vol. 11941, pp. 397–404. Springer, Cham (2019). https://doi.org/10.1007/978-3-030-34869-4_43
20. Mukherjee, J., Mukherjee, J., Chakravarty, D., Aikat, S.: Seasonal detection of coal overburden dump regions in unsupervised manner using Landsat 8 OLI/TIRS images at jharia coal fields. Multimedia Tools Appl. 80(28), 35605–35627 (2021)
21. Mukherjee, J., Mukhopadhyay, J., Chakravarty, D.: Investigation of seasonal separation in mine and non mine water bodies using local feature analysis of land sat 8 OLI/TIRS images. In: 2018 IEEE International Geoscience and Remote Sensing Symposium, Valencia, Spain, pp. 8961–8964 (2018)
22. Petropoulos, G.P., Partsinevelos, P., Mitraka, Z.: Change detection of surface mining activity and reclamation based on a machine learning approach of multi-temporal Landsat TM imagery. Geocarto Int. 28(4), 323–342 (2013)
23. Popelková, R., Mulková, M.: Multitemporal aerial image analysis for the monitoring of the processes in the landscape affected by deep coal mining. Eur. J. Remote Sens. 49(1), 973–1009 (2016)
24. Ranjan, A.K., Sahoo, D., Gorai, A.: Quantitative assessment of landscape transformation due to coal mining activity using earth observation satellite data in Jharsuguda coal mining region, Odisha, India. Environ. Dev. Sustain. 23(3), 4484–4499 (2021)
25. Schölkopf, B., Williamson, R.C., Smola, A., Shawe-Taylor, J., Platt, J.: Support vector method for novelty detection. Adv. Neural Inf. Process. Syst. 12, 582–588 (1999)
26. Tracher, G.B., T.T.: Coal fire burning out of control around the world: thermodynamic recipe for environmental catastrophe. Int. J. Coal Geol. 59, 7–17 (2004)
27. USGS: Using the USGS Landsat Level-1 Data Product. https://www.usgs.gov/land-resources/nli/landsat/using-usgs-landsat-level-1-data-product/ Accessed 11 Sep 2019
28. Xu, H.: Modification of normalized difference water index (NDWI) to enhance open water features in remotely sensed imagery. Int. J. Remote Sens. 27(14), 3025–3033 (2006)
29. Zeng, X., Liu, Z., He, C., Ma, Q., Wu, J.: Detecting surface coal mining areas from remote sensing imagery: an approach based on object-oriented decision trees. J. Appl. Remote Sens. 11(1), 015025 (2017)
30. Zhang, M., Zhou, W., Li, Y.: The analysis of object-based change detection in mining area: a case study with pingshuo coal mine. ISPRS - International Archives of the Photogrammetry, Remote Sensing and Spatial Information Sciences XLII-2/W7, 1017–1023 (2017). https://doi.org/10.5194/isprs-archives-XLII-2-W7-1017-2017

Brain Tumor Grade Detection Using Transfer Learning and Residual Multi-head Attention Network

Jagadeesh Kakarla and Isunuri Bala Venkateswarlu[✉]

Indian Institute of Information Technology, Design and Manufacturing,
Kancheepuram, India
{jagadeeshk,coe19d001}@iiitdm.ac.in

Abstract. Brain tumor grade detection is one of the perpetual tasks in brain image classification. Deep learning models are the most successful for multi-class classification which are trained for non-medical image classification. Thus, there is a need for re-training and feature enhancement for better performance in medical image classification. In this paper, we have proposed a residual multi-head attention network to uplift the re-training process with polished feature extraction. The proposed model consists of three parts including a pre-trained EfficientNetB4, a residual multi-head attention network, and a dense network. The residual multi-head attention network utilizes the attention block with three convolution layers for better tumor detection. The residual connection used in the network avoids the vanishing gradient problem. We have extracted a two-class (low-grade/high-grade) dataset from REMBRANDT repository. The proposed model has attained an accuracy of 96.39% and outperforms its competing models in vital metrics.

Keywords: Brain tumor grade detection · Transfer learning · Residual multi-head attention · Feature enhancement

1 Introduction

Brain caner is one of the most serious and potentially fatal diseases in the world. The early stage detection of cancer can survive the life of patients with proper medication. Medical imaging especially magnetic resonance (MR) imaging is the widely used technique for brain visualization and diagnosis [9]. Recent brain image processing has expanded into a wide range of applications, including tumor classification [16], tumor segmentation [4], and diffuse low-grade glioma monitoring [1]. However, binary classification of brain image is the fundamental and primary task in early stage diagnosis of cancer. It can be further divided into two types as tumor detection and grade detection as shown in Fig. 1. The details are as follows.

D. Gupta et al. (Eds.): CVIP 2022, CCIS 1777, pp. 205–215, 2023.
https://doi.org/10.1007/978-3-031-31417-9_16

- **Grade detection**: It mainly focuses on the binary classification of tumor grades including low-grade and high-grade. It also includes the task of distinguishing healthy/low-grade and healthy/high-grade depending on requirements.
- **Tumor detection**: It consists only classification of healthy/tumorous images.

However, the tumor detection is also referred to as pathological brain detection which focuses on identification of abnormality of brain. There were many proposals, Zhang *et al.* [21] have developed a system for detecting brain pathology using the estimation of fractal dimension and Minkowski-Buligand method. An optimized feature fusion with fisher criterion has formulated by Kaur *et al.* [12]. Nayak *et al.* [15] have combined a modified sine cosine algorithm with an extreme learning machine for the detection of pathology of brain. Siyuan *et al.* [14] have used pre-trained AlexNet to detect brain pathology from MR images. Similarly, Shankar *et al.* [10] have devised an adaptive fuzzy neural interface system to classify MR images of the brain as benign or malignant.

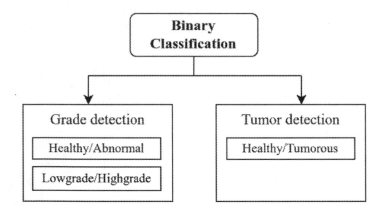

Fig. 1. Binary classification of brain images

Kalpana *et al.* [11] have utilized a machine learning approach for segregation of benign and malignant brain images. They have used discrete wavelet transform and principle component analysis for feature extraction and optimization, respectively. Then, the radial basis function network has employed for the final classification. Emrah Irmak [8] has designed a custom 13 weighted layers convolution network two address binary classification. Kumar *et al.* [13] has proposed another machine learning approach for glioma detection. The pre-processed images are segmented using fuzzy centroid-based region growing. Then, statistical features are extracted, and final results are produced with deep belief network. Table 1 lists out summary of the existing tumor detection models. Recently, discrimination of low-grade and high-grade detection has received great attention. The low-grade tumors are non-cancerous while high-grade tumors are cancerous in nature. Thus, segregation of low-grade and high-grade is the critical task as

Table 1. Summary of literature

Reference	Year	# of Samples	Accuracy
Zhang *et al.* [21]	2016	255	98.08
Kaur *et al.* [12]	2018	50	93.72
Nayak *et al.* [15]	2018	255	99.73
Siyuan *et al.* [14]	2019	215	100.00
Shankar *et al.* [10]	2020	85	96.23
Kalpana *et al.* [11]	2020	120	98.75
Irmak [8]	2021	2990	99.33
Kumar *et al.* [13]	2022	270	95.23

the structural differences are very low. There are very scant number of proposal on low-grade and high-grade detection. Moreover, the existing methods have reported on small datasets except Irmak [8]. It motivated us to implement a grade (low/high) detection model that can produce better performance on large datasets. Thus, we have proposed transfer learning and residual multi-head attention network for the grade detection.

The remaining paper has structured as follows; Sect. 2 elaborates the proposed methodology. Section 3 provides performance analysis in detail and Sect. 4 concludes the findings of the work.

2 Methodology

Deep neural networks (DNN) have received great attention in computer vision and image classification. A large number of models are popular in DNN research including ResNet [5], GoogleNet [17], and MobileNet [6]. Recently, EfficientNet models have been introduced by Mingxing [18] *et al.* for image classification. These models have reported best Top-1 accuracy (%) than their contemporary models on Imagenet dataset. Nowadays, transfer learning has become popular with its substantial use in image classification applications. Thus, the pre-trained weights of the ImageNet dataset of the above models are available for transfer learning. In this process, weights or knowledge gained during solving a problem is reused to solve other related problems. The proposed model have utilized the transfer learning and residual multi-head attention network for brain pathology detection.

2.1 Transfer Learning

In our experiments, we have observed that EfficientNetB4 has reported better performance with optimal parameters. Thus, we have considered EfficientNetB4 as the backbone model for the feature extraction network. The EfficientNetB4 consists of seven convolution blocks preceded by a stem block. Initially, the stem block takes the input image through the input layer with three channels. The given image is processed with seven convolution blocks with a varying number of filters. Then, the final constitutional block of EfficientNetB4 produces a feature map consisting of 1792 channels.

2.2 Residual Multi-head Attention Network

The main purpose of this network is to enhance feature learning for improved performance. The proposed residual multi-head attention network consists of two blocks as follows.

– **Residual convolution block** consists of three convolution layers with a residual connection. The re-convolution of deep convolution features will leads to a vanishing gradient problem. It motivated us to devise the residual convolution to address the problem. Further, we have reduced the number of filters from 1792 to 448. To optimize computational cost, a 1×1 kernel has been utilized for each convolution. However, the number of filters for the three convolutions are 448, 896, and 448, respectively.
– **Multi-head attention block**: performs parallel attention mechanism several times as given in eq. 1 .

$$MA(Q, K, V) = [head_1, head_2, head_3]W_0 \qquad (1)$$

Where $head_i = Attention(Qw_i^Q, KW_i^K, VW_i^V)$ [20]. The expected dimension will be generated through concatenation of independent attention outputs. In this block, we have employed one multi-head attention with three heads and two key dimensions. The multi-head attention block has included with in the residual convolution block after third convolution. From the results, it is observed that the attention block produces low activation for abnormal brain images and high activation for a normal images. The final, feature map will be produced through the Leaky ReLU activation and then global average pooling as shown in Fig. 2.

2.3 Proposed Model

The proposed transfer learning and residual multi-head attention network consist of three parts as shown in Fig. 2. The details of each part are as follows.

1. **Pre-trained EfficientNetB4**:
   Initially, the given input images of size (128, 128, 3) are transformed to feature map of size (4, 4, 172) using pre-trained EfficientNetB4 model. This part of the model will be initialized with imagenet weights for transfer learning. Then, the complete network is retrained with a dataset for improved performance.

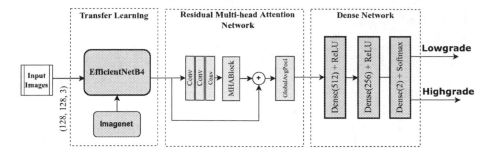

Fig. 2. Proposed Transfer Learning and Residual Multi-head Attention Network

2. **Residual Multi-head Attention Network**:
   This network has been proposed to enhance the feature map obtained from the pre-trained model. The attention layer included in this network is helpful for the detection of the tumor. This network generates a one-dimensional feature vector from a multi-dimensional feature map with global average pooling.

3. **Dense Network**:
   It is the classification network of the proposed model which produces classification results. We have included two dense layers with ReLU activation in addition to the output dense layer. The number of neurons employed for the two dense layers are 512 and 256, respectively. The output dense layer uses two neurons with softmax activation for binary classification.

3 Results and Discussion

The performance analysis of the proposed Transfer learning and Residual Multihead Attention (TLRMA) model has reported in this section. In order to compare the results, the contemporary state-of-the-art model proposed by Irmak *et al.* [2] has been considered. The pre-trained models are reporting the best results and hence we have compared our results with the popular models including EfficientNet, InceptionRestNet, DenseNet, GoogleNet, MobileNet, and RestNet. The performance metric plays a significant role in the evaluation of a model. Thus, we have adopted four vital metrics including accuracy, precision, recall, and jaccard score which can be computed using the following equations.

$$Accuracy = \frac{TP + TN}{TP + FP + TN + FN} \tag{2}$$

$$Precision = \frac{TP}{TP + FP} \tag{3}$$

$$Recall = \frac{TP}{TP + FN} \tag{4}$$

$$Jaccard = \frac{TP}{TP + FP + FN} \tag{5}$$

3.1   Dataset Description

We have extracted the binary classification dataset from the molecular brain neoplasia Data (REMBRANDT) repository. The repository has been published by the cancer imaging archive (TCIA) [3]. It contains pre-surgical magnetic resonance (MR) images of around 130 patients and is in DICOM format having an image resolution of (256, 256). We have extracted a total of 7414 t1-weighted MR images and performed a general pre-processing operation including min-max normalization and resizing to (128, 128). Then, the dataset has segregated into two classes namely low-grade (images of grade 2) and high-grade (images of grade 3 and 4). After segregation, the dataset contains 3568 low-grade and 3846 high-grade images.

3.2   Experimental Setup

We have conducted our experiments using GPU-enabled google colab and the models have been simulated using Python and Keras. We have used the basic Adam optimizer to train the models as it is simple and time-efficient for deep neural networks. The optimizer has associated with a sparse categorical cross-entropy function for computation of loss. Table 2 lists the complete set of hyper-parameters used for training.

Table 2. Training parameters

Hyperparameter	Value
Optimizer	Adam
Initial learning rate	0.0003
Batch size	4
Number of epochs	5

Table 3. Ablation study

Model	Accuracy
EfficientNetB4 + Multi-head attention (MHA)	93.48
EfficientNetB4 + Residual Convolution (RC)	96.26
EfficientNetB4 + RC + MHA	96.39

Table 4. Five-fold stratified cross-validation results

Fold	Accuracy	Precision	Recall	Jaccard
1	96.02	96.04	96.1	92.35
2	95.41	95.74	95.28	91.19
3	96.83	96.81	96.87	93.85
4	96.29	96.28	96.35	92.84
5	97.44	97.44	97.43	94.99
Avg.	96.39	96.46	96.41	93.04
Std.	0.69	0.6	0.73	1.3

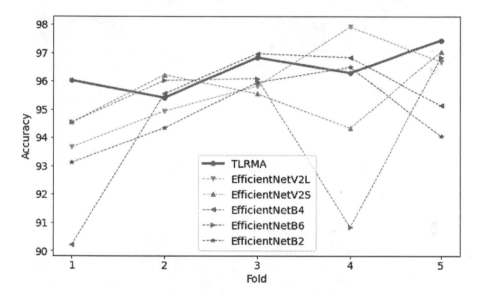

Fig. 3. Fold-wise comparison of accuracy of top-5 pre-trained models

3.3   Performance Analysis

Initially, we have experimented with two different blocks namely multi-head attention and residual convolution. We have computed the performance with different combinations of the blocks for optimal performance as shown in Table 3. EfficientNetB4 with multi-head attention has produced least performance of 93.48%. On the other hand, EfficientNetB4 with residual convolution and multi-head attention has reported the best performance with 96.39%. In our experiments, a stratified five-fold cross-validation has considered to compute the mean performance of the models. Table 4 lists out the cross-validation results of proposed model. In fifth fold, we have achieved best performance while in second fold our model has reported least performance. However, the proposed model has attained a mean jaccard score of 93.04% with a deviation of 1.3%. Figure 3 visualizes the fold-wise comparison of accuracy of top-5 pre-trained models with propose model. The proposed model has exhibited best performance in first and fifth folds. Our model has reported competing performance in other folds. It can be observed that the existing models experiences high deviation while the proposed model exhibits low deviation.

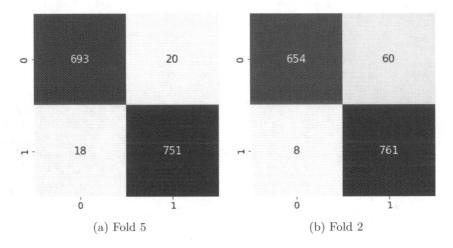

(a) Fold 5   (b) Fold 2

Fig. 4. Confusion matrix of proposed model

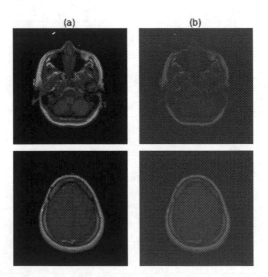

Fig. 5. Class prediction map of proposed model

The confusion matrix captures the class-wise performance along with wrong predictions. Figure 4 (a) visualizes the confusion matrix obtained in fold 5. Here, class 0 and class 1 are represented by low-grade and high-grade, receptively. Our model has predicted 751 high-grade and 658 low-grade images correctly which leads best performance. Similarly. Figure 4 (b) visualizes the confusion matrix obtained in fold 2 that has least performance with 68 wrong predictions. The performance of the proposed model can be further analyzed with class prediction maps of the model as shown in Fig. 5. This figure visualizes sample MR images of low-grade and high-grade tumors in first and second rows, respectively. The class prediction map visualizes low in case of low-grade tumor and high in case of high-grade tumor as shown in second column of Fig. 5.

Table 5. Performance comparison

Reference	Accuracy	Precision	Recall	Jaccard
ResNet50 [5]	86.07	86.49	86.14	76.30
ResNet101 [5]	76.21	78.12	76.01	61.44
MobileNet [6]	93.22	93.76	93.16	87.31
MobileNetV2 [6]	61.05	76.87	62.35	41.01
DenseNet121 [7]	72.51	76.23	72.77	57.33
DenseNet201 [7]	66.05	66.98	65.90	49.48
GoogleNet [17]	84.07	86.16	83.90	72.50
InceptionResNet [17]	93.26	93.74	93.32	87.40
EfficientNetB0 [18]	94.83	94.93	94.86	90.20
EfficientNctB1 [18]	94.71	94.92	94.66	89.95
EfficientNetB2 [18]	94.79	94.97	94.78	90.11
EfficientNetB3 [18]	93.78	94.09	93.73	88.32
EfficientNetB4 [18]	94.94	95.22	94.97	90.45
EfficientNetB5 [18]	94.42	94.68	94.39	89.43
EfficientNetB6 [18]	94.86	95.10	94.91	90.29
EfficientNetB7 [18]	94.24	94.71	94.27	89.18
EfficientNetV2S [19]	95.54	95.65	95.58	91.46
EfficientNetV2M [19]	93.65	93.84	93.67	88.07
EfficientNetV2L [19]	95.80	95.91	95.80	91.97
Irmak [8]	91.44	92.04	91.61	84.31
TLRMA	**96.39**	**96.46**	**96.41**	**93.04**

3.4   Comparison and Discussion

From the contemporary literature, it is observed that Irmak [8] model has reported best performance on large dataset. Thus, we have considered Irmak [8] model for the performance evaluation. In addition to that, we have also considered recent EfficientNetV2 models along with popular models. Table 5 compares the performance of proposed model with its competing models. EfficientNetV2L model has reported best perform in the competing models. However, our model outperforms EfficientNetV2L in all metrics with 1% improvement. Further, we have achieved and improvement of 5% than state-of-the-art models. The residual convolution with multi-head attention used in the proposed model has improved the tumor detection rate.

4   Conclusions

Brain tumor grade detection is the primary task in brain tumor classification. The segregation of low-grade and high-grade tumors is a critical task due to minor changes in texture of the brain images. In this paper, we have presented transfer learning and residual multi-head attention network for brain tumor grade detection. We have extracted two-class (low-grade/high-grade) dataset from REMBRANDT repository. The proposed model has reported 96.39% and 93.04% of accuracy and jaccard score, respectively. The proposed model outperforms its competing pre-trained models in all metrics with 1% improvement. Further, we have achieved an improvement of 5% than state-of-the-art models.

References

1. Abdallah, M.B., et al.: Data-driven predictive models of diffuse low-grade gliomas under chemotherapy. IEEE J. Biomed. Health Inform. **23**(1), 38–46 (2018)
2. Chowdary, G.J., Punn, N.S., Sonbhadra, S.K., Agarwal, S.: Face mask detection using transfer learning of inceptionv3 (2020)
3. Clark, K., et al.: The cancer imaging archive (TCIA): maintaining and operating a public information repository. J. Digital Imaging **26**(6), 1045–1057 (2013)
4. Ding, Y., et al.: Mvfusfra: a multi-view dynamic fusion framework for multimodal brain tumor segmentation. IEEE J. Biomed. Health Inform. **26**(4), 1570–1581 (2021)
5. He, K., Zhang, X., Ren, S., Sun, J.: Deep residual learning for image recognition. In: 2016 IEEE Conference on Computer Vision and Pattern Recognition (CVPR), pp. 770–778 (2016)
6. Howard, A.G., et al.: MobileNets: Efficient convolutional neural networks for mobile vision applications. (2017) arXiv preprint arXiv:1704.04861
7. Huang, G., Liu, Z., Van Der Maaten, L., Weinberger, K.Q.: Densely connected convolutional networks. In: Proceedings of the IEEE conference on computer vision and pattern recognition, pp. 4700–4708 (2017)
8. Irmak, E.: Multi-classification of brain tumor MRI images using deep convolutional neural network with fully optimized framework. Iranian J. Sci. Technol. Trans. Electr. Eng., pp. 1–22 (2021)
9. Isunuri, B.V., Kakarla, J.: Three-class brain tumor classification from magnetic resonance images using separable convolution based neural network. Concurrency Comput. Pract. Experience **34**(1), e6541 (2022)
10. Elhoseny, M., et al.: Optimal feature level fusion based ANFIS classifier for brain MRI image classification. Concurrency and Computation: Practice Experience 32(1), e4887 (2020)

11. Kalpana, R., Chandrasekar, P.: An optimized technique for brain tumor classification and detection with radiation dosage calculation in MRI image. Microprocess. Microsyst. **72**, 102903 (2020). https://doi.org/10.1016/j.micpro.2019.102903

12. Kaur, T., Saini, B.S., Gupta, S.: An optimal spectroscopic feature fusion strategy for MRI brain tumor classification using fisher criteria and parameter-free bat optimization algorithm. Biocybernetics Biomed. Eng. **38**(2), 409–424 (2018)

13. Kumar, T.S., Arun, C., Ezhumalai, P.: An approach for brain tumor detection using optimal feature selection and optimized deep belief network. Biomed. Signal Process. Control **73**, 103440 (2022)

14. Lu, S., Lu, Z., Zhang, Y.D.: Pathological brain detection based on AlexNet and transfer learning. J. Comput. Sci. **30**, 41–47 (2019)

15. Nayak, D.R., Dash, R., Majhi, B., Wang, S.: Combining extreme learning machine with modified sine cosine algorithm for detection of pathological brain. Comput. Electr. Eng. **68**, 366–380 (2018)

16. Sekhar, A., Biswas, S., Hazra, R., Sunaniya, A.K., Mukherjee, A., Yang, L.: Brain tumor classification using fine-tuned google net features and machine learning algorithms: IOMT enabled cad system. IEEE J. Biomed. Health Inform. **26**(3), 983–991 (2021)

17. Szegedy, C., Sergey Ioffe, V.V., Shlens, J., Wojna, Z.: Rethinking the inception architecture for computer vision. CoRR abs/1512.00567 (2015)

18. Tan, M., Le, Q.: Efficientnet: rethinking model scaling for convolutional neural networks. In: International conference on machine learning, pp. 6105–6114. PMLR (2019)

19. Tan, M., Le, Q.V.: Efficientnetv2: smaller models and faster training. CoRR abs/2104.00298 (2021). https://arxiv.org/abs/2104.00298

20. Vaswani, A., et al.: Attention is all you need. Adv. Neural Inf. process. Syst. 30 (2017)

21. Zhang, Y., et al.: Fractal dimension estimation for developing pathological brain detection system based on minkowski-bouligand method. IEEE Access **4**, 5937–5947 (2016)

A Curated Dataset for Spinach Species Identification

R. Ahila Priyadharshini$^{(\boxtimes)}$, S. Arivazhagan, and M. Arun

Centre for Image Processing and Pattern Recognition, Mepco Schlenk Engineering College, Sivakasi, India
rahila@mepcoeng.ac.in

Abstract. India has a large population of spinach eaters. Despite this fact most people and young generation have difficulty in distinguishing the spinach species because of the structure similarity of many plant species. So, automated spinach recognition will support the people community to a greater extent. In this study, we present spinach dataset, a freely accessible annotated collection of images of spinach leaves in Indian scenario. We propose three different custom designed convolutional neural networks (CNN) and compare the performance of the same. Also we apply the transfer learning approach using MobileNetV2 pretrained model for this spinach species recognition. Using transfer learning approach we got an accuracy of 92.96%.

Keywords: Spinach · CNN · Transfer learning · Leaf

1 Introduction

Worldwide, spinach is grown as a healthy leafy vegetable. Ancient Persia is where spinach was initially identified as a necessary vegetable. Iran is the modern name for the ancient Persian Empire. It first spread to India and then, thanks to a prehistoric Chinese who called it "Persia vegetable," to China. Later, it spread to the rest of the nations, including Spain, England, and France. Soldiers in France who were bleeding during the First World War were treated with spinach juice. Since that time, spinach has gained popularity throughout the world.

Spinach has huge levels of iron, calcium, folic acid, vitamins A, C, and K1, and all of these minerals. Additionally, it has potent antioxidants including lutein, zeaxanthin, and quercetin. Carotenoids found in spinach help prevent cancer and oxidative stress. Additionally, the fibre in it encourages fullness and may aid with diabetic management. Lutein and zeaxanthin enhance vision, and calcium helps maintain bone health. Spinach can be added directly to salads or used as a stand-alone vegetable to make soups, stews, steamed food, and dishes that are fried in oil [1].

India's rural areas are home to a large population of spinach eaters. Only a few species of spinach are found in urban settings, despite the fact that numerous species are sold at markets in rural areas. The majority of people and youngsters of the new generation typically struggle to distinguish the spinach because some of the species look similar.

© The Author(s), under exclusive license to Springer Nature Switzerland AG 2023
D. Gupta et al. (Eds.): CVIP 2022, CCIS 1777, pp. 216–228, 2023.
https://doi.org/10.1007/978-3-031-31417-9_17

Even they are unaware of the name of spinach. Therefore, it is required to automatically identify several kinds of spinach based on their leaves.

By examining spinach leaves, it is possible to accurately identify the species of spinach. Numerous researchers have focused on the identification of plant leaves, but there is currently no publicly accessible database of spinach species for Indian context. The primary objective of this research is to recognize spinach species using a deep learning approach and to introduce a publicly accessible spinach leaves database.

Many methods have been put forth to automatically distinguish plant leaves. A significant portion of these efforts involved the extraction of leaf features, followed by the training of a model using these features. The feature extraction and categorization processes frequently employ shape, color, and textural features. Im et al. used polygon based boundary descriptors to represent the shape of the leaves [2]. Kulkarni et al. [3] proposed a method based on vein, colour, texture, and shape properties combined with Zernike moments. Prasvita and Herdiyeni achieved a classification accuracy of 90% by using shape features in association with neural network classifier [4]. Ekshinge and Andore used elliptic Fourier analysis and shape features to reach 85% accuracy [5]. Neto et al. considered the following geometrical properties of leaf for plant species identification: length, width, perimeter, area, & diameter [6]. Using SVM classifier, Priya et al. extracted vein structure features, morphological features, and geometric features to classify plants [7].

Zulkifli used a neural network based on regression [8] to classify ten distinct types of plants with leaves of varying shades of green. Anami et al. [9] proposed a classification system for leaves based on histograms of the leaf's edge and colour, and surface area. Bama et al. [10] proposed a method for retrieving leaf images based on texture and colour. Man et al. [11] proposed shading as a key factor for leaf recognition and classified twenty-four plant species with a 92.2% degree of accuracy. [12] Using Gray level co-occurrence matrix texture features, Chaki and Parekh classified plant leaves with an accuracy of 78%. Zhang et al. [13, 14] detected plant species using a two-stage local similarity-based classification learning method.

Recently, deep learning techniques made major advancements in machine learning, particularly in the area of visual object categorization. The most recent studies on plant identification make use of these strategies and significantly outperform approaches developed a decade earlier. Pawar et al. used the deep learning framework to investigate the effects of multiple data-augmentation techniques for the plant classification problem [15]. Pawar et al. compared both the scratch and fine-tuned versions of the GoogleNet and AlexNet architectures with the local feature descriptor and the bag of visual words combined with SVM and MLPs (multi-layer perceptron) [16]. A deep convolutional neural network (CNN)-based architecture (modified LeNet) has been proposed for maize leaf disease classification [17]. Ahila Priyadharshini et al. proposed a six level convolutional neural network for Ayurvedic medicinal plant identification and reported an accuracy of 87.25% [18]. Islam et al. used four different deep learning architectures to classify the five different species of spinach [19].

We need a huge collection of verified leaf images for developing a perfect classification model for the identification of spinach species. A leaf database for Indian spinach species was not publicly accessible until very recently. As a part of the Kaggle Open Data Research, we have collected 25 distinct species of spinach leaves from the southern region of India in order to address this issue. This data is made freely accessible for researchers to carry out their research works and this dataset is accessible through the link https://www.kaggle.com/datasets/ahilaprem/mepco-tropic-leaf. Moreover, identifying the different species of spinach is a tough task because of its interclass similarity. In this study, we compare three different custom made deep architectures for spinach species recognition and also we compare their performance with transfer learning of MobileNetV2.

2   Materials and Methods

2.1   Spinach Leaf Database – Subset of MepcoTropicLeaf

Spinach Species dataset has 25 different spinach species, including shrubs, herbs, vines, trees, & water plants. Each species contains a minimum of fifty images. To make the database robust, the leaf images are captured under varying lighting conditions and orientations using various mobile cameras. For the database to be more comprehensive, it includes single and compound leaves, as well as front and back views of the leaves. Table 1 contains information about the various types of spinach, and Fig. 1 depicts the species.

2.2   Custom Made Deep Architecture

Deep Convolutional Neural Networks (DCNN) are a type of neural network that has excelled in a number of computer vision and image processing competitions. It is widely acknowledged that Convolutional Neural Networks can automatically learn image recognition features. Therefore, CNNs are used to identify the spinach species using leaf images. Figure 2 depicts the custom CNN architectures used in the proposed work. The proposed architectures differ in terms of the depth (number of filters and kernels) of each convolution layer. After each convolutional layer, a pooling layer and batch normalization layer are introduced in all architectures to reduce the dimension of the feature maps and enhance the network's stability. The output layer is a fully connected layer with 25 neurons that represent class labels.

Deep CNN uses multiple phases of feature extraction to automatically learn data representations, which contributes to its robust learning capabilities. Convolution and pooling layers are interspersed with one or more fully connected layers at the conclusion of a typical CNN architecture. Each neuron in the set of convolutional kernels that comprise the convolutional layer serves as a convolutional kernel. Convolution nevertheless becomes a correlation operation if the kernel is symmetric [20]. The method utilised by convolutional kernels involves slicing the image into receptive fields, which are tiny slices. Kernel convolves with the images by multiplying its elements with the corresponding elements of the receptive field to generate feature maps. CNN parameters are more effective than those of fully connected networks due to the fact that convolutional operations can share their weights, allowing for the extraction of multiple sets of image features using kernels with the same set of weights.

Fig. 1. Sample Images of Spinach species

Table 1. Spinach Species Details.

S.No	Spinach Name	Scientific Name	Count
1.	Amaranthus Green	Amaranthus viridis	123
2.	Amaranthus Red		89
3.	Balloon vine	Cardiospermum halicacabum	123
4.	Betel Leaves	Piper betle	127
5.	Black Night Shade	Solanum nigrum	108
6.	Celery	Apium graveolens	82
7.	Chinese Spinach	Amaranthus dubius	60
8.	Coriander Leaves	Coriandrum sativum	120
9.	Curry Leaf	Murraya koenigii	109
10.	Dwarf Copperleaf (Green)	Alternanthera sessilis	88
11.	Dwarf copperleaf (Red)		79
12.	False Amarnath	Digera muricata	101
13.	Fenugreek Leaves	Trigonella foenum-graecum L	80
14.	Giant Pigweed	Trianthema portulacastrum	103
15.	Gongura	Hibiscus sabdariffa	53
16.	Indian pennywort	Indian pennywort	64
17.	Lagos Spinach	Celosia Spicata Flamingo	84
18.	Lamb's Quarters	Chenopodium album	69
19.	Lettuce Tree	Pisonia grandis	64
20.	Malabar Spinach (Green)	Basella alba	106
21.	Mint Leaves	Mentha spicata	125
22.	Mustard	Brassica juncea	80
23.	Palak	Spinacia oleracea	84
24.	Siru Keerai	Amaranthus campestris	68
25.	Water Spinach	Ipomoea aquatica	55
Total number of Images			2244

The network is given non-linearity by using the activation function. A bias term is added to the output of the convolution process before it is sent through a non-linear activation function. We employ the Rectified Linear Unit (ReLU) activation function due to the non-linear nature of the input data. Convolution procedure produces feature maps that can appear in various places throughout the image. As long as a feature's approximate position in relation to other features is kept once it has been retrieved, its precise location becomes less crucial. The pooling or down sampling, a local operation, compiles similar data nearby the receptive field and generates the reaction that prevails in this particular small area [21]. Using a pooling technique permits the extraction of a

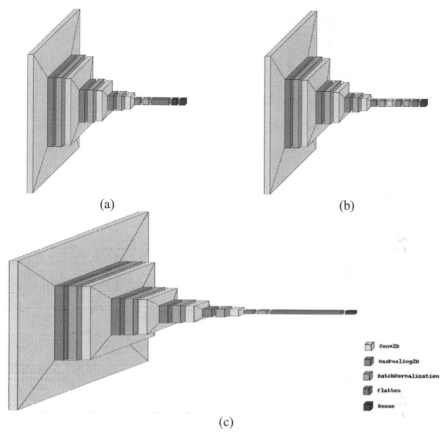

Fig.2. Architecture of the proposed CNN (a) CNN_Arch1 (b) CNN_Arch2 (c) CNN_Arch3

combination of features that are resistant to minor distortions and translational shifts. By reducing the size of the feature map to an invariant feature set, we can control the complexity of the network and also improve the generalization by reducing overfitting. Although there are numerous types of pooling functions, including average, max, min, L2, spatial pyramid pooling, etc...., the most common, max pooling is utilized in this work.

A batch normalizing layer is required to overcome the problems caused by the internal covariance shift in feature maps. The internal covariance shift modifies the distribution values of the hidden units, which slows the convergence by lowering the learning rate. Batch normalization for a transformed feature-map F_i^k is given in Eq. 1.

$$N_i^k = \frac{F_i^k - \mu_B}{\sqrt{\sigma_B^2 - \varepsilon}} \tag{1}$$

where, N_i^k - normalized feature map
   F_i^k - Input feature map.

μ_B - mean of mini batch.

σ_B^2 - Variance of mini batch.

ε - Constant added for numerical stability.

By establishing the feature-map values to have a zero mean and unit variance, batch normalization unifies the distribution of their values. Additionally, it functions as a regulator and smoothens the gradient flow, which enhances the generalization of the network.

The final fully connected layer contains the same number of neurons as the number of classes to be predicted. The categorical cross entropy loss function is used to compute the prediction error in the output layer and is mentioned in Eq. 2.

$$J(\Phi) = -\frac{1}{N} \sum_{\forall X} \sum_j y_j log o_j^k + (1 - y_j)\log(1 - o_j^k) \tag{2}$$

where N denotes the number of classes, y_j and o_j denote the actual and predicted labels respectively. k indicates the corresponding layer. The back propagation algorithm modifies the weight and biases for error and loss reduction after the prediction.

2.3   Transfer Learning Approach

The MobileNetV2 is an inverted residual structure, where the connections between the bottleneck layers are the residual connections. Lightweight depthwise convolutions are used in the intermediate expansion layer as a source of non-linearity to filter features. The architecture of MobileNetV2 includes an initial fully convolution layer with 32 filters as well as 19 additional bottleneck layers [22]. The Google-developed MobileNetV2 model was pre-trained on the ImageNet dataset, which contains 1.4 million images and 1000 classes of web images. To train with our spinach species dataset and categorize the leaf images of spinach species, we use MobileNetV2 as our base model.

3   Experiments and Discussions

Initially the experimentations are done using three various custom made Deep CNN architectures. In all the architectures, the filter size used in all convolutional layers is set to 3×3, the stride to one and padding to zero. For performing maxpool operation, the stride used is 2×2. The dimensions of output feature maps in all convolutional layers for 3 different architectures are given in Table 2. For all the architectures, the activation function used is ReLU, optimizer is Rmsprop, learning rate is 0.001, and the batch size is 16.

As the sizes of the images in the database vary, they are resized to 125×125 pixels for the first two architectures and 224×224 for the third. For experimental purposes, train test ratio of 75:25 is maintained. Table 3 displays the classification accuracy obtained for three architectures at different epochs. The highest accuracies are highlighted in bold. Table 3 demonstrates that CNN Arch3 outperforms CNN Arch1 and CNN Arch2. As the number of filters in CNN Arch3's convolutional layers increases, it acquires stable features. Figure 3 depicts the first nine feature maps obtained at each convolutional layer of CNN Arch3.

Table 2. Dimensions of output feature maps of three different architectures.

Layer	CNN_Arch1	CNN_Arch2	CNN_Arch3
Input	$125 \times 125 \times 3$	$125 \times 125 \times 3$	$224 \times 224 \times 3$
Conv1	$123 \times 123 \times 25$	$123 \times 123 \times 125$	$222 \times 222 \times 64$
Maxpool1	$61 \times 61 \times 25$	$61 \times 61 \times 125$	$111 \times 111 \times 64$
Batch norm 1	$61 \times 61 \times 25$	$61 \times 61 \times 125$	$111 \times 111 \times 64$
Conv2	$59 \times 59 \times 125$	$59 \times 59 \times 125$	$109 \times 109 \times 128$
Maxpool2	$29 \times 29 \times 125$	$29 \times 29 \times 125$	$54 \times 54 \times 128$
Batch norm 2	$29 \times 29 \times 125$	$29 \times 29 \times 125$	$54 \times 54 \times 128$
Conv3	$27 \times 27 \times 125$	$27 \times 27 \times 125$	$52 \times 52 \times 192$
Maxpool3	$13 \times 13 \times 125$	$13 \times 13 \times 125$	$26 \times 26 \times 192$
Batch norm 3	$13 \times 13 \times 125$	$13 \times 13 \times 125$	$26 \times 26 \times 192$
Conv4	$11 \times 11 \times 25$	$11 \times 11 \times 125$	$24 \times 24 \times 128$
Maxpool4	$5 \times 5 \times 25$	$5 \times 5 \times 125$	$12 \times 12 \times 128$
Batch norm 4	$5 \times 5 \times 25$	$5 \times 5 \times 125$	$12 \times 12 \times 128$
Conv5		$3 \times 3 \times 125$	$10 \times 10 \times 64$
Maxpool5		$1 \times 1 \times 125$	$10 \times 10 \times 64$
Batch norm 5		$1 \times 1 \times 125$	$10 \times 10 \times 64$
FC1	650		
# Learnable parameters	279,850	570,900	633,305

Table 3. Classification accuracy of three different architectures.

Epochs	Accuracy (%)		
	CNN_Arch1	CNN_Arch2	CNN_Arch3
50	68.13	68.13	65.85
100	68.55	72.36	67.96
150	69.37	69.19	71.83
200	66.73	70.07	75.70
250	61.62	71.83	75.53
300	60.92	**74.12**	76.41
350	68.13	71.30	76.05
400	67.25	72.71	**76.94**
450	68.13	63.38	**76.94**
500	**70.07**	73.94	76.06

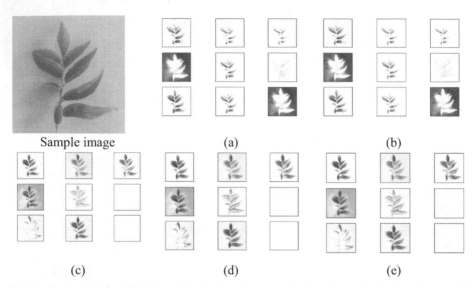

Fig. 3. Feature maps of CNN_Arch3 (a) Conv Layer 1 (b) Conv Layer 2 (c) Conv Layer 3(c) Conv Layer 4(c) Conv Layer 5

To improve the accuracy, the experiment is further carried out using transfer learning approach by considering MobileNetV2 pretrained model. We freeze the weights of all the layers except the final output layer. The number of neurons in the output layer is kept as 25 and experimentation is performed using Rmsprop and Adam optimizer. The classification accuracy of transfer learning approach is tabulated in Table 4. From Table 4, it is inferred that Rmsprop optimizer performs well compared to Adam for this transfer learning approach. The confusion matrix and the performance measures for individual species using Rmsprop optimizer for transfer learning approach is depicted in Fig. 4 and Table 5 respectively. Sirukeerai and Amaranthus Green are getting confused False Amarnath due to their structural similarity. Similarly, Amaranthus Red and Palak are getting confused with Amaranthus Green and Lamb's Quarter.

Table 4. Classification accuracy of transfer learning approach.

Epochs	Accuracy (%)	
	Adam	**Rmsprop**
5	89.61	87.32
10	91.72	91.02
15	92.25	92.08
20	**92.42**	**92.96**
25	92.07	**92.96**

									Predicted Class																
		1	2	3	4	5	6	7	8	9	10	11	12	13	14	15	16	17	18	19	20	21	22	23	24	25
	1	24	0	0	1	1	0	0	0	0	1	0	2	0	0	0	0	0	0	0	1	0	0	0	1	0
	2	2	19	1	1	0	0	0	0	0	0	0	0	0	0	0	0	0	0	0	0	0	0	0	0	0
	3	0	0	30	0	0	0	0	1	0	0	0	0	0	0	0	0	0	0	0	0	0	0	0	0	0
	4	1	0	0	27	0	0	0	0	0	0	0	2	0	0	0	0	0	0	1	0	0	0	0	0	0
	5	1	1	0	0	22	0	0	0	0	0	0	1	0	0	0	0	0	0	0	2	0	0	0	0	0
	6	0	0	0	0	0	21	0	0	0	0	0	0	0	0	0	0	0	0	0	0	0	0	0	0	0
	7	0	0	0	0	0	0	14	0	0	0	0	0	0	0	0	0	0	0	0	0	0	0	0	1	0
	8	0	0	0	0	0	0	0	30	0	0	0	0	0	0	0	0	0	0	0	0	0	0	0	0	0
	9	1	0	0	0	0	0	0	0	27	0	0	0	0	0	0	0	0	0	0	0	0	0	0	0	0
Actual Class	10	0	0	0	0	0	0	0	0	0	22	0	0	0	0	0	0	0	0	0	0	0	0	0	0	0
	11	0	0	0	1	0	0	0	0	0	0	18	0	1	0	0	0	0	0	0	0	0	0	0	0	0
	12	0	1	0	0	0	0	0	0	0	0	0	25	0	0	0	0	0	0	0	0	0	0	0	0	0
	13	0	0	0	0	0	0	0	0	0	0	0	0	20	0	0	0	0	0	0	0	0	0	0	0	0
	14	0	0	0	0	0	0	0	0	0	0	0	0	0	26	0	0	0	0	0	0	0	0	0	0	0
	15	1	0	0	0	0	0	0	1	0	0	0	0	0	0	12	0	0	0	0	1	0	0	0	0	0
	16	0	0	0	0	0	0	1	0	0	0	0	0	0	0	0	15	0	0	0	0	0	0	0	0	0
	17	0	0	0	0	0	0	0	0	0	0	0	0	9	1	0	0	20	0	0	0	0	0	0	0	0
	18	0	0	0	0	0	0	0	0	0	0	0	0	0	0	0	0	0	17	0	0	0	0	0	0	0
	19	0	0	0	0	0	0	0	0	0	0	0	0	0	0	0	0	0	0	16	0	0	0	0	0	0
	20	0	0	0	0	0	0	0	0	0	0	0	0	0	0	0	0	0	0	0	27	0	0	0	0	0
	21	0	0	0	0	0	0	0	0	0	0	0	0	0	0	0	0	0	0	0	0	32	0	0	0	0
	22	0	0	0	0	0	0	0	0	0	0	0	0	0	0	0	0	0	0	0	0	1	19	0	0	0
	23	0	0	0	0	1	0	0	0	0	0	0	1	0	0	0	1	2	0	1	0	0	15	0	0	
	24	0	0	0	0	1	0	0	0	0	0	2	0	0	1	0	0	0	0	0	0	0	0	13	0	
	25	0	0	0	0	0	0	0	0	0	0	0	0	0	0	0	0	0	0	0	0	0	0	0	0	14

Fig. 4. Confusion Matrix of transfer learning approach

Transfer learning is a remarkably effective method, despite its apparent simplicity. With very little data and resources, engineers will be able to complete deep learning works. Using a good pre-trained model will hasten the training process and aid to provide more accurate results. Negative transfer occurs when the new model's performance or accuracy declines as a result of the transfer learning. The initial and goal issues of both models must be sufficiently comparable for transfer learning to be effective. Since the plant images are available in Imagenet database, this transfer learning approach produces good recognition accuracy for our problem.

Table 5. Performance measures of transfer learning approach.

Spinach	Precision	Recall	F1-score
Amaranthus Green	0.79	0.87	0.83
Amaranthus Red	0.9	0.83	0.86
Balloon vine	0.97	1	0.98
Betel Leaves	0.97	0.88	0.92
Black Night Shade	0.92	0.81	0.86
Celery	1	1	1
Chinese Spinach	0.93	0.93	0.93
Coriander Leaves	0.97	1	0.98

(*continued*)

Table 5. (*continued*)

Spinach	Precision	Recall	F1-score
Curry Leaf	0.96	0.93	0.95
Dwarf Copperleaf (Green)	0.96	1	0.98
Dwarf copperleaf (Red)	0.91	1	0.95
False Amarnath	0.88	0.85	0.86
Fenugreek Leaves	0.87	1	0.93
Giant Pigweed	0.96	1	0.98
Gongura	1	0.86	0.92
Indian pennywort	1	0.94	0.97
Lagos Spinach	0.95	0.95	0.95
Lamb's Quarters	0.85	0.94	0.89
Lettuce Tree	1	1	1
Malabar Spinach (Green)	0.9	1	0.95
Mint Leaves	0.97	1	0.98
Mustard	1	0.95	0.97
Palak	0.88	0.71	0.79
Siru Keerai	0.81	0.76	0.79
Water Spinach	0.93	1	0.97

4   Conclusion

In this study, we created a database of specific, standardized Indian spinach leaves for the identification of different spinach varieties. In addition, we evaluated the performance of three distinct Deep CNN architectures for identifying distinct spinach species. Deep CNN, CNN architecture with additional convolutional layers and filters within the layers, outperforms shallow CNN. Using a trained MobileNetv2 model, the potential efficiency of transfer approaches is also investigated. We have discussed our preliminary findings regarding the identification of spinach species; however, the problem tends to be quite difficult and could benefit from further research.

Acknowledgement. This study is done as a part of Kaggle's Open Data Research Grant 2020.

References

1. Singh, A., et al.: Indian spinach: an underutilized perennial leafy vegetable for nutritional security in developing world. Energy Ecol. Environ. **3**(3), 195–205 (2018). https://doi.org/10.1007/s40974-018-0091-1

2. Im, C., Nishida, H., Kunii, T. L : A hierarchical method of recognizing plant species by leaf shapes, In: Proc. IAPR Workshop Mach. Vis. Appl., pp. 158–161 (1998)
3. Kulkarni, A.H., Rai, H.M., Jahagirdar, K.A., Upparamani, P.S.: 'A leaf recognition technique for plant classification using RBPNN and Zernike moments'. Int. J. Adv. Res. Comput. Commun. Eng. 2(1), 984–988 (2013)
4. Prasvita, D.S., Herdiyeni, Y.: MedLeaf: mobile application for medicinal plant identification based on leaf image, Int. J. Adv. Sci., Eng. Inf. Technol., 3(2), pp. 5–8, (2013)
5. Ekshinge, S., Sambhaji, I., Andore, M.D.: 'Leaf recognition algorithm using neural network based image processing'. Asian J. Eng. Technol. Innov. 2(2), 10–16 (2014)
6. Neto, J.C., Meyer, G.E., Jones, D.D., Samal, A.K.: Plant species identification using Elliptic Fourier leaf shape analysis. Comput. Electron. Agricult. 50(2), 121–134 (2006)
7. Priya, C.A., Balasaravanan, T., Thanamani, A.S.: An efficient leaf recognition algorithm for plant classification using support vector machine In: Proc. Int. Conf. Pattern Recogn. Inform. Med. Eng. (PRIME), pp. 428–432(2012)
8. Zulkifli, Z.: Plant leaf identification using moment invariants & general regression neural network, M.S. thesis, Univ. Teknologi Malaysia, Johor Bahru, Malaysia (2009)
9. Anami, B.S., Nandyal, S.S., Govardhan, A.: A combined color, texture and edge features based approach for identification and classification of Indian medicinal plants. Int. J. Comput. Appl. 6(12), 45–51 (2010)
10. Bama, B.S., Valli, S.M., Raju, S., Kumar, V.A.: Content based leaf image retrieval (CBLIR) using shape, color and texture features. Indian J. Comput. Sci. Eng. 2(2), 202–211 (2011)
11. Man, Q.-K., Zheng, C.-H., Wang, X.-F., Lin, F.-Y.: Recognition of plant leaves using support vector machine, In: Proc. Int. Conf. Intell. Comput., pp. 192–199 (2008)
12. Chaki, J., Parekh, R.: Plant leaf recognition using shape based features and neural network classifiers. Int. J. Adv. Comput. Sci. Appl. 2(10), 41–47 (2011)
13. Zhang, H., Yanne, P., Liang, S.: Plant species classification using leaf shape and texture. Amer. J. Eng. Technol. Res., vol. 11(9), pp. 2025–2028 (2011)
14. Zhang, S., Wang, H., Huang, W.: Two-stage plant species recognition by local mean clustering and weighted sparse representation classification. Cluster Comput. 20(2), 1517–1525 (2017)
15. Pawara, P., Okafor, E., Schomaker, L., Wiering, M.: Data Augmentation for Plant Classification. In: Blanc-Talon, J., Penne, R., Philips, W., Popescu, D., Scheunders, P. (eds.) ACIVS 2017. LNCS, vol. 10617, pp. 615–626. Springer, Cham (2017). https://doi.org/10.1007/978-3-319-70353-4_52
16. Pawara, P., Okafor, E., Surinta, O., Schomaker, L., Wiering, M.: Comparing Local Descriptors and Bags of Visual Words to Deep Convolutional Neural Networksfor Plant Recognition. In: Proceedings of the 6th International Conference on Pattern Recognition Applications and Methods. ICPRAM, pp. 479–486 (2017)
17. Ahila Priyadharshini, R., Arivazhagan, S., Arun, M., Mirnalini, A.: Maize leaf disease classification using deep convolutional neural networks. Neural Comput. Appl. 31(12), 8887–8895 (2019). https://doi.org/10.1007/s00521-019-04228-3
18. Ahila Priyadharshini, R., Arivazhagan, S., Arun, M.: Ayurvedic Medicinal Plants Identification: A Comparative Study on Feature Extraction Methods. In: Singh, S.K., Roy, P., Raman, B., Nagabhushan, P. (eds.) CVIP 2020. CCIS, vol. 1377, pp. 268–280. Springer, Singapore (2021). https://doi.org/10.1007/978-981-16-1092-9_23
19. Islam, M., Ria, N.J., Ani, J.F., Masum, A.K.M., Abujar, S., Hossain, S.A.: Deep Learning Based Classification System for Recognizing Local Spinach. In: Troiano, L., et al. (eds.) Advances in Deep Learning, Artificial Intelligence and Robotics. LNNS, vol. 249, pp. 1–14. Springer, Cham (2022). https://doi.org/10.1007/978-3-030-85365-5_1
20. Goodfellow, I., Bengio, Y., Courville, A.: Deep learning. Nat Methods 13, 35 (2017). https://doi.org/10.1038/nmeth.3707

21. Lee, C-Y, Gallagher, PW, Tu, Z.: Generalizing pooling functions in convolutional neural networks: Mixed, gated, and tree. In: Artificial Intelligence and Statistics, pp 464–472 (2016)
22. Sandler, M., Howard, A., Zhu, M., Zhmoginov, A., Chen, L-C.:MobileNetV2: inverted residuals and linear bottlenecks, EEE Conference on Computer Vision and Pattern Recognition (CVPR), pp. 4510–4520 (2018)

Mobile Captured Glass Board Image Enhancement

Boddapati Mahesh, Ajoy Mondal$^{(\boxtimes)}$, and C.V. Jawahar

Centre for Visual Information Technology, International Institute of Information Technology, Hyderabad, India
boddapati.mahesh@research.iiit.ac.in, {ajoy.mondal,jawahar}@iiit.ac.in

Abstract. Note-taking methods and devices have improved tremendously over the past few decades, and people are finding new ways to write notes and take photos. Automatic extraction, recognition, and retrieval are necessary to process the huge chunk of digitized document data. However, an important step in all of these pipelines is the pre-processing step, mainly image enhancement or clean-up, which enhances the text regions and suppresses the non-text regions. In this article, we look at the problem of image enhancement or clean-up on one such important class of images (i.e., mobile captured glass board images). We present a simple yet efficient algorithm using the concepts of classical image processing techniques to solve the problem, and the obtained results are promising in comparison to the Office Lens.

Keywords: Image enhancement · image binarization · specular highlight removal · glass board document images

1 Introduction

Recent technological advancements in computer engineering have led to the development of several applications which changed the way we take notes. We moved on from storing the text in hard copies to taking notes on an electronic device. It means that a lot of text documents today are being circulated on the Internet, which is either scanned copies of the documents or electronically handwritten document images. For instance, several people take photos of slides, whiteboards, and glass boards containing text during conferences, class, etc., and scan the handwritten or printed papers directly using mobile.

Given the considerable number of these images, automatic recognition, extraction, and retrieval of text information from these images are significant in today's world. A couple of techniques have been proposed for this purpose. The performance of all these techniques heavily relies on pre-processing stage. This stage includes various tasks: (i) reduce noise (ii) remove specular highlights (iii) increase the contrast level between foreground (text) and background regions

© The Author(s), under exclusive license to Springer Nature Switzerland AG 2023
D. Gupta et al. (Eds.): CVIP 2022, CCIS 1777, pp. 229–241, 2023.
https://doi.org/10.1007/978-3-031-31417-9_18

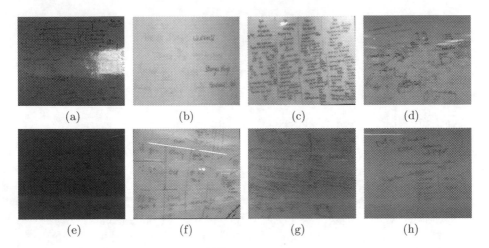

Fig. 1. Shows sample images containing (a) highlight text and background regions, (b) non-uniform color in text, (c) smudged text, (d) multi-color text, (e) different light condition, (f) non-uniform background, (g) non-uniform text density and (h) varying stroke of same character.

(iv) separate text and non-text components, etc. Various techniques have been proposed in the literature to recover textual content (cleaning-up or enhancement) of heavily degraded document images.

Mobile scanned or captured glass board images containing text information make clean-up or enhancement more difficult due to several factors: (i) reflection of the glass board creates highlights on both the background and the handwritten text regions (ii) due to reflection and improper clean-up of the glass board, text are smudged (iii) multi-colored (black, red, blue, green, etc.) handwritten text (iv) non-uniform density of the color in text and stroke of the same character is not constant due to handwriting (v) non-uniform reflection of the glass board creates non-uniform smudged text (vi) non-uniform density of text in the image, and (vii) non-uniform background. Figure 1 highlights the effects of all these factors on mobile captured glass board images.

In this article, we propose a pipeline for cleaning up or enhancing glass board images using classical image processing techniques. The proposed pipeline includes three individual tasks: (i) specular highlight detection and removal from glass board images (ii) segmentation of glass board images into the foreground (text) and background regions, and (iii) color assignment and enhancement of text region.

The first step includes detecting and removing specular highlight regions from the glass board images. A specular highlight is detected using the concept presented in [5]. Then highlight removal is done by proposing a heuristic concept based on local image processing. Therefore, this specular free glass board image is segmented into foreground (text) and background regions, using the adaptive thresholding technique with Gaussian weight. In the final step, the colors of pixels of the specular free glass board image are assigned to the foreground region, and a constant (near to white) color is assigned to the background region of the segmented image. A linear intensity transformation function is considered to enhance the text region. Since the performance analysis of the clean-up task is subjective, we decide to objectively analyze the solution with experts in the loop. The proposed algorithm is tested on 90 mobile captured glass board images, and it provides promising results compared to the existing techniques.

The rest of the article is organized as follows: Sect. 2 describes the related work. The proposed algorithm is explained in detail in Sect. 3. Section 4 presents experimental results and analysis. Finally, the conclusive remark is drawn in Sect. 5.

2   Related Work

Generally, document image enhancement techniques look at the problem as some form of binarization method. The problem of binarization can be solved by global or local processing techniques. The prevalent global thresholding method is Otsu's algorithm [9], which uses a single threshold value that maximizes the inter-class variance and minimizes the intra-class variance. It fails to segment the document images containing illumination variation and non-uniform background (i.e., various local changes in images) due to consideration of global image statistics. In order to address the problems of global thresholding based on document image binarization methods, many pioneering approaches using local image statistics were proposed in the literature [7,8,10,11]. Niblack's [7] method considered local image statistics such as mean and standard deviation within a small image region to determine the local threshold. Under a well-conditioned environment, it obtained highly accurate results. However, its performance is sensitive to local image contrasts. Inspired by Niblack's method, Sauvola modified Niblack's linear decision to the non-linear decision by considering local variance [10]. It provides improved results over Niblack's method when the background contains light texture and non-uniform illuminated documents. In the same direction, Bernsen [8] proposed a modified local adaptive thresholding method based on the mean value of the minimum and maximum intensities of pixels within a small image region. Performance of this method reduces on documents with complex backgrounds. Su et al. [11] improve Bernsen's algorithm by introducing a normalization factor with local contrast terms to handle documents with complex backgrounds. It is called the Local Maxima Minima (LMM) method. The limitation of this technique is that it can not handle document images with bright text on bright background.

Disadvantages of the LMM method are overcome by Gatos's method [3]. Its performance does not require any parameter tuning. It contracts the background by interpolating neighboring background intensities. Therefore, the thresholding technique is applied by integrating the estimated background surface with the original image. It is an advantageous method for the binarization of degraded document images. However, it fails to binarize low-resolution images. Similarly,

Wolf et al. also modified Niblack's method to provide better results on low-contrast images [6,13]. Khurshid *et al.* [4] also modified Niblack's method and maned it as NICK to reduce the black noise in results obtained by Niblack's method. It provides good results for low-contrast images but fails for minimal and low-contrast conditions of thin pen stroke text. In a similar direction, Bataineh *et al.* proposed a robust local thresholding approach based on the mean and standard deviation for each current window and the global image [1]. It can able to produce good results for low-contrast images. It also overcomes the challenges of thin pen stroke text in the image. Feng *et al.* [2] also invented a local thresholding technique by considering local image statistics: minimum and standard deviations of two local windows. It is a modified wolf's method and solves the problem of low performance due to sharp variation in the background. Minor changes in parameter values could drastically affect the binarization results is the limitation of this method. Furthermore, Su *et al.* [12] proposed an adaptive contrast technique for binarization of degraded document images. It solves the problem of high inter/intra variation between the document background and the foreground text of different document images by considering both local image contrast and local image gradient. It is simple and robust, and it requires minimum parameter tuning. The performances of these discussed methods are highly dependent on the window parameters. In order to avoid manually adjusting the window size to the content and take advantage of Sauvola's algorithm, Lazzara and Géraud described a multi-scale binarization approach in [12].

It is proven that local thresholding techniques work well for images having local image variation, whereas global thresholding performs better for images having global variation. Each of these techniques has its advantages. Several techniques have been proposed in literature to segment document images using both concepts. In this direction, Biswas *et al.* applied global thresholding followed by local thresholding to perform binarization of document images in [6]. The authors constructed edge images using a Canny edge detector. The valley of the two peaks of the histogram of the non-edge pixel is chosen as a global threshold. The pixel values exceeding this threshold are turned as background. The remaining pixels are classified as foreground or background depending upon the local threshold using the average of the highest and lowest gray value of the window.

All methods are designed based on global thresholding, local thresholding, and combining both for binarization of degraded (printed, handwritten and historical) document images. Performances of such approaches reduce the processing of camera captures whiteboard images due to various complex factors: illumination variation, shadows, multi-colored handwritten text, etc. In [14,15], Zhang and He proposed a technique to enhance the text regions of the whiteboard images. However, whiteboard images are similar to the established document image enhancement techniques.

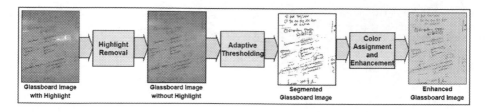

Fig. 2. Present the proposed algorithm for enhancement of camera captured glass board images.

3 The Proposed Algorithm

This section presents the proposed algorithm to enhance the quality of glass board images. Figure 2 displays the block diagram of the proposed algorithm. The input to our algorithm is a rectified glass board image. Office Lens App[1] does image rectification. It is already mentioned that due to the reflection, the glass board images contain a lot of specular highlight regions. Our first job is to remove those specular regions by using a simple yet efficient specular highlight removal technique. After removing those specular regions, adaptive thresholding is applied to segment images into the foreground (text) and the background regions. Then foreground region is assigned with the color of the corresponding region in the specular free image, and the background region is assigned with constant color (i.e., near to white). Finally, a linear transformation is applied to obtain an enhanced cleaned-up glass board image. Each of these steps is elaborated on in the following subsections.

3.1 Highlight Removal

Segmentation of images containing specular highlights is challenging due to its complex nature. Therefore, removing specular highlights from the input glass board image is an essential task before the segmentation of the glass board image. Inspired by the work presented in [5], the specular free (SF) and modified specular free (MSF) images of the input glass board image are estimated using the following equations.

$$SF_c(x, y) = I_c(x, y) - min\{I_1(x, y), I_2(x, y), I_3(x, y)\}. \tag{1}$$

$$MSF_c(x, y) = SF_c(x, y) - \bar{I}_{min}. \tag{2}$$

$I_c(x, y)$ is the value of cth color channel at $(x, y)^{th}$ pixel position of the original glass board image I. $c \in \{1, 2, 3\}$ indicates Red, Green, and Blue channel; and

---

[1] https://play.google.com/store/apps/details?id=com.microsoft.office.officelens&hl=en_IN.

$\bar{I}_{min} = \frac{1}{MXN} \sum_{x=1}^{M} \sum_{y=1}^{N} min\{I_1(x,y), I_2(x,y), I_3(x,y)\}$. The highlight region is detected by thresholding the difference image between the original glass board image I and the modified specular free image MSF. Therefore, the highlight detected image (HDI) is obtained by

$$HDI(x,y) = \begin{cases} 1 \text{ if } D_c(x,y) > TH \ \forall \ c \\ 0 \text{ otherwise,} \end{cases}$$

where $D_c(x,y) = I_c(x,y) - MSF_c(x,y)$. In [5], the authors discussed the selection of the threshold value TH. However, this threshold value (obtained using [5]) is not working for our (glass board image) dataset. Therefore, we manually select the value of TH as 20, which is best suited for our dataset.

After detecting highlight regions in the input image, our goal is to remove those specular (highlight) parts from the image using the concept of local image processing. Color values of a pixel with highlight are replaced by the average color value of all pixels without highlights within a small region in the input image around this particular pixel with highlight. Thus, a highlight-free glass board image ($\bar{I}$) is obtained using the following equation.

$$\bar{I}_c(x,y) = \begin{cases} I_c(x,y) \text{ if } HDI(x,y) = 0 \ \forall \ c \\ I_c^{avg}(x,y) \text{ if } HDI(x,y) = 1 \ \forall \ c, \end{cases}$$

where $I_c^{age}(x,y)$ is average color of $(x,y)^{th}$ position in the input image (I). I_c^{avg} is obtained using

$$I_c^{avg}(x,y) = \frac{\sum_{(i,j) \in w} I_c(i,j)}{l}, \ \forall \ (i, \ j), \ HDI(i,j) = 0, \tag{3}$$

where w is a small region around the center pixel (x,y) and l is many pixels without highlights within this small region. Here, it is noted that the small region w is selected in such a way that it contains at least one highlight-free pixel. The highlight-free image is considered as an input for adaptive thresholding to segment the image into two possible regions: foreground (text) and background.

3.2   Image Segmentation

The next step of the proposed algorithm is to segment specular highlight-free glass board images into two different regions: foreground (text) and background. Various algorithms have been developed to segment images in the literature. However, thresholding-based approaches are quite popular for segmenting camera-based document images due to their simplicity and good performance. In this work, we have explored the adaptive thresholding technique for segmenting specular free glass board images. For this purpose, the specular free color image glass board image ($\bar{I}$) is transformed into a grayscale specular free image using the following equation

$$I_G(x,y) = 0.2989 * \bar{I}_1(x,y) + 0.5870 * \bar{I}_2(x,y)$$
$$+ 0.1140 * \bar{I}_3(x,y). \tag{4}$$

This grayscale specular free glass board image is considered as an input for the thresholding technique. Instead of the global thresholding technique, adaptive thresholding with Gaussian weight is considered to segment images into two regions: foreground (text) and background. For this purpose, each image is divided into many smaller regions. Therefore, pixels of each of these small regions are classified into foreground or background according to the equation

$$I_w(x, y) = \begin{cases} 1 \text{ if } I_w(x, y) > TH_w \\ 0 \text{ otherwise.} \end{cases}$$

Here, I_w is the small image patch, and TH_w is the local threshold value corresponding to this small region w. The threshold value TH_w is calculated as

$$TH_w = \frac{\sum_x \sum_y W(x,y)*I_w(x,y)}{Z}, \tag{5}$$

where $z = \sum_x \sum_y W(x, y)$ and $W(x, y)$ is the weight of a pixel at location (x, y) based on Gaussian distribution. We get different threshold values for different regions of an image. The adaptive thresholding technique provides better segmentation results for the glass board images containing various complex factors.

Furthermore, the results of adaptive thresholding depend on the size of the image patch (i.e., the window). Different windows provide different segmentation results as it contains varying image information. The window also varies from image to image. Therefore, selecting a proper window is crucial for the adaptive thresholding technique. In the subsequent subsection, we will discuss the selection of a proper window for adaptive thresholding.

3.3   Selection of Proper Window

The proper window is selected based on the statistical feature (variance) of the small image region. We first calculate the variance of an initial window. Then, we increase the window size in every step and select the best window for which variance exhibits a maximum local behavior. It can be mathematically expressed as

$$w_{best} = max_i\{V_{w_i}\} \ \forall \ i, \tag{6}$$

where V_{w_i} is the variance of the image patch corresponding to window w_i. The variance of a window will be maximum if it contains both the foreground and background information in a good ratio. It is also noted that we may find multiple windows having equal (maximum) variance in some cases. In such a case, we consider the window as the average of all these windows. It can be mathematically expressed as

$$w_{best} = g\left(int\left[\frac{\sum_{i=1}^{l} w_i}{l}\right]\right), \tag{7}$$

where l is the number of windows having equal (maximum) variance, and g is defined as

$$g(x) = \begin{cases} x+1 \text{ , if } x \text{ is even} \\ x \text{ , if } x \text{ is odd.} \end{cases}$$

Sometimes, it happens that there is no window having a maximum variance. For such a case, we chose the default window as 81×81.

3.4 Color Assignment and Enhancement

In the final step of the proposed algorithm, the colors of the pixels of the specular free glass board image, corresponding to the foreground region of the segmented image, are assigned to pixels in the foreground region of the segmented image. Background regions of the segmented image are assigned with unique (i.e., near to white) color. It is mathematically represented as

$$J_c(x,y) = \begin{cases} I_c(x,y) \text{ , if } I_{seg}(x,y) = 1 \\ 220 \text{ , if } I(x,y) = 0, \ \forall \ c, \end{cases}$$

where I_{seg} is the segmented (binary) image of the specular free glass board image $\bar{I}$. Finally, a linear transformation function is applied to the saturation component of the color assigned (RGB) image (J) to enhance the contrast between the foreground and the background regions. For this purpose, RGB color image J is converted into HSV color image J^{hsv} using standard RGB to HSV conversion. Thus

$$J^{hsv} = F(J) \text{ and } \bar{J}_S^{hsv}(x,y) = T\left[J_S^{hsv}(x,y)\right], \tag{8}$$

where F is the RGB to HSV conversion function, $J_S^{hsv}(x,y)$ is the saturation value of the $(x,y)^{th}$ pixel of the HSV color image (J^{hsv}), $\bar{J}_S^{hsv}(x,y)$ is the enhanced saturation value and T is the enhancement function. Therefore, an enhanced HSV image is obtained using

$$\bar{J}_c^{hsv}(x,y) = \begin{cases} J_c^{hsv}(x,y) \text{ , if } c \in \{H,V\} \\ \bar{J}_S^{hsv}(x,y) \text{ , if } c \in S. \end{cases}$$

Finally, this enhanced HSV image $\bar{J}^{hsv}$ is converted to enhanced RGB image $\bar{J}^{rgb}$ using standard HSV to RGB conversion function. Therefore,

$$\bar{J}^{rgb} = F\left(\bar{J}^{hsv}\right), \tag{9}$$

where $\bar{J}^{hsv}$ is enhanced HSV image, $\bar{J}^{rgb}$ is the enhanced cleaned-up RGB glass-board image and F is standard HSV to RGB conversion function.

4 Experiments

4.1 Datasets

For experimental purposes, a dataset containing 90 glass board images is collected. A few of the sample images are displayed in Fig. 3. We have captured these glass board images by a mobile camera by varying zoom, angle of the camera, and light conditions. These factors increase the complexity of the dataset for the clean-up problem. Each image contains handwritten text with multi-color (black, red, blue, and green) font. The density of the color is not uniform for all text, and the stroke of the same character is not constant due to handwriting. The density of the text is also non-uniform for the images. Due to the reflection of the glass board and improper clean-up of the glass board, the text is smudged. Non-uniform reflection of the glass board creates non-uniform smudged text in the images. Reflection of the glass board also creates highlight regions on both the background and handwritten text regions. All of these factors make the clean-up task more difficult for the glass board images. Each of these images in Fig. 3 illustrates the complexity level of the clean-up task for the mobile captured glass board images.

4.2 Evaluation Measure

Since the performance analysis of the clean-up task is subjective, we decided to analyze the solution with experts in the loop objectively. Since the images are large to display on monitors and for experts to see comfortably, images are split into smaller patches. A total of 582 patches are selected randomly, with all the important parts of the 90 images being covered.

For this purpose, a simple approach for evaluating the performance of the method is proposed by asking questions to the experts. Each expert is asked a simple question, "Compare the outputs obtained by two different algorithms, A and B, for a given input," and the possible answers to this question are: (i) A is better than B (ii) A is arguably better than B (iii) A is similar to B, and (iv) A is less than B. The objective score of the algorithm is calculated as the ratio of the total number of positive votes (images) for each answer over the total number of images. Respective normalization is done to make sure that there is no bias in the expert's evaluation. Mathematically, it can be expressed as

$$S_{h(i)} = \frac{\sum_i g(h(i))}{n}, \tag{10}$$

where $h(i) \in \{r1, r2, r3, r4\}$, $r1 = $ "A is better than B", $r2 = $ "A is arguably better than B", $r3 = $ "A is similar to B", $r4 = $ "A is less than B" and $g(h(i) = r1) = 1$ if $h(i) \in r1$ otherwise 0.

Therefore, success rate of algorithm A and B are obtained using

$$\begin{aligned} S_{rate}^A &= S_{h(r1)} + S_{h(r2)} \\ S_{rate}^B &= S_{h(r4)}. \end{aligned} \tag{11}$$

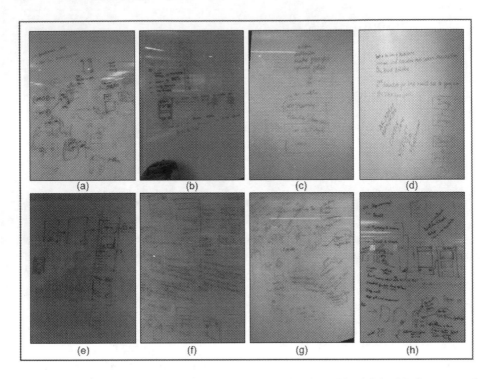

Fig. 3. Show few sample images containing several factors like (a) highlight text and background regions (b) non-uniform color in text (c) smudged text (d) multi color text (e) different light condition (f) non-uniform background (g) non-uniform text density, and (h) varying stroke of same character.

Therefore, gain of algorithm A over B is obtained using

$$G_A = \frac{S^A_{rate}}{S^B_{rate}}. \tag{12}$$

In our experiments, "A" is the proposed algorithm and "B" is any existing algorithm.

Table 1. Objective comparison of the proposed method with the Office Lens with human in the loop.

Name of B	A is better than B	A is arguably better than B	A is similar to B	A is less than B
Office Lens	117/582 = 20%	295/582 = 51%	124/582 = 21%	46/582 = 8%

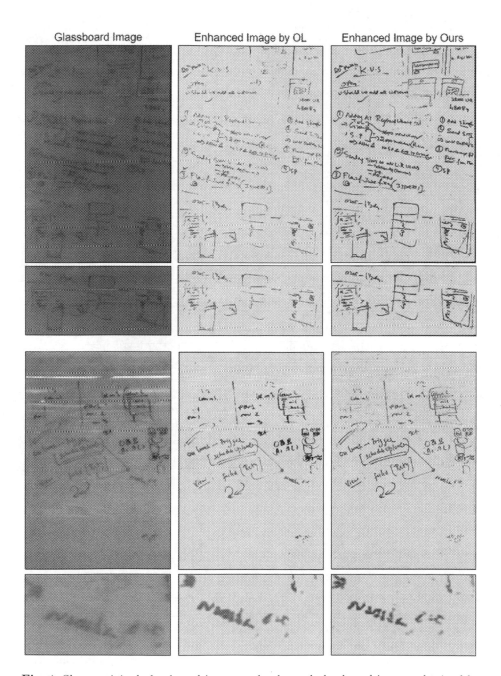

Fig. 4. Shows original glassboard image and enhanced glassboard images obtained by Office Lens (OL) and Ours, respective.

4.3 Quantitative Results Analysis

Cleaned-up glass board images obtained by the proposed algorithm are compared with Office Lens' existing algorithm. The quantitative result obtained using this algorithm is given in Table 1. The table shows that among 582 image patches, the proposed algorithm produced better results for 117 and arguably better results for 295 image patches than Office Lens. In contrast, Office Lens produced better results only for 46 image patches. This numeric value underlined the superiority of the proposed algorithm over Office Lens. Here A is the proposed algorithm. Therefore, a gain of the proposed algorithm over the Office Lens is $412/46 = 8.96$.

4.4 Qualitative Results

Figure 4 shows the qualitative results. In the case of images in the 1st row, the glass board image contains a few white spots due to improper cleaning of the board. We also observe that most text is blurred due to taking pictures far away from the board. It is challenging to recognize the text without cleaning the image. The cleaned image obtained by the Office Lens destroys most of the text. Due to that, it is very difficult to recognize the text. For example, "1", "2", are "3" are written at the lower of the board image. The Office Lens fails to preserve those digits while enhancing the board image. Please see the smaller image below the bigger image for better visualization. While our method enhances the board images by preserving text content. The smaller image below the larger image indicates that our method preserves text while enhancing. The user can easily recognize the text "1", "2", and "3" written within a small region. In the Second example, due to the reflection of the glass board, some background and text parts are highlighted. It creates a significant problem for the enhancement of glass board images. The highlight removal module in our proposed method takes care of this issue. The proposed method obtains better results than the Office Lens.

5 Conclusions

We have presented a simple and efficient algorithm for character enhancement in colored glass board images. The specular highlight removal process heavily influences the system's accuracy before the binarization. A roust specular highlight removal can be used here to boost the performance further. Also, given its failures, the next available solution would be to use deep networks and improve the accuracy of the enhancement. However, the amount of data we currently have is not enough. So, assuming that the deep model would scale up to a small dataset. We should also be able to come up with new metrics to measure the algorithm's effectiveness, thereby reducing human intervention in the system.

References

1. Bataineh, B., Abdullah, S.N.H.S., Omar, K.: An adaptive local binarization method for document images based on a novel thresholding method and dynamic windows. Pattern Recogn. Lett. **32**(14), 1805–1813 (2011)
2. Feng, M.L., Tan, Y.P.: Contrast adaptive binarization of low quality document images. IEICE Electron. Express **1**(16), 501–506 (2004)
3. Gatos, B., Pratikakis, I., Perantonis, S.J.: Adaptive degraded document image binarization. Pattern Recogn. **39**(3), 317–327 (2006)
4. Khurshid, K., Siddiqi, I., Faure, C., Vincent, N.: Comparison of niblack inspired binarization methods for ancient documents. In: Document Recognition and Retrieval XVI. 7247, pp. 267–275 (2009)
5. Koirala, P., Hauta-Kasari, M., Parkkinen, J.: Highlight removal from single image. In: International Conference on Advanced Concepts for Intelligent Vision Systems, pp. 176–187 (2009)
6. Lazzara, G., Géraud, T.: Efficient multiscale sauvola's binarization. Int. J. Doc. Anal. Recogn. (IJDAR) **17**(2), 105–123 (2014)
7. Niblack, W.: An Introduction to Digital Image Processing. Strandberg Publishing Company (1985)
8. Nurhadiyatna, A., Jatmiko, W., Hardjono, B., Wibisono, A., Sina, I., Mursanto, P.: Background subtraction using gaussian mixture model enhanced by hole filling algorithm (GMMHF). In: International Conference on Systems, Man, and Cybernetics, pp. 4006–4011 (2013)
9. Otsu, N.: A threshold selection method from gray-level histograms. IEEE Trans. Syst. Man Cybern. **9**(1), 62–66 (1979)
10. Sauvola, J., Seppanen, T., Haapakoski, S., Pietikainen, M.: Adaptive document binarization. In: International Conference on Document Analysis and Recognition (ICDAR). vol. 1, pp. 147–152 (1997)
11. Su, B., Lu, S., Tan, C.L.: Binarization of historical document images using the local maximum and minimum, pp. 159–166 (2010)
12. Su, B., Lu, S., Tan, C.L.: Robust document image binarization technique for degraded document images. IEEE Trans. Image Process. **22**(4), 1408–1417 (2012)
13. Wolf, C., Jolion, J.M.: Extraction and recognition of artificial text in multimedia documents. Formal Pattern Anal. Appl. **6**(4), 309–326 (2004)
14. Zhang, Z., He, L.w.: Note-taking with a camera: whiteboard scanning and image enhancement. In: IEEE International Conference on Acoustics, Speech, and Signal Processing. vol. 3, pp. 111–533 (2004)
15. Zhang, Z., He, L.W.: Whiteboard scanning and image enhancement. Digital Signal Process. **17**(2), 414–432 (2007)

Computing Digital Signature
by Transforming 2D Image to 3D:
A Geometric Perspective

Ananda Upadhaya[✉] and Arindam Karmakar

Department of Computer Science and Engineering, Tezpur University,
Tezpur, Assam, India
anandaupadhaya@gmail.com, arindam@tezu.ernet.in

Abstract. Recently 2D to 3D face reconstruction has attracted a lot of interest in the area of Computer vision. There has been a recent increase in research into various 3D reconstruction techniques using neural nets, with the majority of approaches producing high-quality results and efficiency. This paper presents an approach to convert 2D facial images to 3D and then use the 3D data and features to construct a unique digital signature. The proposed solution eliminates the need for several pictures and reduces the calculation load. The main objective of this research is to understand the progress that has already been made in this domain and we came up with an open question of whether the generation of a face mesh is possible using a Feature Vector. This would reduce the storage space required for the 3D Facial data. If Face mesh reconstruction is possible using the feature vector only, it would drastically reduce time and space for various 2D and 3D image analysis applications. The feature vector would later be compressed to create a unique digital signature. Accessing any information on the database with a key will be efficient and fast.

Keywords: 3D face Mesh · Digital signature · SIFT · MVGD · backtracking

1 Introduction

Due to the limiting applications of 2D photos, 3D Face reconstruction has received a lot of interest recently in the field of computer vision [1–5]. Numerous image processing professionals are interested in 3D image study since it has attracted major contributions from a number of industries, including security, robotics, and the medical field. When compared to 2D photographs, 3D images give us greater flexibility [6]. Since face matching in 3D is so accurate and effective, face recognition is the most challenging application for 3D reconstruction. Recent studies have revealed encouraging quality and efficiency results for deep learning-based 3D face reconstruction methods [2,4,8,9].

Deep neural networks need a lot of data to train, but it's difficult to find ground-truth 3D face forms [8,9]. It's crucial to bear the following in mind

D. Gupta et al. (Eds.): CVIP 2022, CCIS 1777, pp. 242–252, 2023.
https://doi.org/10.1007/978-3-031-31417-9_19

while employing a deep learning approach: Use a robust, hybrid loss function for weakly supervised learning that integrates both low-level and perception-level information for supervision, and perform multiple-image face reconstruction by combining complementary information from many pictures for shape aggregation [8]. Rapidity, accuracy, and tolerance for occlusion and large postures are required in the technique [9]. Blanz and Vetter proposed and handled numerous secondary problems, and the solutions were regarded as ground-breaking [1]. In recent years, 3DMM have been developed in the context of deep learning and are currently used in several cutting-edge face analysis applications. A beginning point for new researchers, a reference manual for the 3DMM community, and intriguing open research issues are all objectives of this study [8,9].

1.1   Why 3D Reconstruction and Digital Signature?

By carefully reconstructing a 3D mesh from 2D facial photos, 3D face reconstruction we seek to end the gap between the 2D and 3D modalities. As a result, there is less need for time and money-consuming 3D imaging technologies, and 2D facial data may be used in instances where it is already accessible [1]. Learning how to recreate 3D facial data from front and side-on facial photos and creating Digital Signature was the study's main objective. These two inputs were chosen since the bulk of law enforcement and investigation agencies have databases with similar combinations of facial photographs. We wanted to produce 3D faces with higher accuracy by enhancing a previous traditional single-image approach and utilising synthetic data.

In an effort to determine the geometrical layout of a scene captured by a sequence of images, multi-view 3D reconstruction is used [8]. The camera's internal properties and position are typically thought to be known or can be roughly inferred from a collection of images. A pixel-wise correspondence problem involving numerous pictures can be resolved in order to (partially) obtain 3D information. It is crucial to have additional knowledge (previous knowledge) about the object because automatic correspondence estimates are typically imprecise and incomplete [1]. The 3D Mesh's geometrical layout may later be utilised to either identify the person or save the data in a database. A mesh or digital signature would be an effective approach to store information because 3D information has a tendency to increase storage size, which could be wasteful from a space and cost perspective.

1.2   Motivation and Applications

Researching 3D reconstruction has always been difficult. By using 3D reconstruction, it is possible to determine the 3D profile of any object as well as the 3D coordinates of any point on the profile [9]. A fundamental technique in many different industries, such as computer graphics, computer animation, computer vision, medical imaging, computational science, virtual reality, digital media, and others, the 3D reconstruction of objects is a general scientific problem. For instance, the ability to display patient lesion information in 3D on a computer allows for a novel and precise method of diagnosis, which has significant clinical benefit. Digital elevation models can be rebuilt using synthetic aperture radar or airborne laser altimetry [6]. Along with facial recognition and animation, these are some of the use cases.

The production of digital signatures is a relatively recent development in the field of digital security. It stops the creation of extra accounts or ones used fraudulently [6]. By keeping a person's visual identification as a compressed textual signature rather than the more conventional approach of storing an image file, which takes up less space and is more effective in terms of searching, retrieving, and editing, it also lowers database storage overhead.

1.3   Related Work

Existing 3D dense face alignment algorithms are focused on precision, which limits their practical applications [8,9]. Although current monocular 3D face reconstruction methods can restore fine geometric details, they have several drawbacks [8]. Some methods produce faces that cannot be properly animated because they do not mimic how wrinkles change with expression [6]. Other methods rely on high-resolution facial scans and do not translate well to real-world photographs [6].

In face recognition from photos, the gray-level or colour values provided to the recognition system are dependent not only on the person's identity, but also on factors such as head posture and illumination [6]. The most significant issue for face identification is variation in position and illumination, which can cause differences greater than the differences between different people's photos [9] (Fig. 3).

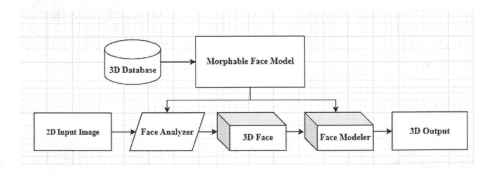

Fig. 1. Volker Blanz and Thomas Vetter in the year 1999 introduced the concept of 3D Morphable Models.

The goal of recognition algorithms is to separate a face's intrinsic form and color (texture) from the random conditions of image production. In contrast to pixel noise, these conditions can be defined consistently across the entire image

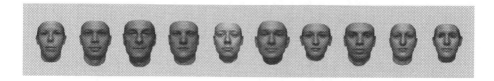

Fig. 2. The BFM Database of 3D Face Scans

by a few extrinsic characteristics such as camera and scene geometry, illumination direction, and intensity (Fig. 2).

Face recognition techniques are classified into two types: One approach is to treat these variables as independent variables and model their functional purpose explicitly. The other method does not distinguish between intrinsic and extrinsic factors and only statistically captures the fact that extrinsic parameters are not diagnostic for faces [10]. In recent years, information security has advanced rapidly, with the rise of social media playing an important role. Individual safety is prioritised in order to standardise this discipline. According to projections, there will be more than 3.6 billion social media users globally by 2025. Unfortunately, anonymous identification has become a major concern for security advisers. Because of technological advancements, phishers can now gain access to confidential information. Numerous solutions, such as biometric identity, facial and audio recognition, and other types of authentication before accessing any highly secured forum on the internet, have been proposed to address these issues (Fig. 3).

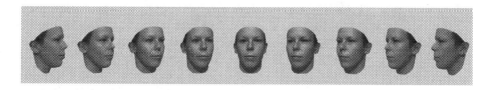

Fig. 3. Pose variations in the BFM Database

Initially, Blanz and Vetter [1999] [1,3] proposed developing separate, independent models for shape and texture. Surprisingly, the Active Appearance Model [Cootes et al. 1998] [4] was first proposed in 2D with a combined shape and appearance model. The benefit of a joint model like this is that correlations between shape and texture can be learned and used as a constraint during fitting with fewer parameters. Separate models, on the other hand, are more flexible, and because shape and texture parameters can be adjusted independently, sequential algorithms can fit the two models independently. However, 3DMMs that model both shape and texture have since been considered. Schumacher and Blanz [2015] [5] investigate shape/texture correlations as well as correlations between face parts using canonical correlation analysis. Egger et al. [2016a] [6]

employ copula component analysis, which can handle data at various scales of shape and texture. Zhou et al. [2019] [7] propose a deep convolutional coloured mesh auto-encoder that learns a nonlinear shape and texture model jointly.

H.M. Rehan Afzal et al. [2] basically had three primary steps. Extraction of features from the 2D image, Calculation of Depth in the 2D Image to fit the image into the model and 3D Mesh production. In their research work done, Facial feature computation and SIFT feature calculation are two types of feature extraction techniques. Multivariate Gaussian Distribution and Shape from Shading approaches are used to calculate depth. The last they have used is the Basel Face model to make 3D photos.

1.4   Organization of the Paper

We start with face detection in the input 2D Image, and then a description of the database of 3D face scans i.e. the Basel Face Model which is the morphable model used. We then discuss the features such as SIFT and other Facial features which are extracted from the 2D Facial data. Then MVGD is used to find the depth in the Facial image. Upon completion of this we proceed to supply this data to the Model to construct a 3D Mesh. In the last stage, the features from the 3D mesh such as number of triangles, number of Vertices, the facial landmarks will be used to construct a Digital Signature which will be unique for every individual.

2   Proposed Method

The system uses a single 2D picture as its input, identifies the face there, and then carries out several operations including Face Detection, Landmark Finding, and Building Face Mesh. A 3D reconstructed face is produced by using those Landmarks and other features that are mentioned in the flow Fig. 4, as seen in the figure below.

The five processes in the suggested technique are face detection, feature extraction, depth calculation, 3D picture construction, and computing digital signatures using the extracted features. Facial feature computation and SIFT feature calculation are subcategories of feature extraction. The MVGD and Shape From Shading (SFS) approaches are used to calculate depth. The Basel face model is used in the third phase to generate a 3D mesh from the 2D picture input, which will then be used as an input for a 3-Dimensional object file.

The next step is to use the scale-invariant feature transform (SIFT) to identify distinguishing features [13]. These attributes will make it easier to recreate a 3D form.

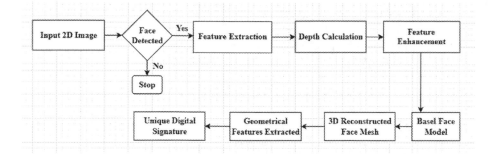

Fig. 4. Flow Chart of the Proposed Method.

The mesh construction uses Delaunay triangulation [11,12], often known as Delone triangulation. There must exist a set of triangles T formed from a discrete set of points P such that none of the triangles in the set contain any other points of P and every point must be a vertex of at least one triangle of T. A circle that passes through the vertices of a triangle is said to be its circumcircle. For a given set of discrete points in a general domain, there exists a triangulation such that no point in the set is inside the boundary of any triangle in that set. Triangulation of point set is not unique. Delaunay triangulation is a kind of triangulation that maximizes the smallest possible angle for each triangle. A group of points along the same line does not form a Delaunay triangle. Since each of the two potential triangulations that divide the quadrilateral into two triangles satisfies the Delaunay condition, which states that all triangles must have empty interior circles circumscribing them. If the given point set is in general position, Delaunay triangulation is unique. Considering the circumscribed spheres, the Delaunay triangulation can be extended to three dimensions and above. Metrics other than Euclidean distance can be generalized under certain circumstances. There is no certainty that Delaunay triangulation exists or is unique in these situations.

Once the 3D Mesh is generated from the 2D Image, then we extract other features such as number of triangles, number of vertices, angle of a triangle between your left eye, right side of the Lip, etc. These details are important to find the uniqueness or type of face an Individual has. For example, a person with a long face will have skinny angled Triangles between the eyes and lips and the person with round face will have equally angles triangles. Only these features are not enough though. The idea is that if we store sufficient data so that a face mesh could be re-generated from the Feature vector only, it would be a very efficient task to do.

The idea that if backtracking were possible, the efficiency in terms of storage, accessing, computing, etc. would reduce to a large extent. It would then be possible to even process facial data in hand held devices.

3   Results and Experiments

This section includes the implementation results of the research work's steps as well as the discussion. The pre-trained BFM Model was used to test the Images. To test the model we used images from multiple sources such as LFW [15], 300W-LP [14]. In the 300W-LP Dataset, there are 300 pictures of people inside and 300 pictures of people outside that were taken in the wild. Diverse identities, emotions, lighting, positions, occlusions, and face sizes are covered. Images were annotated with 68 point markers using a semi-automatic method. The images are between 48 KB and 2 MB in size (Fig. 5).

The first step in this research work was to detect a face in the input 2D image. We were able to detect faces in nearly all of the images. However, in images with multiple faces, any face with insufficient lighting may be missed (Fig. 6). The first step was to detect a face in an image. In the image above, you can see that some noise has been detected as well. To eliminate noise, a threshold value for the bounding box is set. The face detection model was unable to detect one face in one of the images with multiple faces. The cause was poor surface lighting. These factors cause disruption, which may necessitate additional attention. Once the face was detected, the next step was to find Landmarks in the image so that only the mesh of the face could be extracted for feeding into the Basel Face model (Fig. 7).

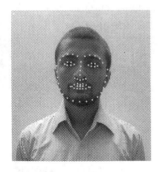

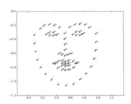

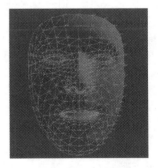

Fig. 5. Landmarks of the Face   **Fig. 6.** Landmarks plotted in 2D   **Fig. 7.** Face Mesh

On the face, various landmarks are located and used to calculate the face mesh later. We were able to detect 68 Landmarks points in the Face as shown in Fig. 5. These Landmarks are also used to draw triangles and find the possible type of faces. For example, a triangle created using leftmost landmark of the eye, center of the lip and the rightmost landmark of the eye would give details such as if the face of the person is long or if the face is more round, etc. using the angles calculated from the triangle drawn between these points (Fig. 8).

Once these Landmarks are plotted in 2D, drawing these triangles becomes easier and the angles can be calculated easily. In one of the research work done by Pradhan et al. [10] they had concluded that the production of the digital signature to individually identify people becomes less difficult when we finish with the smile exclusion and feature recognition steps. After that six separate triangles, each with three data values (perpendicular from top point to opposing vertex and the two opposite angular measures), result in the production of 18 (six triangles, three for each of them) distinct data points for a given face. This was discovered to be particularly unique to every face (Fig. 9).

Fig. 8. Landmarks and other details Extracted

Fig. 9. Face Mesh extracted in 3D

So once the Facial Landmarks points are calculated, the next step is extracting the facial details from the Input image so that these details can be fed into the Basel Face Model. Using the landmark values and other features such as facial features and SIFT features, we calculate the face mesh using a point to point correspondence between the features and the model. In the work done by Yu Deng et al. [9] we had seen that they had used a customizable renderer. For rasterization-based differentiable rendering, we have used the same renderer named Nvdiffrast, a PyTorch package that offers high-performance primitive operations (Fig. 10).

We compute perceptual loss using Arcface, a cutting-edge face recognition model. In the training phase, which involves random picture scaling, rotation, and flipping, data augmentation is used. To stabilise the training process, we additionally increase the training batch size. To expand the variety of training data, we employ a face picture dataset of extra high quality (FFHQ) (Fig. 11).

Computation of Digital Signature: Once the Face Mesh and Facial Landmarks are calculated, the next step is computing digital Signature from the features that were already extracted earlier. We have extracted features such as number of triangles, number of vertices, facial Landmarks data. This research's core hypothesis is that if we could save enough information, a face mesh could be recreated using nothing but a feature vector i.e. with the extracted features only

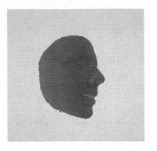

Fig. 10. Left View of the Face Mesh   **Fig. 11.** Right View of the Face Mesh

if reconstruction were possible. The purpose of creating a unique feature vector to store the face mesh information will be so efficient. As we know that to store a 3D image is a very space consuming task. Also a lot of computational power is required to process the 3D images. But Despite the fact that this research is still in its early stages, if enough features are retrieved, it would be able to use those data to create a face mesh (Fig. 12).

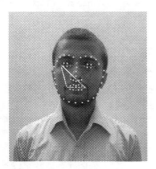

Fig. 12. Triangles calculated from the Landmarks

Fig. 13. Other Features of the Face Mesh

In the Work done by Pradhan et al. [10] we had seen that they had used Facial Landmarks to draw rectangles. Now according to that idea, the area of triangles would give us lots of details about the Facial structure of the Individual. Suppose the person had a long face, this would mean that we would find angles of the triangles created between the eyes and the lips to be skinny. In the same way, we could extract multiple details about the face mesh using these triangles created using the Facial landmarks. We also have extracted other Features such as number of vertices and number of Triangles calculated from the face Mesh (Fig. 13).

The number of Triangles in the face mesh can be kept a constant number as well as variable. The reason we have kept the triangles in the face mesh to be dynamic is because it gives us better results. If the triangles in the face mesh are kept constant then, sometimes in some portion of the face, the mesh generated would be very geometrically shaped in nature which might lead to non-favoured results. At this point we know that the Features extracted would be a feature vector with huge length. So, we will have to shorten/compress the feature vector.

4   Conclusion and Future Work

This paper proposes an automatic end-to-end system that starts with a single image and ends with a 3D image. And the 3D generated Mesh is used to calculate a unique digital signature based on the Geometrical Features. There are three main processes in 3D face rebuilding. Face detection is followed by the extraction of facial features and dense features. The depth of it is then determined by applying a multivariate Gaussian distribution. It is possible to find the high-resolution details that are often required to record the expression details using the shape from shading technique. Later the processed data is aligned with a Basel face model, a 3D face model that is readily accessible. Results indicate that this technique is effective and capable of successfully reconstructing a 3D image. During this research we realised that the preparation of highly 3D scan databases itself is a costlier process. Although there are some freely available Datasets, those datasets are specific to certain region or a community of people. So, datasets with more diversity would be helpful. This would mean merging of 3D scans of people.

The main idea behind this research work is that if we could store sufficient data that a face mesh could be re-generated from the Feature vector only. Although we are at the beginning stage of this research, if enough number of features are extracted it would be possible using those features to generate the Face Mesh.

Acknowledgements. I would like to express my heartfelt appreciation and gratitude to my respected mentor, Dr. Arindam Karmakar, Assistant Professor, Department of Computer Science & Engineering, Tezpur University, Assam, for his unwavering support, patience, motivation, enthusiasm, immense knowledge, and timely support and appropriate suggestions despite his hectic schedule. I would also like to express my heartfelt gratitude to all of my teachers and friends who have directly or indirectly assisted me in completing this project work. Finally, I am grateful to all of my family members, especially my parents, brother, and sister, for their moral support, timely cooperation, and encouragement in carrying out this research work.

References

1. Blanz, V., Vetter, T.: A morphable model for the synthesis of 3D faces, Max-Planck-Institut für biologische Kybernetik, Tübingen, Germany. IEEE Trans. Pattern Anal. Mach. Intell. **25**(9) (1999)
2. Rehan Afzal, H.M., Luo, S., Afzal, M.K., Chaudhary, G., Khari, M., Sathish, A.P.K.: Senior member. In: IEEE 3D Face Reconstruction From Single 2D Image Using Distinctive Features. https://doi.org/10.1109/ACCESS.2020.3028106
3. Blanz, V., Vetter, T.: Face recognition based on fitting a 3D morphable model member, IEEE. IEEE Trans. Pattern Anal. Mach. Intell. **25**(9), 1063–1074 (2003)

4. Cootes, T.F., Edwards, G.J., Taylor, C.J.: Active appearance models. In: Burkhardt, H., Neumann, B. (eds.) ECCV 1998. LNCS, vol. 1407, pp. 484–498. Springer, Heidelberg (1998). https://doi.org/10.1007/BFb0054760
5. Schumacher, M., Piotraschke, M., Blanz, V.: Hallucination of facial details from degraded images using 3D face models. Image Vis. Comput. (2015)
6. Egger, B., et al.: 3D Morphable Face Models-Past, Present, and Future (2019)
7. Zhou, S., Xiao, S.: 3D face recognition: a survey. Hum. Centric Comput. Inf. Sci. 8(1), 1–27 (2018). https://doi.org/10.1186/s13673-018-0157-2
8. Feng, Y., Feng, H., Black, M.J., Bolkart, T.: Learning an animatable detailed 3D face model from in-the-wild images. ACM Trans. Graph. 40 (2021)
9. Deng, Y., Yang, J., Xu, S., Chen, D., Jia, Y., Tong, X.: Accurate 3D face reconstruction with weakly-supervised learning, Beijing Institute of Technology From Single Image to Image Set Microsoft Research Asia Tsinghua University (2019)
10. Galantucci, L.M., Ferrandes, R., Percoco, G.: Digital photogrammetry for facial recognition, 6, 390–396 (2006)
11. Delaunay, B.: Sur la sphère vide. Bulletin de l'Académie des Sciences de l'URSS, Classe des Sciences Mathématiques et Naturelles. 6, 793–800 (1934)
12. Aurenhammer, F., Klein, R., Lee, D-T.: Voronoi diagrams and delaunay triangulations. World Scientific Publishing Company, p. 197 (2013). ISBN 978-981-4447-65-2
13. Chen, S., Zhong, S., Xue, B., Li, X., Zhao, L., Chang, C.-I.: Iterativescale-invariant feature transform for remote sensing image registration, IEEE Trans. Geosci. Remote Sens. 1–22 (2020)
14. Sagonas, C., Tzimiropoulos, G., Zafeiriou, S., Pantic, M.: A semi-automatic methodology for facial landmark annotation (2013)
15. Huang, G.B., Ramesh, M., Berg, T., Erik, L-M.: Labeled faces in the wild: a database for studying face recognition in unconstrained environments. Technical report 07-49, University of Massachusetts, Amherst (2007)

Varietal Classification of Wheat Seeds Using Hyperspectral Imaging Technique and Machine Learning Models

Nitin Tyagi[1]([⊠])(iD), Balasubramanian Raman[1](iD), and Neerja Mittal Garg[2](iD)

[1] Computer Science and Engineering Department, Indian Institute of Technology, Roorkee, India
{nitin_t,bala}@cs.iitr.ac.in
[2] CSIR-Central Scientific Instruments Organisation, Chandigarh, India
neerjamittal@csio.res.in

Abstract. Classification, recognition, and authentication of wheat grain varieties are essential because their high purity results in high yield and quality guarantee. In the present study, sixteen (16) wheat varieties harvested from the Punjab region were chosen for classification. The images of the wheat seeds were captured from both sides using a near-infrared hyperspectral imaging system that covers all the spectral bands from 900–1700 nm wavelength. Two machine learning models, support vector machine (SVM) and linear discriminant analysis (LDA), were implemented to classify wheat varieties. The models were trained separately on raw spectral data and preprocessed spectral data. Three preprocessing techniques pretreated the mean spectra: standard normal variate (SNV), Multiplicative Scatter Correction (MSC), and Savitzky-Golay Smoothing (SG Smoothing) to abolish the interference caused by instrumental and environmental factors. The support vector machine obtained the best result on the raw spectral data with a test accuracy of 93%.

Keywords: Hyperspectral Imaging (HSI) · Preprocessing · Support Vector Machine(SVM) · Linear Discriminant Analysis (LDA)

1 Introduction

Wheat is an essential food source around the world. India is ranked second for wheat production in the world after China, and its production and exportation were about 106.41 million tonnes and 8.2 million tonnes, respectively, in March 2022. Wheat is the most nutritious food, rich in carbohydrates and protein, and ranked first among all the healthy and consumed food. The purity of wheat is a big concern for planters, breeders, and consumers. It is tough to separate the wheat varieties manually through the naked eye. It takes a lot of time and requires more professional knowledge [3]. When some wheat kernels are arranged

Supported by the Ministry of Human Resource Development (MHRD) INDIA with reference grant number: OH-3123200428.

in an array, it is very challenging to distinguish them because of the similarities in their appearance. There are various traditional approaches for identifying seeds, like protein electrophoresis [8], mass spectroscopy, and high-performance liquid chromatography. All these methods are destructive and require expensive instruments.

Nowadays, computer vision technology plays a vital role in identifying varieties of seeds. Fayaz *et al.* [4] used the machine vision technique to classify three rice varieties based on morphological and textural features. Manickavasagan *et al.* [11] used the machine vision technique to classify eight wheat varieties by selecting textural features using a monochrome camera. The machine vision technique alone could not provide adequate results using external appearances like morphological and textural features. The internal characteristics could be considered for the classification of the seeds. Combining imaging and spectroscopic technique could provide the sample data's interior characteristics, compensating for the machine vision technique's flaw. So there is a need to combine both imaging and spectroscopic technique. Hyperspectral imaging (HSI) combines both imaging and spectroscopic technique. It is an emerging non-destructive technique that simultaneously acquires spatial and spectral information of the sample data and stores that complete information in the form hypercube having dimension (width × height× no_of_channels). HSI technique is widely applied for the classification of seeds because of its non-destructive nature [10]. For example, Zheng *et al.* [16] used a hyperspectral imaging technique in combination with a convolutional neural network to classify a single rice seed. The results were compared with the standard machine learning model like support vector machine (SVM) and K-nearest neighbors (KNN). Huang *et al.* [9] differentiated seventeen varieties of maize seeds by hyperspectral imaging integrating with feature transformational method and least square support vector machine. Bao *et al.* [2] classified five wheat varieties using hyperspectral imaging and chemometric methods together. Three machine learning models, SVM, LDA, and extreme learning machine (ELM), were used for the classification. The extreme learning machine got the best accuracy of 91.3.%

The previous study indicates that hyperspectral imaging is a powerful emerging technique for classifying and determining the quality of seeds. In the present research, sixteen(16) wheat varieties were chosen for the classification, and to the best of our knowledge, no one has worked on such a large no of wheat varieties. The main contribution of this paper is: (1) To capture the hyperspectral image of both sides, front side (crease up), and the back side (crease down) of the wheat seed using a HSI system covering a spectral range from 900–1700 nm wavelength (2) To develop machine learning models and evaluate their performance on the raw spectral data and preprocessed spectral data (3) To compare the performance of the machine learning models using performance metrics precision, recall, and F1-score.

The remaining content of the paper is constructed as follows. Discussed the data collection and methods of preparing the dataset in Sect. 2. The proposed methodology has been discussed in Sect. 3. The experiment and results are presented in Sect. 4. The paper concludes in Sect. 5, along with highlighting the directions for future research.

2   Materials and Methods

2.1   Samples Selection and Preparation

For this research activity, 16 wheat varieties were collected from certified wheat growers (University Seed Farm Ladhowal (Ludhiana), Punjab) in India. The name of the varieties are DBW 222, DBW 187, HD_3086, PBW 291, PBW 343, PBW 343 Unnat, PBW 373 , PBW 658, PBW 677, PBW 725, PBW 752, PBW 771, PBW 824, PBW_550_UNNAT, PBW_Zn, PBW 766. Around 1008 seeds were chosen from each variety for capturing the hyperspectral image of sample seeds; therefore, the total number of seeds used in this research activity is 16,128 (16 varieties × 1008 seeds). The seeds were put in a plastic bag to mitigate the effect of the environmental factors and stored in the refrigerator at a temperature 4° celsius. The seeds were kept outside of the refrigerator 24 h before the acquisition of the image.

2.2   Hyperspectral Imaging System

The images of the wheat sample were captured using a line-scan hyperspectral imaging system in the reflectance mode [19]. The system used for capturing images includes a line scan imaging spectrograph, InGaAs (Indium Gallium Arsenide) camera, a linear translation stage, and a stepping motor. The spectrograph (Pika NIR-320, Resonon Inc., Bozeman) has a spectral range of 900–1700 nm, a spectral resolution of 4.9 mm, and contains a total of 168 wavelengths. The distance between the InGaAs camera (Allied Goldeye G-008, PA) and the target was 300 mm. A linear translation stage was handled by a stepping motor at a fixed speed with the help of software (SpectrononPro 2.96 software, Resonon Inc., Bozeman) for capturing images. Before acquiring the images of the wheat data, the scanning speed, frame rate, and camera exposure/integration time were adjusted and had the values of 14.22 mms^{-1}, 41 Hz, and 2.16 ms, respectively. All these values were tuned using a concentric circles image on a white sheet (A4 Size). The system has four halogen bulbs of 35 W, which emit light in the range of 400–2500 nm. The distance between the bulb and the translation stage was 250 mm. In order to maintain the thermal stability inside the chamber and to mitigate any spectrum error that occurred by baseline shift, the halogen bulbs were switched on 45 min before capturing the images. The dark chamber was used to enclose all the components to prevent stray light from coming inside the chamber.

The entire structure was connected by a laptop (Latitude E7470, Dell Inc., Round Rock, TX), having a windows ten(10) operating system and intel vPro processor. The spectrum reflected from the one row of the seeds was received by a two-dimensional photodetector of array 320 × 164 pixels. The hyperspectral image was stored in the form of a hypercube of dimension p × q × λ, where p and q denote spatial coordinates and λ denotes spectral coordinates. The first fourteen (14) and last seven(7) spectral bands show a low signal-to-noise ratio due to the low sensitivity of the InGaAs sensors. Therefore, noisy images were found in those regions. The spectral bands lying in the spectral range 887.46–950.74 nm and 1,694.04–1,725.06 nm were discarded and the spectral bands lying in the spectral range 955.62–1,688.87 nm were taken for the present study. A total of 147 spectral bands were used in the experimentation.

2.3   Hyperspectral Image Acquisition and Correction

For capturing the hyperspectral image, 1008 seeds of each of the 16 varieties were taken, and at a time, 72 seeds were placed manually on a tray of size 200 × 300 mm(Fig 1a). The tray is made of aluminum metal, coated with black non-reflective paint to mitigate the background reflection. For taking the hyperspectral image, the tray was placed on the translational stage. The seeds were scanned from both sides; first, they were scanned from the front side (crease up), and after that, the tray was rotated manually to scan the image of seeds from the back side (crease down). For converting the digital intensities into the reflectance values, the HSI images were corrected using black and white references. The black reference was obtained by blocking the mouth of the lens with a cap, and the white reference was collected using a fluorilon tile having more than 98% reflectance. The images were corrected automatically by the software using the Eq. 1 given below.

$$Img_c = \frac{S_{raw} - S_{dark}}{S_{white} - S_{dark}} \tag{1}$$

where Img_c denotes the corrected hyperspectral image of the data sample, S_{raw} denotes hyperspectral image, S_{dark} denotes dark reference image, S_{white} denotes the white reference image.

3   Proposed Methodology

In the first step, the hyperspectral image was read using the spectral library. A median filter of size 5×5 was applied to remove all the dead or insensitive pixels from the image produced by sensor defects inside the NIR camera. The median filter replaces the reflectance values of all the insensitive pixels with the median values of all the neighboring pixels.The thresholding technique is widely used for the segmentation of the images [17]. In the second step, the region of interest (ROI) was segregated using the thresholding technique. The spectral band at wavelength 1127.65 nm was selected visually based on the best contrast between the seed sample and tray. From the selected band, a binary mask was generated by applying the threshold value 0.19 to all the reflectance values. The pixels having a reflectance value of more than 0.19 were replaced by 1 (white pixel) otherwise by 0 (black pixel). The reflectance threshold value was selected after performing a series of preliminary test in such a way that it retains the seed pixel value and remove the background effect of the tray used for holding the sample data. In the next step, the generated binary mask was multiplied by all the 147 spectral bands to obtain the region of interest. For obtaining the spectral data from the image, two approaches are mostly used, i.e., pixel-wise and mean spectrum [5]. The pixel-wise approach provides more detailed information about the image and is generally used to quantify the chemical composition inside the sample data. This approach is not suitable for the classification process because it leads to misclassification due to the differences in the size of the seeds [18]. The mean spectrum of all the pixels present in the region of interest was computed to find the spectral data from the ROI. The mean spectrum of raw data was passed as an input to the machine learning models, and the results were calculated. The hyperspectral image might have random noise and scattering effects, which would influence the classification process [20]. Therefore the images were preprocessed by three techniques like SNV, MSC, and SG smoothing. The preprocessed mean spectrum was passed as input into the machine learning model, and the results were calculated. The results obtained from raw spectral data and preprocessed spectral data were compared.

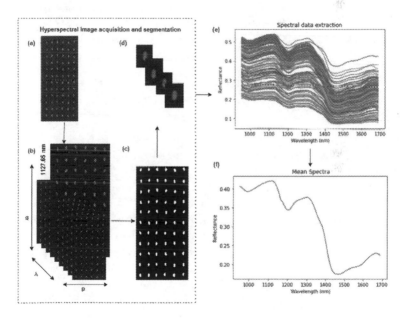

Fig. 1. Description of spectral data extraction (a) Wheat sample data in a matrix of 12 rows×6 columns (b) Image of hypercube after applying median filter (5×5) and selection of image band of wavelength 1127.65 nm for generating binary mask(c) Binary image after applying thresholding technique (used threshold value 0.19) on the selected image band of wavelength 1127.65 nm (d) Extraction of the region of interest after applying binary mask to all spectral bands (e) Image showing pixel-wise spectra (f) Image showing mean spectra of seed

3.1   Machine Learning Models

The present study used two machine learning models, support vector machine and linear discriminant analysis. SVM is a nonlinear modeling method that uses a multidimensional hyperplane or a set of hyperplanes to separate classes [14]. A kernel function is used for those classes which cannot be linearly separated. The kernel function transforms the original data to higher dimensional space. The radial basis function is generally used for handling nonlinear data efficiently. In the present study, the radial basis kernel function is used. The hyperparameters, C and γ, denote the penalty parameter, and the kernel function parameter, respectively, was adjusted using the grid search method and five-fold cross-validation technique.

Linear Discriminant Analysis (LDA) is a supervised algorithm used as a discrimination model for classification purposes [1]. The basic approach behind the LDA algorithm is to make the points within the classes as close as possible and among the classes as far as possible. LDA makes a reference index, which is obtained by dividing the value of the covariance matrix between different matrices and the covariance value within the classes bigger to reach our needs.

4   Experiment and Results

4.1   Software Tools

For the experimentation, python 3 programming language with a jupyter notebook was used. The hyperspectral image was saved using the ".bil" extension and read by the "spectral" library. Image processing operations like thresholding, labeling, separating background parts, and removing dead pixels from the image were implemented using "Scikit-image" and "OpenCV" libraries. For extracting the spectral information, the "Numpy" library was used. For implementing the machine learning model (SVM and LDA), the Scikit-learn package was used. For preprocessing the hyperspectral image, python codes were implemented using scikit-learn, Scipy, and Numpy packages. The experimental work was done on a Windows workstation (64-bit windows 10) with Intel(R) Core(TM) i7- 10750H CPU @ 2.60GHz, 16 GB of RAM, and NVIDIA Geforce RTX 2070 graphics card.

4.2   Performance Evaluation Matrix

The classifier's effectiveness is measured using a confusion matrix that gives precise and wrong predictions based on known truth values. It includes the following terms likes true positive (TP): which means the model figure out the true value and, in reality, the actual value is true; true negative (TN): means the model figure out the false value and, in reality, the actual value is false, false positive (FP): means model figure out the true value and in reality actual value is false, False negative (FN): means model figure out the false value and the actual value is true [6].

Accuracy: it signifies how often a classification model can predict the correct value for the given input value. It is calculated using the Eq. 2.

$$accuracy = \frac{TP + TN}{TP + TN + FP + FN} \tag{2}$$

Precision: it is the ratio between the true positives over true and false positives. It is calculated using the Eq. 3.

$$precision = \frac{TP}{TP + FP} \tag{3}$$

Recall: it signifies how often a classification model can predict false negatives. It is calculated using the Eq. 4.

$$recall = \frac{TP + TN}{TP + FN} \tag{4}$$

F1-Score: it combines both precision and recall evaluation parameter and calculated by harmonic mean of both the parameters using the equation Eq. 5.

$$F1 - score = 2 \times \frac{precision \times recall}{precision + recall} \tag{5}$$

4.3   Analysis of Spectral Bands

The pixel wise spectra of a wheat seed is shown in Fig 2. It is clear from the figure that there is a noise at the beginning and end of the spectral curves. The noise is observed due to the instability of the instrument and various other factors. Therefore the spectral bands from 955.62–1688.87 nm (a total of 147 bands) are taken for the present study, and the rest of the bands have been discarded.

The mean spectra and corresponding standard deviation of all the 16 wheat varieties are shown in Fig 3. It is seen from the figure that the pattern of all the spectral curves is similar for all the varieties, but some discrepancies in the reflectance of all the varieties are also observed. These discrepancies are observed due to the differences in the internal physiological and biochemical constituents. In Fig 3, three absorption peaks were seen at wavelengths 980 nm, 1200 nm nm, and 1450 nm nm. The NIR spectra give the chemical information of the constituents such as protein, starch, and moisture present inside the organic compound [13]. The small absorption peak at wavelength 980 nm was seen due to the second overtone of the O-H bond present in moisture and carbohydrate. The second wide absorption peak was seen at a wavelength of 1200 nm nm. This is due to the second overtone of the C-H bond present in the carbohydrate or starch. The third wide absorption peak was seen at wavelength 1450 nm nm. This is obtained due to the combined effect of the first overtone of the N-H bond present in protein and the O-H bond present in moisture [7].

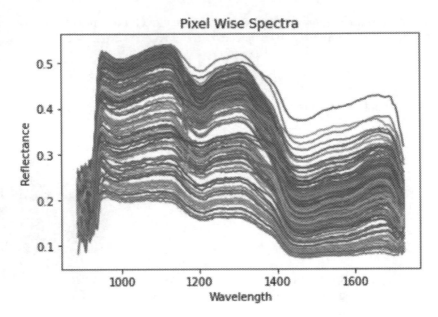

Fig. 2. Pixel wise spectra of wheat seed sample

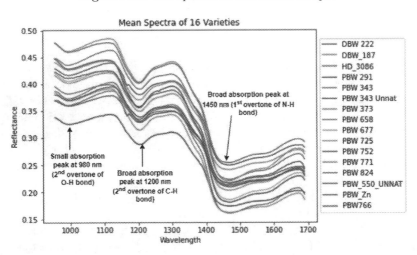

Fig. 3. Mean spectra of 16 wheat varieties

4.4 Development of Classification Model

In the present study, the mean spectra of 16,128 (16 varieties × 1008 seeds)seeds were extracted for the classification. The mean spectra were computed from both sides of the seed. The dataset contains around 32,256 mean spectra (16 varieties × 1008 seeds × 2 sides). For evaluating the machine learning model, the dataset was divided into 80% training set and a 20% testing set. The classes of all the sixteen wheat varieties were assigned numbers as 0,1,2,...15. The SVM and LDA classifiers were used for the classification of wheat seeds. The hyperparameters of the support vector machine (C and γ) were tuned using a grid search algorithm and a five-fold cross-validation technique. The kernel function is used for those classes which can not be classified linearly. In this study, the Radial basis kernel function is chosen for the experimentation.

The machine learning models were trained separately by using both raw spectral data and preprocessed spectral data. The pretreatment of the hyperspectral images was done by three preprocessing techniques, SNV, MSC, and SG Smoothing [15]. These techniques were chosen by trial and error strategy. The models were trained with the same training set, and performance was determined with the same testing set. The performance of the models was evaluated based on performance metrics precision, recall, and F1-score. Table no 1 and 5 show the results of 16 wheat varieties using a support vector machine and linear discriminant analysis model on raw spectral data. Table no; 2, 3, 4, 6, 7, and 8 shows the result of machine learning models on preprocessed spectral data. Table 9 shows the comparison of precision, recall, and F1-score of the machine learning models on raw data and different spectral preprocessing techniques. The results show that the best accuracy, 93%, was obtained by the support vector machine on the raw spectral data. Fig 4 shows the confusion matrix of the support vector machine. It is observed that the spectral preprocessing techniques have less effect on the accuracy of the machine learning models than the raw spectral data [12].

Table 1. Results of classification using SVM on raw spectral data

Class	Precision	Recall	F1-score	Support
0	0.92	0.94	0.93	403
1	0.89	0.91	0.90	403
2	0.95	0.97	0.96	403
3	0.94	0.95	0.94	403
4	0.92	0.93	0.92	403
5	0.92	0.96	0.94	404
6	0.96	0.95	0.95	403
7	0.91	0.90	0.91	403
8	0.98	0.96	0.97	404
9	0.92	0.92	0.92	403
10	0.93	0.94	0.93	403
11	0.95	0.94	0.95	404
12	0.92	0.93	0.93	404
13	0.86	0.86	0.86	403
14	0.95	0.90	0.92	403
15	0.96	0.95	0.96	403
Avg	0.93	0.93	0.93	6452

Table 2. Results of classifications using SNV and SVM

Class	Precision	Recall	F1-score	Support
0	0.91	0.95	0.93	403
1	0.89	0.92	0.90	403
2	0.93	0.96	0.95	403
3	0.95	0.94	0.95	403
4	0.93	0.94	0.93	403
5	0.90	0.94	0.92	404
6	0.97	0.96	0.97	403
7	0.90	0.91	0.91	403
8	0.98	0.96	0.97	404
9	0.91	0.92	0.91	403
10	0.94	0.94	0.94	403
11	0.94	0.94	0.94	404
12	0.94	0.92	0.93	404
13	0.87	0.84	0.85	403
14	0.93	0.90	0.91	403
15	0.97	0.94	0.95	403
Avg	0.93	0.93	0.93	6452

Table 3. Results of classification using MSC and SVM

Class	Precision	Recall	F1-score	Support
0	0.92	0.93	0.93	403
1	0.87	0.90	0.88	403
2	0.94	0.97	0.95	403
3	0.95	0.94	0.94	403
4	0.92	0.91	0.91	403
5	0.93	0.95	0.94	404
6	0.96	0.96	0.96	403
7	0.91	0.89	0.90	403
8	0.96	0.96	0.96	404
9	0.90	0.91	0.91	403
10	0.92	0.93	0.92	403
11	0.95	0.94	0.94	404
12	0.93	0.93	0.93	404
13	0.84	0.85	0.84	403
14	0.94	0.87	0.91	403
15	0.96	0.96	0.96	403
Avg	0.92	0.92	0.92	6452

Table 4. Results of classification using SG Smoothing and SVM

Class	Precision	Recall	F1-score	Support
0	0.81	0.85	0.83	403
1	0.81	0.86	0.83	403
2	0.90	0.90	0.90	403
3	0.87	0.90	0.89	403
4	0.85	0.87	0.86	403
5	0.87	0.91	0.89	404
6	0.94	0.94	0.94	403
7	0.80	0.80	0.80	403
8	0.93	0.93	0.93	404
9	0.84	0.84	0.84	403
10	0.89	0.87	0.88	403
11	0.92	0.86	0.89	404
12	0.89	0.88	0.89	404
13	0.79	0.79	0.79	403
14	0.87	0.80	0.83	403
15	0.96	0.92	0.94	403
Avg	0.87	0.87	0.87	6452

Table 5. Results of classification using LDA on raw spectral data

Class	Precision	Recall	F1-score	Support
0	0.92	0.88	0.90	403
1	0.85	0.90	0.87	403
2	0.92	0.90	0.91	403
3	0.94	0.90	0.92	403
4	0.95	0.89	0.92	403
5	0.93	0.92	0.92	404
6	0.98	0.91	0.94	403
7	0.92	0.87	0.89	403
8	0.88	0.94	0.91	404
9	0.91	0.92	0.92	403
10	0.98	0.93	0.95	403
11	0.88	0.90	0.89	404
12	0.90	0.94	0.92	404
13	0.67	0.82	0.74	403
14	0.89	0.86	0.88	403
15	0.96	0.92	0.94	403
Avg	0.90	0.90	0.90	6452

Table 6. Results of classification using SNV and LDA

Class	Precision	Recall	F1-score	Support
0	0.92	0.88	0.90	403
1	0.84	0.89	0.87	403
2	0.94	0.90	0.92	403
3	0.94	0.91	0.93	403
4	0.94	0.89	0.91	403
5	0.93	0.90	0.91	404
6	0.97	0.91	0.94	403
7	0.88	0.87	0.87	403
8	0.84	0.95	0.89	404
9	0.90	0.92	0.91	403
10	0.98	0.92	0.95	403
11	0.91	0.90	0.90	404
12	0.88	0.94	0.91	404
13	0.70	0.77	0.73	403
14	0.88	0.85	0.86	403
15	0.95	0.93	0.94	403
Avg	0.90	0.89	0.90	6452

Table 7. Results of classification using MSC and LDA

Class	Precision	Recall	F1-score	Support
0	0.86	0.89	0.87	403
1	0.91	0.80	0.85	403
2	0.93	0.91	0.92	403
3	0.98	0.82	0.90	403
4	0.92	0.88	0.90	403
5	0.96	0.86	0.91	404
6	0.99	0.86	0.92	403
7	0.83	0.83	0.83	403
8	0.89	0.92	0.91	404
9	0.81	0.92	0.86	403
10	0.98	0.91	0.94	403
11	0.89	0.92	0.90	404
12	0.98	0.81	0.89	404
13	0.59	0.78	0.67	403
14	0.74	0.94	0.83	403
15	0.93	0.94	0.93	403
Avg	0.89	0.87	0.88	6452

Table 8. Results of classification using SG Smoothing and LDA

Class	Precision	Recall	F1-score	Support
0	0.86	0.89	0.87	403
1	0.91	0.80	0.85	403
2	0.93	0.91	0.92	403
3	0.98	0.82	0.90	403
4	0.92	0.88	0.90	403
5	0.96	0.86	0.91	404
6	0.99	0.86	0.92	403
7	0.83	0.83	0.83	403
8	0.89	0.92	0.91	404
9	0.81	0.92	0.86	403
10	0.98	0.91	0.94	403
11	0.89	0.92	0.90	404
12	0.98	0.81	0.89	404
13	0.59	0.78	0.67	403
14	0.74	0.94	0.83	403
15	0.93	0.94	0.93	403
Avg	0.89	0.87	0.88	6452

Table 9. Comparison of Precision,Recall and F1-Score of Machine Learning Models using different preprocessing techniques

Classifier	Spectral Preprocessing	Parameters (C,γ)	Precision	Recall	F1-score
SVM	Raw	(1000000,0.1)	0.93	0.93	0.93
SVM	SNV	(10000,1)	0.93	0.93	0.93
SVM	MSC	(100000,1)	0.92	0.92	0.92
SVM	SG Smoothing	(100000,1)	0.87	0.87	0.87
LDA	Raw		0.90	0.90	0.90
LDA	SNV		0.90	0.89	0.90
LDA	MSC		0.89	0.87	0.88
LDA	SG Smoothing		0.90	0.89	0.89

Table 10. Comparison with state-of-the-art methods

Method	Author	Accuracy
Extreme Learning Machine	Bao et al. [2]	91.3%
Proposed Method		93%

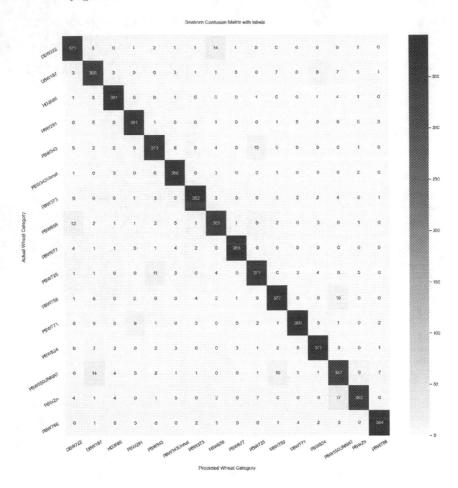

Fig. 4. Confusion Matrix of Support Vector Machine

4.5   Comparison with State-of-the-art Methods

Bao *et al.* [2] classified five wheat varieties. For the experimentation, the images were taken by the hyperspectral imaging system of the spectral range 874–1734 nm. Three machine learning models, SVM, LDA, and extreme learning machine, were used for the classification. The extreme learning machine got an accuracy of 91.3%. In the present study, sixteen wheat varieties were chosen for the classification. The images were captured by a hyperspectral imaging system of the spectral range 900–1700 nm. Two Machine learning models, SVM and LDA, were used for the classification. SVM on raw spectral data got the best accuracy of 93%. Table 10 shows the comparison of the proposed method with the state-of-the-art method. The proposed method outperformed the state-of-the-art method.

5   Conclusion and Future Work

Machine learning methods play a vital role in seed analysis and classification. In this study, sixteen(16) wheat varieties were collected from the certified agriculture department of India. A non-destructive technique using hyperspectral imaging has been investigated to classify wheat seeds. SVM and LDA classifiers were used for the classification. The classifiers were trained separately on raw spectral data and preprocessed spectral data. The mean spectra were pretreated by SNV, MSC, and SG smoothing preprocessing techniques. It was observed from the experimental results that the SVM on raw spectral data outperformed and got an accuracy of 93%. The result shows that the hyperspectral imaging technique combined with machine learning approaches has the potential to identify a variety of seeds. In the future, we will extend our dataset by adding more varieties of different regions of different years and applying a deep learning model to improve accuracy.

References

1. Bandos, T.V., Bruzzone, L., Camps-Valls, G.: Classification of hyperspectral images with regularized linear discriminant analysis. IEEE Trans. Geosci. Remote Sens. **47**(3), 862–873 (2009)
2. Bao, Y., Mi, C., Wu, N., Liu, F., He, Y.: Rapid classification of wheat grain varieties using hyperspectral imaging and chemometrics. Appl. Sci. **9**(19), 4119 (2019)
3. Choudhary, R., Mahesh, S., Paliwal, J., Jayas, D.: Identification of wheat classes using wavelet features from near infrared hyperspectral images of bulk samples. Biosyst. Eng. **102**(2), 115–127 (2009)
4. Fayyazi, S., Abbaspour-Fard, M., Rohani, A., Sadrnia, H., Monadjemi, S.A.H., et al.: Identification and classification of three Iranian rice seed varieties in mixed samples by morphological features using image processing and learning vector quantization neural network. Iran. Food Sci. Technol. Res. J. **10**(3), 211–218 (2014)
5. Feng, L., Zhu, S., Liu, F., He, Y., Bao, Y., Zhang, C.: Hyperspectral imaging for seed quality and safety inspection: a review. Plant methods **15**(1), 1–25 (2019)
6. Hadimani, L., Garg, N.M.: Automatic surface defects classification of kinnow mandarins using combination of multi-feature fusion techniques. J. Food Process. Eng. **44**(1), e13589 (2021)
7. He, X., Feng, X., Sun, D., Liu, F., Bao, Y., He, Y.: Rapid and nondestructive measurement of rice seed vitality of different years using near-infrared hyperspectral imaging. Molecules **24**(12), 2227 (2019)
8. Heisel, S.E., Peterson, D.M., Jones, B.: Identification of united states barley cultivars by sodium dodecyl sulfate polyacrylamide gel electrophoresis of hordeins. Cereal Chem. **63**(6), 500–505 (1986)
9. Huang, M., He, C., Zhu, Q., Qin, J.: Maize seed variety classification using the integration of spectral and image features combined with feature transformation based on hyperspectral imaging. Appl. Sci. **6**(6), 183 (2016)
10. Lim, J., et al.: Application of near infrared reflectance spectroscopy for rapid and non-destructive discrimination of hulled barley, naked barley, and wheat contaminated with fusarium. Sensors **18**(1), 113 (2018)

11. Manickavasagan, A., Sathya, G., Jayas, D., White, N.: Wheat class identification using monochrome images. J. Cereal sci. **47**(3), 518–527 (2008)
12. Manley, M., McGoverin, C.M., Engelbrecht, P., Geladi, P.: Influence of grain topography on near infrared hyperspectral images. Talanta **89**, 223–230 (2012)
13. Mishra, P., Nordon, A., Tschannerl, J., Lian, G., Redfern, S., Marshall, S.: Near-infrared hyperspectral imaging for non-destructive classification of commercial tea products. J. Food Eng. **238**, 70–77 (2018)
14. Nie, P., Zhang, J., Feng, X., Yu, C., He, Y.: Classification of hybrid seeds using near-infrared hyperspectral imaging technology combined with deep learning. Sens. Actuators B: Chem. **296**, 126630 (2019)
15. Osae, R., Essilfie, G., Alolga, R.N., Bonah, E., Ma, H., Zhou, C.: Drying of ginger slices-evaluation of quality attributes, energy consumption, and kinetics study. J. Food Process. Eng. **43**(2), e13348 (2020)
16. Qiu, Z., Chen, J., Zhao, Y., Zhu, S., He, Y., Zhang, C.: Variety identification of single rice seed using hyperspectral imaging combined with convolutional neural network. Appl. Sci. **8**(2), 212 (2018)
17. Sahoo, P.K., Soltani, S., Wong, A.K.: A survey of thresholding techniques. Comput. Vis. Graph. Image process. **41**(2), 233–260 (1988)
18. Sendin, K., Manley, M., Baeten, V., Fernández Pierna, J.A., Williams, P.J.: Near infrared hyperspectral imaging for white maize classification according to grading regulations. Food Anal. Methods **12**(7), 1612–1624 (2019)
19. Sun, D.W.: Hyperspectral imaging for food quality analysis and control. Elsevier (2010)
20. Tujo, T., Kumar, D., Yitagesu, E., Girma, M.: A predictive model to predict seed classes using machine learning. Int. J. Eng. Tech. Res **6**, 334–344 (2019)

Customized Preview Video Generation Using Visual Saliency: A Case Study with Vision Dominant Videos

Shivani Madan[✉], Shantanu Singh Chauhan, Afrah Khan, and Subhash Kulkarni[iD]

Department of Electronics and Communication Engineering,
PES University Electronic City Campus, Bangalore 560100, India
sskul@pes.edu

Abstract. Provisioning preview video for long duration videos has always been an expectation. This paper proposes an approach for user-defined customizable preview video generation using visual saliency by extracting some of the fundamental features of the human visual system such as color, intensity and motion. This motivation led to investigating this option for Vision Dominant videos viz., sports videos, wild-life videos, sea world videos etc. Our proposal for visual saliency computation follows the PQFT (Phase Spectrum of Quaternion Fourier transform) model for feature extraction where phase information is used to detect motion(activity)within the frame. The proposed methodology comprises three main stages, with the pre-processing stage that operates on the dataset to reduce the overall computational complexity. The intermediate stage, the saliency detection stage involves feature extraction algorithm to compute saliency values for each frame generating saliency maps and curves that helps in classifying the videos as low, medium and high activity videos. In the final stage, customization is provisioned based on the user's choice of percentage or duration reduction of the original duration of the video to generate preview with keyframe extraction based on maximum saliency values. The PQFT Model deployed is independent of prior knowledge and other parameters making it computationally simple. The experimental results indicate that the proposed method is capable of generating stable and good results. This novel method finds application in different fields towards automatic summarization facilitating preview video on video hosting and streaming websites.

Keywords: Visual Saliency · Vision dominant videos · Video summarization · Key-frames · Preview video generation · User defined customization

1 Introduction

Abstracted short-duration videos provide people with a fast and easy way to absorb information. This innovative way of communication is aimed to excite and inspire people. With the high demand for visual content videos, the scope for research and advancement in this area has exponentially increased. Video summarization produces short summaries preserving significant segments of the original video, thereby significantly reducing the

© The Author(s), under exclusive license to Springer Nature Switzerland AG 2023
D. Gupta et al. (Eds.): CVIP 2022, CCIS 1777, pp. 267–280, 2023.
https://doi.org/10.1007/978-3-031-31417-9_21

video duration. In this work, we dive deeper into the concepts of video summarization as seen in [1, 2] by examining the role of Human Visual System in detecting salient objects. To predict human attention, saliency detection has been widely studied in recent years, with multiple applications in object recognition, object segmentation, image/video compression, etc. We explore the concept of pixel level visual saliency, which models attention embedded in each video frame. The authors in [3] have provided detailed understanding of visual saliency and preview generation through saliency curve thresholding. Feature cues such as - color, intensity, motion, and detecting keyframes based on these feature cues are discussed in [4]. Various algorithms modeling the HVS (Human Visual System) exists, one such successful model PQFT has been widely accepted [5] that analyzes the phase spectrum of the quaternion representation of an image. Various keyframe extraction and clustering techniques are proposed in [6] and [7]. In this present work, a visual saliency-based model for the generation of video summaries is proposed, that can be extended to facilitate the generation of customizable preview videos.

2   Proposed Method using Visual Saliency for Preview Video Generation

Various factors affect human visual attention. However, the most sought after includes that of visual stimuli and objects that are distinct as compared to those that surround them thereby grabbing our attention. Over the years different methods have been proposed in the literature that model and give insights about this innate attractiveness, termed as visual saliency of various capricious segments embedded in the scene. In this work, we present the idea of working with the phase spectrum of an image representing through its quaternion to determine the saliency map of the image.

2.1   Phase Spectrum

In [8] the authors noted that the spectral representation of an image in terms of its amplitude and phase hold information about the magnitude of the sinusoidal elements existing and also the location of these sinusoid elements respectively. Hence, we can say the spectral representation of an image in terms of its phase tells us the relative position of each component with respect to others. The fact that Phase Spectrum alone can be used for the reconstruction of an image is exploited here. The PFT (Phase Spectrum of Fourier Transform) representation of an image no doubt gives a straightforward and swift approach to compute the saliency maps. However, it does not consider few principal clues such as motion and color. This led us to work with the image in its quaternion form and make use of the quaternion Fourier transform to generate the saliency maps [6].

2.2   Quaternion Representation of an Image

Quaternions are a 4-channel representation of an image that comprises one channel corresponding to motion, two channels holding information regarding color (in this case RG and BY), and finally the last channel containing intensity information.

$$q = a + bi + cj + dk \tag{1}$$

where a, b, c, d ϵ R and the Hamilton product of the quaternions are described by i, j, and k [9]

The Quaternion is made up of features like color, intensity, and motion. Every pixel present in the image is represented by this quaternion, distinct from other models, in a way that there exists an additional dimension of motion that yields spatiotemporal saliency by virtue of its phase spectrum representation [6]. This examines not only important spatial cues over color and orientation among others in a static frame but also interframe temporal features cues like motion.

2.3 Opponent Color Scheme

The opponent-process theory states that humans need four unique colors to characterize perception of color namely - blue, yellow, red, and green. The theory suggests that the way humans perceive colors is controlled by three opposing systems which are.

a) Blue versus Yellow
b) Red versus Green
c) Black versus White

The neurons in the visual cortex, if sensitized by blue or red then yellow or green band are inhibited respectively. This distinct quality of Human Visual System facilitates the computation of saliency features which are independent of every frame.

2.4 Saliency Features Using Opponent Color Scheme

Salient features like color, intensity are acquired from the opponent color space using

$$RG = R - G$$
$$BY = B - Y \tag{2}$$

where

$$R = r - \frac{g+b}{2}$$

$$R = g - \frac{r+b}{2}$$

$$B = b - \frac{r+g}{2} \tag{3}$$

$$Y = \frac{r+g}{2} - \frac{|r-g|}{2} = b$$

Intensity can be obtained by:

$$I = (r + g + b)/3 \tag{4}$$

Hence by using one of the opponent color channels from (2) we compute the Feature vectors using the following equations.

$$myfft = FT[RG] = \sum \sum \forall(m, n)RG(m, n)e^{-j2\pi(mk+nl)}$$
$$= |mag|e^{j\theta} \tag{5}$$

The Phase spectrum of the opponent color channel image inherently possess the ability to grasp static virtual motion information. To maximize the dynamic range as well as the discernment of motion feature, fourier transform of the phase spectrum is used. By replacing the magnitude as unity and then taking inverse fourier transform conserves the motion element appreciably [3]. Additionally, to steer clear of any kind of loss in the fourier domain, a Gaussian filter is used.

Let |mag|=1

$$\text{Myfft} = e^{j\theta} \tag{6}$$

$$\text{Sph} = \text{IFFT}(e^{j\theta}) \tag{7}$$

$$\text{Smask} = \text{GlobalThreshold}(\text{Sph} * e^{j\theta}) \tag{8}$$

$$\begin{aligned} F1 &= S_{mask} * r \\ F2 &= S_{mask} * g \\ F3 &= S_{mask} * b \end{aligned} \tag{9}$$

The visual saliency corresponding to individual frames is then obtained by taking the mean of the feature vectors

$$S = \frac{1}{3}\sum_{k=1}^{3} Fk \tag{10}$$

2.5 Saliency Map

Saliency map corresponds to a feature image showing the motion content amongst pixels. Saliency map can be called as an overlapped mask of red, blue and green channels. Some of the extracted frames from the original videos implemented in this work are given in Fig. 1 with nil or no motion being represented by blue and fair motion being represented by yellow color.

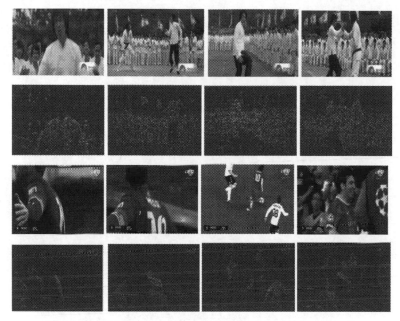

Fig. 1. Saliency Map of input video "Bruce Lee" and "Football"

3   Saliency Curve

The saliency curve is plotted with the saliency values against the frame numbers as can be seen in Fig. 2. These saliency values are computed by feature cues holding more attention in the observed scene. The feature cues we consider here to compute saliency values are - color, intensity, and motion. In a saliency curve, if the curve has more variations with consequent peaks and falls then it reflects higher activity or more scene changes.

In this work, we have considered,
Avg Saliency Values(S):

- $S < 2500$ - Low Activity
- $2500 < S < 5000$ - Medium Activity
- $S > 5000$ - High Activity

Saliency curve analysis for different sample videos used in our work is presented in Table 1.

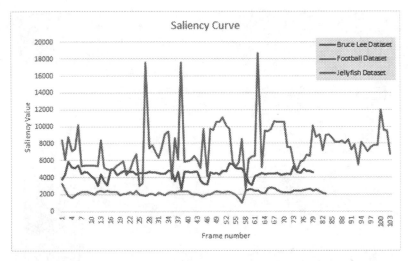

Fig. 2. Comparison of saliency curves of 3 different datasets

Table 1. Saliency Curve Analysis

Dataset	Saliency Value Range	Inference from the curve	Observation	Conclusion
Jellyfish	1000–3200	Saliency curve shows nearly no variations or peaks/falls	– Static background scene and minimal foreground activity – Distinct salient object (Jellyfish)	Low activity video
Bruce Lee	2500–5900	The saliency curve has moderate peaks and falls. No drastic variations	– Minimal background scene changes and a lot of foreground activity – Ambiguous objects in the background. Two salient objects in the foreground	Medium activity video
Football	2500 to 18700	The saliency curve shows a lot of drastic variations and multiple high peaks and falls	– Constant background and foreground changes – Ambiguous salient objects	High activity video

4   Key Frame Extraction

In the saliency curve plots, the significant crests or peaks give us information about those frames which contain high saliency values, known as keyframes. Key frames signify those portions of the signal (in this case the video) which stand out from the rest in terms of high amount of attention that they seek.

5   Preview Generation

In order to generate a preview video, we put a threshold on the number of key frames to be considered for a particular video. Since the previews can be customized, we let the user decide between reducing the video to a percentage of its original or to a duration of their choice. According to the user's input, the preview is then created by applying a threshold on 'K', where K denotes the number of key frames to be used.

The thresholding can be done using the equation:

$$K = d \times f / C \tag{11}$$

where d is the **target duration** of the preview to be generated as specified by the user, f is the **frame rate** to be applied. C is 'cluster of frames' which refers to accumulation of a fixed number of frames on either side of the selected key frames which are compiled to generate the preview.

E.g., In the video 'Bruce Lee.mp4 ', with frame #1000 being identified as a key frame, we select 10 frames ahead as well as before this key frame. This results in a cluster of 21 frames (#990–#1010). This cluster of frames for a given key frame is also a variable and is fixed to 21 in our implementation.

If the user is interested to reduce the video to a percentage P of its original duration d' we find d as –

$$d = P/100 \times d' \tag{12}$$

The number of key frames in consideration is estimated on similar lines using Eq. (11).

Once the number of key frames are decided for a given video, we select those 'K' image frames of the video which correspond to the highest saliency values amongst all the frames. After which we select the clusters of 20 frames for every key frame resulting in the total frames to be used for the preview. These selected frames are then compiled with the frame rate as f, generating the preview video. For.eg to reduce a 65 s video to its 50%, we first compute the number of key frames required using the equations above –

$$K = (65 * 0.5) * 24/21 \tag{13}$$

Here $P = 50\%$; $d' = 65$ s; $C = 21$; $f = 24$

From which we get K to be 37. Now for each of these 37 keyframes we extract their respective clusters of 21 frames and compile to generate the required preview with f = 24 as the frame rate.

6 Block Diagram

Detailed algorithmic steps involved in our experimentation is summarily presented in the block diagram in Fig. 3.

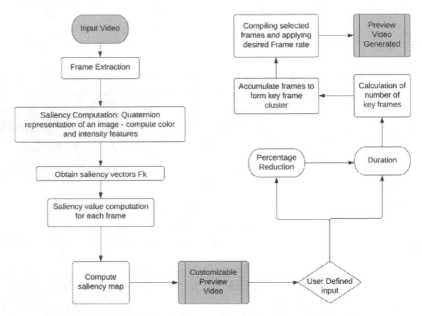

Fig. 3. End to end block diagram illustrating the entire algorithm

7 Experimental Results and Analysis

Evaluating the efficiency of video summaries is difficult mainly because the metrics are subjective that differs from one observer to the next. In the following subsections, we have analyzed the preview video that has been generated through qualitative, quantitative, and subjective analysis.

7.1 Qualitative Analysis

Qualitative analysis of preview video generated involves dual perspective based on scene change detection and data generated preview video.

Analyzing the Scene Changes Detected
Few of the sample video database employed in our experimentation are tabulated in Table 2 considering customizable parameters - duration, frame rate and the number of keyframes secured after sorting the saliency values.

    The preview video is generated by setting a custom duration with different frame rates. To verify if the preview video indeed includes the salient actions, we compare the

Table 2. Data to show the credibility of the preview video generated

Dataset	Duration (sec)		Frame rate (fps)	Total Frames	Total number of scene changes		Number of keyframes
	Original video	Preview video			Original video	Preview video	
Jellyfish	53	15	24	1621	13	10	17
Football	82	30	24	2052	28	19	34
Bruce Lee	65	45	24	1563	19	17	51
Deep Ocean	36	4	30	1087	12	10	7
Birds	70	7	30	1680	6	5	7

scene changes in the original and the preview video. From the table we can see that the preview generation is in fact the accurate summarization of the original video.

Analyzing the Data Obtained from the Generated Preview Video
The customizable parameters in experimentation are preset to the following.

Duration: 15 s, 30 s and 45 s
Percentage reduction: 25%, 50% and 75%

Further, the user can define the parameters to generate desired preview video using any preset values. The results are presented in Table 3.

Table 3. Customizable preview generation parameters

Customizable Parameters	Input Parameter	Dataset	Duration (sec)			Key Frames	Number of frames in preview video		Frame rate (fps)
			Original video	Preview video			Expected	Achieved	
				Expected	Achieved				
Duration	15 s	Jellyfish	53	15	11	17	360	336	24
	30 s	Football	82	30	26	34	714	628	24
	45 s	Bruce Lee	65	45	41	51	1071	1005	24
Percentage Reduction	25%	Jellyfish	53	13.5	13	15	305	284	24
	50%	Football	82	41	38	47	1026	916	24
	75%	Bruce Lee	65	48	46	55	1152	1123	24

After obtaining key frames and performing forward-backward accumulation we see that it leads to overlapping of the cluster of frames, as a result, the total no of frames obtained reduces, leading to a reduction in the duration of the video as inferred from Table 3.

7.2 Quantitative Analysis

Considerable work in literature has been reported on quantitatively analyzing the efficiency of the preview video generated. In this paper, we have resorted to the F-score method [10] to gauge the precision of the preview video generated by comparing it to random reference summary videos (which will be considered as the ground truth).

The F-score Method

In our work, we took $y_i \epsilon$ {0,1} that represents a tag specifying the frames from the original video which are selected for the preview video i.e. $y_i = 1$ if ith frame is selected for preview generation else $yi = 0$ similarly $y_i^* = \{0, 1\}$ represents a tag specifying which frames from the original video are selected for a reference video.

For F-Score, the parameters precision and recall are estimated using the expressions defined below.

Precision: ratio of all frames chosen correctly to all frames in the preview video.

Recall: ratio of all frames chosen correctly to that of frames in the reference video, it shows how accurately our model identifies the correct frames.

Mathematical formulae for precision and recall:

$$PRE = \frac{\sum_{i=1}^{N} y_i * y_i^*}{\sum_{i=1}^{N} yi}, \tag{14}$$

$$REC = \frac{\sum_{i=1}^{N} y_i * y_i^*}{\sum_{i=1}^{N} y_i^*} \tag{15}$$

F Score Formula:

$$F1 = 2 * \frac{PRE * REC}{PRE + REC} \tag{16}$$

where,

PRE -frame-level precision score, REC - frame level recall score.

N - Total frames present in the input video.

F1 scores can range from 0 to 1. Where F1 score of 1 denotes a perfect model.

Steps to analyze preview video using F-Score method:

1. Generate Reference summary videos from the original video manually based on the visual cues and ability of human visual system to detect salient objects.
2. These reference videos serve as a baseline for comparison with the preview video generated using F Score method
3. Further, the F Scores obtained are averaged to secure the final F Score (In this paper we have generated four F Scores and averaged them to secure the final F Score)

Closer the F Score is to 1, higher will be the accuracy.

Table 4. Fscore Table for various datasets

	Filename	Reference video length	Preview video length	F-score
1	Jellyfish.mp4	21s	21s	0.89
2	Brucelee.mp4	26s	27s	0.76
3	Football.mp4	33s	32s	0.64

Results are consolidated in Table 4.

Inference: From Table 4 we can see that we obtained highest F1 score for the Jellyfish video and lowest for the Football video. This is because the Jellyfish video is a low activity video and has lesser scene changes, due to this the generated preview video rightly captures key segments same as that of the reference summary. The ambiguous salient objects, increased activity and drastic scene changes in the Football video led to poor capturing of key activity moments in the preview video.

7.3 Subjective Analysis

We conducted a survey amongst 110 people to learn more about human behavioral characteristics with regards to video content consumption and to perform subjective analysis for our feature. From the survey we learnt that people prefer shorter length videos over longer videos and would like to customize their preview for a full-length video rather than watching the original video. We obtained satisfactory responses for the feature we built.

The results from the survey are as follows:
Video content consumption statistics:

- 37.1% spent 4 h or more on video streaming platforms.
- 87% felt like they have wasted time watching entire videos and gained no entertainment/knowledge.
- Only 38.3% watched the entire original video till the end.
- 94.3% preferred watching the shorter preview video.

User response on our feature:

- 70.1% think that the key aspects of the original video were efficiently captured through the preview video.
- 86.9% would prefer to watch just the preview first rather than a longer original video.
- 80.4% would like the freedom of having to choose their own preview video duration rather than having to choose from a fixed set of durations.
- 84.1% said that they would benefit from having this feature of customizing the preview video on their streaming platform.

8 Related Work and Comparative Analysis

A substantial amount of work has been done in the area of visual saliency and video summarization, some relevant to our paper include [11] where the authors put together the video summarization problem using the temporal collaborative representation (TCR) model in which instead of individual frames, adjacent frames are considered to skip selecting transitional frames. While TCR approach gave better keyframe selection results as compared to some of the state of art algorithms like DT, STIMO, VSUMM, MSR, AGDS, Our method outperforms these given approach in terms of F score and better keyframe selection. Furthermore In [12] they have used a Constraint based summarization model allowing the user to specify the constraints. However, there is a lack of a high-level language which can make this process transparent and user friendly. In [13] the entire saliency detection model uses RGBD concepts and faces challenges to accurately detect keyframes, inter frame relations and are unable to include high level features such as motion. We have overcome this problem by incorporating the use of opponent color scheme which accounts for the motion cue and is computationally simpler and more accurate. Another method explored in [14] was that of RPCA-KFE (Key Frame Extraction for Video using Robust Principal Component Analysis). In this method the resulting description (visual comparison) and subjective metric (quantitative comparison) approaches were exploited. The key frames were chosen using dictionary learning and clustering algorithm. Which resulted in an error of at least 30% in every attempt in contrast to our model that yields less than 25% error. Similarly, there are many more methods and models used to obtain video summaries, each of which has its own advantages and drawbacks. Moreover, absence of common and public video datasets of realistic size poses difficulty in comparing different approaches found in the literature.

9 Limitations

One of the drawbacks of this method can be observed in the results which shows that some of the preview durations achieved are lesser than the expected duration. This can be accounted by the fact that the number of frames selected for the preview are lesser than the desired number of frames. This deficit in the number of frames is due to overlapping of frames in the key frame clusters i.e., when two key frames are close to each other with the number of frames between them being lesser than C then there are common frames present in both, which result in duplicate frames being dropped thereby reducing the total frame count. This causes the achieved preview to be of a shorter length than expected and fails to achieve the exact target duration. Work can be carried out to minimize this deviation from the expected duration of the preview videos by exploring other techniques for keyframe extraction. One possible solution to this problem can be an iterative approach of keyframe selection, where the number of key frames chosen for a video is increased according to the difference in the desired total no of frames for the preview and the obtained number of frames. This will allow the algorithm to achieve the exact expected preview video duration.

10 Conclusion and Future Scope

In this paper, we have proposed an end-to-end mechanism to generate customizable preview videos for Vision Dominant videos. An efficient algorithm is proposed to quantify the visual saliency corresponding to each image frame of a video. Using this algorithm, we have also implemented an effective way to generate saliency maps for frames. Further, we have also come up with a novel method of user-defined preview video generation, which involves putting a threshold on the number of key frames to be extracted. Frames having the highest saliency values are eligible candidates for key frames, The thresholding of which is done based on the user's input specifications i.e. percentage or duration reduction of the original video. Once the number of key frames is identified, a cluster of these key frames is formed. Finally, after choosing a suitable frame rate all the key frame clusters are compiled to generate the desired preview video.

Future scope involves exploring other saliency models and testing them out on an extensive database to compare their efficiency. Identification of key frames with increased precision will be possible by exploring alternate methods for keyframe extraction rather than choosing the top frames with respect to their saliency values. Another direction to better this work could be smart preview video generation for multimedia content driven videos.

References

1. Evangelopoulos, G., et al.: Video event detection and summarization using audio, visual and text saliency. In: 2009 IEEE International Conference on Acoustics, Speech and Signal Processing, pp. 3553–3556 (2009). https://doi.org/10.1109/ICASSP.2009.4960393
2. Cong, R., Lei, J., Fu, H., Cheng, M.M., Lin, W., Huang, Q.: Review of visual saliency detection with comprehensive information. IEEE Trans. Circuits Syst. Video Technol. **29**(10), 2941–2959 (2018)
3. Ramya, G., Kulkarni, S.: Visual saliency based video summarization: a case study for preview video generation. In: Mandal, J.K., Bhattacharya, K., Majumdar, I., Mandal, S. (eds.) Information, Photonics and Communication. LNNS, vol. 79, pp. 155–165. Springer, Singapore (2020). https://doi.org/10.1007/978-981-32-9453-0_16
4. Evangelopoulos, G., Rapantzikos, K., Maragos, P., Avrithis, Y., Potamianos, A.: Audiovisual attention modeling and salient event detection. In: Maragos, P., Potamianos, A., Gros, P. (eds.) Multimodal Processing and Interaction. Multimedia Systems and Applications, vol. 33. Springer, Boston (2008). https://doi.org/10.1007/978-0-387-76316-3_8
5. Treisman, A.M., Gelade, G.: A feature-integration theory of attention. Cognit. Psychol. **12**(1), 97–136 (1980). ISSN 0010-0285. https://doi.org/10.1016/0010-0285(80)900055
6. Guo, C., Zhang, L.: A novel multiresolution spatiotemporal saliency detection model and its applications in image and video compression. IEEE Trans. Image Process. **19**(1), 185–198 (2010). https://doi.org/10.1109/TIP.2009.2030969
7. Jadon, S., Jasim, M.: Unsupervised video summarization framework using keyframe extraction and video skimming. In: 2020 IEEE 5th International Conference on Computing Communication and Automation (ICCCA), pp. 140–145 (2020). https://doi.org/10.1109/ICCCA4 9541.2020.9250764
8. Castleman, K.: Digital Image Processing. Prentice-Hall, New York (1996)

9. Schauerte, B., Stiefelhagen, R.: Quaternion-based spectral saliency detection for eye fixation prediction. In: Fitzgibbon, A., Lazebnik, S., Perona, P., Sato, Y., Schmid, C. (eds.) ECCV 2012. LNCS, pp. 116–129. Springer, Heidelberg (2012). https://doi.org/10.1007/978-3-642-33709-3_9

10. Otani, M., Nakashima, Y., Rahtu, E., Heikkila, J.: Rethinking the evaluation of video summaries. In: Proceedings of the IEEE/CVF Conference on Computer Vision and Pattern Recognition, pp. 7596–7604 (2019)

11. Ma, M., Met, S., Hou, J., Wan, S., Wang, Z.: Video summarization via temporal collaborative representation of adjacent frames. In: 2017 International Symposium on Intelligent Signal Processing and Communication Systems (ISPACS), pp. 164–169 (2017). https://doi.org/10.1109/ISPACS.2017.8266466

12. Boukadida, H., Berrani, S.A., Gros, P.: Automatically creating adaptive video summaries using constraint satisfaction programming: Application to sport content. IEEE Trans. Circuits Syst. Video Technol. 27(4), 920–934 (2017)

13. Cong, R., Lei, J., Fu, H., Cheng, M.-M., Lin, W., Huang, Q.: Review of visual saliency detection with comprehensive information. IEEE Trans. Circuits Syst. Video Technol. 29(10), 2941–2959 (2019). https://doi.org/10.1109/TCSVT.2018.2870832

14. Dang, C., Radha, H.: RPCA-KFE: key frame extraction for video using robust principal component analysis. IEEE Trans. Image Process. 24(11), 3742–3753 (2015). https://doi.org/10.1109/TIP.2015.2445572

Deep Dilated Convolutional Network for Single Image Dehazing

S. Deivalakshmi$^{(\boxtimes)}$ and J. Sudaroli Sandana

Department of Electronics and Communication Engineering, National Institute of Technology,
Tiruchirappalli, India
`deiva@nitt.edu`

Abstract. The visual quality of the images gets decreased due to bad weather conditions. The image captured under hazy weather conditions have serious attenuation in terms of color and saturation. In addition, these hazy images have very low contrast and the visual quality will be drastically poor. Moreover, object detection in hazy environment is too challenging. So, single image dehazing is a demanding, challenging and ill-posed problem. In this paper, we propose a 9-layer convolutional neural network with deep dilated filters of different dilation rates to achieve an end-to-end mapping from haze image to haze free image. Exponential expansion of receptive field is possible with the dilated filters without increasing the model complexity. Furthermore, the dilated convolutional layers help for efficient model compactness. We did experiments on synthetic dataset and on naturally obtained hazy images. The results show that our network achieves outstanding performance over the existing algorithms in terms of PSNR, SSIM and visual quality.

Keywords: dehazing · dilated filters · receptive field

1 Introduction

The visual quality of the image's acquired outdoors is decreased due to dust, smoke and other small particles accumulated in atmosphere. This type of traditional atmospheric situation is known as haze and it attenuates the light reflected by the objects along its path towards the camera. Haze causes a serious problem in terrestrial photography, as it becomes difficult to image distant objects because the light penetration of dense atmosphere is necessary. The light scattered by the hazy particles results in the visual effect of a loss of contrast in the subject. This poor visual quality can inhibit the performance of computer systems which are intended to operate on clear conditions. It also obscures the visual amicability of image contents for the users who use standard cameras. Hazy weather also affects variety of systems such as aerial photography systems [1], image classification [2], satellite remote sensing systems [3] and target recognition systems that depend on optical imaging instruments. In recent years, the need for restoring the quality of the visually degraded images due to poor weather conditions has been increasingly gaining the attention.

D. Gupta et al. (Eds.): CVIP 2022, CCIS 1777, pp. 281–291, 2023.
https://doi.org/10.1007/978-3-031-31417-9_22

It is hard to detect haze because concentration of the haze differs from place to place. Haze is a depth dependent phenomenon. So, image dehazing is thus an ill-posed problem. The existing techniques of image processing which uses a variety of visual information to capture both statistical and deterministic properties of hazy images such as histogram based [4, 5] contrast based and saturation-based image dehazing methods are used by the early researchers to obtain hazy free image from a single image. Later, researchers try to achieve the same performance with multiple images. In [6], polarization-based image dehazing methods are used. In polarization based dehazing, multiple images are taken with different degrees of polarization. In [7], multiple images of the same scene are captured under distinct weather conditions. These are multi constraint based dehazing methods. Dehazing has been carried out based on the depth information from the user inputs. But practically, multiple hazy images or information related to depth are not always available. To overcome this difficulty, single image dehazing approaches were introduced. In recent years, single image dehazing based on the physical model achieved significant progress. It was carried out under the assumption that the local contrast of the haze-free image is very much higher than that in the image captured under haze. Recently, convolutional neural network (CNN) shows promising solutions on many vision tasks, including dehazing. CNNs have shown an explosive popularity because of capability in producing state-of-the-art performance. DehazeNet [8] has been proposed for single image haze removal with bilateral rectified linear unit as nonlinear activation function. The DehazeNet [9] models mapping functions between hazy image and their medium transmissions. The DehazeNet [9] assumed the atmospheric light as a global constant which must be learned along with medium transmission. Recently, Artificial Multiple Exposure Fusion (AMEF) [9] has been proposed for haze removal. The AMEF method [9] used two steps to remove haze. First of all, a sequence of gamma correction operations is used to artificially under-expose the hazy image. Secondly, a multi-scale Laplacian blending scheme is used to merge the resulting set of under-exposed images to yield haze-free image.

The DehazeNet [8] was modeled only using the information of medium transmissions and assumed the atmospheric scattering as a global constant, but in this paper both medium transmission and atmospheric scattering are considered and the network is trained in an end-to-end manner using deep dilated filters. The end-to-end training between hazy image and haze free image learns a single and unique mapping function which is able to remove haze from any real-world hazy image.

The major contributions of the proposed work are as follows.

- A novel 9-layer convolutional neural network is proposed for robust dehazing in an end-to-end manner by considering both medium transmissions and atmospheric scattering.
- The layers are constructed in symmetrical structure with respect to dilation rates. The dilation rate increases the receptive field thereby giving network more scope to exploit contextual information efficiently.
- The network is compactly modeled by selecting proper dilatation rates without causing gridding effect in the produced haze-free images.

The rest of this paper is summarized as follows. Section 2 provides the work related to dehazing. Section 3 presents the proposed methodology adopted to achieve image dehazing. Experimental analysis is presented in Sect. 4. The concluding remarks of the proposed work are provided in Sect. 5.

2 Related Work

Although wide variety of Image dehazing literature is available, it is still an open topic to investigate. There are three types of dehazing methods seen in current research: image enhancement-based methods, image fusion-based methods and image restoration methods based on physical modelling. The image enhancement-based method does not consider the specific cause of the image degradation. Fog is not removed from the image to restore the original appearance. So, these methods cannot be adaptable for different scenes and images. Image restoration methods based on physical modelling analyses the specific causes of image degradation. This method also establishes a deteriorate model of images degraded under fog. The physical modelling image restoration methods are based on the atmospheric scattering theory. According to this theory, the scattering of atmosphere is divided into two parts: one is due to the attenuation of light reflected from the surface of the object to the camera; and the second one is due to the air-light scattering reaching to the camera. To describe how a hazy image is formed, the atmospheric scattering model, which is proposed in 1976 [10], is mainly used in image processing and in computer vision [7]. Image fusion based methods maximize beneficial information from multiple sources to finally form a high quality image. These methods do not need a physical model, but the fusion strategy for multiple sources of information is complex. Image fusion is the process of combining relevant information from multiple source channels into a high quality image. Fusion strategies extract the information from each channel to improve the utilization of image information. These methods have also been used in image dehazing in recent years. A single image dehazing algorithm that removes the visual degradation due to haze is described in [9]. It does not depend on the

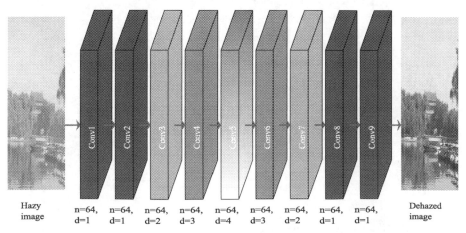

Fig. 1. Architecture of the proposed network

inversion of a physical model of haze formation but considered a few main underlying assumptions to get a haze-free image. A trainable end-to-end model to estimate medium transmission called DehazeNet has been proposed in [8]. It takes a degraded image due to haze as its input, and outputs its transmission matrix. It estimates the global atmospheric light by some empirical rules and haze-free image is recovered using the atmospheric scattering model.

3   Method

In this section, we present the architecture of the deep learning model used for dehazing and the benefits of dilated convolutions. The training procedure and model complexity are also explained.

3.1   Architecture

The deep dilated network used for dehazing is shown in Fig. 1. The proposed network contains 9 convolutional layers. The first two and the last two convolutional layers perform standard convolutions. All remaining layers have specified dilation rates (d) as shown in Fig. 1. Starting layers learns low-level features especially edges and blobs from the hazy image. Dilated convolution with rate d introduces (d − 1) spaces between the adjacent pixels while performing convolution operation. The early layers especially, first layer will learn high frequency information like edges. While applying dilated convolution some of the information about edges may be lost. So, we used normal convolutional filters in the first layer. Similarly, to reconstruct dehazed image accurately, we used normal convolution in reconstruction layer. After each convolutional layer the haze is removed step-by step and at the final layer the dehazed image is produced. Different from the works in [8, 9], our proposed network learns an end-to-end mapping function (F) directly from hazy image to haze-free image. As the deep learning model learns features automatically, there might be a possibility of feature redundancy. Same features may be learned by network in different layers. To avoid feature redundancy, we used dilated filters with different dilation.

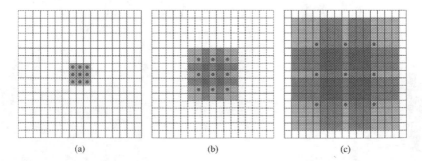

(a)   (b)   (c)

Fig. 2. Dilated convolution operation

rates (d). All the convolutional layers in the proposed network have 64 filters. Each filter has a size of 3 × 3. The first layer learns 64 feature maps from the hazy color image. In the second layer these 64 features are mapped to another feature space. In the third layer, the d of 2 is used. So, the effective filter size (f_e) becomes 5. Therefore, the third layer can exploit more information by expanding receptive field.

3.2 Dilated Convolution

The benefit of using dilated convolution is three folds. First, the dilated convolution can exploit more contextual information. Secondly, by using dilated filters computational complexity will not increase but receptive field can be increased. Thirdly, model can be designed as compactly as possible with a smaller number of convolutional layers. Basically, in low-level vision, exploiting more contextual information is essential to yield better performance. This is possible only with filters of large sizes. Employing large size filters will increase the computational complexity of the model. The dilated filters will consider spaces between each pixel in the image while doing convolution operation. The dilated convolution operation is shown in Fig. 2.

Figure 2(a) represents the standard convolution with filter of size 3 × 3. Figure 2(b) represents dilated convolution with d = 2. A single space is considered while doing convolution operation between each pixel. So, the dilated convolution introduces corresponding spaces (d − 1 spaces) between pixels depending upon d and performs standard convolution thereafter. Similarly, Fig. 2(c) represents dilated convolution with d = 7. So, the effective filter size becomes 15. We generalize the effective filter size (f_e) with d as follows:

Table 1. Proposed Network Specifications

Layer Index (l)	F	d	fe	RF
1	3	1	3	3
2	3	1	3	5
3	3	2	5	9
4	3	3	7	15
5	3	4	9	23
6	3	3	7	29
7	3	2	5	33
8	3	1	3	35
9	3	1	3	37

$$f_e = f + (f - 1)(d - 1) \tag{3}$$

where f is the standard filter size. Similarly, the receptive field (RF) of the network can be formulated based on the depth (D) of the network as follows:

$$RF = f + (f - 1)(D - 1) \tag{4}$$

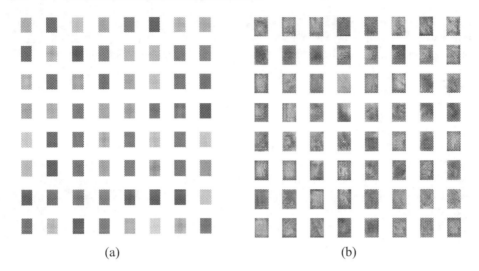

(a)   (b)

Fig. 3. Visualization of different layers

Equation 4 represents the RF for fully convolutional neural network. If dilated filters are used in the network, then the Eq. 4 is modified as follows:

$$RF = f_e + (f_e - 1)(D - 1) \tag{5}$$

In the proposed network, total 9 convolutional layers are used. The dilation rate (d), filter size (f) effective filter size (f_e) and receptive field (RF) are tabulated as shown in Table 1. The total receptive field of the proposed network is 37. So, we cropped patches of size 37×37 from the hazy and haze free images to generate training samples. From Table 1, 9 layers are enough to exploit the whole content in the 37×37 image patch. Adding extra layers will increase the model complexity. Moreover, performance improvement is also marginal. So, we used only 9-layers in the proposed network for dehazing.

3.3   Computational Complexity

Computational complexity is one of the key factors while designing any network. It will decide the real time deployment of the network. Theoretically, computational complexity is the number of parameters that the network must be optimized.

The computational complexity of any fully convolutional neural network is calculated by using the following formulation:

$$C = \sum_{l=1}^{D} n_{l-1} \times f^2 \times n_l \times S_l^2 \tag{6}$$

where l is the layer index, D is the depth of the network and n_l is the number of filters in l^{th} layer. Here, n_0 is equals to number of channels (3 color channels) in input patch. S is the size of the image to be dehazed. The practical computational complexity varies from the theoretical complexity as it depends on the hardware and type of framework used for implementation.

3.4 Loss Function

Let $\{H^i, D^i\}$ represents the training samples. Where i stands for the ith training sample. Similarly, let $^l = \{W^l, B^l\}$ represents the network parameters of individual layers. We minimize the Mean Squared Error (MSE) $L(\Theta)$ as follows:

$$L(\Theta) = \frac{1}{K}\sum_{i=1}^{K} \left\| f\left(H^i, \Theta\right) - D^i \right\|^2 + \lambda\|\Theta\|^2 \qquad (7)$$

where λ denotes the regularization factor. We used Adam optimizer [12] with the parameters β_1, β_2 and ϵ are set to $0.9, 0.999$ and 10^{-8} respectively. We used standard mini-batch gradient descent with each batch size of 64. The gradients with respect to l^{th} layer are computed as:

$$g_t = \nabla_{\Theta_t} L(\Theta_t - 1) \qquad (8)$$

The momentum vectors are formulated as below:

$$m_t = \beta_1 m_{t-1} + (1 - \beta_1)g_t$$

$$v_t = \beta_2 v_{t-1} + (1 - \beta_2)g_t^2 \qquad (9)$$

Finally, the parameter update is as follows:

$$\Theta_t = \Theta_{t-1} - \frac{\eta \widehat{m}_t}{\sqrt{\hat{v}_t} + \epsilon} \qquad (10)$$

where $\hat{m}_t$ and $\hat{v}_t$ are used to counteract the occurrence of zero vectors due to zero initialization of m_t and v_t and computed as:

$$\widehat{m}_t = \frac{m_t}{1 - \beta_1^t}$$

$$\hat{v}_t = \frac{v_t}{1 - \beta_2^t} \qquad (11)$$

3.5 Visualization of the Network

The proposed network adopts standard and dilated convolution operations in different layers, we analyzed the features learned by different convolutional layers in this subsection. In Fig. 3(a), we show the features learned by first convolutional layer. It contains mostly the edges and colors which are required for later convolutional layers in removing haze efficiently. Figure 3(b) represents the features learned in convolutional layer with d $= 4$. These features are combination of lower layer features, and the representations are very complicated as shown in Fig. 3(b). The high-level features can be seen as features that are encoded by higher levels of visual cortex. The size of the features learned in both the layers is same (i.e., 3×3) but the layer with dilated filter exploited contextual information of size 9×9 by inserting d $- 1$ spaces (i.e., 3) between each pixel. The number of parameters of each filter in both the layers are the same.

4 Experiments

In this section, we explain the experimental analysis for dehazing. The datasets, network parameters, comparison with latest dehazing methods and finally, the quantitative and qualitative analysis are also the part of this section.

4.1 Dataset

For training, validation and testing, we used the RESIDE [11] benchmark dehaze dataset. The RESIDE dataset contain synthesized images from depth and stereo datasets as large-scale training and testing hazy image pairs. We considered 100 images for training from the training pairs of RESIDE dataset. A total of 18960 training samples each with a size of 37×37 is cropped from the 100 images. 20 separate images are cropped to produce validation set. Two different datasets test1 and test2 with 100 and 500 images respectively from [11] are considered for testing.

4.2 Training Details

In each layer 64 filters of size 3×3 is used. Initial learning rate is set to 10^{-4}. The learning rate is reduced by 10% after 50 epochs. We trained our network for 100 epochs. The validation error is constant after 50 epochs. So, we reduced learning rate by 10% and terminated learning after 100 epochs. The validation error plateaus after 100 epochs. The regularization factor (λ) is set to 10^{-5}. Gradient clipping is not used as there is no chance of gradient explosion because of using low learning rate. The network is trained on a machine with 32 GB RAM, Intel core I5 processor and NVIDIA GeForce 710 GPU. MATLAB is used for both training and testing.

4.3 Metrics and Compared Methods

The widely used peak signal to noise ratio (PSNR) and Structural SIMilarity (SSIM) index measure are used for quantitative performance comparison. AMEF [9] and DehazeNet [8] methods are used for comparison.

$$PSNR(I_G, I_D) = 10\log_{10} \frac{I_{G_{max}}^2}{\frac{1}{N}\sum_{i=1}^{N}(I_{G_i} - I_D)^2} \tag{12}$$

$$SSIM(I_G, I_D) = \frac{(2\mu_{I_G}\mu_{I_D} + C_1)(2\sigma_{I_G I_D} + C_2)}{(\mu_{I_G}^2 + \mu_{I_D}^2 + C_1)(\sigma_{I_G}^2 + \sigma_{I_G}^2 + C_2)} \tag{13}$$

where $\mu_{I_G}, \mu_{I_D}, \sigma_{I_G}^2, \sigma_{I_D}^2, \sigma_{I_G I_D}$ are local mean, variance and cross-covariance for images I_G and I_D respectively.

4.4 Quantitative Metrics

Tables 2 and 3 represents the quantitative metrics comparison on two different test sets with test1 and test2 containing 100 and 500 test images respectively. The proposed method is consistently the top performer for both the metrics PSNR and SSIM. An improvement of 1.69 dB PSNR is achieved with the proposed method when compared to the next best DehazeNet [8]. AMEF [9] and DehazeNet [10] are the state of-the-art methods for dehazing. Moreover, for fair comparison with AMEF [9] and DehazeNet [10], the proposed network is trained with the same training dataset.

4.5 Qualitative Analysis

Figures 4 and 5 represents the visual comparison of dehazed images with different methods. The visual quality of the image produced with the proposed method is good when compared to the images produced with other methods. As one can see from Figs. 4 and 5, the AMEF restored images contain color artifacts.

Table 2. Average Performance Analysis on Test1

Metrics	Hazy	AMEF [9]	DehazeNet [8]	Proposed Method
PSNR (dB)	15.97	17.68	23.48	25.17
SSIM	0.7992	0.8349	0.8915	0.9393

Table 3. Average Performance Analysis on Test2

Metrics	Hazy	AMEF [9]	DehazeNet [8]	Proposed Method
PSNR (dB)	14.77	17.32	22.92	24.87
SSIM	0.7932	0.8149	0.8715	0.9182

Original   Hazy   AMEF   DehazeNet   Proposed

Fig. 4. Qualitative comparison with different methods for sample image 1

| Original | Hazy | AMEF | DehazeNet | Proposed |

Fig. 5. Qualitative comparison with different methods for sample image 2

4.6 Run Time

For real time applications, the run time is as important as performance. In this subsection, we present the testing times of compared methods on an image of size 512×512 in Table 4. The testing is performed on CPU. The proposed method is ≈ 1.8 and 2.57 times faster than the AMEF [9] and DehazeNet [8] respectively.

Table 4. Testing Time (In Seconds) for a 512×512 Image

Method	AMEF [8]	DehazeNet [7]	Proposed method
Run time	2.65	3.78	1.47

5   Conclusion

In this paper, we proposed a novel deep dilated convolutional neural network for single image dehazing. Furthermore, we considered dilated convolutions in different layers to exploit more image content without increasing the network complexity. We avoided adopting higher dilation rates (e.g., 5, 6 etc.) to overcome the gridding effect caused due to leaving more spaces between pixel elements. The proposed method produced superior performance in terms of quantitative metrics and perceptual quality when compared to other competitive methods in terms of quantitative metrics like PSNR and SSIM. In future, the proposed network will be modified with dense skip connections to achieve further improvement in the performance without increasing the network complexity.

References

1. Woodell, G., Jobson, D.J., Rahman, Z., Hines, G.: Advanced image processing of aerial imagery. In: Proceedings of the SPIE 6246, Visual Information Processing XV, 62460E, 12 May 2006
2. Shao, L., Liu, L., Li, X.: Feature learning for image classification via multiobjective genetic programming. IEEE Trans. Neural Networks Learn. Syst. **25**(7), 1359–1371 (2014). https://doi.org/10.1109/TNNLS.2013.2293418

3. Liu, Q., Gao, X.,He, L., Lu, W.: Haze removal for a single visible remote sensing image. Signal Processing **137**, 3343 (2017). ISSN 0165-1684, https://doi.org/10.1016/j.sigpro.2017.01036

4. Kim, T.K., Paik, J.K., Kang, B.S.: Contrast enhancement system using spatially adaptive histogram equalization with temporal filtering. IEEE Trans. Consumer Electron. **44**(1), 82–87 (1998). https://doi.org/10.1109/30.663733

5. Stark, J.A.: Adaptive image contrast enhancement using generalizations of histogram equalization. IEEE Trans. Image Process. **9**(5), 889–896 (2000). https://doi.org/10.1109/83.841534

6. Schechner, Y., Narasimhan, S., Nayar, S.: Polarization-based vision through haze. Appl. Opt. **42**, 511–525 (2003)

7. Narasimhan, S.G., Nayar, S.K.: Contrast restoration of weather degraded images. IEEE Trans. Pattern Analysis and Machine Intell. **25**(6), 713–724 (2003). https://doi.org/10.1109/TPAMI.2003.1201821

8. Cai, B. Xu, X., Jia, K., Qing, C., Tao, D.: DehazeNet: an End-to-End system for single image haze removal. IEEE Trans. Image Process. 25(11), 5187–5198 (2016). https://doi.org/10.1109/TIP.2016.2598681

9. Galdran, A.: Image dehazing by artificial multiple-exposure image fusion. Signal Process. **149**, 135–147 (2018). ISSN 0165-1684, https://doi.org/10.1016/j.sigpro.2018.03.008

10. Cantor, A.: Optics of the atmosphere–scattering by molecules and particles. IEEE J. Quant. Electron. **14**(9), 698–699 (1978). https://doi.org/10.1109/JQE.1978.1069864

11. Li, B., et al.: Benchmarking single-image dehazing and beyond. IEEE Trans. Image Process. **28**(1), 492–505 (2019). https://doi.org/10.1109/TIP.2018.2867951

12. Kingma, D., Ba, J.: Adam: a method for stochastic optimization. In: International Conference on Learning Representations (2014)

T2CI-GAN: Text to Compressed Image Generation Using Generative Adversarial Network

Bulla Rajesh[1,2]([envelope]) [ID], Nandakishore Dusa[1], Mohammed Javed[1] [ID], Shiv Ram Dubey[1] [ID], and P. Nagabhushan[1,2]

[1] Department of IT, IIIT Allahabad, Prayagraj 211015, U.P, India
{rsi2018007,iwm2016002,javed,srdubey,pnagabhushan}@iiita.ac.in
[2] Department of CSE, Vignan University, Guntur 522213, A.P, India

Abstract. The problem of generating textual descriptions for the visual data has gained research attention in the recent years. In contrast to that the problem of generating visual data from textual descriptions is still very challenging, because it requires the combination of both Natural Language Processing (NLP) and Computer Vision techniques. The existing methods utilize the Generative Adversarial Networks (GANs) and generate the uncompressed images from textual description. However, in practice, most of the visual data are processed and transmitted in the compressed representation. Hence, the proposed work attempts to generate the visual data directly in the compressed representation form using Deep Convolutional GANs (DCGANs) to achieve the storage and computational efficiency. We propose GAN models for compressed image generation from text. The first model is directly trained with JPEG compressed DCT images (compressed domain) to generate the compressed images from text descriptions. The second model is trained with RGB images (pixel domain) to generate JPEG compressed DCT representation from text descriptions. The proposed models are tested on an open source benchmark dataset Oxford-102 Flower images using both RGB and JPEG compressed versions, and accomplished the state-of-the-art performance in the JPEG compressed domain. The code will be publicly released at GitHub after acceptance of paper.

Keywords: Compressed Domain · Deep Learning · DCT Coefficients · T2CI-GAN · JPEG Compression · Compressed Domain Pattern Recognition · Text to Compressed Image

1 Introduction

Generating visually realistic images based on the natural text descriptions is an interesting research problem that warrants knowledge of both language processing and computer vision. Unlike the problem of image captioning that generates

© The Author(s), under exclusive license to Springer Nature Switzerland AG 2023
D. Gupta et al. (Eds.): CVIP 2022, CCIS 1777, pp. 292–307, 2023.
https://doi.org/10.1007/978-3-031-31417-9_23

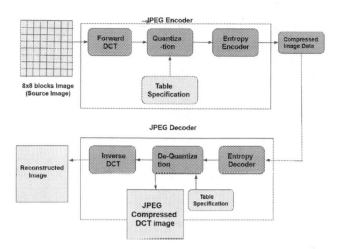

Fig. 1. JPEG Compression and Decompression architecture and extraction of JPEG Compressed DCT image which is used in the proposed approach.

text descriptions from image, the challenge here is to generate semantically suitable images based on proper understanding of the text descriptions. Many interesting techniques have been proposed in the literature to explore the problem of generating pixel images from the given input texts [16,20,26,27]. Moreover, a very recent attempt by [11] is aimed to generate images in the compressed format. The whole idea here is to avoid synthesis of RGB images and subsequent compression stage. In fact, in the current digital scenario, more and more images and image frames (videos) are being stored and transmitted in compressed representation. The compressed data in the internet world has reached more than 90% [19] of traffic. On the other hand, different compressed domain technologies are being explored both by the software giants, like Uber [4] and Xerox [17], and academia [2,9,13,23], that can directly process and analyse compressed data without decompression and re-compression. Some of the prominent works in compressed document images are discussed in [7,8,10] and [18,19]. This gives us strong motivation for exploring the idea of generating compressed images directly from natural text descriptions, and that is attempted in this research paper.

Recently, Generative Adversarial Network (GAN) models have been successfully used for generating realistic images from diverse inputs such as layouts [5], texts [25], and scenes [1]. However, early GAN models [20] have generated images of low resolutions from the input text. In [20], the GAN model was used to generate image from a single sentence. This method was implemented in two stages. Initially the text sentence was encoded into a feature matrix using deep CNNs and RNNs to extract the significant features. Then those features were utilized to generate a picture. In order to improve the quality, a stacked GAN was reported in [27]. It generated the output picture using two GANs. In the first step, GAN-1 produced a low resolution image with basic shape and colors along with the background generated from a random noise vector. In the second step, GAN-2 improvised the produced image by adding details and making some required corrections. MirrorGAN was reported in [16] for text to image translation through re-description. This model has reported the improved semantic consistency between text and produced output image. In [26], authors proposed a Semantics Disentangling Generative Adversarial Network (SD-GAN) which exploited the semantics of text description. However, all the GAN based techniques discussed above were trained using RGB pixel images meant to generate RGB images. Hence, our work is focused on employing the significant features of GAN for generating compressed images directly from the given text descriptions.

In the recent literature, a GAN model was proposed for generating direct compressed images from noise vector [11]. Since JPEG compression was the most used format, the authors attempted to generate direct JPEG compressed images rather than generating RGB images and compressing them separately. Their GAN framework consists of Generator, Decoder and Discriminator sub networks. The Generator consists of locally connected layers, quantization layers, and chroma subsampling layers. These locally connected layers perform the block based operations similar to JPEG compression methods to generate JPEG compressed images. In between the Generator and the Discriminator, a Decoder was used to decompress the image to facilitate the comparison with ground truth RGB image by the Discriminator network. In specific, this decoder performed de-quantization and Inverse Discrete Cosine Transformation (IDCT) followed by YCbCr to RGB transformations on the compressed images generated by the Generator. Unlike [11] which generates the compressed images from noise, our model generates the compressed images based on the given input text descriptions.

Overall, this research paper propose two novel GAN models for generating compressed images from text descriptions. The first GAN model is trained directly with JPEG compressed DCT images to generate compressed images from text description. The second GAN model is trained with RGB images to generate compressed images from text descriptions. The proposed models have been tested on Oxford-102 Flower images benchmark dataset using both the RGB and JPEG compressed versions, reporting state-of-the-art performance in the compressed domain. Rest of the paper is organized as follows: Sect. 2 presents the preliminaries of used concepts. Section 3 discusses the proposed methodology and GAN architectures. Section 4 reports the detailed experimental results and analysis. Finally, Sect. 5 concludes the paper with a summary.

2 Preliminaries

In this section, a brief description of JPEG compression, GAN model and GloVe model is presented.

2.1 JPEG Compression

JPEG compression algorithm achieves compression by discarding the high frequency components. Firstly, the RGB channels of the image are converted into YCbCr format to separate the luminance (Y) and chrominance (CbCr) channels as,

$$Y = (0.299 \times r + 0.587 \times g + 0.114 \times b) \tag{1}$$

$$Cb = (-0.1687 \times r - 0.3313 \times g + 0.5 \times b + 128) \tag{2}$$

$$Cr = (0.5 \times r - 0.4187 \times g - 0.0813 \times b + 128). \tag{3}$$

Then each channel is divided into 8×8 non-overlapping pixel blocks. Forward Discrete Cosine Transform (DCT) is applied on each block in each channel to convert the 8×8 pixel block (let's say $P(x, y)$) from spatial domain to frequency domain. Each DCT block, i.e., $F(u, v)$, is quantized to keep only the low frequency coefficients. Then Differential pulse code modulation (DPCM) is applied on the DC components and Run Length Encoding (RLE) on AC components. Huffman Coding is used to encode the DC and AC components in smaller number of bits. In order to perform the decompression, Entropy decoding, De-Quantization, and Inverse DCT (IDCT) are applied in the given order on the compressed image to obtain the uncompressed image. The compression and decompression stages are illustrated in Fig. 1. In the proposed work, the JPEG compressed DCT images are directly extracted from the JPEG compressed stream and used for training the deep learning model. The decompression is done only for the performance analysis, otherwise it is not required in practice.

2.2 Generative Adversarial Network (GAN)

Generative Adversarial Network (GAN) [3] is a deep learning model built with two networks, including Generator and Discriminator. The Generator (G) generates new images in the training images distribution and the Discriminator (D) classifies the images between actual and generated images into real and fake categories, respectively. These two sub models are trained alternatively such that Generator(G) tries to fool the Discriminator by generating data similar to real domain, whereas the Discriminator is optimized to distinguish the generated images from the real images. Overall, the Generator and the Discriminator play a two player min-max game. The objective function of the GAN is given as follows:

$$\min_{G} \max_{D} F(G, D) = E_{y \sim k_d}[\log D(x)] + E_{z \sim k_z}[\log(1 - D(G(z)))] \tag{4}$$

where y indicates real image sampled from k_d (true data distribution), z indicates noise vector sampled from k_z (uniform or Gaussian distribution).

The Conditional GAN model [12] makes use of some additional information along with the noise. Both Generator (G) and Discriminator (D) use this additional information which is referred as conditioning variable 'c' that can be text or any other data. Thus, the Generator on Conditional GAN generates the images conditioned on variable 'c' as depicted in Fig. 2.

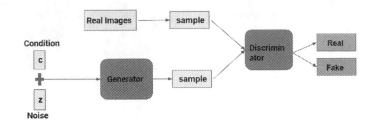

Fig. 2. Conditional GAN architecture [12].

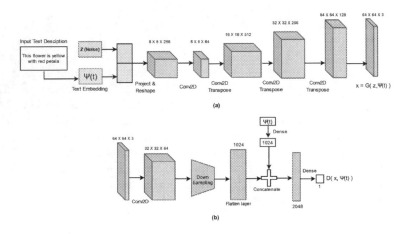

Fig. 3. The proposed T2CI-GAN Model-1 architecture using the backbone networks of [20]. (a) Generator network and (b) Discriminator network.

2.3 GloVe Model

GloVe stands for Global Vectors [15]. GloVe is an unsupervised learning algorithm. It is used for obtaining vector representations of words. It is an Open Source project developed at stanford. Word vectors make words having same meaning to cluster together and dissimilar words to repel. Word2Vec depends on local context information of words. The advantage of GloVe is that, unlike Word2vec to exctract or produce word vectors, it incorporates global statistics.

3   Proposed Methodology

In this section, we present the details of the proposed T2CI-GAN models for text to compressed image translation. We propose two variants of T2CI-GAN with simple Generator and customized Generator, respectively. First, we discuss the base network architecture of the proposed T2CI-GAN models which is adapted from T2I-GAN [20].

3.1   Network Architecture

The Deep Convolutional GAN (DC-GAN) architecture shown in Fig. 3 is used for the implementation of text to image synthesis. This is our base architecture (T2CI-GAN) for implementation of text to compressed image generation. First, the Word Embeddings $\psi(t)$ of given text-descriptions are obtained using the GloVe model. It is concatenated with the Noise Vector 'z' and used as input to the Generator. Hence we provide a pair of both Text Embedding vectors $\psi(t)$ and noise (z) as the input to T2CI-GAN model, instead of only noise.

Generator Network. The embedding of size 300 and the noise of size 100 are concatenated and given as input to the Dense layer. After Reshaping the output of the Dense layer, a series of Convolutions and Batch Normalization are performed, respectively for 4 times. It is then followed by Convolution2D Transpose and finally a Convolution with 'Tanh' activation function. The 'LeakyReLU' activation function is used after every Batch Normalization. It produces a image tensor of shape $64 \times 64 \times 3$ which is given as input to the Discriminator.

Discriminator. Discriminator takes the output of Generator ($64 \times 64 \times 3$ image tensor) and word embedding of size 300 as input. A series of 2D strided Convolutions are performed on image tensor. Batch Normalization is applied after all Convolutions except for first one. Before applying last Convolution, embedding is concatenated with previous output. The 'LeakyReLU' activation function is used and followed by 'Dropout' layer to all Convolution layers except for last layer where 'Sigmoid' is used.

3.2   Proposed T2CI-GAN Model-1: Training with JPEG Compressed DCT Images

Preparing JPEG Compressed DCT Image Dataset. This is an important step for the proposed model. The JPEG compressed entropy encoded images of the dataset are partially decompressed to obtain DCT Compressed version by applying entropy decoding and De-Quantization steps in the decoder as shown in Fig. 1. Sample images from the dataset in RGB and JPEG Compressed DCT image formats are shown in Fig. 5 and Fig. 6, respectively. Note that after conversion of RGB image into JPEG compressed DCT form, the images will be in the form of coefficients upon which a custom transformation is applied where a specified coefficients such as $F01, F10, F11$ etc., are selected to decrease the computational complexity and ease the training process. In this transformation, since JPEG is applied block wise (8×8 blocks) on an image, first 5 coefficients from first row, first 3 coefficients from the second row, and the first coefficient from the third row are extracted from every 8×8 block and making other values to zero. From Fig. 7 shown, we observe very slight decrease in image quality compared to the one before transformation.

Normalization of the JPEG Compressed DCT Image. It is important to normalize the DCT coefficients extracted from above paragraph for training the model. Unlike the original RGB dataset whose pixel values range from 0 to 255, the exact range of values in the compressed image are not known. So, maximum and minimum values are computed from all the DCT values of all images in the dataset. Then, using this maximum and minimum values, the DCT pixel values in the range from [-1, +1] are generated.

Loss Function. Binary Cross-Entropy loss function is used in binary classification tasks. It is also known as log loss [24] and given as,

$$BCE\_Loss = (-\frac{1}{N}) \sum_{i=1}^{N} x_i(\log p(x_i)) + (1 - x_i)(\log 1 - p(x_i)) \tag{5}$$

where x_i represents the actual class and $\log p(x_i)$ is the probability of that class and N is the total number of instances.

3.3   Training T2CI-GAN Model-1

Noise vector of size 100 concatenated with word-embedding vector of size 300 is given as input to the Generator network which performs Up-samplings and Convolutions, and produces a $64 \times 64 \times 3$ image as output. This image-tensor is passed to Discriminator to classify it as fake (generated) or real (original). Training a GAN is a very challenging task, because both Generator and Discriminator networks are trained simultaneously. The main goal of GAN training is to find a point of equilibrium between the Generator and Discriminator models. So, it makes training of GAN unstable. For stable training [6], Batch-normalization is used in both Generator and Discriminator networks. The 'LeakyReLU' activation function is used in all layers of Generator and Discriminator except for output layer. The 'tanh' activation function is used for last layer in case of Generator and the 'Sigmoid' activation function in case of Discriminator.

For training the proposed GAN Model-1, GAN-INT method [20] is used, where the Discriminator is prepared on three pairs of inputs (original images, original captions), (generated images, original captions), and (original images, wrong captions). Binary Cross Entropy (BCE) loss function with ADAM optimizer is used for both Generator and Discriminator networks with learning rate = 0.0002 and momentum = 0.5. The BCE loss of generator is measured by first decoding the output of generator into RGB channels. The network is trained for 500 epochs with a mini-batch size of 64. After training the Discriminator network is discarded. For calculation of Generator loss, right descriptions is passed to the model as input. Then, loss is computed on the outputs from Discriminator (ranges between 0 and 1) and tensor of 1's. For calculation of Discriminator loss, three pairs of inputs (original images, original captions) for real loss, (generated images, original captions) and (original images, wrong captions) for fake loss are

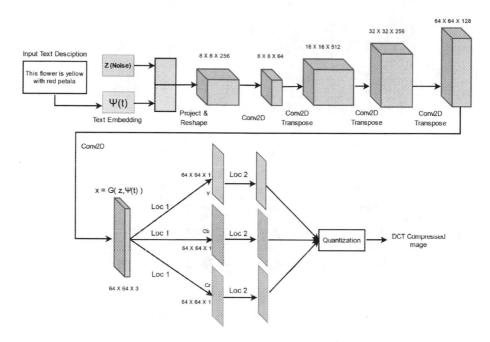

Fig. 4. The Generator network of the proposed T2CI-GAN Model-2. The Discriminator is same as used in T2CI-GAN Model-1.)

considered. The sum of the real loss and fake loss is regarded as the Discriminator loss. Overall, the T2CI-GAN model-1 uses same architecture as used by T2I-GAN Fig. 3, but trained with JPEG compressed DCT images.

The proposed model is able to generate good JPEG Compressed DCT images close to the ones in the dataset, but on decompression to the RGB domain, the images either get distorted or suffers with the mode collapse problem by generating the similar images as shown in Fig. 10. We conclude that the T2CI-GAN Model-1 fails to learn the RGB image information from JPEG Compressed DCT images. Hence, we propose T2CI-GAN Model-2 next which solves this problem.

3.4   Proposed T2CI-GAN Model-2: With Modified Generator and Training with RGB Images

It is noticed in T2CI-GAN Model-1 and in [11] that while training on compressed images directly, DCT values fluctuate to a greater extent within the blocks and also across the blocks. Thus, the Discriminator gives sub-par quality gradients to the Generator and makes it difficult to train a decent Generator. Therefore, in this backdrop, we propose T2CI-GAN Model-2 for text to compressed image translation with modified Generator having the manual compression and decode modules as utilized by [11] for compressed image generation from noise. The Discriminator network in T2CI-GAN Model-2 is same as in T2CI-GAN Model-1.

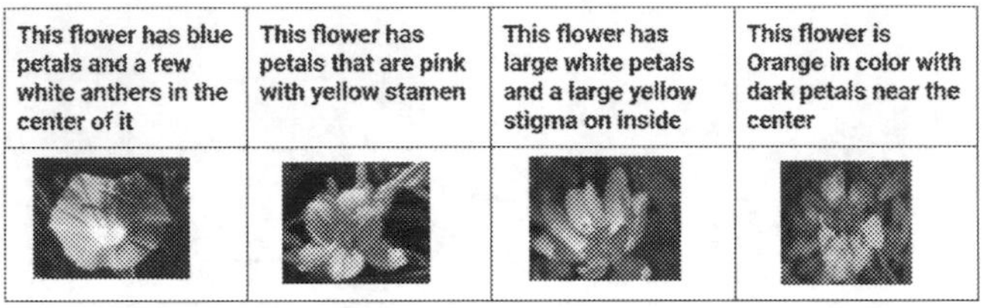

Fig. 5. Sample RGB images from Oxford 102 Flowers dataset with input text descriptions.

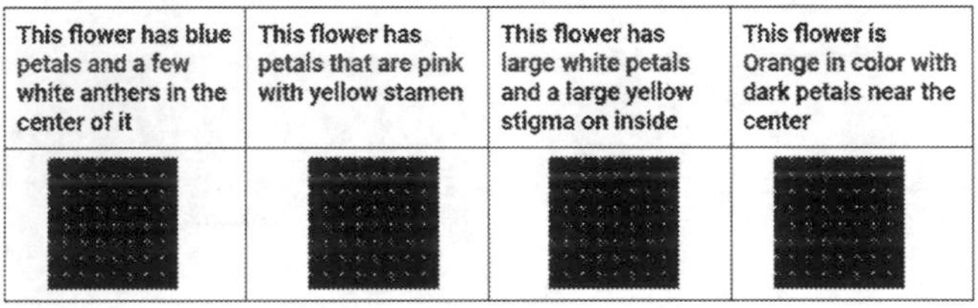

Fig. 6. Corresponding sample JPEG Compressed DCT images generated from Oxford-102 Flower images shown in Fig. 5 and input text descriptions.

Modified Generator. In this proposed model, the Generator is modified such that it implements the idea of a JPEG encoder as used by [11]. Basically, we develop the Generator of T2CI-GAN Model-2 by adding 6 locally connected layers along with a quantization layer and an entropy encoder layer in the Generator of T2CI-GAN Model-2. The modified Generator is shown in Fig. 4. After the Generator generates a $64 \times 64 \times 3$ image tensor from text and noise, the image tensor is divided into 3 channels, and each channel is passed through a Locally connected layer (Loc1) to generate Y, Cb, and Cr channels, respectively. Block size 1×1 is used in Loc1 layer. The Y, Cb, and Cr channels are then passed through another Locally connected layer (Loc2) which performs 8×8 block-wise operation like DCT. Basically, the Loc2 layer produces amplitudes of DCT for Y, Cb, and Cr channels, respectively. Next, the quantization is performed using the standard JPEG quantization method, where DCT block values are divided by a quantization matrix (based on quality factor). Finally an entropy encoder layer is used after the training.

Decoder. In the proposed T2CI-GAN Model-2, the Generator network generates the compressed versions of images (upto quantization) while trained using RGB image dataset. So, during training it is needed to decompress the compressed images into the RGB domain. For this, we use a non-trainable decoder (H) which takes input from the Generator and converts it into RGB pixel values and transfers the output to the Discriminator. In the decoder, De-quantization, Inverse Discrete Cosine Transform (2D IDCT) and color transformation are performed from YCbCr to RGB. At last, pixel values are clipped to range [0,255], and this is given as input to the Discriminator network.

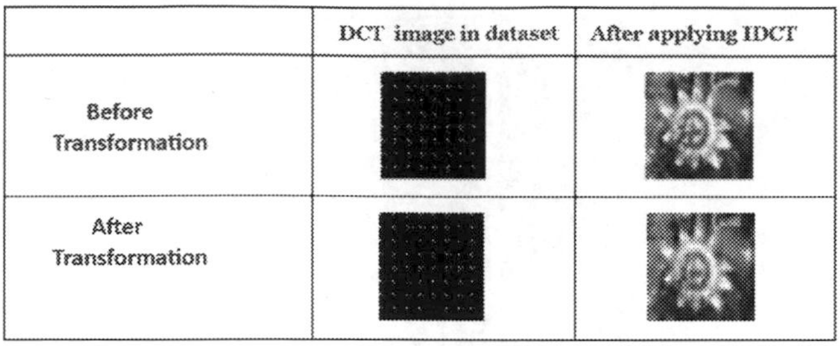

	DCT image in dataset	After applying IDCT
Before Transformation		
After Transformation		

Fig. 7. The significance of applying the simple transformation on JPEG Compressed DCT images.

Loss Function. The loss function remains same for Discriminator, but for Generator extra loss term $\gamma|H(G(z,t))-\hat{G}(z,t)|$ is added to guide the locally connected layers similar to [11]. Here H is the decoder, G is Generator, z is noise vector, $\hat{G}$ indicates the layers of Generator before any Locally connected layer has been used, and γ is a hyperparameter as weight between original Generator loss and the modified Generator loss. The value of γ used in the experiments is 0.1.

4   Experimental Results

4.1   Oxford-102 Flowers Dataset

Oxford-102 flowers dataset [14] has 102 flower categories in RGB format. Each class contains around 40 to 258 pictures with total 8189 images. Each image of the dataset has around 10 text-descriptions or captions portraying that image. To train the proposed models 2500 flower images are JPEG compressed to generate JPEG compressed Oxford-102 flowers dataset. Some sample images and captions of 102-flowers dataset are shown in Fig. 5. The corresponding sample captions with JPEG Compressed Oxford-102 flowers dataset are shown in Fig. 6. The above transformation is applied on JPEG Compressed flowers dataset to ease the training process. Figure 7 shows sample flower image before and after transformation.

4.2   Text to Compressed Image Results

T2CI-GAN Model-1 Results The T2CI-GAN Model-1 is trained with 2500 JPEG Compressed DCT Oxford-102 flowers dataset and corresponding captions. The model is trained for 500 epochs. Figure 8 shows the generated compressed images during training of the model. As mentioned earlier, the quality of generated DCT images is good, but after decompressing them to RGB format, the resultant images are either distorted or the same kind of images are generated for different input captions. Figure 10 shows different input texts, their corresponding generated JPEG compressed images, and their corresponding decompressed

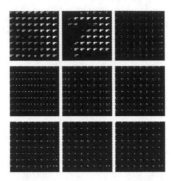

Fig. 8. Sample output images generated for the text descriptions during training with T2CI-GAN Model-1.

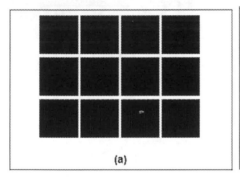
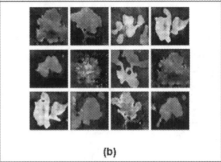

Fig. 9. Performance of T2CI-GAN Model-2, where (a) sample JPEG compressed DCT images generated during training and (b) their corresponding decompressed images in the RGB domain.

Input Text Description	Generated DCT Image	Decompressed RGB Image
This flower is white in color with petals are oval shaped		
This flower is pink and white in color with petals are oval shaped		
This flower has petals that are pink and has pointy tips		
This flower is orange in color with petals that are oval shaped		

Fig. 10. Sample output images generated for the text descriptions during training with the T2CI-GAN Model-1.

RGB images. It can be seen that only in a few cases the model gives correct results irrespective of the generated compressed images which look very similar for different input texts.

Input Text Description	Generated DCT Image	Decompressed RGB Image
Two bright Red flowers whose petals are not separated but a whole	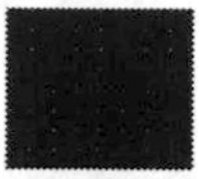	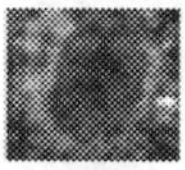
This particular flower has petals that are light purple and white	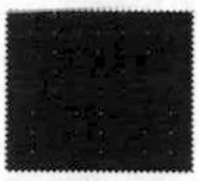	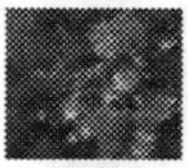
This flower is blue and white in color with oval shaped petals	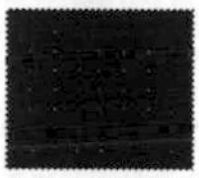	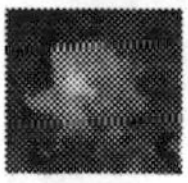
This flower consists of a cluster of orange small flowers	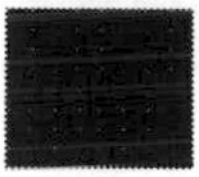	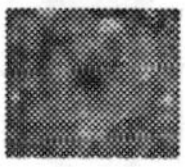

Fig. 11. Sample output images generated for the input text descriptions with the T2CI-GAN Model-2.

T2CI-GAN Model-2 Results. In T2CI-GAN Model-2, the decoder is used to convert the compressed version of images generated by the Generator back into RGB format to feed them to the Discriminator network during training. This model is trained for 500 epochs. Figure 9 shows the compressed images (Quantized DCT images) generated and corresponding decoded RGB images during training. Figure 11 shows the sample Input text descriptions, Generated compressed version of image (Quantized DCT image) and its corresponding decoded RGB image. It can be observed that quality of the generated and decompressed images using T2CI-GAN Model-2 is much better than quality of the generated and decompressed images using T2CI-GAN Model-1.

4.3 Quantitative Evaluation of the Model

In order to perform the quantitative evaluation, We compute the InceptionScore [21] for the proposed models. Inception score is a metric which evaluates the quality of generated images. It is mostly used for GANs evaluation which uses a pre-trained InceptionV3 model [22]. Using this model we calculate conditional probability of each generated image $p(y|x)$) and average of these conditional probabilities which is marginal probability $p(y)$. Next, we calculate KL divergence for each generated image as follows:

$$KL = p(y|x) \times (log(p(y|x)) - log(p(y)). \tag{6}$$

Summation of KL divergence over all images and average over all classes and exponent of this result is inception score. Inception score captures quality of images and image diversity (i.e., whether a wide range of images are generated or not).

Table 1. Performance comparison of T2I-GAN, T2CI-GAN Model-1 and T2CI-GAN Model-2 on Oxford-102 Flower dataset images with output and Inception Score measured in their respective domains.

Model	Input Domain	Generator Output	Domain	Inception Score
T2I-GAN	RGB	RGB	RGB	2.38 ± .17
Model-1	Compressed	Compressed	Compressed	1.08 ± .01
Model-2	RGB	Compressed	Compressed	1.01 ± .01

Table 2. Performance of the proposed compressed domain models, i.e., T2CI-GAN Model-1 and T2CI-GAN Model-2, on Oxford-102 Flower dataset with output in compressed domain and Inception Score measured in RGB domain.

Model	Input Domain	Generator Output	Domain	Inception Score
Model-1	Compressed	Compressed	RGB	1.42 ± .02
Model-2	RGB	Compressed	RGB	2.01 ± .12

Table 3. Comparison of the proposed compressed domain models with the state-of-the-art models such as GAN-INT-CLS [20], StackGAN [27] and T2I-GAN [20] using inception score measured in RGB domain on Oxford-102 dataset.

Model	Input Domain	Generator Output	Inception Score
GAN-INT-CLS [20]	RGB	RGB	2.66 ± .03
StackGAN [27]	RGB	RGB	3.20 ± .01
T2I-GAN [20]	RGB	RGB	2.38 ± .17
T2CI-GAN Model-1	Compressed	Compressed	1.42 ± .02
T2CI-GAN Model-2	RGB	Compressed	2.01 ± .12

Table 1 shows the experimental of T2I-GAN [20], T2CI-GAN Model-1 and T2CI-GAN Model-2, where input domain for training of the model, domain of Generated images, domain of images to calculate inception score and inception scores are shown. Table 2 shows inception scores of methods proposed for text to compressed image generation. Here, instead of calculating Inception score directly with generated images in compressed domain, we first decompress them into RGB domain and then calculate the Inception score. From the results, it is clear that T2CI-GAN Model-2 performs better compared to T2CI-GAN Model-1 and achieves promising and state-of-the-art results in the compressed domain.

4.4   Comparative Study

The proposed T2CI-GAN models translate the text descriptions into compressed domain images. Although there is no existing GAN framework that generates compressed images directly from the input text, to compare our proposed models with state-of-the-art text to image GAN models, we first decompress the generated compressed images to RGB domain, and then evaluate and compare them with state-of-the-art models using Inception score. In Table 3, we can see that inception score of the proposed models are low when compared with the state-of-the-art models like GAN-INT-CLS [20], StackGAN [27] and T2I-GAN [20] working in RGB domain because Inception score is usually calculated with 20k-50k images in the existing models. However, we train the model only with 2500 images and the corresponding captions to decrease the training time. So the Inception score reported with the models is low.

5   Conclusion

In this paper, we achieve the objective of generating compressed versions of images directly from text descriptions instead of generating raw RGB images and compressing it later as a post-processing step. We present two T2CI-GAN frameworks that generate compressed versions of images. We demonstrate the training and testing on Oxford flower-102 dataset. We observe a promising performance by the proposed T2CI-GAN Model-2. The performance of the proposed T2CI-GAN Model-1 is also satisfactory in compressed domain, but suffers to get the qualitative uncompressed images. The proposed models can be further improved by using the state-of-the-art text to image GAN models and optimization techniques to improve the quality of generated images in the compressed domain.

References

1. Ashual, O., Wolf, L.: Specifying object attributes and relations in interactive scene generation. In: Proceedings of the IEEE/CVF International Conference on Computer Vision, pp. 4561–4569 (2019)
2. Bell, T., Adjeroh, D., Mukherjee, A.: Pattern matching in compressed texts and images (2001)
3. Goodfellow, I., et al.: Generative adversarial nets. In: Advances in Neural Information Processing Systems, vol. 27 (2014)
4. Gueguen, L., Sergeev, A., Kadlec, B., Liu, R., Yosinski, J.: Faster neural networks straight from jpeg. In: Advances in Neural Information Processing Systems, pp. 3933–3944 (2018)
5. He, S., et al.: Context-aware layout to image generation with enhanced object appearance. In: Proceedings of the IEEE/CVF Conference on Computer Vision and Pattern Recognition, pp. 15049–15058 (2021)
6. Jason, B.: Tips for training stable generative adversarial networks (2019). https://machinelearningmastery.com/how-to-train-stable-generative-adversarial-networks/

7. Javed, M., Nagabhushan, P., Chaudhuri, B.B.: Extraction of line-word-character segments directly from run-length compressed printed text-documents. In: 2013 Fourth National Conference on Computer Vision, Pattern Recognition, Image Processing and Graphics (NCVPRIPG), pp. 1–4. IEEE (2013)
8. Javed, M., Nagabhushan, P., Chaudhuri, B.: Extraction of projection profile, run-histogram and entropy features straight from run-length compressed text-documents. arXiv preprint arXiv:1404.0627 (2014)
9. Javed, M., Nagabhushan, P., Chaudhuri, B.B.: A review on document image analysis techniques directly in the compressed domain. Artif. Intell. Rev. **50**(4), 539–568 (2018)
10. Javed, M., Nagabhushan, P., Chaudhuri, B.B.: A direct approach for word and character segmentation in run-length compressed documents with an application to word spotting. In: 2015 13th International Conference on Document Analysis and Recognition (ICDAR), pp. 216–220. IEEE (2015)
11. Kang, B., Tripathi, S., Nguyen, T.Q.: Generating images in compressed domain using generative adversarial networks. IEEE Access **8**, 180977–180991 (2020). https://doi.org/10.1109/ACCESS.2020.3027800
12. Mirza, M., Osindero, S.: Conditional generative adversarial nets. arXiv preprint arXiv:1411.1784 (2014)
13. Mukhopadhyay, J.: Image and video processing in the compressed domain. Chapman and Hall/CRC (2011)
14. Nilsback, M.E., Zisserman, A.: 102 category flower dataset (2008). https://www.robots.ox.ac.uk/~vgg/data/flowers/102/
15. Pennington, J., Socher, R., Manning, C.D.: Glove: Global vectors for word representation. In: Proceedings of the 2014 conference on empirical methods in natural language processing (EMNLP), pp. 1532–1543 (2014)
16. Qiao, T., Zhang, J., Xu, D., Tao, D.: MIRRORGAN: learning text-to-image generation by redescription. In: Proceedings of the IEEE/CVF Conference on Computer Vision and Pattern Recognition, pp. 1505–1514 (2019)
17. de Queiroz, R.L., Eschbach, R.: Fast segmentation of the jpeg-compressed documents. J. Electron. Imaging **7**(2), 367–378 (1998)
18. Rajesh, B., Javed, M., Ratnesh, Srivastava, S.: DCT-compCNN: a novel image classification network using jpeg compressed DCT coefficients. In: 2019 IEEE Conference on Information and Communication Technology, pp. 1–6 (2019). https://doi.org/10.1109/CICT48419.2019.9066242
19. Rajesh, B., Javed, M., Nagabhushan, P.: Automatic tracing and extraction of text-line and word segments directly in jpeg compressed document images. IET Image Processing, April 2020
20. Reed, S., Akata, Z., Yan, X., Logeswaran, L., Schiele, B., Lee, H.: Generative adversarial text to image synthesis. In: International Conference on Machine Learning, pp. 1060–1069. PMLR (2016)
21. Salimans, T., Goodfellow, I., Zaremba, W., Cheung, V., Radford, A., Chen, X.: Improved techniques for training GANs. Adv. Neural. Inf. Process. Syst. **29**, 2234–2242 (2016)
22. Szegedy, C., Vanhoucke, V., Ioffe, S., Shlens, J., Wojna, Z.: Rethinking the inception architecture for computer vision. In: Proceedings of the IEEE Conference on Computer Vision and Pattern Recognition, pp. 2818–2826 (2016)
23. Tompkins, D.A., Kossentini, F.: A fast segmentation algorithm for bi-level image compression using jbig2. In: Proceedings. 1999 International Conference on Image Processing, 1999. ICIP 99, vol. 1, pp. 224–228. IEEE (1999)

24. Vovk, V.: The fundamental nature of the log loss function. In: Beklemishev, L.D., Blass, A., Dershowitz, N., Finkbeiner, B., Schulte, W. (eds.) Fields of Logic and Computation II. LNCS, vol. 9300, pp. 307–318. Springer, Cham (2015). https://doi.org/10.1007/978-3-319-23534-9_20
25. Xu, T., et al.: ATTNGAN: fine-grained text to image generation with attentional generative adversarial networks. In: Proceedings of the IEEE Conference on Computer Vision and Pattern Recognition, pp. 1316–1324 (2018)
26. Yin, G., Liu, B., Sheng, L., Yu, N., Wang, X., Shao, J.: Semantics disentangling for text-to-image generation. In: Proceedings of the IEEE/CVF Conference on Computer Vision and Pattern Recognition, pp. 2327–2336 (2019)
27. Zhang, H., et al.: Stackgan: text to photo-realistic image synthesis with stacked generative adversarial networks. In: Proceedings of the IEEE International Conference on Computer Vision, pp. 5907–5915 (2017)

Prediction of Fire Signatures Based on Fractional Order Optical Flow and Convolution Neural Network

Shreya Gupta, Muzammil Khan$^{(\boxtimes)}$, and Pushpendra Kumar

Department of Mathematics, Bioinformatics and Computer Applications, Maulana Azad National Institute of Technology, Bhopal 462003, India
{mk.193104002,pkumarfma}@manit.ac.in

Abstract. As we know that thousands of indoor and outdoor fires break out every day in different parts of the world, which result in a large number of serious causalities and threat to property safety. Therefore, it becomes of extreme importance to detect the fire in its very early stage, because once it is spread it becomes disastrous and difficult to control. The early detection of fire is associated with smoke, which is small at the beginning and have different colors, shape and textures. The initial stage of smoke can be seen easily through digital cameras installed in many locations. This paper proposed a smoke detection algorithm based on dynamical features of smoke using convolutional neural network (CNN). The dynamical features are considered in the form of optical flow color map. The estimation of optical flow is performed based on a fractional order variational model, which is capable in preserving dynamical discontinuities in the optical flow. Optical flow helps to find the active region of the images (video). The estimated color map is further dissected into its RGB channels and the channel with more sensitivity towards smoke motion is segmented with the help of binary mask. Finally, the segmented optical flow color maps are fed into a random forest based CNN architecture and a proposed ensemble learning based CNN architecture. Different accuracy metrics are considered for performance evaluation and comparison with other techniques. A variety of datasets consisting of 10 smoke (4576 frames) and 10 non-smoke (3219 frames) videos are considered for experiments.

Keywords: Convolutional neural networks · Fractional order derivative · Optical flow · Smoke detection · Variational model

1 Introduction

Fires are frequently abrupt, impact a wide area and are difficult to extinguish. Therefore, to protect any building, offices, forest or workplace from fire, early detection of fire becomes very important. The early detection of fire can be done with the help of smoke because it is a starting stage of fire before the flames and highly visible from long distance through digital cameras installed in many locations. However, smoke is small at the beginning and have different colors,

D. Gupta et al. (Eds.): CVIP 2022, CCIS 1777, pp. 308–321, 2023.
https://doi.org/10.1007/978-3-031-31417-9_24

shape and textures compare to fire. Hence, detection of smoke is a crucial step in early prevention of fire [24].

Nowadays, with recent rapid advancements in the digital video camera technology, these video cameras have become highly affordable and economical [26]. These video cameras are mounted at hilltop, walls and ceilings of the various buildings and continuously record videos in the form of image sequences. Since, manually processing of this huge amount of video data is extremely tedious, therefore an automatic approach to classify such events is an inevitable requirement of the time. Computer vision and deep learning algorithms together have constituted one sort of sophisticated technology that is becoming more prevalent in various areas of image processing such as face recognition, image retrieval, surveillance, object detection and classification [4, 7, 15, 16, 30, 32]. Detection of fire signatures such as smoke in videos is one of its fruitful application.

A considerable amount of work over detection of smoke in videos is available in the literature. Generally, smoke detection framework can be categorized into two groups: (1) traditional computer vision based approach and (2) deep learning based approach [18]. Computer vision based approaches rely on mathematical formulation, while deep learning approaches are based on training [3]. In [9], Hanh et al., performed fire detection using aerial forest videos in which the fire regions are detected with the help of RGB, YCbCr and HSI color spaces. Xu et al., [34] proposed a framework based upon deep domain adaptation technique which utilized synthetic data in smoke characterization using CNN. Moreover, Muhammad et al. [23] discussed a fine tuned GoogleNet architecture with low computing complexity. Detection of fire and smoke in natural videos faces a basic hurdle of recognising dynamic texture. For this purpose, pre-trained CNN models with SVM or random forest classifiers were employed in [5]. Luo et al. [19] identified the suspicious region based on a dark channel obtained from dynamic update of background. Pundir et al., [27] used the local extrema co-occurrence pattern to characterise foreground regions, intensity and hue of smoke in HSV color space. All such deep learning techniques utilize image datasets.

In vision based techniques, object motion detection is generally extracted with optical flow [3]. The optical flow field is estimated by assuming that same object on different image frames does not show any alteration in its intensity value. Optical flow-based approaches try to find the value of motion velocities at pixel level. In [2], optical flow is used for classifying moving blobs with an adaptive background subtraction algorithm. Dual deep learning framework presented in [28], employed optical flow calculation for characterising motion based on features. In [22], Mueller et al., developed two methods for optical flow estimation which estimate dynamic texture of fire and saturated flames. Their methods provide feature vectors for neural network for classification task. Wu et al., [33] employed local binary pattern with dense optical flow estimator for video smoke detection, where color maps are converted to HSV color space with specified values of HSV parameters. All these techniques rely upon integer order derivatives based variational models for the extraction of dynamical features of fire through optical flow. However, integer order derivatives are known to work with local and smooth variations functions, whereas fire manifests large and discontinuous variations in the features such as texture, color, shapes, etc. [8,21,25]. Therefore, in this paper, we evaluate the dynamic features of fire using fractional order derivative based variational model, this generalizes the traditional models which are based on integer order derivatives.

Fractional order derivatives deal with differentiation of arbitrary order in $(0, 2)$ and provide a long-term memory, which allows to calculate non-local variations in the function [14]. Literature has several definitions of these derivatives amongst them quite renowned are Riemann-Liouville, Marchaud, Grünwald-Letnikov fractional derivatives [10,20,29].

This paper proposed a novel fire-smoke detection system based on fractional order optical flow and convolution neural network. The estimation of the optical flow is performed using a fractional order variational model. Optical flow color map is used to demonstrate the region of interest and collect the dynamic features of smoke. Color maps utilize distinct colors to represent distinct motion directions and same color represents no motion of smoke. Since, smoke contains different textures and discontinuity in the flow, therefore the fractional order variational model is capable in preserving dynamical discontinuities in the flow field. The segmentation of region of interest is carried out with the help of binary mask used in the green channel of the RGB color map. The green channel of color map can represent smoke features very effectively. The segmented color maps are used for the training of random forest based CNN and the proposed CNN architecture for features vector extraction and classification. Different accuracy metrics are employed for performance evaluation and a detailed comparison is provided. A dataset consisting of 10 smoke (4576 frames) and 10 non-smoke (3219 frames) videos is used for the experiment purposes.

The paper is composed of: Sect. 2 that discusses the overall methodology of the proposed work, followed by the fractional order optical flow model, feature extraction using binary mask and deep CNN architecture. Section 3 that gives the details about the datasets used for experiments and discusses the experimental results with different classifiers. Finally, Sect. 4 that concludes the proposed work.

2   Methodology

The complete methodology of the proposed framework is depicted in Fig. 1. First, two consecutive image frames of a video are considered for optical flow estimation using the fractional order variational model as illustrated in the next

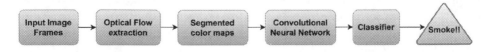

Fig. 1. Proposed framework for fire-smoke motion detection.

subsection. The extracted dynamic features are now collected and fed into a deep CNN architecture and classified with random forest.

2.1   Proposed Fractional Order Variational Optical Flow Model

Let at any pixel position, intensity values be $\mathcal{J}(\mathcal{X}, \mathcal{Y}, \mathcal{T})$ and $\mathcal{J}(\mathcal{X} + \delta\mathcal{X}, \mathcal{Y} + \delta\mathcal{Y}, \mathcal{T} + \delta\mathcal{T})$ at spatiotemporal coordinates $(\mathcal{X}, \mathcal{Y}, \mathcal{T})$ and $(\mathcal{X} + \delta\mathcal{X}, \mathcal{Y} + \delta\mathcal{Y}, \mathcal{T} + \delta\mathcal{T})$, respectively. By employing the data conservation assumption [12], we obtain

$$\mathcal{J}(\mathcal{X}, \mathcal{Y}, \mathcal{T}) = \mathcal{J}(\mathcal{X} + \delta\mathcal{X}, \mathcal{Y} + \delta\mathcal{Y}, \mathcal{T} + \delta\mathcal{T}) \tag{1}$$

where, $\mathcal{J} : \Omega \subset \mathbb{R}^3 \to \mathbb{R}$ is a volume representing a rectangular image sequence. Therefore, using Taylor series expansion in (1), we have

$$(\nabla \mathcal{J})^T \boldsymbol{u} + \mathcal{J}_{\mathcal{T}} = 0 \tag{2}$$

where, $\nabla \mathcal{J} = (\mathcal{J}_{\mathcal{X}}, \mathcal{J}_{\mathcal{Y}})^T$ stands for the intensity gradient in spatial region, $\mu(\mathcal{X}, \mathcal{Y})$ and $\nu(\mathcal{X}, \mathcal{Y})$ as components of optical flow in $\mathcal{X}$ and $\mathcal{Y}$ directions, respectively and $\boldsymbol{u} = (\mu, \nu)^T$ is the desired optical flow field. Here, $\mathcal{J}_{\mathcal{T}}$ denotes the intensity temporal derivative. The problem of optical flow estimation using (2) is referred to as an ill-posed problem. To convert this problem into a well-posed one, it is needed to be regularized by introducing an additional constraint called the smoothness constraint [12]. This constraint is laid down on the assumption that all the neighboring pixel of any pixel in an image plane moves coherently.

In order to estimate the optical flow field, a variational model based on Riemann-Liouville (RL) fractional derivative is presented as follows

$$E(\boldsymbol{u}) = \int_{\Omega} \left[((\nabla \mathcal{J})^T \boldsymbol{u} + \mathcal{J}_{\mathcal{T}})^2 + \beta^2 |\boldsymbol{u}|^2 + \lambda(|D^\alpha \mu|^2 + |D^\alpha \nu|^2) \right] d\boldsymbol{X} \tag{3}$$

where, $\alpha \in (0, 2)$ and $D^\alpha = (D_{\mathcal{X}}^\alpha, D_{\mathcal{Y}}^\alpha)^T$ denotes the left RL fractional derivative, and $|D^\alpha \mu| = \sqrt{(D_{\mathcal{X}}^\alpha)^2 + (D_{\mathcal{Y}}^\alpha)^2}$. It can be noticed that for $\alpha \in \mathbb{Z}^+$, the proposed model (3) reduces to an integer order variational model.

2.2   Minimization

Euler-Lagrange Equation: Now, we have to find out the iterative equations for optical flow $\boldsymbol{u} = (\mu, \nu)^T$ using (3). Therefore, select $\mu^*(\mathcal{X}, \mathcal{Y})$ and $\nu^*(\mathcal{X}, \mathcal{Y})$ to denote the solutions for the Euler-Lagrange equations of (3). Hence, the deviation functions μ and ν from $\mu^*(\mathcal{X}, \mathcal{Y})$ and $\nu^*(\mathcal{X}, \mathcal{Y})$ are defined with the help of arbitrary mappings $\eta(\mathcal{X}, \mathcal{Y})$ and $\phi(\mathcal{X}, \mathcal{Y}) \in C^\infty$ as follows

$$\mu(\mathcal{X}, \mathcal{Y}) = \mu^*(\mathcal{X}, \mathcal{Y}) + \epsilon\eta(\mathcal{X}, \mathcal{Y}) \tag{4}$$

$$\nu(\mathcal{X}, \mathcal{Y}) = \nu^*(\mathcal{X}, \mathcal{Y}) + \epsilon\phi(\mathcal{X}, \mathcal{Y}) \tag{5}$$

On substituting the values of (4) and (5) into (3), we have

$$E(\epsilon) = \int_{\Omega} [(\mathcal{J}_{\mathcal{X}}(\mu^* + \epsilon\eta) + \mathcal{J}_{\mathcal{Y}}(\nu^* + \epsilon\phi) + \mathcal{J}_T)^2 + \beta^2((\mu^* + \epsilon\eta)^2 + (\nu^* + \epsilon\phi)^2)$$
$$+ \lambda(|D_{\mathcal{X}}^{\alpha}\mu^* + \epsilon D_{\mathcal{X}}^{\alpha}\eta|^2 + |D_{\mathcal{Y}}^{\alpha}\mu^* + \epsilon D_{\mathcal{Y}}^{\alpha}\eta|^2 + |D_{\mathcal{X}}^{\alpha}\nu^* + \epsilon D_{\mathcal{X}}^{\alpha}\phi|^2$$
$$+ |D_{\mathcal{Y}}^{\alpha}\nu^* + \epsilon D_y^{\alpha}\phi|^2)]\, d\mathbf{X} \tag{6}$$

Equation (6) is differentiated with respect to ϵ, then in order to have the extremum, ϵ is set equal to zero and that gives,

$$E'(0) = \int_{\Omega} [\eta\{\Psi\mathcal{J}_{\mathcal{X}} + \beta^2\mu^* + \lambda(D_{\mathcal{X}}^{\alpha*}D_{\mathcal{X}}^{\alpha}\mu^* + D_{\mathcal{Y}}^{\alpha*}D_{\mathcal{Y}}^{\alpha}\mu^*)\}$$
$$+ \phi\{\Psi\mathcal{J}_{\mathcal{Y}} + \beta^2\nu^* + \lambda(D_{\mathcal{X}}^{\alpha*}D_{\mathcal{X}}^{\alpha}\nu^* + D_{\mathcal{Y}}^{\alpha*}D_{\mathcal{Y}}^{\alpha}\nu^*)\}]\, d\mathbf{X} \tag{7}$$

where, $\Psi = \mathcal{J}_{\mathcal{X}}\mu^* + \mathcal{J}_{\mathcal{Y}}\nu^* + \mathcal{J}_T$ and $D^{\alpha*}$ stands for the RL right fractional order derivative. In $E'(0)$, the setting of coefficients of η and ϕ to zero gives

$$(\mathcal{J}_{\mathcal{X}}\mu^* + \mathcal{J}_{\mathcal{Y}}\nu^* + \mathcal{J}_T)\mathcal{J}_{\mathcal{X}} + \beta^2\mu^* + \lambda(D_{\mathcal{X}}^{\alpha*}D_{\mathcal{X}}^{\alpha}\mu^* + D_{\mathcal{Y}}^{\alpha*}D_{\mathcal{Y}}^{\alpha}\mu^*) = 0 \tag{8}$$

$$(\mathcal{J}_{\mathcal{X}}\mu^* + \mathcal{J}_{\mathcal{Y}}\nu^* + \mathcal{J}_T)\mathcal{J}_{\mathcal{Y}} + \beta^2\nu^* + \lambda(D_{\mathcal{X}}^{\alpha*}D_{\mathcal{X}}^{\alpha}\nu^* + D_{\mathcal{Y}}^{\alpha*}D_{\mathcal{Y}}^{\alpha}\nu^*) = 0 \tag{9}$$

Now, we have to discretize the above system of equations as given in (8) and (9) for $\mathbf{u} = (\mu, \nu)^T$.

Numerical Discretization and Implementation: For discretizing the fractional order derivative, Grünwald-Letnikov(GL) derivative [20] definition is utilized. If a pixel position is represented by (l, m) and the size of the mesh grid by δh, then

$$\mu(l, m) = \mu(l\delta h, m\delta h), \quad \nu(l, m) = \nu(l\delta h, m\delta h)$$

Employing the GL fractional derivative definition with order α on μ, we obtain

$$D_{\mathcal{X}}^{\alpha}\mu(l, m) = \sum_{s=0}^{\infty} w^{(\alpha)_s}\mu(l - s, m) \tag{10}$$

Here, the following recursion formula defines $w^{(\alpha)_s}$ as follows

$$w^{(\alpha)_0} = 1, \quad w^{(\alpha)_s} = \left(1 - \frac{\alpha + 1}{s}\right)w^{(\alpha)_{s-1}} \text{ with } s = 1, 2, \dots \tag{11}$$

Thus, the right RL fractional order derivative of the expression in (10) is

$$D_{\mathcal{X}}^{\alpha*}D_{\mathcal{X}}^{\alpha}\mu(l, m) = \sum_{s=-\infty}^{0} w^{(\alpha)_{|s|}}\Delta\mu(l - s, m) + \sum_{s=0}^{\infty} w^{(\alpha)_s}\Delta\mu(l - s, m) \tag{12}$$

So, for the image window, the expression in (12) is approximated by

$$D_{\mathcal{X}}^{\alpha*}D_{\mathcal{X}}^{\alpha}\mu(l, m) \approx \sum_{s=-W}^{0} w^{(\alpha)_{|s|}}\Delta\mu(l - s, m) + \sum_{s=0}^{W} w^{(\alpha)_s}\Delta\mu(l - s, m) \tag{13}$$

where, $\Delta\mu(l-s,m) = \mu(l-s,m) - \mu(l,m)$ and W is the size of the kernel. Similarly, the fractional order derivative with respect to $\mathcal{Y}$ for u is written as

$$D_{\mathcal{Y}}^{\alpha *} D_{\mathcal{Y}}^{\alpha} \mu(l,m) \approx \sum_{s=-W}^{0} \omega^{(\alpha)_{|s|}} \Delta\mu(l,m-s) + \sum_{s=0}^{W} \omega^{(\alpha)_s} \Delta\mu(l,m-s) \quad (14)$$

Hence, discrete form of complete fractional order derivative for μ can be given as

$$D_{\mathcal{X}}^{\alpha *} D_{\mathcal{X}}^{\alpha} \mu(l,m) + D_{\mathcal{Y}}^{\alpha *} D_{\mathcal{Y}}^{\alpha} \mu(l,m) \approx \sum_{(\bar{l},\bar{m})\in\chi(l,m)} \omega^{(\alpha)_{s_{\bar{l}\bar{m}}}} \left(\mu(\bar{l},\bar{m}) - \mu(l,m)\right) \quad (15)$$

where, $\chi(l,m)$ stands for a pixel set with pixels lying in the neighborhood of (l,m) pixel location and $r_{\bar{l}\bar{m}} = max(|\bar{l}-l|, |\bar{m}-m|)$. Similarly, the discrete form of fractional order derivative for ν can be provided as

$$D_{\mathcal{X}}^{\alpha *} D_{\mathcal{X}}^{\alpha} \nu(l,m) + D_{\mathcal{Y}}^{\alpha *} D_{\mathcal{Y}}^{\alpha} \nu(l,m) \approx \sum_{(\bar{l},\bar{m})\in\chi(l,m)} \omega^{(\alpha)_{r_{\bar{l}\bar{m}}}} \left(\nu(\bar{l},\bar{m}) - \nu(l,m)\right) \quad (16)$$

Using equations (15) and (16) into (8) and (9), a sparse system of equations is obtained as follows

$$(\mathcal{J}_{\mathcal{X}\mathcal{X}} + \beta^2)\mu + \mathcal{J}_{\mathcal{X}\mathcal{Y}}\nu + \lambda \sum_{(\bar{l},m)\in\chi(l,m)} w_{plm}^{(\alpha)} (\bar{\mu} - \mu) = -\mathcal{J}_{\mathcal{X}T}$$

$$\mathcal{J}_{\mathcal{X}\mathcal{Y}}\mu + (\mathcal{J}_{\mathcal{Y}\mathcal{Y}} + \beta^2)\nu + \lambda \sum_{(\bar{l},\bar{m})\in\chi(l,m)} w_{plm}^{(\alpha)} (\bar{\nu} - \nu) = \mathcal{J}_{\mathcal{Y}T} \quad (17)$$

where,

$$\begin{aligned}
\mathcal{J}_{\mathcal{X}\mathcal{Y}} &= \mathcal{J}_{\mathcal{X}}(l,m)\mathcal{J}_{\mathcal{Y}}(l,m) & \mathcal{J}_{\mathcal{X}\mathcal{X}} &= \mathcal{J}_{\mathcal{X}}^2(l,m) & \bar{\mu} &= \mu(\bar{i},\bar{j}) \\
\mathcal{J}_{\mathcal{X}T} &= \mathcal{J}_{\mathcal{X}}(l,m)\mathcal{J}_{T}(l,m) & \mathcal{J}_{\mathcal{Y}\mathcal{Y}} &= \mathcal{J}_{\mathcal{Y}}^2(l,m) & \bar{\nu} &= \nu(\bar{i},\bar{j}) \\
\mathcal{J}_{\mathcal{Y}T} &= \mathcal{J}_{\mathcal{Y}}(l,m)\mathcal{J}_{T}(l,m)
\end{aligned}$$

Equation (17) is solved to have the iteration expressions for μ and ν, which are as follows

$$\mu^{n+1} = \bar{\mu}^n + \frac{\left\{\begin{array}{c}(\lambda\varrho\mathcal{J}_{\mathcal{X}\mathcal{X}} - \beta^2\mathcal{J}_{\mathcal{X}\mathcal{X}} - \beta^2\mathcal{J}_{\mathcal{Y}\mathcal{Y}} + \beta^2\lambda\varrho - \beta^4)\bar{\mu}^n \\ +\lambda\varrho\mathcal{J}_{\mathcal{X}\mathcal{Y}}\bar{\nu}^n + (\lambda\varrho - \beta^2)\mathcal{J}_{\mathcal{X}T}\end{array}\right\}}{D} \quad (18)$$

$$\nu^{n+1} = \bar{\nu}^n + \frac{\left\{\begin{array}{c}\lambda\varrho\mathcal{J}_{\mathcal{X}\mathcal{Y}}\bar{\mu}^n + (-\beta^2\mathcal{J}_{\mathcal{X}\mathcal{X}} + (\lambda\varrho - \beta^2)\mathcal{J}_{\mathcal{Y}\mathcal{Y}} \\ +\beta^2\lambda\varrho - \beta^4)\bar{\nu}^n + (\beta^2 - \lambda\varrho)\mathcal{J}_{\mathcal{Y}T}\end{array}\right\}}{D} \quad (19)$$

where, $\varrho = \sum_{(\bar{l},\bar{m})\in\chi(l,m)} w^{(\alpha)_{r_{lm}}}$ and D represents the determinant of (17). The above system of equations provides the optical flow color map for two consecutive image frames, which is further segmented and trained with the help of binary mask and CNN, respectively.

2.3   Binary Mask

The optical flow color map is used to detect the region of interest. This color map illustrates different RGB colors and intensities, which correspond to different motion directions and motion magnitudes, respectively. Figure 2 represents the optical flow color maps corresponding to the two sample datasets used in experiments. Since, smoke generally tends to diffuse upwardly [31], therefore the green channel of the color map shows more susceptibility to smoke motion as compared to blue and red channels. Figure 4 demonstrates the R,G and B channels of the color map for the smoke and non-smoke images. Now, the segmentation of active region is performed using binary mask based on the green channel, defined as

$$I_{BM} = \begin{cases} 1, & I_g > I_r. \\ 1, & I_g > I_b. \\ 0, & \text{otherwise.} \end{cases} \qquad (20)$$

where, I_{BM}, I_g, I_b and I_r denote the intensity values of binary mask, green, blue and red channels, respectively. This binary mask has the same dimensions as those of the reference frames. Now, the quality of segmented region is further improved with the help of connected component analysis (CCA) as described

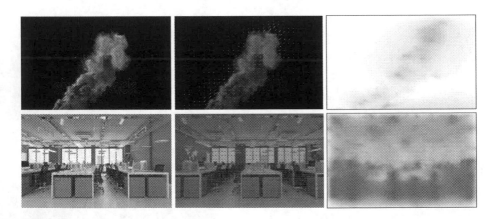

Fig. 2. Reference images of smoke and non-smoke videos and their fractional order optical flow color maps in rows first and second.

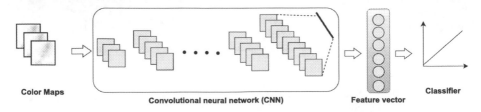

Fig. 3. Fire-smoke detection framework based on optical flow color maps.

Reference Image	Red channel	Green channel	Blue channel

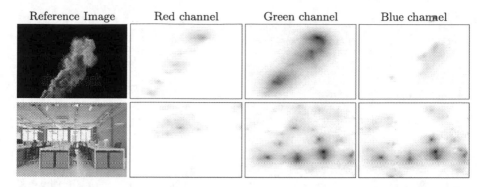

Fig. 4. First and second rows represent the red, green and blue channels of the optical flow corresponding to smoke and non-smoke datasets. (Color figure online)

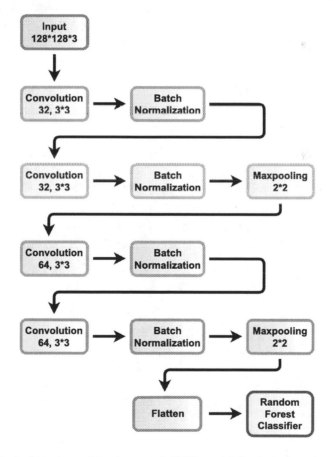

Fig. 5. Architecture of implemented CNN model for features extraction.

in [2]. In CCA, a morphological dilation operation is applied upon the entire binary mask in order to fill the insignificant holes that helps to choose the highly smoky region.

2.4 Feature Extraction: Deep CNN Architecture

The CNNs (convolutional neural networks) have been widely employed in image classification tasks and shown an impressive classification accuracy [13]. In this paper, a CNN architecture as given in Fig. 5 is implemented. This CNN architecture is implemented by fine tuning the model of Bhattiprolu [6] on optical flow color maps. The implemented architecture consists of 4 convolution layers, 4 batch normalization layers and 2 max pooling. The extracted feature vector is classified using random forest (RF) machine learning classifier. The reason to choose RF classifier is its convenient dealing with large datasets [17].

Moreover, an ensemble learning based CNN architecture using VGG16 and DenseNet121 is designed for features extraction from segmented color maps as

Fig. 6. Architecture of proposed CNN model for classification.

Layer (type)	Output Shape	Param #	Connected to
input_6 (InputLayer)	[(None, 8192)]	0	[]
input_7 (InputLayer)	[(None, 16384)]	0	[]
dense (Dense)	(None, 512)	4194816	['input_6[0][0]']
dense_3 (Dense)	(None, 512)	8389120	['input_7[0][0]']
dense_1 (Dense)	(None, 256)	131328	['dense[0][0]']
dense_4 (Dense)	(None, 256)	131328	['dense_3[0][0]']
dense_2 (Dense)	(None, 128)	32896	['dense_1[0][0]']
dense_5 (Dense)	(None, 128)	32896	['dense_4[0][0]']
add (Add)	(None, 128)	0	['dense_2[0][0]', 'dense_5[0][0]']
dropout (Dropout)	(None, 128)	0	['add[0][0]'}
dense_6 (Dense)	(None, 2)	258	['dropout[0][0]']

Total params: 12,912,642
Trainable params: 12,912,642
Non-trainable params: 0

Fig. 7. Summary of the proposed CNN architecture.

shown in Fig. 6. This architecture first extracts features from the estimated color maps using convolution bases VGG16 and DenseNet121, and then fuses the features of these two architectures to produce an improved feature vector for classification purpose. VGG16 efficiently deals with finer details, while DenseNet121 is more focused on abstract properties of an object in an image. This proposed CNN model is composed of convolution bases, dense, add and dropout layers. The complete schematic diagram of the proposed methodology is shown in Fig. 3 (Fig. 7).

3   Experiments, Results and Discussion

3.1   Datasets

Datasets play a vital role for assessment of any algorithm. In this paper, we have used 10 smoke and 10 non-smoke videos of length around 1–3 min as publicly available at [28]. The total number of frames for smoke and non-smoke videos are 4576 and 3219, respectively. These videos are of different indoor and outdoor scenes and have different shapes, environments and structures, etc. These image frames undergo optical flow estimation step and provide us with a total number of 4576 smoke color maps and 3219 non-smoke color maps. The datasets are split into a training and testing set in a ratio of 8:2. Figures 8–9 show sample image frames for all the smoke and non-smoke videos datasets.

3.2   Performance Metrics

The literature has availed several measures for performance evaluation of CNN based models. This paper considers the following metrics based on the requirement of the proposed work,

- **Detection rate (DR):** It demonstrates the proportion of the truly positive samples. It is defined as

$$DR = \frac{TP}{TP + FN} \times 100\%$$

- **Precision (P):** This gives the proportion of true positives among all positive. It is given by

$$P = \frac{TP}{TP + FP} \times 100\%$$

- **F1-score(F):** This is the harmonic mean of DR and P, which lies in the range $(0, 1)$. It helps in finding the optimal values of DR and P. It is written as

$$F = \frac{2 * P * DR}{P + DR} \times 100\%$$
$$= \frac{2 * TP}{2TP + FP + FN}$$

- **Accuracy rate (AR):** It is the proportion of truly positive samples. It is denoted as

$$AR = \frac{TP + TN}{TP + TN + FP + FN} \times 100\%$$

Here, TP, FN, FP and TN stand to denote true positive, false negative, false positive and true negative, respectively. The complete information concerning these measures can be found at [1,35].

3.3 Experimantal Discussion

Experiments have been conducted on an Intel(R) Xeon(R) W-2245 CPU @3.90 GHz with 128 GB of RAM. The implementation of the algorithm is carried out on a MATLAB R2021a platform. All the experiments are carried on by setting $\beta = 0.1$, $\alpha = 0.7$ and $\lambda = 10$ as per the results suitability. The estimated optical flow is described with the help of color maps and vector plots of the flow field. The vector plots are also demonstrated by overlapping with the corresponding image frames to discuss the accuracy as shown in Fig. 2. The fractional order derivatives are evaluated by using the window mask of size 5×5. To validate the superiority of the proposed approach with designed CNN architecture, we conducted two types of experiments. Experiment first was employed on the smoke datasets while second was performed on non-smoke datasets. The estimated results for the given datasets in terms of different metrics is given in Table 1. The results of the proposed algorithm are also compared with the state of the art techniques such as ResNets, dense layers, SVM, deep belief models etc. in Table 1. The results from other techniques are evaluated using the image datasets instead of optical flow color maps. These comparisons show that the proposed algorithm outperfoms other existing models. The F1-score and accuracy rates for the RF classifier are 98.95% and 99.10%, respectively. This shows the significance of the proposed algorithm.

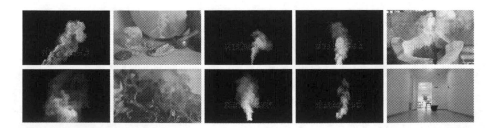

Fig. 8. Ten smoke video sample frames used in experiment.

Fig. 9. Ten non-smoke video sample frames used in experiment.

Table 1. Results comparison between the proposed and existing algorithms.

Classifiers	DR (%)	P (%)	F (%)	AR (%)
ResNet101 model [11]	92.81	95.24	94.01	94.93
ResNet50 model [11]	99.85	80.72	89.27	89.42
Dense layer based model [33]	81.33	98.07	89.32	88.59
CNN based model [28]	94.89	98.05	96.75	97.14
SVM based model [28]	97.53	97.10	97.22	97.49
Deep Belief Network [27]	95.97	92.58	94.21	94.26
RF based CNN model	**99.56**	**98.17**	**98.86**	**98.65**
Proposed CNN model	**99.40**	**98.51**	**98.95**	**99.10**

4   Conclusion

In this paper, an early detection of fire is demonstrated based on smoke features in the video. The smoke detection is carried out based on optical flow. For this purpose, a fractional order variational model has been implemented. The optical flow color maps have been segmented through binary mask using green channel of color map. The segmented color maps are fed into an RF based CNN architecture and the proposed ensemble learning based CNN architecture for classification. The obtained results are comparatively better in case of the proposed model. It is observed that the fractional order model can be scaled to the integer order variational models. The accuracy rate in the presented model is 99.10%, which is satisfactory for real life applications. In future, the proposed model can be further extended for the fog detection and weather forecasting.

Acknowledgement. The authors acknowledge to SERB, New Delhi for supporting the presented work with grant no. EEQ/2020/000154. The third author Muzammil Khan shows gratitude to MHRD, New Delhi, Government of India.

References

1. Aafaq, N., Mian, A., Liu, W., Gilani, S.Z., Shah, M.: Video description: a survey of methods, datasets, and evaluation metrics. ACM Comput. Surv. (CSUR) **52**(6), 1–37 (2019)
2. Ablameyko, S.V., Brovko, N., Bogush, R.: Smoke detection in video based on motion and contrast (2012)
3. Baker, S., Scharstein, D., Lewis, J., Roth, S., Black, M.J., Szeliski, R.: A database and evaluation methodology for optical flow. Int. J. Comput. Vision **92**(1), 1–31 (2011)
4. Balodi, A., Dewal, M., Anand, R.S., Rawat, A.: Texture based classification of the severity of mitral regurgitation. Comput. Biol. Med. **73**, 157–164 (2016)
5. Bansal, R., Pundir, A.S., Raman, B.: Dynamic texture using deep learning. In: Region 10 Conference, pp. 2609–2614 (2017). https://doi.org/10.1109/TENCON.2017.8228302
6. Bhattiprolu, S.: Python for microscopists (2020). https://github.com/bnsreenu/python_for_microscopists. Accessed 30 May 2022
7. Chaturvedi, S., Khanna, P., Ojha, A.: A survey on vision-based outdoor smoke detection techniques for environmental safety. ISPRS J. Photogramm. Remote. Sens. **185**, 158–187 (2022)
8. Chino, D.Y., Avalhais, L.P., Rodrigues, J.F., Traina, A.J.: Bowfire: detection of fire in still images by integrating pixel color and texture analysis. In: Conference on Graphics, Patterns and Images, pp. 95–102 (2015)
9. Dang-Ngoc, H., Nguyen-Trung, H.: Aerial forest fire surveillance-evaluation of forest fire detection model using aerial videos. In: International Conference on Advanced Technologies for Communications, pp. 142–148 (2019)
10. Ferrari, F.: Weyl and marchaud derivatives: a forgotten history. Mathematics **6**(1), 6 (2018)
11. He, K., Zhang, X., Ren, S., Sun, J.: Deep residual learning for image recognition. In: Computer Vision and Pattern Recognition, pp. 770–778 (2016)
12. Horn, B.K., Schunck, B.G.: Determining optical flow. Artif. Intell. **17**(1–3), 185–203 (1981)
13. Huo, Y., et al.: A deep separable convolutional neural network for multiscale image-based smoke detection. Fire Technol. **58**(3), 1445–1468 (2022)
14. Khan, M., Kumar, P.: A nonlinear modeling of fractional order based variational model in optical flow estimation. Optik **261**, 169136 (2022)
15. Kumar, P.: Development of a thermal-visible video surveillance system based on fractional order tv-model. In: Journal of Physics: Conference Series, vol. 1950, p. 012026. IOP Publishing (2021)
16. Kumar, P., Khan, M., Gupta, S.: Development of an IR video surveillance system based on fractional order tv-model. In: 2021 International Conference on Control, Automation, Power and Signal Processing, pp. 1–7 (2021)
17. Liang, J.X., Zhao, J.F., Sun, N., Shi, B.J.: Random forest feature selection and back propagation neural network to detect fire using video. J. Sens. 2022 (2022)
18. Lin, G., Zhang, Y., Zhang, Q., Jia, Y., Xu, G., Wang, J.: Smoke detection in video sequences based on dynamic texture using volume local binary patterns. KSII Trans. Internet Inf. Syst. **11**(11), 5522–5536 (2017)
19. Luo, Y., Zhao, L., Liu, P., Huang, D.: Fire smoke detection algorithm based on motion characteristic and convolutional neural networks. Multimedia Tools Appl. **77**(12), 15075–15092 (2018)

20. Miller, K.S.: Derivatives of noninteger order. Math. Magazine **68**(3), 183–192 (1995)
21. Miller, K.S., Ross, B.: An introduction to the fractional calculus and fractional differential equations. Wiley (1993)
22. Mueller, M., Karasev, P., Kolesov, I., Tannenbaum, A.: Optical flow estimation for flame detection in videos. IEEE Trans. Image Process. **22**(7), 2786–2797 (2013)
23. Muhammad, K., Ahmad, J., Mehmood, I., Rho, S., Baik, S.W.: Convolutional neural networks based fire detection in surveillance videos. IEEE Access **6**, 18174–18183 (2018)
24. Nguyen, V.T., Quach, C.H., Pham, M.T.: Video smoke detection for surveillance cameras based on deep learning in indoor environment. In: International Conference on Recent Advances in Signal Processing, Telecommunications & Computing, pp. 82–86 (2020). https://doi.org/10.1109/SigTelCom49868.2020.9199056
25. Oldham, K., Spanier, J.: The fractional calculus theory and applications of differentiation and integration to arbitrary order. Elsevier (1974)
26. Pincott, J., Tien, P.W., Wei, S., Kaiser Calautit, J.: Development and evaluation of a vision-based transfer learning approach for indoor fire and smoke detection. Building Services Engineering Research and Technology p. 01436244221089445 (2022)
27. Pundir, A.S., Raman, B.: Deep belief network for smoke detection. Fire Technol. **53**(6), 1943–1960 (2017)
28. Pundir, A.S., Raman, B.: Dual deep learning model for image based smoke detection. Fire Technol. **55**(6), 2419–2442 (2019)
29. Riemann, B.: Versuch einer allgemeinen auffassung der integration und differentiation. Gesammelte Werke 62(1876) (1876)
30. Shakya, S., Kumar, S.: Characterising and predicting the movement of clouds using fractional-order optical flow. IET Image Proc. **13**(8), 1375–1381 (2019)
31. Shi, J., Wang, W., Gao, Y., Yu, N.: Optimal placement and intelligent smoke detection algorithm for wildfire-monitoring cameras. IEEE Access **8**, 72326–72339 (2020). https://doi.org/10.1109/ACCESS.2020.2987991
32. Tu, Z., Xie, W., Zhang, D., Poppe, R., Veltkamp, R.C., Li, B., Yuan, J.: A survey of variational and CNN-based optical flow techniques. Signal Process. Image Commun. **72**, 9–24 (2019)
33. Wu, Y., Chen, M., Wo, Y., Han, G.: Video smoke detection base on dense optical flow and convolutional neural network. Multimedia Tools Appl. **80**(28), 35887–35901 (2021)
34. Xu, G., Zhang, Y., Zhang, Q., Lin, G., Wang, J.: Deep domain adaptation based video smoke detection using synthetic smoke images. Fire Saf. J. **93**, 53–59 (2017)
35. Zalpour, M., Akbarizadeh, G., Alaei-Sheini, N.: A new approach for oil tank detection using deep learning features with control false alarm rate in high-resolution satellite imagery. Int. J. Remote Sens. **41**(6), 2239–2262 (2020)

Colonoscopy Polyp Classification Adding Generated Narrow Band Imaging

Nahush V. Bhamre[1]([✉]), Vanshali Sharma[2] [ID], Yuji Iwahori[3] [ID],
M. K. Bhuyan[1] [ID], and Kunio Kasugai[4]

[1] Department of Electronics and Electrical Engineering, Indian Institute
of Technology Guwahati, Guwahati, Assam 781039, India
{v.nahush,mkb}@iitg.ac.in

[2] Department of Computer Science and Engineering, Indian Institute
of Technology Guwahati, Guwahati, Assam 781039, India
vanshalisharma@iitg.ac.in

[3] Department of Computer Science, Chubu University, Kasugai 487-8501, Japan
iwahori@isc.chubu.ac.jp

[4] Department of Gastroenterology, Aichi Medical University,
Nagakute 480-1195, Japan
kuku3487@aichi-med-u.ac.jp

Abstract. Colorectal polyp differentiation is an important clinical assessment to avoid colorectal cancer (CRC). To aid in proper diagnosis from colonoscopy images, a deep learning-based computer-aided analysis system is necessary. This paper first explains why the narrow band imaging technique is a better alternative to conventional white light images for the learning of this system. This is followed by exploring the concept of image-to-image translation using Cycle GAN which was used to acquire narrow band image data distribution via unsupervised learning. This was required because not all colonoscopy equipments are enabled with special optical enhancement tools to return NBIs, and we need more image data from this domain. The paper concludes with a set of experiments that have different combinations of the datasets acquired, to check how and which models should be trained to return the highest classification accuracy.

Keywords: Cycle GAN · NBI · Classification

1 Introduction

Colorectal cancer (CRC) is the third most common malignancy and second leading cancer in terms of mortality [1]. With worldwide 0.9 million deaths reported in 2020, early detection of CRC becomes alarmingly important. To achieve this, frequent screening using colonoscopy is performed to detect the CRC precursors, known as polyps. These polyps are mainly categorized as hyperplastic and adenomatous. The former is benign but the later one is at high risk of malignancy, and hence, it is crucial to timely detect and identify the adenomas.

Despite several efforts to enhance adenoma identification, such as improved bowel preparation, spending adequate time evaluating the colonic mucosa, and

D. Gupta et al. (Eds.): CVIP 2022, CCIS 1777, pp. 322–334, 2023.
https://doi.org/10.1007/978-3-031-31417-9_25

developing revolutionary technology such as cap-assisted and wide-angle cameras methods to flatten colonic folds, the problem of overlooking polyps still remains. A real-time automatic polyp identification and classification system could accommodate for doctor's limited visual field by displaying probable areas on the display and bringing the doctors' visual attention to the matter of concern. Recently many deep learning based methods have thereby been developed. However, varying lighting circumstances, equivalent tissue representation, and occlusion [3], make it difficult for the automated systems as well to classify polyps using traditional white-light (WL) colonoscopy videos and images. Considering these issues, some colonoscopy procedures adopt Narrow band imaging (NBI) for improved visibility of mucosal tissues and blood vessels. Clinical studies have shown the enhanced ability of NBI to WL endoscopy to evaluate lesions in the gastrointestinal tract and to estimate their histology in real time. However, not all colonoscopes are enabled with the proper optical instruments to return NBI images. This puts constraint on the availability of NBI videos and images for appropriate training of the desired systems.

Considering the polyp assessment potential of NBI images and their limited availability, we proposed an image-to-image translation method that converts regular WL images to NBI images. This is followed by polyp classification using the generated NBI images. The NBI conversion not only enhances the classification performance but also increases the count of training images. The first step in image-to-image translation is shifting a sample from one illustration of an endoluminal picture to some other. In the supervised setting, where example image pairs are available, decades of studies in image processing and computer vision have produced highly effective translation frameworks. However, we are unable to use paired training data because the majority of the NBIs that are currently available are not paired with their white light counterpart. We used the CycleGAN [5] framework to address this problem, which identifies unique features of one image collection and determines how these features might be applied to the other image collection in the dearth of any coupled datasets. The generated images are then used for polyp classification. This is done by performing exhaustive experiments using different deep learning based classification models. The reported results show improved classification performance using generated NBI images.

Below is a summary of our proposed work's leading contributions.:

- We proposed a method to convert WL to NBI colonoscopy images that are more capable for polyp assessment. This is achieved without using paired dataset, which is rarely available.
- We performed exhaustive experiments using different deep learning based classification models. This classifies the polyps into hyperplastic and adenoma.
- Our work experimented with different proportions of NBI and WL images and reported thorough analysis on how these varying proportions impact the classification performance.

– The results achieved show that the proposed method of image translation and training enhances the automated polyp classification systems' performance.

The remainder of the paper is structured as follows: Sect. 2 provides some background information on the prior research in polyp classification, and Sect. 3 provides description of the proposed method. Section 4 explains the findings and discussions. Finally, Sect. 5 draws conclusions.

2   Literature Review

2.1   Polyp Classification

Recent studies have used deep learning-based algorithms to produce promising results in colorectal polyp classification (CPC). Others have focused on feature extraction, video tracking to select the best frames, and classifying using deep networks and standard classifiers. Some studies have focused on the detection and segmentation of polyps. Because of the improved visibility and performance of datasets comprising NBI or Blue Light Imaging (BLI) images, most studies preferred to use them [3]. Usami et al. [4], for example, recommended utilising WL, dye, and NBI pictures to identify benign from malignant polyps. The authors of [5] combined WL, BLI, and Linked Color Imaging (LCI) modalities to reach one of the greatest accuracy of 95%. Colorectal polyp diagnosis with simply WL endoscopic images is also important, although it has got little attention. Yang et al. [6] recently published classification findings utilising WL pictures that were accurate up to only 79.5%. This demonstrated that the classification performance between WL endoscopic images and improved images varies significantly.

To optimise the classification of endoscopic images without using enhanced images, Hafner et al. [7] presented a system to describe local texture properties within colour images. They generated a colour vector field from an image and calculated how similar adjacent pixels were. The resulting image descriptor is a compact 1D-histogram that is used in the k-nearest neighbours classifier for classification. An active contour model with bias field correction was presented in [8]. This segmentation technique is widely used to identify tumour areas from brain MRI scan images.

2.2   Image-to-Image Translation

CNNs are being used in some emerging methods for learning a parametric translation function from an image database of input-output samples in image-to-image translation.

Unpaired Image-to-Image Translation: A few techniques address the configuration involving unpaired dataset. Lately, weight-sharing has been used by CoGAN [11] and cross-modal scene networks [12] to identify a shared representation among domains. With the addition of variational autoencoders and generative adversarial networks like the cycleGAN, Liu et al. [13] expanded the structure mentioned above.

The cycleGAN proposal does not depend on any predetermined resemblance or application-specific feature between the input-output, in contrast to the preceding methods. The assumption that the input and output must be in the identical low-dimensional embedding space is also not made.

3 Proposed Method

This section explains the proposed method in detail. Firstly, we describe the WL to NBI conversion and the cycle-GAN involved in this process. This is followed by the description of polyp classification models.

3.1 Proposed WL to NBI Translation Using CycleGAN

The objective is to study mapping functions among domains WL and NBI from training samples $\{x_i\}_{i=1}^{N}$ where $x_i \in WL$ and $\{y_j\}_{j=1}^{M}$ where $y_j \in NBI$. To achieve this objective, we used CycleGAN proposed by Zhu et al. [2]. All with no paired training examples, it can learn how to capture unique aspects of one image collection and determine how those features might be transferred to a different image collection. Even though it has very little guidance in the manner of coupled instances, the model can use it at the level of sets: it is provided a set of images in WL domain and another in NBI domain. A mapping $G : WL \to NBI$ can be trained so that the output $\hat{y} \approx G(x)$, $x \in WL$, is hardly distinguishable from samples $y \in NBI$ by an adversary trained to distinguish y aside from $\hat{y}$. The two adversarial discriminators are D_{WL} and D_{NBI}, where D_{WL} seeks to distinguish between images x and translated images F(y); and D_{NBI} seeks to distinguish between y and G(x).

One of the key features of this framework is that it takes advantage of the property that translation should be "cycle consistent". According to mathematical concepts, if we have two translators, $G : X \to Y$ and $F : Y \to X$, then G and F should be inverse to one another and both mappings ought to be bijections. By simultaneously training the mapping F and G as well as including a cycle consistency loss that promotes $F(G(x)) \approx x$ and $G(F(y)) \approx y$, Zhu et al. [2] applied this structural supposition of inverse mappings. The complete idea of unpaired image-to-image translation is realised when this loss is taken in conjunction with adversarial losses on segments X and Y.

The Adversarial loss can be described as:

$$L_{GAN}(G, D_{NBI}, WL, NBI) = E_{y \sim P_{data}(y)}[log D_{NBI}(y)] \\ + E_{x \sim P_{data}(x)}[log(1 - D_{NBI}(G(x)))] \tag{1}$$

where G attempts to create images G(x) which resemble images from domain NBI, and D_{NBI} attempts to differentiate between these new samples G(x) and the authentic ones y. G seeks to minimise the objective function while D tries

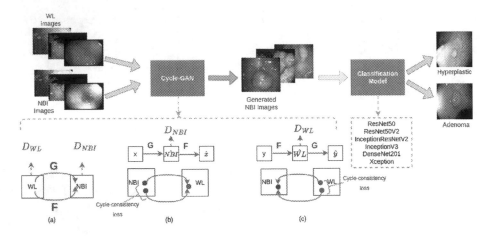

Fig. 1. Proposed approach.

maximising it, i.e., $min_G\,max_{D_{NBI}}\,L_{GAN}(G, D_{NBI}, WL, NBI)$. They also proposed a same adversarial loss for the mapping function F : NBI → WL and its discriminator D_{WL} also: i.e., $min_F\,max_{D_{WL}}\,L_{GAN}(F, D_{WL}, NBI, WL)$.

Adversarial training, theoretically, understands mappings F and G which generate outputs identically distributed as target domains WL and NBI. However, adversarial losses by themselves are unable to guarantee that the trained function can translate a single input x_i to necessary output y_i. To limit range of feasible mappings, as shown in Fig. 1(b), the trained mapping functions must be cycle-consistent in order for the image-to-image translation cycle to be able to return x to the original image, i.e., x → G(x) → F(G(x)) ≈ x. This is termed as forward cycle consistency. For each image y from the domain, G and F should also satisfy backward cycle consistency as shown in Fig. 1(c): y → F(y) → G(F(y)) ≈ y. To encourage this behaviour, we employ a cycle consistency loss:

$$L_{cyc}(G, F) = E_{x \sim P_{data}(x)}[||F(G(x))||_1] + E_{y \sim P_{data}(y)}[||G(F(y))||_1]. \quad (2)$$

Thus, the full objective of the Cycle GAN model is:

$$
\begin{aligned}
L(G, F, D_{WL}, D_{NBI}) &= L_{GAN}(G, D_{NBI}, WL, NBI) \\
&\quad + L_{GAN}(G, D_{WL}, NBI, WL) + \lambda L_{cyc}(G, F)
\end{aligned} \quad (3)
$$

where λ controls the relative importance of the two objectives. We aim to solve:

$$G*, F* = arg\,\underset{G,F}{min}\,\underset{D_{WL}, D_{NBI}}{max}\,L(G, F, D_{WL}, D_{NBI}) \quad (4)$$

3.2 Polyp Classification Using Generated NBI Images

The next step followed after image-to-image translation is binary classification. Our aim is to differentiate polyp images based on whether the polyps are benign (hyperplastic) or pre-cancerous (adenomas). To do so we passed the images to six different models including Xception, DenseNet201, ResNet50, ResNet50V2, InceptionV3, and InceptionResNetV2. The details of these model's architectures are mentioned in rest of this section.

Xception [14] architecture is composed of 36 convolution layers. With the exception of the first and last modules, all of the 14 modules have linear residual connections surrounding them. In short, the Xception architecture can be summed as a linear stack of depth-wise separable convolution layers with residual connections. This makes defining and adapting the architecture extremely convenient.

DenseNet [15] consists of Dense Blocks, where all layers are directly connected to one another, to create dense connections between layers. The DenseNet-201, which has 201 layers, was employed. Each layer's input is the feature-maps of all layers that came before it. The vanishing-gradient problem is eliminated, feature propagation is improved, feature reuse is encouraged, and there are a lot fewer parameters when using dense networks.

ResNet50 is a variant of ResNet [16] model which has 48 Convolution layers along with 1 MaxPool and 1 Average Pool layer. Residual connections between earlier layers and the current layer were proposed by the ResNet architecture. The outputs from earlier layers were essentially added together to create the input for the current layer.

In an Inception v3 [17] model, a number of network optimization techniques have been proposed to relax the restrictions and make model adaptation simpler. The methods include regularisation, dimension reduction, factorised convolutions, and parallelized computations. Factorized Convolutions reduce the number of parameters used in a network, which helps to increase computational efficiency. Faster training is made possible by smaller and asymmetric convolutions.

Inception-ResNet-v2 [18] consists of 164 layers and is constructed using both the Residual connection and the Inception structure. The filter concatenation stage of the Inception architecture is replaced in the Inception-ResNet block by the combination of multiple sized convolution filters and residual connections. In addition to avoiding the degradation issue brought on by deep structures, the use of residual connections shortens training time.

4 Result and Experimental Details

4.1 Datasets

Three datasets are used for evaluating our proposed work. In the image-to-image translation, we used two datasets, CVC-ClinicDB [19] and Aichi Dataset, for training purposes. The obtained trained Cycle-GAN model is then used to convert the images of the third dataset, ISIT-UMR [20] to NBI. The classification task is carried out using WL images (236 Adenomas and 100 Hyperplastic) and generated NBI images (236 Adenomas and 100 Hyperplastic) of ISIT-UMR.

CVC-ClinicDB is a publicly available database of 612 WL image frames extracted from 29 colonoscopy videos. These frames contain several examples of polyps.

ISIT-UMR Multimodal Polyp Classification Dataset comprises of 76 recordings from both white light and NBI modalities. Each video revolves around a lesion, taking different angles to record the texture and colour information. Each video has labels that are based on histopathology as well as on input from a number of gastroenterologists. Only two of the three classes of polyps in the dataset—adenoma and hyperplastic—were used for the task of classification.

Aichi Medical University Hospital Dataset consists of 614 NBI images and 612 WL images provided by Aichi Medical University Hospital, Aichi, Japan.

4.2   Data Pre-processing

Similar to the ISIT-UMR dataset, the CVC-ClinicDB also had many repetitive image frames. So this dataset was reduced manually to 240 distinct polyp images in the WL domain.

From the ISIT-UMR WL videos dataset, we have extracted 236 adenomas and 100 hyperplastic polyps distinct image frames and from the NBI videos dataset we have extracted 318 adenomas and 149 hyperplastic polyps distinct image frames.

Thus we have used a combined 1188 WL images and 1081 NBI images for the cycle-GAN to learn features from both domains and convert ISIT-UMR WL images into NBIs.

4.3   Implementation and Training Details

In order to implement the Cycle GAN networks, PyTorch 0.4 and Cuda 9.0 were used. Kaggle GPU was used for training purposes. The original white light images with their corresponding generated(or converted) narrow band band images followed by the most similar image of the polyp from original narrow band videos have been displayed in Fig. 2. The Generator and the discriminator losses have been plotted in Fig. 3.

All images when used for classification were down sampled from 256×256 to 224×224 for efficient processing. After generating the new NBIs from the ISIT-UMR WL images, we performed following experiments with batch size of 32 for 24 epochs with different classifiers such as ResNet50, ResNet50V2, InceptionResNetV2, InceptionV3, DenseNet201 and Xception with different dataset proportions.

Initially, original WL images were split into 80% training i.e. 269 training images and 20% testing split i.e. 67 testing images. The results are shown in Table 1. To generate more samples and to overcome the scarcity of data, original

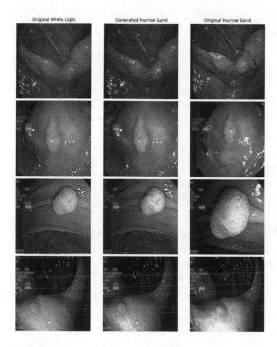

Fig. 2. White Light images followed by corresponding generated narrow band images compared with similar original narrow band images

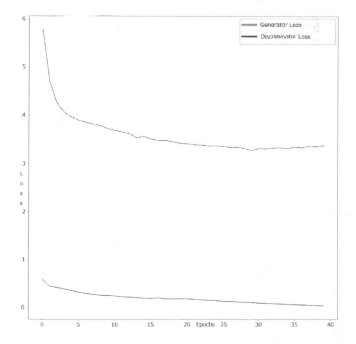

Fig. 3. Generator and Discriminator Losses

WL images were further added with three types of data augmentation to the split. The three types of data augmentations included flipping the image about the X axis, flipping about the Y axis and rotating the training images by 90° clockwise. Thus the training split increased by 4 times than before. So we split the original dataset in 50% training i.e. 168 images and applied augmentations to them increasing it to 672 training images. The remaining 168 images were used for testing. The associated results are shown in Table 2

After the above experiments, we utilized the Generated NBIs in the further experiments. Firstly, all 336 generated NBIs were combined with 60% of the WL dataset i.e. 202 images for training, and after learning the polyps images from both domains, the models were tested on the remaining 40% WL i.e. 134 images. The results are mentioned in Table 3. Similar experiments were done where the all the WL images of 336 size were used and the split was made for the generated NBI dataset with 60% being added with white light images for training and remaining 134 images for testing. The results are provided in 4. It can be observed that most of the models yielded better results in this case when compared to other above cases.

Further, we added augmentations to the Generated NBIs. The complete generated NBI dataset(336 images) was used and combined with 20% of the WL dataset(67 images) added with the data augmentation mentioned(before for training i.e. 1612 images from training, and after learning the polyps images from both domains, the models were tested on the remaining 80% WL dataset i.e. 134 testing images. Table 5 presents the associated results. Similar experiments were done where the complete WL images were used and the split was made for the generated NBI dataset with 20% being added with WL images with augmentations applied for training and remaining 80% for testing. The results are shown in Table 6

Lastly, we performed two experiments using the original NBI. These images were combined with WL first and after that with their Generated NBIs, along with augmentations. For this, 65% original NBIs and 65% Generated NBIs,i.e. 304 images each were augmented and used as training dataset of 2432 training size and the remaining 35% each for testing,i.e. 212 testing split images. The results are depicted in Table 7, 8.

Table 1. Original WL images without adding any data augmentation or without adding Generated NBIs

	Test Error	Accuracy	Precision	Recall	F1 Score	AUC
ResNet50	0.587	0.4029	0.4029	0.4029	0.4029	0.4489
ResNet50V2	0.566	0.4205	0.4205	0.4205	0.4205	0.4187
InceptionResNetV2	0.529	0.4558	0.4558	0.4558	0.4558	0.4743
InceptionV3	0.521	0.4617	0.4617	0.4617	0.4617	0.4828
DenseNet201	0.392	0.5852	0.5852	0.5852	0.5852	0.5948
Xception	0.310	**0.6258**	0.6258	0.6258	0.6258	0.6537

Table 2. Original WL images with data augmentation but without adding Generated NBIs

	Test Error	Accuracy	Precision	Recall	F1 Score	AUC
ResNet50	0.585	0.3684	0.3676	0.3583	0.3625	0.3717
InceptionResNetV2	0.571	0.3916	0.3916	0.3916	0.3916	0.4107
InceptionV3	0.573	0.4095	0.4095	0.4095	0.4095	0.4181
ResNet50V2	0.558	0.4154	0.4154	0.4154	0.4154	0.4397
DenseNet201	0.483	0.4976	0.4976	0.4976	0.4976	0.4979
Xception	0.255	**0.7024**	0.7024	0.7024	0.7024	0.7963

Table 3. All Generated NBIs and 60% of Original WL images without adding any data augmentation for training and 40% of WL for testing

	Test Error	Accuracy	Precision	Recall	F1 Score	AUC
InceptionResNetV2	0.687	0.3007	0.3007	0.3007	0.3007	0.2987
InceptionV3	0.683	0.2977	0.2977	0.2977	0.2977	0.3004
ResNet50V2	0.557	0.3955	0.3955	0.3955	0.3955	0.3911
ResNet50	0.382	0.5288	0.5313	0.5244	0.5277	0.5528
DenseNet201	0.286	0.6725	0.6725	0.6725	0.6725	0.7018
Xception	0.246	**0.6978**	0.6978	0.6978	0.6978	0.7260

Table 4. All WL images and 60% of Generated NBIs without adding any data augmentation for training and 40% of Generated NBIs for testing

	Test Error	Accuracy	Precision	Recall	F1 Score	AUC
InceptionResNetV2	0.6347	0.3466	0.3466	0.3466	0.3466	0.3341
ResNet50V2	0.519	0.4503	0.4503	0.4503	0.4503	0.4580
InceptionV3	0.478	0.4681	0.4681	0.4681	0.4681	0.4927
ResNet50	0.427	0.4918	0.49108	0.47998	0.4852	0.4819
DenseNet201	0.375	0.5896	0.5896	0.5896	0.5896	0.6087
Xception	0.235	**0.7037**	0.7037	0.7037	0.7037	0.7422

Table 5. All Generated NBIs and 20% of WL images with data augmentation for training and 80% of WL images for testing

	Test Error	Accuracy	Precision	Recall	F1 Score	AUC
ResNet50V2	0.218	0.7308	0.7308	0.7308	0.7308	0.7812
InceptionV3	0.203	0.7814	0.7814	0.7814	0.7814	0.8124
ResNet50	0.190	0.8014	0.8014	0.8014	0.8014	0.8523
InceptionResNetV2	0.190	0.8029	0.8029	0.8029	0.8029	0.8299
DenseNet201	0.188	0.8156	0.8156	0.8156	0.8156	0.8572
Xception	0.067	**0.9130**	0.9130	0.9130	0.9130	0.9382

Table 6. All WL images and 20% of Generated NBIs with data augmentation for training and 80% of Generated NBIs for testing

	Test Error	Accuracy	Precision	Recall	F1 Score	AUC
ResNet50	0.227	0.7546	0.7546	0.7546	0.7546	0.7890
DenseNet201	0.196	0.7947	0.7947	0.7947	0.7947	0.7947
InceptionResNetV2	0.164	0.8245	0.8245	0.8245	0.8245	0.8535
ResNet50V2	0.141	0.8557	0.8557	0.8557	0.8557	0.8688
InceptionV3	0.138	0.8747	0.8747	0.8747	0.8747	0.8747
Xception	0.056	**0.9413**	0.9413	0.9413	0.9413	0.9665

Table 7. 65% of Original WL images and 65% of Original NBIs were augmented and used as training dataset and the remaining 35% of each for testing.

	Test Error	Accuracy	Precision	Recall	F1 Score	AUC
DenseNet201	0.2191	0.7659	0.7659	0.7659	0.7659	0.7954
InceptionV3	0.169	0.8028	0.8028	0.8028	0.8028	0.8776
ResNet50V2	0.1675	0.8156	0.8148	0.8156	0.8152	0.8610
ResNet50	0.1104	0.8617	0.8617	0.8617	0.8617	0.9312
Xception	0.106	0.8748	0.8755	0.8737	0.8746	0.9298
InceptionResNetV2	0.0868	**0.8961**	0.8952	0.8971	0.8962	0.9475

Table 8. 65% of Original NBIs and 65% of Generated NBIs with data augmentation for training and 35% of Original NBIs with 35% of Generated NBIs for testing.

	Test Error	Accuracy	Precision	Recall	F1 Score	AUC
DenseNet201	0.2922	0.6950	0.6950	0.6950	0.6950	0.7112
ResNet50V2	0.1641	0.8197	0.8193	0.8203	0.8198	0.8664
ResNet50	0.1568	0.8163	0.8168	0.8156	0.8162	0.8738
InceptionV3	0.1114	0.8673	0.8673	0.8673	0.8673	0.9254
InceptionResNetV2	0.0925	0.8843	0.8844	0.8843	0.8844	0.9520
Xception	0.0828	**0.8960**	0.8958	0.8964	0.8961	0.9550

5   Conclusion

After conducting the various experiments it was observed that the Xception architecture was the best classifier in all cases. When we classified images taken directly from the ISIT-UMR dataset we saw a maximum accuracy of 62.58%. After adding simple data augmentations, we could improve this accuracy to 70.24%. When we combined the NBI images with original WL, without adding any other augmentation, a similar accuracy of 69.78% was observed when tested on WL image and a slightly better accuracy of 70.37% was observed when the test images were of NBI modality. Finally after combining the WL and generated NBI and simple augmentation were added to it, a considerable increase in accuracy was noted. 91.3% accuracy was observed when the model was tested on remaining WL images. And **94.13%** accuracy was observed when the model was tested on NBIs.

It is evident from comparative statistics that the current work outperforms a few of the others. NBI colonoscopy images were studied because they provided more accurate classification. As this research has only been performed on separate manually chosen frame sequences, we intend to connect it with automated frame selection and video tracking in the coming years. Additionally, to further improve accuracy, future study may use even more image modalities and better classification models.

Acknowledgments. Iwahori's research is supported by Japan Society for the Promotion of Science (JSPS) Grant-in-Aid for Scientific Research (C) (20K11873) and by Chubu University Grant.

References

1. Boerin, A., Drasovean, S., Pascarenco, O., Dobru, D.: Narrow-band imaging with magnifying endoscopy for the evaluation of gastrointestinal lesions. World J. Gastrointest Endosc. **7**(2), 110–120 (2015)
2. Zhu, J.-Y., Park, T., Isola,P., Efros, A.A.: Unpaired image to image translation using cycle-consistent adversarial networks (2017)
3. Rondonotti, E., et al.: Blue-light imaging compared with high-definition white light for real-time histology prediction of colorectal polyps less than 1 centimeter: a prospective randomized study. Gastrointestinal Endoscopy **89**(3), 554–564 (2019)
4. Usami, H., et al.: Colorectal polyp classification based on latent sharing features domain from multiple endoscopy images. Procedia Comput. Sci. **176**, 2507–2514 (2020)
5. Fonolla, R., et al.: A CNN CADX system for multimodal classification of colorectal polyps combining WL, BLI, and LCI modalities. Appl. Sci. **10**(15), 5040 (2020)
6. Yang, Y.J., et al.: Automated classification of colorectal neoplasms in white-light colonoscopy images via deep learning. J. Clin. Med. **9**(5), 1593 (2020)
7. Hafner, M., Liedlgrubera, M., Uhl, A., Vecsei, A., Wrba, F.: Color treatment in endoscopic image classification using multi-scale local color vector patterns. Med. Image Anal. **16**(1), 75–86 (2012)
8. Huang, C., Zeng, L.: An active contour model for the segmentation of images with intensity inhomogeneities and bias field estimation. PLoS One **10**(4), e0120399 (2015)
9. Goodfellow, I.J., et al.: Generative adversarial nets. In: Advances in Neural Information Processing Systems (2014)
10. Isola, P., Zhu, J. Y., Zhou, T., Efros, A.A.: Image-to-image translation with conditional adversarial networks. In: Proceedings - 30th IEEE Conference on Computer Vision and Pattern Recognition, CVPR 2017, 2017-January, pp. 5967–5976 (2017)
11. Liu, M.-Y., Tuzel, O.: Coupled generative adversarial networks. In: NIPS (2016)
12. Aytar, Y., Castrejon, L., Vondrick, C., Pirsiavash, H., Torralba, A.: Cross-modal scene networks. In: PAMI (2016)

13. Liu,M.-Y., Breuel, T., Kautz, J.: Unsupervised image-to-image translation networks. In: NIPS (2017)
14. Chollet, F.: Xception: deep learning with depthwise separable convolutions (2017)
15. Huang, G., Liu, Z., Van Der Maaten, L., Weinberger, K.Q.: Densely connected convolutional networks. In: Proceedings of the IEEE Conference on Computer Vision and Pattern Recognition, pp. 4700–4708 (2017)
16. He, K., Zhang, X., Ren, S., Sun, J.: Deep residual learning for image recognition. In: Proceedings of the IEEE Conference on Computer Vision and Pattern Recognition, pp. 770–778 (2016)
17. Szegedy, C., Vanhoucke, V., Ioffe, S., Shlens, J., Wojna, Z.: Rethinking the Inception Architecture for Computer Vision (2015)
18. Szegedy, C., Vanhoucke, V., Ioffe, S., Alemi, A.: Inception-v4, Inception-ResNet and the Impact of Residual Connections on Learning (2016)
19. Bernal, J., Sánchez, F.J., Fernández-Esparrach, G., Gil, D., Rodríguez, C., Vilariño, F.: WM-DOVA maps for accurate polyp highlighting in colonoscopy: validation vs. saliency maps from physicians. Comput. Med. Imaging Graphics **43**, 99–111 (2015)
20. Mesejo, P., et al.: Computer-aided classification of gastrointestinal lesions in regular colonoscopy. IEEE Trans. Med. Imaging **35**(9), 2051–2063 (2016)

Multi-class Weather Classification Using Single Image via Feature Fusion and Selection

Ganesh Deepak[1], Venkat Siddish Gudla[1], and Faheema AGJ[2]($\boxtimes$)

[1] Indian Institute of Technology Kharagpur, Kharagpur, India
{v.ganeshdeepak,durgajp94}@iitkgp.ac.in
[2] Centre for AI & Robotics, Bangalore, India
faheema.cair@gov.in

Abstract. Weather classification using multiple classes is the most sought technique which has many potential applications. It is extremely difficult to get discriminative features from weather images due to diverse nature of weather conditions. In this paper, we have tried to capture the discriminative features by using feature fusion and feature reduction/selection methods. The proposed method uses combination of Histogram of Gradient (HOG) & deep features, feature selection/reduction and classification. Extensive experiments on the benchmark datasets were carried out using various features extraction and selection/reduction methods in conjunction with various classifiers. The extensive experimental evaluation demonstrates fusion of HOG & DenseNet-161 features with linear SVM classifier achieves the best classification accuracy of 99.65% & 95.2% for MCWRD and MWI dataset respectively. Our method has outperformed the state-of-the-art methods for both datasets. Our method is scalable, as it generates variety of solutions. Based on available compute, user can pick & choose the relevant method.

Keywords: ResNet · DenseNet · Vision Transformer (ViT) · Histogram of Gradient (HOG) · SVM · PCA · Mutual Information

1 Introduction

In adverse and severe weather conditions multi-class weather classification system plays critical & an indispensable role in supporting the decisions of self-driving cars. Development of technologies related to self-driving cars is very active research area. A self-driving car requires development of robust and accurate localization, environment perception and behavioral planning. Environment perception is one of the important technology which sense the environment around the vehicle to generate the obstacle map for vehicle navigation. Environment perception enables the vehicle to discern stationary and moving objects. In order to develop a robust perception model for adverse weather conditions, multimodal sensors are employed to capture complementary features. Existing literature in the field of computer vision is mostly based on the assumption that the weather condition in outdoor images or videos is clear. However, in reality different weather conditions such as rain, snow or haze, fog will decrease the quality of images or videos, which will result in degraded performance. In order to develop accurate and robust environment perception algorithm, it is essential to sense the weather conditions and accordingly choose the right set of sensors for obstacle perception. In order to improve the detection of obstacle in adverse weather conditions, a reliable and accurate weather detection/classification system is essential. With advances in deep learning techniques, self-driving cars can effectively identify outdoor weather conditions using single image and thus make appropriate decisions to easily adapt to new conditions and environments. Several researchers have reported good accuracy for weather classification using images. In this paper, we have proposed fusion of deep and conventional features for multi-class weather classification.

Therefore, in this paper, we make use of deep CNN and Histogram of Oriented Gradient (HOG) [1] features for weather detection. The proposed model tends to be accurate, sensitive and precise for efficient deployment on autonomous vehicles for making proper decisions, especially in adverse weather.

The main contribution of this paper are listed as under.

1. Fusion of deep and HOG features for characterization of images
2. Evaluation of statistical, entropy and transform based feature selection methods for feature selection.
3. Weather classification using fusion, selection and reduction of feature vectors with various classifiers.
4. Comprehensive experimental results and analysis to provide more insight into solution, which is supported by various metrics like classification accuracy, confusion matrix, precision, recall, F1-score and support.
5. Comparison of our results on weather classification benchmark datasets with existing related research to show the advantage of our findings

The paper is structured as follows: Sect. 2 describes and discusses the related work. Section 3 describes proposed method and discusses in detail various feature extraction, selection and reduction techniques. Section 4 provides details about experimental environment, dataset, evaluation metrics, and discussion. Finally, Sect. 5 captures the conclusion drawn and future work.

2   Related Work

Weather classification is an active research area in the domain of computer vision. Despite advances in deep CNN, the existing works in this domain still suffer from challenges. Few authors [2, 3] have focused on weather recognition from vehicle camera images for driver assistance system for recognition of rainy weather. These methods focus only on fixed target scene images. The authors of [4] proposed a method to label images of the same scene with three weather conditions including sunny, cloudy, and overcast. In [5], authors has attempted for any scenario multi-class weather classification using multiple features and multiple kernels learning. They extracted multiple features and combine them into high dimensional vector and use multiple kernels learning to learn adaptive classifier. C. Zheng [6] et al. tried weather classification by extracting more comprehensive features for sky and non-sky regions. In addition, they used dictionary learning in conjunction with active learning for labeling images. W. Chu [7] et al. proposed a method which captured various correlations between weather properties and metadata. Using this information, they constructed computational models based on random forests to estimate weather information for any given image. They also described interesting statistics linking weather properties with human behaviors. Z. Zhu [8] et.al proposed novel dual fine-tuning strategy to train the GoogLeNet model. At first, they used ILSVRC-2012 dataset to pre-train GoogLeNet to generate initial model. Then the initial model was fine-tuned on weather dataset. Later they optimized the GoogleNet by truncation. The final recognition model was generated by further fine-tunning the truncated model on dataset. Yi. Shi [9] et al. tried to capture the weather feature using edge deterioration phenomenon in convolution neural network (CNN). They used Mask R-CNN to extract the regions of interest including the foreground and foreground edges in the image, and superimposed them into the same scale matrix which was fed to network for classification. Kang [10] et al. tried solving weather classification by introducing pre-processing stage to automatically determine the weather condition for an input image. Then the corresponding proper de-weathering operations was applied. They used GoogleNet and AlexNet architecture to evaluate their method. AG Oluwafemi [11] et.al presented a new dimension to multi-class weather recognition using stacking ensemble method. Their approach used ensemble model selection and diversity measurement for multi-class weather classification.

Developing their own framework Ibrahim [12] et al. proposed WeatherNet which consisted of parallel Deep CNN models which were used to analyses street-level images of urban scenes. The WeatherNet comprised of four models which were used to detect dawn/dusk, day, night-time, glare, rain, snow, and fog, respectively. Training parallel model on their curation of images from various sources, they achieved class accuracies ranging from 91.6–95.6%.

Whang [13] et al. proposed a method which uses ResNet and DenseNet CNN to build the network structure, and perform probability discrimination on the output results of each model to increase the recognition rate. Another Deep CNN approach was proposed by Xia [14] et al. in which they develop a model called MeteCNN. They created their own dataset, which has 11 classes. The CNN was developed as an optimized version of the VGG-16 which is easy to train and occupies small memory footprint. Their network consisted of 13 convolutional layers, 6 pooling layers and a softmax classifier which was trained on the 6,877 images belonging to 11 classes. The accuracy achieved by the MeteCNN was 92.68%. Haija [15] et al. proposed a deep CNN classification model using ResNet-18 architecture. They employed the use of transfer learning for feature extraction and softmax for classification. Fully connected neural network was run through the network which outputs the numerical probabilities of each class. Their model achieved a classification accuracy of 98.22% for MCWRD dataset.

Zhang [18] et al. tackled the weather image classification using HOG for their feature extraction method. Then combining that with a combination of dictionary learning and multiple kernel learning which attempts to reduce the feature space using feature selection methods and improves the learning capacity of models. They went on to create their own dataset, the Multi-class Weather Image (MWI) [5] containing 20K images and reported classification accuracy of 71.39% on the four classes in the dataset.

We have tried to capture most of the literature which has leveraged MCWRD [19] and MWI dataset [5]. As per our knowledge our method is first one where we tried fusion, selection/reduction of deep and HOG features for accurate and robust weather classification algorithm, which can be deployed on self-driving cars.

3   Proposed Method

We propose a model which uses fusion of deep and conventional features, feature selection, feature reduction/selection techniques in conjunction with classifier to achieve high accuracy on the benchmark datasets. The proposed method uses transfer learning using pre-trained models to extract features and fuse deep features with HOG features. The proposed method is described in detail in Fig. 1.

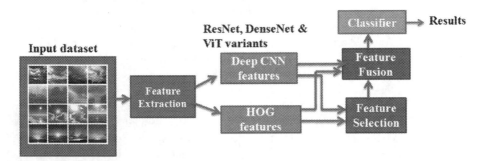

Fig. 1. Proposed Method

Figure 1 describes in detail proposed method. It consists of blocks for feature extraction, feature selection, feature fusion and classification. Input to feature extraction is dataset. Feature extraction module deal with feature extraction from images. In this case we extracted deep features from various variants of ResNet, DenseNet, ViT and HOG features. Feature selection module select only relevant features and thereby enable in handling curse of dimensionality. As part of this module, we tried statistical, entropy, transform and manifold-based feature selection methods. Finally, the feature fusion model concatenates the feature vectors from both deep and HOG to generate fused feature vector. The feature selection module takes the input feature vector applies relevant feature selection method to generate low dimension feature vector. The classification module uses various classifiers ranging from; K-Nearest Neighbor (KNN), Linear SVM, Decision trees (DT), Random Forest (RF) and Gaussian Naïve Bayes (GNB).

3.1   Feature Extraction

Accurate weather classification system is hugely dependent on strong environmental features. It is very important to capture discriminative and robust features for weather detection from single image. This section describes various feature extraction methods which are described in detail.

Histogram of Oriented Gradients (HOG)

The HOG [1] descriptor focuses on the structure or the shape of an object. In case of edge features, we only identify if a pixel is an edge or not. HOG is able to provide the edge direction as well. This is done by extracting gradients and orientation of the edges. To obtain features using HOG, the images are first resized into the shape of where the ratio of height is to width is 1:2. Before extracting features, all the images undergo pre-processing process. The dimensionality of HOG feature vector is 3780. One drawback with HOG features is that it is very sensitive to image rotation. To improve the results, deep learning-based features are leveraged.

Deep Features

Transfer learning is leveraged to extract deep features from pre-trained model. We have only chosen top performing deep architectures which include DenseNet, ResNet and ViT. HOG features (non-DL) chosen due to its good performance on weather images.

Residual Networks (ResNet).

In order to solve the problem of vanishing gradient, this architecture introduced the concept called residual blocks. Skip connections technique was introduced in this method. The skip connection connects activations of a layer to further layers by skipping some layers in between. This forms a residual block. ResNet are made by stacking these residual blocks together. The approach behind this network is instead of layers learning the underlying mapping, we allow the network to fit the residual mapping.

So, instead of say H(x), initial mapping, let the network fit,

$$F(x) := H(x) - x \text{ which gives } H(x) := F(x) + x. \tag{1}$$

To extract features from ResNet models, we imported the pre-trained ResNet models from Pytorch. After importing the models, we replaced *model.fc* with *nn.Identity*. Identity () will just return the input without any clone usage or manipulation of the input and since the features are its input, the output of the entire model will be the features. We have leveraged pre-trained models of various variants of ResNet model such as ResNet-18, ResNet-34, ResNet-50, ResNet-101 and ResNet-152 for extracting deep features for our experiments.

DenseNetworks (DenseNets).

Each layer in DenseNet receives inputs from all preceding levels, implying that each layer has access to the cumulative knowledge of all preceding layers. They solve the vanishing-gradient problem, improve feature propagation, promote feature reuse, and cut the number of parameters. DenseNet has better accuracies over SOTA methods and requires less memory and computation to attain good performance. To extract features from DenseNet models, we imported four pre-trained DenseNet models from Pytorch.

After importing the models, we replaced *model.classifier* with *nn.Identity*. We have leveraged DenseNet-121, DenseNet-161, DenseNet-169 and DenseNet-201.

Vision Image Transformers (ViT).
The Vision Transformer (ViT), is a model for image classification that employs a transformer-like architecture over patches of the image. An image is split into fixed-size patches, each of them are then linearly embedded, position embeddings are added, and the resulting sequence of vectors is fed to a standard transformer encoder. In order to perform classification, the standard approach of adding an extra learnable "classification token" to the sequence is used. Again, using the similar approach, we extracted the feature vectors from ViT models. The pre-trained ViT models which were leveraged are: Vit_b_16, Vit_b_32, Vit_l_16 and Vit_l_32.

3.2 Feature Selection

Selection of important features is extremely crucial for weather recognition. Feature selection aims at choosing a subset of relevant features for effective classification of weather images. In high dimensional data classification, the performance of a classifier often depends on the feature subset. Feature selection methods are broadly classified into unsupervised and supervised methods. Unsupervised methods do not use the target variable for selecting the feature importance of input variable. Correlation, entropy, and variance are few examples. Supervised methods use target variable to remove irrelevant features. Supervised methods are further categorized into wrapper, filter and intrinsic methods. Wrapper method search for subsets which are well performing. Filter methods select subset of features based on their relationship with target variable. Intrinsic method selects automatically relevant features during training. We evaluated statistical, entropy and transform based feature selection methods to reduce the dimensionality.

Statistical & Entropy Based Methods
As part of statistical based feature selection, variance was computed for each feature element. The features whose variance is above some threshold were retained and remaining features were dropped to get low dimension feature vector. This selection method was tried for both dataset for different combination of training feature vectors. In entropy-based methods, both entropy and mutual information were used to select the relevant features. Variance & Entropy based feature selection methods were not able to select of discriminative features. As these methods did not improve the accuracy, they were dropped from further experiments. Mutual information (MI) based features selection was employed to select the relevant features. It is based on feature–feature mutual information to determine an optimal subset of features to minimize redundancy and to maximize relevance among features. The effectiveness of the selected feature subset is evaluated using multiple classifiers on both datasets. MI based feature selection enabled in selection of discriminative features. We call MI based feature selection as feature selection (F.S) in the remaining sections of paper.

The mutual information between two random variables X and Y can be stated formally as follows:

$$I(X:Y) = H(X) - H(X \mid Y) \tag{2}$$

where I (X: Y) is the mutual information for X and Y, H(X) is the entropy of X and H (X|Y) is the conditional entropy for X given Y. Mutual information is a measure of dependence between two random variables.

Dimensionality Reduction Using Transform-Based Methods

The curse of dimensionality basically means that the error increases with the increase in the number of features. Algorithms are harder to design in high dimensions and often have a running time exponential. Principal Component Analysis (PCA) helps us to identify patterns in data based on the correlation between features. PCA aims to find the directions of maximum variance in high-dimensional data and projects it onto a new subspace with equal or fewer dimensions than the original one. We also tried manifold based methods like Uniform Manifold Approximation and Projection(UMAP) and t-distributed Stochastic Neighbor Embedding (t-SNE) for selection of relevant features. These methods also did not help in improving the accuracy. PCA based feature vector reduction enabled in retaining good features, which has discriminative power, thereby improving the accuracy.

In our extensive experiments, we found that the dimensions of the raw features were quite high owing to the fact that the features obtained through HOG were of the dimension. This contributed to a high dimension feature space which slows down the execution of the classification model. During our experiments, we found out that the best results were obtained when we fused the features obtained through a DL and a non-DL method. The non-DL features obtained through HOG were able to enrich the information of the feature space which previously contained the feature vectors from the DL models. We used different approaches to reduce dimensionality and apply feature selection. First was to apply PCA to the individual feature vectors from DL models and HOG and thereby concatenating them to obtain the final features. The second approach was to apply feature selection (MI) to the individual features after applying PCA and then concatenating them. A different approach was to first apply feature selection and concatenating them to obtain the final features. Also, a variation of this would be to apply PCA after feature selection and finally concatenating them to obtain the feature vector.

3.3   Classification

Feature vectors are fed to the classifier for categorizing weather images into relevant classes. Combining the features of the DL models, DL models and HOG along with the four aforementioned feature spaces, we trained our classifier models on these six feature spaces. We used Random forest, K-Nearest Neighbors, Decision trees, Support Vector Machines and Gaussian Naïve Bayes classifier to classify the weather dataset images. Experimental evaluation of various features and classifiers is discussed in detail in experiment section.

All the different feature spaces obtained through the mentioned methods were shuffled randomly to reduce the model bias towards a particular class. For the features obtained through fusion of two different kinds of features, shuffling was performed after the fusion of features. We split the data into training and testing set in a 75–25% train-to-test fashion for both the benchmark dataset discussed in next section. We did this so that our model could be tested first on unseen data before being deployed into real-world scenarios.

3.4 Implementation &Data Set Details

The experiments were conducted using Pytorch open-source framework on Ubuntu 20.04 LTS operating system. The experimental platform uses high end workstation 64GB memory & 4TB hard disk with NVIDIA GeForce RTX 1080ti graphics card. Pre-trained deep models & vision transformers are used for feature extraction from the weather images. The algorithms are implemented using Pytorch, OpenCV and Scikit-learn libraries.

We have utilized two benchmark datasets for evaluation of proposed method: Multi-class Weather Image (MWI) [5] and Multi-class Weather Recognition Dataset (MCWRD) [17].

MWI dataset consists of 20K images obtained from many web albums and films such as Flicker, Picasa, MojiWeather, PoCo, Fengniao. The main motivation of authors of this dataset was to generate an extensive test bed for the evaluation. We have used around 4K images of this dataset for the experiments. This dataset comprises of four categories; Sunny, rainy, snowy and Haze.

Multi-Class Weather Recognition Dataset (MCWRD) comprises of multi-classification of the outdoor weather condition images into four categories: cloudy, rain, shine, and sunrise. This dataset is one of the benchmark dataset which is publicly available. It is a comprehensive dataset composed of 1125 colored images with different image dimensions and bit-depths. The dataset consists of Cloudy (300 images), Rainy (215 images), Shine (253 images), and Sunrise (356 images).

4　Experiments Results

Extensive experiments are carried out to evaluate the performance of the multi-class weather classification using various feature extraction, selection/reduction and fusion in conjunction with variety of classifiers. As discussed in feature selection we found variance and entropy did not help much in improving accuracy. Combining the features of the DL models, DL models and HOG along with the four aforementioned feature spaces, we trained our classifier models on these six feature spaces.

4.1 Evaluation of Classifier

We tried various classifiers with different feature extraction techniques as discussed in Sect. 3.1. We can draw conclusion from Fig. 2 that Support Vector Classifier was giving the best results as compared to Random Forest (RF), Decision trees Classifier (DTC), K-nearest neighbor (KNN) and Gaussian Naïve Bayes (GNB). In our subsequent experiments we have selected Support Vector Machine classifier

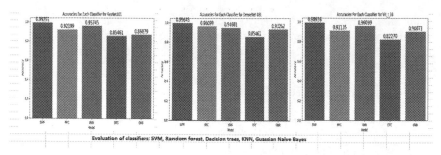

Fig. 2. Evaluation of classifiers using ResNet-101, DenseNet-161 & Vit_l_16

4.2 Classification Using Various Features

We chose only state-of-the-art network architecture like ResNet and DenseNet and ViT for features extraction. We tried weather classification techniques only with various deep model features, fusion of deep model and HOG, application of PCA on fused feature vector of deep model and HOG, PCA followed by feature selection using fused feature vector of deep model and HOG, feature selection on fused deep model and HOG feature vector and lastly feature selection followed by PCA on fused feature vector of deep model and HOG. The results of our experiments are depicted by Fig. 3 and Table 1.

From Fig. 3 & Table 1 it is clear that for MCWRD dataset, DenseNet161 + HOG (fv = 5988) gave 99.65% accuracy, this is followed by ResNet101 + HOG + PCA (fv = 757) which has recorded 99.29% accuracy. Both these methods have outperformed the state-of-the-art method. Among Vision transformer variants ViT-l-32 + HOG + PCA + FS (fv = 875) & ViT-l-16 + HOG + PCA + FS (fv = 909) and Vit-b-32 + HOG + PCA + FS (fv = 853) gave accuracy of 98.93% & 98.58% respectively.

For MWI dataset DenseNet-161 + HOG (feature vector size = 5988), DenseNet-161 + HOG + PCA + FS (feature vector size = 853) and DenseNet-169 + HOG + PCA (feature vector size = 838) gave accuracy 95.2%, 94.44% and 94.4% respectively. Among the vision transformer variants ViT-l-32 + HOG + PCA + F.S (fv = 875) gave the best accuracy of 92.4% and among ResNet variants ResNet-101 + HOG + PCA + FS (fv = 757) gave 94.2% accuracy.

From the above analysis it is very clear that DenseNet-161 + HOG model has outperformed for both the datasets. This shows that fusion of deep and HOG features captures distinguishing features which enables in achieving higher accuracy. One more insight we can draw from above analysis is that PCA followed by feature selection on fused feature vectors of various deep model and HOG has resulted in promising accuracy. It can be noted that dimensionality of feature vector with plane fusion of deep model and HOG is very high as compared to the deep model + HOG + PCA + FS. Section 4.3 captures the details of various feature vector size for various variants of deep model & HOG along with PCA and feature selection. Our claim of using feature tapping from pre-trained model is validated by [18]. It is evident from the extensive experiments that the tapped features using various variants of pre-trained deep models in conjunction with HOG has captured robust and discriminative features which has resulted in getting good accuracy. Figure 4 shows visual results for both datasets using top performing model.

Our detail experiments enable us to select right set of feature vector dimension based on available compute. Tradeoff between accuracy and feature vector dimensions is depicted in Table 1 & Table 2.

4.3 Accuracy & Feature Vector Size

Table 1 shows accuracy for both dataset for various models. Table 2 shows the number of features classifier model is trained with in different approaches as discussed above. F.S stands for Feature Selection in below table.

Table 1. Accuracy of various variants of ResNet, DenseNet and ViT with feature fusion, PCA and F.S

Model		Model + HOG	Model+ HOG+PCA	Model+HOG + PCA + F.S	Model + HOG + F.S	Model + HOG + F.S + PCA
Resuts with MCWRD dataset						
ResNet models	ResNet-18	98.22	98.22	98.22	98.22	98.22
	ResNet-34	96.81	97.16	97.52	96.45	96.81
	ResNet-50	98.22	97.87	98.22	97.52	97.16
	ResNet-101	98.58	99.29	98.93	98.22	98.22
	ResNet-152	98.22	97.87	98.22	97.52	97.16
DenseNet models	DenseNet-121	98.22	96.45	97.16	96.81	96.45
	DenseNet-161	99.65	98.93	98.58	98.58	98.22
	DenseNet-169	98.58	98.58	98.58	98.22	98.22
	DenseNet-201	98.93	98.58	98.93	98.22	97.87
ViT models	ViT_b_16	97.51	97.16	97.51	97.87	97.87
	ViT_b_32	97.87	98.22	98.58	97.87	98.22
	ViT_l_16	98.58	98.58	98.93	98.22	98.22
	ViT_l_32	98.22	98.58	98.93	98.22	98.22
	Max	99.65	99.29	98.93	98.58	98.22
	Avg	98.27769231	98.1148138	98.33153848	97.84153846	97.75848154
Resuts with MWI dataset						
	Model	Model + HOG	Model + HOG + PCA	Model + HOG + PCA + F.S	Model + HOG + F.S	Model + HOG + F.S + PCA
ResNet models	ResNet-18	91.4	90	90.4	90.2	90.2
	ResNet-34	91.4	90.4	90.2	89.6	89
	ResNet-50	93.4	93.4	93	93.6	93.6
	ResNet-101	94.2	93.4	94.2	93.4	93.8
	ResNet-152	92.4	92.2	92.8	92.8	92.4
DenseNet models	DenseNet-121	92.6	91	92.6	90.8	91.2
	DenseNet-161	95.2	94	94.44	92	91.8
	DenseNet-169	94	94.4	93.8	92.22	92.22
	DenseNet-201	93.2	92.2	93.4	91	91.2
ViT models	ViT_b_16	91.4	90	90.4	89.6	89.6
	ViT_b_32	91.2	91.6	91.8	90.6	90.6
	ViT_l_16	90.6	91	90.6	89.6	90
	ViT_l_32	90.8	91.6	92.4	90.8	90.2
	Max	95.2	94.4	94.44	93.6	93.6
	Avg	92.44615385	91.93846154	92.31076923	91.74769231	91.20153846

4.4 Comparison with Other Methods

We carried out comparison with related methods on MCWRD [17] and MWI [5] datasets. Table 3(a) & (b). Depicts the classification accuracies reported by various papers as discussed in the related work section & our proposed method. It is clearly seen that for both the datasets our method has outperformed the other proposed methods. Even our various combination of DL and non-DL with PCA & feature selection has also outperformed methods reported in literature.

Table 2. Feature vector size for various variants of ResNet, DenseNet & ViT.

Model	Model + HOG	Model + HOG + PCA	Model + HOG + PCA + F. S	Model + HOG + F. S	Model + HOG + F.S + PCA
ResNet-18	512+3780= 4292	181+556= 737	181+556=737	256+1890=2146	114+397=511
ResNet-34	512+3780= 4292	184+556=740	184+556=740	256+1890=2146	116+397=513
ResNet-50	2048+3780=5828	204+556=760	204+556=760	1024+1890=2914	153+397=550
ResNet-101	2048+3780=5828	201+556=757	201+556=757	1024+1890=2914	151+397=548
ResNet-152	2048+3780= 5828	192+556=748	192+556=748	1024+1890=2914	145+397=542
DenseNet-121	1024+3780=4804	216+556=772	216+556=772	512+1890=2402	79+397=476
DenseNet-161	2208+3780=5988	297+556=853	297+556=853	1104+1890=2994	103+397=500
DenseNet-169	1664+3780=5444	282+556=838	282+556=838	832+1890=2722	105+397=502
DenseNet-201	1920+3780=5700	298+556=854	298+556=854	960+1890=2850	103+397=500
ViT_b_16	768+3780=4548	274+556=830	274+556=830	384+1890=2274	185+397=582
ViT_b_32	768+3780=4548	273+556=820	273+556=829	384+1890=2274	185+397=582
ViT_l_16	1024+3780=4804	353+556=909	353+556=909	512+1890=2402	247+397=644
ViT_l_32	1024+3780=4804	319+556=875	319+556=875	512+1890=2402	222+397=619

Table 3. (a) Comparison with other methods for both MCWRD (left) and (b) MWI (right) datasets.

MCWR dataset		MWI dataset	
Method/Year	Accuracy	Method/Year	Accuracy
C. Zheng et. al. [6] [2016]	94.00%	M. Roser, F. Moos ann[2]/2008	0.2267
W. Chu, et. Al[7][2017]	96.30%	X. Yan, Y. Luo, X. Zheng[3]/2009	0.1889
Z. Zhu et. al.[8][2017]	95.46%	Z. Chen, F. Yang, A. Lindner et al. [4]/2012	0.4158
Y. Shi et. al.[9][2018]	94.71%	Z. Zhang, H.D. Ma[5]/2015	0.7139
L. Kang et. al.[10][2018]	92.00%	Proposed Method	0.952
O. Luwafemi et. al.[11][2019]	86.00%		
M. Ibrahim et. al.[12][2019]	97.69%		
Y. Wang et. al.[13][2020]	81.25%		
J. Xia et. al.[14][2020]	96.03%		
Qasem Abu Al-Haija[15] [2020]	98. 22%		
Proposed Method	99.65%		

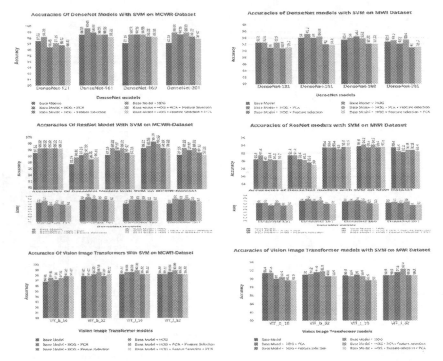

Fig. 3. Classification results on MCWRD dataset & classification results on MWI dataset

Fig. 4. Visual Results on MCWRD & MWI dataset using HOG + DenseNet161 model

4.5 Evaluation Metrics

The well-known metrics for evaluating classification algorithms comprises of computation of confusion matrix, precision, recall, F1-score and support. Precision is the number of relevant images retrieved with respect to total number of retrieved images & Recall is number of relevant images retrieved with respect to total relevant images.

Figure 5(a) captured the confusion matrix and classification support report for top two performing model; 1). DenseNet + 16 + HOG and 2) ResNet101 + HOG + PCA

	Predicted Class				Classes	Precision	Recall	F1-score	Support
	Cloudy	Rain	Shine	Sunrise	Cloudy	1	0.99	0.99	80
Cloudy	79	1	0	0	Rain	0.98	1	0.99	46
Rain	0	46	0	0	Shine	1	1	1	65
Shine	0	0	65	0	Sunrise	1	1	1	91
Sunrise	0	0	0	91	Average	0.995	0.9975	0.995	282

(Actual Class)

	Predicted Class				Classes	Precision	Recall	F1-score	Support
	Cloudy	Rain	Shine	Sunrise	Cloudy	0.99	0.99	0.99	80
Cloudy	79	0	1	0	Rain	1	1	1	46
Rain	0	46	0	0	Shine	0.98	0.98	0.98	65
Shine	1	0	64	0	Sunrise	1	1	1	91
Sunrise	0	0	0	91	Average	0.9925	0.9925	0.9925	282

(Actual Class)

(a). Confusion matrices & classification report for DenseNet-161+HOG & Re-seNet101+HOG+PCA for MCWRD dataset

	Predicted Class				Classes	Precision	Recall	F1-score	Support
	Haze	Rainy	Sunny	Snowy	Haze	0.92	0.94	0.93	127
Haze	120	1	4	2	Rainy	0.93	0.96	0.95	114
Rainy	4	110	0	0	Sunny	0.97	0.98	0.97	134
Sunny	1	2	131	0	Snowy	0.98	0.92	0.95	125
Snowy	5	5	0	115	Average	0.95	0.95	0.95	500

(Actual Class)

	Predicted Class				Classes	Precision	Recall	F1-score	Support
	Haze	Rainy	Sunny	Snowy	Haze	0.92	0.94	0.93	127
Haze	120	1	4	2	Rainy	0.93	0.96	0.95	114
Rainy	4	110	0	0	Sunny	0.97	0.98	0.97	134
Sunny	1	2	131	0	Snowy	0.98	0.92	0.95	125
Snowy	5	5	0	115	Average	0.95	0.95	0.95	500

(Actual Class)

(b). Confusion matrices and classification report DenseNet-161+HOG & DenseNe-161+HOG+PCA for MWI dataset

Fig. 5. (a) Confusion matrices & classification report for DenseNet-161 + HOG & ReseNet101 + HOG + PCA for MCWRD dataset.(b) Confusion matrices and classification report DenseNet-161 + HOG & DenseNe-161 + HOG + PCA for MWI dataset.

and Fig. 5(b) has depicted the top two performing confusion matrix; 1) DenseNet + 161 + HOG and 2) DenseNet-161 + HOG + PCA.

It is evident from the results that the DenseNet-161 variants captured most robust, accurate and discriminative features in conjunction with HOG as compared to other deep variants. We will discuss in detail confusion matrix and classification report of DenseNet161 + HOG for both MCWRD and MWI datasets.

Figure 5(a) demonstrates the four-class confusion matrix and classification report for top 2 best performing methods for MCWRD dataset. The confusion matrix analysis for the testing dataset for DenseNet-161 + HOG based method indicates its robustness which is visible through the large number of correctly predicted samples represented in the diagonal of the matrix as compared to only one incorrectly predicted sample represented in the upper diagonal. Figure 5(b) depicts the classification summary report for DenseNet-161 + HOG based & DenseNet-161 + HOG + PCA methods for MWI dataset. It shows Precision, recall, F1-score and support for each class for MWI dataset. The classification report of DenseNet-161 + HOG shows the precision for 3 classes out 4 is 1, which indicates the ability of classifier not to label a positive instance as negative. We can also notice that Recall of 3 classes out of 4 is 1, which indicates the ability of classifier to find all positive instances, which is very good.

F1-score is a weighted harmonic mean of precision and recall. F1-score for both MCWRD and MWI dataset with DenseNet + 161 is near to 0.99 & 0.95 which is best score.

5 Conclusion

This study investigates the performance of various DL based features and HOG features for weather classification. Exhaustive experiments demonstrate that the fusion of transfer learned deep feature and HOG has outperformed the SOTA methods. We have evaluated various DL, HOG features and fusion/selection of features using various methods with a various classifier. It was evident from our study that PCA followed by feature selection on fused features vector of various deep model and HOG has resulted in promising accuracy with a very low dimension feature vector. It is clearly evident with minor reduction in accuracy fused feature, PCA and feature selection combination has given very good performance. Another insight we can draw from the above study is that the deep models have outperformed the ViT variants. In future, we will utilize the model for weather classification to select the relevant sensors for multimodal obstacle detection for environment perception.

References

1. Dalal, N., Triggs, B.: Histogram of oriented gradients for human detection. In: IEEE Computer Society Conference on Computer Vision and Pattern recognition (CVPR'05) (2005)
2. Roser, M., Moosmann, F.: Classification of weather situations on single color images. In: Proceedings of IEEE Intelligent Vehicles Symposium, pp. 798–803 (2008)
3. Yan, X., Luo, Y., Zheng, X.: Weather recognition based on images captured by vision system in vehicle. In: Yu, W., He, H., Zhang, N. (eds.) ISNN 2009. LNCS, vol. 5553, pp. 390–398. Springer, Heidelberg (2009). https://doi.org/10.1007/978-3-642-01513-7_42
4. Chen, Z., Yang, F., Lindner, A., Barrenetxea, G., Vetterli, M.: How is the weather: automatic inference from images. In: Proceedings of IEEE ICIP (2012)
5. Zhang, Z., Ma, H.D.: Multi-class weather classification on single images. In: Proceedings of IEEE International Conference on Image Processing (2015)
6. Zheng, C., Zhang, F., Hou, H., Bi, C., Zhang, M., Zhang, B.: Active discriminative dictionary learning for weather recognition. Math. Probl. Eng. **2016**, 8272859, 12 (2016)

7. Chu, W., Zheng, X., Ding, D.: Camera as weather sensor: estimating weather information from single images. J. Vis. Commun. Image Represent. **46**, 233–249 (2017)
8. Zhu, Z., Li, J., Zhuo, L., Zhang, J.: Extreme weather recognition using a novel fine-tuning strategy and optimized GoogLeNet. In: 2017 International Conference on Digital Image Computing: Techniques and Applications (DICTA), Sydney, NSW (2017)
9. Shi, Y., Li, Y., Liu, J., Liu, X., Murphey, Y.L.: Weather recognition based on edge deterioration and convolutional neural networks. In: 2018 24th International Conference on Pattern Recognition (ICPR), Beijing, pp. 2438–2443 (2018)
10. Kang, L., Chou, K., Fu, R.: Deep learning-based weather image recognition. In: International Symposium on Computer, Consumer & Control (IS3C), Taichung, Taiwan (2018)
11. Oluwafemi, A.G., Zenghui, W.: Multi-class weather classification from still image using said ensemble method. In: Southern African Universities Power Engineering Conference, South Africa, pp. 135–140 (2019)
12. Ibrahim, M.R., Haworth, J., Cheng, T.: WeatherNet: recognizing weather and visual conditions from StreetLevel images using deep residual learning. ISPRS Int. J. Geo-Inf. (2019)
13. Wang, Y., Li, Y.: Research on multi-class weather classification algorithm based on multi-model fusion. In: IEEE 4th Information Technology, Networking, Electronic and Automation Control Conference (ITNEC), China, pp. 2251–2255 (2020)
14. Xia, J., Xuan, D., Tan, L., Xing, L.: ResNet15: weather recognition on traffic road with deep convolutional neural network. Adv. Meteorol., Hindawi, (2020)
15. Al-Haija, Q.A., Smadi, M.A., et al.: Multi-class weather classification using resnet-18 CNN for autonomous IoT and CPS applications. In: International Conference on Computational Science and Computational Intelligence (CSCI) (2020)
16. Zhang, Z., et al.: Scene-free multi-class weather classification on single images. Neurocomputing **207**, 365–373 (2016)
17. Ajayi, G.: Multi-class weather dataset for image classification. Mendeley Data **V1**, (2018). https://doi.org/10.17632/4drtyfjtfy.1
18. Chanda, S., Okafor, E., Hamel, S., Stutzmann, D., Schomaker, L.: Deep learning for classification and as tapped-feature generator in medieval word-image. In: 13th IAPR International Workshop on Document Analysis Systems (2018)

Scene Text Detection with Gradient Auto Encoders

S. Raveeshwara[1]($\boxtimes$) (iD) and B. H. Shekar[2] (iD)

[1] Government First Grade College Uppinangady, Uppinangady 574241, Karnataka, India
raveeshwara@gmail.com
[2] Department of Computer Science, Mangalore University, Mangalore 574199, Karnataka, India

Abstract. Text serves as an excellent persistent communication medium for unambiguous and precise information exchange. Text could help us to describe any scene. Hence, it would be ideal to understand scene text to accurately identify and understand a scene image or video. Variations such as script, font, color, scale, lighting, angle of view and other distortions make scene text understanding a challenge. Detecting and localizing the possible text, could improve the task of text understanding. Though decades of research had attempted to address the problem, still it is an open area. For instance, requirement of high-performance computation platform, large training dataset and longer training process. We have attempted to train our auto encoder based text detector to precisely localize text with minimum training on a small dataset and limited computational resources. The idea involves computation of morphological gradient to enhance text on the scene image and to feed it to a gradient auto encoder neural network to locate possible text components. The proposed detector can detect text across multiple languages and it is robust against the variations such as scale, orientation, font, and lighting. The results are promising. The proposed method achieves an F-measure of 0.75 and 0.76 on MRRC dataset and MSRA-TD500 dataset respectively, after training with 167 images.

Keywords: Efficient text spotting · Reducing training · Gradient auto encoders

1 Introduction

Text detection and recognition is easy and intuitive task to most humans. It is spontaneous and natural skill. The same could be a highly complex job to be done by a machine. The task of understanding text is also known as text reading or text spotting. This task of text reading generally requires text detection and text localization. Text detection and localization is the process determining text regions from an image. This task is also complex due to the variations such as font, color, size, shape and due to presence of variety of distortions such as perspective, noise, occlusion, poor illumination and low contrast [40].

Text reading is a high value research area to computer vision. Text provides rich communication platform which is precise yet, is simple. Research community has spent decades of research effort in identifying and understanding text present in natural scene

D. Gupta et al. (Eds.): CVIP 2022, CCIS 1777, pp. 350–361, 2023.
https://doi.org/10.1007/978-3-031-31417-9_27

and documents. Due to the presence of variations and distortions present in the text, the problem of text reading is still an important open area of research [20].

Though few modern methods are fairly accurate in locating text, these techniques generally rely on an extreme training process that require a very large dataset consisting tens of thousands of samples and need a huge amount of computational time for training iterations. The procedure of improving and fine tuning of the training process is mostly heuristic and extremely complex. Even with powerful computational infrastructure, the process of training may demand days to weeks to complete.

This work is motivated by fairly simple image enhancement techniques such as morphological gradient. We hope to decrease the amount of training required using these enhancements. Our proposed novel semi-supervised approach aims to utilize benefits of using image gradients and an unsupervised auto encoder network to detect and enhance text regions. Image gradient is likely to eliminate few of variations such as color and some changes in brightness. Text usually has a contrasting background and gradient operation make high contrast regions more prominent. These merits of gradients would likely to reduce training time significantly and improve the overall results. The proposed method is resilient over differences in font, scale, orientation, and script of the text.

We have fined tuned the proposed method based on the merits and limits of the few early and/or prominent works. Rule based text detection was implemented in early works. Some works have imposed rules on upon a set of extracted features from the image [7, 14, 30, 38]. Supervised learning approaches proposed later, significantly improve coded rules. Inception of neural networks and allied learning approaches have shown substantial improvements in the results in comparison to all early approaches. Hence, most of the recent works use neural network based learning models for predicting text regions [11, 22, 34]. The promising results have also boosted interest of the researchers in text spotting, in the recent years. All these efforts have resulted in considerable developments in text detection and recognition in natural scene imagery and video. Neural network based classifiers, especially deep learning models [19] in text localization and text recognition has promised a considerable improvement in results. Generally, these approaches demand long hours of training and are extremely resource hungry. Most of these techniques could not be executed in ordinary systems and in embedded environments.

2 Related Work

Scene text detection, localization and understanding are explored by eminent research scholars due to precious information that could be obtained. This problem of text spotting is still considered as an open area due to the challenges involved. Finding the presence of text i.e., text detection and marking up possible area i.e., text localization are preliminary steps in understanding the text. The references [8, 10, 11, 14, 24, 30, 33, 38] discuss rule-based methodologies that are prominent in the early days of scene text understanding. Neural network based classifiers in the recent years have given text spotting a new spotlight. Deeper neural networks have shown greater ability to detect and understand text with greater precision. References [13, 16–18, 28, 29, 31, 39] explore some such efforts. Survey works found in the reference [14, 19, 20, 35, 41] list and compare various works related to scene text detection and understanding.

Intra class variations in the text such as script, font, scale and distortions make text detection extremely complex task. Detection of characters belonging to a specific language or its subset, specific font, orientation or character set was explored in the early works [14]. These conditions would help to limit the computational complexity caused by the variations in the text. The condition also reduced requirement of computational resources to a reasonable level. More advanced, robust and accurate methods with multilingual text detection abilities could be seen as computational infrastructure and research efforts expanded. For instance, generic text detection was attempted by estimating edge level features by methods such as MSER [8] and SWT [11]. These methods define specific features such as stroke width feature. Text regions are estimated by processing these features with other allied parameters. On the other hand, scene image can be perceived in a different domain. For instance, frequency domain representation of an image can aid text detection. Efforts such as [24] has explored text detection from this perspective. Efforts such as reference [10] have tried to reduce supervision required in the process of training.

Convolutional neural networks and deep learning introduced new possibilities in text detection and recognition. Efforts such as [13, 16–19, 28, 29, 31, 39] present substantially improved results from the early efforts. Improvements in accuracy and robustness along with multi-scale, multi-script, multi-orientation text recognition capabilities in more challenging scene imagery are now realized. This improvement is offered at the cost of vast amount of training time, high-end computational platform and a large set of relevant training images. Though some ways to improve training process [12] are explored, the gain in efficacy had costed substantially by reduction of text detection accuracy or reduced robustness. For instance, reducing training efforts by limiting scale of the text or orientation.

Researchers have located horizontal text by using morphological gradients [24, 27]. Composite image contrast enhancement is utilized by Text CNN and similar text attentional convolutional neural networks [13]. Neural network based text detectors are more prone to variations such as angle and scale. Detection of text in different orientations is explored by Rotation-Sensitive Regression [17]. The method featured Rotation-sensitive Regression Detector (RRD) intended to compute oriented bounding box regression. Context modelling and semantic segmentation approach attempts to understand the scene. Scene understanding could boost text detection performance. One of such method is discussed in TextScanner [28]. Text line detection in multiple orientation is explored by EAST [39] text detector. It also featured improvements in both performance and results against earlier approaches. Like Rotation-Sensitive Regression, multi-orientation text detection is explored in Inceptext [31] with performance enhancement. Text detection, localization and recognition capabilities of Inceptext is available online with opensource implementation. Text might appear in arbitrary shapes in scene imagery. This variety of text localization with adaptive text region representation has been discussed in the work referenced in [29]. A technique exclusively designed for detecting curved text that are featured in some signboards, shirts is explored in the work [18]. The approach works by estimating transverse and longitudinal sequence connection. The work also proposes a curved scene text dataset. Language and script cause greater variations in text. Multilingual text detection is an important research avenue. Text detection with fixed brightness and contrast adjustments across multiple languages is explored in the following reference [5]. Extracting text by assembling text components from higher level annotations and a has discussed in the work [16] with multilingual and multiple orientation resilience.

Implementing most of the above techniques demand high-end computational facility. The neural networks may demand greater amounts of memory and training iterations require parallel computations which usually is possible with high end graphics processing units having machine learning support. Even then, most of these techniques require a time consuming training process – spanning from days to weeks. There is no doubt that we need to improve the process of training. Hence, we have focused on improvement of training process in this work and attained a promising result while reducing a substantial amount of training effort.

3   Dataset Description

Multi-script Robust Reading Competition (MRRC) [15] scene text dataset consists scenic images containing text. The dataset set is captured around India roads and it includes multi-script diversity found commonly in India, for example bilingual/trilingual sign-boards. Also, the dataset is a good mixture of distortions found in scene images. Text in different orientation, blur, low contrast, low light, day/night captures are found in the set.

The dataset consists 167 images for training and 167 images testing purpose. It is a small dataset and generally considered insufficient for training deep neural networks. We choose this challenging dataset to demonstrate the possibility of detecting and localizing text using our proposed technique.

We have also used Microsoft Research Asia Text Detection 500 dataset (MSRA-TD500) [32] dataset for testing our model. The dataset includes real world challenges to be faced by a text detection system with its 300 training and 200 testing images.

4   Proposed Method

In an attempt to minimize the amount of training required to achieve a decent text localization result, we propose a semi-supervised method for text detection and localization. Our aim is to realize an efficient technique that produces promising results with small dataset, minimal training and limited computational ability without losing the ability to detect text across multiple languages and to maintain robustness against variations in the text such as scale, orientation and color. Image processing technique such as edge detection, contour features [25] and gradients are generally help in the tasks of computer vision. We have observed in our experiments that the morphological gradient analysis (MGA) enhances textual regions. These enhanced images are likely to improve the task of text detection.

On the other hand, auto encoder networks generally used for image compression or to achieve an improved representation. With some modification and appropriate training, we aim to feed an auto encoder network with scene text image and to obtain possible text regions as the result. These results may be further processed to achieve better results in the task of recognizing the text.

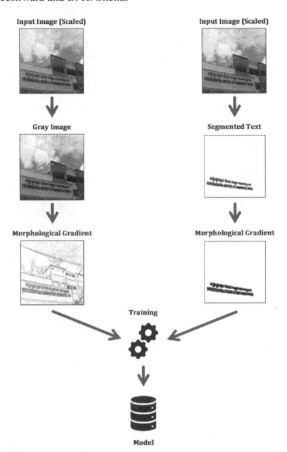

Fig. 1. The training phase: Input image is scaled down and converted to gray scale. Gradient of this image and actual text regions are used for training.

Combination of gradient processing and auto encoders are likely to be a good combination for text reading. Auto encoder networks are provided with gradient images. The task of the neural network to eliminate non-textual regions. Result of the network is expected to text candidates with minimal noise.

The detection noise can be reduced by simple techniques including morphological opening. And also, elimination of extreme high frequency components. The result is likely to contain text regions across the languages. Text boundary or regions could be used directly or could be merged together based on neighborhood analysis for example, dilation.

4.1 Phase 1: Training

During the phase of training, two major activities are performed. First, image is pre-processed and morphological gradient [23] operation is applied on it. Morphological gradient operation would enhance variations of pixel intensity. Second, gradients are fed to an encoder-decoder network. Sequence of these operations are shown in Fig. 1. Segmented text and gradient images are inverted to enhance visibility.

We have scaled down input images to the resolution of 348x348 to reduce dimensionality. This would also reduce our results but would offer excellent performance. Reducing images to any lower dimension would reduce the results substantially. Increasing resolution up to 512x512 has not improved the results considerably. Hence all images are reduced to 348x348 size.

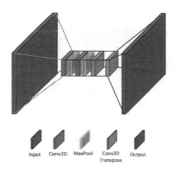

Fig. 2. Distribution of layers in the auto encoder neural network. The network is supposed to enhance the text components present in the input gradient image. Input and output are images of 348x348. Neural network layers would contain 48 neurons.

To compute morphological gradient of the reduced input image, first image is converted to gray scale. Noise is reduced using 3x3 median filtering and Gaussian blur. Image is binarized. Then, morphological gradient $G(i)$ is computed as the difference between dilation ($\oplus$) and erosion ($\ominus$) operations using 3x3 kernel.

$$G(i) = (i \oplus \delta) - (i \ominus \delta) \tag{1}$$

Gradient images prepared as per the above equation are used in the further processing. Gradient image is fed to auto encoder network. The auto encoder is trained to enhance possible text components and suppress the rest. The encoder neural network is designed with 48 neurons at each Conv2D layer of 3x3 dimension as shown in Fig. 2. Max pooling is applied after each convolutional layer. The appropriate decoder is designed to invert the encoding. The network is pretrained for 200 iterations and fine-tuned to achieve maximum detection results by further iterations of training.

We have trained our model using only 167 images of MRRC dataset. Gradient images of training samples and segmented images are computed. Further these gradients are fed into the auto encoder. We have observed that the model optimally fits after around 200 iterations. This generated model is used for scene text detection and localization across image and video frames.

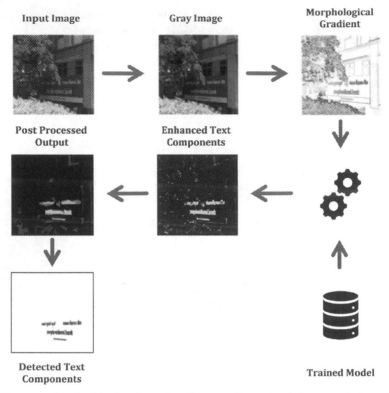

Fig. 3. Processes involved in the phase of testing – gradient of scaled gray scale input image is used text localization by the neural network.

4.2 Phase 2: Testing

During testing, an image under goes similar phases as that of training. However, instead of updating the training model, a classification decision is produced to identify text components and locate text in the input image. Text regions such as words and lines are formed by grouping text candidates.

For testing, we have preprocessed image or frame by computing gradient. This gradient is fed to the model to further enhance possible text components. These text candidates are filtered for noise to obtain localization results. The steps involved are shown in Fig. 3.

5   Experimental Results

We have trained proposed method with training images of MRRC scene text dataset. The results are evaluated against MRRC test set and test set of MSRA-TD500 dataset. The method has shown promising results. The obtained result and comparison with the standard result can be seen in Table 1 and Table 2. We have conducted our experiments using Google Colaboratory, Keras [9]-TensorFlow [21], Python OpenCV [2], NumPy

[8] array image data and tools available with Scikit Learn [6]. We have achieved 14fps using Colab GPU.

Table 1. Experiment results comparison with MRRC dataset

Method	F-score	Precision	Recall
Yin et. al [15]	0.51	0.64	0.42
LoG&Struct – Basavaraju et. al [4]	0.75	0.69	0.81
DWT&MSER – Ajay et. al [1]	0.79	0.82	0.76
Neighborhood – Basavaraju et. al [2]	0.71	0.74	0.75
LoG & Connected Component – Basavaraju et. al [3]	0.72	0.65	0.81
Gradient Auto Encoder (proposed)	**0.75**	**0.69**	**0.81**

Table 2. Experiment results comparison with MSRA-TD500 dataset

Method	F-score	Precision	Recall
LoG&Struct	0.78	0.73	0.84
DWT&MSER	0.80	0.83	0.78
SWT Epshtein et al. [11] [16]	0.25	0.25	0.25
Text Detection-ICDAR [32]	0.50	0.53	0.52
Text Detection-Mixture [32]	0.60	0.63	0.63
MGA [26]	0.69	0.71	0.69
AT-Text Li et al. [16]	0.73	0.77	0.69
Zhang et al. [37]	0.74	0.83	0.67
Text-Attentional CNN He et al. [13]	0.74	0.77	0.70
CFL [25]	0.75	0.84	0.67
Zhang et al. [36]	0.76	0.81	0.72
MGA + CFL [26]	0.77	0.85	0.71
Gradient Auto Encoder (proposed)	**0.76**	**0.73**	**0.79**

The proposed method works best with contrasting background. The method has produced promising results against variations in script, color, font, size, input dimension, orientation of text, blur introduced in natural scene images with limited training of 167 images. Detection results of MRRC dataset can be seen in Fig. 4 and Fig. 5 shows localization results against MSRA-TD500 dataset. However, we have observed that the method may not always yield good results when text is not clearly distinguishable from the background. Some of the such instances of failure are shown in Fig. 6 and Fig. 7.

Fig. 4. Some random successful detection results of the proposed method on MRRC dataset. Input image (color) and enhanced gradient images (dark) from the auto encoder network are shown above.

Fig. 5. Some random successful detection results of the proposed method on MSRA-TD500 dataset. Input image (color) and enhanced gradient images (dark) from the auto encoder network are shown above.

Fig. 6. Failure cases from MRRC dataset

Fig. 7. Failure cases from MSRA-TD500 dataset

6   Conclusion

The proposed method has shown promising results, considering that it is trained with only 167 training images of MRRC dataset. Method has performed well on the testing set of MRRC images and also against MSRA-TD500 dataset. The method has successful results in multiple scripts/languages, fonts, styles, different scales, different input image size and in multiple orientations, Amount of training time required is reduced from weeks and days to minutes. Yet, the results of the method are comparable with works of recent literature. The method stands out with the ability to learn detecting text with limited training.

References

1. Ajay, B.N., Naveena, C.: A mechanism for detection of text in images using DWT and MSER. In: Krishna, A.N., Srikantaiah, K.C., Naveena, C. (eds.) Integrated Intelligent Computing, Communication and Security. SCI, vol. 771, pp. 669–676. Springer, Singapore (2019). https://doi.org/10.1007/978-981-10-8797-4_68
2. Basavaraju, H., et al.: Neighborhood structure-based model for multilingual arbitrarily-oriented text localization in images/videos (2021)
3. Basavaraju, H.T., Manjunath Aradhya, V.N., Guru, D.S.: A novel arbitrary-oriented multilingual text detection in images/video. In: Satapathy, S.C., Joao Manuel, R.S., Tavares, V.B., Mohanty, J.R. (eds.) Information and decision sciences. AISC, vol. 701, pp. 519–529. Springer, Singapore (2018). https://doi.org/10.1007/978-981-10-7563-6_54
4. Basavaraju, H.T., et al.: LoG and structural based arbitrary oriented multilingual text detection in images/video. Int. J. Nat. Comput. Res. (IJNCR). **7**(3), 1–16 (2018)
5. Basu, S., et al.: Multilingual scene text detection using gradient morphology. Int. J. Comput. Vis. Image Process. **10**(3), 31–43 (2020). https://doi.org/10.4018/IJCVIP.2020070103
6. Buitinck, L., et al.: API design for machine learning software: experiences from the scikit-learn project. In: ECML PKDD Workshop: Languages for Data Mining and Machine Learning, pp. 108–122 (2013)

7. Chen, D., Luettin, J.: A survey of text detection and recognition in images and videos (2000)
8. Chen, H., et al.: Robust text detection in natural images with edge-enhanced maximally stable extremal regions. In: 2011 18th IEEE International Conference on Image Processing, pp. 2609–2612 (2011). https://doi.org/10.1109/ICIP.2011.6116200
9. Chollet, F.: Others: Keras (2015)
10. Coates, A., et al.: Text detection and character recognition in scene images with unsupervised feature learning. In: 2011 International Conference on Document Analysis and Recognition, pp. 440–445 (2011). https://doi.org/10.1109/ICDAR.2011.95
11. Epshtein, B., et al.: Detecting text in natural scenes with stroke width transform. In: 2010 IEEE Computer Society Conference on Computer Vision and Pattern Recognition, pp. 2963–2970 (2010). https://doi.org/10.1109/CVPR.2010.5540041
12. Fu, K., et al.: Text detection for natural scene based on MobileNet V2 and U-Net. In: 2019 IEEE International Conference on Mechatronics and Automation (ICMA), pp. 1560–1564 (2019). https://doi.org/10.1109/ICMA.2019.8816384
13. He, T., et al.: Text-attentional convolutional neural network for scene text detection. IEEE Trans. Image Process. 25(6), 2529–2541 (2016). https://doi.org/10.1109/TIP.2016.2547588
14. Jung, K., et al.: Text information extraction in images and video: a survey. Pattern Recogn. 37(5), 977–997 (2004). https://doi.org/10.1016/j.patcog.2003.10.012
15. Kumar, D., et al.: Multi-script robust reading competition in ICDAR 2013. In: Proceedings of the 4th International Workshop on Multilingual OCR. Association for Computing Machinery, New York, NY, USA (2013). https://doi.org/10.1145/2505377.2505390
16. Li, H., Lu, H.: AT-Text: assembling text components for efficient dense scene text detection. Future Internet. 12(11), 1–14 (2020). https://doi.org/10.3390/fi12110200
17. Liao, M., et al.: Rotation-sensitive regression for oriented scene text detection. In: Proceedings of the IEEE Computer Society Conference on Computer Vision and Pattern Recognition, pp. 5909–5918 (2018). https://doi.org/10.1109/CVPR.2018.00619
18. Liu, Y., et al.: Curved scene text detection via transverse and longitudinal sequence connection. Pattern Recogn. 90, 337–345 (2019). https://doi.org/10.1016/j.patcog.2019.02.002
19. Long, S., He, X., Yao, C.: Scene text detection and recognition: the deep learning era. Int. J. Comput. Vision 129(1), 161–184 (2020). https://doi.org/10.1007/s11263-020-01369-0
20. Manjunath Aradhya, V.N., Basavaraju, H.T., Guru, D.S.: Decade research on text detection in images/videos: a review. Evol. Intel. 14(2), 405–431 (2019). https://doi.org/10.1007/s12065-019-00248-z
21. Abadi, M., et al.: TensorFlow: large-scale machine learning on heterogeneous systems. https://www.tensorflow.org/ (2015)
22. Matas, J., et al.: Robust wide-baseline stereo from maximally stable extremal regions. In: Image and Vision Computing (2004). https://doi.org/10.1016/j.imavis.2004.02.006
23. Rivest, J.-F., et al.: Morphological gradients. J. Electron. Imaging 2(4), 326–336 (1993). https://doi.org/10.1117/12.159642
24. Shekar, B.H., et al.: Discrete wavelet transform and gradient difference based approach for text localization in videos. In: Proceedings - 2014 5th International Conference on Signal and Image Processing, ICSIP 2014, pp. 280–284 (2014). https://doi.org/10.1109/ICSIP.2014.50
25. Shekar, B.H., Raveeshwara, S.: Contour feature learning for locating text in natural scene images. Int. J. Inf. Technol. 14, 1–6 (2022). https://doi.org/10.1007/s41870-021-00851-3
26. Shekar, B.H., Raveeshwara, S.: Morphological gradient analysis and contour feature learning for locating text in natural scene images. In: International Conference on Computer Vision and Image Processing, pp. 254–261 (2022)
27. Shekar, B.H., Smitha M., L.: Morphological gradient based approach for text localization in video/scene images. In: 2014 International Conference on Advances in Computing, Communications and Informatics (ICACCI), pp. 2426–2431 (2014). https://doi.org/10.1109/ICACCI.2014.6968426

28. Wan, Z., et al.: TextScanner: reading characters in order for robust scene text recognition. arXiv (2019). https://doi.org/10.1609/aaai.v34i07.6891
29. Wang, X., et al.: Arbitrary shape scene text detection with adaptive text region representation. In: Proceedings of the IEEE Computer Society Conference on Computer Vision and Pattern Recognition, 2019-June, pp. 6442–6451 (2019). https://doi.org/10.1109/CVPR.2019.00661
30. Wu, V., et al.: Textfinder: an automatic system to detect and recognize text in images. IEEE Trans. Pattern Anal. Mach. Intell. **21**(11), 1224–1229 (1999). https://doi.org/10.1109/34.809116
31. Yang, Q., et al.: Inceptext: a new inception-text module with deformable PSROI pooling for multi-oriented scene text detection. In: IJCAI International Joint Conference on Artificial Intelligence, pp. 1071–1077 (2018). https://doi.org/10.24963/ijcai.2018/149
32. Yao, C., et al.: Detecting texts of arbitrary orientations in natural images. In: Proceedings of the IEEE Computer Society Conference on Computer Vision and Pattern Recognition, vol. 8, pp. 1083–1090 (2012). https://doi.org/10.1109/CVPR.2012.6247787
33. Yao, C., et al.: Scene text detection via holistic, multi-channel prediction, pp. 1–10 (2016)
34. Ye, Q., Doermann, D.: Text detection and recognition in imagery: a survey. IEEE Trans. Pattern Anal. Mach. Intell. **37**(7), 1480–1500 (2014)
35. Yin, X.C., et al.: Text detection, tracking and recognition in video: a comprehensive survey. IEEE Trans. Image Process. **25**(6), 2752–2773 (2016). https://doi.org/10.1109/TIP.2016.2554321
36. Zhang, Y., Huang, Y., Zhao, D., Wu, C.H., Ip, W.H., Yung, K.L.: A scene text detector based on deep feature merging. Multimedia Tools Appl. **80**(19), 29005–29016 (2021). https://doi.org/10.1007/s11042-021-11101-w
37. Zhang, Z., et al.: Multi-oriented text detection with fully convolutional networks. In: 2016 IEEE Conference on Computer Vision and Pattern Recognition (CVPR), pp. 4159–4167 (2016). https://doi.org/10.1109/CVPR.2016.451
38. Zhong, Y., et al.: Locating text in complex color images. Pattern Recogn. **28**(10), 1523–1535 (1995). https://doi.org/10.1016/0031-3203(95)00030-4
39. Zhou, X., et al.: EAST: an efficient and accurate scene text detector. In: Proceedings - 30th IEEE Conference on Computer Vision and Pattern Recognition, CVPR 2017, pp. 2642–2651 (2017). https://doi.org/10.1109/CVPR.2017.283
40. Zhu, A.: Scene text detection and recognition. Front. Comp. Sci. **10**(1), 19–36 (2017)
41. Zhu, Y., Yao, C., Bai, X.: Scene text detection and recognition: recent advances and future trends. Front. Comp. Sci. **10**(1), 19–36 (2016). https://doi.org/10.1007/s11704-015-4488-0

A Novel Scheme for Adversarial Training to Improve the Robustness of DNN Against White Box Attacks

N. Sai Mani Rohith and P. P. Deepthi[(⊠)]

Department of Electronics and Communication Engineering,
National Institute of Technology Calicut, Kozhikode 673601, India
`deepthi@nitc.ac.in`

Abstract. Deep Neural Networks (DNNs) are found to give excellent results in many applications including image classification. DNNs are found to have reduced efficiency in their performance when exposed to adversarial attacks. An adversarial attack is a phenomenon that is used to fool the DNN, by adding imperceptible perturbations to the input. Under white-box attack conditions, when an adversary has complete knowledge of the network and may produce substantial perturbations via repeated iterations, the robustness of current defense methods against these assaults is severely compromised. By observing learned feature space of a DNN it is noted that different class samples are within close proximity due to which by adding imperceptible perturbations, the feature map of input in the learned feature space is being mapped away from its respective class samples. This forces the model to completely change its decision when an unnoticeable perturbation is added to the input. To counter such attacks, this work attempts to force the DNN to learn how to maximize the distance between different class samples.

Keywords: Deep Neural Network · perturbations · adversarial attack · adversarial defense · feature map

1 Introduction

Deep Neural Networks (DNNs), used in field of computational science, analyses and interprets information like patterns and structures in data to enable learning, reasoning, and decision making. DNN can be used for a variety of classification tasks, such as sorting email spam, putting images into groups, and putting documents into groups. Some areas in which DNN based classification outperforms conventional classification are computer vision and natural language processing. Though DNN is giving excellent results, their performance is reduced drastically to adversarial instances generated because of adding small, human unnoticeable intentional perturbations to conventional examples. This property of DNNs raises concerns about their appropriateness for security sensitive applications such as facial recognition and self-driving vehicles. As a result, for safe

D. Gupta et al. (Eds.): CVIP 2022, CCIS 1777, pp. 362–376, 2023.
https://doi.org/10.1007/978-3-031-31417-9_28

deep learning, defense techniques that increase the robustness of DNN against hostile situations have become important.

An adversarial attack is a phenomenon that is used to fool the DNN by adding imperceptible perturbations to the input. This perturbation is not a random noise, but rather a purposefully generated vector that results in misclassification of the inputs. Basically, adversarial attacks deliberately push the data point into the nearest neighbourhood region by adding an unnoticeable perturbation to the input so that the data point value will vary in a particular direction, causing errors in the output of the classifier. Due to the openness of the classification models, it is very easy for an adversary to add the perturbations to the input. A powerful defense mechanism is required to counter these attacks.

In recent years, a variety of empirical defence strategies, such as adversarial training [4], input/feature denoising [9,14,25], and defensive distillation [7], have been proposed as ways to protect CNNs from the adversarial perturbations that they suffer. One of the most effective approaches is adversarial training, which involves generating adversarial data on the go for the purpose of training CNNs. Adversarial training is a useful method for making CNNs more robust; however, it results in a significant decline in the accuracy of the predictions made for natural data [22] and suffers from the issue of over-fitting to the adversarial data that is used for training. Different forms of AT, such as TRADES [23] and Friendly Adversarial Training (FAT) [24], have been offered by researchers as potential solutions to these issues. Many works have been published that seek to suggest innovative defensive mechanisms to offset the impacts of adversarial data on feature extraction in CNNs in the hopes of making CNNs even more robust under AT. Most of this research tried to improve robustness by trying to locate and suppress irregularities at specific positions throughout channels (generally referred to as feature maps in CNNs) [1,2], whereas the relationship between robustness and significant overlap of feature maps of distinct class samples in the learnt feature space has received very little attention.

By analysing feature maps of a DNN in the learned feature space, it is observed that there is a significant amount of overlap between features of different class samples after adversarial training. We noticed that by adding perturbations to the input leads to mapping of input sample away from its respective class samples in the high-dimensional feature space. Based upon this observation, we worked on defense method by introducing a loss function in the training process which tries to maximally separate different class feature samples in the corresponding feature space.

This research presents a defensive approach based on a unique training process that optimally isolates the learnt feature representations of different classes of the model, an idea is shown in Fig. 1. Major contributions of this work are following:

– We formulated expressions for within class sum of squares (WCSS) and between class sum of squares (BCSS) as weighted Euclidean distance by suitably choosing weights based on the covariance matrix of learned feature samples. The covariance matrix of learned feature samples is used to derive the

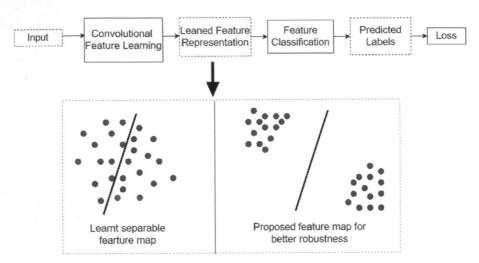

Fig. 1. A typical framework of CNN and an idea of feature map before and after training with proposed defense method.

weights because more correlated dimension will be given high weight compared to less correlated dimension thereby helping to minimize variance of the dimension that is more correlated with each other.

- We proposed a new custom loss function based on the derived WCSS and BCSS to minimize WCSS and maximize BCSS. This loss function helps to optimally isolate the distinct class samples such that the overlap between any two classes in the learnt feature space is minimal. This makes it difficult for an attacker to generate adversarial perturbations within a limited budget.
- We proposed to use an extra layer in the CNN to apply the proposed loss function. Initial class clusters are formed with the cross-entropy loss function and further class separation is ensured with the proposed loss function.
- The proposed adversarial training is applied on various popular datasets and the improved robustness against adversarial attacks is validated.

Our method gives strong evidence that adversarial perturbations can fool DNNs not just because of the properties of the data (like high dimensionality) and the architecture of the network, but also because of the objective function used in optimization of training process. This proposed defence gives a large increase in robustness under the most extreme attack circumstances. These include white-box attacks and iterative opponents, as well as the most powerful first-order attacks (Projected Gradient Descent). Extensive testing on three publicly accessible datasets shows that the proposed defence is robust against the PGD-20 attack ($\epsilon = 0.03$), with a robustness of 51.61% for the CIFAR10 dataset. It is a greater level of robustness against a wide variety of powerful adversarial attacks, to the best of our understanding.

2   Related Work

There is good amount of recent research literature focused on creating adversarial instances and establishing defences against them in order to fool a deep network. The authors in [15] first developed an adversarial perturbation by using L-BFGS-based optimization approach, then followed by the Fast Gradient Sign Method (FGSM) [3] and its iterative form [16]. DeepFool [17] generates the adversarial instance by projecting the input iteratively over the decision boundary until the input crosses the boundary and is mistakenly classified. The Projected Gradient Descent (PGD) [4] attack, which generates adversarial example for input by iteratively adding perturbation (within the ϵ-ball around input) in the direction of gradient of prediction loss *wrt* input such that the prediction loss of the adversarial image is maximised, is one of the most effective attacks that have been developed recently.

In the literature, two primary defensive techniques have been suggested to defend adversarial attacks. First, by applying various pre-processing methods and change the input at the time of inference [9,10]. The second group of defences enhances the training process of the network to resist adversarial attacks. Effective in this area is adversarial training, in which input data is augmented by adversarial data [4,19]. Ensemble adversarial training is used in [5] to soften the decision bounds of the classifier. Virtual Adversarial Training [8] uses a regularisation term to smooth the model distribution. The authors in [7] used distillation to improve the performance of the model by re-training using soft labels. [13] proposes a defensive quantization strategy to regulate the network's Lipschitz constant in order to limit perturbations during testing. Stochastic Activation Pruning was suggested in [26] as a protection against adversarial assaults. Min-Max optimization [4], which includes first-order attacked samples in the training data, is currently the most effective protection approach. Recent research [6] demonstrates that the present state-of-the-art defences [11,12] may be effectively evaded in white-box situations, despite the enormous research work devoted to developing defences against adversarial assaults. In our experiments, we extensively compare our findings to those of [4] and establish a strong argument by achieving substantial improvements.

3   Proposed Defense Method

In the following, we will first explain the notations used in this paper, then offer a quick summary of the traditional cross entropy loss, and finally provide a detailed explanation of the technique that we have proposed.

Notations: Let x and y are an input-label pair, and DNN is represented as $\mathcal{F}_\theta(x)$, where θ denotes the DNN parameters. Feature representation of input x is denoted by the notation $f \in \mathcal{R}^d$, is the intermediate output of a DNN. This representation is then utilised by a fully connected layer to carry out classification task. Let's say that there are K different classes. In order to train the model, we need to identify the ideal value for θ, which will minimise the value of a specific objective function.

3.1 Cross-entropy Loss Function

Cross-entropy objective is used as a distance metric between predicted labels and the true-class labels. To put it another way, in order to maximise the projection onto the real class labels, the model must learn a mapping from input to output space which is forced by cross-entropy loss.

$$\mathcal{L}_{CE} = \sum_{i=1}^{m} -log \underbrace{\frac{exp(\mathcal{F}_\theta(x_i)_{y_i} + b_{y_i})}{\sum_{j=1}^{K} exp(\mathcal{F}_\theta(x_i)_{y_{i_j}} + b_{y_{i_j}})}}_{softmax\ activation} \tag{1}$$

where m denotes the total inputs and b is the bias term for classification layers.

Adversarial Objective: The primary objective of an attack algorithm is to make a trained DNN $\mathcal{F}_\theta(.)$ into making incorrect classification. The objective of attack algorithms is to do this with minimal perturbation. The aim of the attacker is indicated by:

$$\underset{\delta}{argmax}\ \mathcal{L}(\mathcal{F}_\theta(x + \delta), y) \qquad s.t.\ ||\delta||_p \le |\epsilon| \tag{2}$$

where δ represents adversarial perturbation, $\mathcal{L}(.)$ represents the loss function, $||.||_p$ represents the p-norm, that is often thought of as a l_∞-ball that is centred around x, and ϵ represents the available perturbation budget.

To train a model robust to adversarial attacks, the learning method has to take into consideration of the allowed perturbations in the input domain and it needs to train such that it can map input that have been perturbed into true class. The following min-max (saddle point) problem, which reduces empirical risk when there is a perturbation present, may be used to achieve this:

$$\underset{\theta}{min}\ \underset{(x,y)\sim\mathcal{D}}{\mathbf{E}}[\underset{\delta}{max}\ \mathcal{L}(\mathcal{F}_\theta(x + \delta), y)], \qquad s.t.\ ||\delta||_p \le |\epsilon| \tag{3}$$

where the variable $\mathcal{D}$ represents the data distribution.

CE Loss in Adversarial Perspective: When it comes to typical classification jobs, a CE loss is the default option. In practical terms, it is only possible to assign a given input sample to one of the classes that have already been specified. Because of this, it does not enable one to differentiate between normal and adversarial data. In addition, it will not impose any boundary limits between the learnt classification region. As shown in Eq. 1, the objective of an adversary is to maximise $\mathcal{L}(.)$ while staying within a specified perturbation limit. Let the adversarial polytope in the learnt feature space of a DNN with respect to input x is provided by the following equation:

$$\mathcal{P}_\epsilon(x; \theta) = \{\mathcal{F}_\theta(x + \delta)\ s.t.\ ||\delta||_p \le |\epsilon|\} \tag{4}$$

If there is significant overlap of different adversarial polytopes in the learned feature space, the input will require minimal perturbations to fool the model. To counter this if we can somehow make it difficult for the adversary to find feasible perturbation within the budget, we can improve robustness of the model.

Proposition: The adversary will be unable to find a feasible modification within the perturbation budget limit if the adversarial polytopes for different classes of samples are maximally separated. For an ith input sample x_i with class label y_i, the adversary's success would be decreased for a small perturbation $||\delta||_p \leq |\epsilon|$ if the separation between a ith input sample's polytope, $\mathcal{P}_\epsilon(x_{y_i}^i; \theta)$, and the polytopes of other class samples, $\mathcal{P}_\epsilon(x_{y_j}^j; \theta)$, s.t., $y_j \neq y_i$, are improved. Therefore, the task to fool the DNN can be made more difficult for an adversary by introducing a simple maximum separation restriction in the training process. The traditional CE loss does not imply any such constraint and in absence of such a limitation, the resultant models are more vulnerable to adversarial attacks.

3.2   Proposed Loss Function

In this work, we introduce a new custom loss function that tries to minimize within class sum of squares (WCSS), by reducing the weighted Euclidean distance between within class feature samples, so that the variance of the learned features of the similar class samples in the feature map decreases, and to maximize between class sum of squares (BCSS), as we increase the distance between different class samples even by adding perturbations, input is mapped nearer to its respective class samples. WCSS equation is given by

$$WCSS = \sum_{k=1}^{K} \sum_{i=1}^{n} (f_{k_i} - \mu_k)^T . \Sigma_k . (f_{k_i} - \mu_k) \tag{5}$$

where n represents number of samples in each class, Σ_k represents the co-variance matrix of k class. In the above equation we use co-variance matrix of learned feature samples as weights because we need to minimize variance of that particular dimension that is more overlapped with other polytopes. So, the covariance matrix serves as weights so that more correlated dimension is given high weight compared to less correlated dimension.

By minimizing WCSS, we are trying to reduce the variance of each cluster (Fig. 2).

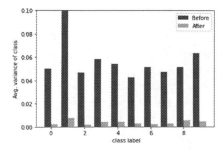

Fig. 2. Average variance plot of each class before and after training model with proposed loss function (Eq. 7).

Between Class Sum of Squares (BCSS) addresses the problem of overlap of different class samples by maximally separating the different class samples from each other. BCSS equation is given by

$$BCSS = \sum_{k=1}^{K} \sum_{i=k+1}^{K} (\mu_k - \mu_i)^T . \Sigma . (\mu_k - \mu_i) \qquad (6)$$

where $\Sigma = \frac{\Sigma_k + \Sigma_i}{2}$.

The proposed loss function to introduce in model training process is given by

$$L_{prop} = \frac{WCSS}{BCSS} \qquad (7)$$

3.3   Model Training

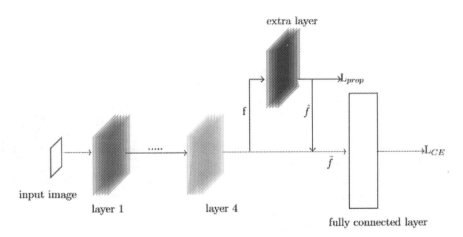

Fig. 3. An illustration of our model which is trained with both L_{CE} and L_{prop}. ($\tilde{f} = f + \hat{f}$)

The loss function defined in Eq. 7 is used to train the extra layer of the model in Fig. 3, whereas the rest of the model is trained using cross-entropy loss (L_{CE}).

By training the extra layer with the proposed loss in Eq. 7, the layer maps the input sample to its intermediate representation $\hat{f}$ in the learned feature space, which is more closely located to its respective class samples and maximally separated from different class samples.

4   Adversarial Attack

Let the normal input-label pair be (x, y) and a DNN $\mathcal{F}_\theta$, the objective of an attacker is to find an adversarial examples (AE) x' that forces the DNN to

---

Algorithm 1: Model Training with proposed loss function.

Input: Training data $\{x_i, y_i\}_{i=1,2,\ldots,n}$, Trained DNN $\mathbf{F}(\theta)$, maximum training epochs T.

Output: Robust Network $\mathbf{F}$ with updated parameters θ.

for $t=0$ to T-1 **do**

    for *minibatch* $x_1, x_2, \ldots, x_b$ **do**

        Adversarial instances are generated as:

        if FGSM **then:** $x_{adv} = x + \epsilon.sign(\nabla_x L(x,y))$

        if PGD **then:** $x_{adv}^{i+1} = x^i + \epsilon.sign(\nabla_{x^i} L(x^i, y))$

        Augment x with x_{adv}.

        Compute the losses $(L_{CE}\&L_{prop})$

        Update parameters of extra layer by calculating gradients of L_{prop} w.r.t θ_{extra}.

        Update parameters of rest of the model by calculating gradients of L_{CE} w.r.t θ.

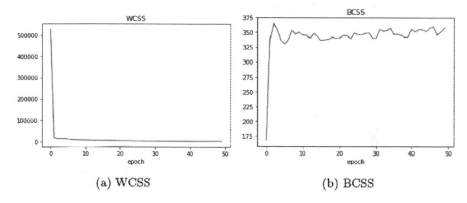

(a) WCSS   (b) BCSS

Fig. 4. Model shown in Fig. 3 trained with Eq. 7 for 50 epochs on CIFAR-10 dataset as mentioned in Algorithm.1

make an incorrect prediction $(\mathcal{F}_\theta(x) \neq y)$. The general formulation of adversarial example can be formulated as

$$minimise \; \mathcal{D}(x, x') \; ; \quad x' = x + \delta$$
$$suchthat \; \mathcal{F}(x') \neq y \; ; \quad x' \in [0, 1]^n$$

where the goal is to find δ that minimises $\mathcal{D}(x, x')$. Here $\mathcal{D}(.)$ is any distance metric (i.e., either L_2 or L_0 or L_∞ norm).

4.1 Fast Gradient Sign Method (FGSM)

FGSM [3] is a single step attack in which the adversary generates the perturbations for normal examples x^0 by taking the scaled (by amount of ϵ) sign gradient of loss *wrt* input.

$$x^1 = x^0 + \epsilon.sign(\nabla_x l(\mathcal{F}_\theta(x^0), y)) \tag{8}$$

4.2 Projected Gradient Descent (PGD)

PGD [4] is an iterative attack which generates perturbations for normal example x^0 for K steps iteratively with smaller step size α, such that the prediction loss of the adversarial image is maximised.

$$x^k = \pi(x^{k-1} + \alpha.sign(\nabla_{x^{k-1}} l(\mathcal{F}_\theta(x^{k-1}), y)) \tag{9}$$

where α is the step size, $\pi(.)$ is the projection function that maps adversarial example back to ϵ-ball of x^0 after each iteration, and x^k is the adversarial example at the kth step. PGD-K represents adversarial example is generated iteratively for K steps.

4.3 Carlini and Wagner (CW) Attack

In CW [18] attack, we try to search for an auxiliary variable Ψ that minimises

$$min. \; ||\frac{1}{2}(tanh(\Psi) + 1) - x||_2 + c.g(\frac{1}{2}(tanh(\Psi) + 1)) \tag{10}$$

where $\frac{1}{2}(tanh(\Psi) + 1) - x$ is the perturbation δ, c is the constant and $g(.)$ is defined as

$$g(x') = max(max \mathcal{Z}(x')_i : i \neq y - \mathcal{Z}(x')_y, -k) \tag{11}$$

Here k controls the adversarial example confidence and $\mathcal{Z}(.)_k$ are the logits (is an array of non-normalized predictions the classifier generates. This is generally given as input to softmax function to get probability of prediction) of corresponding class k.

5 Results

5.1 Experimental Settings

We experimented with the proposed methods on three publicly available datasets: FMNIST, CIFAR-10/100. For FMNIST we use the ResNet-9 model, and for CIFAR-10/100 we use the ResNet-18 model. The deep features of the model are obtained from the penultimate layer using an auxiliary branch. Initially we train the model for T_0 epochs ($T_0 = 50$ for FMNIST, $T_0 = 200$ for CIFAR-10/100) using cross-entropy loss function (L_{CE}). Further training details using proposed defense method (for $T = 50$ epochs) are summarised in Algorithm 1.

5.2   Results and Analysis

Figure 5 represents feature maps of adversarial trained model and model trained by proposed defense method. From Fig. 5b, there is a clear distinguishment of different class samples in the learnt feature map.

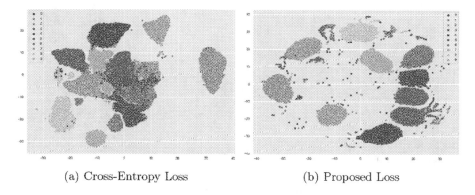

(a) Cross-Entropy Loss   (b) Proposed Loss

Fig. 5. Feature map obtained from penultimate layer activations of adversarially trained model with cross-entropy loss and proposed method on CIFAR-10 dataset (t-SNE algorithm is used for data visualization).

White *vs* Black box Settings: Two basic threat models exist when dealing with an adversary: white-box settings, the adversary has complete information about the targeted model, and black-box settings, the adversary provides perturbed data (produced without being aware of the target model) during testing. Table 1 displays our results for the various attacks discussed in Sect. 4 under both white-box and black-box settings. Robustness of the model is evaluated for a maximum allowed perturbation of $\epsilon = 0.3$ for FMNIST and $\epsilon = 0.03$ for CIFAR-10/100 datasets. The number of iterations for C&W attack are 1000 with a learning rate of 0.01.

Recent research [3,16,19] has shown that adversarial data are powerful even on models for which they were not originally generated. Therefore, an adversary may utilise this property of DNN to produce adversarial examples that works effectively even against the targeted models. For the safe deployment of machine learning models, defence versus black-box attacks is therefore particularly desired [27]. To show the robustness of our suggested defence in black-box environments, pre-trained VGG-19 model is used to generate adversarial examples and given to model trained with our proposed method during inference. Robustness of proposed defense method under black-box settings is reported in Table 1.

Adversarial Training: Several newly suggested defensive strategies have been shown to be enhanced by adversarial training (AdvTrain). Additionally, we examine the effect of adversarial training on our proposed defence. For this we augment the input data with adversarial samples. These samples are generated by using FGSM and PGD, with $\epsilon = 0.3$ for FMNIST, and $\epsilon = 0.03$ for CIFAR-10/100 to train our model. It is clear from Table 1 that AdvTrain enhances our method's robustness against both black box and white box assault conditions.

Baseline: We compare our proposed defense method with normal training (no defense) and few adversarial training methods.

- No defense. Model is trained using cross-entropy loss only on clean data.
- Standard Adversarial Training (SAT) [4]. Clean data along with adversarial data, generated along the training process using the PGD variant, are used to train the model.
- Ensemble Adversarial Training (EAT) [5]. Clean data along with adversarial data, generated using pre-trained models using the PGD variant, are used to train the model.
- Friendly Adversarial Training (FAT) [24]. Clean data along with adversarial data, generated along the training process, are used to train the model. Adversarial examples generated are not maximum loss sample but instead a weak adversarial example is used so as to not lose the generalization of clean samples.

5.3   Comparison with Existing Defenses

Our approach is compared with some of the state-of-the-art defensive mechanisms that change the model architecture or employ modified loss functions in training process (Table. 2). In order to do this, we conduct a comparison using [19], which includes hostile instances in the training data and creates new data for every iteration. We also do comparison with [20], which incorporates an ADP regularizer to enhance adversarial robustness. In addition, an input gradient regularizer mechanism proposed by [21] that penalises the degree to which input perturbations may alter the predictions of a model by regularising the gradient of the cross-entropy loss is also used for comparison. The last comparison is with Min-Max optimization-based defence [4], which includes the adversarial data in the training data.

Table 1. Classification accuracy (%) of different defense methods compared with proposed method different datasets. The defense method that is more robust to adversarial attacks have been highlighted.

Training	No attack	White-box settings				black-box settings			
		FGSM	CW	PGD-20	PGD-40	FGSM	CW	PGD-20	PGD-40
FMNIST($\epsilon = 0.3$, $c = 1$)									
No defense	**90.21**	38.64	0.0	0.0	0.0	40.57	38.21	38.53	37.89
SAT	81.37	55.1	52.41	39.32	39.01	72.71	71.82	71.27	70.94
EAT	82.64	58.39	53.67	40.24	40.01	73.49	71.68	72.36	71.53
FAT	83.06	59.27	55.25	39.07	38.21	**73.86**	72.59	**73.54**	**72.31**
SAT + Ours	83.43	**69.16**	**67.84**	**47.35**	**45.87**	72.67	**72.64**	72.27	72.03
CIFAR-10($\epsilon = 0.03$, $c = 0.1$)									
No defense	**95.09**	32.19	0.0	0.01	0.0	39.54	28.37	27.35	27.68
SAT	84.73	52.73	46.67	44.39	42.86	66.27	66.31	65.49	65.13
EAT	85.64	55.27	49.25	43.87	43.21	70.63	69.46	69.11	69.14
FAT	89.34	**65.52**	46.82	46.13	45.31	73.42	72.18	73.04	72.95
SAT + Ours	85.71	61.27	**62.47**	**51.61**	**49.76**	**82.57**	**82.41**	**80.43**	**80.09**
CIFAR-100($\epsilon = 0.03$, $c = 0.1$)									
No defense	**79.22**	3.52	0.0	0.0	0.0	28.41	26.37	23.91	23.16
SAT	59.78	29.57	23.05	22.78	22.44	53.19	52.67	53.76	52.49
EAT	59.1	29.15	22.37	23.59	22.04	52.73	53.07	51.97	51.64
FAT	59.54	**35.68**	23.08	22.95	22.09	54.81	53.54	51.38	51.29
SAT + Ours	61.24	35.67	**31.51**	**30.42**	**29.13**	**56.82**	**55.21**	**55.37**	**54.18**

Table 2. Performance of different defense methods evaluated on CIFAR-10 dataset under white-box adversarial setting (values represents the robustness). * represents models trained under adversarial settings.

Attacks	Params.	Base Model	Adv Train [19]*	Madry et. al [4]*	Pang et. al [20]*	Ross et. al [21]*	Ours*
No attack	-	**95.09**	84.5	87.3	90.6	86.2	85.71
FGSM	$\epsilon = 0.02$	47.61	44.3	**71.6**	61.7	39.5	68.47
	$\epsilon = 0.04$	22.37	31.0	47.4	46.2	20.8	**55.28**
C&W	$c = 0.01$	20.87	40.9	65.7	54.9	47.8	**76.27**
	$c = 0.1$	0.0	25.4	47.9	25.6	19.9	**62.47**
PGD	$\epsilon = 0.01$	6.35	24.3	67.7	48.4	24.5	**70.49**
	$\epsilon = 0.02$	0.27	7.8	48.5	30.4	8.5	**60.32**

5.4   Identifying Obfuscated Gradients

The authors in [6] managed to circumvent a variety of defense techniques under white-box attack settings by showing that these defense techniques are exhibiting a false hope of security. This phenomenon is called as *gradient masking*. Few main characteristics (mentioned in [6]), which proves proposed defense method does not rise gradient masking problem, are given below.

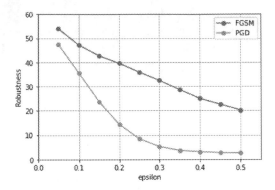

Fig. 6. Robustness of proposed model evaluated under different white-box attacks for wide range of perturbation budgets (ϵ) on CIFAR-10 dataset.

Iterative Attacks *vs* One-step Attacks: The success rate of adversarial examples generated by iterative attacks (*e.g.* PGD) should be more compared to one-step attacks (FGSM) at fooling defense method under white-box attack settings. Our evaluations in Fig. 6 proves this.

Black-box *vs* White-box Settings: As the adversary has total information about the model, under white-box attack settings, the attack success should be higher compared to black-box settings. Performance of our defense model under different white-box and black-box settings has been reported in Table 1, shows that our defense method overcomes gradient masking problem.

Effect of Distortion Bound (ϵ) on Model Robustness: The success rate of an attack should increase as we increase the perturbation budget (ϵ). For an unbounded ϵ attack, the robustness of the model should approach near zero, which is satisfied by our defense method (Fig. 6).

6   Conclusion

This work shows that by inclusion of maximal separation restriction in the training process of DNNs, which is not provided by standard cross-entropy loss, makes the task of the adversary more difficult. From our study, it is safe to say that the adversary task to identify a perturbation within the given budget is made more difficult if the adversarial samples from different classes are non-overlapping. We have tested the proposed defense method extensively in white-box conditions for a wide range of attack methods (both single-step and iterative). Results in Table 1 shows that proposed defense method maintains high robustness in almost all instances.

Acknowledgement. Authors sincerely acknowledge the contributions of Dr. Renu M Rameshan, Assistant Professor, IIT Mandi in bringing out this work.

References

1. Bai, Y., Zeng, Y., Jiang, Y., Xia, S.-T., Ma, X., Wang, Y. Improving adversarial robustness via channel-wise activation suppressing. In: ICLR 2021. OpenReview.net (2021)
2. Yan, H., Zhang, J., Niu, G., Feng, J., Tan, V.Y.F., Sugiyama, M.: CIFS: improving adversarial robustness of CNNs via channel-wise importance-based feature selection. In: ICLR (2021)
3. Goodfellow, I. J., Shlens, J., Szegedy, C.: Explaining and harnessing adversarial examples. In: ICLR (2015)
4. Madry, A., Makelov, A., Schmidt, L., Tsipras, D., Vladu, A.: Towards deep learning models resistant to adversarial attacks. In: ICLR (2018)
5. Tramer, F., Kurakin, A., Papernot, N., Goodfellow, I., Boneh, D., McDaniel, P.: Ensemble adversarial training: attacks and defenses. In: ICLR (2018)
6. Athalye, A., Carlini, N., Wagner D.: Obfuscated gradients give a false sense of security: circumventing defenses to adversarial examples. arXiv preprint arXiv:1802.00420. In: ICML (2018)
7. Engstrom, L., Ilyas, A., Santurkar, S., Tsipras, D., Tran, B., Madry, A.: Adversarial robustness as a prior for learned representations. arXiv preprint arXiv:1906.00945 (2019)
8. Miyato, T., Maeda, S.-I., Koyama, M., Nakae, K., Ishii, S.: Distributional smoothing with virtual adversarial training. arXiv preprint arXiv:1507.00677 (2015)
9. Guo, C., Rana, M., Cisse, M., van der Maaten, L.: Countering adversarial images using input transformations. arXiv preprint arXiv:1711.00117 (2017)
10. Xie, C., Wang, J., Zhang, Z., Ren, Z., Yuille, A.: Mitigating adversarial effects through randomization. In: International Conference on Learning Representations (2018)
11. Raghunathan, A., Steinhardt, J., Liang, P.: Certified defenses against adversarial examples. arXiv preprint arXiv:1801.09344 (2018)
12. Kolter, J.Z., Wong, E.: Provable defenses against adversarial examples via the convex outer adversarial polytope. arXiv preprint arXiv:1711.00851, $1(2)$, 3 (2017)
13. Hein, M. Andriushchenko, M.: Formal guarantees on the robustness of a classifier against adversarial manipulation. In: NeurIPS (2017)
14. Guo, C., Rana, M., Cisse, M., van der Maaten, L.: Countering adversarial images using input transformations. In: ICLR (2018)
15. Szegedy, C., et al.: Intriguing properties of neural networks. arXiv preprint arXiv:1312.6199 (2013)
16. Kurakin, A., Goodfellow, I., Bengio, S.: Adversarial examples in the physical world. arXiv preprint arXiv:1607.02533 (2016)
17. Moosavi-Dezfooli, S.-M., Fawzi, A., Frossard, P.: DeepFool: a simple and accurate method to fool deep neural networks. In: Proceedings of the IEEE Conference on Computer Vision and Pattern Recognition, pp. 2574–2582 (2016)
18. Carlini, N., Wagner, D.: Towards evaluating the robustness of neural networks. In: 2017 IEEE Symposium on Security and Privacy (SP), pp. 39–57. IEEE (2017)
19. Kurakin, A., Goodfellow, I., Bengio, S.: Adversarial machine learning at scale. arXiv preprint arXiv:1611.01236 (2016)
20. Pang, T., Xu, K., Du, C., Chen, N., Zhu, J.: Improving adversarial robustness via promoting ensemble diversity. arXiv preprint arXiv:1901.08846 (2019)
21. Ross, A.S., Doshi-Velez, F.: Improving the adversarial robustness and interpretability of deep neural networks by regularizing their input gradients. In: Thirty-Second AAAI Conference on Artificial Intelligence (2018)

22. Tsipras, D., Santurkar, S., Engstrom, L., Turner, A., Madry, A.: Robustness may be at odds with accuracy. In: ICLR 2019. OpenReview.net (2019)
23. Zhang, H., Yu, Y., Jiao, J., Xing, E.P., Ghaoui, L.E., Jordan, M.I.: Theoretically principled trade-off between robustness and accuracy. In: ICML 2019. PMLR (2019)
24. Zhang, J., et al.: Attacks which do not kill training make adversarial learning stronger. In: ICML 2020 (2020)
25. Xie, C., Wu, Y., van der Maaten, L., Yuille, A. L., He, K.: Feature denoising for improving adversarial robustness. In: CVPR 2019. Computer Vision Foundation/IEEE (2019)
26. Dhillon, G.S., et al.: Stochastic activation pruning for robust adversarial defense. arXiv preprint arXiv:1803.01442 (2018)
27. Papernot, N., McDaniel, P., Jha, S., Fredrikson, M., Celik, Z.B., Swami, A.: The limitations of deep learning in adversarial settings. In: 2016 IEEE European Symposium on Security and Privacy (EuroS&P), pp. 372–387. IEEE (2016)

Solving Diagrammatic Reasoning Problems Using Deep Learning

Himanshu Choudhary[1], Debi Prosad Dogra[1], and Arif Ahmed Sekh[2]([✉])

[1] Indian Institute of Technology, Bhubaneswar, India
{hc11,dpdogra}@iitbbs.ac.in
[2] XIM University, Bhubaneswar, India
skarifahmed@gmail.com

Abstract. Diagrammatic Reasoning (DR) questions are very common in competitive examinations. However, construction of interesting and fresh DR questions can be a tedious job even for the experts. We explore the possibility of using Artificial Intelligence (AI) and computer vision (CV) for construction and solving DR problems. In this paper, we have proposed a new deep learning-based framework that can be used to solve certain types of DR problems. The research also shows that a similar framework can be used to generate new DR problems of similar characteristics. We formulate the DR problem with an extension of conventional 4×1 Raven's Progressive Matrix (RPM) by keeping 4 outputs. Thus, each problem sample has eight images, where the first four images are part of the input in a sequence and the last four images are options for the correct output. The first four images create a valid sequence and the target is to choose the fifth image from the next four images. To find the correct option, we have proposed a deep learning framework that consists of an LSTM, an Encoder and a fully connected classifier unit. The framework has also been used to generate new DR problems. We have tested our framework on Rotational DR problems. A new DR dataset has been generated using automated scripts to train the framework. The framework performs better as compared to SOTA deep learning frameworks.

Keywords: Diagrammatic Reasoning · Raven's Progressive Matrix · LSTM · Encoder · Image Analysis

1 Introduction

Diagrammatic reasoning (DR) problems are well known. A DR problem consists of a sequence of images with some logical relation in between them. The goal is to choose the next image from a set of given options that fits correctly into the sequence. Thus, solving DR problems using AI and CV requires visual representations of the objects or diagrams. It involves understanding of the concepts and ideas from images with the patterns that are used in visual IQ tests.

D. Gupta et al. (Eds.): CVIP 2022, CCIS 1777, pp. 377–387, 2023.
https://doi.org/10.1007/978-3-031-31417-9_29

Solving diagrammatic reasoning problems using artificial intelligence can help to understand complex patterns of objects. It can also be used to generate new DR problems that can be used in tests. We have chosen to solve a class of diagrammatic reasoning problems that involve rotated objects. Such problems are referred to as rotational DR problems. In such DR problems, an object is rotated by certain angle to create a valid sequence. We are given with four options to choose the correct one in the sequence. The problems we chose contain a sequence of 4 images and we need to find out the 5th image from the given four options.

1.1 Related Work

Reasoning is the ability to make sense of things by verifying facts and applying logic. We refer to machine learning-based methods for reasoning as artificial reasoning (AR). AR uses knowledge completion, value approximation, and goal-oriented reasoning to solve different forms of reasoning [3]. Zhou et al. [4] have explored the use of knowledge graphs, that capture general or commonsense knowledge, to augment the information extracted from images by the state-of-the-art methods for image captioning. Value approximation is a method for extracting numeric facts. It is used in quantitative question answering from natural language texts and images [5]. Goal-oriented reasoning is a top-down approach that heuristically searches for a solution to achieve a goal. It is popular in robotics, intelligent agent, and case-based reasoning [6]. Data and knowledge-driven statistical methods [7], logic programming [8], and neural network-based approaches [9] are also popular for solving various reasoning problems.

Artificial reasoning methods are complex in nature and such methods require a logical representation of data, common sense, statistical information, and learning techniques. In the past few years, Deep learning has been widely used to learn and represent the features. However, majority of the existing representations rely on low-level features and they do not consider high-level representations such as logic or knowledge, etc. Recently, Serafini et al. [10] have proposed a logic tensor network (LTN) to learn the data-driven logic. LTN converts real logic formulas into TensorFlow computational graphs. Such formulas can express complex queries about the data. Kazemi et al. [11] have also proposed a deep neural network known as relational neural networks (RelNNs) to learn the reasoning directly from the FOL. Garcez et al. [12] have proposed a neural-symbolic computing approach to combine neural networks with symbolic representation and a reasoning-based learning approach. Mao et al. [13] have proposed a Neuro-Symbolic Concept Learner, a model that learns visual concepts, words, and semantic parsing of sentences without explicit supervision. This model learns by simply looking at images and reading paired questions and answers.

However, visual reasoning is not straightforward as compared to the other types of reasoning due to the difficulty in interpreting the objects and relations between them. Therefore, logical and statistical AI methods cannot directly be applied to solve visual reasoning problems. Two similar domains of reasoning that have received the attention of the CV research community are visual question answering and visual reasoning. Visual question answering consists of images and questions that can be answered from the images. To answer the questions, we may require prior knowledge about the objects, their color, position, etc. In addition to these features, visual reasoning may also require shape information, count, orientation, etc. Johnson et al. [5] have released a CLVR dataset that tests a range of visual reasoning abilities. It is used for reasoning color, shape, quantity, and size. Visual IQ questions that are based on RPM [2] vary in nature and are diverse in complexities. Answers to RPM-based reasoning require common sense, the idea about the shapes, and knowledge of mathematics. A recent work in this field by Arif et al. [1] introduces a new deep learning-based approach to solve DR problems. A knowledge acquisition module has been used that constructs a knowledge-base from the sequence of images given in the problem and answer options. The authors have used relation features such as rotation, counting, and scaling to prepare the knowledge-base. After this, the active features are chosen. Based on the active features, an LSTM network is used to find the correct option. For other types of DR problems, a ConvLSTM network has been used.

1.2 Contributions

The existing work discussed earlier have some limitations. For example, the work proposed in [1] cannot generate new sets of DR problems. Moreover, the architecture proposed cannot handle complex DR problems. Even for the rotation-related DR problems, the maximum accuracy has been reported to be around 76.2% using RF-LSTM framework. This can be further improved with encoder-decoder architecture. To mitigate some of the aforementioned problems, we have made the following technical contributions in this paper:

(a) We have proposed a new deep learning-based architecture that can solve rotational DR problems with better accuracy. The model predicts a score between [0, 1] for each options given. The correct option is the one that gets the highest score.

(b) We have created a new DR dataset using automated scripts. The dataset contains newly generated 1500 rotation DR problems. Each sample contains 8 images of size $(64 \times 64 \times 3)$. We have implemented and tested the model architecture and the new dataset. We have achieved better accuracy as compared to other known models suitable for solving rotational DR problems.

The rest of the paper is organized as follows. In Sect. 2, we present the proposed method. Section 3 summarizes the dataset and the experiment results. We conclude in Sect. 4.

2 Proposed Framework

We present the proposed architecture in this section. There are three main components in the architecture, namely a VGG16 feature extractor module, an LSTM module to encode the spation-temporal relation of the sequence of images, and a classifier. The first four images are given as inputs in the question sequence. The last image is one of the given options. The idea is to first extract the relation from this sequence of 5 images and then classify it into a valid or invalid relation.

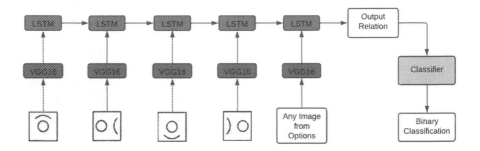

Fig. 1. The architecture of the proposed DR problem solving framework.

The VGG16 module has been used in the image encoder part. It takes a $64 \times 64 \times 3$ dimension image as input and produces a feature vector of size 2048. Once the encoder-decoder is trained, the decoder is discarded during the testing. The LSTM module takes the feature vector produced using the VGG16 as input and produces a relation vector of size 128. The last module (classifier) is a fully connected neural network. It takes a relation vector extracted by LSTM as input and performs a binary classification. It predicts a score in the range of [0,1]. The higher score an option gets, better the option. We then choose the option with the highest score as the correct option.

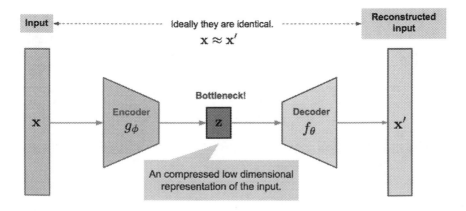

Fig. 2. The Encoder-Decoder training architecture.

2.1   Encoder-Decoder Training

We have trained the VGG16 encoder using a total of 12000 (1500×8) images. This has ensured that the module learns to encoder the shapes and arrangement of images. Figure 2 depicts the encoder-decoder architecture that has been used to train the encoder model from the scratch. A reconstruction loss as formulated using (1–6), has been used to regenerate the encoded images. Since this is an unsupervised step, we have trained the encoder on every image of the training set.

$$g_\psi : \text{Encoder (VGG16)} \tag{1}$$

$$f_\theta : \text{Decoder} \tag{2}$$

$$z = g_\psi(x) \tag{3}$$

$$x' = f_\theta(z) \tag{4}$$

$$\mathcal{L}(x, x') = ||x - x'||^2 \tag{5}$$

$$\mathcal{L}_{\text{total}} = \frac{1}{n} \sum_{\forall x \in \text{dataset}} \mathcal{L}(x, x') \tag{6}$$

2.2   LSTM Training

After training the VGG16-based encoder-decoder architecture, we have fixed the weights of VGG16 model. In the next step, we have trained the LSTM and the classifier parts of the model using the training set. Each sample in the dataset contains 8 images. Out of which, the first four are given as the input sequence and the other four are given as options from which the correct answer is selected. First, we encode a given sequence images using the VGG16-based encoder and the encoded features are given as input to the LSTM as shown in Figure 1. After this, we chose one of the options at a time and gave it's encoding as input to the LSTM. We take the output vectors of the LSTMs. These time-step outputs are used as inputs to the classifier. It performs as a binary classifier to check if the given sequence of 5 images is correct or not. The expected output of the classifier is 1 if the chosen option is correct, else 0. We have trained the classifier using binary cross-entropy loss. Since there is only 1 correct option and 3 incorrect options, we have multiplied the loss of the correct option by 3 to solve the class imbalance problem. The whole process is described in (7–13).

$$I_i : i^{th} \text{ image from the given question} \tag{7}$$

$$Op_i : i^{th} \text{ image from the given options} \tag{8}$$

$$[z_1^i, z_2^i, z_3^i, z_4^i] = [En(I_1^i), En(I_2^i), En(I_3^i), En(I_4^i)] \tag{9}$$

$$[\bar{z}_1^i, \bar{z}_2^i, \bar{z}_3^i, \bar{z}_4^i] = [En(Op_1^i), En(Op_2^i), En(Op_3^i), En(Op_4^i)] \tag{10}$$

$$R = LSTM(z_4^i, LSTM(z_3^i, LSTM(z_2^i, LSTM(z_1^i)))) \tag{11}$$

$$y_1^i = LSTM(\bar{z}_1^i, R), \quad y_2^i = LSTM(\bar{z}_2^i, R) \tag{12}$$

$$y_3^i = lstm(\bar{z}_3^i, R), \quad y_4^i = lstm(\bar{z}_4^i, R) \tag{13}$$

The loss is calculated using (14–15) when the first option is correct.

$$\mathcal{L'}_i = 3 * BCE(y_1^i, 1) + \sum_{j=2}^{4} BCE(y_j^i, 0) \tag{14}$$

$$\mathcal{L}_{total} = \frac{1}{n} \sum_{i=1}^{n} \mathcal{L'}_i \tag{15}$$

3   Experiments and Results

3.1   Dataset

Figure 3 is a sample from our created dataset. It contains 8 images. First four images are given as a question which create a sequence of rotating images. These images and an image from options (one at a time) will be given as input to LSTM after encoding to encode the relation used to created this sequence. Our goal is to find the correct option from given options which fits correctly as 5th image in the sequence. So the option for which our model will predict the most score will be chosen as correct option.

Our dataset contains total 1500 samples, each of which has 8 images. We have used 1050 (70%) samples for training and rest 450 (30%) were used for testing the model.

3.2   Accuracy

We have achieved an accuracy of 94.66% on train set and 85.55% on test set. Table 1 contains the our model accuracy and size of train and test dataset.

3.3   Model Predictions

Below are some predictions from our model. We have included few of correctly and incorrectly predicted examples from our test set. Figures 4 and 5 are correctly predicted by our model a high score for the correct option. Figures 7 and 6 are negative samples in which wrong option is getting more score than correct option. Also in Fig. 7, we can see that option 1 and option 4 are very similar and option 4 is getting a slightly better score than option 1.

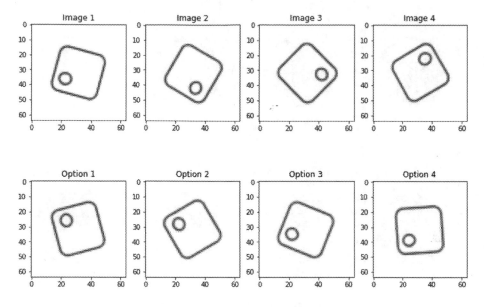

Fig. 3. Dataset Example

Table 1. Train and Test Set Description

	Train Set	Test Set
Accuracy	94.66 %	85.55 %
Size	1050	450

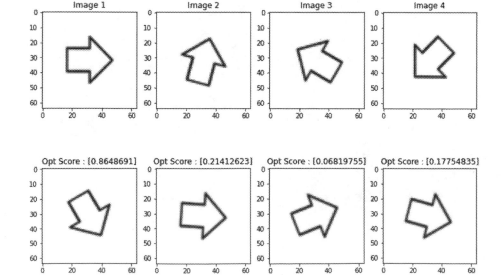

Fig. 4. Correctly Predicted Example

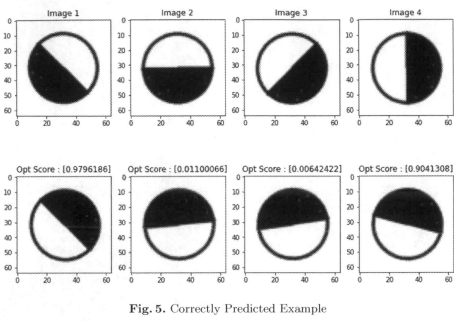

Fig. 5. Correctly Predicted Example

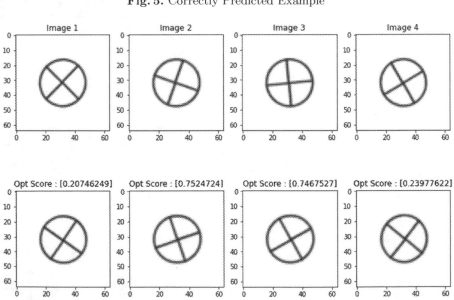

Fig. 6. Incorrectly Predicted Example

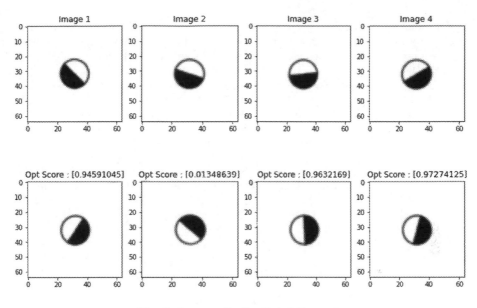

Fig. 7. Incorrectly Predicted Example

4   Conclusion

This article contributes towards the challenges and the possibilities of cognitive learning. We considered Raven's Progressive Matrix for experiment. The article proposed a solution towards imitating the visual cognitive reasoning of a person. We solve a simple visual reasoning problem using AI. There are many questions and possibilities, we hope the research will attract more CV researchers in this domain.

References

1. Dogra, D.P., Sekh, A.A., Kar, S., Roy, P.P., Prasad, D.K.: Can we automate diagrammatic reasoning, October (2020)
2. Burke, H.R.: Raven's progressive matrices: a review and critical evaluation. J. Genet. Psychol. **93**(2), 199–228 (1958)
3. Diamantini, C., Freddi, A., Longhi, S., Potena, D., Storti, E.: A goal-oriented, ontology-based methodology to support the design of AAL environments. Expert Syst. Appl. **64**, 117–131 (2016)
4. Zhou, Y., Sun, Y., Honavar, V.: Improving image captioning by leveraging knowledge graphs. In: IEEE Winter Conference on Applications of Computer Vision, pp. 283–293 (2019)

5. Johnson, J., Hariharan, B., van der Maaten, L., Fei-Fei, L., Zitnick, C.L., Girshick, R.: CLEVR: a diagnostic dataset for compositional language and elementary visual reasoning. In: IEEE Conference on Computer Vision and Pattern Recognition, pp. 1988–1997 (2017)
6. Giorgini, P., Mylopoulos, J., Nicchiarelli, E., Sebastiani, R.: Reasoning with goal models. In: Spaccapietra, S., March, S.T., Kambayashi, Y. (eds.) ER 2002. LNCS, vol. 2503, pp. 167–181. Springer, Heidelberg (2002). https://doi.org/10.1007/3-540-45816-6_22
7. Mineau, G.W., Godin, R.: Automatic structuring of knowledge bases by conceptual clustering. IEEE Trans. Knowl. Data Eng. **7**(5), 824–829 (1995)
8. Raedt, L.D., Kersting, K., Natarajan, S., Poole, D.: Statistical relational artificial intelligence: logic, probability, and computation. Synth. Lect. Artif. Intell. Mach. Learn. **10**(2), 1–189 (2016)
9. Shin, C.-U., Cha, J.-W.: End-to-end task dependent recurrent entity network for goal-oriented dialog learning. Comput. Speech Lang. **53**, 12–24 (2019)
10. Serafini, L., d'Avila Garcez, A.S.: Learning and reasoning with logic tensor networks. In: Adorni, G., Cagnoni, S., Gori, M., Maratea, M. (eds.) AI*IA 2016. LNCS (LNAI), vol. 10037, pp. 334–348. Springer, Cham (2016). https://doi.org/10.1007/978-3-319-49130-1_25
11. Kazemi, S.M., Poole, D.: ReINN: a deep neural model for relational learning. In: 32nd AAAI Conference on Artificial Intelligence, pp. 6367–6375 (2018)
12. Garcez, A., Gori, M., Lamb, L., Serafini, L., Spranger, M., Tran, S.: Neural-symbolic computing: an effective methodology for principled integration of machine learning and reasoning. J. Appl. Logics **6**(4), 611–632 (2019)
13. Mao, J., Gan, C., Kohli, P., Tenenbaum, J.B., Wu, J.: The neuro-symbolic concept learner: interpreting scenes, words, and sentences from natural supervision. In: International Conference on Learning Representations, pp. 1–28 (2019)
14. Wang, J., Wang, W., Wang, L., Wang, Z., Feng, D.D., Tan, T.: Learning visual relationship and context-aware attention for image captioning. Pattern Recogn. **98**, 107075–107086 (2020)
15. Wang, W., Huang, Y., Wang, L.: Long video question answering: a matching-guided attention model. Pattern Recogn. **102**, 107–248 (2020)
16. Santoro, A., Hill, F., Barrett, D., Morcos, A., Lillicrap, T.: Measuring abstract reasoning in neural networks. In: International Conference on Machine Learning, pp. 4477–4486 (2018)
17. Hill, F., Santoro, A., Barrett, D., Morcos, A., Lillicrap, T.: Learning to make analogies by contrasting abstract relational structure. In: International Conference on Learning Representations, pp. 1–14 (2019)
18. Kunda, M., McGreggor, K., Goel, A.: Addressing the ravens progressive matrices test of general intelligence. In: AAAI Fall Symposium Series, pp. 22–27 (2009)
19. Lovett, A., Forbus, K., Usher, J.: A structure-mapping model of raven's progressive matrices. In: Proceedings of the Annual Meeting of the Cognitive Science Society, vol. 32, pp. 2761–2766 (2010)
20. Ragni, M., Neubert, S.: Solving Raven's IQ-tests: an AI and cognitive modeling approach. In: Proceedings of the 20th European Conference on Artificial Intelligence, pp. 666–671. IOS Press (2012)
21. Lovett, A., Forbus, K.: Modeling visual problem solving as analogical reasoning., Psychol Rev. **124**(1), 60 (2017)
22. Zhang, C., Gao, F., Jia, B., Zhu, Y., Zhu, S.-C.: Raven: a dataset for relational and analogical visual reasoning. In: Proceedings of the IEEE Conference on Computer Vision and Pattern Recognition, pp. 5317–5327 (2019)

23. Sutskever, I., Vinyals, O., Le, Q.V.: Raven, sequence to sequence learning with neural networks. Accessed 10 Sep 2014
24. Bank, D., Koenigstein, N., Giryes, R.: Autoencoders, v1. Accessed 12 Mar 2020
25. Ronneberger, O., Fischer, P., Brox, T.: U-Net: convolutional networks for biomedical image segmentation (2021)

Bird Species Classification from Images Using Deep Learning

Manoj Kumar, Arun Kumar Yadav, Mohit Kumar$^{(\boxtimes)}$ ⓘ, and Divakar Yadav

National Institute of Technology Hamirpur, Hamirpur 177005, H.P, India
{ayadav,mohit}@nith.ac.in, dsy99@rediffmail.com

Abstract. Learning about the birds improve the understanding of the world, and provides valuable information about the natural world. To assess the quality of the living environment, accurate data on the species of birds is important. Birds species classification and identification is a difficult task, even for expert biologists and ornithologists. The unavailability of experts, along with human limitations, further pose an upper limit on manual identification of birds and their species. Using an automated approach to identify birds and their species could be a significantly important idea in this scenario. In this paper, we evaluate several deep learning based models including SSD, YOLOv4 and YOLOv5 for birds species classification and identification. All the models are evaluated on publicly available CUB-200-2011 dataset. The YOLOv4 model outperforms the recent state-of-art methods with 95.43% accuracy, 93.94% precision, 94.34% recall and 94.27% F-1 score for 20 classes, along with 96.99% mAP score.

Keywords: Bird Species · Species classification · Classification · Deep Learning · YOLO · SSD

1 Introduction

Birds play a vital role in environmental balance and serve as an excellent indicator of biodiversity [6]. To assess the quality of the living environment, accurate data on the species of birds and animals is important. In ecological study, monitoring animal populations is crucial, especially in light of the ongoing danger of climate change [24]. Birds are abundant and sensitive to environmental changes. The study of birds can help us comprehend the world around us and nature, but the identification of birds manually is a tedious and time consuming process. The unavailability of experts along with human limitations pose an upper limit on manual identification of birds and their species. In the past, many efforts have been carried out for environmental conservation and the rescue of endangered animals. Using an automated approach to identify bird species is a smart idea in this scenario. Analyzing the diversity and abundance of birds can be simplified with the help of an automated bird identification system. Using the technique, researchers no longer need to study through thick textbooks to organize and categorize their photographic images. A combination of the bird species detector with other forms of cultural knowledge, such as poetry and mythology, may be a lot of fun in a community. Public interest in birds may be sparked, that might have a positive effect on conservation programs.

Image categorization is one of the most important area of research in machine learning and deep learning. The categorization of the many species of birds presents a hard challenge for both human beings and computer programs. Birds of varying shapes and sizes, surroundings, lighting situations, and extreme postures all provide obstacles for object detection algorithms during attempt to accomplish this work automatically.

In the past, various bird species classification methods have been proposed. In literature, it was found that majority of the work done on bird species categorization relies on one of two inputs modalities — image or sound-based. In recent years, most of appearance-based research identifies species from a single image using the properties of birds In broad areas, there are two types of image-based classification methods: one employs the entire picture for feature extraction, called as "non part-based" while the other uses the structural properties of each bird called as "part-based" [24]. To execute specific operations, such as categorization and species identification, non-part-based approaches employed the colour and shape attributes of the complete bird [14]. A research was conducted in the paper [9] to detect and categorize bird species of Bangladesh. They used VGG-16 model to identify the categories of bird species.

The main concentration of this work is to classify and identify birds using deep learning models. To evaluate the various models, this study uses publicly available dataset *CUB-200-2011* and their results are compared on standard evaluation metrics. The contributions of the paper may be summarized as follows:

- In the previous paragraphs, we have discussed about the lack of significant amount of work specifically with birds species classification. This study uses the CUB-200-2011 dataset [27] for evaluation the proposed model.
- We have considered 4 different deep learning models with CSPDarknet53 as feature extractor. The YOLOv4 model achieves an accuracy of 95.43% on the provided test dataset for 20 classes of birds on above mentioned, publicly available dataset.
- Due to the comprehensive set of methods used in experiments, the authors report the best performance that outperforms the recent state-of-art methods for bird species classification.

The rest of the paper is organized into the following sections. Section 2 discusses the recent contributions on bird species classification and identification in the literature, especially using machine learning and deep learning methods. Section 3 describes the methodology used in the experiments. Section 4 reports and discusses the results obtained, and shows comparison of the results obtained in the study with recent state-of-art approaches. Section 5 concludes the paper with final thoughts and future directions.

2   Literature Survey

This section describes the work done on bird species classification and identification in the past. In the past, mainly birds are classified in on the basis of sound and image features. Automated identification of birds based on aural rather than visual signals has been used in a number of previous studies [10,17,29]. In the paper [17], the authors used convolutional neural networks to recognize bird species from audio. In this paper, the authors used three CNN-based network structures and a basic ensemble model with a mean average accuracy of 41.2%. Again, in the paper [10], the authors use ResNet and Inception networks on Bird-CLEF2019 dataset for classification and achieve a mAP of 0.23% for Inception model. In the paper [29], the authors discuss the comparative analysis of bird classification experiments. They concluded that experiments on a total of 43 bird species yielded an overall accuracy of 86.31%. Audio signals, however, are only relevant for species with unique calls and no line of sight. If the audio stream has noise, it will be harder to recognize and categorize. Furthermore, auditory signals have some restrictions, making it difficult to differentiate species.

Due to limitations for classification in audio signals, the authors of the paper [15] implemented classification by combining appearance features on caltech-ucsd birds-200-2011 dataset [27] with acoustic signal taken from Xeno-Canto dataset. In the paper [14], the authors compared the appearance features and achieved a higher classification rate, with improvements between 1.2% and 15.7% on machine learning models.

In order to classify birds based on their appearance, several studies have been carried out based on other approaches. In the paper [4], the authors propose appearance features and follow the two-step prediction methods to estimate the object. In this paper, the authors uses the object properties for classification by using the cluster-based method with 84.5% accuracy. In the paper [11], the authors used RNN model with Inception Net, train it on CVIP dataset and achieve F-1 score of 55.67%. The authors of the paper [16] worked on part-based categorization and created a framework using discriminative features. They experimented on the CUB-200-2011 dataset and attained an accuracy of 64.6% mAP.

The authors of the paper [5] used deep learning algorithms to solve the problem of identifying and classify bird species on caltech-ucsd birds-200-2011 dataset. They used a DCNN-like layered structure to extract features from the input images. To maximize classification accuracy, various alignments or features such as head, color, body, form, beak, and whole bird image was extracted using a deep network that achieves 90.93% classification accuracy. Another deep learning-based model was used in the paper [9] to identify Bangladeshi bird species. For bird species classification, they have employed Random Forest, kNN, and SVM with VGG-16. They utilized a data collection that have images of 27 species and 1600 images of Bangladesh without any annotations. SVM was the most accurate of the algorithms tested in this study, with an accuracy of 89%. In the paper [30], the authors worked on a manually constructed dataset of 32,442 images taken by a camera. They employ Haar-like image features, HOG, AdaBoost, and CNN algorithms to categorize bird species surrounding a wind farm. They used thee types of recognition tasks — bird detection, species filtering, and bird species classification — and tested using images collected at the wind farm. This study concluded that LeNet correctly identified 83% of the hawks with an FPR of 0.1. In another paper [2], the authors used a video dataset of 13 bird species. They used classification using Random Forests with 90% accuracy. In the paper [12], the authors compare different SVM, K-Means Clustering, deep learning algorithms and commented that deep learning methods outperform as compare to machine learning methods in general. In the paper [18], the authors discuss classification on 12 bird species using machine learning techniques and obtain 96% accuracy subsequently. In the research [1], the researchers employed regularized softmax with broad classes and achieved 70% accuracy using the regularized softmax, SVM, and transfer learning algorithms for classifying bird species.

In the literature review, it was observed that there are considerable scope of improvement in research on bird species classification and identification. Three major issues were identified and addressed as described here. First, most of the research have done experiments on different datasets with limited data. Second, the researchers used limited classes to classify the identify the bird species. Finally, we evaluate the methods comprehensively using all available performance metrics and compare with recent state-of-art methods for 20 classes.

3   Methodology

This section describes the methodology used for bird species classification and identification while addressing the issues identified in the literature. It includes discussion on the dataset, proposed methodology and the overall layout for bird species identification.

3.1   Dataset Description

This study uses the one of most popular and publicly available image datasets, CUB-200-2011 [27]. This dataset contains 200 categories of birds, each with 40 to 60 images, and total 11,788 images of North American bird species. In the analysis of dataset, it was found that the image collection has not been cleaned or filtered in any way, and the images were shot in the actual surroundings. In the background, there are leaves and branches, adding to the natural feel of the image along with complexity in identification. Figure 1 depicts a few sample images from the dataset.   The dataset is labeled manually using LabelImg annotation tool [26]. Figure 2 demonstrates an example bounding box labelling along with choosing the corresponding class. After labelling, it produces an XML/TXT annotation file with object description.

Fig. 1. Images of Dataset [27]

Fig. 2. Labelling of image

3.2 Model Architecture

This subsection describes the architecture of the proposed model, used for bird species identification and classification. This study uses YOLOv4 [3] object detection model, a real-time CNN-based system. In a single stage, the YOLOv4 network can predict the object's bounding boxes and class. Objects are directly detected by applying model to image [3, 19–21]. YOLOv4 comprises of backbone, neck, and head. Backbone extracts features, neck gathers feature maps from network stages, and head makes the predictions. Figure 3 illustrates YOLOv4 architecture.

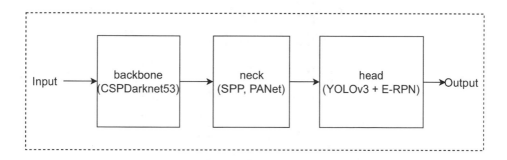

Fig. 3. Basic Architecture of YOLOv4 [3]

In the backbone, the network first extracts image features by utilizing CSP-Darknet53. CSPDarknet53 is an upgraded version of YOLOv3's darknet53. It used skip connections in the Darknet53 network's consecutive 3×3 and 1×1 convolutional layers [8]. YOLOv4 modified Darknet53 with Cross Stage Partial (CSP) networks, renaming it CSPDarknet53. CSP improves gradient combination to minimize model calculation cost. It distributes computational tasks to each CNN layer to improve model computation and decrease memory cost. Neck contains the additional features of YOLOv4. It is mainly used to gather feature map from different stage of backbone. PaNet [13] has developed an architecture that allows for improved propagation of layer data.

CNN generally requires scaling of all images of dataset to make them fixed size. During the scaling, the required region may be distorted or cropped away. To overcome such types of issues, the YOLOv4 uses the SPP [7]. It doesn't matter how big or small a picture is, SPP produces a fixed-length representation. Also, it uses Max pooling to generate a feature map with a fixed size and a variety of representations. A Spatial Attention Module (SAM) block [28] is used in this model to enhance the representation of an interested region by considering only relevant features. In Yolov4, head acts as object detector.

Bounding Box Prediction: The original YOLO has four parameters for each bounding box: x, y, w, and h, where (x,y) coordinates denote the box centre. The width and height are determined in relation to the total picture size. The second version of YOLO uses anchors and projected offsets. Predicting offsets instead of coordinates simplifies the model and facilitates the network's learning process. Predicted objects' tx,ty coordinates are calculated by the network using two anchor dimensions: height and width. Figure 4 represent the anchor box.

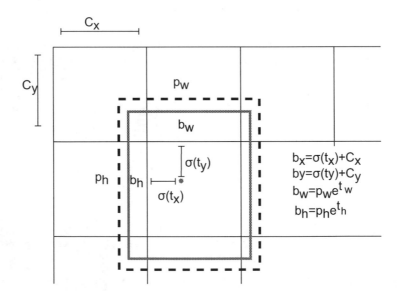

Fig. 4. Anchor Box [20]

3.3   Other Models Used

Even though the YOLOv4 model performed the best among all, the following other models were also used during the study and are described briefly.

ResNet [8] contains the residual block to avoid the problem of vanishing gradient in CNN based model having large number of CNN layers. It helps to build a very deep CNN based model without compromising with gradient. Residual blocks have some CNN layer connected in a series and have a skip connection.

MobileNetV2 [23] is a deep learning model that uses the depth-wise separable convolution and the residual connections. Through the integrating residual connections and the utilization of depth-wise Separable Convolution, MobileNetV2 enhances operating speed over MobileNetV1.

Faster R-CNN [22] contains 2 main components. **Region Proposal Network (RPN)** – Convolution feature map generated by the backbone layer is the input for region proposal network and this RPN outputs the coordinates of interested objects that are produced by the convolutional operation on entire input feature map. **Object Detection** – Faster R-CNN uses an object detection network that uses the RoI pooling layer for making fixed-size region proposals, and a dual layer of softmax classifier with the bounding box regressor to predict the objects and object's coordinates.

Inception model [25] uses 1×1 convolutional layer to reduce the computation cost. Deep Convolutional Networks require high computation, but 1×1 convolution reduces computation effectively. Inserting a 1×1 convolution between the 3×3 and 5×5 convolutions limits the input channels. Inception Net delivers high accuracy with less processing than earlier CNN models.

Single Shot Multibox Detector (SSD) classifies and localizes objects using feature maps from the feature extraction network using feed-forward neural networks. SSD utilizes VGG-16 with 6 additional layers to lower the feature map size to distinguish large and tiny items. Merging these layers' feature maps provides the required detection.

4   Results and Analysis

This section elaborates the experimental results and discussion on the results, along with various experimental decisions considered during the study.

4.1   Training

The default configuration file for yolov4 has undergone several modifications, including the dataset, number of classes, label map, max epochs, step size, and batch size. Training and testing sets of data are created from the entire dataset. Training and testing datasets comprise 80% and 20% original images. This is the strategy most researchers use to separate the dataset into two part. Experiments are conducted for the 20 class dataset. The values of various hyper parameters

used in experiments include 0.001 learning rate, 0.0005 decay, and 0.95 momentum. Three activation types are used – most levels employ mish activation to
transport signal back and forth, linear activation for skip connections, and leaky
activation at deep layers.

4.2   Model Loss Trend

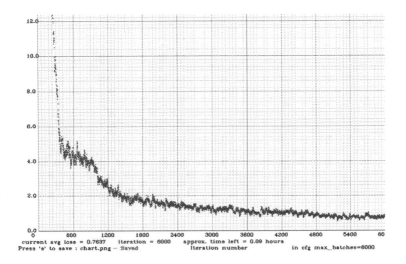

Fig. 5. Yolov4 loss graph for 20 classes

Figure 5 shows the total loss graph of model. Google Colab Pro was used to
train the model for around 10 h and 6000 iterations. The loss graph showed a
significant drop after the 400th iteration. Further iterations show a linear decline
in the loss graph. Loss curve changes become negligible after step 4800 that
indicate the completion of training.

4.3   Result

The results obtained using various models are shown in Table 1. The graphical
comparison of accuracy is depicted in Fig. 6. As can be seen, the YOLOv4 model
is the best performing among all the models used in the work with 95.43%
accuracy and 94.27% F-1 score in bird species identification. Furthermore, SSD
turned out to be the worst performing model for the current task of bird species
classification.

Evaluation of object detection models is generally also done by using mean
average precision (mAP) based metrics. **Average Precision (AP)** is calculated
by area under the precision recall (r) curve for recall value of 0 to 1.

$$AP = \int_0^1 p(r)dx \tag{1}$$

Mean Average Precision (mAP) is achieved by average of Average Precision of M classes. Mathematically mAP is defined as:

$$mAP = \frac{1}{M} \sum_{j=1}^{j=M} APj \qquad (2)$$

By comparing the ground-truth bounding box to the detected box, the mAP score is calculated. The greater the score, the better the model will be able to identify the objects. Table 1 also depicts the mAP comparison of the various models. Finally, a few sample outputs for classification and detection by YOLOv4 and YOLOv5 models are also shown in Fig. 7.

Table 1. Results obtained using various deep learning methods utilized in this work

Model	Accuracy	Precision	Recall	F-1 Score	mAP
YOLOv4	95.43	93.94	94.34	94.27	96.99
YOLOv5	86.45	85.54	84.96	85.25	87.65
SSD ResNet101v1	82.74	81.22	81.86	81.63	84.42
Faster R-CNNv2	88.16	87.98	87.74	87.86	90.11
SSD MobileNetv2	35.64	35.26	35.54	35.40	36.08

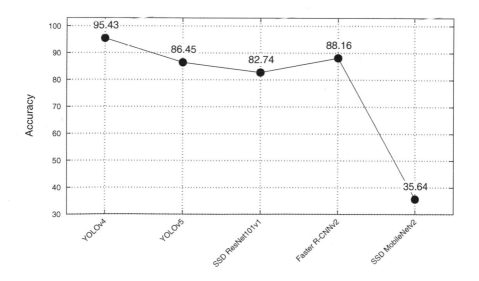

Fig. 6. Graph showing results of various methods used in this work

(a) YOLOv4 result   (b) YOLOv5 result

Fig. 7. Sample outputs of YOLOv4 and YOLOv5

4.4 Comparison with State-of-Art

The proposed methodology outperforms other recent research works for 20 class automatic bird species classification, on similar datasets. There is one research [18] that has a slightly better accuracy but it considers only 12 classes and on a different dataset. So this difference is an outcome of less number of classes. With each additional class, the accuracy of models begins to decline and this model may not scale well when the number of classes are increased to 20 or more. The comparison of the proposed work with recent state-of-art is shown in Table 2 and Fig. 8.

Table 2. Comparison of the proposed methodology with recent state-of-art

Paper	Dataset	Classes	Accuracy	Method
[18]	The Caltech-UCSD birds 200-2011 & CIFAR-10	12	96.00	Softmax Classifier with CNN
[11]	CVIP 2018, 150 images	16	92.29	Inceptionv3, Inception ResNetv2, Mask R-CNN
[5]	CUB-200-2011	7	92.90	GoogLenet
[9]	Self made, 1600 images	27	89.00	VGG-16 with KNN, SVM, Random Forest
[2]	Self made video dataset	12	90.00	Random Forest, VGG-19, MobileNet
[12]	CUB-200-2011	20	86.50	CNN, RNN, InceptionV3
This study	CUB-200-2011	20	95.43	YOLOv4 with CSPDarknet53 backbone

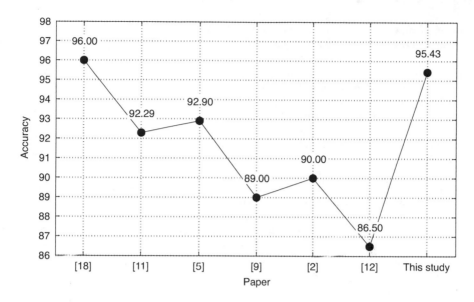

Fig. 8. Comparison of the proposed methodology with recent state-of-art

5   Conclusion and Future Work

In this paper, the authors have investigated the task of bird species classification and detection. The dataset used in this work [27] contains 20 bird species
for classification purposes. Several deep learning models including YOLOv4,
ResNet101, YOLOv5 and SSD are evaluated to classify bird species from images.
The YOLOv4 model achieves better performance than other utilized models and
outperforms recent state-of-the-art models for 20 classes bird species classification. There are opportunities in several directions to enhance the effectiveness
of the proposed methodology. Firstly, data augmentation methods can add more
images per class to a dataset. This contributes to the enhancement of training
robustness and influences the model's overall performance in a positive way. Secondly, other recent transformers-based model may be investigated in future to
further improve performance. Finally, the developed models may be converted
into a smartphone app that the public can use to identify birds in real time.

References

1. Alter, A.L., Wang, K.M.: An exploration of computer vision techniques for bird
   species classification (2017)
2. Atanbori, J., Duan, W., Shaw, E., Appiah, K., Dickinson, P.: Classification of bird
   species from video using appearance and motion features. Ecol. Inform. **48**, 12–23
   (2018)
3. Bochkovskiy, A., Wang, C.-Y., Mark Liao, H.-Y.: YOLOV4: optimal speed and
   accuracy of object detection. arXiv preprint arXiv:2004.10934 (2020)

4. Branson, S., Van Horn, G., Belongie, S., Perona, P.: Bird species categorization using pose normalized deep convolutional nets. arXiv preprint arXiv:1406.2952 (2014)
5. Gavali, P., Saira Banu, J.: Bird species identification using deep learning on GPU platform. In: 2020 International Conference on Emerging Trends in Information Technology and Engineering (ic-ETITE), pp. 1–6. IEEE (2020)
6. Gregory, R.: Birds as biodiversity indicators for Europe. Significance **3**(3), 106–110 (2006)
7. He, K., Zhang, X., Ren, S., Sun, J.: Spatial pyramid pooling in deep convolutional networks for visual recognition. IEEE Trans. Pattern Anal. Mach. Intell. **37**(9), 1904–1916 (2015)
8. He, K., Zhang, X., Ren, S., Sun, J.: Deep residual learning for image recognition. In: Proceedings of the IEEE Conference on Computer Vision and Pattern Recognition, pp. 770–778 (2016)
9. Islam, S., Khan, S.I.A., Abedin, M.M., Habibullah, K.M., Das, A.K.: Bird species classification from an image using VGG-16 network. In: Proceedings of the 2019 7th International Conference on Computer and Communications Management, pp. 38–42 (2019)
10. Koh, C.-Y., Chang, J.-Y., Tai, C.-L., Huang, D.-Y., Hsieh, H.-H., Liu, Y.-W.: Bird sound classification using convolutional neural networks. In: CLEF (Working Notes) (2019)
11. Kumar, A., Das, S.D.: Bird species classification using transfer learning with multistage training. In: Arora, C., Mitra, K. (eds.) WCVA 2018. CCIS, vol. 1019, pp. 28–38. Springer, Singapore (2019). https://doi.org/10.1007/978-981-15-1387-9_3
12. Kumar, S., Dhoundiyal, V., Raj, N., Sharma, N.: A comparison of different techniques used for classification of bird species from images. Smart Sustain. Intel. Syst., 41–50 (2021)
13. Liu, S., Qi, L., Qin, H., Shi, J., Jia, J.: Path aggregation network for instance segmentation. In: Proceedings of the IEEE Conference on Computer Vision and Pattern Recognition, pp. 8759–8768 (2018)
14. Marini, A., Facon, J., Koerich, A.L.: Bird species classification based on color features. In: 2013 IEEE International Conference on Systems, Man, and Cybernetics, pp. 4336–4341. IEEE (2013)
15. Marini, A., Turatti, A.J., Britto, A.S., Koerich., A.L.: Visual and acoustic identification of bird species. In: 2015 IEEE International Conference on Acoustics, Speech and Signal Processing (ICASSP), pp. 2309–2313. IEEE (2015)
16. Pang, C., Yao, H., Sun, X.: Discriminative features for bird species classification. In: Proceedings of International Conference on Internet Multimedia Computing and Service, pp. 256–260 (2014)
17. Piczak, K.J.: Recognizing bird species in audio recordings using deep convolutional neural networks. In: CLEF (working notes), pp. 534–543 (2016)
18. Pillai, S.K., Raghuwanshi, M.M., Shrawankar, U.: Deep learning neural network for identification of bird species. In: Peng, S.-L., Dey, N., Bundele, M. (eds.) Computing and Network Sustainability. LNNS, vol. 75, pp. 291–298. Springer, Singapore (2019). https://doi.org/10.1007/978-981-13-7150-9_31
19. Redmon, J., Divvala, S., Girshick, R., Farhadi, A.: You only look once: unified, real-time object detection. In: Proceedings of the IEEE Conference on Computer Vision and Pattern Recognition, pp. 779–788 (2016)
20. Redmon, J., Farhadi, A.: YOLO9000: better, faster, stronger. In: Proceedings of the IEEE Conference on Computer Vision and Pattern Recognition, pp. 7263–7271 (2017)

21. Redmon, J., Farhadi, A.: YOLOv3: an incremental improvement. arXiv preprint arXiv:1804.02767 (2018)
22. Ren, S., He, K., Girshick, R., Sun, J.: Faster R-CNN: towards real-time object detection with region proposal networks. In: Advances in Neural Information Processing Systems, vol. 28 (2015)
23. Sandler, M., Howard, A., Zhu, M., Zhmoginov, A., Chen, L.-C.: MobileNetv2: inverted residuals and linear bottlenecks. In: Proceedings of the IEEE Conference on Computer Vision and Pattern Recognition, pp. 4510–4520 (2018)
24. Şekercioğlu, Ç.H., Primack, R.B., Wormworth, J.: The effects of climate change on tropical birds. Biol. Conserv. **148**(1), 1–18 (2012)
25. Szegedy, C., Vanhoucke, V., Ioffe, S., Shlens, J., Wojna, Z.: Rethinking the inception architecture for computer vision. In: Proceedings of the IEEE Conference on Computer Vision and Pattern Recognition, pp. 2818–2826 (2016)
26. Tzutalin, D.: tzutalin/labelimg (2015)
27. Wah, C., Branson, S., Welinder, P., Perona, P., Belongie, S.: The caltech-ucsd birds-200-2011 dataset (2011)
28. Woo, S., Park, J., Lee, J.-Y., Kweon, I.S.: CBAM: convolutional block attention module. In: Proceedings of the European Conference on Computer Vision (ECCV), pp. 3–19 (2018)
29. Xie, J., Kai, H., Zhu, M., Jinghu, Yu., Zhu, Q.: Investigation of different CNN-based models for improved bird sound classification. IEEE Access **7**, 175353–175361 (2019)
30. Yoshihashi, R., Kawakami, R., Iida, M., Naemura, T.: Bird detection and species classification with time-lapse images around a wind farm: dataset construction and evaluation. Wind Energy **20**(12), 1983–1995 (2017)

Statistical Analysis of Hair Detection and Removal Techniques Using Dermoscopic Images

Apurva Shinde[iD] and Sangita Chaudhari[(✉)][iD]

Ramrao Adik Institute of Technology, D.Y. Patil Deemed to be University, Nerul,
Navi Mumbai, India
{apurva.karkhanis,sangita.chaudhari}@rait.ac.in

Abstract. Deaths due to various types of cancers have increased to a greater extent in decades. Computer-aided diagnosis is the fast and efficient way used in the medical field all around the globe for early diagnosis and treatment of cancer. The design of such automated systems is a major challenge in the medical field due to various aspects and the availability of data for testing these systems. Skin cancer is one such type of cancer that if treated at an early stage helps to reduce the mortality rate. Many technological solutions have been provided by researchers in the last decade for the early detection and classification of skin cancer. Hair detection and removal is one of the primary pre-processing step in the skin cancer detection process. Dull Razor, Adaptive Principal Curvature, E-shaver, etc. are common techniques used for hair detection and removal. These methods aim to remove the hairs from the lesion image, but some artifacts and background abnormalities are left behind in the resultant images. In this paper, slight functional modification using different color spaces and hybridization of various existing techniques for hair detection and removal has been proposed. The proposed techniques are evaluated on standard dermoscopic datasets using different standard performance metrics like Accuracy, Sensitivity, Specificity, False Positive Rate, Peak Signal to Noise Ratio, and Structural Similarity Index Measure. The proposed pre-processing methods are tested for classification accuracy using VGG-16 model. The evaluation results indicate that Modified E-shaver and Modified Dull Razor methods perform better than existing systems.

Keywords: Skin Cancer · Dull Razor · E-shaver · Principal Curvature

1 Introduction

The medical field is continuously striving for developing computer-aided techniques for the detection of different types of cancers in their early stages. One such type of cancer that needs attention is skin cancer. In skin cancer, the cell grows in an abnormal manner leading to serious cancerous tissues in the body. These cells spread from the primary location to different parts of the body and affect those parts leading to cancer. More than 90% of skin cancer cases around the globe are the result of harmful UV radiation exposure. One of the major types of skin cancer due to radiation exposure is melanoma skin cancer which is witnessed prominent evidence in white skinned population across the globe [7,13]. Early detection of this cancer helps in reducing the mortality rate. Preventive solutions include the design of a non-invasive computer-aided system to analyze dermoscopic images of skin lesions [2] for early detection. These dermoscopic images contain artifacts such as hairs and unwanted spots that need to be removed before the classification process. Asymmetry, Border, Color, and Diameter (ABCD) features are widely used for skin cancer detection. Many existing methods are based on the detection of lesion boundaries using segmentation, but these lesions are hindered due to the hairs present in the images. If the color of hair is similar to the lesion, they are considered a lesion else considered a split in the lesion. Several techniques have been developed for addressing this kind of issue, One of the common techniques is an application of a low pass filter to remove hairs as they detect low-intensity pixels i.e. thin and light hairs. However, it does not remove thick hair. Similarly, averaging filter results in smoothing which leads to the loss of necessary information from the image [6].Deep learning models have been used widely for detection of skin lesion and disease. VGG-16 pretrained model is used for skin cancer detection and compared with RESNET-50 by the authors [10] This paper presents enhanced methods for the detection and removal of hairs from dermoscopic images and a comparative analysis of those methods with existing hair removal approaches. The paper is organized as follows: Sect. 2 presents an overview of existing approaches, the Proposed system is presented in Sect. 3, results are illustrated in Sect. 4, and conclusions are drawn in Sect. 5.

2   Related Work

Hair detection and removal is a primary and important stage in skin cancer detection, if not handled properly, greatly affects the classification accuracy leading to a wrong diagnosis. Therefore, there is a need to design an automated technique for the same while preserving lesion features. Some of the well-known approaches used in literature are Dull Razor (DR) [8], Adaptive Principal Curvature (APC) [18] and E- shaver [6], etc. Related work introduces the basic and most widely used hair detection and removal approaches stated above. The Dull Razor algorithm involves steps such as bottom hat filtering, thresholding, and inpainting. Commonly extracted features include ABCD features, Gray-Level Co-occurrence Matrix (GLCM) texture features, Deep features, etc. from the Dull Razor applied images. Multi-class classification is performed to classify cancer into various categories [4,5,11,17] after extraction of texture and statistical features. Dull Razor is fast and efficient at hair removal but fails to detect and remove thin hairs or hairs in the shade from dermoscopic images. E-shaver algorithm utilizes edge detection operators for detecting hairs in combination with different filters to detect dark and light hairs. Basic image processing operations of averaging and thresholding are also applied to obtain the mask to be applied for the inpainting task. Inpainting is performed using the interpolation method, the E- shaver algorithm leaves a grey shadow at the hair location as smoothing was not performed. Another approach similar to E-shaver is Virtual shave [3], which uses a top hat filter to detect the hairs followed by the application of morphological operations. Inpainting is performed using PDE based approach that replaces hair pixels with its neighborhood pixels, the virtual shave was applied on 20 images, test on a large dataset is required to generalize the methodology used.

Some of the researchers used APC technique for hair detection and removal. The APC algorithm uses the hessian matrix for hair detection and removal, segmentation is performed using Otsu's thresholding. ABCD features are extracted and further used for classification [18], a subset of images was used which have a different set of resolutions so there is difficulty in defining the diameters of skin lesions across images. A similar approach was utilized for the early detection of skin cancer using the Adaptive Contour Technique (ACT) and ABCD features [16]. Many researchers adapted image processing operations such as noise reduction, grayscale conversion, and thresholding for hair detection and removal followed by lesion segmentation. ABCDE features are extracted and classification is done using KNN. However, this technique does not give good accuracy [9, 20].

3   Hair Removal Techniques

This section presents 8 different methods which include variations in terms of the color space such as RGB, HSV, and YCbCr, and hybridization of existing methods to improve the performance of the hair detection and removal process. The Dataset images are resized to 512×512 before being fed to the below algorithms for processing.

1. Modified Dull Razor with RGB Plane:- In this, DR [8] algorithm is applied on RGB planes separately, and further the output is enhanced by additional morphological operations (dilation & erosion) to generate individual plane masks. The individual mask is used to obtain the final mask by performing a logical AND operation between Red and Green plane values followed by an OR operation with the Blue plane values, steps shown in Algorithm 1.

Algorithm 1. Modified Dull Razor with RGB Plane

1: Select Red plane from RGB Image
    i.Blackhat(img)= (img ∘ Y) - img where ∘ = (A ⊕ B) ⊖ B (closing operation)
    Blackhat(img) represents Blackhat output image
    ii. F = f(x) > T then 255 else 0.
      where T: Threshold, T is initialized to (10,255)
    iii. Perform Morphological operations on Red plane to generate the binary Mask
2: Select Green plane from RGB Image.
    i. Repeat step 1.(i) to 1.(iii) on Green plane
3: Select Blue plane from RGB image.
    i. Repeat step 1.(i) to 1.(iii) on Blue plane
4: **Create a mask by performing Bitwise AND operation between Red and Green plane binary mask followed by OR operation with Blue plane mask.**
5: Mask obtained in above step is used for inpainting on original image.

---

2. Modified Dull Razor with HSV Plane:- In the hair detection and removal process, color description plays an important role which is very well represented by the HSV model and the RGB model. V plane is selected for further process. This methodology involves the use of HSV instead of RGB along with Modified DR as shown in Algorithm 2.

Algorithm 2. Modified Dull Razor with HSV Plane

1: Perform conversion of RGB image to HSV .
2: **Perform Denoise on processed HSV image.**
3: Apply Blackhat filtering   i.Blackhat(img)= (img ∘ Y) - img where ∘ = (A ⊕ B) ⊖ B (closing operation)
    Blackhat(img) represents Blackhat output image
4: Threshold   ii. F = f(x) > T then 255 else 0.
      where T: Threshold, T is initialized to (10,255)
5: Convert thresholded image into binary image that represents binary mask.

---

3. Modified Dull Razor with YCbCr Plane:- YCbCr representation produces better results compared to RGB in many skin segmentation approaches [14]. This methodology uses the information from the Y plane of YCbCr im- age. The Y plane is fed as input to the Modified DR algorithm. The steps of Modified DR on the Y plane enhance the process of hair removal as represented in Algorithm 3.

Algorithm 3. Dull Razor with YCbCr Plane

1: Perform conversion of image from RGB to YCbCr plane.
    i. Y= 16 + 65.738*R/256 + 129.057*G/256 + 25.064*B/256.
    ii. Cb = 128-37.945*R/256 - 74.494*G/256 + 112.439*B/256.
    iii. Cr = 128+112.439*R - 94.154*G/256 - 18.285*B/256.
2: Y-plane is considered for further processing.
3: Apply Blackhat filtering (Algorithm 1).
4: Apply Thresholding on filtered image (Algorithm 1).
5: Inpaint using the Threshold image from step 4.

4. Dull Razor based Adaptive Principal Curvature:- The original RGB image is processed using the DR algorithm and the output of DR is fed to the APC algorithm for further processing. The mask of APC is used for inpainting and producing the final hair-removed image. The steps are shown in Algorithm 4.

Algorithm 4. Dull Razor based Adaptive Principal Curvature

1: Convert Input image to Grayscale.
2: Apply Blackhat Filtering (Algorithm 1).
3: Apply Thresholding on filtered image (Algorithm 1).
4: Perform inpainting of Dull Razor image and feed as input for APC.
5: **Threshold the inpainted image, using OTSU thresholding.**
6: Obtain hessian matrix on threshold image.
7: Invert image and use mask for Inpainting operation.

5. Modified Dull Razor with RGB Plane based Adaptive Principal Curvature:- The steps of the Modified DR algorithm are applied to the input image and the inpainted image is fed to the APC. The Combination of Modified DR and APC yields improved resultant hair-removed images (Algorithm 5).

Algorithm 5. Modified Dull Razor with RGB Plane based Adaptive Principal Curvature

1: Select Red plane from RGB image.
    i. Perform blackhat filtering on Red plane (Algorithm 1).
    ii. Perform Thresholding on Red Plane (Algorithm 1).
    iii. Perform Morphological operations on Red plane.
2: Select Green plane from RGB image.
    i. Repeat step 1.(i) to 1.(iii) on Green plane.
3: Select Blue plane from RGB image.
    i. Repeat step 1.(i) to 1.(iii) on Blue plane.
4: **Combine the mask obtained in step (iii) for each plane to generate a new mask.**
5: Perform inpainting and save the image as output of stage 1.
6: Use the image from above step as input to the APC algorithm.
7: The output of above step is the final inpainted image.

6. HSV Plane based Adaptive Principal Curvature:- In this methodology, the RGB image is converted to HSV and V plane is selected for next stages. The Modified DR is applied on V plane, inpainted image is passed to APC algorithm as represented in Algorithm 6.

Algorithm 6. HSV Plane based Adaptive Principal Curvature

1: Convert RGB image to HSV Color space.
2: **Split Hue, Saturation and Value plane and consider the value plane as grayscale.**
3: Obtain Hessian matrix for value plane.
4: Invert the obtained matrix using bitwise not.
5: Inpaint Original image using inverted mask.

---

7. YCbCr Plane based Adaptive Principal Curvature:- The RGB image is converted to YCbCr and Y plane is selected for further processing. Filtering is performed on Y plane using prewitt edge detection mask followed by thresholding. Prewitt mask provides clear detection of hair pixels so prewitt operator is used as discussed by the authors [3]. Hessian image is generated using APC algorithm and morphological dilation is applied which is followed by image cleaning to obtain the final mask. This mask is inpainted on original image to obtain the hair removed image. This process is demonstrated in Algorithm 7.

Algorithm 7. YCbCr Plane based Adaptive Principal Curvature

1: Convert the input image from RGB to YCbCr and consider Y plane.
2: **Perform filtering using a edge detection mask.**
3: Threshold the filtered image to perform hair detection.
4: Obtain hessian matrix of above image.
5: Perform dilation of hessian image.
6: **Reduce the noise pixel of the image by removing disconnected small noise pixels.**
7: **Use the noise reduced image as a mask for inpainting.**

---

8. Modified E-shaver Algorithm:- The E-shaver Algorithm discussed in literature section uses edge detection operations and threshold mechanism for detecting presence of light hairs and dark hairs. Experimentation was carried on 5 operators and one was chosen for analysis . The proposed Modified E-shaver algorithm uses the operator analysed by the researchers in E-shaver algorithm with addition of steps such as image blurring, removing noise pixels to enhance hair detection and morphological operations. The steps of the algorithm are stated in Algorithm 8.

Algorithm 8. Modified E-shaver Algorithm

1: Convert input RGB image to grayscale.
2: **Perform image blur on the above obtained image.**
3: Perform Blackhat filtering followed by thresholding (Algorithm 1).
4: Use the prewitt mask of E-shaver algorithm and obtain horizontal and vertical mask.
5: **Combine the masks obtained in step 4 by performing OR operation.**
6: **This combined mask undergoes dilation operation followed by image cleaning.**
7: Use the mask obtained in above step for inpainting operation.

4   Implementation Details

The proposed system is implemented in Google Colab Environment using Keras library. The VGG-16 [10] network was trained from scratch with randomly initialized weights and using the Adam optimizer with a learning rate experimentally set to 10-4. Input shape of image is set to (224,224,3), no of epochs used in training is 30. The loss function applied is the categorical cross entropy and metrics considered is accuracy.

5   Result Analysis and Discussion

The results of different proposed techniques for hair detection and removal are presented using visual and statistical representations along with classification using VGG-16 pre-trained model. Classification results are calculated on 1489 images from ISIC-2020 dataset [15] which consists of 488 melanoma images and 1001 non melanoma images. Sample visual results for proposed hair removal techniques are presented for images shown in Fig. 1.

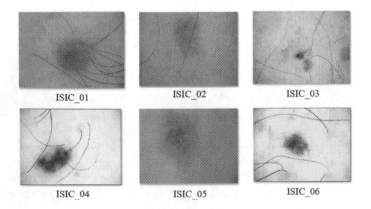

Fig. 1. Sample Images from ISIC 2020 Dataset [15]

Figure 2 shows results of DR and variants of DR respectively with intermediate steps. The Input image undergoes grayscale conversion, black hat filtering and thresholding as shown in the Fig. 2a. Final image represents the inpainted output with proper hair removal image. Similarly, Fig. 2b shows all intermediate results for Modified DR. Figure 2c shows all the results for Modified DR with HSV. This method produces some noisy effect in the final hair removed image. In Fig. 2d, Y plane undergoes steps of DR that yields useful mask for final step of inpainting with clear hair removed output.

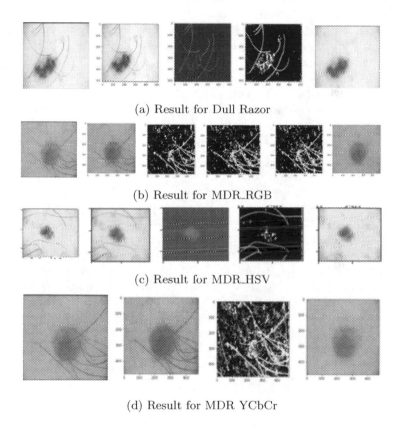

(a) Result for Dull Razor

(b) Result for MDR_RGB

(c) Result for MDR_HSV

(d) Result for MDR YCbCr

Fig. 2. Visual Results of Dull Razor and Variants

Figure 3 shows output of APC and its variants applied on the dermoscopic images for hair detection and removal. The Fig. 3a shows visual results of all the steps of APC. The final inpainted image still consists of presence of some hair artifacts. Similarly, Fig. 3b shows output of hybridization of DR and APC. It is observed that the final inpainted image shows skin lesion clearly but with blur background. Figure 3c shows steps of Modified DR applied on input image followed by APC on the mask of Modified DR with RGB plane. The final inpainted image is clear. Figure 3d shows intermediate steps of HSV based APC. Here also inpainted image shows few hair artifacts. The Fig. 3e shows visual results of YCbCr based APC. In the final hair removed image skin lesion is clearly visible with no background noise. The results of Modified E-shaver are shown in Fig. 3f. This algorithm also gives clear visualization of skin lesion.

The set of proposed algorithms are also evaluated using statistical parameters such as Accuracy (ACC), Sensitivity (SENS), Specificity (SPEC), False Positive Rate (FPR), Peak to Signal Noise Ratio (PSNR) & Structural Similarity Index (SSIM) on various input images [1,12,19]. Analysis is done in terms of performance metrics for various method on input images as shown in Fig. 1. Accuracy of 79% is achieved for Modified E-shaver and DR algorithm as shown in Fig. 4a, b and e. Sensitivity of 100% is achieved for Modified DR_YCbCr as shown in Fig. 4b, c and for Modified DR_HSV based APC as shown in Fig. 4e. Specificity of 95% and 94% is achieved for DR based APC algorithm as in Fig. 4f and d respectively. FPR value achieved is 5% for DR based APC for ISIC_06, followed by 9% for ISIC_01 as shown in Fig. 4f and a respectively. PSNR obtained is 45% for Modified E-shaver algorithm and 42% for APC algorithm as shown in Fig. 4e and a respectively. Highest SSIM of 99% is obtained for Modified E-shaver algorithm for ISIC_05, followed by 95% is obtained for Modified E-shaver and Modified DR_RGB algorithm for ISIC_02 as shown in Fig. 4b. Overall analysis indicates that Modified E-shaver and Modified DR variants combination yields better results for all the selected sample images. The other combinations or hybridisation show satisfactory performance for all the performance metrics that indicates a successful outcome of the proposed algorithms.

Table 1 presents classification results of proposed techniques and original dataset obtained for VGG-16. Analysis indicates that proposed hair detection and removal methods performed with better efficiency compared to original dataset.

Table 1. Classification Results of VGG-16

Algorithm	Accuracy	Sensitivity	Specificity	False Positive Rate
Original Dataset Classification	74.83	65.78	77.87	22.12
Dull Razor	75.49	68.57	77. 58	21.48
APC-YCbCr	**78.14**	64.91	**86.17**	**13.82**
MDR-YCbCr	74.17	62.79	**78.70**	23.12

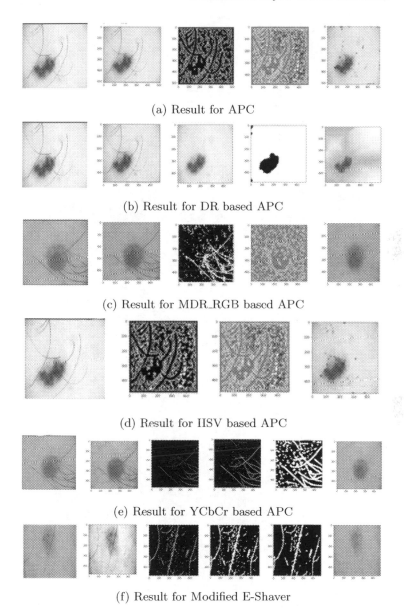

(a) Result for APC

(b) Result for DR based APC

(c) Result for MDR_RGB based APC

(d) Result for IISV based APC

(e) Result for YCbCr based APC

(f) Result for Modified E-Shaver

Fig. 3. Visual Results of Adaptive Principal Curvature, its Variants and Modified E-shaver

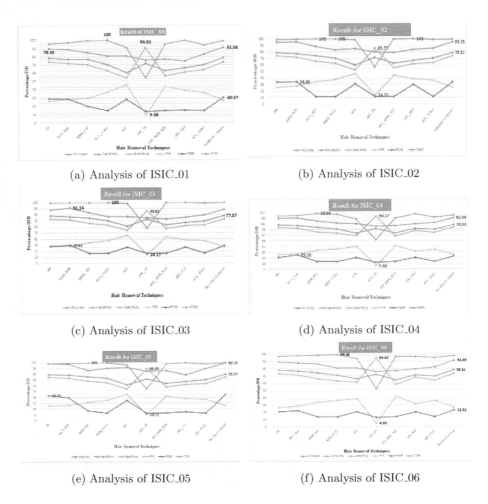

(a) Analysis of ISIC_01   (b) Analysis of ISIC_02

(c) Analysis of ISIC_03   (d) Analysis of ISIC_04

(e) Analysis of ISIC_05   (f) Analysis of ISIC_06

Fig. 4. Statistical Analysis of ISIC Images.

6   Conclusion

Skin cancer has been studied for decades and many tools and techniques have been developed for accurate and fast detection of the same. The first stage of skin cancer detection involves the detection and removal of hairs present in the skin region. Different techniques available include DR, E-shaver, APC, etc. The analysis of these existing methods provides insights into the need for improvement in the first stage for improved performance. Hybridization of various existing techniques with different color spaces such as HSV, RGB, and YCbCr are presented. The algorithms are evaluated using standard performance metrics which indicate the higher performance of the proposed algorithms. The classification results for sample images from ISIC-2020 dataset is obtained using the VGG-16 model for the proposed methods. The Hybridization methods have higher results compared to the original dataset images. Future work includes designing background invariant algorithms for hair detection and removal along with fused feature extraction methods and its impact on classification accuracy.

References

1. Abhishek, K., Hamarneh, G.: Matthews correlation coefficient loss for deep convolutional networks: Application to skin lesion segmentation. In: 2021 IEEE 18th International Symposium on Biomedical Imaging (ISBI), pp. 225–229. IEEE (2021)
2. Abuzaghleh, O., Barkana, B.D., Faezipour, M.: Noninvasive real-time automated skin lesion analysis system for melanoma early detection and prevention. IEEE J. Transl. Eng. Health Med. 3, 1–12 (2015)
3. Fiorese, M., Peserico, E., Silletti, A.: VirtualShave: automated hair removal from digital dermatoscopic images. In: 2011 Annual International Conference of the IEEE Engineering in Medicine and Biology Society, pp. 5145–5148. IEEE (2011)
4. Huang, A., Kwan, S.Y., Chang, W.Y., Liu, M.Y., Chi, M.H., Chen, G.S.: A robust hair segmentation and removal approach for clinical images of skin lesions. In: 2013 35th Annual International Conference of the IEEE Engineering in Medicine and Biology Society (EMBC), pp. 3315–3318. IEEE (2013)
5. Ichim, L., Popescu, D.: Melanoma detection using an objective system based on multiple connected neural networks. IEEE Access 8, 179189–179202 (2020)
6. Kiani, K., Sharafat, A.R.: E-shaver: An improved dullrazor® for digitally removing dark and light-colored hairs in dermoscopic images. Comput. Biol. Med. 41(3), 139–145 (2011)
7. Labani, S., Asthana, S., Rathore, K., Sardana, K.: Incidence of melanoma and nonmelanoma skin cancers in Indian and the global regions. J. Cancer Res. Therap. 17, 906–911 (2020)
8. Lee, T., Ng, V., Gallagher, R., Coldman, A., McLean, D.: Dullrazor®: a software approach to hair removal from images. Comput. Biol. Med. 27(6), 533–543 (1997)
9. Linsangan, N.B., Adtoon, J.J., Torres, J.L.: Geometric analysis of skin lesion for skin cancer using image processing. In: 2018 IEEE 10th International Conference on Humanoid, Nanotechnology, Information Technology, Communication and Control, Environment and Management (HNICEM), pp. 1–5. IEEE (2018)
10. Manasa, K., Murthy, D.: Skin cancer detection using VGG-16. Europ. J. Molecular Clin. Med. 8(1), 1419–1426 (2021)
11. Monika, M.K., Vignesh, N.A., Kumari, C.U., Kumar, M., Lydia, E.L.: Skin cancer detection and classification using machine learning. Mater. Today: Proceed. 33, 4266–4270 (2020)
12. Naeem, A., Farooq, M.S., Khelifi, A., Abid, A.: Malignant melanoma classification using deep learning: datasets, performance measurements, challenges and opportunities. IEEE Access 8, 110575–110597 (2020)
13. Narayanamurthy, V., et al.: Skin cancer detection using non-invasive techniques. RSC Adv. 8(49), 28095–28130 (2018)
14. Rahman, M.A., Haque, M., Shahnaz, C., Fattah, S.A., Zhu, W.P., Ahmed, M.O.: Skin lesions classification based on color plane-histogram-image quality analysis features extracted from digital images. In: 2017 IEEE 60th International Midwest Symposium on Circuits and Systems (MWSCAS), pp. 1356–1359. IEEE (2017)
15. Rotemberg, V., et al.: A patient-centric dataset of images and metadata for identifying melanomas using clinical context. Sci. Data 8(1), 1–8 (2021)

16. Senan, E.M., Jadhav, M.E.: Analysis of dermoscopy images by using ABCD rule for early detection of skin cancer. Global Trans. Proceed. **2**, 1–7 (2021)
17. Tajeddin, N.Z., Asl, B.M.: Melanoma recognition in dermoscopy images using lesion's peripheral region information. Comput. Methods Programs Biomed. **163**, 143–153 (2018)
18. Thanh, D.N., Prasath, V.S., Hien, N.N., et al.: Melanoma skin cancer detection method based on adaptive principal curvature, colour normalisation and feature extraction with the ABCD rule. J. Digit. Imaging **33**, 574–585 (2019)
19. Zaqout, I.S.: An efficient block-based algorithm for hair removal in dermoscopic images. Comput. Opt. **41**(4), 521–527 (2017)
20. Zghal, N.S., Derbel, N.: Melanoma skin cancer detection based on image processing. Curr. Med. Imaging **16**(1), 50–58 (2020)

Traffic Sign Detection and Recognition Using Dense Connections in YOLOv4

Swastik Saxena[✉][iD] and Somnath Dey

Department of Computer Science and Engineering, Indian Institute of Technology
Indore, Indore, India
sswastik630@gmail.com, somnathd@iiti.ac.in

Abstract. A self-driving car is a growing technology in India where detection of traffic sign in an unconstrained environment is a challenging task due to its small size. With the development of deep neural networks, many models for object detection have been developed. In this work, we have used a single-stage detection model YoloV4 with further improvements in detection neck for detection of traffic signs. We have used dense connections in place of normal connections of the model for better feature propagation. This improves the accuracy with less inference time. We have conducted our experiments on bench-marked Chinese traffic sign dataset, Tshigua-Tenscent 100K dataset (TT-100K). We have achieved accuracy of 94.30% with 32 FPS.

Keywords: Traffic sign detection · Deep learning · Object detection · YOLOv4 · TT-100K

1 Introduction

Object detection is a computer vision technique whose aim is to detect different objects such as cars, buildings, and human beings, etc. The objects can generally be identified from either pictures or video feeds. Traffic sign detection and recognition deals with the problem of detecting and recognizing different traffic signs present above or besides the roads, highway or any other pathway. Traffic sign detection and recognition (TSDR) technology plays a very important role in traffic assistance driving systems and automatic driving systems. These systems can assist drivers to provide alert about coming obstacles or information about the road or highways.

There are many challenges involved with traffic sign detection. The change in weather condition can make traffic signs partially visible. Sometimes traffic signs get physically damaged by high winds, the color of traffic signs gets faded with time. Our problem is to detect traffic signs with a moving car so sometimes motion blurring also happens if our model is not fast. Partial occlusion problem can also occur due to trees, person, objects standing in front of traffic signboard. To overcome these challenges, there is a need to develop an automatic system that can detect and recognize traffic signs accurately.

Traffic sign detection is a traditional problem and many work have been done in this field. After recent development in the deep neural network, this problem gets new approaches to solve. Traditionally traffic sign detection process consists of mainly two stages i. e. detection of traffic signs and recognition of traffic signs to the class they belong to. Detection of traffic signs can be done on common properties of traffic signs like color and shape. Many approaches using color segmentation [1–5], Histogram of Gradient (HOG) [5] and using other hand crafted features are proposed. The limitation of color based approach is illumination change over the course of day. To overcome this, shape-based techniques were used in many works [6–8]. Shapes such as triangular, circular, square, etc. were used to detect and recognize traffic signs. Though, these methods were not affected by illumination change but were computationally expensive and were not suitable for real-time detection.

After the evolution of the deep neural network, the whole process of traffic sign detection gets a boost. Many object detection models have been used in traffic sign detection. Region-based Convolutional Neural Network (RCNN) [9], Fast-RCNN [10], Faster-RCNN [11], Mask-RCNN [12], Single-Shot Detector (SSD) [13], You Only Look Once (YOLO) [14], YOLOv2 [15], YOLOv3 [16] and YOLOv4 [17] are some models which are used for traffic sign detection. These detectors can be divided into two categories, single-stage detectors, and two-stage detectors. Two-stage detectors have good accuracy as first it proposes the regions which can contain a sign and after that classification and bounding box regression is performed. However, in a single-stage detector, this whole process of region proposing, classification and bounding box regression is done in a single step. Single-stage detector are fast in comparison to two-stage detectors whereas two-stage detectors are more accurate then single-stage detectors.

In this paper, we have addressed issues of learning and detecting traffic sign categories for the road-based automatic driving system. For our work, we have used YoloV4 [17]. YoloV4 is a recently developed model in the single-stage category. As our main contribution, we have improved the detection neck of the model to reduce traffic sign detection speed and increase accuracy in comparison to original model. We have performed our experiments on TT-100K dataset as it mostly used in previous work of traffic sign detection and recognition.

2 Related Work

A lot of research has been done on traffic sign detection and recognition. The traditional approach of traffic sign detection consists of using manual feature extraction to detect regions that can contain a traffic sign. Authors in [1–3], used color based segmentation for detecting different traffic signs. For segmentation, different color spaces are used to take advantages of different color spaces. In [4], they used thresholding-based segmentation in HSI color space for detecting traffic signs as RGB color space is sensitive to illumination change. In the work proposed by Romdhane et al. [5], possible candidates for traffic signs were detected from HSV color space by thresholding each channel. These detected signs are further fed into SVM based classifier to predict the class of detected traffic signs. In shape based detection methods, different methods are proposed for detection of circles, triangles and rectangles. P. Yakimov and V. Fursov [6], used Generalized Hough transformation to detects triangular-shaped traffic signs and in [7], radial symmetry transform was utilized to detect circular speed signs. Further, methods based on both color and shape are also used in some work. Zheng et al. [8] used color and shape-based techniques to detect traffic signs. First segmentation in RGB color space is used followed by shape based detection. They used two different methods for shapes that are fast radial symmetry transform, which is used to detect circles, and the Douglas-Peucker algorithm to identify triangles, rectangles, and octagons. In the work proposed by [18], a color probability model was used to enhance the input image, and a Maximally Stable Extremal Regions (MSERs) detector was used to find traffic signs proposal. They used SVM for classifying into a higher label which was further classified into specific sub-classes by employing CNN. Further, there are several other approaches of [19–21] which also used Histogram of Gradient (HoG) and SVM for classifying traffic signs.

Recent work consists of neural network based methods for detection and recognition of traffic sign. Convolutional Neural Network (CNN) are used for feature extraction from images using different filters for different features. Most popular CNN models used for feature extraction are VGG16 [22], Resent [23], DenseNet [24]. These features are further used for recognizing the class of detected object. In [25], two modules based on CNN are used for locating and classifying traffic signs. Tang et al. [26] proposed Integrated Feature Pyramid Network with Feature Aggregation (IFA-FPN). To address the imbalance problem of ROIs in pyramid levels, an Integrated Operation (IO) was introduced and to improve the feature representation capacity of feature maps, a Feature Aggregation (FA) structure was used. General object detection models consists of Region-based Convolutional Neural Network (RCNN) [9], Fast-RCNN [10], Faster-RCNN [11], and Mask-RCNN [12]. These models are used in many work for traffic signs detection and recognition. Tabernik et al. [27] used Mask RCNN with various modifications in training data which consists of online hard-example mining, distribution of selected training samples, sample weighting, and adjusting region pass-through during detection. A Multi-scale Region-based Convolutional Neural Network (MR-CNN) detection framework that simultaneously employs fused feature representations in the detection and classification stage is proposed by Liu et al. [28]. Other category of object detection models comprises of Single-Shot Detector (SSD) [13], YOLO [14], YOLOv2 [15], YOLOv3 [16] and YOLOv4 [17]. These models does detection and recognition in a single step. Jin et al. [29] employed MF-SSD, an improved SSD algorithm, which jointly exploited feature fusion and enhanced SSD algorithm. This work proposed an improved SSD algorithm through feature fusion and enhancement, named Multi-Feature Fusion and Enhancement Single Shot Detector (MF-SSD). Luo et al. [30] introduced a contextual network called Contextual-YOLOv3, which utilized contextual information to detect small objects for better performance. Authors in

[31] proposed an improved lightweight algorithm based on YOLOv4-Tiny. It used an enhanced k-means algorithm and proposed large-scale feature map optimization. Further, the non-maximum suppression algorithm was improved based on soft non-maximum suppression (NMS). Improved YOLOv4 was utilized by [32] which comprises one extra feature layer for detection and anchor box creation according to small and medium traffic signs.

3   Proposed Work

In our proposed work for problem of traffic sign detection and recognition, we have used the YOLOv4 model. We have further improved the detection neck of YOLOv4 model for better features utilization and improve the performance of model for traffic signs. In the following subsections, we have provided an overview of YOLOv4 model and then details of our proposed modifications in the architecture of model.

3.1   YOLOv4 Model

YOLOv4 model is a single-stage object detection model which belongs to YOLO family. First model in this family was proposed in [14]. Further, YOLOv2 [15] and YOLOv3 [16] were introduced with different improvements over the previous models. Currently YOLOv4 [17] is the most efficient and fastest model for object detection among all YOLO models. Single-stage object detectors can be divided into three parts, as shown in Fig. 1, that are: the backbone, neck, and head. Feature extraction from images is done by backbone which are further propagated using Neck of the model. Finally, the detection head is used to perform detection and classification of objects. YOLOv4 uses CSPDarknet53 as backbone and neck of YOLOv4 consists of Spatial Pyramid Pooling (SPP) block and Path Aggregation Network (PANet). YOLOv4 uses same head as YOLOv3 model which performs detection at three different scales for different sizes of objects. Figure 1 shows the YOLOv4 model as a single object detector.

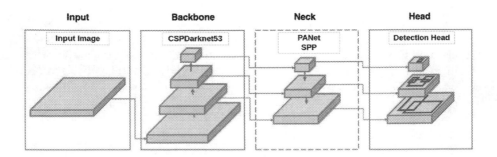

Fig. 1. YOLOv4 model as single-stage object detector architecture [17]

Though, the current YOLOv4 model is used for general object detection and does not perform well in the case of traffic sign images due to complex objects and the small size of signs. So, to overcome that issues in the conventional YOLOv4 model, we have made improvements in the neck of the YOLOv4 model. We have used dense connections in the detection neck in place of normal connections for better feature propagation.

3.2   Dense Connection in Detection Neck

YOLOv4 model consists of the head part of YOLOv3 model, which has a detection block followed by an output layer for three different feature scales. These detection blocks consist of features from the previous layers and the initial layers of the model. In a conventional YoloV3 head, there is no skip or partial connections between layers. It consists of convolution followed by batch normalization and Leaky Relu activation function, which we have termed as CBL block. We have improved these blocks for better utilization of information by improving the connections in CBL blocks. We have used dense connection in the head, inspired by DenseNet [24]. Dense connection is shown in Fig. 2. The input to the $(i+1)^{th}$ layer will be concatenation of input and output feature maps of the ith layer. Equations given in Eq. 1 express the dense connections.

$$x_1 = w_1 * x_0$$
$$x_2 = w_2 * [x_1, x_0]$$
$$\cdot$$
$$\cdot \quad (1)$$
$$\cdot$$
$$x_k = w_k * [x_1, x_0, ..., x_{k-1}]$$

In Eq. 1, $[x_0, x_1...]$ denotes the concatenation of x_0, x_1 and so on, w_i and x_i denote the weights and output of the ith and $*$ denotes the convolutional oper-

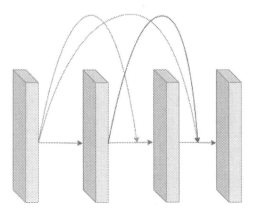

Fig. 2. Dense Connection in DenseNet.

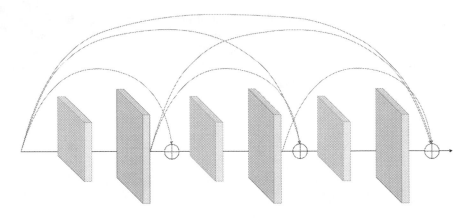

Fig. 3. Dense Connection in Detection Head.

ation layer, respectively. Changing the normal convolutional block with dense connection results in better feature utilization, increasing the model's accuracy. Figure 3 shows the CBL block of YOLOv4 with dense connections. The orange block shows the layers with 1×1 kernel, and the blue blocks show the 3×3 kernel operation. Grey lines show the new dense connections, and the circle with $(+)$ shows the concatenation operation. In this new head, the feature to current layers consists of features from the output of previous layers and input of previous layers. The detection head gives a vector as output which consists of the confidence score of the prediction, the label and the coordinates of the predicted bounding box (center, width, height). To increase the accuracy of predicted bounding boxes, it uses CIoU loss which is defined in Eq 2,

$$L_{CIoU} = 1 - IoU + \frac{\rho^2(b, b^{gt})}{c^2} + \alpha * \nu \qquad (2)$$

where B and B^{gt} denotes the predicted box and target box and central points of these boxes are denoted by b and b^{gt}, respectively. The Euclidean distance is defined by $\rho(.)$, the diagonal length of the smallest box that covers the two boxes is represented by c, a positive trade-off parameter is represented by α, and aspect ratio consistency is represented by ν.

$$\nu = \frac{4}{\pi^2} (arctan\frac{w^{gt}}{h^{gt}} - arctan\frac{w}{h})^2 \qquad (3)$$

$$\alpha = \frac{\nu}{(1 - IoU) + \nu} \qquad (4)$$

where w is the width and h is the height of the bounding box. In Eq 3, w^{gt} and h^{gt} represent the width and height of the ground truth box, respectively.

4   Experiment Results and Analysis

4.1   Experimental Setup

All experimental evaluations of this work are performed on Intel(R) Xeon(R) Silver 4214 CPU @ 2.20GHz with 128GB memory and Nvidia RTX 3090 GPU with 24GB memory. We have used publicly available implementation of the YOLOv4 model on the Darknet framework[1] as a base architecture in our experiments.

4.2   Evaluation Metrics

We have evaluated the proposed model with commonly used object detection performance metrics. We have considered precision, recall, f1-score, average precision, and mean average precision for evaluation of our work. The equations for calculating precision, recall and F1-Score are given in Eq. (5) (6) and (7), respectively.

$$Precision = \frac{TP}{TP + FP} \tag{5}$$

$$Recall = \frac{TP}{TP + FN} \tag{6}$$

$$F1 = 2 * \frac{precision * recall}{precision + recall} \tag{7}$$

TP, FP and FN in Eq. (5) (6), denotes True Positive, False Positive and False Negative, respectively. TP refers to the case when model predicts the true instances as true while FP refers to the case when model predicts the false instances as true. FN refers to the case in which model predicts true as false. FP cases are not considered for object detectection evaluation as it denotes every part of the image where no object is present. Each category's Average Precision (AP) is calculated using the precision-recall area under the curve (AUC). All classes' APs are used to calculate mean Average Precision (mAP).

4.3   Dataset

We have used Tsinghua-Tencent 100k (TT-100K) dataset [33] for our work. It is a Chinese traffic sign dataset which consists of 100K images having 200 different classes of traffic signs. Figure 4 shows the different category of traffic signs present in TT-100K. These traffic signs are captured in different challenging conditions and all images have a resolution of 2048×2048. This dataset has 6753 images for training and 2984 images for testing. For a fair comparison of accuracy with previous work, we have considered top 44 categories with the most traffic signs. Figure 5 shows input image in our dataset which consists of different type of traffic signs. In this dataset, multiple instances of traffic signs are present in a single image. Table 1 shows the number of images in each category. We have used at least 200 instances of each category for proper training of the proposed model.

---

[1] https://github.com/AlexeyAB/darknet.

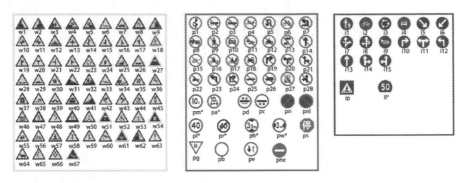

Fig. 4. Different category of traffic signs in TT-100K dataset.

Table 1. Number of images in each top 44 classes of TT-100k dataset.

Class	Pn	Pne	I5	P11	Pl40	Pl50	Pl80	Pl60	P26	I4	Pl100
Number of images	6601	4974	3605	3338	2992	2232	1877	1777	1771	1679	1419
Class	Pl30	Pl5	Il60	I2	P5	I2r	P10	P13	Ip	I4l	P23
Number of images	1334	1155	1041	989	914	911	874	814	771	727	710
Class	Il80	Pl120	W59	Pr40	P12	Ph4.5	W55	Pm20	P3	Pg	Pl20
Number of images	629	620	488	428	404	402	369	359	354	334	327
Class	Pl70	Pm55	P27	P19	Il100	W13	Ph5	Ph4	W32	P6	Pm30
Number of images	314	281	278	274	270	269	268	266	263	238	231

4.4   Results and Analysis

We have reported results with YOLOv3, original YOLOv4 and modified YOLOv4 models. We have trained our model for 20000 iterations with learning rate of 0.00261, which is increased after training for 80% and 90% iterations.

(a)   (b)

Fig. 5. Input image in TT-100K dataset having different type of traffic signs.

The input image size is kept at 640×640 pixels to reduce the training time. For better feature extraction, image resolution is increased during testing. Hence, final results are reported on the image with resolution 1024×1024. Table 2 shows the precision, recall, f1-score and mAP achieved using different models. We have received an overall mAP of 94.30% with improved YOLOv4. Our model achieved an increase of 1.30% and 9% in overall mAP in comparison to original model and YOLOv3. Further, the Frames Per Second (FPS) of both models are same making it compatible for real time performance. We have further reported the per-class results in Table 3. From the Table 3, it is shown that our model has performed good and have more than 85% average precision for most category. Only $p3$ have AP of 79.87%. Figure 6 shows the output images of our model. As shown in Fig. 6((a)), our model detected traffic signs of $pl40$ and $p23$ with 100% confidence. Similarly, in Fig. 6((b)), the traffic signs of category pne, $i4$, $pl50$ and pn are accurately detected.

Table 2. mAP achieved using original and improved YOLOv4 model.

Model	Precision	Recall	F1-Score	mAP
YOLOv3	85%	89%	87%	85.65%
Original YOLOv4	82%	95%	88%	93%
Improved YOLOv4	83%	95%	88%	94.30%

We have compared our work with previous work to show the effectiveness of our model. In traffic sign detection, different metrics are used to report results in existing work. We have compared our work using precision, recall, F-1 score, and mAP, which are used by the most of the works. If authors did not report results on any parameters, we have kept them as a dash $(-)$. Table 4 compares our work with previous work on the TT-100K dataset. The offered findings are a comparison of accuracy in the top 42 classes. Our model has achieved an mAP of 94.30%. The technique reported in [33] have an 89% recall, but our model has a 95% recall, indicating that we have fewer false-negative cases. Our model consists of convolutional layers with additional blocks for better feature propagation, resulting in better recall than method used in [33]. Our proposed method is fast compared to method used in [28], as this method is a two-stage network in which different modules are used for classification and regression and our model is a single-stage model. Center point estimation [34] has similar accuracy to our model, but our model's F1-score and recall for many classes is high in comparison to this method. The accuracy achieved by using an integrated feature pyramid network with feature aggregation [26] is 94.50%. This method uses RCNN model which is two-stage detector so inference speed is low in comparison to our model. All the comparisons are reported on test images with resolution 1024×1024 for a fair comparison of accuracy.

(a)   (b)

Fig. 6. Output image of our model having different detected traffic signs.

Table 3. Average Precision on each category of TT-100K dataset.

Class	pn	pne	i5	p11	pl40	pl50	pl80	pl60	p26	i4	pl100
Precision	0.79	0.96	0.95	0.73	0.79	0.78	0.82	0.85	0.82	0.90	0.90
Recall	0.96	0.99	0.96	0.95	0.94	0.92	0.94	0.91	0.94	0.98	0.97
F-1 Score	0.94	0.97	0.96	0.90	0.91	0.92	0.92	0.91	0.90	0.94	0.97
AP	98.02%	98.45%	97.97%	93.38%	95.14%	93.79%	94.78%	94.84%	94.50%	98%	98.11%
Class	pl30	pl5	il60	i2	p5	i2r	p10	p13	ip	i4l	p23
Precision	0.83	0.82	0.88	0.85	0.91	0.79	0.79	0.84	0.92	0.82	0.89
Recall	0.92	0.95	0.98	0.94	0.95	0.95	0.90	0.88	0.93	0.99	0.95
F-1 Score	0.86	0.89	0.96	0.89	0.93	0.88	0.90	0.86	0.95	0.89	0.88
AP	94.35%	95.06%	98.16%	95.13%	94.92%	93.75%	91.64%	87.47%	95.95%	97.46%	95.83%
Class	il80	pl120	w59	pr40	p12	ph4.5	w55	pm20	p3	pg	pl20
Precision	0.94	0.91	0.79	0.91	0.77	0.82	0.88	0.80	0.82	0.94	0.74
Recall	0.96	0.98	0.91	0.98	0.93	0.86	0.89	0.90	0.74	0.94	0.91
F-1 Score	0.94	0.98	0.86	0.93	0.76	0.74	0.80	0.63	0.82	0.93	0.81
AP	97.52%	97.79%	89.84%	99.84%	93.18%	91.52%	95.84%	93.64%	79.87%	97.16%	95.17%
Class	pl70	pm55	p27	p19	il100	w13	ph5	ph4	w32	p6	pm30
Precision	0.77	0.84	0.82	0.72	0.84	0.59	0.65	0.75	0.87	0.76	0.68
Recall	0.89	0.97	0.98	0.91	0.97	0.87	0.84	0.89	0.92	0.97	0.88
F-1 Score	0.78	0.79	0.89	0.69	0.96	0.72	0.61	0.62	0.91	0.70	0.57
AP	89%	95.68%	98.45%	92.19%	96.13%	89.17%	82.74%	89.32%	95.60%	97.62%	89.74%

Table 4. Comparison with previous work on TT-100K dataset.

Model	Precision	Recall	F1-score	MAP
Zhu et al. [33]	87.7%	89%	88%	-
Liu et al. [28]	89%	91%	89%	-
Wei et al. [34]	94.9%	93.6%	94.33%	
Xiao and Liu [35]	-	-	-	88%
Liu et al. [36]	-	-	91.55%	-
Tang et al. [26]	-	-	-	94.5%
Luo et al. [30]	-	-	-	94%
Ours	**83%**	**95%**	**88%**	**94.30%**

5   Conclusion and Future Work

In this work, we have proposed model for traffic sign detection and recognition. We have improved the YOLOv4 model in our work. For improving the performance of YOLOv4 model for complex and small traffic signs, we have modified the detection neck of the model for better feature propagation. Dense connections are used in place of normal convolutional layers which help in more features utilization and increasing accuracy by keeping less detection time. Our experiments are conducted on TT-100K dataset and we have achieved 94.30% mAP with 32 FPS which is good for real time performance.

In our future work, we will try to further improve our model and will conduct experiments on more challenging datasets.

Acknowledgements. We are thankful to Ministry of Higher Education (MHE) for providing the Teaching Assistantships (TA) to carry out the research work. We would also like to acknowledge Department of Computer Science and Engineering, Indian Institute of Technology Indore, for providing the laboratory support and research facilities to carry out this research work.

References

1. Gomez-Moreno, H., Maldonado-Bascon, S., Gil-Jimenez, P., Lafuente-Arroyo, S.: Goal Evaluation of Segmentation Algorithms for Traffic Sign Recognition, In: IEEE Transactions on Intelligent Transportation Systems 11, pp. 917–930 (2010)
2. Ruta, A., Li, Y., Liu, X.: Real-time traffic sign recognition from video by class-specific discriminative features. Pattern Recogn. **43**(1), 416–430 (2010)
3. Salti, S., Petrelli, A., Tombari, F., Fioraio, N., Stefano, L.D.: Traffic sign detection via interest region extraction. Pattern Recogn. **48**, 1039–1049 (2015)
4. Nguwi, Y.-Y., Kouzani, A.: Automatic Road Sign Recognition Using Neural Networks, In: The 2006 IEEE International Joint Conference on Neural Network Proceedings, pp. 3955–3962, (2006)

5. Romdhane, N.B., Mliki, H., Hammami, M.: An improved traffic signs recognition and tracking method for driver assistance system In: 2016 IEEE/ACIS 15th International Conference on Computer and Information Science (ICIS), pp. 1–6 (2016)
6. Yakimov, P., Fursov, V.: Traffic Signs Detection and tracking using modified Hough transform, In: 2015 12th International Joint Conference on e-Business and Telecommunications (ICETE), pp. 22–28 (2015)
7. Barnes, N., Zelinsky, A., Fletcher, L.S.: Real-Time speed sign detection using the Radial symmetry detector. IEEE Trans. Intell. Transp. Syst. **9**, 322–332 (2008)
8. Zheng, Z., Zhang, H., Wang, B., Gao, Z.: Robust traffic sign recognition and tracking for advanced driver assistance systems, In: 2012 15th International IEEE Conference on Intelligent Transportation Systems, pp. 704–709 (2012)
9. Girshick, R., Donahue, J., Darrell, T., Malik, J.: Rich feature hierarchies for accurate object detection and semantic segmentation (2014) arXiv [cs.CV]
10. Girshick, R.: Fast R-CNN, In: 2015 IEEE International Conference on Computer Vision (ICCV), pp. 1440–1448 (2015)
11. Ren, S., He, K., Girshick, R., Sun, J.: Faster R-CNN: towards real-time object detection with region proposal networks. IEEE Trans. Pattern Anal. Mach. Intell. **39**(6), 1137–1149 (2017)
12. He, K., Gkioxari, G., Dollár, P., Girshick, R.: Mask R-CNN, In: 2017 IEEE International Conference on Computer Vision (ICCV), pp. 2980–2988 (2017)
13. Liu, W., et al.: SSD: Single Shot MultiBox Detector. In: Leibe, B., Matas, J., Sebe, N., Welling, M. (eds.) ECCV 2016. LNCS, vol. 9905, pp. 21–37. Springer, Cham (2016). https://doi.org/10.1007/978-3-319-46448-0_2
14. Redmon, J., et al.: You Only Look Once: unified, real-time object detection, In: 2016 IEEE Conference on Computer Vision and Pattern Recognition (CVPR), pp. 779–788 (2016)
15. Redmon, J., Farhadi, A.: YOLO9000: better, faster, stronger, In: 2017 IEEE Conference on Computer Vision and Pattern Recognition (CVPR), pp. 6517–6525 (2017)
16. Redmon, J., Farhadi, A.: YOLOv3: an incremental improvement (2018)
17. Bochkovskiy, A., Wang, C.-Y., Liao, H.-Y. M.: YOLOv4: optimal speed and accuracy of object detection (2020)
18. Yang, Y., Luo, H., Xu, H., Wu, F.: Towards real-time traffic sign detection and classification. IEEE Trans. Intell. Transp. Syst. **17**, 2022–2031 (2016)
19. Berkaya, S.K., Gunduz, H., Ozsen, O., Akinlar, C., Gunal, S.: On circular traffic sign detection and recognition. Expert Syst. Appl. **48**, 67–75 (2016)
20. Zaklouta, F., Stanciulescu, B.: Real-Time traffic-sign recognition using tree classifiers. IEEE Trans. Intell. Transp. Syst. **13**(4), 1507–1514 (2012)
21. Gomez-Moreno, H., Maldonado-Bascon, S., Gil-Jimenez, P., Lafuente-Arroyo, S.: Goal evaluation of segmentation algorithms for traffic sign recognition. IEEE Trans. Intell. Transp. Syst. **11**, 917–930 (2010)
22. Simonyan, K., Zisserman, A.: Very Deep Convolutional Networks for Large-Scale Image Recognition (2014)
23. He, K., Zhang, X., Ren, S., Sun, J.: Deep Residual Learning for Image Recognition (2015)
24. Huang, G., Liu, Z., Van Der Maaten, L., Weinberger, K.Q.: Densely Connected Convolutional Networks In: 2017 IEEE Conference on Computer Vision and Pattern Recognition (CVPR), pp. 2261–2269 (2017)
25. Kamal, U., Tonmoy, T.I., Das, S., Hasan, M.K.: Automatic traffic sign detection and recognition using Segu-net and a modified Tversky loss function with l1-constraint. IEEE Trans. Intell. Transp. Syst. **21**, 1467–1479 (2020)

26. Tang, Q., Cao, G., Jo, K.-H.: Integrated feature pyramid network with feature aggregation for traffic sign detection. IEEE Access **9**, 117784–117794 (2021)
27. Tabernik, D., Skočaj, D.: Deep learning for large-scale traffic-sign detection and recognition. IEEE Trans. Intell. Transp. Syst. **21**(4), 1427–1440 (2020)
28. Liu, Z., Du, J., Tian, F., Wen, J.: MR-CNN: a multi-scale region-based convolutional neural network for small traffic sign recognition. IEEE Access **7**, 57120–57128 (2019)
29. Jin, Y., Fu, Y., Wang, W., Guo, J., Ren, C., Xiang, X.: Multi-Feature fusion and enhancement single shot detector for traffic sign recognition. IEEE Access **8**, 38931–38940 (2020)
30. Luo, H.-W., Zhang, C.-S., Pan, F.-C., Ju, X.-M.: Contextual-YOLOV3: implement better small object detection based deep learning In: 2019 International Conference on Machine Learning, Big Data and Business Intelligence (MLBDBI), pp. 134–141 (2019)
31. Wang, L., Zhou, K., Chu, A., Wang, G., Wang, L.: An improved light-weight traffic sign recognition algorithm based on YOLOv4-tiny. IEEE Access **9**, 124963–124971 (2021)
32. Wang, H., Yu, H.: Traffic sign detection algorithm based on improved YOLOv4, pp. 1946–1950 (2020)
33. Zhu, Z., Liang, D., Zhang, S., Huang, X., Li, B., Hu, S.: Traffic-Sign Detection and Classification in the Wild In: 2016 IEEE Conference on Computer Vision and Pattern Recognition (CVPR), pp. 2110–2118 (2016)
34. Wei, L., Xu, C., Li, S., Tu, X.: Traffic sign detection and recognition using novel center-point estimation and local features. IEEE Access **8**, 83611–83621 (2020)
35. Xiao, D.,Liu, L.: Super-Resolution-Based traffic prohibitory sign recognition, In: 2019 IEEE 21st International Conference on High Performance Computing and Communications IEEE 17th International Conference on Smart City; IEEE 5th International Conference on Data Science and Systems (HPCC/SmartCity/DSS), pp. 2383–2388 (2019)
36. Liu, L., Wang, Y., Li, K., Li, J.: Focus First: Coarse-to-fine traffic sign detection with stepwise learning. IEEE Access **8**, 171170–171183 (2020)

Novel Image and Its Compressed Image Based on VVC Standard, Pair Data Set for Deep Learning Image and Video Compression Applications

Rohan lal[1]([✉])[ID], Prashant Sharma[1][ID], and Devendra Kumar Patel[2][ID]

[1] Indian Institute of Technology Madras, Chennai, India
rohan.lal709@gmail.com
[2] Samrat Ashok Technological Institute Vidisha, Vidisha, India

Abstract. More than 80 percent of online traffic is video and image traffic and this will likely rise in the upcoming years. Images and video have multiple dimensions to grow data rate via increasing frame resolution, frame depth, multi-view representation etc. Thus it is very crucial to compress these images and videos efficiently. Lack of sufficient experimental data is a major setback for the development of image and video compression based on deep learning models.

This study presents a new kind of data set for the research community with the goal of advancing the state-of-the-art in image compression using deep learning models. The proposed data set consists of the image and its corresponding VVC (Versatile Video Coding) standard based compressed image as a label of the input image for two quantization parameters. Images from different states of Indian subcontinent area has been captured, containing common objects in their natural context, the beautiful campus of Indian Institute of Technology Madras, which is blessed with rich flora and fauna, and is home to several rare wildlife species, scenes from Himalayas, Clouds in Cherrapunji, Indoor scenes etc. has been captured. The data set will be made publicly to the research community. Statistical analysis of the data set is presented along with VVC compression standard coding analysis.

Keywords: Data set · Compression · VVC

1 Introduction

There has been a dramatic advancement in the computer vision and image processing domain due to training of deep learning models using colossal realistic image datasets. In the studies motivated by computational neuroscience, it has been found that the representations in these task-trained models exhibit striking similarities to those in the primate visual system [1] [2] [3]. Through the retina

Indian Institute of Technology Madras.

D. Gupta et al. (Eds.): CVIP 2022, CCIS 1777, pp. 428–442, 2023.
https://doi.org/10.1007/978-3-031-31417-9_33

Fig. 1. Building

Fig. 2. Doll

Fig. 3. Fruit

Fig. 4. Flower

Fig. 5. Sky

(a)

Fig. 6. Architectural Monuments

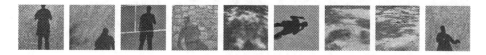

Fig. 7. Shadow

Fig. 8. People

Fig. 9. Vehicle

Fig. 10. Object

Fig. 11. Tree

Fig. 12. Valley

Fig. 13. Railway Tracks

Fig. 14. Animals

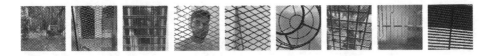

Fig. 15. Fence Occlusion

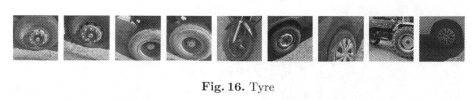

Fig. 16. Tyre

Fig. 17. Cat

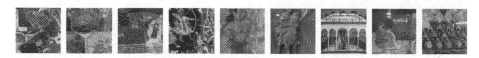

Fig. 18. Painting

Fig. 19. Sculpture

Fig. 20. Bodies of water

Fig. 21. Cattle

the visual information flows to the human brain where the visual cortex transforms the sensory visual input into coherent perceptions. A part of the visual cortex called the inferotemporal cortex and subsets of the inferotemporal cortex regions in the human brain are responsible for distinguishing different objects [4].

Before the advent of deep learning it was elusive for the computers to prognosticate the visual features which a human can do effortlessly. The prediction of deep learning models depends to a large extent on the colossal scale datasets and thus these dataset should be designated such that it can mimic the human viewing experience that will result in better computational modeling of the human visual system. The outbreak of deep learning models emerged in the ImageNet challenge [5] in 2012, performance of deep learning models has been improving at an unparalleled speed. In Open Images V4, a dataset of 9.2 Million images with unified annotations for image classification, object detection and visual relationship detection is presented [6]. Realistic colossal amounts of datasets is the core in the success of these deep learning models.

Most of the IP network traffic today consists of video content. In 2021 the video traffic was estimated to be 80 percent of the Internet traffic and it is expected to rise in future [28] [29]. With high resolution TV, computer monitors and mobile being available to the general consumer, the demand for high quality images and video including high definition and ultra high definition is steadily increasing and thus increasing the bits to represent these quality images and video. In 2003, the Advanced Video Coding (AVC/H.264) [7] standard was released that was made common for video compression standards for video streaming services. Then High Efficiency Video Coding (HEVC/H.265) [8], the successor of AVC was released in 2013 which improved the compression efficiency of HD and UHD videos with around 50 percent bitrate savings for the same observed quality [9] [10]. Thus efficient compression and coding techniques are needed to be updated. The collaboration groups formed by ITU-T VCEG and ISO/IEC MPEG developed AVC and HEVC . The collaboration group for the development of AVC was called Joint Video Team (JVT) and the group developing HEVC was named Joint Collaboration Team on Video Coding (JCT-VC). In July 2020 Versatile Video Coding Standard (H.266/VVC) [11] [12] [13] was completed by Joint Video Expert Team (JVET) of ITU-T and ISO/IEC. This new ITU recommendation, international standard is a successor to the well-known H.265/HEVC video coding standard with roughly doubled compression efficiency that is 50 percent of the bitrate saving with same subjective quality, but also at the cost of an increased computational complexity [14]. Also various studies [20] on image compression based on deep learning models utilize single element in set of images database $\{X\}$ for training the model and exploits the deep learning features to reconstruct the original image as compressed version $\tilde{x}$ with respect to the original image $x \in X$. In [21], a set of training images $\{X\}$ is used to build an image compression method based on a convolutional autoencoder. The encoder $E : \mathbb{R}^n \mapsto \mathbb{R}^f$ transforms a given image $x \in X$ into a latent representation $z = E(x)$. The decoder $D : \mathbb{R}^f \mapsto \mathbb{R}^n$ reconstructs the original image from the latent representation $\tilde{x} = D(z)$.

To compress an image or video each time the codec needs to perform complex computation. Using a deep learning platform provided with a trained network, the computation for prediction would be less complex and thus will make the compression less computational. But to do so we need a large scale dataset with image and its corresponding compressed image pair. Thus we propose a novel image pair data set $\{X, Y\}$, which have two elements in the set, where the element X represent the image and Y represent its compressed image based on VVC encoder, also Y contains two more elements that is quantization parameter of 5 and 10 compressed images. To enable the next generation state-of-the-art image and video compression algorithms, in this paper a larger diverse array of around 0.1 million and its corresponding compressed image pairs (compressed image as a label), a novel data set is proposed in this paper. To the best of our knowledge, this type of data-set is unique or not present in open source for the research community. The proposed data set is not limited and can also be used for classification of images and other domains.

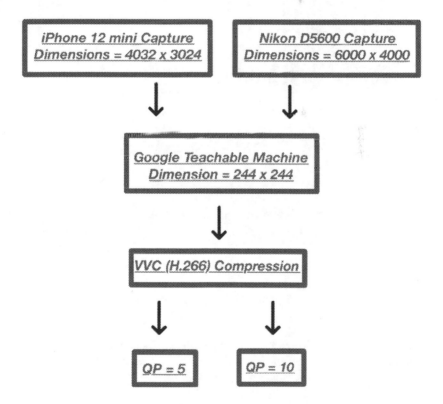

Fig. 22. Data capturing and processing steps

2   Database Capturing and Characteristic

In this section a detailed description of the captured data set is presented. All the data sets are captured using iPhone 12 mini and NIKON D5300 DSLR Camera. Google's Teachable Machine [16] is a web-based resource for training and developing deep learning models for image classification, sound classification, and pose classification. Also large scale data sets can be organized, resized and categorized using Google's Teachable Machine effectively. We used this platform for resizing our captured data-set from 4032×3024 (iPhone 12 mini) , 6000×4000 (NIKON D5300 DSLR Camera) to 224×224 and categorizing the data set that are more appropriate for deep learning training tasks. Figure 22 shows the capturing and organizing the data set captured.

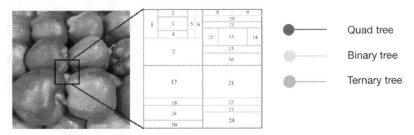

(a) Partitioning of Input image into several frames in VVC

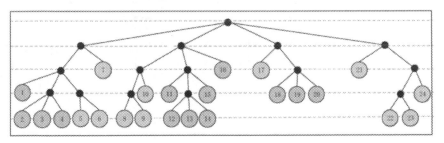

(b) Quad tree node Partitioning Process

Fig. 23. Coding Structure

There is an improved Intra and Inter prediction performance in VVC codec due to introduction of a new inter-prediction mode based on block-based affine transform motion compensation and in loop filter which is not present in the predecessors HEVC and H.264 [12]. In [8] HEVC coding, each frame is divided into small units called coding tree units (CTUs). In VVC (H.266) codec, the concept of CTUs is extended. Later the CTU can measure up to 128×128 pixels and is partitioned with a quad, nested with a multi-type tree diagram (QTMT). The Fig. 23 shows the coding and frame partitioning process used to encode the data set. The input image is divided into 128×128 pixels also called CTU and in Fig. 23a the square shown in apple image is one of these divided pixel. Further partition is done using Quad tree, Binary tree and Ternary tree, the hierarchical partitioning process is shown in Fig. 23. The VVC (H.266) provides the maximum compression, maintaining the same subjective quality as compared to its predecessors [11] [12] [13]. Thus VVC (H.266) codec is chosen to compress the captured data set. One important issue in image and video compression is bit-rate control and in order to achieve target bit rate by adjusting certain coding parameters and one important parameter is quantization parameter (QP) [15]. We have selected two QP settings in VVC to compress the images thus two compressed images of $QP = 5$ and $QP = 10$ are present per captured image. While training a model any one QP compressed image can be chosen to achieve a target quality of compressed image. The random access coding configuration in VVC is used to compress our data set. The other VVC parameters Intra-Period, profile, Group of Pictures (GOP) and frame rate in coding structure are kept to 32, auto, 32 and 60 sec respectively.

Diverse data set has been collected by visiting several parts of the Indian subcontinental region. Various classes of image collection have been shown from Fig. 1 to Fig. 21. From indoor to outdoor, valley to desert, forests, natural scenes, different types of objects etc. has been captured. Our data captured is more classified and diverse so that it can train the weights and biases of deep learning networks effectively and thus precise prediction would be possible. From Figure 24 to Figure 29 shows the image, image compressed with VVC having $QP = 5$ and image compressed with VVC having $QP = 10$ respectively. Note that the images look similar but they are not digitally equal as shown by the Rate distortion curves 30. The features of some of these classes of data set is presented below:

(a) Original Image   (b) Compressed $QP = 5$ (c) Compressed $QP = 10$

Fig. 24. Taj Mahal, a class of Architectural Monuments

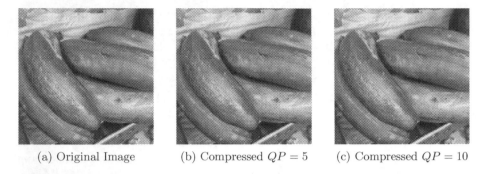

(a) Original Image   (b) Compressed $QP = 5$ (c) Compressed $QP = 10$

Fig. 25. Red Banana, a class of Fruit (Color figure online)

(a) Original Image   (b) Compressed $QP = 5$ (c) Compressed $QP = 10$

Fig. 26. Ocean, a class of Bodies of water

1. **Buildings:** Buildings are the dominant structures in urban environments. Different colors, different heights and different building construction structure scenes are captured. In [17], a study of Building detection from urban SAR images using building characteristics and contextual information is presented. Figure 1 shows randomly selected images from the building category.
2. **Dolls:** Different dolls wearing different color cloths, different looking faces and different posture man made dolls scenes have been captured. Figure 2 shows randomly selected images from the doll category.
3. **Fruits:** Food processing industry in developing nations like India has been growing and thus grading fruits is necessary. Different types of fruits with variation in color, shape and texture have been captured. [18] proposes a study on classification of fruits. Figure 3 shows randomly selected images from the fruits category.
4. **Flowers:** Distinct flowers with variation in color, texture and shape have been captured. Figure 4 shows randomly selected images from the flowers category.
5. **Sky:** In different weather and different time periods of the day and night, the sky scenes are captured. Sky and cloud play an important role in the hydrological cycle and the energy balance of the atmosphere-earth surface

system and in [19], a method of cloud classification is proposed. Figure 5 shows randomly selected images from the Sky category.

6. **Architectural Monuments:** In the development of a region, Architectural style classification [22], of which the purpose is to classify buildings by some algorithms are of great importance. Figure 6 shows randomly selected images from the Architectural Monuments category.

7. **Shadow:** In remotely sensed images, shadows are common features. Clues to the casting object can be obtained using shadows and they can be used for building detection, delineation, and height estimation [23] [24]. In [25] Shadow detection study is presented. Various illumination source shadows and shadows on different surfaces had been captured. Figure 7 shows randomly selected images from Shadow category.

8. **Fence Occlusion:** De-fencing is a challenging task in computer vision. There are various demands where a fence in the foreground is to be removed to get a clear background. [26] shows a study on image de-fencing, segmentation and restoration of occluded fence regions from the images. We have captured different types of background with foreground as fence or occlusion by some array structure. Figure 15 shows randomly selected images from the Fence Occlusion category.

| (a) Original Image | (b) Compressed $QP = 5$ | (c) Compressed $QP = 10$ |

Fig. 27. Pooja function, a class of Doll

| (a) Original Image | (b) Compressed $QP = 5$ | (c) Compressed $QP = 10$ |

Fig. 28. Sky pattern, a class of Sky

(a) Original Image   (b) Compressed $QP = 5$ (c) Compressed $QP = 10$

Fig. 29. Person Shadow a class of Shadow

3   Results and Discussions

Appropriate permissions had been taken while capturing the data sets of some renowned monuments. No harm to the animals has been done while capturing images of animals. We carefully captured the images without harming the environment and flora and fauna of the places we visited. We have collected around 0.1 million of images and we will be still working on capturing different classes of images and will be made public for the research purpose and on demand the data set will be sent via email to the authors for research purposes. Some of the rare images have been captured and one of them is shown in Fig. 31, in the background sun is present but still face is captured clearly, note that no processing is done to the image, this is due to present of cloud in front of the scene and the sun rays reflection from the clouds makes the face illuminated.

Figure 30 shows rate distortion curve for some randomly selected classes having nine images each as shown in Fig. 1 to 21. As QP is increased the bitrate and PSNR decreases as shown in the RD-curve 30. Further we evaluate the quality analysis using HDR-VDP-2 [27]. HDR-VDP-2 is a visual metric that compares a pair of images (a reference and a test image) and predicts, visibility that is the probability that the differences between both images are visible for an average observer and Quality which is the quality degradation with the respect to the reference image, expressed as a mean-opinion-score. The metric prediction Quality scores for Architectural Monument class are summarized in Table 1. We analyzed quality scores considering diagonal display size in 24 and 21 in., display resolution in pixels, and viewing distance of 0.5 m.

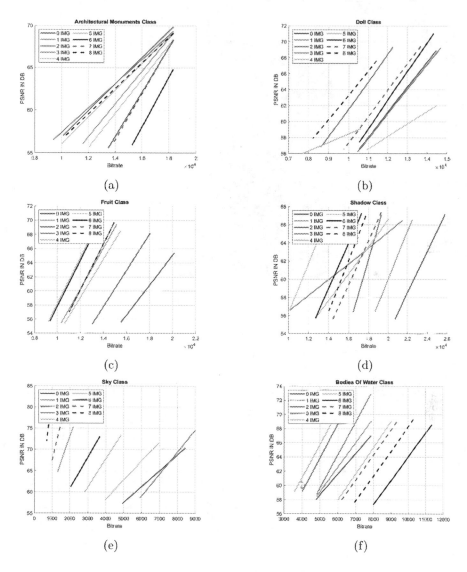

Fig. 30. Rate distortion curves

Fig. 31. Sun light reflected by cloud captured in Cherrapunji

Table 1. Qualitative Analysis for Architectural Monuments

Image	QP=5			QP=10		
Number	BITRATE	HDR-VDP-2 24 (0.5)	HDR-VDP-2 21 (0.5)	BITRATE	HDR-VDP-2 24 (0.5)	HDR-VDP-2 21 (0.5)
0	18331.6800	68.2811	67.3243	13491.8400	68.2900	67.3354
1	16028.1600	65.8416	65.0468	11584.8000	65.8160	65.0223
2	13769.2800	61.3121	60.3269	10107.3600	61.2884	60.2843
3	13404.4800	62.5815	61.7431	9405.1200	62.0765	61.1935
4	14374.0800	65.2482	64.2934	9993.6000	65.2257	64.2589
5	16668.9600	65.0805	63.9580	12039.8400	64.8296	63.6478
6	19769.2800	64.9681	64.1125	15261.1200	65.3574	64.5165
7	18251.5200	66.0829	65.0624	13821.1200	66.0910	65.0713
8	13845.6000	64.7894	63.7492	10190.4000	64.7750	63.7327

4   Conclusion

In this paper a novel image and its compressed version based on VVC encoder has been proposed. Around 0.1 million diverse image data set has been collected and processed for deep learning applications. Further two QP based compressed images are also provided. We explained how the data set is captured and compressed. We hope that the scale, diversity and quality of our data set will foster further research in compression based on deep learning and can also be utilized for the areas of image classification and visual relationship detection, as our data set is well classified and organized.

References

1. Khaligh-Razavi, S.-M., Kriegeskorte, N.: Deep supervised, but not unsupervised, models may explain IT cortical representation. PLoS comput. biol. **10**(11), e1003915 (2014)
2. Güçlü, U., Van Gerven, M.A.J.: Deep neural networks reveal a gradient in the complexity of neural representations across the ventral stream. J. Neurosci. 35(27), 10005–10014 (2015)
3. Martin, S., et al.: Brain-score: which artificial neural network for object recognition is most brain-like?. " BioRxiv407007 (2020)
4. DiCarlo, J.J., Zoccolan, D., Rust, N.C.: How does the brain solve visual object recognition? Neuron **73**(3), 415–434 (2012)
5. Olga, R., et al.: ImageNet large scale visual recognition challenge. Int. J. Comput. Vis. 115(3), 211–252 (2015)
6. Alina, K., et al.: The open images dataset v4. Int. J. Comput. Vis. 128(7) 1956–1981 (2020)
7. Wiegand, T., Sullivan, G.J., Bjontegaard, G., Luthra, A.: Overview of the H.264/AVC video coding standard. IEEE Trans. Circ. Syst. Video Technol. **13**(7), 560–576 (2003). https://doi.org/10.1109/TCSVT.2003.815165
8. Sullivan, G.J., et al.: Overview of the high efficiency video coding (HEVC) standard IEEE Trans. Circuits Syst. Video technol. **22**(12), 1649–1668 (2012)
9. Jens-Rainer, O., et al.: Comparison of the coding efficiency of video coding standards-including high efficiency video coding (HEVC) IEEE Trans. Circuits Syst. Video Technol. **22**(12), 1669–1684 (2012)
10. Thiow Keng, T., et al.: Video quality evaluation methodology and verification testing of HEVC compression performance. IEEE Trans. Circuits Syst. Video Technol. **26**(1), 76–90 (2015)
11. Versatile Video Coding, Standard ISO/IEC 23090–3, ISO/IEC JTC 1 July 2020
12. Benjamin, B., et al.: Overview of the versatile video coding (VVC) standard and its applications. IEEE Trans. Circuits Syst. Video Technol. **31**(10), 3736–3764 (2021)
13. Duolikun, D., et al.: Enhancing VVC with deep learning based multi-frame post-processing (2022) arXiv preprint arXiv:2205.09458
14. Bin, Z., et al.: A software decoder implementation for H. 266/VVC video coding standard (2020) arXiv preprint arXiv:2012.02832
15. Zhenyu, W., et al.: Adaptive initial quantization parameter determination for H. 264/AVC video transcoding. IEEE transactions on broadcasting **58**(2), 277–284 (2021)
16. https://teachablemachine.withgoogle.com/
17. Zhao, L., Zhou, X., Kuang, G.: Building detection from urban SAR image using building characteristics and contextual information. EURASIP Journal on Advances in Signal Processing **2013**(1), 1–16 (2013)
18. Bairwa, D., Sharma, G.: Classification of Fruits Based on Shape, Color and Texture using Image Processing Techniques. Int. J. Eng. Res. **6**, 110–114 (2017)
19. Qingyong, L., et al.: From pixels to patches: a cloud classification method based on a bag of micro-structures. Atmos. Meas. Tech. 9(2), 753–764 (2016)
20. Yasin, H.M., Abdulazeez, A.M.: Image compression based on deep learning: A Review. Asian J. Res. Comput. Sci., 62–76 (2021)
21. Vito Walter, A., et al.: Deep learning-based adaptive image compression system for a real-world scenario. In: 2020 IEEE Conference on Evolving and Adaptive Intelligent Systems (EAIS). IEEE, p. 1–8 (2020)

22. Peipei, Z., et al.: Architectural style classification based on feature extraction module. IEEE Access 6, 52598–52606 (2018)
23. Liow, Y.-T., Pavlidis, T.: Use of shadows for extracting buildings in aerial images. Comput. Vis. Graph. Image Process. **49**(2), 242–277 (1990)
24. Arévalo, V., González, J., Ambrosio, G.: Shadow detection in colour high-resolution satellite images. Int. J. Remote Sens. **29**(7), 1945–1963 (2008)
25. Liu, J., Fang, T., Li, D.: Shadow detection in remotely sensed images based on self-adaptive feature selection. IEEE Trans. Geosci. Remote Sens. **49**(12), 5092–5103 (2011)
26. Varalakshmamma, M., Venkateswarlu, T.: Detection and restoration of image from multi-color fence occlusions. Pattern Recogn. Image Anal. **29**(3), 546–558 (2019)
27. Rafał, M., et al.: HDR-VDP-2: a calibrated visual metric for visibility and quality predictions in all luminance conditions. ACM Trans. Graph. (TOG) 30(4), 1–14 (2011)
28. Cisco Systems. Cisco Visual Networking Index: Forecast and Trends, 2017–2022, Cisco Systems White Paper (2018). http://web.archive.org/web/20181213105003/https://www.cisco.com/c/en/us/solutions/collateral/service-provider/visual-networking-index-vni/white-paper-c11-741490.pdf
29. Cisco Systems. Cisco Annual Internet Report, (2018–2023), (2020). Cisco Systems White Paper. http://web.archive.org/web/20200310054239/https://www.cisco.com/c/en/us/solutions/collateral/executive-perspectives/annual-internet-report/white-paper-c11-741490.html

FAV-Net: A Simple Single-Shot Self-attention Based ForeArm-Vein Biometric

Shitala Prasad[1]([✉])(iD), Chaoying Tang[2], Yufeng Zhang[2], and Biao Wang[2]

[1] Institute for Infocomm Research, A*STAR, Singapore, Singapore
shitala@ieee.org
[2] College of Automation Engineering, Nanjing University of Aeronautics and Astronautics, Nanjing, China
{cytang,wangbiao}@nuaa.edu.cn

Abstract. One of the most challenging tasks in deep feature representation is the amount of data required for training. The fields like forearm-vein biometric, data collection is too difficult plus are too time-consuming. Thus, we proposed a simple yet powerful data augmentation based self-attention method for a biometric system that involves only a single image per subject for feature learning. We call it the FAV-Net (ForeArm-Vein Network). A strong data augmentation method is proposed to extract vascular patterns from the NIR forearm image. Extensive experiments are performed on NTU forearm NIR image database that shows our proposed method can significantly outperform the state-of-the-art methods and is consistent with class incremental learning.

Keywords: ArcFace · Single-Shot Biometrics · Multi-scale · Forearm-Vein

1 Introduction

Under biometrics, there are several biological key features in the human body that can be used for a person's identification, verification and/or authentication. Features such as forearm [2,6], palmprint [4,27], face [48], finger [26], facial emotion [30], ECG, EEG and others [45] are commonly used in biometric systems. We can broadly categorized these biometrics under physiological traits (face, fingerprint, vein, iris and bio-geometries) and behavioural traits (gait, voice, handwritten and brain-psychological) [14,27]. Among these biometrics, the face is the most explored human part for identification/verification. Several face recognition algorithms, including both traditional image processing (IP) and deep convolutional neural network (CNN), are proposed to boost the biometrics performance. For this, authors have proposed many new architectures, new feature space or new loss functions to deal with inter and intra-class similarities [7]. But in the current situation of COVID-19[1], the existing face recognition algorithms show downfall of 5% to 50% due to the use of mask which is now an essential measure in many countries

---

[1] [online] https://www.who.int/emergencies/diseases/novel-coronavirus-2019.

D. Gupta et al. (Eds.): CVIP 2022, CCIS 1777, pp. 443–457, 2023.
https://doi.org/10.1007/978-3-031-31417-9_34

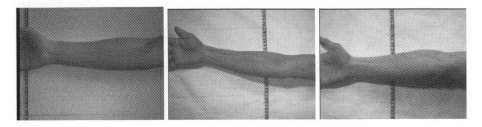

Fig. 1. IR samples of NTU forearm NIR image database focusing vein patterns of subjects 1, 251 and 327, respectively.

to stop/control the spread of virus, as reported by NIST[2]. Thus, mask face detection and recognition has become the hot spot in the past few months [20,28]. Since collecting and annotating faces with a variety of masks is a challenging job, authors have come-up with several synthetic masked face datasets to deal with it [20,28]. However, the gap between a synthetic and a real mask dataset actually limits the capability of existing mask face recognition algorithms in real-world application [18,20]. This drawback piloted several protests against the government in many countries during these COVID-19 pandemic[3], as the faces cannot be recognized.

Consequently, other biological characteristics are exponentially inspected to be potentially used for identification and verification in these pandemic and riot situations. To address these tough biometric problems, we focus on vein pattern based biometric systems for our research. The blood vessels between skin and muscle gaggle unique patterns for a person's identity. Hence, vein recognition is a biometric method which utilizes the vein pattern recognition techniques on blood vessel images of human's visible biological parts. Vascular patterns are unique immunity to be forged and it does not require any contact during registration and authentication [6]. As an observation, it was found that even identical twins who have the same DNA sequence have different vein patterns [17] and that is one of the motivations of this research. The current vein recognition system is based on high quality infrared and laser techniques to clearly capture the patterns from the area where skins are thin; like palms, writs and figures [1,8,15]. Hand, wrist, palm and finger vein recognition systems are proposed by many computer vision (CV) researchers but they all are dependent on high quality near infrared (NIR) images that are captured using high-end NIR cameras in a controlled environment. This is due to the weak penetration capability of visible light in skin compared to NIR. Tang *et al.* proposed optical skin models to uncover the hidden blood patterns from coloured images [39]. They introduced a database of 490 forearms and 460 thighs, which collected a total of 3800 images. They extended their models on various parts of the human body. Parts like hand, arm, chest, breast and abdomen images of men,

---

women and children are recorded in indoor and outdoor environments and are trained for vein pattern extraction for biometrics objectives.

In this COVID-19 pandemic, the face and contact-based identification/ verification are narrowed down. Thus, motivated by [39], in this paper we focus on the forearm-vein based biometrics. The advantage of vein pattern is that it's registrant to forgery, as the patterns are really hidden within the individuals but can be extracted easily at any time. Conversely, it's difficult to acquire images of body parts with thin skin layers to obtain clear vein patterns. Tang *et al.* [39] used image processing (IP) methods such as Gabor features, line enhancement and corner detection successfully to extract the vein patterns from the coloured and NIR (near infrared) images. They achieved a matching performance of vascular extraction from RGB to NIR. In our paper, we inherit such a powerful image enhancement concept as our major data augmentation methods to train the proposed single-shot forearm-vein based deep biometrics, we call it ForeArm-Vein Network (FAV-Net). In this model, we used a single forearm NIR image to learn vascular patterns for the recognition task. For this, we compute Gabor energy and Gabor orient of forearm-vein image along with the forearm boundary and vein lines per subject. Further, the database and experimental settings are detailed in Sect. 4. Thus, the major contributions of this paper are three-fold:

- We proposed a novel single-shot self-attention based deep model for forearm-vein biometrics, which is first of its kind as per our knowledge that uses only one forearm-vein image per subject for recognition.
- By introducing strong data augmentation in deep biometrics we achieved a high accuracy. This approach is further explored and applied on different state-of-the-art (SOTA) CNN backbones and appreciably our approach significantly lifts the baseline performance.
- Extensive experiments are performed on NTU forearm near-infrared image database containing NIR images of 250 subjects ageing from 13 to 69, demonstrating that our method significantly out-performs the SOTA methods by just using a single forearm-vein image per subject. We also tested the claim on other biometric databases such as SDUMLA-finger vein.

Rest of the paper is layered as follows. Section 2 discusses a few related works followed by the proposed methodology in Sect. 3. In Sect. 4, we present experimental results and perform various ablation studies to support our claims. Lastly, Sect. 5 concludes the paper and tail the future objectives.

2   Related Works

Basically vascular or vein pattern based biometrics deals with patterns formed by the haemoglobin in blood which flows inside the human body. Thus, we call these vascular pattern based identification systems as an internal biometric trait. Since these patterns are not visible by naked eyes and are not able to be captured by simple cameras, we use a dedicated designed capturing device to sample such data. The haemoglobin has a higher light absorption coefficient within the NIR spectrum than the surrounding tissue. Hence, they can be rendered and visible as dark lines in the captured images, see Fig. 1. The most common and considered body parts for biometrics include finger [32], hand [41], wrist [25] and forearm [6,39]. In the following subsections, we will aim on vascular recognition of vein patterns inside the human forearm as it is the least explored biometrics and is commonly exposed. We sub-categorized the section in vein-based biometrics using traditional and CNN methods. We also briefly explained the concept behind the single shot self-attention based biometrics. Since CNN is a data greedy method, we will discuss the role of data augmentation in the biometric field in the next Section.

2.1 Vein-Based Traditional Biometrics

Simon-Zorita et al. [33] evaluated an automatic minutiae-based fingerprint verification system on the MCYT Fingerprint Database using traditional methods. In these methods, the effects of a controlled image acquisition for fingerprint matching involves several methods to enhance the quality of imprints and results have been investigated in [29]. On contrary, Stewart et al. considered rugged environmental conditions, especially cold weather, to test the performance of fingerprint recognition technology [36]. Han and Lee [10] used Gabor filter to compute palm-vein based recognition system on 207 identities. On the other hand, Wu et al. used a directional filter bank to extract the palm vein pattern and employed minimum directional code (MDC) to encode the line-based vein features in a binary code [42]. R.S. Choras proposed a biometric system based on forearm-vein patterns using basic IP methods [6] on their own database. Similarly, Olegs et al. used human wrist vascular patterns for recognition in which they involved a fast cross-correlation approach [24]. The major challenge in such traditional methods are feature descriptor design and image enhancement approach.

2.2 Vein-Based CNN Biometrics

In deep learning (DL) era, CNN is the most actively used CV techniques for biometrics and is especially popular in face identification and recognition where they reach up to 99.83% accuracy for LFW database [7]. Liu et al. [21] used VGG-like CNN model with two fully connected layers for finger-vein recognition on SDUMLA-FV database [44]. They achieved 99.53% for 198 identities with total 2970 NIR images. Yang et al. proposed a binary decision diagram based finger-vein biometric using a deep model where they used finger vein images from six fingers of a person [43]. Recently, Kuzu et al. [16] proposed a new loss function for better understanding CNN-based vascular patterns of finger, palm and hand images. They tested their approach on different publicly available finger-vein databases and have achieved 0.02% of equal error rate (EER) on the SDUMLA database. Zhong et al. proposed an end-to-end deep hashing based palm-vein network (DHPN) with a fixed length binary code and achieved 0.0222% EER on PolyU database [47]. Lastly, Sun et al. [37] introduced an improved CNN for

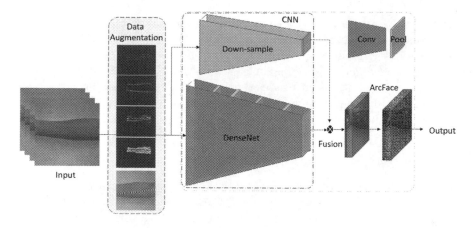

Fig. 2. The overview pipeline of the proposed FAV-Net.

palm-vein recognition and acquired 99.57% accuracy on the PolyU database. For further study, a detailed survey on vein-based biometric systems can be found in [11,15].

2.3   Few-Shot Biometrics

DL algorithms require a huge amount of data in order to successfully learn the patterns to discriminate between the inter-classes. As an outcome, most of the techniques usually lack the ability of learning from a less training database. Thus, a natural solution to attenuate this insufficient training data is to augment the existing samples per class [35]. For data augmentation, researchers have invoked invariant transformation in feature space [5,19,23,40].

2.4   Self-attention Biometrics

Self-attention mechanism is where the mapping function is learned in an unsupervised manner by looking beyond what is immediately perceivable and pays special attention to the spectral characteristics of the pixel itself. In [46], the author proposed a self-attention for gait pattern recognition which significantly performs better than the baseline method and achieves SOTA performance. We refer to our method as an unsupervised self-attention based forearm-vein feature extractor which boost-up the representation learning for biometrics recognition.

3   Proposed Approach

In this section, we discuss details of the proposed single-shot self-attention based forearm-vein biometrics. In particular, we first discuss the base network pipeline used in this paper. Then we introduced the proposed data augmentation methods for single-shot FAV-Net. Next, we detailed the self-attention mechanism followed by the loss function used in FAV-Net training. For better understanding, the overall work flow is shown in Fig. 2. The given input NIR image, I, is first synthesized to another feature domain using data augmentation generators. Then we fuse it with self-attention to generate a blend of original information with feature maps. In order to minimize the loss, we incorporated ArcFace [7]. We detail these modules in the next few sub-sections.

3.1   Base Network

Our method is based upon DenseNet [13] because of its outperforming results in image classification. We train a DenseNet-121 as the backbone network to extract the key features of forearm-vein by influencing it with the original information, as seen in Fig. 2. That is to say, the final output of DenseNet-121 is fused with the down-sampled version of I, which in our case is obtained by a 1×1 convolutional layer $\mathcal{F}(I)$ followed by *BatchNorm* and *ReLu* layers. To match the requirement of DenseNet-121, the final layer output $\mathcal{F}_{dense}(I)$ is kept the same, even after self-attention fusion. This obtains a better vascular pattern representation, because we also learn the down-sampling operation of I for self-attention fusion and not just the *maxpool*. This makes $\mathcal{F}(I)$ stronger and defensible. Note, the proposed network does not involve any fully connected layers and we replayed all by a simple convolutional layer with Xavier initializer [9].

3.2   Data Augmentation

As we know, DL methods are data starving and in CV there are many fields where data acquisition is a big challenge. Basically, data augmentation (DA) in DL is a way to up-samples the data volume by introducing different variations on the existing data or by creating synthetic data from the existing methods like GAN. But GAN is a computationally expensive method and may not be very suitable for vein patterns where thin lines are the critical features. In deep model learning, data augmentation acts as a regularizer and assists to reduce overfitting during the training phase. Thus, in this paper we used four different data augmentation methods to multiply the forearm-vein image database that can boost the network's learning capability. These augmentations are Gabor energy, orient, line and boundary of the forearm-vein NIR image, see Fig. 3.

The frequency and orientation representation of Gabor filters are quite similar to human visual system and are expressively appropriate for texture discrimination. Thus, a set of 16 different Gabor filters of different orientations and scales, covering all the texture details of forearm-veins present in the NIR image are used. Considering the blood vessel as the dark ridge, we only considered the real part of Gabor filters. Next, to deal with the brightness variation, for which we remove the direct current component of Gabor and normalize them to obtain an accurate estimation of the local orientation. Let's say $\mathcal{G}$ denotes the Gabor filter, then it can be defined as:

$$\mathcal{G}_{\lambda,\theta,\omega,\sigma,\rho}(x,y) = \exp(-\frac{x^2 + (\rho y)^2}{2\sigma^2} \cos(2\theta\frac{x'}{\lambda} + \omega)) \tag{1}$$

where, λ is the wavelength of cosine factor of Gabor filter, θ is the orientation of normal to parallel stripes of Gabor, ω is the phase-off of cosine factor in Gabor function, ρ is the spatial aspect ratio of Gabor function that specifies the ellipticity of the support and σ is the standard deviation of Gaussian factor of Gabor function. In Eq. 1, (x, y) are the coordinates of I and (x', y') are defined as:

$$x' = x\cos(\theta) + y\sin(\theta) \ and \ y' = -x\sin(\theta) + y\cos(\theta) \tag{2}$$

To capture the local information and the orientation of vascular patterns, $\mathcal{G}$ is further processed using the details as discussed in [39]. The data augmentation results are shown in Fig. 3, corresponding to original NIR images shown in Fig. 1. For these images, we used masks to obtain the ROIs, as shown in Fig. 4.

Table 1. Database summarization with the proposed DA approaches.

Database	#Session	Train	Test	#Subjects	#Images	Forearm	w/ DA
NTU Forearm NIR image	2	S1	S2	250	500	Right	×
	2	S1	S2	250	2500	Right	✓
Database	**#Session**	**#/class**	**#/class**	**#Subjects**	**#Images**	**Fingers**	**w/ DA**
SDUMLA-FV [44]	1	3 each	3 each	106	0816	Left&Right	×

3.3 Self-attention Mechanism

To further benefit from our learned forearm-vein feature maps, we implement a simple yet productive self-attention (SA) mechanism within the network. Once we obtain the forearm-vein feature map $\mathcal{F}_{dense}$, we down-sample I by a factor of 2^5 to reduce the dimension in respect to it to the match dense output of the original feature map. To attenuate the response of spatial information, we multiply every channel of the feature map $\mathcal{F}_{dense}(I)$ with our original info-map $\mathcal{F}(I)$. Thus, reducing the probability of false positives in unconnected regions within I. That is, $\mathcal{F}_{fuse}$ is defined as Eq. 3:

$$\mathcal{F}_{fuse}(I) = \mathcal{F}(I) \bigotimes \mathcal{F}_{dense}(I) \tag{3}$$

where, $\mathcal{F}$ and $\mathcal{F}_{dense}$ have the same dimension $\rightarrow \mathbb{R}^d$ and $\bigotimes$ fusion operation. This is a very straightforward yet powerful approach to boost-up the network learning.

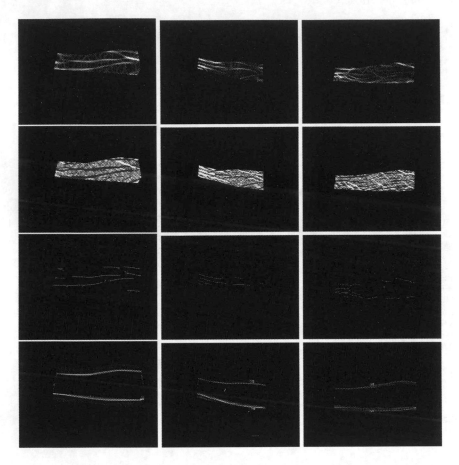

Fig. 3. Data augmentation outcome for images in Fig. 1, respective to subjects 1, 251 and 327 (column-wise). Row-wise: Gabor energy, Gabor orientation, line and boundary.

Fig. 4. Forearm masks used for pre-processing.

3.4   Loss Function and Training Strategy

Inspired by ArcFace [7], we adopted it for our forearm-vein recognition too. ArcFace is an additive angular margin loss designed on the *softmax* loss. Arc-Face loss actually adds an additive angular margin penalty m between I_i and weight W_{y_i} based on the feature and weight normalization. This simultaneously enhances the intra-class compactness and inter-class discrepancy [7].

$$\mathcal{L} = -\frac{1}{N} \sum_{i=1}^{N} \log \frac{e^{s(cos(\theta_{y_i}+m))}}{e^{s(cos(\theta_{y_i}+m))} + \sum_{j=1,j\neq y_i}^{n} e^{cos(\theta_j)}} \tag{4}$$

where N is the number of data samples in database $\mathcal{D}$ and y_i is the output corresponding to i-th sample. For additional elaboration, refer to ArcFace by Deng *et al.* [7]. Secondly, we involved cross-entropy loss for forearm-vein recognition.

After defining all losses, the network is trained in an end-to-end fashion. All the new layers, in FAV-Net, are initialized with Xavier random initializer [9]. The network is pre-trained on LFW face database and then tuned on NTU forearm NIR image database [39].

3.5   Implementation Details

All the experiments were conducted in PyTorch[4] and used a standard Adam optimizer with learning rate $\Lambda = 0.001$, batch size, $b = 32$ and weight decay $w = 0.0005$. The input image size is set to 256 for all the experiments. FAV-Net network is trained for 20 epochs (as the dataset is too small) to learn forearm-vein patterns, see the details in next Section. Note, we performed each experiment three times and then were averaged in the next Section.

Table 2. Accuracy comparison for forearm-vein recognition.

Methods	Accuracy (%)
LM-ICP [39]	10.8
Original-CPD [39]	62.4
Preliminary matching [39]	76.0
Tang *et al.* [39]	80.0
FAV-Net (*our*)	**94.1**

4   Experiments and Results

In this section, we evaluated the proposed FAV-Net on NTU forearm NIR image database for recognition and then performed rigorous experiments to validate our hypothesis on different state-of-the-art networks.

---

[4] [online] https://pytorch.org/.

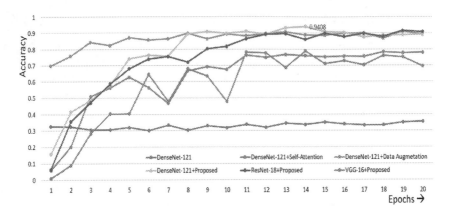

Fig. 5. FAV-Net testing accuracy over training epochs.

Table 3. Accuracy comparison for forearm-vein recognition with different backbones.

Backbones	Accuracy (%)	Size (MB)
ResNet-18 [12]	<u>91.8</u>	43
ResNet-34 [12]	82.6	82
VGG-16 [34]	78.9	81
MNASNet [38]	26.72	92
MobileNet_v2 [31]	88.0	89
ShuffelNet_v2 [22]	42.2	69
FAV-Net (*our*)	**94.1**	91

Table 4. Ablation study on FAV-Net with DenseNet-121 as the backbone.

Settings	Data Augmentation	Self-attention	Accuracy (%)
Train: S1, Test: S2	×	×	35.4
	✓	×	78.3
	×	✓	92.7
	✓	✓	**94.1**
Train: S2, Test: S1	✓	✓	**94.2**

4.1   Database

The database used in this paper is NTU forearm NIR image database [39]. It consists of 500 NIR forearm images for 250 subjects, two sessions per subject. The subjects were chosen from eight different regions and ethnicities to include

Table 5. Accuracy comparison for forearm-vein recognition.

Methods	Accuracy (%)
FAV-Net + *softmax*	80.2
FAV-Net + ArcFace	**94.1**

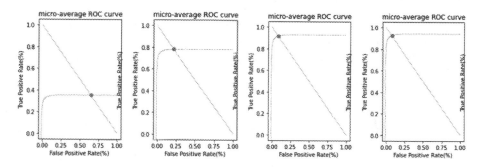

Fig. 6. Micro ROC curve for FAV-Net with DenseNet-121: (a) baseline, (b) *w/* DA and *w/o* SA, (c) *w/o* DA and *w/* SA and (d) *w/* DA and *w/* SA.

different skin tones. The subjects in this database range from 13 years to 69 years old. The images were taken with a JAI-ADC080CL near infrared camera, with at least minimum distance of two meters between the forearm and the lens. Each person in this database gives two shots with an average interval of two weeks. Thus, in this paper we used session one (S1) for training and session two (S2) for testing. The database is further summarized in Table 1. To enhance the vein patterns and suppress noise, the mask processing and the contrast limited adaptive histogram equalization (CLAHE) are utilized. Otsu's methods are adopted for binarization of the vein patterns. Finally, a series of morphological open and close operations followed by skeletonization are applied to obtain the forearm-vein images after following the operations from [39].

4.2   Results

As discussed in previous sections, we used S1 for training and S2 for testing our proposed network and are compared with the state-of-the-art methods. In Table 2, a detailed comparison on NTU forearm NIR image database is shown. It is observed that the proposed FAV-Net outperforms compared to state-of-the-art methods by a margin of 14.1% from the base paper method [39]. The methods reported in [39], are all traditional image processing based and is the only existing work on this database. Deep models do perform best compared to the traditional approaches (Table 2) but in this paper, we showed that even a single forearm-vein NIR image together with strong data augmentation and self-attention mechanism can significantly outperform the state-of-the-art methods.

We further explore the proposed method on different backbone networks to validate the robustness of hypothesis for forearm-vein recognition. Table 3 shows a comprehensive analysis of proposed approaches on different state-of-the-art backbones, pre-trained on LFW face database. In this table, we observe that DenseNet-121 performs the best after ResNet-18 by 2.3%. The table also concludes that the DenseNet network can obtain better forearm-vein representations in contrast with VGG-16, ResNet, MobileNet, ShuffelNet and MNASNet. The model size after incorporating self-attention and ArcFace loss is also differentiated in Table 3. Figure 5 shows the accuracy curve over epochs during training.

4.3 Ablation Study

To pool better understanding of the proposed FAV-Net, we conduct capacious ablation experiments to examine the role of data augmentation and self-attention in forearm-vein recognition. As illustrated in Table 4, we evaluate the performance of several different settings on the NTU forearm NIR image database to focus on the observations of accuracy of different training-testing sets. By applying the DenseNet-121 as the backbone, we set up a strong baseline (94.1%), which is significantly better than DenseNet-121 without self-attention (78.3%). FAV-Net performance drops drastically when both data augmentation and self-attention mechanism are off. The fall reached 35.4%.

Adding self-attention in DenseNet, the forearm-vein representation is significantly improved to discriminate the classes, as the results shown in Table 4. The performance is marginally lowered when training and testing sets are revered, which is very obvious. But still the proposed method works very well. The performance with training-testing S1-S2 is 94.1% while S2-S1 results in 94.2%. We also plot the micro-ROC curve (Fig. 6) for different methods *with* and *without* data augmentation and self-attention, as mentioned in Table 4.

4.4 Loss Functions

Lastly, we evaluated the recognition performance with and without ArcFace loss function. To understand the role of ArcFace, we removed it from FAV-Net and used the same setting to compute the performance and found that it actually immune the network with strong feature representation. Table 5 shows a complete comparison. Noticeably, the improvement with ArcFace is 14.1%, which is significantly a big difference.

4.5 Other Applications

Other than NTU forearm NIR image database, we also tested the proposed network on finger-vein database to compare the domain robustness. We trained and tested the SDUMLA-FV database with similar settings and achieved 99.98% accuracy. The train and test split for this database are shown in Table 1(last row), where 6 fingers are captured per person out of which 3 are used for training.

Compared to Semi-PFVN [3], the proposed method outperforms by 3.37%. Thus, the proposed approach can also be scaled to other vein-based biometrics and significantly improves the results.

5   Conclusion and Future Work

In this paper, we propose the first single-shot self-attention based deep learning model for forearm-vein recognition, called FAV-Net. We demonstrated that our method consistently outperforms the state-of-the-art through comprehensive experiments conducted on NTU forearm NIR image database. Since the database is too small, only one image per subject for training, the proposed approach actually does a great justification to this new trending biometric field. In future work, we can further optimize the computation cost and improve the overall performance.

Acknowledgements. Authors would like to thank the Google Colab team for providing a research platform to test our concepts.

References

1. Aberni, Y., Boubchir, L., Daachi, B.: Palm vein recognition based on competitive coding scheme using multi-scale local binary pattern with ant colony optimization. PRL **136**, 101–110 (2020)
2. Alpar, Orcan, Krejcar, Ondrej: Thermal imaging for localization of anterior forearm subcutaneous veins. In: Rojas, Ignacio, Ortuño, Francisco (eds.) IWBBIO 2018. LNCS, vol. 10814, pp. 243–254. Springer, Cham (2018). https://doi.org/10.1007/978-3-319-78759-6_23
3. Chai, T., Li, J., Prasad, S., Lu, Q., Zhang, Z.: Shape-driven lightweight CNN for finger-vein biometrics. J. Inf. Secur. Appl. **67**, 103211 (2022). https://doi.org/10.1016/j.jisa.2022.103211. https://www.sciencedirect.com/science/article/pii/S2214212622000886
4. Chai, T., Prasad, S., Wang, S.: Boosting palmprint identification with gender information using deepnet. FGCS **99**, 41–53 (2019)
5. Chen, Z., Fu, Y., Zhang, Y., Jiang, Y.G., Xue, X., Sigal, L.: Multi-level semantic feature augmentation for one-shot learning. IEEE TIP **28**(9), 4594–4605 (2019)
6. Choras, R.S.: Personal identification using forearm vein patterns. In: IWOB, pp. 1–5. IEEE (2017)
7. Deng, J., Guo, J., Xue, N., Zafeiriou, S.: ArcFace: additive angular margin loss for deep face recognition. In: CVPR, pp. 4690–4699 (2019)
8. Garcia-Martin, R., Sanchez-Reillo, R.: Vein biometric recognition on a smartphone. IEEE Access **8**, 104801–104813 (2020)
9. Glorot, X., Bengio, Y.: Understanding the difficulty of training deep feedforward neural networks. In: ICAIS, pp. 249–256. JMLR Workshop and Conference Proceedings (2010)
10. Han, W.Y., Lee, J.C.: Palm vein recognition using adaptive Gabor filter. Expert Syst. Appl. **39**(18), 13225–13234 (2012)
11. Hassan, B., Izquierdo, E., Piatrik, T.: Soft biometrics: a survey. In: MTAP, pp. 1–44 (2021)

12. He, K., Zhang, X., Ren, S., Sun, J.: Deep residual learning for image recognition. In: CVPR, pp. 770–778 (2016)
13. Huang, G., Liu, Z., Van Der Maaten, L., Weinberger, K.Q.: Densely connected convolutional networks. In: CVPR, pp. 4700–4708 (2017)
14. Jain, A.K., Flynn, P., Ross, A.A.: Handbook of biometrics. Springer Science & Business Media (2007). https://doi.org/10.1007/978-0-387-71041-9
15. Kuzu, R.S., Piciucco, E., Maiorana, E., Campisi, P.: On-the-fly finger-vein-based biometric recognition using deep neural networks. IEEE TIFS **15**, 2641–2654 (2020)
16. Kuzu, R.S., Maiorana, E., Campisi, P.: Loss functions for CNN-based biometric vein recognition. In: EUSIPCO, pp. 750–754. IEEE (2020)
17. Ladoux, Pierre-Olivier., Rosenberger, Christophe, Dorizzi, Bernadette: Palm vein verification system based on SIFT matching. In: Tistarelli, Massimo, Nixon, Mark S.. (eds.) ICB 2009. LNCS, vol. 5558, pp. 1290–1298. Springer, Heidelberg (2009). https://doi.org/10.1007/978-3-642-01793-3_130
18. Lane, L.: NIST finds flaws in facial checks on people with COVID masks. Biometric Technology Today (2020)
19. Leghari, M., Memon, S., Dhomeja, L.D., Jalbani, A.H., et al.: Analyzing the effects of data augmentation on single and multimodal biometrics. Mehran Univ. Res. J. Eng. Technol. **39**(3), 647 (2020)
20. Li, Y., Guo, K., Lu, Y., Liu, L.: Cropping and attention based approach for masked face recognition. Appl. Intell. **51**(5), 3012–3025 (2021). https://doi.org/10.1007/s10489-020-02100-9
21. Liu, W., Li, W., Sun, L., Zhang, L., Chen, P.: Finger vein recognition based on deep learning. In: ICIEA, pp. 205–210. IEEE (2017)
22. Ma, Ningning, Zhang, Xiangyu, Zheng, Hai-Tao., Sun, Jian: ShuffleNet V2: practical guidelines for efficient CNN architecture design. In: Ferrari, Vittorio, Hebert, Martial, Sminchisescu, Cristian, Weiss, Yair (eds.) Computer Vision – ECCV 2018. LNCS, vol. 11218, pp. 122–138. Springer, Cham (2018). https://doi.org/10.1007/978-3-030-01264-9_8
23. Mekruksavanich, Sakorn, Jitpattanakul, Anuchit: Convolutional neural network and data augmentation for behavioral-based biometric user identification. In: Tuba, Milan, Akashe, Shyam, Joshi, Amit (eds.) ICT Systems and Sustainability. AISC, vol. 1270, pp. 753–761. Springer, Singapore (2021). https://doi.org/10.1007/978-981-15-8289-9_72
24. Nikisins, O., Eglitis, T., Anjos, A., Marcel, S.: Fast cross-correlation based wrist vein recognition algorithm with rotation and translation compensation. In: IWB, pp. 1–7. IEEE (2018)
25. Pascual, J.E.S., Uriarte-Antonio, J., Sanchez-Reillo, R., Lorenz, M.G.: Capturing hand or wrist vein images for biometric authentication using low-cost devices. In: CIIHMSP, pp. 318–322. IEEE (2010)
26. Peng, C., Chen, M., Jiang, X.: Under-display ultrasonic fingerprint recognition with finger vessel imaging. IEEE Sensors J. **21**, 7412–7419 (2021)
27. Prasad, S., Chai, T.: Palmprint for individual's personality behavior analysis. Comput. J. **65**(2), 355–370 (2022)
28. Prasad, S., Li, Y., Lin, D., Sheng, D.: maskedFaceNet: a progressive semi-supervised masked face detector. In: WACV, pp. 3389–3398 (2021)
29. Ratha, N.K., Bolle, R.M.: Effect of controlled image acquisition on fingerprint matching. In: ICPR, vol. 2, pp. 1659–1661. IEEE (1998)
30. Saeed, U.: Facial micro-expressions as a soft biometric for person recognition. PRL **143**, 95–103 (2021)

31. Sandler, M., Howard, A., Zhu, M., Zhmoginov, A., Chen, L.C.: MobileNetV2: Inverted residuals and linear bottlenecks. In: CVPR, pp. 4510–4520 (2018)
32. Shaheed, K., Liu, H., Yang, G., Qureshi, I., Gou, J., Yin, Y.: A systematic review of finger vein recognition techniques. Information $9(9)$, 213 (2018)
33. Simon-Zorita, D., Ortega-Garcia, J., Fierrez-Aguilar, J., Gonzalez-Rodriguez, J.: Image quality and position variability assessment in minutiae-based fingerprint verification. VISP $150(6)$, 402–408 (2003)
34. Simonyan, K., Zisserman, A.: Very deep convolutional networks for large-scale image recognition. arXiv preprint arXiv:1409.1556 (2014)
35. Solano, J., Tengana, L., Castelblanco, A., Rivera, E., Lopez, C., Ochoa, M.: A few-shot practical behavioral biometrics model for login authentication in web applications. In: NDSS Workshop on MADWeb (2020)
36. Stewart, R.F., Estevao, M., Adler, A.: Fingerprint recognition performance in rugged outdoors and cold weather conditions. In: ICB: Theory, Applications, and Systems, pp. 1–6. IEEE (2009)
37. Sun, B., Tao, X., Luo, X., et al.: Research on palm vein recognition algorithm based on improved convolutional neural network. In: CACS, pp. 1–6. IEEE (2020)
38. Tan, M., et al.: MnasNet: platform-aware neural architecture search for mobile. In: CVPR, pp. 2820–2828 (2019)
39. Tang, C., Zhang, H., Kong, A.W.K.: Using multiple models to uncover blood vessel patterns in color images for forensic analysis. Inf. Fusion 32, 26–39 (2016)
40. Wang, H., Gu, J., Wang, S.: An effective intrusion detection framework based on SVM with feature augmentation. KBS 136, 130–139 (2017)
41. Wang, J., Wang, G.: Quality-specific hand vein recognition system. IEEE TIFS $12(11)$, 2599–2610 (2017)
42. Wu, K.S., Lee, J.C., Lo, T.M., Chang, K.C., Chang, C.P.: A secure palm vein recognition system. J. Syst. Softw. $86(11)$, 2870–2876 (2013)
43. Yang, W., Wang, S., Hu, J., Zheng, G., Yang, J., Valli, C.: Securing deep learning based edge finger vein biometrics with binary decision diagram. IEEE TII $15(7)$, 4244–4253 (2019)
44. Yin, Yilong, Liu, Lili, Sun, Xiwei: SDUMLA-HMT: a multimodal biometric database. In: Sun, Zhenan, Lai, Jianhuang, Chen, Xilin, Tan, Tieniu (eds.) CCBR 2011. LNCS, vol. 7098, pp. 260–268. Springer, Heidelberg (2011). https://doi.org/10.1007/978-3-642-25449-9_33
45. Zanlorensi, L.A., Proença, H., Menotti, D.: Unconstrained periocular recognition: Using generative deep learning frameworks for attribute normalization. In: ICIP, pp. 1361–1365. IEEE (2020)
46. Zhang, Y., Qin, J., Lv, L., Wang, Z.: Based on Siamese network with self-attention model for gait recognition. In: ICMA, pp. 1118–1122. IEEE (2020)
47. Zhong, Dexing, Liu, Shuming, Wang, Wenting, Du, Xuefeng: Palm vein recognition with deep hashing network. In: Lai, J.-H., et al. (eds.) PRCV 2018. LNCS, vol. 11256, pp. 38–49. Springer, Cham (2018). https://doi.org/10.1007/978-3-030-03398-9_4
48. Zhong, Y., Deng, W., Hu, J., Zhao, D., Li, X., Wen, D.: SFace: sigmoid-constrained hypersphere loss for robust face recognition. In: IEEE TIP (2021)

Low-Textural Image Registration: Comparative Analysis of Feature Descriptors

Vasanth Subramanyam[1,2]([✉])[ID], Jayendra Kumar[2][ID], Shiva Nand Singh[2], Roshan Kumar[3], and Arvind R. Yadav[4]

[1] Tata Steel Ltd., Jamshedpur, Jharkhand, India
v.subramanyam@tatasteel.com
[2] National Institute of Technology, Jamshedpur, Jharkhand, India
[3] Miami College of Henan University, Henan, China
[4] Parul Institute of Engineering and Technology, Parul University, Vadodara, Gujarat, India

Abstract. Industrial machine-vision (MV) applications require high-speed stitching of low-textural images from multiple high-resolution cameras for Field-of-View expansion. The most vital step in the stitching process is the effective and efficient extraction of features, which becomes challenging for low-textural images. This paper presents a comparative study of five popular feature descriptor algorithms for image stitching viz. Scale Invariant Feature Transform (SIFT), Speeded Up Robust Feature (SURF), Oriented Fast and Rotated BRIEF (ORB), Binary Robust invariant scalable keypoints (BRISK), and Accelerated-KAZE (AKAZE).

The focus of this paper is to present a study of the performance comparison among these feature extraction methods for low-textural images from real-time steel surface inspection systems. Primarily, synchronized images of steel rolled at room temperatures are obtained from a two-camera network with overlapping regions. Feature descriptor algorithms extract features from two images with an overlapping area and further match the features using K-Nearest Neighbour (KNN) algorithm. The performance of the five feature descriptor algorithms is evaluated using a low-textural dataset that consists of a set of 177 images captured from two cameras placed at a fixed distance from each other. The efficiency of these algorithms is quantitatively and qualitatively evaluated using execution time, sensitivity, and specificity. Finally, this paper provides guidelines for future research on problems with FOV expansion in industrial scenarios.

Keywords: Feature Descriptors · Image Stitching · Low textural imaging

1 Introduction

Some key sectors in the manufacturing industry, such as instrumentation, quality improvement, tracking, etc., employ futuristic automation owing to their high accuracy and precision. The most widely used technology among

D. Gupta et al. (Eds.): CVIP 2022, CCIS 1777, pp. 458–473, 2023.
https://doi.org/10.1007/978-3-031-31417-9_35

these is machine-vision [13]. Such applications employ application-specific high-resolution cameras and lenses. Lens selection for such applications depends on the geometry and dimensions of the object [15]. Using a wide-angle or telephoto lens introduces distortions that might cause deformities of the captured object. Thus, the selection of lens impact field-of-view (FOV) and object-to-camera distance.

Limited FOV issues of cameras can be solved using either of these techniques. The first involves Omni Directional cameras [30] arranged with reflective mirrors for enhancing the FOV. The drawback of this technique is the non-uniformity of the output image. The second involves employing a predefined arrangement of multiple cameras known as distributed aperture systems (DAS) [22]. Such DAS systems produce wider FOV outputs with a dynamic view of neighbouring surroundings.

Numerous DAS-based inventions [8] are reported in the literature. The DAS invented by Northrop-Grumman Corporation employs mid-wave infrared (IR) sensors, each covering 30°, thereby requiring six sensors to cover the complete 360° area around a tactical environment. An advanced DAS (ADAS) invented by Raytheon Company [40] uses high-resolution IR sensors for 360° view for situational awareness. Another invention of DAS by Sarnoff Corporation [14] provides a 180° view of the surroundings inside military vehicles, details of which are confidential. Other inventions based on robotic vehicles [34] use numerous visible and IR cameras to produce seamless broader FOV views. The underlying common factor among all these implementations is image stitching of the acquired images to create a seamless output.

To understand the importance of image stitching in industrial DAS implementations, consider continuous rolling processes such as fabric manufacturing [20] and steel manufacturing [27], [38] in which surface aberrations and their location are captured in real-time. Expanded FOVs are created by image stitching algorithms using a three-stage process [39]. In the first stage, the relationships between the pixels in the overlapping areas are defined [18,37]. Alternatively, optical flow algorithms are employed to estimate the pixel-wise motion model [31] and thereby the relationship between the corresponding pixels of the images [16,24,45]. Also, feature matching is another technique applied to estimate the pixel relationships [5,6,9]. In the second stage, the images are projected onto a common plane, so that the output view is assumed to be created by a single camera. The projection onto the common plane is derived through transforming and registering the images from the different cameras. The transformed images are aligned in the common plane without ghosting effects or other artefacts. Finally, in the third stage, the pixels in both images are blended to ensure that the seam between the images is invisible.

Feature descriptor algorithms generally identify and match the common features in the overlapping regions. The eight most popular feature descriptor algorithms are Scale Invariant Feature Transform (SIFT), Speeded Up Robust Feature (SURF), Binary Robust Independent Elementary Features (BRIEF), Oriented Fast and Rotated BRIEF (ORB), Binary Robust invariant scalable keypoints (BRISK), KAZE, Accelerated-KAZE (AKAZE) and Features from

Accelerated Segment Test (FAST). This paper focuses on evaluating the qualitative and quantitative performance of these feature descriptor algorithms for low-textural images of steel surface inspection systems.

The main contributions of this paper are as follows:

- A motivation from the steel industry is presented in this paper that captures information from low-textural images of the steel sheets.
- The experimental setup for capturing the dataset of real-time low-texture images is presented.
- Modern feature descriptor algorithms are evaluated for performance and efficiency using the low-textural image dataset. In this regard,
  - The efficiency of the algorithms is compared in terms of sensitivity and specificity of the low-textural features extracted.
  - The execution times of the algorithms are analysed with respect to usage in low textural applications.
- This paper also presents the limitations of feature descriptor algorithms for low-textural images, thereby paving the way for newer strategies for feature extraction that can be used for low textural images in real-time industrial scenarios.

2   Motivation

This section presents the motivation for this problem to illustrate the advantages of stitching algorithms in machine vision systems. In steel rolling processing, steel surface inspection for defect detection and classification uses high-resolution MV cameras as shown in Fig. 1.

Steel rolling can be classified into hot and cold rolling processes. In hot rolling, a slab of steel is heated and flattened to thin steel strips. Conversely, cold rolling involves drawing hot rolled coils into thinner sections at variable speeds. Generally, the thickness of the strip is inversely proportional to the rolling speeds.

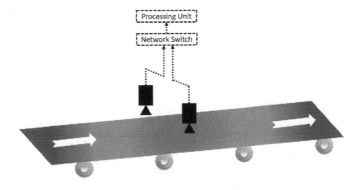

Fig. 1. Illustration of the motivation. Steel sheets are rolled continuously and the machine vision cameras continuously inspect the sheet for detection of surface defects

The minimum and maximum speeds in cold rolling mills are 4 and 10 m per second. Hypothetically, considering strip inspection while rolling, using a machine vision system for surface defects. The cameras used are high-resolution line scan cameras with an appropriate lens. Generally, the strip width is approximately 2 m which would require multiple cameras to capture the total width of the strip for inspection.

Uncaptured defects or inaccurate location information may lead to catastrophic degradation of product quality. For example, sheets of steel are rolled at speeds of approximately 20 m per second, and two cameras are arranged across the width of the sheet, capturing 30 frames per second. The images captured by the synchronized cameras are stitched together to create a digital twin of the steel sheet. Images of the strip as captured by the cameras are shown in Fig. 2 and the textural information available on these images is minimal. Consider the scenario where the images are stitched improperly resulting in missed defects or incorrect location information. Any mismatch in the stitching causes missed defects or improper identification of defects. So the feature descriptor and extraction algorithms play a crucial role in ensuring accurate stitching without any ghosting effects or other artefacts. The above discussion aids in understanding the significance of the image stitching of the images from cameras. Therefore, it would lead to understanding the importance of feature extraction and image stitching for industrial applications can be envisaged and the criticality of the performance of these algorithms in stitching can be understood.

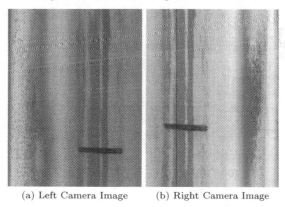

(a) Left Camera Image   (b) Right Camera Image

Fig. 2. Images of steel strips captured with cameras for surface inspection system

3   Related and Relevant Work

Understanding and analysing the performance of feature-descriptors has always been crucial to research in image registration and there have been numerous studies on the same. Performance of feature-descriptors [28] such as SIFT, Steerable filters, PCA-SIFT, Complex Filters, GLOH, etc., have been evaluated over various image transformations such as rotation, varying illumination, compression, blur, etc. in multiple datasets. Nonetheless, this paper deals with variation in the scale between 200 and 250%. In [41], various feature-detector-descriptor combinations such as SIFT, ORB, SURF, SURF-BinBoost, AKAZE-MSURF, etc., have been compared for point-cloud registrations that were obtained using terrestrial laser scanning methods. Moreover, various feature-detectors and feature-descriptors were evaluated for visual tracking applications [10]. A similar quantitative comparison is provided for multiple feature-detectors such as BRISK, FAST, ORB, SIFT, STAR, SURF, AGAST, and AKAZE were applied to different image data sequences but this paper does not compare the computational times of these algorithms [32]. Another attempt compares SIFT, SURF, ORB, and AKAZE features in a monocular visual odometry application [7] using the KITTI benchmark dataset. The next paper describes performance comparison [19] for SIFT and SURF against different image deformations using the feature-matching technique.

In the comparisons of feature descriptors available in the literature, the basic assumption is that there are enough features to be detected. In general, the scenes or applications used for analysing the feature descriptors for image registration have many distinct textures that can be detected as features. Low-textural images present a distinctive challenge of finding and matching features for feature-descriptor and in turn, image registration algorithms. There are many real-time industrial applications such as paper processing, steel manufacturing, etc. in which image registration and stitching do not work due to a dearth of features. In this paper, we aim to analyse the performance and efficiency of various feature-descriptor algorithms where the images captured have the least textural information. Also, this analysis would aid in understanding the shortcomings of the feature descriptor algorithms when dealing with low-textural images, thus making it difficult for image registration in industrial applications.

4   Hardware Configuration and Experimental Setup

The hardware configuration and experimental setup used in the evaluation of the feature descriptors are shown in Fig. 3a. The primary elements of this experimental setup are:

- Sensing element: consists of monochrome line-scan cameras (Dalsa Spyder3) combined with 30 mm focal length F-mount lens.
- Interfacing element: consists of a four-port Peripheral Component Interconnect (PCI) Power-Over-Ethernet (POE) card (Adlink PCIe-GIE64+)
- Processing element: consists of a windows powered workstation using an i7 processor, 16 Gigabytes of RAM, and 4-gigabyte Nvidia graphics card
- Application software: comprises Python environment, an interpreted, high-level, general-purpose programming language

The final hardware configuration and setup are shown in Fig. 3b.

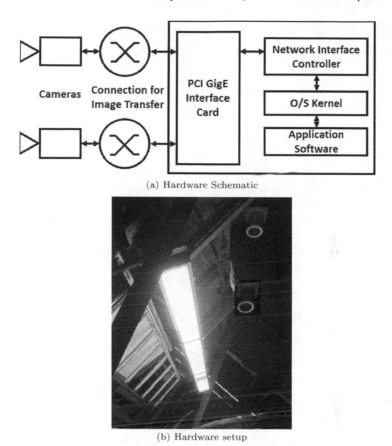

(a) Hardware Schematic

(b) Hardware setup

Fig. 3. Hardware Schematic and setup with Illumination system at Cold Rolling Mill, Tata Steel

5   DataSet Preparation

Using the hardware setup mentioned in Sect. 4, images are captured in real-time for multiple rolling sections at a frame-rate of 30 frames every second. The trigger for image capturing starts whenever the rolling of a coil starts and then, the captured image forms part of a data set. For preparation of the dataset, images are collected for different types of coils that are rolled at varying speeds. Also, the ambient lighting conditions are varied by collecting images in the morning, noon and night. As part of these experiments, we captured images of 12 types of coils that are rolled at different coils, during the morning, noon and night. Hence, a total of 36 coils were captured and mapped in one day and such images were captured for a period of 10 days. Images of 360 coils and approximately 200 images are captured per coil, and hence, total number of images in the dataset is 72000.

6   Understanding Feature Descriptors

The important phases of image stitching are feature descriptors, registration, and blending [44]. Feature descriptors are algorithms that encode unique information in images into matrices that enable differentiation between images and features. Feature descriptor algorithms can be organized into direct, deep learning-based, and feature-based methods

Direct methods compare the pixel intensities and thereby ensuring that the properties depicted by each of the pixel intensities are compared with the others in the overlapping areas of the multiple images [17]. These direct techniques generally minimize the variations in the pixel intensities and ensure optimal usage of image details. Moreover, these techniques aid in evaluating each pixel intensities in the image, thus making these techniques extremely complicated. Some tomography parameters are assessed using phase correlation [4], [29]. After which, the homography matrix is updated to minimize a specific cost function. The major drawback of this class of techniques is that they are limited to flat scenes without parallax, making these algorithms unsuitable for real-time industrial applications such as surface inspection systems.

Recently developed feature descriptor algorithms based on deep learning are detailed. Some attempts [12, 36, 42] utilize Convolutional Neural Network (CNN) for feature detection replacing traditional feature descriptor algorithms. Other variants use neural networks for feature matching [2] for estimating transformational parameters from the detected features [43]. Furthermore, few papers attempt to design for specific criteria such as fixed views [21, 35], wide-angle views using fisheye lenses [25] etc. The major drawback of such deep learning-based methodologies is that these techniques require very high processing times in the order of seconds, thereby making them unusable for real-time applications. Hence, in the purview of this paper, we do not consider deep-learning-based methodologies for evaluation and comparison.

Feature-based techniques focus on ascertaining the relationships between the overlapping areas in the images by comparing a few key feature descriptors extracted from the images [11]. This class of techniques has no restrictions in terms of the scenes and is highly reliable and fast. One of the basic requirements of these techniques is the presence and accurate detection of feature descriptors that are usually textural features in the images. Feature-based techniques operate on matching different features and ensure invariance to noise, scale, translation, and rotation. Some popular feature descriptors in the literature include SIFT, SURF, ORB, BRISK, and AKAZE.

6.1   Scale Invariant Feature Transform (SIFT)

SIFT, proposed by Lowe, extracts key points and evaluates the local descriptor using image gradient and the direction information from the image [26]. We have implemented the SIFT algorithm to the low-textural images shown in Fig. 2. The results, as shown in Fig. 4a, show that the number of distinct features as required by SIFT is unavailable in the images and hence, the algorithm detects keypoints that are not unique and the matching is also inaccurate.

6.2   Speeded Up Robust Feature (SURF)

The SURF algorithm uses multi-dimensional space theory. Furthermore, the key-point detection is improved by monitoring their quality, and keypoint matching is improved by using Hessian matrix [3]. The keypoint detection and matching using SURF for the set of low-textural images is shown in Fig. 4b. The detection and matching accuracy is much better than SIFT but still, some points were erroneously detected and matching, thereby affecting the quality of image stitching.

6.3   Oriented Fast and Rotated BRIEF (ORB)

ORB is a fast binary descriptor that captures the salient features of FAST and BRIEF algorithms using key points of BRIEF and detectors of FAST [33]. The performance of ORB is much better than SIFT and SURF in terms of speed and efficiency. The performance of ORB is shown in Fig. 4c. It can be observed that due to the lack of textural features, the detection accuracy of ORB is poor for image stitching.

6.4   Binary Robust Invariant Scalable Keypoints (BRISK)

The BRISK algorithm employs the grayscale relationship between random pairs of points in the image resulting in the binary descriptor [23]. This algorithm is faster than other algorithms and also the storage memory is lower, but the tradeoff is that robustness is reduced. The results of the BRISK, shown in Fig. 4d, reveal the exact feature points, but the matching algorithm is not effective, thereby making the stitching process inefficient.

6.5   Accelerated-KAZE (AKAZE)

AKAZE uses non-linear diffusion in multi-scale feature detection resulting in better repeatability and performance [1]. The major drawback of this algorithm is that it is computationally expensive. The results using the AKAZE algorithm on low-textural images are shown in Fig. 4e. On observation, it can be seen that the matching accuracy is poor even though, the keypoint detection accuracy is high.

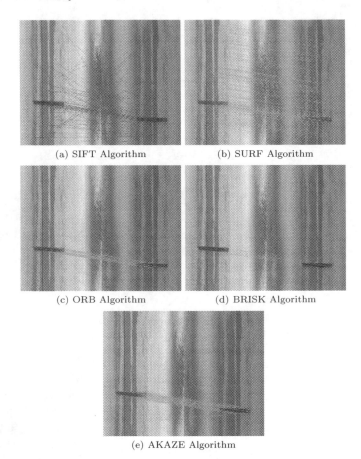

(a) SIFT Algorithm   (b) SURF Algorithm

(c) ORB Algorithm   (d) BRISK Algorithm

(e) AKAZE Algorithm

Fig. 4. Keypoint Matching using various feature descriptor algorithms on Low-Textural Images

7   Performance Comparison of Feature Descriptor Algorithms

This section analyses the performance and efficiency of the feature descriptor algorithms based on usability in low-textural real-time applications. The fundamental requirement for real-time applications is the ability to process at least 15 to 20 frames of images a second so that the digital twin covers maximum areas at the speed of rolling. Higher frame rates are accomplished by understanding the steps that consume the most computational time during processing. Hence, the computational time of each process step of various algorithms is evaluated and shown in Table 1.

The feature descriptor consumes maximum computational time (approximately 50%) of the image stitching algorithm. Moreover, the feature descriptor has been evolving. With each improved algorithm, there is considerable reduction in computation time.

The fastest existing feature description algorithm consumes 39 ms with a total computational time of 79 ms that means that the maximum number of frames processed in a second is around 12.

Table 1. Comparison of step-wise computational time of Stitching Approaches

ALGORITHMIC STEPS	TIME in milliseconds				
	SIFT	SURF	ORB	BRISK	AKAZE
Feature Descriptor	152	128	93	65	39
Keypoint Detection	98	67	45	23	17
Keypoint Matching	7	8	6	8	8
Homography Estimation	6	7	6	7	6
Warping & Stitching	9	8	8	9	9
Total Time	272	218	158	112	79

Feature descriptor algorithms were applied to nearly 3000 images captured from multiple cameras for conducting Monte-Carlo trials. As part of these trials, estimation and statistical analysis of computation times for the five feature descriptor algorithms were conducted to compute parameters such as mean, median, and standard deviation shown in Table 2.

Table 2. Performance Comparison of Feature Descriptor Algorithms

	Time (milliseconds)				
	SIFT	SURF	ORB	BRISK	AKAZE
Mean	151.47	129.96	92.53	67.60	39.03
Median	151	129	92	67	39
Standard Deviation	4.10	5.53	5.14	5.67	3.72

The mean and median of the AKAZE algorithm are the least among all the feature descriptor algorithms followed by BRISK, ORB, SURF, and SIFT. The standard deviation shows that AKAZE is the least followed by SIFT, ORB, SURF, and BRIEF. Upon analysis, the standard deviation values follow a different order than the mean and median. Thus, AKAZE is the best-performing feature descriptor algorithm for low-textural images that is further ascertained by visually studying the box plots shown in Fig. 5.

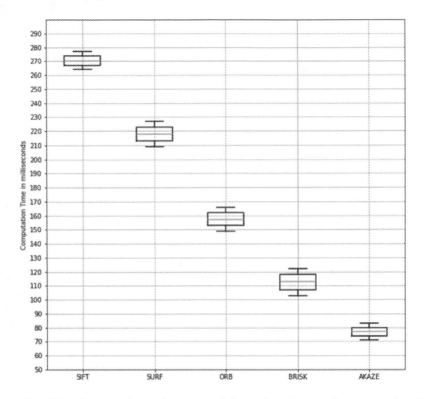

Fig. 5. Box Plot showing the performance of the various feature descriptor algorithm

The efficiency of the algorithms is compared using the sensitivity and specificity of the matched low-textural features extracted from the images. Sensitivity, also known as True Positive Rate (TPR), can be defined as the ratio of true positives to the total number of matched low-textural features extracted from the images. Similarly, specificity, also known as False Positive Rate (FPR), can be defined as the ratio of false positives to the total number of matched low-textural features extracted from the images. Table 3 shows the comparison of TPR and FPR for the matched low-textural features.

Table 3. Efficiency Comparison of Feature Descriptor Algorithms

	TP	FP	TP + FP	TPR	FPR
SIFT	26	146	172	0.15	0.85
SURF	137	243	380	0.36	0.64
ORB	46	19	65	0.71	0.29
BRISK	11	4	15	0.73	0.27
AKAZE	78	8	86	0.91	0.09

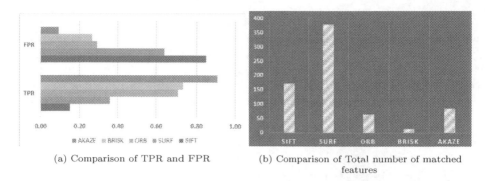

(a) Comparison of TPR and FPR   (b) Comparison of Total number of matched features

Fig. 6. Efficiency Comparison between feature descriptor algorithms

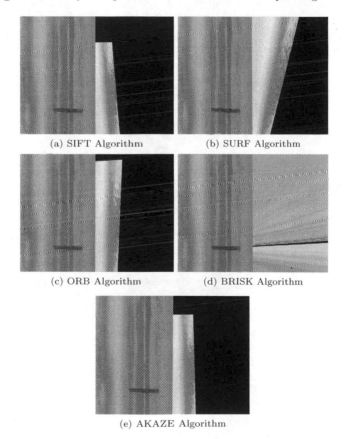

(a) SIFT Algorithm   (b) SURF Algorithm

(c) ORB Algorithm   (d) BRISK Algorithm

(e) AKAZE Algorithm

Fig. 7. Registered Images based on the various feature descriptor algorithm

The TPR increases with every new generation of feature descriptor algorithm while FPR decreases. TPR is maximum and FPR is minimum for AKAZE algorithm. Furthermore, TPR is least and FPR is highest for SIFT algorithm.

Another important inference is that, for SIFT, SURF, ORB, and Brisk algorithms, even though the TPR is increasing, the total number of matched features keeps decreasing, thus proving that the trade-off for increasing TPR is the reduction in the total number of matched features. Hence, the main advantage of the AKAZE algorithm is that it has the highest TPR with a 780% increase in the number of features as compared to the BRISK algorithm that is further established visually in the bar graphs shown in Fig. 6.

8   Comparison of Registration Based on the Various Feature Descriptors

Based on the matched features from the feature descriptors, the next step in the algorithm is registration of the images, that implies that the second image is transformed onto the plane of the first image. After this process, the homography matrix is computed and the second image is warped to finally register the images. The effectiveness, accuracy and efficiency of the feature descriptors can be clearly understood. Figure 7 clearly depicts that the currently available feature descriptors do not perform effectively for low- textural images. The major reason for this, is that the feature descriptor algorithms are designed on the assumption that numerous features are available in the images that can be further matched and registered.

9   Conclusions

This paper presents a detailed comparative analysis of five popular feature descriptors for low textural images. The primary motivation for this study is the application of these algorithms to real-time image and video stitching applications involving low-textural images captured from multiple cameras. Also, the performance and efficiency comparison helps to understand the improvements made in each generation of the feature descriptor algorithms.

Based on the results comparison of the registration using the various feature descriptor algorithms, it can be clearly understood that the currently available descriptors fail to effectively register low-textural images. This paves the way for future work, that is to design feature descriptors specifically for stitching of low-textural images.

References

1. Alcantarilla, P.F., Nuevo, J., Bartoli, A.: Fast explicit diffusion for accelerated features in nonlinear scale spaces. British Machine Vision Conference (BMVC) (2013)
2. Alzohairy, T., El-Dein, E.: Image mosaicing based on neural networks. Int. J. Comput. Appl. **975**, 8887 (2016)
3. Bay, H., Tuytelaars, T., Gool, L.V.: SURF: Speeded-up robust features. Comput. Vis. Image Underst. **110**(3), 346–359 (2008)

4. Bonny, M., Uddin, M.: Feature-based image stitching algorithms. In: IWCI, pp. 198–203 (2016)
5. Brown, M., Lowe, D.G.: Recognizing panoramas. In: Proceedings of the IEEE International Conference on Computer Vision, vol. 3, p. 1218. Nice, France (2003)
6. Brown, M., Lowe, D.G.: Automatic panoramic image stitching using invariant features. Int. J. Comput. Vis. **74**(1), 59–73 (2007)
7. Chien, H.: When to use what feature? sift, surf, orb, or a-kaze features for monocular visual odometry, pp. 1–6. Palmerston North, IVCNZ (2016)
8. Colucci, F.: Keep one eye out (2012). http://www.aviationtoday.com/av/issue/cover/Keep-One-Eye-Out_75101.html. Accessed 1 May 2020
9. Gao, J., Kim, S.J., Brown, M.S.: Constructing image panoramas using dual-homography warping. In: Proceedings of the IEEE Conference on Computer Vision and Pattern Recognition, vol. 201, pp. 49–56. Colorado Springs, CO, USA (2011)
10. Gauglitz, S.: Evaluation of interest point detectors and feature descriptors for visual tracking. Int. J. Comput. Vision **94**(3), 335–360 (2011)
11. Goa, F., Goa, F.: Stitching (2017)
12. Hoang, V.-D., Tran, D.-P., Nhu, N.G., Pham, T.-A., Pham, V.-H.: Deep feature extraction for panoramic image stitching. In: Nguyen, N.T., Jearanaitanakij, K., Selamat, A., Trawiński, B., Chittayasothorn, S. (eds.) ACIIDS 2020. LNCS (LNAI), vol. 12034, pp. 141–151. Springer, Cham (2020). https://doi.org/10.1007/978-3-030-42058-1_12
13. Horst, R., Negin, M.: Vision system for high-resolution dimensional measurements and on-line SPC: web process application. IEEE Trans. Ind. Appl. **28**, 993–997 (1992)
14. Imaging, S.: Distributed aperture systems. http://www.sarnoffimaging.com/research-and-development/vision-technologies/embeddedvision/distributed-aperture-systems. Accessed 16 May 2020
15. Jain, R., Kasturi, R., Schunck, B.G.: Machine vision. McGraw-Hill, Inc. (1995)
16. Jia, J., Tang, K.C.: Eliminating structure and intensity misalignment in image stitching. In: Tenth IEEE International Conference on Computer Vision, ICCV2005, pp. 1651–1658. Beijing, China (2005)
17. Joshi, K.: Open access a survey on real-time image stitching (2020)
18. Kaynig, V., Fischer, B., M, B.J.: Probabilistic image registration and anomaly detection by nonlinear warping. In: Proceedings of the IEEE Conference on Computer Vision and Pattern Recognition, pp. 1–8. Anchorage, Alaska, USA (2008)
19. Khan, N.: Sift and surf performance evaluation against various image deformations on benchmark dataset. In: IEEE International Conference on Digital Image Computing Techniques and Applications, pp. 501–506. DICTA (2011)
20. Kumar, A.: Computer-vision-based fabric defect detection: a survey. IEEE Trans. Ind. Electron. **55**, 348–363 (2008)
21. Lai, W.S., Gallo, O., Gu, J., Sun, D., Yang, M.H., Kautz, J.: Video stitching for linear camera arrays (2019). arXiv preprint arXiv:1907.13622
22. Lamkin, M., Ringgenberg, K., Lamkin, J.: Distributed multi - aperture camera array. US 2019/0246044 A1 (2019)
23. Leutenegger, S., Chli, M., Siegwart, R.: Brisk: Binary robust invariant scalable keypoints. In: International Conference on Computer Vision, pp. 2548–2555 (2011)
24. Levin, A., Zomet, A., Peleg, S., Weiss, Y.: Seamless image stitching in the gradient domain. In: Pajdla, T., Matas, J. (eds.) ECCV 2004. LNCS, vol. 3024, pp. 377–389. Springer, Heidelberg (2004). https://doi.org/10.1007/978-3-540-24673-2_31

25. Li, J., Zhao, Y., Ye, W., Yu, K., Ge, S.: Attentive deep stitching and quality assessment for 360 omnidirectional images. IEEE J. Select. Top. Signal Process **14**, 209–221 (2019)

26. Lowe, D.G.: Distinctive image features from scale-invariant keypoints. Int. J. Comput. Vis. **60**(2), 91–110 (2004). http://link.springer.com/10.1023/B:VISI.0000029664.99615.94

27. Luo, Q., Fang, X., Liu, L., Yang, C., Sun, Y.: Automated visual defect detection for flat steel surface: a survey. IEEE Trans. Instrum. Meas. **69**(3), 626–644 (2020)

28. Mikolajczyk, K., Schmid, C.: A performance evaluation of local descriptors. IEEE Trans. Pattern Anal. Mach. Intell. **27**(10), 1615–1630 (2005)

29. Mistry, S., Patel, A.: Image stitching using Harris feature detection. Int. Res. J. Eng. Technol **03**(04), 1363–1369, (2016). https://www.irjet.net/

30. Nayar, S.: Catadioptric omnidirectional camera. In: Proceedings of IEEE Computer Society Conference on Computer Vision and Pattern Recognition, pp. 482–488 (1997)

31. Peleg, S., Rousso, B., Rav-Acha, A., Zomet, A.: Mosaicing on adaptive manifolds. IEEE Trans. Pattern Anal. Mach. Intell. **22**(10), 1144–1154 (2000)

32. Pusztai, Z., Hajder, L.: Quantitative comparison of feature matchers implemented in opencv3. Computer Vision Winter Workshop (2016)

33. Rublee, E., Rabaud, V., Konolige, K., Bradski, G.: ORB: an efficient alternative to SIFT or SURF. In: IEEE International Conference on Computer Vision (ICCV) (2011)

34. Sanders-Reed, J., Koon, P.: Vision systems for manned and robotic ground vehicles. Proc. SPIE **7692**, 1–12 (2010)

35. Shen, C., Ji, X., Miao, C.: Real-time image stitching with convolutional neural networks. International Conference on Real-time Computing and Robotics (RCAR), pp. 192–197 (2019)

36. Shi, Z., Li, H., Cao, Q., Ren, H., Fan, B.: An image mosaic method based on convolutional neural network semantic features extraction. J. Signal Process. Syst **92**, 435–444 (2020)

37. Silva, R., Bruno, F., Gomes, P., Frensh, T., Monteiro, D.: Real time 360° video stitching and streaming. In: ACM SIGGRAPH 2016 Posters, pp. 1–2. ACM, Anaheim, California (2016)

38. Sugimoto, T., Kawaguchi, T.: Development of a surface defect inspection system using radiant light from steel products in a hot rolling line. IEEE Trans. Instrum. Meas. **47**, 409–416 (1998)

39. Szeliski, R.: Image alignment and stitching: a tutorial. Found. Trend® Comput. Graph. Vis. **2**(1), 1–104 (2007)

40. Technologies, R.: Advanced distributed aperture system (adas). http://www.raytheon.com/capabilities/products/adas/. Accessed 6 May 2020

41. Urban, S., Weinmann, M.: Finding a good feature detector-descriptor combination for the 2D keypoint-based registration of TIS point clouds, pp. 121–128. Annals of Photogrammetry, Remote Sensing and Spatial Information Sciences pp (2015)

42. Wang, L., Yu, W., Li, B.: Multi-scenes image stitching based on autonomous driving. In: 2020 IEEE 4th Information Technology, Networking, Electronic and Automation Control Conference (ITNEC), vol. 1, pp. 694–698 (2020)

43. Yan, M., Yin, Q., Guo, P.: Image stitching with single-hidden layer feedforward neural networks. International Joint Conference on Neural Networks (IJCNN), pp. 4162–4169 (2016)

44. Zhang, J., Chen, G., Jia, Z.: An image stitching algorithm based on histogram matching and sift algorithm. Int. J. Pattern Recognit Artif Intell. **31**(4), 1–14 (2017)
45. Zomet, A., Levin, A., Peleg, S., Weiss, Y.: Seamless image stitching by minimizing false edges. IEEE Trans. Image Process. **15**(4), 969–977 (2006)

Structure-Based Learning for Robust Defense Against Adversarial Attacks in Autonomous Driving Agents

Manoj Kumar Sharma[1], Rudrajit Choudhuri[2]([⊠]), Mayank Dixit[3],
Mrinmoy Sarkar[4], and Bhat Dittakavi[1]

[1] AI4ICPS, IIT Kharagpur, Kharagpur, India
{manoj,ceo}@ai4icps.in
[2] St. Thomas' College of Engineering & Technology, Kolkata, India
rudrajit1729@gmail.com
[3] Netaji Subhas University of Technology, Delhi, India
mayank.ee19@nsut.ac.in
[4] Techno International New Town, Kolkata, India

Abstract. Owing to the recent remarkable advancements in computer vision and artificial intelligence, resilient self-driving cars are now becoming a reality. In this paper, we detail an autonomous car prototype that uses vision-based perception for control and navigation. The car uses a deep neural network to classify traffic symbols based on which motor control decisions are taken. The classification model is tested in various environmental settings and is observed to be robust. In real-world situations, misclassification in autonomous systems can lead to serious accidents. Although the classification model is reliable, there may arise different environmental scenarios where misclassification can occur. In order to simulate such a scenario, we explore the effects of different adversarial attacks on the network. It is observed that the attacks are able to trick the network into misclassifying symbols. Therefore, a network defense mechanism is crucial for handling such scenarios. We present a structure-based learning approach for a robust defense mechanism. The approach is self-supervised and it leverages the use of data augmentations of a sample to have different representations of the same. This ensures that the network is trained to learn the base structure for various environmental settings, thereby nullifying the effect of different adversarial attacks.

Keywords: Adversarial Attack & Defense · Autonomous Vehicles · Deep Learning

1 Introduction

The development of reliable autonomous driving agents has revolutionized the automobile industry. Notable contributions in the intersections of computer vision, machine learning, and deep learning make it possible for autonomous vehicles to be efficient and reliable for deployment in real world scenarios. Vision based perception is one of the key factors that influence decision making for vehicle control and navigation. Deep learning (DL) based systems are incorporated for handling a wide variety of tasks based on perception. Safety is a major consideration when deploying autonomous vehicles, and efficiency flaws in the DL-based controller models can lead to grave accidents.

In recent years, researchers have pointed out that adversarial attacks pose severe hazard to the DL based techniques [1]. Adversarial samples are able to fool deep learning models by perturbing input samples, which sometimes are also indistinguishable by humans [17]. The domain of adversarial attacks is relevant as it places a severe bottleneck in real time deployment of DL-based techniques, especially in autonomous vehicles. Over the span of time, different algorithms were proposed focused on adversarial attacks [7]. Development of defense strategies against adversarial attacks is also an emerging research domain. The defense mechanisms [18] have varying efficiencies for different attacks. In order to circumvent the effect of adversaries in real-world deployed models, it is crucial to develop a robust and scalable defense strategy that caters to different attack types and varied use cases.

In this manuscript, we propose a robust structure-based learning strategy for a defense mechanism generalizable against white box adversarial attacks in autonomous driving agents. First, we detail the development of an autonomous car prototype that incorporates vision based perception for vehicle control and self-navigates based on the classification of traffic signs. The DL model responsible for the classification is tested in various environmental settings and after experimentation, it is observed to be robust. Next, we incorporate different attack techniques to study the effect of adversaries (adversarial traffic signs in this context) on the classifier network. Inferences made from different test runs under a controlled lab environment suggest that the attacks are able to fool the network into misclassifying symbols. We also highlight the challenges in real-time data acquisition and present ways to tackle the same. Finally, we propose a structure-based learning approach for the development of a generalizable robust network defense mechanism. The presented technique is self-supervised and it amalgamates the use of data augmentations of a sample to have multi-faceted sample representations. The technique ensures that the network is trained to identify the base structure for different environmental settings, thereby nullifying the effect of attacks. Furthermore, the defense model is integrated with the autonomous car prototype. On comparing with the other widely used defense techniques, the method emerges to be reliable against the different implemented attack types, thus highlighting resiliency and scalability across a wide gamut of real-world applications.

The major contributions of the paper are threefold:

1. A robust structure-based learning mechanism focused at defense against white box adversarial attacks is proposed.

2. Development of an end-to-end cyber physical autonomous vehicular system for testing the effect of attacks and the resiliencies of the defense strategies is detailed.
3. We propose techniques to overcome the challenges identified in real time data acquisition for vision based perception with respect to an autonomous driving prototype.

The rest of the paper is structured as follows: Sect. 2 summarizes the related works and discusses the background relevant to adversarial attacks. The research design and methodology are presented in Sect. 3. The results are analyzed and inferences are discussed in Sect. 4. Finally, conclusion is derived in Sect. 5.

2   Related Work

The domain of adversarial attacks has been fairly explored in the recent years. Some of the key achievements in the domain include the Fast Gradient Sign Method (FGSM) [10], basic iterative method (BIM) [13], Carlini and Wagner Attack (CW) [6], Projected Gradient Descent (PGD) [14], Deepfool [15], and Fast Adaptive Boundary (FAB) [8]. Research has also been conducted in exploring the effects of physical perturbations [9] in fooling DL models. These attacks among many others have proven to be robust in generating adversarial samples that potentially cause misclassification. We briefly summarize the different attack types incorporated in our experiments targeted at fooling the classifier networks as follows:

Fast Gradient Sign Method (FGSM): FGSM [10] is one of the most trivial methods for generation of adversarial image samples. The method uses a linear cost function and solves for the perturbation that maximizes the same. The formulation is defined as follows:

$$I^{adv} = I + \epsilon * sign(\nabla_I J(\Psi, I, y_{true})) \tag{1}$$

where Ψ is the classifier, y_{true} is the original class label, J is the cost function, ∇_I is the gradient of the objective function with respect to the image (I), and ϵ is a tuning parameter that controls the amount of perturbations. The cost function searches the data point which has the maximum loss with respect to the original class in the ϵ-neighborhood of I, i.e. the point which is most likely to be misclassified by the classifier, thereby generating the adversarial sample I^{adv}. As the method involves calculation of just one back-propagation step, it is measurably faster than the other attacks.

Basic Iterative Method (BIM) and Projected Gradient Descent (PGD): BIM [13] is an extension of the FGSM method. It iteratively applies FGSM method on the image sample with a small step size (α). After each iteration, the pixel values of the intermediate image are clipped, such that it lies in the ϵ-neighborhood of the original image. The BIM technique uses the formulation defined in Eq. 2.

$$I_0^{adv} = I; I_{N+1}^{adv} = Clip_{I,\epsilon}[I_N^{adv} + \alpha * sign(\nabla_I J(\Psi, I_N^{adv}, y_{true}))] \qquad (2)$$

The number of iterations are heuristically chosen, such that the adversarial sample (I^{adv}) reaches the edge of the ϵ-maximum normalization ball while keeping the values restricted to manage the cost of computations. A variation of the technique is referred to as Projected Gradient Descent (PGD) [14]. The iterative techniques focus on multi-step variation instead of single step maximization of the objective function (as in FGSM).

Carlini and Wagner Attack (CW): CW [6] is an improvement over the traditional FGSM attack. It tries to solve an optimization problem (same as in FGSM), by solving for minimally distorted perturbation. The objective function that the method tries to minimize is defined as follows:

$$J(\Psi, I_N^{adv}, t) = ||I - I_N^{adv}||^2 + c * (max_{i \neq t} Z(\Psi, I_N^{adv}, i) - Z(\Psi, I_N^{adv}, t)) \qquad (3)$$

where t is the target class, $Z(\Psi, I_N^{adv}, i)$ represents the probability of the image (I_N^{adv}) belonging to the class i on passing it to the model Ψ, and c is a hyperparameter. The cost function minimization encourages the method to find a sample that has the maximum probability for the target class (t). Finally, line search is performed on c to find an adversarial sample that has the least distance with respect to the original sample. The second term in the objective function resembles margin loss that helps in the direct minimization of the distance between the adversarial and the original sample when the predicted class is the target class itself.

DeepFool: In 2016, Dezfooli et al. [15] proposed a resilient adversarial attack for deep neural networks that focuses on sample misclassification using minimal data point perturbation. The technique utilizes decision boundaries around data points for adversarial sample generation. The study argues that the resiliency of a classifier for an image sample is highlighted by the distance between the image and the decision boundary. Given an image (I), the method tries to find a path such that the data point is able to go beyond the boundary, thereby leading to a different class prediction. In order to achieve the same, the method linearizes the decision boundary in each iteration, and computes the orthogonal vector between the point and the plane. The vector is then used to perturb the point such that it goes beyond the decision boundary, i.e. by moving the point along the direction of the vector, adversarial samples are generated that are misclassified by the prediction model. The formulation for adversarial sample generation using DeepFool technique is defined as:

$$I_0^{adv} = I; I_{N+1}^{adv} = I_N^{adv} - \frac{\Psi(I_N^{adv})}{||\nabla \Psi(I_N^{adv})||_2^2} \nabla \Psi(I_N^{adv}) \qquad (4)$$

where Ψ is an affine classifier. The process continues iteratively till $sign(\Psi(I_N^{adv})) \neq sign(\Psi(I_0^{adv}))$.

Fast Adaptive Boundary (FAB): FAB [8] is a gradient based iterative adversarial attack that builds and improves upon the concept of DeepFool attack. At each iteration, the classifier is linearized to compute the constrained projections of the intermediate and the original image onto the decision hyperplane. Furthermore, the convex combinations of these projections are used depending upon the distance of the adversarial sample and the original sample from the decision boundary. Finally, an extrapolation phase is performed for iterative sample generation. Unlike deepfool, the FAB attack tries to provide a solution close to the original sample, at the same time ensuring misclassification.

Physical Perturbations: In real world scenarios, acquisition devices might not be able to capture subtle changes in the image introduced by the attacks due to pixel intensity quantization. Recent developments in the domain discuss the idea of introducing physical perturbations in the object for producing adversarial samples. Robust physical perturbation (RP2) [9] is such an attack: it perturbs real objects (traffic signs) by attaching stickers on them which in effect is able to fool the classification model. The method incorporates an $L1$ norm based attack on the digital images of the road signs that gives a rough idea about the region to perturb. It then concentrates on the extracted region and uses an $L2$ norm based attack for generating sticker colors. Finally, the perturbed regions are printed out and are stuck on the traffic signs.

Contributions have also been made in the field of developing defense mechanisms [18] for mitigating the effects of these attacks. Adversarial training [2] is one of the most trivial defense mechanisms, where the adversarial samples are included in the training data and the models are trained on a combination of original and perturbed samples. The technique aids the model in the correct classification of the perturbed samples upto a certain extent. The domain of autoencoder based denoising has also been explored for developing a defense model [3]. The perturbed samples are passed through the denoiser which reduces the perturbations and tries to reconstruct the original image. These techniques are somewhat generalizable across different attack types and hence are used as baseline mechanisms.

3   Research Design and Proposed Methodology

This section details the different phases of experimentation performed to test the performances of adversarial attacks and defenses with respect to the autonomous driving car. First, we summarize the working of the car including the performance of the classifier model responsible for motor decisions. Next we discuss the configuration and effects of attacks on the model, and finally we propose a defense strategy that works on all of the attack types in the simulated environment. Figure 1 pictorially summarizes the different phases of the presented workflow.

3.1 Autonomous Vehicular System Prototype

The developed autonomous car (shown in Fig. 2) uses vision based perception for navigation and control. The car detects and distinguishes traffic signs, based on which its motion is determined. We use an IR camera for capturing the real time feed from the car. A primary Raspberry Pi 4 microcontroller is responsible for the processing and decision making. The frame that the car captures in real time is fed into the microcontroller. The traffic symbols are detected using Hough transformations [4]. Next, a deep learning based classification model (discussed in the following subsection) is used to identify the traffic sign. Based on the classification, the Raspberry Pi controller signals an Arduino controller. The arduino controller in turn uses PWM signals to control motors and hence navigates the car.

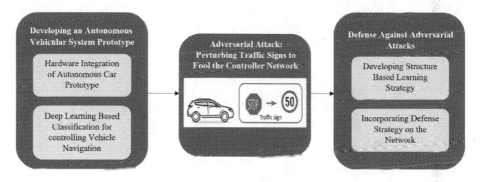

Fig. 1. The different phases of experimentation: First, an autonomous driving agent is developed that relies on a deep learning based classifier for vehicle navigation. Next, the network is fooled by adversaries (perturbed traffic signs). Finally a defense strategy is presented and is incorporated in the vehicle for network defense.

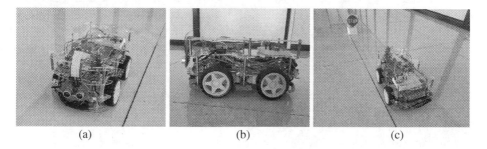

(a)	(b)	(c)

Fig. 2. Autonomous Car Prototype: (a) Frontal view, (b) Side view, and (c) Experimental scenario where the car stops on detecting a stop sign (the rear display shows the controller command)

3.2   Deep Learning Based Classifier for Vehicle Navigation

A fine-tuned ResNet18 [11] model is used as the classification model for traffic sign classification. We train the model to classify between four different traffic signs, i.e. left, right, stop, and speed signs (the data acquisition and splitting steps are reported in the result section). Firstly, the ResNet18 architecture is imported with ImageNet weights. The final dense fully connected layer responsible for class prediction is pruned and replaced with a fully connected dense layer that has 4 outputs. A softmax activation is attached to the fully connected layer. The model is compiled using categorical cross-entropy as the loss function, prediction accuracy as the evaluation metric, and stochastic gradient descent (SGD) as an optimization algorithm for updating the weights. The model is trained for 30 epochs with a batch size of 32 and an initial learning rate of 0.0001, which is reduced by 10% every 5 epochs. It ensures that the model converges and does not overshoot the optimal solution. A momentum of 0.9 is used to accelerate the optimization process. The model attains 99.79% and 99.57% training and validation set accuracies respectively.

Note: Other pre-trained models including VGGNet, MobileNet, and AlexNet were also trained. These models have more parameters and their computation complexity is more as compared to a ResNet-18 model. As computation time plays an important role in embedded systems, thus we use the ResNet-18 model as the classifier network of the vehicle (less complexity, compatibility with Raspberry Pi, and robust results for our use case).

3.3   Adversarial Attacks: Configuration, and Effects

The section discusses the experimentation configuration for different attack types. The samples are able to fool the trained classifier (responsible for motor control in the car prototype) with varying accuracies (misclassification rates are discussed in the result section). The FGSM attack is tested with epsilon values in range of 0.1 to 0.5. The epsilon values control the amount of perturbations in the image sample. BIM attack is incorporated with an alpha value of 0.5 and an epsilon value of 0.05. For CW attack, we use fifty steps with a learning rate of 0.01 and c = 0.5. An alpha value of 0.15 along with 0.15 epsilon and 50 iterations is the configuration used for the PGD attack. The deepfool attack is incorporated with overshoot values in range of 0.02 to 0.06 with fifty steps each. Finally, FAB attack samples are generated with epsilon value of 0.15.

On experimentation, it is observed that the BIM attack performs best, i.e. the generated samples manage to fool the classifier effectively. Next in line, the FAB, CW, and PGD attacks show notable performances. The DeepFool attack also generates samples that is able to fool the classifier upto a certain extent. The FGSM and the physical attack types are observed to be least effective in fooling the classification model. Overall, we observe that the robustness of the classification model is hampered drastically with the introduction of attacks.

3.4   Challenges in Real Time Data Acquisition

In this subsection, we discuss the challenges in real time data acquisition. Experiments are performed using different camera modules (normal cameras, IR cameras). In addition, varied experimental settings are used including different lighting conditions, background, and traffic signs. We observe different problems during image acquisition through cameras. For providing feed to the car, traffic signs had to be printed (Signs shown through a mobile screen posed issues with reflection and illumination and were manipulated by changing display settings). Problems with printed signs are manifold. The samples that successfully attack the model when fed from memory fail to do the same when the printed version is fed from the camera. The major problem is in data quantization, which happens when signs are printed (small pixel intensity changes/perturbations are nullified). Also the image resolution and DPI undergo changes when the signs are printed.

Fig. 3. Adversarial sample generation (FGSM attack): (a) Normal Sample, (b) Perturbed Sample, and (c) Processed Perturbed Sample (suitable for printing).

To overcome the changes introduced during real time data acquisition multiple steps are followed. For ensuring that the printed versions of the adversaries are able to attack the network, image enhancement has to be performed (see Fig. 3). First, we enhance the contrast of the image. Next, the shadows and saturation levels are adjusted. Finally, we cap the lower pixel values (values less than a defined threshold) to 0 (shown in Fig. 3c). Furthermore, while printing the samples, the size of the images are increased such that it can tackle data quantization up to an extent.

3.5   The Defense Strategy

Although the classifier model is robust, we observe that under the influence of the attacks, the resiliency of the model is questioned. In this subsection, we propose a generalizable defense strategy that is focused on nullifying the effect of different attacks. For this purpose, structure based learning is incorporated. The use of data augmentations are leveraged to present different views of the same image. This in effect aids a classification model to focus on the image structure during classification. To simulate aberrations, inhomogeneities, and change in environments, various data augmentations are used. We use the PyTorch, OpenCV, and Numpy libraries for the implementation of the different augmentations listed as follows:

Random Color Jitter: The operation is relevant in the simulation of different lighting conditions. It aids neural networks in focusing on the physical structure of the object rather than the different colors in the images. This is achieved by bringing in random change in the contrast, saturation, hue, and brightness of an image (as shown in Eq. 5).

$$I_{out} = ColorJitter(I, brightness, contrast, saturation, hue) \tag{5}$$

where I and I_{out} signify the input and the augmented image respectively. The color jitter function is implemented in Pytorch. It takes the attribute values as input (float values) and randomly sets the image attributes in the range [1-attribute, 1+attribute].

Random Color Swap: Color swapping operation randomly swaps pixel intensities across different channels. It is relevant because the attacks often swap pixel intensities across channels and the perturbations are able to fool the network. By incorporating the color swap operation, the networks are forced to learn the structure of the object, thus nullifying such attacks.

Image Blurring and Adding Noise: Different aberrations in images result in misclassification. Blurring and noise are the most detrimental aberrations as they have adverse consequences on classification networks. These aberrations prevent convolutional filters in edge detection and feature extraction, thereby reducing the robustness of a model. Gradient based attacks often induce such kind of aberrations, thus blurring and noise addition (Gaussian, Salt & Pepper) augmentation operations are crucial for circumventing the effect of such attacks. The blurring filter follows the Gaussian function. For adding noise, we use a combination of Gaussian and salt and pepper noise as defined in Eq. 6.

$$I_{out} = SPN(GN(I, \alpha), \beta) \tag{6}$$

where SPN and GN represent the functions for adding Salt & Pepper noise and Gaussian noise respectively. The parameters α and β decide the percentage of noise corruption that is to be added to the image.

Image Solarization: The solarization operation (Eq. 7) is relevant as it shifts the network's focus from image color to object shape. Solarization mimics the effect of tone reversal that is observed in cases of overexposure of photographic films. The overexposure aids in highlighting the overall object shape in images.

Therefore, the augmentation in the dataset forces the network to learn the intrinsic features about an object shape (that remains unchanged during most perturbations).

$$I_{out} = solarize(I, \phi) = \begin{cases} \sim I_{i,j}, & \text{if } intensity < \phi. \\ I_{i,j}, & \text{otherwise.} \end{cases}, \; \forall \; pixels \; in \; I \qquad (7)$$

where $I_{i,j}$ represents the pixel intensity located at (i,j), ϕ denotes the threshold attribute, and $\sim I_{i,j}$ represents bitwise negation of the pixel intensity.

Edge Detection: Edge detection is yet another augmentation that accentuates the object edges and eliminates colors in the image. The attacked samples have almost similar structure as the original sample and thus having edge detected images during model training stabilizes the model's ability against color/pixel intensity based adversaries. In this context, we use Canny edge detection [5] as it is currently the widely accepted benchmark.

Image Inversion: The inversion operation inverts all the colors of a provided sample. Colors and textures provide queues to networks in a particular direction. By incorporating the inversion operation, the queues are negated, therefore the network is obligated to learn the structure of a sample rather than digressing into classification based on prominent colors.

Image Water Color: The painting operation mimics data quantization and intensity averaging that gets introduced as an effect of the attacks. The augmentation therefore helps the network understand the key important features in an image sample. On including the augmented data in the training phase, the model's ability in structure based feature extraction is enhanced. The operation is implemented using the predefined functions in the numpy library.

Image Gamma Adjustment: Gamma adjustment operation (Eq. 8) manipulates pixel intensities and brightness, thus simulating different luminances and lighting conditions. For $\gamma < 1$, the image is shifted to the darker side of the image intensity spectrum and vice versa. A classification network is obligated to learn image structure when the same image with varying lighting conditions are fed as training data (thus being effective against attacks).

$$I_{out} = c.I^{\gamma} \qquad (8)$$

where c is a constant that can be treated as a scale parameter.

Affine Transformation: In the context of autonomous cars, object distance and variations in camera viewpoint/angles are the major environment changes. The affine operation caters to such environmental variabilities. It is used to simulate experimental samples involving images under varying distances and angles.

The network learns to detect the object efficiently given different perspectives of the same.

$$I_{out} = affine(I, \theta, shift, shear, zoom, order) \tag{9}$$

Equation 9 denotes the affine function (implemented in the Pytorch library). θ controls the rotations. Shift, shear, and zoom parameters have their usual meanings, and order denotes the interpolation order.

Figure 4 shows augmented traffic signs corresponding to the different data augmentations. Along with the mentioned augmentations, standard rotation and perspective projections are also performed to strengthen classifier resiliency.

Model Training After Augmentation: After the augmentation steps, the original and the augmented images are combined to form a dataset. The data is then randomly split into training, validation, and test set with a ratio of 60:20:20. For the model training phase, a step similar to the original model training (discussed before) is undertaken. A pre-trained ResNet18 model is loaded and the final dense layer is replaced with a fully connected dense layer (4 outputs). Cross-entropy loss along with SGD optimization is used for model compilation. The model is trained for 30 epochs with an initial learning rate of 0.001 (reduced by 10% for every 5 epochs). The model achieves a training set accuracy of 99.82% along with a validation set accuracy of 99.52%.

Fig. 4. Different augmentation operations applied to an image sample: (a) Color Jitter, (b) Color Swap, (c) Image Blurring, (d) Noise Addition, (e) Image Solarization, (f) Edge Detection, (g) Color Inversion, (h) Image Watercolor, (i) Gamma Adjustment, and (j) Affine Transformation

4   Experimental Results and Discussion

The results corresponding to each phase of the experimentation pipeline are detailed in this section. In the following subsections, firstly the data acquisition and splitting steps are reported. For analyzing the performance of the presented defense strategy, we compare it with the adversarial training [2] and denoising autoencoder [3] based defense approaches. Next, the obtained results are examined on a quantitative scale to judge the resiliency of different methods.

4.1 Data Acquisition and Splitting

For training the models, it is crucial to have a standardized dataset. We acquire traffic sign data from two sources: one from kaggle [12], and the other from the German Traffic Sign Recognition Benchmark dataset [16]. Traffic data corresponding to left, right, speed, and stop signs are retained. The amalgamated dataset consists of 2400 images in total. Furthermore, seven attack techniques are applied on 230 samples. The generated adversarial sample set consists of 1610 images. Next, for adversarial training we combine the normal image dataset with the adversarial sample dataset. The total images in the dataset are 4010. For training the denoising autoencoder, 1200 original data samples (equally distributed among 4 classes) are picked and their corresponding perturbed images are generated and are used in the training and validation phase. Finally, for the proposed structured based learning, 400 samples from the original dataset along with its different augmentations are used (4000 images in total). After data acquisition, the data is split into training, validation, and test sets respectively (Splitting ratio - 60:20:20).

Table 1. Quantitative metrics for model evaluation on the original dataset

Class	Precision	Recall	F1-Score
Left	0.992	0.983	0.987
Right	0.983	0.992	0.988
Speed	1	1	1
Stop	1	1	1
Average	0.994	0.994	0.994

4.2 Performance Evaluation

Quantitative metrics are critical in judging robustness of different methods. In this paper, we use the precision, recall, F1-score, and accuracy metrics for the evaluation of the implemented methods. The quantitative performance results related to the ResNet-18 model is tabularized in Table 1. The model attains 99.4% test set accuracy. The acquired precision and recall are high signifying the accurate class prediction ability of the model. Also, the observed specificity highlights the reliability of the model against misclassification.

Next, we study the effect of attacks on the trained model. Different settings are incorporated and the consequences of adversaries on the network are analyzed. Figure 5 shows the adversarial samples corresponding to a stop sign generated by different attack techniques. It can be observed that some of the attacks are subtle up to the extent where the perturbation cannot be determined by the human eye. We report the performance of the trained ResNet model on the adversarial sample set in Table 2. The accuracy and F1-score trends clearly point out that the performance drops significantly and the model robustness is put to question. As observed from Table 2, the FAB attack misleads the network to the point where the accuracy drops to 18.3% although the generated samples (see Fig. 5g) have indistinguishable resemblance with the original samples. In real-world scenarios, misclassification at this scale will severely affect the navigation and control of the car and thus can have tremendous outcomes.

After noting the effects of the attacks on the classifier network, the proposed defense strategy is incorporated to tackle the same. The quantitative metrics corresponding to the defense model is tabulated in Table 3. The metrics highlight the robustness of the classification model. For evaluating the efficiency of the presented mechanism, we compare it with the popular defense paradigms. Figure 6 presents the overall accuracies achieved by the original and the defense models with respect to the adversarial sample set (1610 perturbed samples). The adversarial training based defense strategy achieves decent results across different attack types. The denoising autoencoder based defense works well for

Table 2. Performance evaluation of the model on the adversarial sample set

Approaches	Accuracy	F1-score
Fast Gradient Sign Method (FGSM)	23.809	0.170
Basic Iterative Method (BIM)	16.667	0.153
Projected Gradient Descent (PGD)	20.000	0.140
Carlini & Wagner Attack (CW)	21.875	0.19
Deep-Fool	21.311	0.193
FAB	18.333	0.145
Physical Perturbation	26.833	0.223

Table 3. Quantitative metrics corresponding to the defense model

Class	Precision	Recall	F1-Score
Left	0.998	0.988	0.993
Right	0.985	1	0.992
Speed	1	0.998	0.999
Stop	0.998	0.993	0.996
Average	0.995	0.995	0.995

Fig. 5. Adversarial Stop Sign Samples Corresponding to Different Attack Types: (a) Original Image, (b) FGSM, (c) BIM, (d) PGD, (e) CW, (f) DeepFool, (g) FAB, and (h) Physical Perturbation.

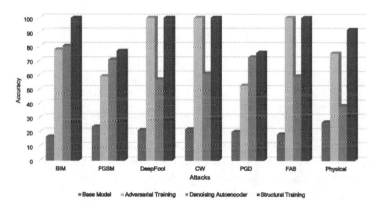

Fig. 6. Performance comparison of the original and defense models on the adversarial sample set based on accuracy metric.

the attacks that induce noticable perturbations in the images. However, it does not perform well against physical perturbations. The presented strategy stands out from its peers and performs best across the different attack types. The resiliency is further defended by its performance on the physical perturbation attack. Figure 7 presents the predicted probabilities corresponding to adversarial samples from each image class. As it can be observed, the original classifier is mislead into predicting the wrong class with a high probability. The defense models have varying performances in their ability to increase the correct class probability out of which the presented strategy emerges to be the winner.

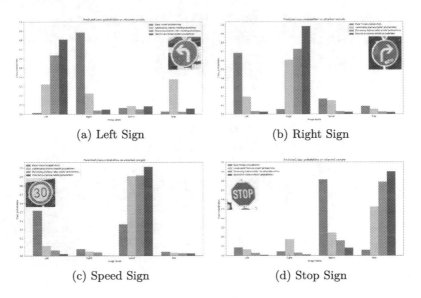

(a) Left Sign   (b) Right Sign

(c) Speed Sign   (d) Stop Sign

Fig. 7. Class probabilities predicted by different models corresponding to adversarial samples from each image class.

5   Conclusion

In this paper, we discuss the effect of adversarial attacks on a vision based autonomous car. The classification accuracy of the model responsible for navigation is hindered when exposed to adversarial image samples. To tackle the same, we propose a defense mechanism fundamented on structure based learning. After rigorous experimentation, it is observed that the defense strategy is robust and generalizable across different attack types. The methodology is simple and can be scaled across varied use cases in industrial applications dealing with adversarial attacks.

References

1. Akhtar, N., Mian, A.: Threat of adversarial attacks on deep learning in computer vision: a survey. IEEE Access **6**, 14410–14430 (2018)
2. Bai, T., Luo, J., Zhao, J., Wen, B., Wang, Q.: Recent advances in adversarial training for adversarial robustness. arXiv preprint arXiv:2102.01356 (2021)
3. Bakhti, Y., Fezza, S.A., Hamidouche, W., Déforges, O.: DDSA: a defense against adversarial attacks using deep denoising sparse autoencoder. IEEE Access **7**, 160397–160407 (2019)
4. Brahmbhatt, S.: Practical OpenCV. Apress (2013)
5. Canny, J.: A computational approach to edge detection. IEEE Trans. Pattern Anal. Mach. Intell. **6**, 679–698 (1986)
6. Carlini, N., Wagner, D.: Towards evaluating the robustness of neural networks. In: 2017 IEEE Symposium on Security And Privacy (SP), pp. 39–57. IEEE (2017)

7. Chakraborty, A., Alam, M., Dey, V., Chattopadhyay, A., Mukhopadhyay, D.: A survey on adversarial attacks and defences. CAAI Trans. Intell. Technol. **6**(1), 25–45 (2021)

8. Croce, F., Hein, M.: Minimally distorted adversarial examples with a fast adaptive boundary attack. In: International Conference on Machine Learning, pp. 2196–2205. PMLR (2020)

9. Eykholt, K., et al.: Robust physical-world attacks on deep learning visual classification. In: Proceedings of the IEEE Conference on Computer Vision and Pattern Recognition, pp. 1625–1634 (2018)

10. Goodfellow, I.J., Shlens, J., Szegedy, C.: Explaining and harnessing adversarial examples. arXiv preprint arXiv:1412.6572 (2014)

11. He, K., Zhang, X., Ren, S., Sun, J.: Deep residual learning for image recognition. In: Proceedings of the IEEE Conference on Computer Vision and Pattern Recognition, pp. 770–778 (2016)

12. Hemateja, A.V.N.M.: Traffic sign dataset - classification (2021). https://www.kaggle.com/datasets/ahemateja19bec1025/traffic-sign-dataset-classification?resource=download

13. Kurakin, A., Goodfellow, I.J., Bengio, S.: Adversarial examples in the physical world. In: Artificial Intelligence Safety and Security, pp. 99–112. Chapman and Hall/CRC (2018)

14. Madry, A., Makelov, A., Schmidt, L., Tsipras, D., Vladu, A.: Towards deep learning models resistant to adversarial attacks. arXiv preprint arXiv:1706.06083 (2017)

15. Moosavi-Dezfooli, S.M., Fawzi, A., Frossard, P.: DeepFool: a simple and accurate method to fool deep neural networks. In: Proceedings of the IEEE Conference on Computer Vision and Pattern Recognition, pp. 2574–2582 (2016)

16. Stallkamp, J., Schlipsing, M., Salmen, J., Igel, C.: The German traffic sign recognition benchmark: a multi-class classification competition. In: The 2011 International Joint Conference on Neural Networks, pp. 1453–1460. IEEE (2011)

17. Szegedy, C., et al.: Intriguing properties of neural networks. arXiv preprint arXiv:1312.6199 (2013)

18. Xu, H., et al.: Adversarial attacks and defenses in images, graphs and text: a review. Int. J. Autom. Comput. **17**(2), 151–178 (2020)

Improvising the CNN Feature Maps Through Integration of Channel Attention for Handwritten Text Recognition

B. N. Shashank[1], S. Nagesh Bhattu[1(✉)], and K. Sri Phani Krishna[2]

[1] Department of Computer Science and Engineering,
National Institute of Technology Andhra Pradesh, Tadepalligudem, India
`nageshbhattu@nitandhra.ac.in`
[2] Department of Electrical Engineering, National Institute of Technology
Andhra Pradesh, Tadepalligudem, India

Abstract. Convolutional Neural Network (CNN) based encoder and Recurrent Neural Network (RNN) based decoder architectures are widely used in the design of Handwritten Text Recognition (HTR) systems. Effective encoder representation plays a vital role in improving the performance of HTR systems. Squeeze and Excitation Networks, used in the context of image classification, object detection and scene classification, capture global inter-channel dependencies. ECA-Net learns channel attention via local Cross Channel Interaction (CCI). The current work proposes an encoder-decoder architecture for HTR which combines the benefits of local and global cross-channel attention for effective encoder representation. Experimental results on the IAM dataset show that there is an 8.98%, 3.24% reduction in Character Error Rate (CER) and an 8.98%, 3.45% reduction in Word Error Rate (WER) when the proposed module is applied to the state-of-the-art HTR Flor model and Puigcerver model respectively. The proposed work also presents a detailed error analysis at the character level on the IAM dataset.

Keywords: Image to sequence models · Handwritten Text Recognition · Channel Attention

1 Introduction

The task of HTR was first addressed by the models designing handcrafted features with Hidden Markov Model (HMM) [3]. These models were designed to extract language-specific handcrafted features for transcription at the character level, performing segmentation, pre-processing, and sequence learning task [12–15]. The pre-processing step is performed to reduce the variability in the handwriting by applying slant skew kind of spatial transformations. These handcrafted features are utilized by HMM for the sequence learning task. But these models suffer from the problem of transcribing the text sequences having long-term dependencies. Another major problem with these models was while transcribing word level or line level images, the inability to understand the character alignment for variable length input and output sequences [16]. These models were not end-to-end trainable. To address the problem of transcribing long-range dependencies, models were developed using HMM combined with Recurrent Neural Networks (RNNs) and Convolutional Neural Networks (CNNs) [4,5] which showed better results compared to the standard HMM architecture. Later Long Short-Term Memory (LSTM) based deep learning models emerged having a higher ability to capture long-term dependencies. The success of these models is mainly because of the use of MDLSTMs [6]. Models used in [2,17–19] use the combination of CNNs and RNN variations for spatial and time-aligned feature extraction. These models overcome the alignment problem by using Connectionist Temporal Classification (CTC) [20] as the output layer and cost function for time sequencing the features that do not require character boundaries in labelled data. This enabled end-to-end training of the model for transcribing line-level and word-level images. Later Long Short-Term Memory (LSTM) based deep learning models emerged having a higher ability to capture long-term dependencies. The success of these models is mainly because of the use of MDLSTMs [6]. However, the use of MDLSTMS incurred high computational costs. Long training time and more parameters made the researchers look for alternative solutions. The solution was to imitate the abilities of MDLSTMs with CNN in the initial layers however the LSTMs are used at later layers for sequence generation task. The idea of partly replacing MDLSTM with CNN present in the initial layers reduced computational cost, achieving state-of-the-art results with no loss of accuracy [2]. Further gating mechanisms were implemented with the convolutional components which are known as Gated Fully Convolutional Neural Networks (GFCN) [1,7]. The approaches implemented using GFCN achieved state-of-the-art results with a decrease in the number of parameters.

The contribution of the proposed work are as follows: The work proposes a channel attention module which combines the benefits of global CCI and local CCI in the context of HTR for improving CNN-based encoder representations. The work presents a detailed error analysis at the character level on the IAM dataset analyzing the impact of the proposed channel attention module on the state-of-the-art HTR architectures presented in [1,2]. The state-of-the-art models developed for HTR use a statistical language model for HTR post-correction for increasing performance. However, the focus of the proposed work is on increasing the text recognition capabilities of the models by improvising the feature representation of the encoder by integrating channel attention mechanisms. Therefore, the proposed work does not employ any statistical language models to perform HTR post-correction.

2   Related Works

In recent years, CRNN [21] kind of architectures which are initially built for Scene Text Recognition resulted in achieving state-of-the-art results and are being extended to the context of HTR. The CRNN-based architectures proved to be effective and efficient in the context of HTR giving state-of-the-art results. These models consist of an encoder network and a decoder network where the encoder part focuses on encoding the image to a feature representation and the decoder part focuses on generating the sequence from the encoded representation by using RNNs. The models use CTC for training the model and decoding the final text.

Figure 1 (a) shows the architecture of the model developed by Puigcerver which follows a CRNN architecture. The encoder part consists of 5 CNN blocks and the decoder part consists of 5 BLSTM layers. Each convolutional block is composed of 3×3 kernels where the number of filters depends on the convolutional block. The number of kernels is fixed to 16n where n represents the nth convolutional block. Max pooling is applied to the first 3 blocks using a 2×2 kernel and dropout is applied to the last 3 blocks with a probability of 0.2. Leaky Rectified Linear Unit (Leaky ReLU) is used as an activation function for all CNN layers and batch normalization is used. The decoder part contains 5 BLSTM layers with a dropout of probability 0.5, each having 256 units. Finally, a dense layer contains the number of neurons equal to the character set size + 1. Figure 1 (b) shows the workflow of Flor architecture [1] for HTR. The encoder part consists of convolutional blocks which comprise traditional convolutions followed by gated convolutions. Parametric Rectified Linear Unit (PReLU) is used as an activation function for the traditional blocks. A dropout of probability 0.2 is added to gated convolutions in the last three convolutional blocks. The decoder part has 2 Bidirectional Gated Recurrence Units (BGRU) having 128 hidden units with alternating dense layers. The size of the last dense layer is equal to the size of the character set + 1.

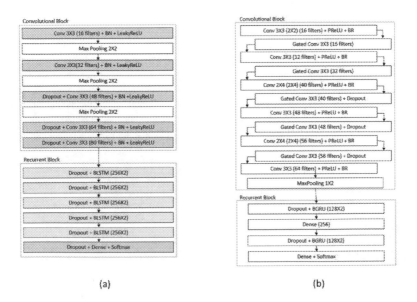

Fig. 1. (a) Workflow of Puigcerver architecture [2] to the left and (b) Workflow of Flor architecture [1] to the right

3   Channel Attention in HTR Architectures

Various channel attention mechanisms are implemented for CNN in recent years which generate attention weights for channels so that the channels which contribute more to the prediction task get higher attention weights. By using these learned attention weights the feature maps are recalibrated. The recalibrated feature map provides a better representation of features which results in better accuracy.

3.1   Squeeze and Excite

The most followed channel attention module is the Squeeze and Excitation Networks (SENet) [8] which squeezes the feature maps channel-wise using global average pooling which is then followed by the excitation phase. The result of performing global averaging pooling generates a vector of dimension equal to the number of channels C. This C dimensional vector is then passed through a dense layer with Relu activation where the dimensionality reduction happens. The vector dimension gets reduced to C/r where r is called the reduction ratio which is a hyper-parameter. It is then passed through one more dense layer with a sigmoid activation function. In this layer, the vector dimension will be scaled back to C. The above process of adaptive recalibration captures channel-wise dependencies. For the purpose of capturing channel-wise dependencies, nonlinear interactions between channels and non-mutual relationships between the channels are learned. The set of operations performing squeeze and excitation is summarized in equation (1) where σ refers to the sigmoid function, δ refers to ReLU activation and z is the feature map generated after global average pooling.

$$s = F_{ex}(z, W) = \sigma(g(z, W)) = \sigma(W_2\delta(W_1z)) \tag{1}$$

The result of squeeze and excitation is obtained by dot-wise multiplication of the generated vector of C dimension with the original CNN feature map as represented by equation (2) where $F_{scale}()$ represents channel-wise multiplication between the generated scalar s_c and the original feature map before the squeeze operation u_c.

$$\tilde{x}_c = F_{scale}(u_c, s_c) = s_c u_c \tag{2}$$

To improve the feature representation of the Flor model, experiments were carried out by integrating the squeeze and excitation operation at various positions of the model architecture. The empirical results show that performing squeeze and excitation operations on the generated CNN feature maps after the first and second CNN blocks resulted in a much improved encoded representation of the features. The reduction ratio is set to 4. At the first CNN block of the Flor model, the feature map has 16 channels. The squeeze operation performed through global average pooling forms a vector of dimension 16. The next layer is a dense layer with ReLU which does the dimensionality reduction resulting in an output dimension of 4. The next layer is again a dense layer with a sigmoid which increases the dimension to 16. These scalar values are used to recalibrate the CNN feature map generated at the first block of CNN which is of size $512 \times 64 \times 16$, by performing element-wise multiplication of the scalar values present in the vector with the channels. The squeeze and excitation operation is performed a second time on the Flor model immediately after the second convolution block, i.e., after the gated convolution layer where the size of the feature map is $512 \times 64 \times 32$. Since the reduction ratio is set to 4, after performing the squeeze operation and passing the feature maps through the first dense layer with ReLU activation, the dimension reduces to 8 which is then rescaled and used to recalibrate the feature map. The newly generated feature map has a much better representation of encoded features since the channels that contribute more to the prediction task are given more weightage.

Similar experimentation is followed to improve the feature representation of the Piugcerver model by integrating squeeze and excite operations. The best results were obtained when the channel attention operations are performed after the first 2 convolution blocks. The last layer of the first convolutional block is a max pooling layer where the dimension of the feature map will be $512 \times 64 \times 16$. Performing squeeze and excitation with the reduction ratio 4 leads to reducing the dimensionality of the generated vector from 16 to 4 which is then rescaled back to 16 after passing through the second dense layer. Using these attention maps the input feature is recalibrated. The squeeze and excite operation is again performed for the second time after the second convolutional block. The max pooling layer, which is the last layer of the second convolutional transforms the feature map to a dimension of size $512 \times 64 \times 16$. This generated feature map is again recalibrated using squeeze and excitation operation as mentioned above.

3.2   Efficient Channel Attention

The Efficient Channel Attention mechanism explained in [9] is similar to [8] which aims to provide channel attention. The major difference is due to the fact that the authors claim the dimensionality reduction phase in the squeeze and excitation process is not necessary for improved performance. Instead of learning non-linear dependencies, allowing direct correspondence between the channel and its weights makes the model capture channel-wise dependencies better. So, this channel attention mechanism does not employ any dimensionality reduction. The main change introduced by this efficient channel attention is the local Cross Channel Interaction (CCI). In SENet, the weights for a query channel are learned by considering all the remaining channels where the CCI is global. But efficient channel attention introduces local CCI where the weight of a query channel is learned by considering k neighbouring channels where k is a hyper-parameter to be selected. However, the authors propose a method for the adaptive selection of value k, in our experiments the results are tested by setting different values for k. The process of Efficient Channel Attention is mathematically shown by equation (3) where the weight of y_i is calculated by considering y_i and its k neighbours and Ω_i^k represents the set of k adjacent channels of y_i

$$\omega_i = \sigma(\sum_{j=1}^{k} \omega^j y_i^j), y_i^j \in \Omega_i^k \tag{3}$$

Squeeze and excitation operations for the Flor model are replaced with efficient channel attention in the first two blocks, i.e., immediately after the gated convolutional layers of the model. For the Puigcerver model, the experimentation is carried out by replacing squeeze and excitation from the first 2 convolutional blocks-i.e., after the max pooling layer.

3.3 Combining Global CCI and Local CCI

When the squeeze and excite operation is performed, the channels are recalibrated by learning attention weights through global CCI. Passing these recalibrated channels to efficient channel attention makes the model learn allowing direct correspondence between the channel and its weights. Since the channels are already recalibrated considering global CCI, the query channel gets proper weightage when weights are learned by grouping the neighbouring channels in a more efficient way. The channel attention modules added for the Flor architecture and Puigcerver architecture are replaced by this sequential combination of SENet and ECA-Net for which better results are obtained.

4   Results and Discussion

4.1   Dataset

IAM database [10]: The database contains unconstrained handwritten English text. The database provides word-level, line-level, paragraph-level, and page-level images. In the proposed work, line-level images are considered for training the model. The data split for training, testing and validation are used as per the Large Writer Independent Text Line Recognition Task which is mentioned on their official website. Data split details are shown in Table 1.

Table 1. Details of IAM dataset split.

Dataset	Training	Validation	Test	Total
IAM	6,161	1,840	1,861	9,862

4.2   Experimental Setup

Puigcerver model [2] and Flor model [1] are considered as reference models for our experimentation purposes. An experimental setup similar to [1] is followed. Since the aim of the proposed work is to improve the encoded feature representation of the model, performing HTR post-correction using a statistical language model is not considered for experimentation. Numbers from 0 to 9, lower case alphabets, upper case alphabets, and special symbols are considered in the character set of size 95. For making a fair comparison, the same hyper-parameters are maintained, CTC loss is employed and RMSprop optimizer is used with a 0.001 learning rate. A batch size of 16 images is considered, Early stopping and Reduced learning rate on the plateau are applied for 20 and 15 epochs respectively. Vanilla Beam search is used to decode the generated CTC sequence. Each variant of the model is run for 5 trials. The training was performed on a Ubuntu system with 32 GB memory and NVIDIA GeForce RTX 2080 TI 12 GB GPU.

4.3 Evaluation Metrics

The error rate is calculated by considering 3 kinds of errors present in the transcribed text: Insertion error refers to the error that occurred because of wrongly inserted symbols or words in the transcribed text when compared to ground truth. Deletion error refers to errors caused by those symbols or words which are missing in the transcribed text when compared to the ground truth. Substitution error refers to the error induced by the model due to wrongly transcribing the symbols or words. Character Error Rate (CER) and Word Error Rate (WER) are the two standard metrics that are used widely by the HTR community. These metrics are based on the concept of Levenshtein distance which measures the edit distance between two sequences. CER specifies the minimum number of insertions, deletions, and substitutions of symbols that are required to convert the ground truth text to predicted text. Equation (4) gives the formula for calculating the CER between two sequences of characters.

$$CER = (S_c + D_c + I_c)/N_c \qquad (4)$$

where S_c indicates the number of characters to be substituted, D_c indicates the number of characters to be deleted and I_c indicates the number of characters to be inserted into the ground truth text for transforming it into predicted text. N_c indicates the total number of characters present in the ground truth text. Similar to CER, WER specifies the minimum number of insertions, deletions, and substitutions at the word level that is required to convert the ground truth text to predicted text. Equation (5) gives the formula for calculating the WER between two sequences of characters

$$WER = (S_w + D_w + I_w)/N_w \qquad (5)$$

where S_w indicates the number of words to be substituted, D_w indicates the number of words to be deleted and I_w indicates the number of words to be inserted into the ground truth text for transforming it into predicted text. N_w indicated the total number of words present in the ground truth text. The error rates are usually normalized so that the error rate value does not exceed 100. Sequence Error Rate (SEQ) is another metric that is used to measure the error at the line level or sequence level. The metric is less used since a single character error in the transcription of a line evaluates the entire line as wrongly predicted. Equation (6) represents the formula for calculating SER.

$$SER = N_c/N \tag{6}$$

where N_c represents the number of correctly predicted line-level images in the test set and N represents the total number of line-level images considered for evaluation. The character level analysis is carried out by implementing Wagner-Fischer algorithm [11] which is a dynamic programming-based approach that calculates the edit distance between two strings. To infer the moves from the edit distance matrix, the backtracking algorithm has been used which selects one path from multiple possible paths. By following the backtracking algorithm, we get all the characters that contribute to insertion, deletion, and substitution errors.

4.4 Results

Table 2. Character Error Rate, Word Error Rate and Sequence Error Rate of the reference models considered and its tried-out variants

Model	CER	WER	SER
Flor	0.071679	0.235825	0.833207
	($\pm$0.002405)	(+0.008603)	($\pm$0.013393)
Flor + SENet	0.066755	0.219639	0.815905
	($\pm$0.001523)	($\pm$0.003073)	($\pm$0.008233)
Flor + ECANet	0.068827	0.227176	0.823320
	($\pm$0.002223)	($\pm$0.005843)	($\pm$0.007253)
Flor + SENet + ECA	**0.065238**	**0.214663**	**0.808167**
	($\pm$0.001152)	($\pm$0.004007)	($\pm$0.009142)
Puigcerver	0.072659	0.222576	0.826652
	($\pm$0.000254)	($\pm$0.006116)	($\pm$0.008586)
Puigcerver + SENet	0.071838	0.219819	0.827190
	($\pm$0.003332)	($\pm$0.008515)	($\pm$0.010171)
Puigcerver + ECA	0.073396	0.223058	0.831810
	($\pm$0.003255)	($\pm$0.012635)	($\pm$0.011949)
Puigcerver + SENet + ECA	**0.070303**	**0.214899**	**0.821494**
	($\pm$0.001758)	($\pm$0.004275)	($\pm$0.004856)

Table 2 shows the average CER and WER for the different configurations of the models over 5 trials conducted. From the results, it can be observed that performing the squeeze and excitation operation on the first two convolutional blocks of the Puigcrever model and Flor model decreases the error rates. When squeeze and excite operation is replaced with efficient channel attention, improvements were found for the Flor model against base configuration but when replaced in the Puigcerver model the error rate worsens. The increase in error rate might be because of the number of neighbouring channels considered for calculating weights for a query channel. Improvements were found in the Puigcerver model by integrating channel attention in other places of the model immediately after the convolutional block. However, the proposed work addresses this by combining both kinds of attention mechanisms. Since all the channels are already recalibrated using squeeze and excite, performing efficient channel attention after that gives much improved results and the number of neighbour channels considered for calculating the attention weights does not degrade the performance.

Table 3. A total of 62286 characters in the ground truth, over the 5 trials conducted for each model variant the table displays average values of TP= True Positive character number, Pred Char= number of predicted characters, and IE=Insertion Error count

Model	TP(avg)	Pred Char(avg)	IE(avg)
Flor Model	57955	61778.6	597
Flor Model + SENet	58291.6	61821.6	581.2
Flor Model +ECA-Net	58127.4	61829.8	607.6
Flor Model + ECA-Net + SENet	58411.2	61880	585
Puigcerver	57748	61890.4	597
Puigcerver + SENet	57766	61846.6	585.8
Puigcerver + ECANet	57740.2	61894.2	597.1
Puigcerver + SENet + ECANet	57913.6	61864.2	585.7

Table 3 shows the statistics related to insertion errors. Insertion error refers to the characters which are to be inserted while converting ground truth to predicted text which indicated the characters that are wrongly inserted in the predicted text. When squeeze and excitation operation is performed on both the Flor model and Puigcerver model, the average number of characters considered for the prediction is increased. The reduction in the average insertion error confirms that the increase in the number of characters considered for prediction is not because of additional characters inserted by the model. An increase in the average true positive rate of characters further confirms that the model performs better with respect to insertion errors when squeeze and excitation operation is integrated into the model. When efficient channel attention is added to the reference models considered, the insertion error increases. The Flor model performs better with the integration of efficient channel attention but the performance is not because of the control of insertion error. When SENet and ECA-Net are combined, both models perform better with decreased average insertion error and increased average true positive rate.

Table 4. Substitution Error of Flor model with the combination of attention mechanisms. The top 10 characters with the highest average substitution error over 5 trials are displayed in increasing order

Flor	Flor + SENet	Flor + ECA-Net	Flor + SENet + ECA-Net
'l': 138.6	'w': 144.2	'l': 131.2	'l': 131.4
'w': 160.2	'l': 146.8	't': 153.6	'w': 138.6
't': 167.2	't': 151.2	'w': 160.0	't': 154.8
'u': 194.8	'u': 179.6	'u': 184.4	'u': 161.6
'n': 202.8	'n': 179.8	'n': 190.8	'n': 182.4
'a': 212.2	'a': 195.4	'a': 206.2	's': 183.2
's': 219.6	's': 204.6	's': 213.2	'a': 186.6
'e': 243.0	'e': 225.6	'o': 233.6	'o': 215.0
'o': 243.4	'o': 226.8	'e': 240.0	'e': 226.4
'r': 267.6	'o': 234.4	'e': 247.2	'e': 241.2

Table 5. Substitution Error of Puigcerver model with the combination of attention mechanisms. The top 10 characters with the highest average substitution error over 5 trials are displayed in increasing order

Puigcrever	Puigcerver + SENet	Puigcerver + SENet + ECA-Net
'h': 124.2	'h': 116.6	'h': 120.4
'l': 141.2	'l': 143.6	'l': 141.6
'u': 156.2	'w': 152.4	'w': 148.4
'w': 161.0	'u': 158.2	'u': 166.2
't': 162.6	't': 165.8	't': 167.8
'n': 219.0	'n': 225.8	'n': 217.8
's': 251.2	'a': 243.6	's': 226.4
'a': 255.6	's': 251.8	'a': 228.2
'o': 263.8	'o': 276.4	'o': 250.8
'e': 281.0	'e': 282.4	'e': 270.2

Table 4 and Table 5 show the top most substituted characters on average for the variants of the Flor model and Puigcerver model respectively. When the squeeze and excite operation is performed on the Flor model, the average substitution error characters 'r', 'e', and 'n' are reduced. On average there are 43 miss-classification of character 'r' corrected out of which 7 times 'r's getting miss-classified as 't' and 6.2 times 'r's getting miss-classified as 'e' gets corrected. For both characters 'e' and 'n' on average 28 miss-classifications are corrected. When ECA-net is integrated with the Flor architecture, on average 26 miss-classifications of character 'r', 18 miss-classifications of character 'i', and 16 miss-classifications of character 't' gets corrected. When both SENet and

ECA-Net have added together the characters that contribute to the improvement in substitution error are 'r', 's', and 'e'. Majorly 'r's getting miss-classified as 's', and 'r's getting miss-classified as 'n' gets corrected. Adding SENet to the Puigcerver model majorly corrected the substitution error of characters 'a', 'd', and 'h'. Adding ECA-Net further worsened the substitution error because of which the character error rate gets high. The combination of SENet and ECA-Net on the Puigcerver model improves the average substitution error and the characters that are majorly corrected are 'd' and 's'.

Table 6. Deletion Error of Flor model with the combination of attention mechanisms. The top 10 characters with the highest average deletion error over 5 trials are displayed in increasing order

Flor	Flor + SENet	Flor + ECA-Net	Flor + SENet + ECA-Net
'o': 51.6	'o': 44.8	'i': 45.0	'i': 42.0
't': 53.8	'i': 48.0	'o': 49.0	'o': 46.0
'i': 57.2	't': 53.8	't': 52.2	't': 52.0
'n': 69.0	'': 57.4	'': 56.6	'': 61.6
'': 69.2	'n': 65.4	'l': 71.4	'n': 65.6
'l': 71.8	'l': 76.4	'n': 76.2	'l': 75.8
's': 91.2	's': 87.0	's': 93.2	's': 79.8
'e': 124.4	'e': 115.2	'e': 117.2	'e': 103.8
'r': 134.2	'r': 125.4	'r': 128.8	'r': 116.6
'': 328.4	'': 296.8	'': 309.2	'': 280.6

Table 7. Deletion error of Puigcerver model with the combination of attention mechanisms. The top 10 characters with the highest average deletion error over 5 trials are displayed in increasing order

Puigcrever	Puigcerver + SENet	Puigcerver + SENet + ECA-Net
'i': 37.8	'i': 39.6	'i': 36.2
't': 51.0	'o': 49.6	't': 48.8
'o': 54.2	't': 51.6	'o': 50.8
'': 62.4	'': 61.0	'': 60.0
'n': 64.2	'n': 67.0	'n': 64.4
'l': 72.0	'l': 74.8	'l': 67.8
's': 94.4	's': 92.8	's': 87.8
'e': 118.6	'e': 122.6	'e': 115.4
'r': 141.6	'r': 144.0	'r': 146.0
'': 251.2	'': 255.4	'': 240.0

Table 6 and Table 7 show the top deletion error of the base model and its variants. Deletion error refers to those characters which are to be deleted when transforming the ground truth text to predicted text. It indicated the characters that are present in the ground truth but left out of prediction. Combining SENet with the Flor model majorly reduces the deletion error of characters 'e' and 'r'. Integrating ECA-Net to the Flor model majorly reduces the deletion error of characters 'e' and 'i'. Combining both channel attention mechanisms addresses all three characters 'e', 'i', and 'r'. Integrating SENet with the Puigcerver model improves the deletion error rate of characters 'o' and 'f' but for a few characters, the deletion error was found to be increasing. ECA-Net added to the Puigcerver model worsens the deletion error. When both SENet and ECA-Net are combined on Puigcerver model characters 'e', 'o', and 's'.

5   Conclusion

The reference models have experimented with different channel attention mechanisms. The idea of learning weights through global CCI followed by local CCI by combining squeeze and excitation with efficient channel attention contributes to a better representation of the feature maps because of which the transcription can be done more effectively. The results showed a reduced Character Error Rate, Word Error Rate, and Sequence Error Rate for the addition of the integrated module. The analysis part shows the contribution of the attention module towards reducing insertion, substitution, and deletion errors.

References

1. Neto, d.S., Flor, A., et al.: HTR-Flor: a deep learning system for offline handwritten text recognition. In: 2020 33rd SIBGRAPI Conference on Graphics, Patterns and Images (SIBGRAPI). IEEE (2020)
2. Joan. P.: Are multidimensional recurrent layers really necessary for handwritten text recognition?. In: 2017 14th IAPR International Conference on Document Analysis and Recognition (ICDAR). Vol. 1. IEEE (2017)
3. Plötz, T., Fink, G.A.: Markov models for offline handwriting recognition: a survey. Int. J. Doc. Anal. Recogn. (IJDAR) **12**(4), 269–298 (2009)
4. Frinken, V., Peter, T., Fischer, A., Bunke, H., Do, T.-M.-T., Artieres, T.: Improved Handwriting Recognition by Combining Two Forms of Hidden Markov Models and a Recurrent Neural Network. In: Jiang, X., Petkov, N. (eds.) CAIP 2009. LNCS, vol. 5702, pp. 189–196. Springer, Heidelberg (2009). https://doi.org/10.1007/978-3-642-03767-2_23
5. Bluche, T., Ney, H., Kermorvant, C.: Tandem HMM with convolutional neural network for handwritten word recognition. In: 2013 IEEE International Conference on Acoustics, Speech and Signal Processing. IEEE (2013)
6. Alex, G., Schmidhuber, J.: Offline handwriting recognition with multidimensional recurrent neural networks. Adv. Neural Inf. Proc. Syst. 21 (2008)
7. Théodore, B., Messina, B.: Gated convolutional recurrent neural networks for multilingual handwriting recognition. In: 2017 14th IAPR International Conference on Document Analysis and Recognition (ICDAR). Vol. 1. IEEE (2017)

8. Jie, H., Shen, L., Sun, G.: Squeeze-and-excitation networks. In: Proceedings of the IEEE Conference on Computer Vision and Pattern Recognition (2018)

9. Qilong, W., et al.: Supplementary material for 'ECA-Net: efficient channel attention for deep convolutional neural networks. In: Proceedings of the 2020 IEEE/CVF Conference on Computer Vision and Pattern Recognition, IEEE, Seattle, WA, USA (2020)

10. Marti, U-V., Horst Bunke, H.: The IAM-database: an English sentence database for offline handwriting recognition. Int. J. Doc. Anal. Recog. **5**, 39–46 (2002)

11. Wagner, R.A., Fischer, M.J.: The string-to-string correction problem. J. ACM (JACM) **21**(1), 168–173 (1974)

12. Nafiz, A., Fatos, Y.V.: An overview of character recognition focused on off-line handwriting. IEEE Trans. Syst. Man Cyber. Part C (Appl. Rev.) **31**, 216–233 (2001). https://doi.org/10.1109/5326.941845

13. Marti, U.-V., Bunke, H.: Using a statistical language model to improve the performance of an hmm-based cursive handwriting recognition system. IJPRAI. **15**, 65–90 (2001). https://doi.org/10.1142/S0218001401000848

14. Sauvola, J., Seppänen, T., Haapakoski, S., Pietikäinen, M.: Adaptive Document Binarization. Pattern Recognition. 33. vol 1, pp. 147–152 (1997). https://doi.org/10.1109/ICDAR.1997.619831

15. de Zeeuw, F.: Slant Correction Using Histograms, Bachelor's Thesis in Artificial Intelligence (2006)

16. Marti, U.-V., Bunke, H.: Handwritten sentence recognition. 3. vol 3, pp. 463–466 (2000). https://doi.org/10.1109/ICPR.2000.903584

17. Voigtlaender, P., Doetsch, P., Ney, H.: Handwriting Recognition with Large Multi-dimensional Long Short-Term Memory Recurrent Neural Networks. In: 2016 15th International Conference on Frontiers in Handwriting Recognition (ICFHR), pp. 228–233 (2016) https://doi.org/10.1109/ICFHR.2016.0052

18. Vu, P., Christopher, K., Jérôme, L.: Dropout Improves Recurrent Neural Networks for Handwriting Recognition. In: Proceedings of International Conference on Frontiers in Handwriting Recognition, ICFHR (2014) https://doi.org/10.1109/ICFHR.2014.55

19. Krishnan, P., Dutta, K., Jawahar, C.V.: Word Spotting and Recognition Using Deep Embedding. 1–6 (2018). https://doi.org/10.1109/DAS.2018.70

20. Alex, G., Santiago, F., Faustino, G., Jürgen, S.: Connectionist temporal classification: Labelling unsegmented sequence data with recurrent neural 'networks. In: ICML 2006 - Proceedings of the 23rd International Conference on Machine Learning, pp. 369–376 (2006). https://doi.org/10.1145/1143844.1143891

21. Baoguang, S., Xiang, B., Cong,Y.: An End-to-End trainable neural network for image-based sequence recognition and its application to scene text recognition. In: IEEE Transactions on Pattern Analysis and Machine Intelligence (2015). https://doi.org/10.1109/TPAMI.2016.2646371

XAIForCOVID-19: A Comparative Analysis of Various Explainable AI Techniques for COVID-19 Diagnosis Using Chest X-Ray Images

Nisarg Patel[1]([✉]), Siddhraj Parmar[1], Priyanka Singh[1],
and Manoranjan Mohanty[2]

[1] Dhirubhai Ambani Institute of Information and Communication Technology,
Gandhinagar, Gujarat, India
{201801013,201801466,priyanka_singh}@daiict.ac.in
[2] University of Technology Sydney, Sydney, Australia
Manoranjan.Mohanty@uts.edu.au

Abstract. The World Health Organization (WHO) declared a pandemic in response to the global spread of the coronavirus SARS-CoV-2, which was discovered in 2019. The test, used to identify the presence of this virus in humans, utilises sputum or blood samples, and results are often available in a few hours or days. To assist the medical professionals in the diagnosis process, advanced Artificial Intelligence (AI) models are proposed that work on medical imaging, such as Computed Tomography (CT) and X-rays. As it is a crucial application that involves life and death implications, the trust of the people is gained by explaining the results of the model. Despite the excellent results of AI models in terms of precision and performance, they are black boxes as they don't provide significant insights behind their working, their decisions are not always interpretable and explainable. Here comes the domain Explainable AI (XAI) which attempts to provide insights underneath these black box models. Various XAI techniques exist today with certain differences in the parameters such as reliability, causality and usability. Thus, in this paper we apply different available XAI techniques and try to rank them for the task of distinguishing covid-19 infection and viral pneumonia patients from healthy people based on chest X-ray images by investigating and obtaining the results from these techniques that are then shown to the domain experts. We also compute a Mean Opinion Score (MOS) to validate them.

Keywords: Covid-19 Diagnosis · Explainable AI · Resnet · Gradcam · Lime · Saliency

1 Introduction

The ongoing pandemic caused by a sudden outbreak of coronavirus disease has posed significant challenges to medical professionals, as the virus has rapidly

D. Gupta et al. (Eds.): CVIP 2022, CCIS 1777, pp. 503–517, 2023.
https://doi.org/10.1007/978-3-031-31417-9_38

spread throughout the world. As of 17 July 2022, over 559 million confirmed cases and over 6.3 million deaths have been reported globally [20]. The reverse transcription polymerase chain reaction (RT-PCR) test is the most commonly used method for detecting Covid-19. The disadvantage of real-time RT-PCR is that it sometimes misses the covid positive, which can have serious consequences in critical situations [17]. Also, it is a manual and labor-intensive method, so other screening techniques that can assist this diagnosis are encouraged to relieve pressure on healthcare professionals. One such method of diagnosis is from the chest X-ray of a person, which has a high sensitivity (around 89 percent) on real-world data [6]. The rapid advancement of Artificial Intelligence (AI) has facilitated it's adoption in many fields like developing new tools for cybersecurity, handling deepfakes, military applications and above all, the crucial healthcare adoption. Deep learning algorithms are frequently used in medical imaging, with promising results [8].

2   Related Work

Researchers made diagnostic suggestions for the Covid-19 infection in response to the pandemic. Using chest X-rays and Computed Tomography (CT) scans, many deep learning models were put forth to identify Covid-19. In [1], a CNN model was suggested to categorise chest X-ray pictures of pneumonia into Covid-19, pneumonia viral, pneumonia bacterial, and normal (Non-covid19).

Wang et al. proposed COVID-Net, a deep learning network for recognising covid-19 [19]. They were able to obtain an accuracy of 93.3% using a pooled data-set from five repositories. They further investigated how COVID-Net makes decision using an explainability method called GSInquire(an atribution based technique). Another deep learning model DarkCovidNet was proposed in [13] where they generated heatmaps using the Grad-CAM method. These heatmaps were further evaluated by a radiologist. It achieved a classification accuracy of 87.02% when classifying into three classes: Covid 19, Pneumonia and Normal.

Application of transfer learning to a pre-trained, VGG-16 CNN was proposed in [3]. Here, they used a total of 6523 X-ray images in their study: 250 Covid, 2753 other pulmonary diseases and 3520 healthy people. They trained two models: first model to distinguish between healthy individuals and patients with lung diseases (Pneumonia and Covid-19 combined), and second model to distinguish between pneumonia and Covid-19. They achieved an accuracy of 96% with the first model and an accuracy of 98% for the second model. They used Grad-CAM to visualise the key areas that the model considers, when predicting a given class label.

DeepCovidExplainer compared various CNN networks: VGG-16, ResNet-34, DenseNet-201, ResNet-18, VGG-19, and DenseNet-161 [12]. DenseNet-161 out-performed all other models with a precision of 0.952. They also used two techniques: prediction maximisation and softmax posterier averaging to deploy model ensemble. VGG-19 + DenseNet-161 outperformed other model ensembles with a maximum precision of 0.937 in prediction maximisation and 0.946 in softmax posterier averaging. They used GradCam and Grad-CAM++ to create heatmaps for explainability, as well as Layer-wise Relevance Propagation (LRP) for interpretability.

So, as we can see that many deep learning models have been developed which can assist with much better accuracies in diagnosing covid-19, but they lack reliability. Thus, in this paper we take a step forward and try to explore the explainability aspect of these models by comparing the results obtained after applying different XAI techniques and see how they perform.

3 Explainable AI

Deep learning algorithms are now used in many AI applications because they provide high accuracy, but humans find it difficult to trust them because they are a black box. Understanding the black-box nature of algorithms sparked a new branch of research known as XAI. Many applications require explanations from deep learning algorithms rather than just yes or no responses to ensure trust and transparency. In fields such as medicine, explainability is essential for trust and adoption. AI can produce potentially biased results because of the type of data used to train the model. These biases could be identified using the explanations provided by the XAI system.

XAI may alleviate concerns about transparency, bias, and reliability, thereby hastening AI adoption. We will now try to explain each of the techniques used in this paper in brief.

3.1 LIME

In 2016, Ribeiro et al. [15] published Local Interpretable Model- Agnostic Explanations(LIME). In order to provide a human-readable representation, LIME tries to assess the significance of consecutive superpixels (a patch of pixels) in a source image to the output class. As a result, LIME discovers a binary vector x' $\in \{0, 1\}$ to indicate the absence or presence of a superpixel or a continuous patch for image classification. An explanation is defined as a model g $\in$ G, where G is a class of models which are potentially interpretable such as linear models, decision trees etc.Let $\Omega(g)$ be a measure of the complexity of the explanation g $\in$ G and π x(z) is proximity measure between an instance z to x. In the locality defined by πx, $(f, g, \pi x)$ denotes how unfaithful g is in approximating f. Lime then generates the explanation by minimising the following objective function:

$$\xi(x) = argmin(f, g, \pi x) + \Omega(g) \tag{1}$$

3.2 Occlusion

A straightforward interpretability method called occlusion finds the input stimuli that cause particular feature maps to light up at any layer of the model. In the visualisation method, to project the feature activations back to the input pixel space, a multi-layered deconvolutional network is used. By hiding portions of the input image, it also demonstrates the classifier output's sensitivity analysis, highlighting the crucial portions of the image for categorization [21].

3.3 Saliency

Saliency map creation in deep neural networks was created by Simonyan et al. in 2013 as a method of figuring out the gradient of the output class category with respect to an input image. In the context of gradient visualisation, examining the positive gradients that had the most influence on the outcome might help determine how important a pixel is. For an image I_0, a classification ConvNet with the class score function $S_c(I)$, and a class c, we can rank the pixels of I_0 based on their impact on the score $S_c(I_0)$ using the following linear score model.

$$S_c(I) = \omega_c^T I + b_c \tag{2}$$

where b_c is the bias of the model and ω_c is the weight vector [16].

3.4 LRP

LRP is a method for decomposing a classification decision into pixel-wise relevances, which show how each pixel contributes to the overall classification score. Bach et al. proposed a model in 2015 that is based on the conservation principle, according to which every neuron receives a portion of the network output and distributes it precisely to its forerunners until the input variables are reached.

$$\sum_i R_i^{(l)} = \sum_j R_j^{(l+1)} \tag{3}$$

$R_i^{(l)}$ denotes relevance associated with ith neuron of layer l and $R_j^{(l+1)}$ denotes the relevance associated with the jth neuron in the next layer [2].

3.5 Deconvolution

Deconvolutional networks were first introduced as a method for unsupervised feature learning by Zeiler et al. in 2010.. It is used to visualise image patterns in a CNN that strongly activate any given neutron. The Deconvolutional Network is a top-down algorithm that aims to generate the input signal using learned filters and a sum of feature map convolutions (rather than the input) [22].

3.6 GradCAM++

While gradient-based methods, like Grad-CAM, produce visualisations that explain the prediction produced by the CNN model with fine-grained features of the projected class, these methods have drawbacks. For instance, their performance suffers when localising numerous instances of the same class. Grad-CAM heatmaps frequently fail to capture the entire item in completeness in single object photos, which is necessary for higher performance on the associated recognition task. Grad-CAM++, a generalised visualisation tool for explaining CNN judgments, was presented to solve these drawbacks. It addresses the aforementioned issues and offers a more comprehensive solution [4].

3.7 AlbationCAM

Ablation-CAM is a gradient-free technique for producing class-discriminative localization maps that can be used to explain individual CNN-based model decisions [7].

3.8 XGrad-CAM

Axioms are characteristics that are thought to be required for the CNN decision visualisation approach. Continuity [17], implementation invariance [30], sensitivity [30], and conservation [17] are examples of existing axioms. A unique visualisation technique called XGrad-CAM is inspired by the axioms of sensitivity and conservation. It primarily focuses on proving these two fundamental principles.

4 Experiments Setup

We started by getting a data-set of lung x-ray images. Then, we applied pre-processing techniques and prepared it to train our models. After the training, we applied a comprehensive set of XAI techniques to our trained models and analysed the outputs qualitatively and quantitatively. Each of these steps are explained in detail in upcoming subsections. The overall flow of the process has been outlined in the Fig. 1 below.

4.1 Data-set

We have used the Covid-19 Radiography Database[1] for our experiments [5,14]. This data-set contains four classes of labeled chest X-ray images: Normal cases, Covid-19 cases, viral pneumonia cases and lung opacity cases. It contains 3616 chest X-ray images for Covid-19 cases, 10, 192 for normal, 6012 lung opacity (Non-Covid lung infection), and 1345 viral pneumonia images.

4.2 Data Pre-processing

The Covid-19 Radiography Database has highly imbalanced image classes. Thus, prior to using this data-set, we did image augmentation and image deletion to balance the classes in order to keep the model balanced. Image augmentation was done by changing the parameters like rotation of image, horizontal and vertical shifting, brightness range, sheer range and zoom range. We augmented every image in such a way that each class now contains around 5000 images. Chest X-ray images were resized to 256×256 before being fed into the network. The images were then normalised using the pre-trained model standards. The data-set also included images for Lung Opacity (Non-Covid lung infection), which were removed as we were focusing only on distinguishing covid, normal, and viral pneumonia images. We have divided the data-set into three subsets - training(64% of the data-set), validation(16% of the data-set) and testing(20% of the data-set).

---

[1] data-set available at: https://www.kaggle.com/tawsifurrahman/covid19-radiography-database.

4.3   Network Model

We have used CNN models for classification of the covid, non covid and viral pneumonia images. We selected pre-trained(on ImageNet Data) ResNet18 and ResNet50 [10] for the classification after experimenting with various neural networks. In this initial experiment, some models failed due to lower accuracy after training while on other models, the interpretability techniques could not be used owing to the different architectures of the models. Thus, ResNets proved to be the best models for comparing these XAI techniques.

4.4   Model Training

We trained ResNet18 and ResNet50 individually on Tesla P100-PCIE GPU by using Google Colab Pro. We employed transfer learning using pytorch[2]. Input Features were changed based on the model requirements, while output classes were set to 3. We loaded the above models, which were pre-trained on ImageNet data-set. We then used Adam optimizer for each of the models, fine tuned its learning rate and set to 0.00003, using cross entropy loss as the criterion. We used cuda method to utilize GPUs's power properly and get lesser training times.

4.5   Interpretability Pipeline

An interpretability pipeline for PyTorch-based classification models was developed with the help of captum[3]. Occlusion, saliency, integrated gradients, deconvolution and LRP were implemented using the captum library. Lime was implemented using lime library in python[4] . All the class activation maps were implemented using gradcam and pytorch-gradcam libraries[5]. Then, for getting validation from the radiologists, we prepared images to show them. Images were prepared for covid, normal and viral pneumonia classes each consisting a ground truth image, the prediction of the model with probability for that class, and the results of different XAI techniques.

5   Results and Interpretability Analysis

To better understand the decision-making behavior and performance on detecting important areas of an image, we used both qualitative and quantitative analysis.

---

[2] https://pytorch.org/.
[3] https://captum.ai/.
[4] https://github.com/marcotcr/lime.
[5] https://github.com/jacobgil/pytorch-grad-cam.

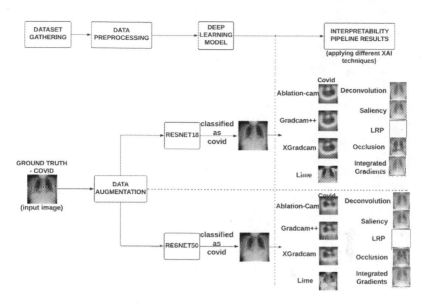

Fig. 1. A visual representation of the process

5.1   Qualitative Analysis

For the interpretability analysis, we have used following techniques: Ablation-CAM, Grad-CAM++, XGrad-CAM, LIME, Deconvolution, Saliency, LRP, Occlusion, and Integrated Gradients. We have analysed the output of these techniques for a normal case (Non-Covid), Covid, and viral pneumonia as depicted in Fig. 7 to Fig. 4 respectively. The ground truth for each case is shown in the top row as the single image. The other rows depict the output of the respective techniques obtained for each of the three classes with respect to the ground truth using ResNet18 and ResNet50 models. These techniques demonstrate that the areas focused by model differ for covid, normal, and viral pneumonia images.

According to medical findings of [18] from the COVID-19 image data, the most common CXR lesions were Ground-glass opacity (GGO) and reticular pattern, either alone or in combination with other alterations. Consolidation was less common, but it did show an increasing trend over time. GGO is defined as a hazy, increased lung opacity that is usually widespread and the margins of pulmonary vessels become indistinct. Reticular alteration is characterised as an accumulation of countless tiny linear opacities that, when combined, provide the impression of a net. A steady rise in pulmonary attenuation, known as consolidation, obstructs the margins of the arteries and the walls of the airways [9]. Lesions are most commonly found in the lower lobes. Involvement in the lower fields occurred substantially more frequently than in the middle fields, and in the lower and middle fields than in the upper fields. [18]. These areas are highlighted in the corresponding covid-19 images in our work in Fig. 5.

5.2   Quantitative Analysis

For quantitative analysis, we computed F1 score, precision and recall for each infection type. We also calculated test accuracy for both CNN architectures. Table 1 portrays the performance of ResNet18 and ResNet50. On the testing data-set containing 2986 images of all three classes, ResNet18 obtained an accuracy of 97.82% and ResNet50 an accuracy of 98.2%.

We showed our prepared images to the expert radiologists, discussed these findings, and got their opinions based on a questionnaire about the performance of the XAI techniques. It was evaluated on a scale of 1 to 5, where 1 is "I disagree strongly" and 5 is "I agree strongly". The MOS for the inputs obtained from three radiologists is presented in Table 2. It was determined that Ablation-CAM, Grad-CAM++, and XGrad-CAM are targeting the right areas where virus affected the most. Even though these techniques accurately identified the regions, explanations are far from complete.

In comparison to Ablation-CAM and GradCAM++, it was determined that XGrad-CAM was more satisfying and provided better details when compared to other techniques.

Results for the following techniques: deconvolution, saliency, integrated gradients, and LRP are shown in Fig. 2, Fig. 3, and Fig. 4. They highlight the key regions responsible for classification but are less consistent than Class Activation Maps (CAM).

Table 1. Performance of the classifiers

Model	Class	Precision	Recall	F1-score
ResNet18	covid	0.97	0.98	0.98
	normal	0.97	0.97	0.97
	viral pneumonia	0.99	0.98	0.99
ResNet50	covid	0.98	0.98	0.98
	normal	0.97	0.97	0.97
	viral pneumonia	0.99	0.98	0.99

6   Discussions and Conclusion

Our findings provide a thorough understanding of the classification task of covid-19. We used CAM techniques to generate heat maps for all possible output classes, which can be useful even if the CNN models misclassify a specific instance. As we show the probabilities of the various classes along with their explanations, radiologists can make better decisions.

Explanation Quality: We have used 5-point Likert Explanation Satisfaction Scale developed by [11] Table 2 shows metrics (Understand, Satisfying, Sufficient detail, Complete, Accurate) and MOS calculated with the help of 3 expert radiologists. We can conclude that Ablation-CAM, Grad-CAM++, and XGrad-CAM are more reliable and trustworthy overall. Because hr-ct scans have higher specificity and sensitivity for detecting covid-19 infection, XGrad-CAM may be useful in predicting covid-19 infection when hr-ct scans are not available. A little more improvisation is required for this technique.

Table 2. Mean Opinion Scores (MOS) of different techniques from 3 Radiologists using explanation scale

Metric	Ablation-Cam	Grad-Cam++	XGrad-Cam	Lime	Occlusion
Understand	4	4	4	3.66	3.66
Satisfying	4	4	4	3.66	3.66
Sufficient detail	3	3	3.33	3.33	3.66
Complete	1.33	1.33	2.66	2.33	2.66
Accurate	3.33	3	3.66	2.66	3

In the future, we plan to overcome these limitations by incorporating hr-ct data and training a multimodal neural network with segmented images which only have the lung areas.We would also like to integrate more explainable components and provide more detailed explanations so that we can build more reliable models for crucial applications. Also, we will work towards improving the scalability of the pipeline.

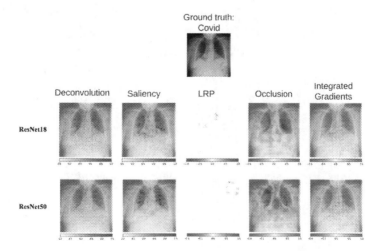

Fig. 2. These techniques highlight the significant areas which they believe were important for the respective models to classify the image as a **covid** image.

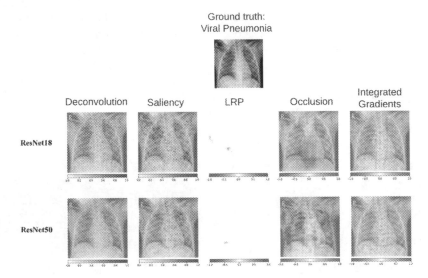

Fig. 3. These techniques highlight the significant areas which they believe were important for the respective models to classify the image as a **viral pneumonia** image.

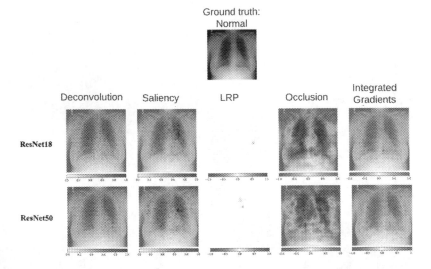

Fig. 4. These techniques highlight the significant areas which they believe were important for the respective models to classify the image as a **normal** image.

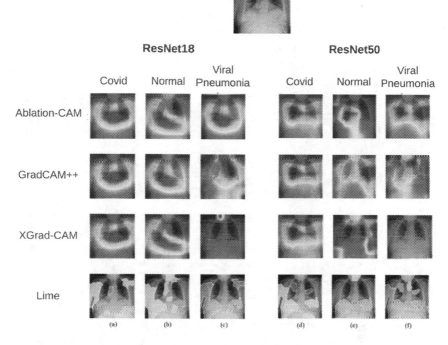

Fig. 5. In the case of CAMs, the colour scale is red to blue in order of increasing importance. For Lime technique, Green, and Red colours represent areas that influence model decision making positively and negatively. (a)(d) Resnet18 and Resnet50 classified the given image as **covid** infected with 93.7017% and 99.916% certainty. The techniques in the respective rows highlight the significant areas of the input image that they believe were important for the respective models to classify the image as a covid image. (b),(e) Resnet18 and Resnet50 classified the given image as **normal** with 06.2975% and 0.586% certainty. The techniques in the respective rows highlight the significant areas of the input image that they believe were important for the respective models to classify the image as a normal image. (c),(f) Resnet18 and Resnet50 classified the given image as **viral pneumonia** infected with 0.0009% and 0.0038% certainty. The techniques in the respective rows highlight the significant areas of the input image that they believe were important for the respective models to classify the image as a viral pneumonia image. (Color figure online)

Ground truth:
Viral Pneumonia

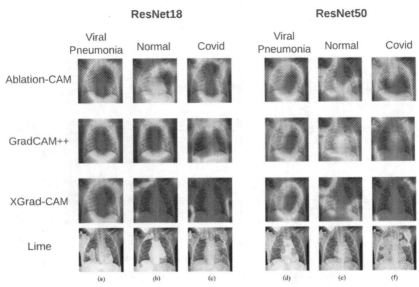

Fig. 6. (a),(d) Resnet18 and Resnet50 classified the given image as **viral pneumonia** infected with 99.9567% and 69.2812% certainty. The techniques in the respective rows highlight the significant areas of the input image that they believe were important for the respective models to classify the image as a viral pneumonia image. (b),(e) Resnet18 and Resnet50 classified the given image as **normal** with 0.0321% and 30.6947% certainty. The techniques in the respective rows highlight the significant areas of the input image that they believe were important for the respective models to classify the image as a normal image. (c),(f) Resnet18 and Resnet50 classified the given image as **covid** infected with 0.0112% and 0.0242% certainty. The techniques in the respective rows highlight the significant areas of the input image that they believe were important for the respective models to classify the image as a covid image.

Ground truth:
Normal

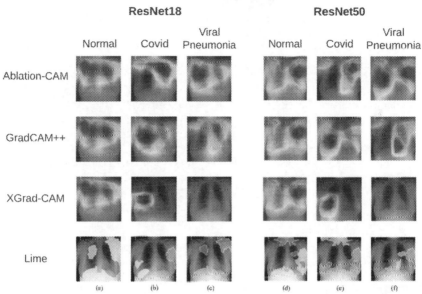

Fig. 7. (a),(d) Resnet18 and Resnet50 classified the given image as **normal** with 99.916% and 99.997% certainty. The techniques in the respective rows highlight the significant areas of the input image that they believe were important for the respective models to classify the image as a normal image. (b),(e) Resnet18 and Resnet50 classified the given image as **covid** infected with 0.0838% and 0.003% certainty. The techniques in the respective rows highlight the significant areas of the input image that they believe were important for the respective models to classify the image as a covid image. (c),(f) Resnet18 and Resnet50 classified the given image as **viral pneumonia** infected with 0.0002% and 0% certainty. The techniques in the respective rows highlight the significant areas of the input image that they believe were important for the respective models to classify the image as a viral pneumonia image.

References

1. Apostolopoulos, I.D., Mpesiana, T.A.: Covid-19: automatic detection from x-ray images utilizing transfer learning with convolutional neural networks. Phy. Eng. Sci. Med. 43(2), 635–640 (2020)
2. Bach, S., Binder, A., Montavon, G., Klauschen, F., Müller, K.-R., Samek, W.: On pixel-wise explanations for non-linear classifier decisions by layer-wise relevance propagation. PloS one **10**(7), e0130140 (2015)

3. Brunese, L., Mercaldo, F., Reginelli, A., Santone, A.: Explainable deep learning for pulmonary disease and coronavirus COVID-19 detection from x-rays. Comput. Methods Prog. Biomed. **196**, 105608 (2020)
4. Chattopadhay, A., Sarkar, A., Howlader, P., Balasubramanian, V.N.: Grad-cam++: Generalized gradient-based visual explanations for deep convolutional networks. In: 2018 IEEE winter conference on applications of computer vision (WACV), pp. 839–847. IEEE (2018)
5. Chowdhury, E.M., et al.: Can AI help in screening viral and COVID-19 pneumonia?. IEEE Access **8**, 132665–132676 (2020)
6. Cozzi, A., et al.: Chest x-ray in the COVID-19 pandemic: radiologists' real-world reader performance. Eur. J. Radiol. **132**, 109272 (2020)
7. Desai, S., Ramaswamy, H.G.: Ablation-cam: visual explanations for deep convolutional network via gradient-free localization. In: 2020 IEEE Winter Conference on Applications of Computer Vision (WACV). pp. 972–980 (2020)
8. Greenspan, H., Ginneken, B.V., Summers, R.M.: Guest editorial deep learning in medical imaging: Overview and future promise of an exciting new technique. IEEE Trans. Med. Imaging **35**(5), 1153–1159 (2016)
9. Hansell, D.M., et. al.: Fleischner society: glossary of terms for thoracic imaging. Radiology **246**(3), 697–722 (2008)
10. He, K., Zhang, X., Ren, S., Sun, J.: Deep residual learning for image recognition. In: Proceedings of the IEEE Conference on Computer Vision and Pattern Recognition, pp. 770–778 (2016)
11. Hoffman, R.R., Mueller, S.T., Klein, G., Litman, J.: Metrics for explainable AI: Challenges and prospects. arXiv preprint arXiv:1812.04608 (2018)
12. Karim, M.R., Cochez, T.M., Beyan, O., Rebholz-Schuhmann, D., Decker, S.: Deep-covidexplainer: Explainable COVID-19 diagnosis from chest x-ray images. In: 2020 IEEE International Conference on Bioinformatics and Biomedicine (BIBM), pp. 1034–1037. IEEE (2020)
13. Ozturk, T., Talo, M., Yildirim, E.A., Baloglu, U.B., Yildirim, O., Acharya, U.R.: Automated detection of COVID-19 cases using deep neural networks with x-ray images. Comput. Bio. Med. **121**, 103792 (2020)
14. Rahman, T., et al.: Exploring the effect of image enhancement techniques on COVID-19 detection using chest x-ray images. Comput. Bio. Med. **132**, 104319 (2021)
15. Ribeiro, M.T., Singh, S., Guestrin, C.: why should i trust you? explaining the predictions of any classifier. In: Proceedings of the 22nd ACM SIGKDD International Conference on Knowledge Discovery and Data Mining, pp. 1135–1144 (2016)
16. Simonyan, K., Vedaldi, A., Zisserman, A.: Deep inside convolutional networks: Visualising image classification models and saliency maps. arXiv preprint arXiv:1312.6034 (2013)
17. Tahamtan, A., Ardebili, A.: Real-time RT-PCR in COVID-19 detection: issues affecting the results. Expert Rev. Mol. Diagn. **20**(5), 453–454 (2020)
18. Vancheri, S.G., et al.: Radiographic findings in 240 patients with COVID-19 pneumonia: time-dependence after the onset of symptoms. Eur. Radiol. **30**, 6161–6169 (2020)
19. Wang, L., Lin, Z.Q., Wong, A.: COVID-net: a tailored deep convolutional neural network design for detection of COVID-19 cases from chest x-ray images. Sci. Reports **10**(1), 1–12 (2020)
20. WHO et al. COVID-19 weekly epidemiological update, 17 July 2022. https://www.who.int/publications/m/item/weekly-epidemiological-update-on-covid-19---20-july-2022, 2022

21. Zeiler, M.D., Fergus, R.: Visualizing and Understanding Convolutional Networks. In: Fleet, D., Pajdla, T., Schiele, B., Tuytelaars, T. (eds.) ECCV 2014. LNCS, vol. 8689, pp. 818–833. Springer, Cham (2014). https://doi.org/10.1007/978-3-319-10590-1_53

22. Zeiler, M.D., Krishnan, D., Taylor, G.W., Fergus R.: Deconvolutional networks. In: 2010 IEEE Computer Society Conference on Computer Vision and Pattern Recognition, pp. 2528–2535 (2010)

Features Assimilation via Three-Stream Deep Networks for Spam Attack Detection from Images

Shubham Kumar, Anirudh Chaudhary, Devansh Goyal, Amanjit Singh, Ashish Yadav, Samarth Roday, and Tushar Sandhan[✉]

Indian Institute of Technology, Kanpur, India
{kshubham20,anirudhc20,devanshg20,samanjit20,ashisy20, samarthr20,sandhan}@iitk.ac.in

Abstract. Spam filters typically use optical character recognition (OCR) for extracting the text from images. These days spammers have circumvented optical scanning by fracturing the text within the images thereby improving their attacks and finally reaching to the users. This paper proposes a three-stream deep learning-based model which uses Convolutional Neural Networks (CNN), Transfer Learning, SIFT and HOG features via hybrid fusion framework. Transfer learning alone can only achieve an accuracy of 95% but our hybrid model shows improved performance and obtains an accuracy of 96%, eclipsing the existing techniques. We have created our dataset of challenging HAM images which will be publicly available. On our challenging dataset as well, the proposed method outperforms other existing methods for effectively detecting the spam attacks targeted via images.

Keywords: Convolutional neural networks · Transfer learning · Spam image · Hybrid 3-stream model · Bag of words model

1 Introduction

E-Mail has become a ubiquitous communication medium and widely popular nowadays. According to the report released by the Radicati group [1], as of April 2022, there are 4.26 billion email users worldwide, which is approximately fifty percent of the world population. However, the effectiveness of email has often been reduced due to compromised security by spam attacks via emails. Spam emails, also known as junk emails, are uninvited email messages that are typically delivered to a large number of recipients. Every day, hackers, invaders, and attackers seek to exploit consumers by sending several unsolicited emails containing unwanted information. To combat this problem, a number of Machine Learning (ML)-based spam detectors were created. Initially, spam from e-mail was in the form of text. ML models such as K-Nearest Neighbors (KNN), Support Vector Machines (SVM) and Naive Bayes (NB), among others, are used to filter email spam based on textual content and have achieved up to 95% accuracy [2].

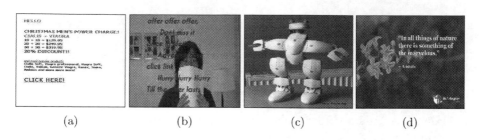

(a)   (b)   (c)   (d)

Fig. 1. Spam text in form of image is shown in (a), while in (b) spam text is embedded over natural image to make it more challenging. Ham image is shown in (c), while it is more challenging to recognize (d) as a ham image because useful texts are embedded over the natural image.

With the technology enhancement of spam detection, the attackers are always finding a new way to spam the users even with the multiple layers of security mechanisms. They find the bugs, vulnerabilities and exploit them by actively improving their spam attacks on a day-to-day basis. In recent times, they have found a new way of sending spam emails through embedding all the information inside a single image. Whereas the real word normal image containing genuine information is called as Image Ham.

Email spam in which the spam text is embedded in an image is known as 'Image spam', as shown in Fig. 1a. To improve the spam attack further, spammers have made image spam more challenging by embedding spam text over natural images like Fig. 1b. Now the problem is that, the distinction between spam and ham images became so narrow that even human can not separate them easily. In challenging ham images, useful texts are embedded over the natural images Fig. 1d. With dire need of strong Cybersecurity in this digital age, the image spam detection is very crucial problem to be solved.

In the initial stages, the text is embedded within an email in the form of HTML, and to counter that researchers have started using optical character recognition(OCR) techniques [3]. OCR is a technology that recognizes text in digital images. But later spammers started using captcha-based techniques to obfuscate the text in the images which was difficult to read by OCR algorithms. This problem motivated the researchers to propose several machine learning and deep learning based algorithms for effective classification of image spams [4]. Numerous researchers have developed approaches based on deep learning for diverse cyber security applications [5], including malicious domain discovery [8], malware detection [6,7], intrusion detection [9] etc. Transfer learning and many pre-trained CNN models, such as Xception, VGG19 etc., have been utilised in the work presented in [10]. Transfer learning alone is not sufficient to protect against sophisticated spam image attacks. In addition to the framework for transfer learning, we suggest fusing a multi-feature hybrid three-stream deep convolutional neural network for efficient spam detection.

The main contribution of this work is the following: Firstly, four models SIFT feature CNN, SIFT image CNN, HOG feature CNN, and Hog image CNN models are proposed and their effectiveness is analyzed for image spam detection. Secondly, the ability of the transfer learning techniques are studied by utilizing pre-trained CNN model VGG19. Lastly, the features extracted by HOG [11], SIFT [12], and VGG19 [13] are combined using a 3-stream hybrid CNN model and used for the detection of spam images. The remaining sections of this work are organized as follows; Sect. 2 presents the literature review, Sect. 3 contains the proposed model architecture and Sect. 4 presents the dataset, experiments, and results. Finally, the Sect. 5 concludes our work.

2   Literature Review

The recent state-of-the-art methods employ deep neural networks for spam image classification. Image spam classification based on CNN [14] method proposes a novel deep architecture, where a linear support vector machine (LSVM) is used in the output layer, and parameters are tuned by minimizing a loss which is marginal in nature correspondingly. They trained the network with hinge-loss instead of softmax-loss i.e. they placed the classic softmax layer with L2-SVM while optimizing parameters via backpropagation from the last SVM layer focusing on assessing feature representation performance on the spam classification task. The network compromises of five convolutional layers and three fully-connected layers. Images are rescaled to 256×256 and a crop of 227×227 is passed to the network. Finally, the output obtained from the last layer which was fully connected is passed to a SVM layer to train the network for classification. Back-propagation of gradients from the top linear SVM layer is used to train the lower layer weights. Unlike the previous methods the method in [15] uses the multi-estimating points to enhance the standard moment estimation and ADAM [16] a stochastic gradient optimization algorithm. It also proposes WDSP-net combined with SPR and ADAM algorithms. The WDSP-net achieves very high accuracy in image spam recognition.

In [10], two DCNN and hybrid models are studied on 3 different datasets for image spam classification. Balanced class weights is used to study the effects of cost-sensitive learning on model accuracy and pre-trained CNN architectures like Xception [18], VGG19 [17], etc. are used to study effects of transfer learning. Some parts of CNN models are trained on several combinations of Dredze Image-Spam dataset for 100 epochs in various input sizes. Then these models are trained and tested on the ISH dataset for improving the performance. Hybrid models are also employed which extracted the features from the last hidden dense layer of the base model to enhance the performance.

Color Model Based CNN is proposed in [19] for image spam classification. It consists of two steps- image preprocessing and CNN. Their CNN model for image spam detection is tiny for speed improvement and it has an input layer, three convolutional layers, three max-pooling layers, a flatten layer, a drop-out unit, and two dense fully connected layers. Their color space analysis, RGB experiments did not obtain as good accuracy as YCbCr, YUV, and XYZ. According to [19] the XYZ color model achieved the highest accuracy among all color models. In comparison to other related works, their XYZ model-based CNN was able to increase the accuracy up to 98.4% on ISH dataset where previous best performance reported was 98%. From the results, it can be said that different color models obtained different accuracy.

Keeping this in mind, we have performed extensive experiments on different color models. Three machine learning techniques were tested in [20] SVM and two techniques based on neural-net, CNN and multilayer perceptrons (MLP). [20] also studied the features based on Canny images, row images [21], and their combination. Their detailed experiments were based on three datasets established the effectiveness of the proposed approaches, and concluded that a SVM model achieved high accuracy on a public image spam dataset, a CNN technique performed better on challenging image spam dataset. On the ISH dataset all three techniques described in this paper performed well, with SVM achieving an accuracy of 98.72 while a CNN achieving even more at 99.02, while an MLP showed an accuracy of 95.57. For challenging dataset 1, CNN surpassed other methods with an accuracy of 83.13, while none of the techniques can achieve an accuracy greater than 71.83 on the more challenging challenge dataset 2. Moreover these challenging datasets are not publicly available. Nevertheless it shows how dramatically the best performing model on easier spam dataset can show reduced performance on just slightly challenging spam image dataset.

The above discussion has shown some important feature extraction techniques that have been used to extract important features from an image. Some methods are manual i.e. employ image processing techniques like HOG and SIFT while some methods are based on learning feature extraction from training like CNN. These techniques have been used in many previous works. Now let's analyze some of these techniques as they form a building block for our three-stream network framework:

Scale Invariant Feature Transform (SIFT): SIFT [12] is a image processing algorithm which describes and detects local features in images. For each image, SIFT is applied to extract the key-points from the image. After locating the key-points, the magnitude and direction of the gradient are calculated using neighboring pixels of the key point. To identify the dominant directions, the gradient histogram is formed. The number of key-points obtained is different for different images. So, it cannot be used directly to give input to a CNN model. So for this we perform, and then for clustering of key-points we employed the Bag of Words model [22].

Bag of Words (BOW): The BOW model [22] is used for vectorization of text, i.e. it turns random text into fixed-length vectors by counting the number of times each word appears. This is done because machine learning algorithms is incompatible to work with the raw text directly, the text needed to be converted into numbers. Similar concept is used for obtaining visual words inside an image and a dictionary is declared to hold the bag of words and tokenize each feature into words. Now for each word in an image, it is checked that if the word exists in the dictionary. If it does, then count is incremented by 1. If it doesn't, it is added to the dictionary and count is set as 1.

Histogram-Oriented Gradients (HOG): The HOG [11] is a powerful element descriptor utilized broadly in object identification and recognition. While the HOG features are essentially utilized for object identification, object recognition can also be performed using the extracted features. The fundamental difference among HOG and other feature descriptors, for example, shape contexts, SIFT, and histograms which are edge oriented, is that dense uniformly dispersed grids are utilized for the calculation of HOG and nearby contrast normalization is utilized for improvement of accuracy. The HOG descriptor is photometric and geometric transformation invariant. These characteristics enabled us to investigate the assimilation of two different features viz. SIFT and HOG for detecting spam pictures.

Support Vector Machines: The following details will explain the key concepts of SVM as mentioned in [23]:

Separating Hyperplane - During training, SVM tries to find a hyperplane that separate different classes by acting as a decision boundary. Obviously, such a hyperplane need not exist, which leads us to think about spaces which are higher dimensional.

Maximize the Margin - Classes are separated using a hyperplane, in that case there will be endless numbers of such hyperplanes. In SVM, a hyperplane is picked that enable it to maximizes the margin. Here the least distance between the class of data and hyperplanes are referred as margin. We have employed SVM at the final stage for the classification.

3   Proposed Method

3.1   Pre-processing

Dataset is randomly divided into train and test dataset for training and testing purpose. The training dataset contains 70% images of the whole dataset i.e. 2690 images while the test dataset contains 30% of the total images i.e. 1154. Each image from the train and test dataset is converted from RGB to grayscale. The train and test grayscale images are used to extract SIFT and HOG features.

SIFT Feature: The SIFT descriptor [12] is obtained by dividing an image into 4×4 squares. For each of these sixteen squares, a vector of length eight is obtained. By merging all the vectors, a vector of size 128 is formed for each key point. To utilize the generated key-point descriptors in classification, a fixed size vector is required. For this purpose, bag of words model is employed which uses K-means to cluster the descriptors into a group. Then, a bag of key-points is created by calculating descriptors number that are enclosed in every cluster. The resulting feature vector has a definite size (Fig. 2).

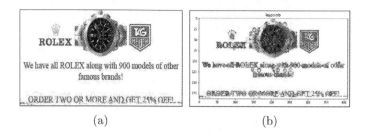

(a)   (b)

Fig. 2. Embedded key-points are shown in (b) of spam Image shown in (a) using SIFT features.

HOG feature: In HOG [11], the histogram of oriented gradients is used as feature. Gradients which are calculated in x and y directions are features that represent complex shapes like edges and corners. The gradient's direction represents the directional change in intensity of pixels in an image, whereas the amount of the change is represented by pixels.

$$\nabla f = \begin{bmatrix} f_x \\ f_y \end{bmatrix} = \begin{bmatrix} \frac{\delta f}{\delta x} \\ \frac{\delta f}{\delta y} \end{bmatrix} \tag{1}$$

Here, the derivative of the image with respect to x and y is given by $\frac{\delta f}{\delta x}$ and $\frac{\delta f}{\delta y}$ respectively. The derivative can further be calculated as shown in 2 and 3:

$$f_x(x) = \frac{\delta f}{\delta x} = f(x+1) - f(x-1) \tag{2}$$

$$f_y(y) = \frac{\delta f}{\delta y} = f(y+1) - f(y-1) \tag{3}$$

After calculation of gradients, the magnitude and direction of the gradients can be obtained using the Eq. 4:

$$f = \sqrt{f_x(x)^2 + f_y(y)^2}, \quad \theta = \arctan \frac{f_x(x)}{f_y(y)} \tag{4}$$

In cases of corners and edges there are sudden large changes in intensity making the magnitude of gradient to be large. In smooth regions there are no sudden changes in intensity as a result the gradient magnitude is zero. Thus, while calculating the gradients various redundant information in the in image background is eliminated [11]. The Normal ham Image is shown in Fig. 3a while Fig. 3b shows the HOG image extracted from the given ham image.

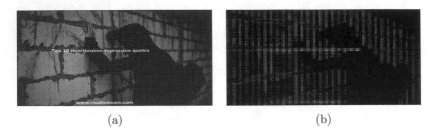

(a)   (b)

Fig. 3. A ham image is shown in (a) and its corresponding transformed HOG feature image is shown in (b), which becomes an input for HOG-CNN.

Algorithm 1: Image Spam Classification

---

    input   : A set of images obtained from emails
    output   : Labels $y_1 \ldots y_N$
                    (0 for Ham and 1 for Spam)
    preprocessing: Duplicates are removed and images are resized to desired sizes
                                as mentioned in Table1

1 **for** *Every image* **do**
2   Convert from RGB to GRAY
3   **for** *GRAY image* **do**
4   Extract SIFT descriptors
5   Apply Bag of Words model on SIFT descriptor to capture all key-points
6   Extract HOG image
7   Pass RGB image to VGG19 feature extractor containing VGG19 to extract optimal feature vector v_i^1
8   Compute $d_i^1 =$ Dense layer(v_i^1)
9   Pass SIFT descriptors to SIFT CNN to extract optimal feature vector v_i^2
10   Compute $d_i^2 =$ Dense layer(v_i^2)
11   Pass HOG images to HOG CNN to extract optimal feature vector v_i^3
12   Compute $d_i^3 =$ Dense layer(v_i^3)
13   Concatenate $D_i = [d_i^1 ; d_i^2 ; d_i^3]$
14   Compute $D_i^1 =$ Dense layer(D_i)
15   Calculate $y_i =$ Sigmoid(D_i^1)

Network Architecture: We propose a three-stream network as shown in Fig. 4 using pre-trained VGG-19 and custom CNN layers with modifications and finally classification is done using SVM as a classifier. Our network consists of three CNN models applied to the transformed data from the SIFT, HOG, and normal image respectively and the features from three streams are concatenated to form the final model. The description of each individual model is given below as well as summarized in Algorithm 1.

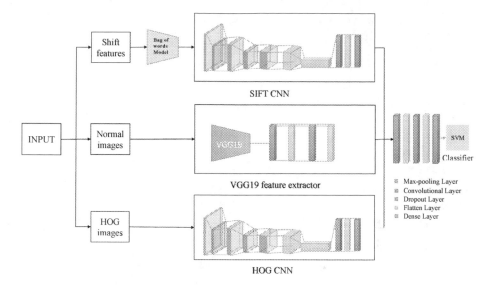

Fig. 4. Proposed Pipeline of Three-Stream Hybrid Model.

Top-stream (SIFT CNN: Input Size $50 \times 128 \times 1$*):* It takes resized SIFT descriptors as input and applies convolutional layers for feature extraction. It also has 3 Convolutional layers and 2 Max-pooling layers for feature extraction and downsampling of the feature space respectively. Finally, the features are flattened and passed through a dense layer with appropriate dropouts. Top and bottom stream's CNN architecture is kept similar for symmetry and throughput improvement but models are having different filter weights. The features obtained from all these models are concatenated and passed through a dense layer with an intermediate dropout layer to avoid overfitting the model. The output from the dense layer is passed to SVM for the final classification.

Mid-stream (VGG19 transfer learning features :Input size $156 \times 156 \times 3$*):* This model is based on the concept of transfer learning. It takes the image as input and passes through the pre-trained VGG-19 model trained on the 'imagenet' dataset. The features extracted from VGG-19 are flattened and passed through dense layers. Appropriate dropouts have been applied between dense layers.

Bottom-stream (HOG CNN :Input size $156 \times 156 \times 1$*):* It takes grayscale HOG images as input and applies convolutional layers to extract features from the input. It has 3 Convolutional layers and 2 Max-pooling layers for feature extraction and downsampling of the feature space respectively. Finally, the features are flattened and passed through a dense layer with appropriate dropouts. The model summary of the entire unified framework is discussed in Table 1.

Table 1. Model summary describing each layer with output shape and number of parameters.

Layer Type	Outputs	Parameters	Layer Type	Outputs	Parameters
Input Layer	(-,156,156,1)	0	Flatten	(-,36992)	0
Input Layer	(-,50,128,31)	0	Flatten	(-,49152)	0
Conv2D	(-,156,156,32)	320	Dense	(-,512)	4194816
Conv2D	(-,50,128,32)	320	Dense	(-,512)	18940416
Maxpooling2D	(-,52,52,32)	0	Dense	(-,512)	25166336
Maxpooling2D	(-,25,64,32)	0	Droupout	(-,512)	0
Conv2D	(-,52,52,64)	18496	Droupout	(-,512)	0
Conv2D	(-,25,64,64)	18496	Droupout	(-,512)	0
Maxpooling2D	(-,17,17,64)	0	Dense	(-,128)	65664
Maxpooling2D	(-,12,32,64)	0	Dense	(-,128)	65664
Input Layer	(-,156,156,3)	0	Dense	(-,128)	65664
Conv2D	(-,17,17,128)	73856	Concatenate	(-,384)	0
Conv2D	(-,12,32,128)	11	Dense	(-,384)	147840
VGG19(Funtional)	(-,4,4,512)	20024384	Droupout	(-,384)	0
Droupout	(-,17,17,128)	0	Dense	(-,128)	48280
Droupout	(-,12,32,128)	0	Droupout	(-,128)	0
Flatten	(-,8192)	0	Dense	(-,1)	129

Total Parameter count = 68,905,537

4   Experiments

All of our experiments have been performed using NVDIA RTX 3660 GPU with 12GB of RAM. We have used Python, OpenCV, and the Tenserflow library. We have experimented with different image color spaces like BGR, YCbCr, LAB, etc. We tested various techniques, other features amd classifiers like pure HOG features, K-means clustering and SVM with our dataset. The following is the description of the datasets used in our research and Fig. 5 shows some of the samples images.

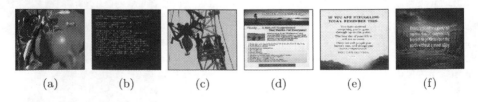

(a)   (b)   (c)   (d)   (e)   (f)

Fig. 5. Ham image in (a) and spam text embedded image in (b) are from Dredze Image Spam dataset. Ham image in (c) and spam text embedded image in (d) are from ISH dataset. Ham image (e) and (f) with embeddded useful text to make it more challenging to be recognized as Ham image are from our dataset.

4.1   Datasets

Dredze Image Spam Dataset: The dataset [24] contains images in 3 sets. Personal Spam has 3,298 images in total out of which the number of unique images are 1,274. Personal Ham has 2,021 images out of which the number of unique images are 1,517. And, the Spam Archive has files of various formats like PNG, JPEG, GIF etc., in total it has 16,028 files in which the number of unique images are 3,039.

Image Spam Hunter Dataset (ISH): The ISH dataset [25] contains both ham and spam images collected from original emails and images are in in JPEG format. There are 929 spam and 810 ham images in total. The number of unique ham and spam images found in the dataset after processing is 810 and 879 respectively.

Our HAM Dataset: This dataset is created by web crawling to get more challenging HAM images with embedded text, challenging images will allow us to train our model more efficiently which will increase the efficiency of the model in differentiating between challenging HAM and spam images with embedded text. There are 2533 ham images in this dataset. Our dataset will be publicly available.

4.2   Multidataset Unification

The datasets that are used in this work contain several duplicate images and corrupted files. At first, the corrupted files are deleted and then to avoid duplicated files, hashing is done to convert each image into a hash and stored in hashlist. In this way, whenever a duplicate image is encountered, its hash will be matched with the images present in the hashlist. If the match is confirmed, then the image will be skipped. Lastly, all unique images are resized into (156,156,3) shapes.

4.3   Ablation Study

Effectivness of the Top Stream: (Only top-stream from Fig. 4 is used for this study) Grayscale dataset was obtained from original dataset. Then SIFT feature vector was constructed after resizing extracted SIFT descriptor to (50,128,1). Resizing is required as we obtain a different number of key-points for a different image.

SIFT key-points were plotted to the corresponding image and stored to check the accuracy of the model on both the SIFT image and feature. SIFT feature and SIFT image both dataset was divided into 30% test and 70% train. Test model was trained on both SIFT feature and SIFT image and tested its accuracy respectively. The test model shows higher accuracy 82% accuracy on SIFT feature for predicting spam and ham image than on SIFT image which has an accuracy of 80% as given in Table 2 and Fig. 6.

Table 2. Percentage accuracy of test CNN on SIFT image vs SIFT feature.

Model	Accuracy
SIFT Image + CNN	80
SIFT Descriptor +CNN	82

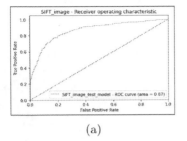 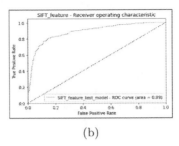

(a)   (b)

Fig. 6. ROC of SIFT-CNN with (a) SIFT image and (b) SIFT feature as input.

Effectivness of the Bottom Stream: (Only bottom-stream from Fig. 4 is used here) Grayscale was obtained from original dataset. Both the HOG feature vector and HOG image was obtained. Obtained size of the HOG feature array was resized as the required input size. Both the HOG feature array and HOG image array are divided into 30% test and 70% train. CNN model is trained and tested on both datasets separately. Obtained accuracy was 80% for the HOG features and 90% for HOG images. So clearly, the HOG image performed better than the HOG feature for spam image classification. This accuracy is given in Table 3 and Fig. 7.

Table 3. Percentage accuracy of test CNN with HOG image vs HOG feature.

Model	Accuracy (%)
HOG Image + CNN	90
HOG Feature + CNN	80

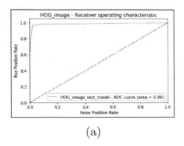 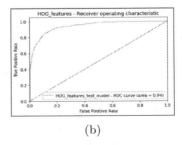

(a)   (b)

Fig. 7. ROC of HOG-CNN with (a) HOG image and (b) HOG feature as input.

SVM with Linear and RBF Kernel: Our test model is tested on SVM as a classifier. Linear and RBF kernels of SVM are used to check the model accuracy one by one. In Table 4 LSVM refers to SVM with linear kernel while RSVM refers to SVM with RBF as kernel. SVM with RBF as kernel gave higher accuracy as compared to linear kernel as shown in Table 4.

Table 4. Percentage accuracy of SVM using linear and RBF kernels.

Classifier	Accuracy (%)
LSVM (Linear kernel)	95
RSVM (RBF kernel)	96

Color Space Analysis: Pre-trained test model was tested after transforming our image dataset from RGB to other image types like LAB, HSV, YCbCr, etc. Pixel value of GRAY images captures the intensity of light according to a particular weighted combination of frequencies. The HLS color space module converts the image into a hue, saturation, and lightness components. The Hue is the color of the image, the Saturation is the pureness of the hue, and the lightness is the strength of the hue. LAB contains a mix of one channel with no color (L), plus two channels that have no contrast but with a dual color combination (A+B). In YCbCr, Y is the luma, the brightest component of the color. It represents the brightness of the color. Cr and Cb are the red and blue component relative to the green component respectively. Accuracy of different color models are given in Table 5.

Table 5. Performance of test CNN on different Color spaces.

Model	Precision	Recall	F1-Score	Support
BGR2GRAY	0.86	0.82	0.82	1147
BRG2HLS	0.69	0.63	0.59	1147
BGR2LAB	0.73	0.58	0.49	1147
BGR2YCbCr	0.23	0.38	0.28	1142

4.4 Quantitative Analysis Comparison with Other Methods

After pre-processing, the whole dataset containing 1937 spam images and 1907 ham images is divided into 30% test and 70% train. SIFT and HOG features are extracted from the train and test dataset. Bag-of-words model using K-means clustering is applied on SIFT descriptors. Finally, all three train datasets are used to train our model upto 100 epochs with batch size of 32. A learning rate of 0.001 is applied with Adam as optimizer and cross-entropy as loss function. Testing of our proposed method gave an accuracy of 96% as shown in

Table 6. Performance of various transfer learning methods like VGG19, Xception, ResNet251 and DenseNet201 are studied on our dataset. ResNet251 and Xception have resulted in accuracy of only 77% and 93% respectively while DensNet201 and VGG19 performed decently having the same accuracy of 95%. The method discussed in [10] closely performed as compared to our model but failed in terms of recall and F1-score. Moreover it needs higher supports (1160) than other methods as shown in the Table 6.

Table 6. Accuracy of different methods in classifying spam and ham images.

Model	Precision	Recall	F1-Score	Support
VGG19 [17]	0.95	0.95	0.95	1154
CNN [10]	0.96	0.95	0.95	1160
Xception [18]	0.93	0.93	0.93	1154
ResNet251 [26]	0.78	0.77	0.77	1154
DenseNet201 [27]	0.95	0.95	0.95	1154
Our Model	**0.96**	**0.96**	**0.96**	**1154**

5   Conclusion

In this work the effectiveness of the proposal 3-stream neural network in classifying whether a given image is spam or ham is studied. Individual effectiveness of the features like SIFT and HOG is studied and appropriately fused in our 3-stream model for improving the accuracy of transfer learning methods. We have employed the transfer learning technique by employing pre-trained CNN architecture VGG-19 in our model. We have experimented with the effectiveness of the SIFT feature vs SIFT image with our test image dataset. Similarly, we have tested the effectiveness of HOG feature vs HOG image in spam image classification. We have also employed the Bag-of-words model to capture all key-points of the SIFT features. Our model performs better than previous methods. It can be concluded that in order to build a better image spam classifier, additional feature information like SIFT and HOG should also be used in model training and testing. In future works, we will try to extract local features from images using faster RCNN and study its effectiveness.

References

1. Radicati group email statistics report 2021–25. https://www.radicati.com/wp/wp-content/uploads/2021/Email_Statistics_Report,_2021-2025_Executive_Summary.pdf. Accessed 2 Jun 2022
2. Lai, C.-C., Tsai, M.-C.: An empirical performance comparison of machine learning methods for spam e-mail categorization. In: Fourth International Conference on Hybrid Intelligent Systems (HIS'04), pp. 44–48. IEEE (2004)

3. Image spam classification using OCR technique. January 2017. Sunita V. Dhavale: https://www.researchgate.net/publication/315388437_Image_Spam_Filters_ Based_on_Optical_Character_Recognition_OCR_Techniques
4. Kumar, A.D., Vinayakumar, R., Soman, K.P.: Deep Learning based Image Spam Detection 3 Oct 2018. https://arxiv.org/abs/1810.03977
5. Vinayakumar, R., Soman, K., Poornachandran, P., Akarsh, S.: Application of deep learning architectures for cyber security. In: Hassanien, A., Elhoseny, M. (eds) Cybersecurity and Secure Information Systems, pp. 125–160. Springer, Cham (2019). https://doi.org/10.1007/978-3-030-16837-7_7
6. Venkatraman, S., Alazab, M., Vinayakumar, R.: A hybrid deep learning image-based analysis for effective malware detection. J. Inf. Secur. Appl. **47**, 377–389 (2019)
7. Vinayakumar, R., Alazab, M., Soman, K., Poornachandran, P., Venkatraman, S.: Robust intelligent malware detection using deep learning. IEEE Access **7**, 46 717-46 738 (2019)
8. Mohan, V.S., Vinayakumar, R., Soman, K., Poornachandran, P.: Spoof net: syntactic patterns for identification of ominous online factors. In: 2018 IEEE Security and Privacy Workshops (SPW), pp. 258–263. IEEE (2018)
9. Vinayakumar, R., Alazab, M., Soman, K., Poornachandran, P., AlNemrat, A., Venkatraman, S.: Deep learning approach for intelligent intrusion detection system. IEEE Access **7**, 41 525-41 550 (2019)
10. https://ieeexplore.ieee.org/document/9044249
11. https://doi.org/10.1007/s42979-021-00762-x
12. https://www.researchgate.net/publication/306186011_Facial_Expression_ Recognition_Using_a_Hybrid_CNN-SIFT_Aggregator
13. https://www.researchgate.net/publication/355152280_Image-Based_Malware_ Classification_Using_VGG19_Network_and_Spatial_Convolutional_Attention
14. https://ieeexplore.ieee.org/document/7860934
15. https://link.springer.com/article/10.1007/s00779-018-1168-8
16. ADAM: Kingma, D., Adam, B.J.: A method for stochastic optimization. Comput. Sci. (2014)
17. Bansal. https://doi.org/10.1007/s12652-021-03488-z
18. Xception: 7 Oct 2016: François Chollet: arXiv:1610.02357v3
19. https://www.researchgate.net/publication/346534797_Color_Model_Based_ Convolutional_Neural_Network_for_Image_Spam_Classification
20. https://arxiv.org/abs/2204.01710
21. https://docs.opencv.org/4.x/da/d22/tutorial_py_canny.html
22. https://www.researchgate.net/publication/338511771_An_Overview_of_Bag_ of_WordsImportance_Implementation_Applications_and_Challenges
23. Introduction to machine learning with applications in information security. Chapman & Hall/CRC
24. Dredze, M., Gevaryahu, R., Elias-Bachrach, A.: Learning fast classifiers for image spam. In: CEAS, pp. 2007–487 (2007)
25. Gao, Y., et al.: Image spam hunter. In: 2008 IEEE International Conference on Acoustics, Speech and Signal Processing, pp. 1765–1768. IEEE (2008)
26. ResNet251: He, K., Zhang, X., Ren, S., Sun, J.:10 Dec 2015: arXiv:1512.03385
27. DenseNet201: https://arxiv.org/abs/1608.06993v5

A Transformer-Based U-Net Architecture for Fast and Efficient Image Demoireing

Densen Puthussery[1] , P. S. Hrishikesh[1]([⊠]) , and C. V. Jiji[2]

[1] Founding Minds Software, Trivandrum, India
{densen,hrishikesh}@foundingminds.com
[2] SRM University-AP, Amaravati, Andhra Pradesh, India
jiji.c@srmap.edu.in
https://www.foundingminds.com, https://srmap.edu.in

Abstract. Recently, transformer based deep neural networks have been found useful in solving various image restoration tasks like image denoising, deblurring, deraining etc., producing significant improvement in PSNR and SSIM over CNN based techniques on benchmark datasets. These networks have effectively addressed quadratic computational complexity issue with increasing image resolution by making use of novel self attention strategies on local image windows. In this paper, we propose a fast and efficient UNet based architecture using transformer modules for the image demoireing task. The proposed architecture is computationally very efficient as the transformer blocks perform non-overlapping window-based self-attention instead of global self attention. We further improve upon the computational complexity by using decreasing window sizes across scales under the proposed U-Net multi resolution framework. To the best of our knowledge, ours is the first deep network architecture using transformer blocks for the image demoireing problem producing comparable results with state of the art techniques both visually and quantitatively on the CFAMoire challenge dataset [23].

Keywords: Image Restoration · Transformer · Demoireing · U-Net

1 Introduction

Digitalization has brought about a great change in the field of photography. The miniaturization of camera modules has made it possible for them to be integrated into handheld devices like smartphones. It has become habitual that people take pictures using handheld devices like smartphones or digital cameras to save information for later reference or to keep records of precious moments in life. In addition, taking pictures from digital screens have also become very common. However, all such digital images are prone to diverse degradation like noise, blur, moire etc.

All the authors have equally contributed.

© The Author(s), under exclusive license to Springer Nature Switzerland AG 2023
D. Gupta et al. (Eds.): CVIP 2022, CCIS 1777, pp. 532–542, 2023.
https://doi.org/10.1007/978-3-031-31417-9_40

Moire patterns are image artifacts that occur when a repetitive pattern is overlaid on a similar pattern but with some degree of misalignment. The misalignment could be displacement along an arbitrary angle of the image or it could be a rotation effect. Whenever there is a misalignment, the two patterns interfere and thus generate moire fringes. Depending on the degree of misalignment the moire pattern generated also varies. The image sensors are arranged in a grid architecture in digital cameras. Thus, moire artifacts appear in digital images when the scene being captured has a grid pattern as the scene is overlaid on sensor array that has a similar pattern. It is commonly found in images of fabrics, feathers, metal gratings, camera captured images of digital screens etc. In color images, the moire fringes often appear as repetitive coloured bands. Moire artifacts affect the perceptual quality of the image as the interference results in a corrupt representation of the scene being captured and the artifacts are easily visible.

The demoireing task is very challenging as the moire artifacts vary over a wide range of frequencies, colour and shape. Moreover, the interference pattern varies with image scale, distance between scene and the camera, rotation etc. Although much research have been done on image restoration like image super resolution [4,8,26], image denoising [1,6,17], image deblurring [7,25] etc., a similar in-depth study has not been done in image demoireing. But, recently many works have been reported on the demoiering problem using CNN based deep neural networks giving rise to cutting edge results.

The transformer architecture [15], originally developed for addressing NLP problems have been successfully ventured for various high level vision problems like recognition, detection, etc. making effective use of the attention mechanism under a computationally efficient framework. Recently, the transformer architecture have been successfully attempted for solving various image restoration tasks like denoising, deblurring, deraining, etc. producing state of the art results in benchmark datasets. In this work we propose a computationally efficient, multi resolution UNet architecture making use of transformer blocks instead of CNN blocks to effectively solve the demoiring problem. The transposed version of the attention computation on non overlapping blocks across feature channels as well as varying block size across resolutions make the proposed network computationally efficient and also produce better results on benchmark datasets.

2   Related Work

Image demoireing is a restoration task that has not received much attention when compared with other restoration problems like image super resolution [4,8, 26], image deblurring [7,25] etc. A conventional image processing method called layer decomposition on polyphase components (LPDC) was proposed by Yang [20] for demoireing. The technique fails to remove moire fringes that have large spatial extent and tends to over-smooth the details of the image [11]. Deep learning based methods have proved to be promising for solving many challenging image restoration tasks in the recent past.

Recently, many deep learning based methods have been proposed for the demoireing problem making use of large amounts of annotated clean and moire image pairs. Such public datasets include [5,14]. [14] dataset was developed to address the demoireing problem in real world images, along with which they proposed a multi-scale CNN architecture called DMCNN. [5] introduced a high-definition dataset FHDMi to address the availability of high-resolution image pairs for demoering and developed deep learning architecture called FHDe2Net.

Moire photo restoration using multi-resolution CNN was proposed by Sun [14] in which the moire image is converted into multiple feature maps at various resolutions. The moire at different frequency bands is removed by introduction separate branches for feature maps at different scales and then fusing them to restore the image. This network used deconvolution or transposed convolution for upsampling the feature maps and hence is prone to introduction of image artifacts. Additionally, these networks have poor feature expression ability [2]. Liu [11] proposed a deep CNN based method to remove moire artifacts from camera-captured screen images. The method performed moire removal at coarse scale and at a fine scale and integrated generative adversarial network (GAN) based training to increase the robustness of the model. However, the demoireing is done only at a specific resolution and hence is effective only in removing moire with a given frequency band. Thus the network fails to generalise and additionally, the upsampling of coarse scale demoired image is done by bicubic interpolation which could result in information loss. Exclusive studies were done by the research community on the demoireing problem at the advances in image manipulation workshop (AIM 2019) and the new trends in image restoration and enhancement (NTIRE 2020) workshop with the challenge event on demoireing [21,24]. Two novel synthetic datasets namely LCDMoire [22] and CFAMoire [21] were introduced respectively in each workshop as a part of the demoireing challenge. A number of solutions were proposed by researchers with notable works like [13,27].

Vision Transformers: Initially, transformer achitecture was introduced by [15] in the field of natural language processing (NLP). After its introducton in 2017 it has revolutionised the field of NLP and currently all the state of the art architectures for different fundamental problems in NLP are based on transformers. The main advantage with transformer is its ability to learn the long range dependencies in data and the learnable weigths are dynamic and adaptable based on the input.

CNNs were the de facto base for many vision based architecture till the vision transformer [3] was introduced, where a transformer based architecture was proposed for image recognition/classification tasks. The network divided the input images to patches and along with the position embedding and was passed through a transformer network. The aim here was to address the main issue of local receptive fields of CNN with global attention that can be achieved with transformer architectures. But one of the main issue faced by vannila transformer architecture is the quadratic increase in the complexity which makes it unsuitable for low level vision problems like image restoration.

After the success of [3], several transformer based architectures have been proposed for both low and high level vision tasks. One of the main issue to be tackled with these architecture where to reduce the model complexity. In [12], this issue was successfully solved using non-overlapping local windows with cross window connection instead of global attention. Transformer architectures that were proposed for high level vision tasks include [18,28] etc. In [28], a set based global losses that force unique predictions based on bipartite matching and a transformer model were introduced. The main advantage with such a loss is that it does not require any anchor boxes which are generated based on prior information about the data. This makes the architecture more generalisable. The method was able to generate results in par with current state of the art in object detection based on CNNs. Recently, several works have been proposed for image restoration problems based on transformer architectures. In [10], the authors proposed an architecture that uses a shifting window scheme that computes self attention on non-overlapping local windows with cross window connection which reduced the computational complexity faced when working on high resolution images. Here, the total number of parameters were reduced by 67% when compared with vannila transformers, with an increase in PSNR between 0.14 dB $\sim$ 0.45 dB from the SOTA in different restoration tasks. [19] developed a transformer based architecture for super resolution using images with texture priors. The method proposed a learnable transformer based texture extractor which enabled joint feature embedding of low resolution and reference image aiding the attention mechanism for better performance. [16] proposed U-Net shaped transformer architecture which have a non-overlapping window-based self-attention module at each spatial scale.

3   Proposed Method

The basic framework of the proposed network is based on the U-Net Architecture. Very recently, it has been demonstrated in the literature that the transformer based architectures are very effective in solving various restoration tasks producing state of the art results on benchmark datasets. Hence, in order to take advantage of the attention mechanism which is capable of capturing the long range pixel interactions, we replace the CNN blocks in the U-Net by transformer blocks. The proposed network is similar to the Uformer network proposed in [16] which could effectively solve restoration problems like image denoising, deraining and deblurring. In the proposed approach, we perform block wise self attention across scales using varying window sizes to capture the global dependencies to solve the demoiering problem in a computationally efficient manner (Fig. 1).

The proposed method uses the skip connection and encoder-decoder architecture, but instead of convolution blocks it uses transformers [12,15] as the basic block of the encoder-decoder architecture. Here, the feature maps are extracted from 5 levels at scales ranging from 1 to $\frac{1}{16}$. Each level has a combination of strided convolution and Transformer Attention Non-Spatial Convolution (TrANSConv) block as shown in Fig. 2. The TrANSConv block is basically a transformer and CNN based block that utilises the advantages of both transformers and CNNs. Tranformer is used to capture the long range dependencies

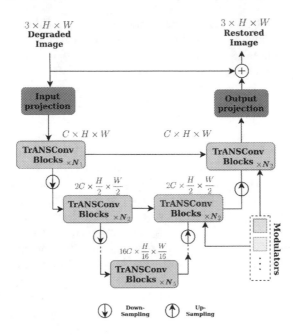

Fig. 1. Model Architecture

from the features using the self-attention mechanism and CNN helps in understanding the local relationship between the pixels. The use of non-overlapping windows based on [12] reduces the computational cost present in vanilla transformer architecture. TrANSConv block is followed by a 4×4 convolution block with stride 2. At the end of encoder section a series of TrANSConv blocks are used as a bottleneck layer. For image restoration from the encoder feature space, the decoder section consists of a combination of deconvolution and TrANSConv block. The deconvolution at each level doubles the spatial size and reduces the number of feature maps by half, each level is connected to the encoder at same spatial resolution using skip connections.

3.1   TrANSConv Block

The TrANSConv block is the fundamental building block in the proposed architecture and it combines the advantages of both transformers and convolution modules. It consists of two main sub blocks 1. Window based self-attention(WinSA) and 2. Feed Forward Network(FFN) based on CNN. WinSA block reduces the computational cost of vanilla transformers by not applying global attention on the whole image instead applying it on non-overlapping windows. Consider the 2D input features obtained from the convolution blocks as $P \epsilon \mathbb{R}^{C \times H \times W}$, before passing it to the WinSA block the feature P is split into N non-overlapping windows of size $W \times W$. Then each window is flattened and transposed to obtain $P^i \epsilon \mathbb{R}^{W^2 \times C}$ on which the self attention is performed.

Considering there are H heads in the attention module, the following equations represent the attention calculation for each head $h\epsilon H$.

$$Attention(Q, K, V) = Softmax(\frac{QK^T}{\sqrt{d_k}} + B)V \qquad (1)$$

$$P = \{P^1, P^2, P^3, ...P^N\} \qquad (2)$$

$$O_k^i = Attention(P^i W_k^Q, P^i W_k^K, P^i W_k^V), k = 1, 2, ...H \qquad (3)$$

$$O_h = \{O_k^1, O_k^2, O_k^2......O_k^N\} \qquad (4)$$

Q, K and V respectively represent queries, keys, and values of the attention block, d_k is the dimension of the keys and B represents the relative position bias [12]. Attention is the mapping of a query and a set of key-value pairs to an output, where a set of weights are generated for corresponding values based on a compatibility function between query and its corresponding key. Then the weighted sum of the values are used to compute the output. WinSA block reduces the computational cost to a significant level by computing self attention within local windows. Apart from this, across various scales in the U-Net architecture we use decreasing window sizes which further reduces the computations required.

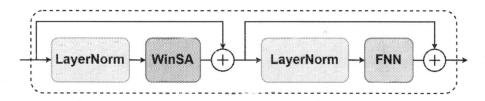

Fig. 2. TraNSConv Block

3.2 Feed Forward Net

Although the self-attention mechanism in transformers is very efficient in capturing the inherent information of the image at a global scale, it falls short in capturing the local context. The local context carries crucial information that aids in restoration of the image. For example, the local information of a small area within the image defines whether the signal is of a low or a high spatial frequency in that region. We can remove salt and pepper noise through approximation of the actual value of spiky pixels by interpolating from its noise-free neighbourhood. Many other image restoration tasks like deblurring, super-resolution etc. heavily rely on the local context of an image for effective results. Following [9], we also employ Depthwise convolution on the normalized feature vectors of the transformer output to capture the local information of the pixels. Figure 3b depicts the convolutional neural network used in this work. It essentially consists of two 1×1 convolutions and a depthwise convolution. The initial 1×1 convolution is used to expand the feature map. The new feature set is then reshaped

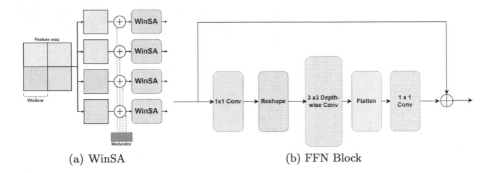

(a) WinSA   (b) FFN Block

Fig. 3. Basic Blocks

into two dimensional feature map so that these are now structured in the same manner as the feature maps in fully convolutional networks. Following this, the depthwise convolution is applied on the feature map which would capture the local context across different channels. These features are then reshaped back to tokens. The second 1×1 convolution which acts as a bottleneck, is applied on the tokens to make the number of output channels of the feed forward network equal to its number of input channels.

3.3   Restoration Modulator

The modulators employed functions as a bias vector added to the non-overlapping feature windows before applying the transformer based self-attention. Since the network follows the U-Net architecture, the resolution of the modulator is different for each feature scale in the U-Net structure.

4   Experimental Results

4.1   Dataset and Training Details

The dataset used for the experiment is CFAMoire dataset [23] provided as part of the NTIRE 2020 Challenge on Image Demoireing. There are a total of 11000 clean and moire image pairs, of which 1000 is in training set, 500 in the validation set and 500 in the test set all of resolution 128×128. Since the test set ground truths are not publicly available, we perform the experiments on the validation set. The training set was divided into two different sets. 9500 image pairs were used for training the model and 500 for validation. s the images of the dataset is of size 128×128, non-over lapping window at initial feature scale is trivial as the window is also of size 128. The patches of size of 16×16 was used as the input to the self-attention module and 12 attention heads were used. The model was trained for 1500 epochs with an initial learning rate of 0.0002 and Adam optimiser was used with cosine annealing. The model was optimised for L1 loss.

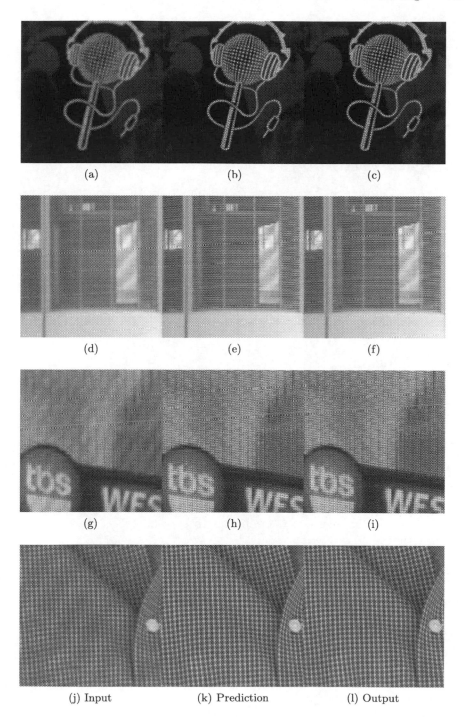

(a)   (b)   (c)

(d)   (e)   (f)

(g)   (h)   (i)

(j) Input   (k) Prediction   (l) Output

Fig. 4. Sample results of moire, prediction and ground truth images from CFAMoire dataset (Color figure online)

Table 1. Performance of proposed method on validation set of CFAMoire dataset

Method	PSNR	SSIM	Parameters(M)
RCAN	41.71	0.99	15.29
AWUDN+	42.22	0.99	144.3
Ours	**41.32**	**0.993**	50

4.2   Result Analysis

Four examples from the predictions on 500 images in the evaluation set used while training are depicted in Fig. 4. The colored moire fringes are readily visible in the input as shown in the figure. The color and texture pattern of the reconstructed image is much alike the ground truth that their distinction is not apparent as evident from the figure. Hence the perceptual quality is maintained in the proposed method with same reflecting in the PSNR metric. The quantitative assessment of the proposed method is shown in Table 1. The proposed method generates quality results in terms of the perceptual appeal when compared with the ground truth.

5   Conclusion

The nature of moire interference is that it is a dynamic texture that varies with image scale and covers a wide frequency range. The transformer based multi-scale image reconstruction approach as proposed is capable of suppressing the moire patterns that appear along several frequency ranges efficiently. The ability of proposed method to learn both global and local information at different scale helps in achieving the same. Overall, the proposed transformer-based approach is computationally very efficient due to the new model architecture utilized. Currently the method has only been tested with smaller images available in [23] and hence the performance of the same has to be validated in images of larger size in future

References

1. Anwar, S., Barnes, N.: Real image denoising with feature attention. CoRR abs/1904.07396 (2019). http://arxiv.org/abs/1904.07396
2. Cheng, X., Fu, Z., Yang, J.: Multi-scale dynamic feature encoding network for image demoireing (2019)
3. Dosovitskiy, A., et al.: An image is worth 16x16 words: transformers for image recognition at scale. In: 9th International Conference on Learning Representations, ICLR 2021, Virtual Event, Austria, May 3–7, 2021. OpenReview.net (2021). https://openreview.net/forum?id=YicbFdNTTy
4. Haris, M., Shakhnarovich, G., Ukita, N.: Deep back-projection networks for super-resolution (03 2018)

5. He, B., Wang, C., Shi, B., Duan, L.Y.: Mop moire patterns using MOPNET. In: Proceedings of the IEEE/CVF International Conference on Computer Vision (ICCV), October 2019

6. Kim, Y., Soh, J.W., Park, G.Y., Cho, N.I.: Transfer learning from synthetic to real-noise denoising with adaptive instance normalization. In: IEEE/CVF Conference on Computer Vision and Pattern Recognition (CVPR), June 2020

7. Kupyn, O., Budzan, V., Mykhailych, M., Mishkin, D., Matas, J.: Deblurgan: blind motion deblurring using conditional adversarial networks. CoRR abs/1711.07064 (2017). http://arxiv.org/abs/1711.07064

8. Ledig, C., et al.: Photo-realistic single image super-resolution using a generative adversarial network. In: 2017 IEEE Conference on Computer Vision and Pattern Recognition (CVPR), pp. 105–114 (2017)

9. Li, Y., Zhang, K., Cao, J., Timofte, R., Van Gool, L.: Localvit: bringing locality to vision transformers (2021). https://doi.org/10.48550/ARXIV.2104.05707, https://arxiv.org/abs/2104.05707

10. Liang, J., Cao, J., Sun, G., Zhang, K., Van Gool, L., Timofte, R.: Swinir: image restoration using swin transformer. In: 2021 IEEE/CVF International Conference on Computer Vision Workshops (ICCVW), pp. 1833–1844 (2021). https://doi.org/10.1109/ICCVW54120.2021.00210

11. Liu, B., Shu, X., Wu, X.: Demoiréing of camera-captured screen images using deep convolutional neural network (2018)

12. Liu, Z., et al.: Swin transformer: hierarchical vision transformer using shifted windows. In: 2021 IEEE/CVF International Conference on Computer Vision, ICCV 2021, Montreal, QC, Canada, October 10–17, 2021. pp. 9992–10002. IEEE (2021). https://doi.org/10.1109/ICCV48922.2021.00986

13. Luo, X., Zhang, J., Hong, M., Qu, Y., Xie, Y., Li, C.: Deep wavelet network with domain adaptation for single image demoireing. In: 2020 IEEE/CVF Conference on Computer Vision and Pattern Recognition Workshops (CVPRW), pp. 1687–1694 (2020). https://doi.org/10.1109/CVPRW50498.2020.00218

14. Sun, Y., Yu, Y., Wang, W.: Moiré photo restoration using multiresolution convolutional neural networks. IEEE Trans. Image Process. **27**, 4160–4172 (2018)

15. Vaswani, A., et al.: Attention is all you need. CoRR abs/1706.03762 (2017). http://arxiv.org/abs/1706.03762

16. Wang, Z., Cun, X., Bao, J., Liu, J.: Uformer: a general u-shaped transformer for image restoration. CoRR abs/2106.03106 (2021). https://arxiv.org/abs/2106.03106

17. Xia, Z., Chakrabarti, A.: Identifying recurring patterns with deep neural networks for natural image denoising. In: IEEE Winter Conference on Applications of Computer Vision, WACV 2020, Snowmass Village, CO, USA, March 1–5, 2020, pp. 2415–2423. IEEE (2020). https://doi.org/10.1109/WACV45572.2020.9093586

18. Xie, E., Wang, W., Yu, Z., Anandkumar, A., Alvarez, J.M., Luo, P.: Segformer: simple and efficient design for semantic segmentation with transformers. In: Ranzato, M., Beygelzimer, A., Dauphin, Y., Liang, P., Vaughan, J.W. (eds.) Advances in Neural Information Processing Systems, vol. 34, pp. 12077–12090. Curran Associates, Inc. (2021). https://proceedings.neurips.cc/paper/2021/file/64f1f27bf1b4ec22924fd0acb550c235-Paper.pdf

19. Yang, F., Yang, H., Fu, J., Lu, H., Guo, B.: Learning texture transformer network for image super-resolution. In: Proceedings of the IEEE/CVF Conference on Computer Vision and Pattern Recognition (CVPR), June 2020

20. Yang, J., Liu, F., Yue, H., Fu, X., Hou, C., Wu, F.: Textured image demoiréing via signal decomposition and guided filtering. IEEE Trans. Image Process. **26**(7), 3528–3541 (2017)
21. Yuan, S., et al.: Ntire 2020 challenge on image demoireing: methods and results. In: 2020 IEEE/CVF Conference on Computer Vision and Pattern Recognition Workshops (CVPRW), pp. 1882–1893 (2020)
22. Yuan, S., Timofte, R., Slabaugh, G., Leonardis, A.: Aim 2019 challenge on image demoireing: Dataset and study. In: 2019 IEEE/CVF International Conference on Computer Vision Workshop (ICCVW), pp. 3526–3533 (2019)
23. Yuan, S., Timofte, R., Leonardis, A., Slabaugh, G.: Ntire 2020 challenge on image demoireing: methods and results. In: Proceedings of the IEEE/CVF Conference on Computer Vision and Pattern Recognition (CVPR) Workshops, June 2020
24. Yuan, S., et al.: Aim 2019 challenge on image demoireing: methods and results (2019). https://doi.org/10.48550/ARXIV.1911.03461
25. Zhang, H., Dai, Y., Li, H., Koniusz, P.: Deep stacked hierarchical multi-patch network for image deblurring. In: 2019 IEEE/CVF Conference on Computer Vision and Pattern Recognition (CVPR), pp. 5971–5979 (2019)
26. Zhang, Y., Li, K., Li, K., Wang, L., Zhong, B., Fu, Y.: Image super-resolution using very deep residual channel attention networks. CoRR abs/1807.02758 (2018). http://arxiv.org/abs/1807.02758
27. Zheng, B., Yuan, S., Slabaugh, G., Leonardis, A.: Image demoireing with learnable bandpass filters (2020). https://doi.org/10.48550/ARXIV.2004.00406. https://arxiv.org/abs/2004.00406
28. Zhu, X., Su, W., Lu, L., Li, B., Wang, X., Dai, J.: Deformable DETR: deformable transformers for end-to-end object detection. In: 9th International Conference on Learning Representations, ICLR 2021, Virtual Event, Austria, May 3–7, 2021. OpenReview.net (2021). https://openreview.net/forum?id=gZ9hCDWe6ke

Auxiliary CNN for Graspability Modeling with 3D Point Clouds and Images for Robotic Grasping

Priyanka Varun[1]([✉]), Laxmidhar Behera[2], and Tushar Sandhan[1]

[1] Electrical Engineering, IIT Kanpur, Kanpur, U.P., India
{priyankav20,sandhan}@iitk.ac.in
[2] Electrical Engineering, IIT Mandi, Mandi, Himachal Pradesh, India
director@iitmandi.ac.in

Abstract. Automatic object grasping is a challenging problem and has numerous applications in various fields. Currently, researchers have developed models that use only 3D point cloud data which is not sufficient to capture a complete grasping ability (graspability), because many visual features related to objects are missing in the 3D points. So here we propose an auxiliary convolutional neural network pipeline (CNN) for graspability modeling via simultaneously using visual information from RGBD images and 3D point clouds. For training the auxiliary CNN, we have created new dataset where the most graspable object has been placed in class 5, whereas the least graspable object has been placed in class 1. Our graspability modeling includes, 12 object features, where 9 are extracted from elliptic Fourier descriptors, the other 3 features are Euclidian distance from the centroid, compactness of an object and category of an object. We have thoroughly evaluated our proposed approach by incorporating it into state-of-the-art grasping method Graspnet [8], which has further improved the overall average grasp precision. Additionally, we performed an ablation study on various network elements and loss functions (cross entropy, mean square loss) for obtaining the best accuracy and graspability scores.

Keywords: Convolutional neural networks CNN · Deep learning · 3D point clouds · Object grasping · GraspNet

1 Introduction

Humans can manipulate objects rather easily, but it is still difficult for robots to properly grasp a wide variety of objects. Various industrial applications like part assembly of machines, container binning and sorting, mainly rely on the accuracy of automatic robotic grasping. Perception and planning are required in robotic grasping [6]. Perception is to find the position and orientation of the object which needs to be grasped. The planning phase determines where and how to position the manipulator for a grasp [26].

© The Author(s), under exclusive license to Springer Nature Switzerland AG 2023
D. Gupta et al. (Eds.): CVIP 2022, CCIS 1777, pp. 543–557, 2023.
https://doi.org/10.1007/978-3-031-31417-9_41

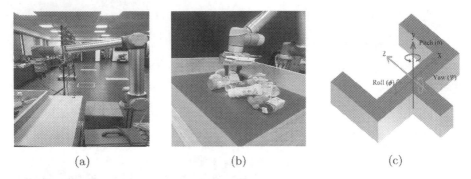

(a)   (b)   (c)

Fig. 1. Robotic manipulator interacting with outside environment to carry out specific tasks (a) Complete setup of the robotic manipulator, (b) robotic manipulator performing grasping task, (c) 6D pose of an end-effector.

A robot manipulator is an electronic device having numerous segments that interact with its surroundings to carry out multiple automation tasks. They are also known as robotic arms. In addition to having numerous specialized uses, robot manipulators are widely utilized in the general purpose industrial settings, where they can be programmed for any new task. Links and joints are assembled to form manipulators as the Fig. 1a. The assembly is made up of rigid pieces called links. Joints are the points where two links are connected. The end-effector is the component of the manipulator that interacts with the outside world to carry out tasks as shown in the Fig. 1b. There are five types of joints i.e. Revolute, Cylindrical, Prismatic, Spherical and Planar. The research of robot manipulators entails analyzing the positions and orientations of the various manipulator segments. The roll, pitch and yaw angles are a series of rotations about the axes x, y and z respectively. The order in which the rotation roll, pitch and yaw are done is also important.

In industrial robots, the roll-pitch-yaw angles can be combined to determine orientation of the end-effector. The roll-pitch-yaw angles for a spherical wrist, which is a frequent feature of 6-axis industrial robots and comprises the fourth, fifth and sixth joints with their axes of rotation intersecting at one location (known as the wrist center) are shown in the Fig. 1c.

In recent studies grasp pose estimation was done without object pose estimation [7,15,32]. These approaches used point cloud data to obtain all feasible grasps. A large number of grasps were estimated, and top grasp was selected among them based on the probability of grasping. These techniques effectively generalize grasp information to new objects because they identify grasps irrespective of the identify of an object. Although these approaches are promising, their accuracy decreases with real-world scenarios and cluttered scenes [26]. Recent developments in grasp synthesis for unidentified items have been made possible by deep learning approaches. Its main advantage is the ability to learn effective representations from vast amounts of labelled and unlabelled data without manually constructing the feature spaces [6]. Most of the time, sampling and ranking of the grasp candidates [17,23] result in lengthy computation times that range from a second to tens of seconds. These methods rely on (RGB) or (RGBD) and could have side effect of grasp planning, especially when an accurate and responsive sensor is not available [22].

To alleviate these drawbacks, we have proposed an auxiliary CNN for graspability modelling with simultaneously using 3D point clouds as well as 2D visual features from RGBD input images. We predict the intermittent graspability score for a wide range of items based on 5 grasping categories. The most graspable object has been placed in category 5, whereas the least graspable object has been placed in category 1. Object has been classified based on 12 features, elliptic Fourier descriptors, compactness measure, distance map and object categorization. In our method we emphasize on including inherent properties of the object such as shape, compactness and size for prediction of our graspability score which distinguishes our work from previous work in this domain.

2 Related Work

Algorithms for identifying grasps can be categorized into multiple groups based on the input used, method of classification and type of sensor data modalities. The most common one is to use RGB-D image input to find a rectangle-based grasps [1,6,13,17,20,23,25,27]. A two-step learning algorithm was proposed by Y. Jiang et al. [13], the second step was more accurate but slow in terms of computation, whereas the initial step was fast but less accurate and more prone to errors. In the first-step, the features were applied to facilitate quick search during the inference. The second step employed more sophisticated attributes to produce a more precise forecast on the rankings of the grasping rectangles given a few top-ranked rectangles. D. Park et al. [25] suggested a single, multi-task deep neural network that, with only a minimal amount of post-processing, may provide data on grasp detection, object detection and object reasoning. L. Pinto et al. [27] demonstrated that large-scale trial-and-error studies are now feasible and have provided a framework for self-supervising robot grasping tasks.

S. Levine et al. [20] described a technique for developing hand-eye coordination for robotic grasping that uses deep learning to create a grasp success prediction network and a continuous servoing mechanism to continually operate a robotic manipulator. Such techniques do not have orientation restrictions, but they do necessitate prior object geometry information. U. Asif et al. [1] proposed EnsembleNet, a deep learning framework that combines a variety of CNN models that have been trained using various objective functions to yield the grasps.

To directly learn features from unprocessed point cloud inputs, Qi et al. first presented the PointNet [28]. Then many techniques [2,21,29–31] for point cloud categorization and segmentation are suggested in the literature. C. R. Qi et al. [29] proposed the PointNet++, a robust neural network design, to handle point sets sampled from metric spaces. H. Su et al. [30] proposed SPLAT-Net which computes spatially aware and hierarchical features using a sparse and effective lattice directly considering point clouds as the inputs. Additionally,

SPLAT-Net makes it simple to convert 2D data into 3D and vice-versa, creating a cutting-edge network architecture for the simultaneous processing of point clouds and multi-view images.

M. Atzmon et al. [2] introduces PCNN, a method for defining convolution of functions over point clouds that is fast, translation invariant and resilient to point sampling, density and invariant to point cloud order. Y. Li et al. [21] proposed PointCNN, a generalization of CNN that uses spatially-local correlation using point cloud data. To provide high-resolution 3D outputs represented as octrees, M. Tatarchenko et al. [31] have developed a novel convolutional decoder architecture. This architecture proved to be versatile in terms of the precise layer configuration and to offer the same accuracy as dense voxel grids. In terms of memory usage and run time, it also scales significantly better to higher resolutions.

Our proposed auxiliary CNN for graspability modelling, simultaneously uses 3D point clouds as well as 2D visual features from RGBD input images. It predicts the intermittent graspability score to boost the performance of grasp prediction networks.

3   Method

Graspnet [8] is an end-to-end grasp pose prediction network that takes only point cloud as input and it learns approaching direction and parameters for operation independently. The analytical computations used here can evaluate any type of grasp pose without thoroughly labeling the ground truths and directly reports whether a grasping was successful or not. Our auxiliary CNN and graspability modeling pipeline improves the Graspnet via intermittently fusing graspable scores to objectness score inside Graspnet. So first we briefly introduce few modules of the Graspnet in the Sect. 3.1.

3.1   GraspNet

Graspnet is composed of Approach Net, Operation Net, and Tolerance net.

Approach Net: Given that some paths in 3D space are inaccessible due to obstruction or occlusion, the Approach Network estimates the approaching vectors and potential grasp spots concurrently. PointNet++ has been adopted as a backbone network [29] to effectively capture point cloud geometric information to provide a strong foundation for viewpoint classification. It outputs a new collection of points with C channel features from an input raw point cloud with size N × 3. M points have been sub-sampled by using farthest point sampling to cover the whole scene. Approaching vectors have been classified into V predefined viewpoints. The Approach Network generates two values for each point to indicate whether it is confident in being graspable or not. As a result, the output of the proposal generation network is M × (2 + V), where V stands for the number of predetermined approaching vectors and 2 represents the binary class indicating the object is graspable or not.

Operation Net: Operation Net predicts in-plane rotation, approaching distance, gripper width and grasp confidence after obtaining approaching vectors from graspable locations. For each grasp candidate, an unified representation obtained before passing across the operating network. Previous research [6] has demonstrated that classification could outperform regression at predicting in-plane rotation. As a result of this configuration, the rotation network uses aligned point cloud as input to predict classification scores, normalised residuals for each binned rotation and the appropriate grasp width and confidence. Notably, the predicted rotations are between 0 and $180°C$ because the gripper is symmetric.

Tolerance Net: This network can already predict precise grasp positions as a result of earlier sub-networks. In addition, a representation known as grasp affinity fields (GAF) is utilized to strengthen the reliability of grasp pose prediction [8]. Humans typically choose grasp poses that can accommodate larger inaccuracies because possible grasp poses are endless. This serves as inspiration for GAF, which learn to anticipate each grasp's tolerance to disruption. When given a ground truth grasp pose, its neighbor in the sphere space is sought to determine the farthest distance at which the grasp is still secure with a grasp score s > 0.5 and set it as the target for GAF.

Graspnet [8] estimates an Objectness score which is further used in the pipeline to estimate whether an object is graspable or not. The network uses only 3-D point cloud data which is not sufficient to capture a graspability score because many features related to objects are missing in 3D points. So we have proposed to extract relevant information from RGBD input in terms of the graspability score.

3.2   Our Method

Our method has three main parts feature generation, model formation and appropriately fusing graspability modelling framework with the existing pipeline as shown in Fig. 2. Various modules of the proposed framework are explained below.

Object Categorization: Image structures are grouped into many classes using semantic segmentation. This is accomplished by classifying each pixel into predefined categories. Allowing the algorithm to divide the image pixels into classes is the purpose of image segmentation [14]. High-Resolution Network (HRNet) [34] is a convolutional neural network used for image segmentation. It maintains various high-resolution representations of an image by connecting high-to-low resolution convolutions simultaneously. It also uses repeated multiscale feature fusions across parallel convolutions to produce better quality segmented masks. In our dataset, every distinct 88 objects has a unique id. This unique id is also used as a class label and which is assigned to every pixel occupied by that object in our network. Since this gives us a unique 2D identification of each object.

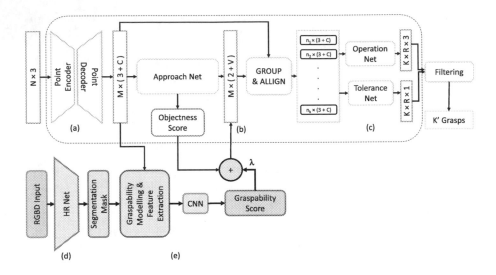

Fig. 2. Overview of an upgraded end-to-end network: (a) A point encoder-decoder collects cloud features from a scene point cloud with N input 3D cloud points before sampling M points with C-dim features, (b) ApproachNet predicts approaching vectors, which are then applied to groups of points in cylindrical volumes, (c) ToleranceNet and OperationNet make predictions about the operating parameters and reliability of the grasps, (d) HRNet converts RGBD inputs into a segmentation mask where every object has been provided with a unique id, (e) 3D points have been remapped into 2D spatial points and used in graspability modelling whose output is given to the CNN which predicts our graspability scores.

Spatial Mapping: In Graspnet, only 3D point cloud information is used. That means the features of the objects are attached with these 3D points and passed to approach Net. Whereas in our method, since the features are extracted using the RGBD input image as well, the 3D point clouds have to be mapped to corresponding 2D points to synchronize our model with the ongoing pipeline. We have utilized fixed camera parameters and back-projection matrix to obtain corresponding 2D mappings for each 3D point.

Grapability Modelling and Feature Extraction: Our model uses twelve features from which nine are generated using elliptic Fourier descriptors, one from HRNet and other two compactness measure and distance map are obtained via object silhouette modeling and processing.

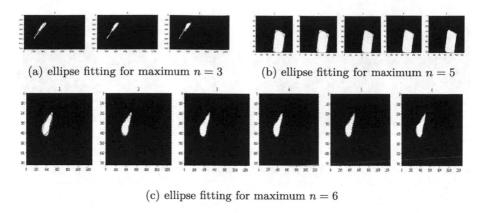

(a) ellipse fitting for maximum $n = 3$ (b) ellipse fitting for maximum $n = 5$

(c) ellipse fitting for maximum $n = 6$

Fig. 3. Fourier ellipse fitting for different objects at distinct value of coefficients.

Elliptic Feature: Many researchers [11,33] have successfully employed Fourier descriptors to characterise the closed contours. Fourier descriptors retain all of the information about the shape of a contour, despite being invariant with rotation, dilation and translation of the contour [16]. Since a closed curve is a continuous periodic function of a parameter, it can also be written as the combination of sine and cosine functions with increasing frequencies, each of which is influenced by a set of coefficients known as 'Fourier descriptors' (FD). As the number of harmonics rises, the total of these cosine and sine functions converges towards the starting contour. Every harmonic is an ellipse that has its period and FD entirely defines it. In multivariate analysis, the FD can be employed as morphometric variables, enabling the separation of groups within a set of shapes [10]. The majority of two-dimensional applications deal with biological topics [18], such as anthropology [3], anatomy [5] and evaluating how well orthodontic therapy [19] is working. Other applications include algorithms for reading handwriting [11] or identifying the aircraft [16].

A series of piecewise linear fits made up of eight standardized line segments, as first described by Freeman [9], are used to approximate a continuous contour using the chain code [16], so the chain U of length k becomes the code for a contour as $U = p_1 p_2 \cdots p_k$.

Each link in this structure, p_i, is an integer between 0 and 7, oriented in the direction $\frac{\pi}{4} p_i$, (measured counterclockwise from the X axis of an X-Y coordinate system), and it has a length of either 1 or $\sqrt{2}$, depending on whether it is even or odd. The following is the definition of the Fourier series expansion for the entire contour's x projection of the chain code:

$$x(t) = A_0 + \sum_{n=1}^{\infty} a_n \cos \frac{2n\pi t}{T} + b_n \sin \frac{2n\pi t}{T} \tag{1}$$

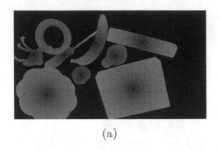 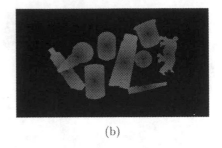

(a)   (b)

Fig. 4. Distance maps for different scenes. The intensity of every pixel is directly proportional to the euclidean distance from the centroid of the object.

$$A_0 = \frac{1}{T} \int_0^T x(t)dt, \quad a_n = \frac{2}{T} \int_0^T x(t) \cos \frac{2n\pi t}{T} dt, \quad b_n = \frac{2}{T} \int_0^T x(t) \sin \frac{2n\pi t}{T} dt. \tag{2}$$

It is relatively easy to find the Fourier coefficients for the nth harmonic a_n and b_n, $(B_0, \equiv 0)$, because $x(t)$ is piecewise linear and continuous throughout time. Thus a_n and b_n obtained from the Fourier series expansion are used as the features in our work. Fourier series is applied to the shape of an object returns the coefficient a_n, b_n, c_n and d_n as given in Eq. 2 and Eq. 4. As the maximum harmonic n increases the elliptic Fourier description becomes more and more accurate and closely represents shape of the counter as shown Fig. 3. Similarly we obtain the coefficient for $y(t)$ as follows,

$$y(t) = C_0 + \sum_{n=1}^{\infty} c_n \cos \frac{2n\pi t}{T} + d_n \sin \frac{2n\pi t}{T} \tag{3}$$

$$C_0 = \frac{1}{T} \int_0^T y(t)dt, \quad c_n = \frac{2}{T} \int_0^T y(t) \cos \frac{2n\pi t}{T} dt, \quad d_n = \frac{2}{T} \int_0^T y(t) \sin \frac{2n\pi t}{T} dt \tag{4}$$

Distance Map: We obtain the distance map feature in two steps. The first we determine the centroid of an object as given in Eq. 5. In the subsequent step, Euclidean distance of each pixel from that object instance's centroid is calculated as given in Eq. 6. The y axis is pointing downward and origin of the coordinate system is in the upper-left corner as in Fig. 4.

Step 1 - Obtaining the Centroid for Each Instance
The arithmetic mean or average, of each point within a shape, is known as the centroid. Assuming a structure has n unique points, $x_1, ..., x_n$ and $y_1, ..., y_n$, the centroid is given by

$$c_x = \frac{1}{n} \sum_{i=1}^{n} x_i, \quad c_y = \frac{1}{n} \sum_{i=1}^{n} y_i. \tag{5}$$

Step 2 - Computing Map with Euclidean Distance
In this step euclidean distance is calculated for each pixel (x_p, y_p) from centroid obtained in previous step (c_x, c_y),

$$D = \sqrt{(x_p - c_x)^2 + (y_p - c_y)^2} \tag{6}$$

Compactness: Compactness is a fundamental characteristic of items. As a result, geometric adjustments like translation, rotation and scaling do not affect the compactness measure. Since object graspability depends upon the shape of the object, compactness can be used to predict the graspability of the object. The dimensionless ratio of contour length (L) and contour area (A) can be used to calculate the object's degree of compactness (C),

$$C = \frac{(L)^2}{(A)}. \tag{7}$$

Model: A Convolutional Neural Network (ConvNet/CNN) takes in an input image, obtain importance (learnable weights and biases) to various aspects/objects in the image and be able to distinguish one from the other. In comparison to other classification methods, CNN requires substantially less pre-processing. They can learn these filters and features from the data, whereas in primitive techniques filters are hand-engineered.

We have used a convolutional neural network to exploit correlation among our graspability features. Our model as shown in Fig. 5a, uses 1D convolutions, batch normalization and ReLU activation function. The number of filters are kept in each layer is (12,24,48) respectively. Sigmoid is used as the activation function in the output layer. The learning rate was kept at 0.01. The training data was divided into 80:20 ratio, where 80% was used for training and 20% was used for validation. For visual depiction in Fig. 5b, only 60 points were randomly sampled out of 921600 original 2D mapped points from an image. Green points in the images are the points which are correctly classified.

4   Experimental Results

Previous approaches used the rectangle metric, which checks whether a grasp is correct or not, to assess the prediction performance of the grasp pose. The algorithms for grasp position prediction are anticipated to predict numerous grasps in cluttered scenes. The percentage of true positives is particularly significant because we typically carry out implementation after predicting all grasp positions. The precision of the top-k ranked grasps is an evaluation metric. For various range of the k, average precision (AP) is calculated.

We have implemented our model with PyTorch and trained with a stochastic gradient descent optimizer on NVIDIA GeForce GTX 1080Ti GPU. 20000 3D points were sampled from each scene and the they were down-sampled to 1024 points. The learning rate was kept at 0.01. Time taken for the 1K epoch was 1 min 13 s and the 10K epoch was 13 min 26 s. 12 features were extracted from an object

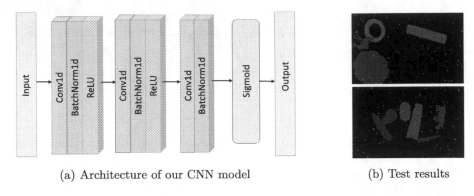

(a) Architecture of our CNN model   (b) Test results

Fig. 5. CNN model and its result on two test images. Green points in the images are correctly predicted points whereas red shows incorrect predictions. (Color figure online)

where 9 features were extracted from elliptic Fourier descriptor, the other 3 features were Euclidian distance from the centroid, compactness of an object and object category. 50 points from each object were sampled from 100 segmented masks, and 87700 of those points were used for training and validation.

4.1 Dataset

We have chosen 13 adverse objects from DexNet 2.0 [23], 43 objects from grasp-Net [8] and 32 objects that are appropriate for grasping from the YCB dataset [4]. The items are sized appropriately for grasping and feature a variety of shapes, textures, sizes, materials, etc. This diversified local geometry will improve the algorithm's capacity for generalization. The dataset includes 88 common objects with exquisite 3D mesh models, where we did not use 3D mesh information in our framework. The 160 cluttered scenes provide 256 RGBD images each, in which 100 scenes are being used for training and 60 scenes are being used for testing. Out of 60 scenes, 30 scenes are labeled as seen and 30 scenes are labeled as similar.

4.2 Evaluation

We have divided objects into 5 classes based on their graspability. The object which is easily graspable has been assigned to class 5 and object which is the least graspable has been assigned to class 1. So instead of regression, our framework focuses on classification problem which is more effective as evident from our experiments as well.

We report classification performance in terms of accuracy percentage and robotic grasping performance in terms of average precision. Classification performance analysis is given in detailed ablation studies performed in Sect. 4.5, and grasping performance is analyzed in below sections.

Table 1. Comparison of graspNet and our method for every 10 scenes where the best results are shown in boldfaces.

Methods/	AP (Seen)			AP (Simiar)		
Scenes	100-109	110-119	120-129	130-139	140-149	150-159
GraspNet [8]	41.224	48.534	39.054	37.173	40.962	37.281
Our Method	**45.309**	**51.886**	**41.609**	**39.877**	**44.481**	**39.919**

Table 2. Comparison of AP for different methods and best results are shown in boldfaces.

Methods	AP (Seen)	AP (Similar)
GG-CNN [24]	24.103	19.531
Multiobject [6]	24.860	22.693
GPD [26]	35.611	31.428
PointNet GPD [22]	40.042	33.407
GraspNet [8]	42.938	38.472
Our Method	**46.268**	**41.426**

4.3 Quantitative Analysis

In this section we have compared our results with existing models for different scenes. In Table 1 our modified pipeline is compared with the existing one. Results have been compared for two different types of scenes. The models were evaluated for every 10 scenes. In Table 2 our method has been compared with existing state-of-the-art pipelines. These models have been compared for two different scene types containing 30 scenes each.

In Table 1 we have done comparison of graspNet with our proposed pipeline having auxiliary CNN. For detailed comparison we have evaluated AP for every 10 scenes to show sectional improvement of our method over state-of-the-art method. Our method has shown minimum improvement of 6.54% for average precision which is in scene 120–129 and maximum improvement of 9.9% which is in scene 100–109 as compared to the best performing method in the literature.

In Table 2 our method is being compared with multiple previous models for robotic grasping. As we can see in the table graspNet showed the significant improvement over other grasping models. Whereas our model has shown an average precision improvement of 7.7% over state-of-the-art method. For the scene numbers 110-119 our method has surpassed 51% average precision.

The best performance of our method can be attributed to appropriate graspability modelling via important object features which can directly capture ability-to-grasp for that object; and efficient auxiliary CNN which can predict accurate graspability scores synchronized with the objectness score of the graspNet.

4.4   Qualitative Analysis

Grasp pose visualization has been shown on different objects in Fig. 6. Objects having greater cubic measure will be having more number of feasible grasp poses whereas flat objects have lesser feasible grasp poses since they are difficult to grasp. As seen in Fig. 6c, Since drill is having greater cubic measure, it has more number of grasp poses while scissor is having comparatively lesser volume hence it has less number of grasp poses.

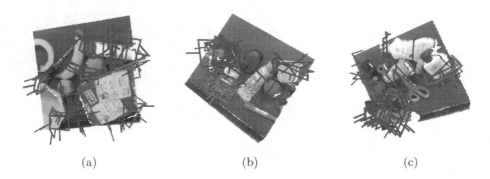

(a)   (b)   (c)

Fig. 6. 6D grasp pose visualization to show quality of grasp for different objects.

4.5   Ablation Study

We have evaluated the effects of differently trained models with various epochs and different loss functions in our framework. Finally, we have conducted an ablation study on components of our network. Model is tested with two different types of the loss function, Cross entropy, and Mean-square error as shown in Table 3. Figure 7 shows relation of loss and accuracy with number of epochs.

Table 3. Comparison of MSE and Cross-entropy loss for different epochs.

Type of loss	No. of Epoch	Training	Validation
MSE	100	60.02	60.36
	1000	68.34	67.93
	10000	74.52	74.61
Cross Entropy	100	68.64	68.63
	1000	77.45	76.92
	10000	95.54	90.26

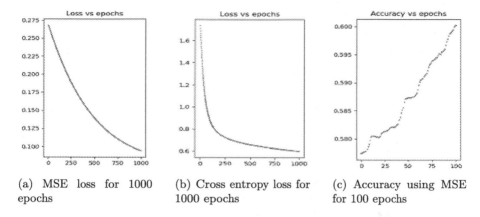

(a) MSE loss for 1000 epochs

(b) Cross entropy loss for 1000 epochs

(c) Accuracy using MSE for 100 epochs

Fig. 7. Optimization loss and accuracy at different epochs for our model.

5   Conclusion

We have introduced the auxiliary CNN with graspability modelling with 3D point clouds and 2D visual image data for obtaining the improved robotic grasping as compared to state-of-the-art model graspNet [8]. With the aid of five classes ranked from 1 to 5, where 5 being easily graspable and 1 being least graspable, auxiliary CNN can be trained efficiently. Thus our proposed method has improved average precision significantly as compared to graspNet. We have effectively merged the objectness scores from an existing pipeline to the graspability scores of the proposed network to increase the grasping capability of the gripper for all 88 objects. Due to the shorter pre-processing time and compact 1D convolutions, the training period for even large epochs of our model was sufficiently short. Moreover our graspability modelled features can be saved in advance for future modifications to further improve on training time for the entire unified network.

References

1. Asif, U., Tang, J., Harrer, S.: Ensemblenet: improving grasp detection using an ensemble of convolutional neural networks. In: BMVC, p. 10 (2018)
2. Atzmon, M., Maron, H., Lipman, Y.: Point convolutional neural networks by extension operators. arXiv preprint arXiv:1803.10091 (2018)
3. Bailey, S.E., Lynch, J.M.: Diagnostic differences in mandibular p4 shape between neandertals and anatomically modern humans. Am. J. Phys. Anthropology Official Publication Am. Assoc. Phys. Anthropologists **126**(3), 268–277 (2005)
4. Calli, B., et al.: Yale-cmu-berkeley dataset for robotic manipulation research. Int. J. Robot. Res. **36**(3), 261–268 (2017)
5. Chen, S.Y., Lestrel, P.E., Kerr, W.J.S., McColl, J.H.: Describing shape changes in the human mandible using elliptical fourier functions. Europ. J. Orthodontics **22**(3), 205–216 (2000)

6. Chu, F.J., Xu, R., Vela, P.A.: Real-world multiobject, multigrasp detection. IEEE Robot. Autom. Lett. **3**(4), 3355–3362 (2018)
7. Detry, R., Ek, C.H., Madry, M., Kragic, D.: Learning a dictionary of prototypical grasp-predicting parts from grasping experience. In: 2013 IEEE International Conference on Robotics and Automation, pp. 601–608. IEEE (2013)
8. Fang, H.S., Wang, C., Gou, M., Lu, C.: Graspnet-1billion: a large-scale benchmark for general object grasping. In: Proceedings of the IEEE/CVF Conference on Computer Vision and Pattern Recognition, pp. 11444–11453 (2020)
9. Freeman, H.: Computer processing of line-drawing images. ACM Comput. Surv. (CSUR) **6**(1), 57–97 (1974)
10. Godefroy, J.E., Bornert, F., Gros, C.I., Constantinesco, A.: Elliptical fourier descriptors for contours in three dimensions: a new tool for morphometrical analysis in biology. C.R. Biol. **335**(3), 205–213 (2012)
11. Granlund, G.H.: Fourier preprocessing for hand print character recognition. IEEE Trans. Comput. **100**(2), 195–201 (1972)
12. Guo, D., Sun, F., Liu, H., Kong, T., Fang, B., Xi, N.: A hybrid deep architecture for robotic grasp detection. In: 2017 IEEE International Conference on Robotics and Automation (ICRA), pp. 1609–1614. IEEE (2017)
13. Jiang, Y., Moseson, S., Saxena, A.: Efficient grasping from rgbd images: Learning using a new rectangle representation. In: 2011 IEEE International Conference on Robotics and Automation, pp. 3304–3311. IEEE (2011)
14. Jordan, J.: An overview of semantic image segmentation. Data Science, pp. 1–21 (2018)
15. Kappler, D., Bohg, J., Schaal, S.: Leveraging big data for grasp planning. In: 2015 IEEE International Conference on Robotics and Automation (ICRA), pp. 4304–4311. IEEE (2015)
16. Kuhl, F.P., Giardina, C.R.: Elliptic fourier features of a closed contour. Comput. Graphics Image Process. **18**(3), 236–258 (1982)
17. Lenz, I., Lee, H., Saxena, A.: Deep learning for detecting robotic grasps. Int. J. Robot. Res. **34**(4–5), 705–724 (2015)
18. Lestrel, P.E.: Fourier descriptors and their applications in biology. Cambridge University Press (1997)
19. Lestrel, P.E., Kerr, W.J.S.: Quantification of function regulator therapy using elliptical fourier functions. Europ. J. Orthodontics **15**(6), 481–491 (1993)
20. Levine, S., Pastor, P., Krizhevsky, A., Ibarz, J., Quillen, D.: Learning hand-eye coordination for robotic grasping with deep learning and large-scale data collection. Int. J. Robot. Res. **37**(4–5), 421–436 (2018)
21. Li, Y., Bu, R., Sun, M., Wu, W., Di, X., Chen, B.: Pointcnn: convolution on x-transformed points. Advances in neural information processing systems 31 (2018)
22. Liang, H., et al.: Pointnetgpd: detecting grasp configurations from point sets. In: 2019 International Conference on Robotics and Automation (ICRA), pp. 3629–3635. IEEE (2019)
23. Mahler, J., et al.: Dex-net 2.0: Deep learning to plan robust grasps with synthetic point clouds and analytic grasp metrics. arXiv preprint arXiv:1703.09312 (2017)
24. Morrison, D., Corke, P., Leitner, J.: Closing the loop for robotic grasping: a real-time, generative grasp synthesis approach. arXiv preprint arXiv:1804.05172 (2018)
25. Park, D., Seo, Y., Shin, D., Choi, J., Chun, S.Y.: A single multi-task deep neural network with post-processing for object detection with reasoning and robotic grasp detection. In: 2020 IEEE International Conference on Robotics and Automation (ICRA), pp. 7300–7306. IEEE (2020)

26. ten Pas, A., Gualtieri, M., Saenko, K., Platt, R.: Grasp pose detection in point clouds. Int. J. Robot. Res. **36**(13–14), 1455–1473 (2017)
27. Pinto, L., Gupta, A.: Supersizing self-supervision: learning to grasp from 50k tries and 700 robot hours. In: 2016 IEEE International Conference on Robotics and Automation (ICRA), pp. 3406–3413. IEEE (2016)
28. Qi, C.R., Su, H., Mo, K., Guibas, L.J.: Pointnet: deep learning on point sets for 3d classification and segmentation. In: Proceedings of the IEEE Conference on Computer Vision and Pattern Recognition, pp. 652–660 (2017)
29. Qi, C.R., Yi, L., Su, H., Guibas, L.J.: Pointnet++: Deep hierarchical feature learning on point sets in a metric space. Advances in neural information processing systems 30 (2017)
30. Su, H., et al.: Splatnet: sparse lattice networks for point cloud processing. In: Proceedings of the IEEE Conference on Computer Vision and Pattern Recognition, pp. 2530–2539 (2018)
31. Tatarchenko, M., Dosovitskiy, A., Brox, T.: Octree generating networks: efficient convolutional architectures for high-resolution 3d outputs. In: Proceedings of the IEEE International Conference on Computer Vision, pp. 2088–2096 (2017)
32. Ten Pas, A., Platt, R.: Using geometry to detect grasp poses in 3d point clouds. In: Robotics Research, pp. 307–324. Springer (2018)
33. Wallace, T.P., Wintz, P.A.: An efficient three-dimensional aircraft recognition algorithm using normalized fourier descriptors. Comput. Graphics Image Process. **13**(2), 99–126 (1980)
34. Wang, J., et al.: Deep high-resolution representation learning for visual recognition. IEEE Trans. Pattern Anal. Mach. Intell. **43**(10), 3349–3364 (2020)

Face Presentation Attack Detection Using Remote Photoplethysmography Transformer Model

Haoyu Zhang[1](✉)[iD], Raghavendra Ramachandra[1][iD], and Christoph Busch[1,2][iD]

[1] Norwegian University of Science and Technology,
Teknologivegen 22, 2815 Gjøvik, Norway
{haoyu.zhang,raghavendra.ramachandra,christoph.busch}@ntnu.no
[2] Darmstadt University of Applied Sciences, Schöfferstraße 3,
64295 Darmstadt, Germany

Abstract. Face Presentation Attack Detection (PAD) is essential for face recognition systems to achieve reliable verification in secured authentication applications. The face Presentation Attack Instruments include the printed photo, electronic display, wrap-photo and custom 3D masks. With the evolving technologies to generate the novel face PAI the generalisable PAD is of paramount importance. In this paper, we proposed a novel face PAD algorithm to achieve reliable detection of presentation attacks by quantifying the liveness using the remote photoplethysmography (rPPG) signal. The proposed method is developed by augmenting the PhysFormer model with an additional Temporal Difference Multi-Head Self-attention (TD-MHSA) block to obtain the reliable rPPG signal. We also proposed a novel classifier using 3DCNN to effectively capture the spatio-temporal to achieve a reliable PAD across different un-seen PAI. Extensive experiments are conducted on the publicly available OULU-NPU dataset comprised of four different PAI and six different smartphones. The proposed method is benchmarked with nine different existing PAD techniques on two different evaluation protocols and indicates considerable performance compared with the existing PAD techniques.

Keywords: Biometrics · Face Recognition · Face Presentation Attack Detection · Remote Photoplethysmography · Deep Learning

1 Introduction

Face Recognition Systems (FRS) have been widely deployed in the magnitude of security applications and have become part of our daily life. Meanwhile, concerns have been raised because of the vulnerability of the FRS against different types of attacks. Presentation attacks are one type of the attacks where the facial artefact is presented to the biometric sensor. Following the definition from ISO/IEC 30107-1: 2016 [12], it indicates the presentation to the biometric capture subsystem with the goal of interfering with the operation of the biometric system.

Since presentation attacks can be easily generated and the cost-effective attacks on the FRS are increasing exponentially. This has motivated the researchers to devise the techniques to automatically detect the presentation attacks on the FRS.

Face PAD is extensively addressed in the literature that has resulted in the magnitude of techniques [1, 8, 33] that are generally classified into hardware-based methods and software-based methods. The hardware-based methods use dedicated hardware to capture the liveness cues from the data subjects. The software-based approaches will use the images/videos recorded from the dedicated camera to determine the attacks. Software-based PAD approaches are widely used and developed because of their interoperability and are easy to install and to use. The available software approaches can be broadly classified as: hand-crafted features, deep features, deep networks, hybrid methods and liveness methods. Each of these techniques has its own characteristics in terms of the detection performance and the generalisabality to unknown (or un-seen) presentation attacks. Among these techniques, the use of hybrid features that can include different types of cues has indicated the robust performance with un-seen attacks on FRS.

Among these approaches, the measure of liveness from the recorded video using rPPG signal [9, 20, 23, 31]. Early work on detecting the rPPG from the video streaming is proposed in [37] that has indicated the reliable liveness measure in the ambient lighting. Motivated by this, researchers explored the rPPG for the face PAD as it can provide the liveness measure by recording the heartbeat and thus, can generalise on the different PAI that may result in the reliable PAD. The rPPG signal can be estimated based on hand-crafted algorithms [25, 34] and deep learning based approaches [28].

Table 1 indicates the existing rPPG techniques evaluated for face PAD. The available techniques are based on hand-crafted features and also deep learning techniques. Hand-crafted features like frequency estimation [9, 23, 31], correlation analysis [23] and temporal filtering [20], correspondence filtering [22], long term spectral statistics [10] and perfusion analysis [15]. With the evolving of deep learning techniques, the rPPG signals are estimated using deep learning techniques based on both 1-D and 2D information. The deep learning approaches include patch-based CNN [21] and CNN-RNN model [24]. Even though the goal of rPPG measurement is to provide the vital information on the heart functionality by utilising the skin pixels, its application to face PAD is inevitable. Recent progress in rPPG generation is based on the temporal difference transformer (PhysFormer) [39] where the video transformer-based architecture is proposed to aggregate spatio-temporalfeatures both locally and globally to achieve the enhancing of rPPG representations. The rPPG signal generation using PhysFormer has indicated improved performance over the existing techniques, especially in the variation of data capture. Motivated by this, in this work, we adapted and improved the PhysFormer model to achieve the reliable face PAD. To effectively analyse and adapt the PhysFormer, we propose the following research questions:

Table 1. Existing methods based on rPPG for face PAD

Authors	Approach
Liu et al. [23]	CHROM [4], Fourier transform, cross-correlation, and SVM with RBF kernel and learned confidence map
Suh et al. [36]	Skin color magnification, frequency and amplitude analysis
Li et al. [20]	[19,32], temporal filtering, power spectral density (PSD) patterns, and SVM with linear kernel
Nowara et al. [31]	[18], using local background signal and spectral feature extraction to overcome the global noise, and SVM with RBF kernel
Hernandez-Ortega et al. [9]	RGB and NIR videos, detrending filter, moving-average filter, band-pass filter, and extracting PSD patterns for SVM classifier.
Liu et al. [22]	CHROM [4], self-learned spectrum template from face region and background, correspondence filtering, and SVM with linear kernel
Liu et al. [24]	CNN-RNN framework to apply auxiliary supervision with depth map and estimate rPPG signal
Heusch et al. [10]	LTSS [26] in multi-scale, SVM
Lin et al. [21]	LTSS [26] in multi-scale, contextual patch-based CNN
Kossack et al. [17]	Pulse transit time (PTT) maps and signal-to-noise ratio (SNR)
Yu et al. [39]	MSTmap [30], rPPG-based multi-scale spatio-temporal maps and transformer framework
Kossack et al. [39]	POS [38], reliability determination [16], then calculate reference correlation, SNR, and magnitude of heart frequency as features for cubic SVM classifier.

- Does the PhysFormer can achieve reliable face PAD performance, especially on the un-seen attacks and environment conditions?
- Does the multiple regions from the face region can contribute to the face PAD?

To effectively answer the research questions. We proposed a novel scheme for the face PAD by augmenting the PhysFormer with an additional Temporal Difference Multi-Head Self-attention (TD-MHSA) layer to extract the reliable feature representing rPPG signal. Then, we proposed a novel classifier architecture based on the serial network using 3DCNN to effectively capture the spatio-temporal information for face PAD. Thus following are the main contribution of this paper:

- Proposed a novel framework for face PAD based on rPPG features and 3DCNN-based spatio-temporal classifier to reliably detect face presentation attacks.
- Comprehensive experiments are performed on the publicly available face PAD detection. Experimental protocols are designed to evaluate the face PAD techniques for un-seen PAI and environment.
- Proposed method is benchmarked with nine different existing face PAD techniques.

2 Proposed Face PAD Method

Figure 1 shows the block diagram of the proposed method. The proposed method consists of three main functional units. Given the face image, we first pre-process

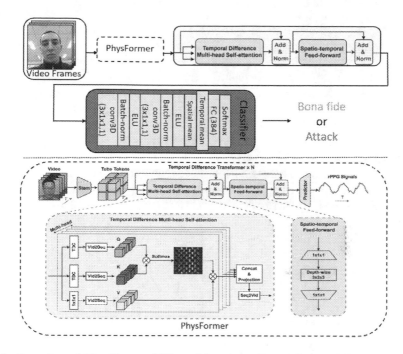

Fig. 1. Overview of PhysFormer [40] model and our Face PAD model based on Phys-Former.

the video frames and crop them into different face regions. Then, we apply a pre-trained PhysFormer model augmented with an additional Temporal Difference Multi-Head Self-attention (TD-MHSA) layer. Finally, features are classified using a novel 3DCNN classifier to detect the face presentation attacks.

2.1 Cropping Face Regions

This step will extract the face and its corresponding regions that will be used to extract the features. The face region extraction is carried out using dlib [14] landmark detection model and extracting 68 landmark points. Given the face image video, we crop it to have six different regions such as face, background, forehead, eye, nose, and cheek. In addition, video in the full face region following the alignment configuration of the pre-trained model is extracted using MTCNN [42]. In the next step, features are extracted from the augmented PhysFormer model as described below.

2.2 PhysFormer

The architecture of PhysFormer [40] is shown in the bottom part of Fig. 1. The PhysFormer architecture is designed to learn from the temporal information in order to fit the final task of estimating rPPG signals. Given RGB input video

$X \in \mathbb{R}^{D \times T \times H \times W}$, Shallow stems with 3DCNN are applied to extract local coarse features $X_{Stem} = E_{Stem}(X)$. D, T, W, H denotes channels of input, sequence length, width, and height of the input size, respectively. Then, the extracted X_{Stem} will be split into tube tokens to reduce the computational complexity of further Transformer blocks: $X_{tube} = E_{tube}(X_{Stem})$. Then, after stacked transformer blocks, the outputted transformer feature X_{trans} will be spatially upsampled by 3DCNN to fit the original length of time and then spatially averaged to fuse the features. Finally, a 1DCNN is applied to use all channels of learned features to estimate the rPPG signal.

To reuse the learned representation with rPPG information, we extract the inferenced X^3_{trans} features from pre-trained PhysFormer model after the last Temporal Difference Multi-Head Self-attention (TD-MHSA) blocks. As for the pre-trained PhysFormer model, it is provided by Yu et al. and trained on VIPL-HR dataset [29]. The model uses $4 \times 4 \times 4$ patch size, 96 dimension size for the projection MLP in each 4-head TD-MHSA block, and 144 dimension size for the spatio-temporal Feed-forward block. In total, 3 Temporal Difference Transformer blocks are stacked in the applied PhysFormer model.

Then, we build our PAD model by augmenting an additional TD-MHSA layer with the same hyper-parameters to enable the model to learn the transformation of feature vectors that are required for further detecting presentation attacks. Finally, the output will be fed to a classifier, as explained below.

2.3 Classification: 3DCNN Network

The classifier module is designed to have 2 3DCNN layers with $3 \times 1 \times 1$ kernel size, padding size $1 \times 0 \times 0$ and stride length of 1. Each 3DCNN layer will double the dimension of the feature channel and will be attached with a 3D batch normalization layer and ELU activation layer sequentially. Finally, the features will be averaged first spatially and then temporally as pooling and fed to a 384-dimension MLP with a 0.1 dropout rate to output the final classification score.

The cross-entropy loss is used to supervise the classification task. To handle the unbalanced data, we apply weight w on different classes calculated by:

$$w_i = \frac{\sum_j N_j}{C * N_i}, \tag{1}$$

where N_i indicates the number of samples for class i and $C = 2$ denotes the number of classes.

During training, we applied ADAM optimiser with 5×10^{-4} weight decay. The learning rate is initially searched within 5×10^{-3}, 1×10^{-3}, 5×5^{-4}, 1×10^{-4}, 5×10^{-5} and then scheduled to decay into half every 5 epochs.

3   Experiments and Results

3.1   Dataset

In this section, experiments and quantitative results of the proposed method on the publicly available face PAD dataset will be introduced. We perform the experiments on the OULU-NPU dataset [3] which is widely used to benchmark the face PAD task. The OULU-NPU dataset consists of 4950 real access and attack videos. The videos are recorded with six different mobile phones (HTC Desire EYE, Samsung Galaxy S6 edge, ASUS Zenfone Selfie, MEIZU X5, OPPO N3, and Sony XPERIA C5 Ultra Dual) and three sessions of different capturing conditions (illumination condition and background scenes). In the OULU-NPU dataset, the attack were created by two printers (Printer 1 and Printer 2) and two replay devices (Display 1 and Display 2). Figure 2 shows the examples of the OULU-NPU dataset, and statistics of the database are given the Table 2.

Meanwhile, it is essential to evaluate the generalisability of the model and make the PAD algorithm robust against varied conditions and types of attacks. We benchmark the performance of the proposed method with protocol I and II provided in the dataset. In protocol I, the videos in the Train set and the Dev set are captured in session 1 and 2, while the Test set is captured in session 3. Hence the protocol evaluates the algorithm's generalisability to unknown illumination conditions and background scenes. Similarly, protocol 2 evaluates the algorithm's testing performance on attacks generated by unknown printers and display devices. Thus, in this work, we benchmark the performance of the proposed method for both un-seen attacks and environments.

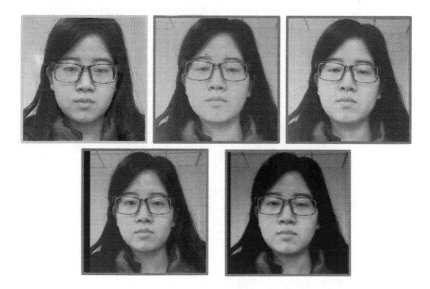

Fig. 2. Examples of samples in OULU dataset. Green box: bona fide presentations Red box: attack presentations (Color figure online)

Table 2. Information of protocol I and protocol II in OULU-NPU dataset [3] [35]

Protocol	Subset	Session	Phones	Subjects	Attacks generated by	# Bona fide	# Attack	# All
Protocol I	Train	1,2	6	1-20	Printer 1,2; Display 1,2	240	960	1200
	Dev	1,2	6	21-35	Printer 1,2; Display 1,2	180	720	900
	Test	3	6	36-55	Printer 1,2; Display 1,2	240	960	1200
Protocol II	Train	1,2,3	6	1-20	Printer 1; Display 1	360	720	1080
	Dev	1,2,3	6	21-35	Printer 1; Display 1	270	540	810
	Test	1,2,3	6	36-55	Printer 2; Display 2	360	720	1080

3.2 Visualisation of rPPG Signals Extracted from Different Face Regions

In this section, we present the qualitative results of the rPPG signals corresponding to six different regions from face. Figure 3 shows one input frame and rPPG results of different face regions in one bona fide sample. The first and the last 20 frames are cut out to avoid disturbing padding frames. Correspondingly Fig. 4 shows the qualitative results from the presentation attack sample. From Fig. 4(a) it is shown that the proposed method has outputted a relatively flat signal as expected for the background input. Minor noise can be noticed in the bona fide example but much stronger in the attack example. In Fig. 4(b), (e), and (f), it is shown that the signals of the bona fide example are less noisy than the attack example and can be roughly approximated to heart rate signals. Compared to the cheek and nose, the signal extracted from the forehead region tends to have less noise but a stronger variation in amplitude. This might be because the forehead region has less movement during expressions but is also usually covered by hair. However, for the full face region, the proposed method outputs the most well-shaped heart rate signal in Fig. 3(d). In Fig. 4(d), the model also estimated a signal for the presentation attack but is visibly more noisy than the bona fide one. For the eye region and mouth region in Fig. 4(c) and (g) respectively, both signals are quite noisy and not distinguishable. Thus, based on the obtained results, it is clear that the rPPG estimate from the full face when compared to the different facial regions that have indicated the noisy signals.

3.3 Quantitative Results of the Proposed PAD Model

To benchmark our results with other existing works, we selected standardised metrics attack presentation classification error rate (APCER), bona fide presentation classification error rate (BPCER), and average classification error rate (ACER) [13]. During each training process, the model is validated and selected based on the lowest classification loss on the development set and then evaluated on the test set.

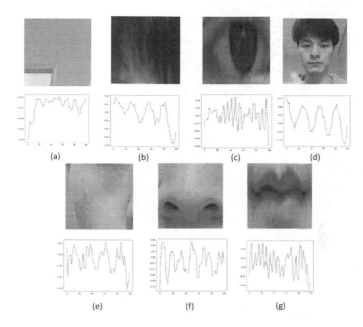

Fig. 3. Bona fide example with cropped regions and their rPPG signal extracted by the proposed method: (a) background (b) forehead (c) eye (d) full face (e) cheek (f) nose (g) mouth

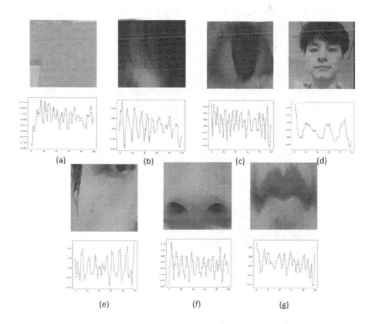

Fig. 4. PAD attack example with cropped regions and their rPPG signal extracted by the proposed method: (a) background (b) forehead (c) eye (d) full face (e) cheek (f) nose (g) mouth

Ablation Study. In this section, the ablation study of the proposed PAD model is presented. Given the extracted features from the pre-trained Phys-Former model, we present the results on two different configurations (1) *Config-I: PhysFormer model with proposed classifier* (2) *Config-II: PhysFormer model augmented with TD-MHSA layer and the proposed classifier*. The Config-II is the proposed PAD scheme. Thus, the ablation study is targeted to empirically evaluate the effectiveness of augmenting the PhysFormer model for the application of face PAD. Table 3 and Table 4 illustrate the quantitative results of these two Configs respectively, and the ACER are visualised as a bar graph in Fig. 5. The quantitative results are presented to full face and also independently with six different regions. Based on the obtained results, it can be noted that:

- The full face gives the best performance on detecting attacks as it approximately follows the similar alignment configuration as the training data of the pre-trained PhysFormer. However, it has a decreased performance in protocol II while similar behaviour is observed with other face regions such as the cheek, nose and forehead. This indicates that different face regions may not be suitable for presentation attack detection, and the use of full face can provide the best detection performance. Further, for the background regions, they are less suitable for extracting rPPG signals and classifying presentation attacks as expected. The eye region is also not performing well, and this might be influenced by glasses or the tight cropping and approximated alignment from only the first frame of the face. The forehead region has a poor performance in protocol I, but the error rate is significantly decreased in protocol II. Similar to the observation in the example of rPPG signals, the cheek and the nose regions have shown acceptable performances and perform better in protocol II than protocol I. Finally, the mouth region is shown to have a stable performance in protocol I and II.
- Config-II indicates consistent high performance on both face and associated regions when compared to Config-I on both protocol I and II. For the best performances within each protocol, the Config-II (or proposed method) improves the ACER with 4.44% and 5.76%, respectively for protocol I and II. These results justify the proposed method with the augmentation.

Table 3. Detection Performances on OULU-NPU dataset with different face regions: Config-I

Protocol	Model	APCER	BPCER	ACER	Protocol	Model	APCER	BPCER	ACER
I	Full Face	10.26	15.15	12.71	II	Ours (Full Face)	28.15	13.02	20.59
	Background	73.27	13.13	43.20		Background	56.22	10.59	33.41
	Eye	57.85	14.41	36.13		Eye	57.49	22.65	40.07
	Cheek	55.37	9.69	32.53		Cheek	38.87	8.27	23.57
	Nose	46.51	6.54	26.53		Nose	34.91	7.25	21.08
	Forehead	65.77	9.12	37.45		Forehead	44.89	12.50	28.70
	Mouth	46.51	6.54	26.525		Mouth	34.91	7.25	21.08

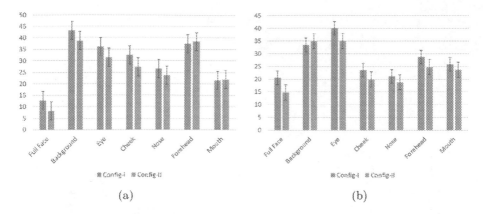

Fig. 5. Bar graph of the ACER (%) of our approach using different face region as input: (a) Protocol I (b) Protocol II

Table 4. Detection Performances on OULU-NPU dataset with different face regions: Config-II

Protocol	Model	APCER	BPCER	ACER	Protocol	Model	APCER	BPCER	ACER
I	Full Face	2.38	14.16	8.27	II	Ours Full Face	18.34	11.32	14.83
	Background	61.74	15.67	38.71		Background	56.75	12.99	34.87
	Eye	50.78	12.08	31.43		Eye	52.08	18.03	35.01
	Cheek	40.51	14.01	27.26		Cheek	29.54	10.34	19.94
	Nose	39.26	8.17	23.72		Nose	32.16	5.52	18.84
	Forehead	69.25	7.55	38.40		Forehead	37.69	11.92	24.81
	Mouth	33.95	9.78	21.87		Mouth	41.46	5.98	23.72

Comparison with SOTA Methods. In this section, we compare the detection performance of the proposed method (with full face) with the nine different SOTA face PAD techniques. The quantitative performance is shown in Table 5, and the proposed method has achieved the 8.27% ACER on the protocol I and ACER = 14.83% on the protocol II. When compared to protocol I, the performance of the proposed method is degraded in protocol II, indicating that the proposed method is more sensitive to unknown PAI compared to the unknown environment conditions. When compared to other SOTA methods, the proposed method did not show improved results with several SOTA algorithms since most of the SOTA methods are trained directly on the training set of the dataset. However, the proposed method is based on the pre-trained PhysFormer as the backend and only features are extracted. Thus, the proposed method is less computational and reliable for deployment.

Table 5. Detection Performances on OULU-NPU dataset

Protocol	Model	APCER	BPCER	ACER	Protocol	Model	APCER	BPCER	ACER
I	CPqD [2]	2.9	10.8	6.9	II	MixedFASNet [2]	9.7	2.5	6.1
	GRADIANT [2]	1.3	12.5	6.9		FAS-BAS [24]	2.7	2.7	2.7
	FAS-BAS [24]	1.6	1.6	1.6		GRADIANT [2]	3.1	1.9	2.5
	IQM-SVM [6]	19.17	30.83	25		IQM-SVM [6]	12.5	16.94	14.72
	LBP-SVM [7]	12.92	51.67	32.29		LBP-SVM [7]	30	20.28	25.14
	DeepPixBiS [7]	0.83	0	0.42		DeepPixBiS [7]	11.39	0.56	5.97
	A-DeepPixBis [11]	1.19	0.31	0.75		A-DeepPixBis [11]	4.35	1.29	2.82
	Bi-FAS [35]	2.92	3.33	3.12		Bi-FAS [35]	2.36	1.11	1.73
	TSS with ResNet [27]	0.60	10.30	5.50		TSS with ResNet [27]	2.00	2.10	2.10
	TSS with ResNet-BiLST [27]	0.00	0.20	0.10		TSS with ResNet-BiLST [27]	0.40	0.80	0.60
	Proposed Method	2.38	14.16	8.27		Proposed Method	18.34	11.32	14.83

4 Conclusions

Reliable detection of the face presentation attacks on FRS is essential to ensure reliable secure applications. In this work, we have presented a novel framework for the face PAD based on the rPPG features. The proposed method is based on the PhysFormer as the backbone network which is augmented with an additional Temporal Difference Multi-Head Self-attention (TD-MHSA) layer. Further, we have also proposed a novel classifier network based on the 3DCNN. Extensive experiments are carried out on the OULU-NPU dataset to benchmark the performance of the proposed method for unknown PAI and environment. The proposed method is also benchmarked with the nine different SOTA face PAD techniques. Overall, we've shown that using the full face as input is more reliable for face PAD detection using transformer-based rPPG features, and the proposed method can achieve a considerable detection performance.

References

1. Abdullakutty, F., Elyan, E., Johnston, P.: A review of state-of-the-art in face presentation attack detection: from early development to advanced deep learning and multi-modal fusion methods. Inf. Fusion **75**, 55–69 (2021)
2. Boulkenafet, Z., et al.: A competition on generalized software-based face presentation attack detection in mobile scenarios. In: 2017 IEEE International Joint Conference on Biometrics (IJCB), pp. 688–696. IEEE (2017)
3. Boulkenafet, Z., Komulainen, J., Li, L., Feng, X., Hadid, A.: Oulu-npu: a mobile face presentation attack database with real-world variations. In: 2017 12th IEEE International Conference on Automatic Face & Gesture Recognition (FG 2017), pp. 612–618. IEEE (2017)
4. De Haan, G., Jeanne, V.: Robust pulse rate from chrominance-based rppg. IEEE Trans. Biomed. Eng. **60**(10), 2878–2886 (2013)
5. Fouad, R., Omer, O.A., Ali, A.M.M., Aly, M.H.: Refining roi selection for real-time remote photoplethysmography using adaptive skin detection
6. Galbally, J., Marcel, S., Fierrez, J.: Image quality assessment for fake biometric detection: application to iris, fingerprint, and face recognition. IEEE Trans. Image Process. **23**(2), 710–724 (2013)

7. George, A., Marcel, S.: Deep pixel-wise binary supervision for face presentation attack detection. In: 2019 International Conference on Biometrics (ICB), pp. 1–8. IEEE (2019)

8. Hernandez-Ortega, J., Fierrez, J., Morales, A., Galbally, J.: Introduction to face presentation attack detection. In: Marcel, S., Nixon, M.S., Fierrez, J., Evans, N. (eds.) Handbook of Biometric Anti-Spoofing. ACVPR, pp. 187–206. Springer, Cham (2019). https://doi.org/10.1007/978-3-319-92627-8_9

9. Hernandez-Ortega, J., Fierrez, J., Morales, A., Tome, P.: Time analysis of pulse-based face anti-spoofing in visible and nir. In: Proceedings of the IEEE Conference on Computer Vision and Pattern Recognition Workshops, pp. 544–552 (2018)

10. Heusch, G., Marcel, S.: Pulse-based features for face presentation attack detection. In: 2018 IEEE 9th International Conference on Biometrics Theory, Applications and Systems (BTAS), pp. 1–8. IEEE (2018)

11. Hossain, M.S., Rupty, L., Roy, K., Hasan, M., Sengupta, S., Mohammed, N.: A-deeppixbis: attentional angular margin for face anti-spoofing. In: 2020 Digital Image Computing: Techniques and Applications (DICTA), pp. 1–8. IEEE (2020)

12. ISO/IEC JTC1 SC37 Biometrics: ISO/IEC 30107-1. Information Technology - Biometric presentation attack detection - Part 1: Framework. International Organization for Standardization (2016)

13. ISO/IEC JTC1 SC37 Biometrics: ISO/IEC 30107-3. Information Technology - Biometric presentation attack detection - Part 3: Testing and Reporting. International Organization for Standardization (2017)

14. King, D.: Dlib c library. http://dlib.net/

15. Kossack, B., Wisotzky, E., Eisert, P., Schraven, S.P., Globke, B., Hilsmann, A.: Perfusion assessment via local remote photoplethysmography (rppg). In: Proceedings of the IEEE/CVF Conference on Computer Vision and Pattern Recognition (CVPR) Workshops, pp. 2192–2201 (June 2022)

16. Kossack, B., Wisotzky, E., Hilsmann, A., Eisert, P.: Automatic region-based heart rate measurement using remote photoplethysmography. In: Proceedings of the IEEE/CVF International Conference on Computer Vision, pp. 2755–2759 (2021)

17. Kossack, B., Wisotzky, E.L., Hilsmann, A., Eisert, P.: Local remote photoplethysmography signal analysis for application in presentation attack detection. In: VMV, pp. 135–142 (2019)

18. Kumar, M., Veeraraghavan, A., Sabharwal, A.: Distanceppg: robust non-contact vital signs monitoring using a camera. Biomed. Opt. Express 6(5), 1565–1588 (2015)

19. Li, X., Chen, J., Zhao, G., Pietikainen, M.: Remote heart rate measurement from face videos under realistic situations. In: Proceedings of the IEEE Conference on Computer Vision and Pattern Recognition, pp. 4264–4271 (2014)

20. Li, X., Komulainen, J., Zhao, G., Yuen, P.C., Pietikäinen, M.: Generalized face anti-spoofing by detecting pulse from face videos. In: 2016 23rd International Conference on Pattern Recognition (ICPR), pp. 4244–4249. IEEE (2016)

21. Lin, B., Li, X., Yu, Z., Zhao, G.: Face liveness detection by rppg features and contextual patch-based cnn. In: Proceedings of the 2019 3rd International Conference on Biometric Engineering and Applications, pp. 61–68 (2019)

22. Liu, S.-Q., Lan, X., Yuen, P.C.: Remote photoplethysmography correspondence feature for 3D mask face presentation attack detection. In: Ferrari, V., Hebert, M., Sminchisescu, C., Weiss, Y. (eds.) ECCV 2018. LNCS, vol. 11220, pp. 577–594. Springer, Cham (2018). https://doi.org/10.1007/978-3-030-01270-0_34

23. Liu, S., Yuen, P.C., Zhang, S., Zhao, G.: 3D mask face anti-spoofing with remote photoplethysmography. In: Leibe, B., Matas, J., Sebe, N., Welling, M. (eds.) ECCV 2016. LNCS, vol. 9911, pp. 85–100. Springer, Cham (2016). https://doi.org/10. 1007/978-3-319-46478-7_6

24. Liu, Y., Jourabloo, A., Liu, X.: Learning deep models for face anti-spoofing: binary or auxiliary supervision. In: Proceedings of the IEEE Conference on Computer Vision and Pattern Recognition, pp. 389–398 (2018)

25. McDuff, D.J., Estepp, J.R., Piasecki, A.M., Blackford, E.B.: A survey of remote optical photoplethysmographic imaging methods. In: 2015 37th Annual International Conference of the IEEE Engineering in Medicine and Biology Society (EMBC), pp. 6398–6404. IEEE (2015)

26. Muckenhirn, H., Korshunov, P., Magimai-Doss, M., Marcel, S.: Long-term spectral statistics for voice presentation attack detection. IEEE/ACM Trans. Audio Speech Lang. Process. **25**(11), 2098–2111 (2017)

27. Muhammad, U., Yu, Z., Komulainen, J.: Self-supervised 2d face presentation attack detection via temporal sequence sampling. Pattern Recogn. Lett. **156**, 15–22 (2022)

28. Ni, A., Azarang, A., Kehtarnavaz, N.: A review of deep learning-based contactless heart rate measurement methods. Sensors **21**(11), 3719 (2021)

29. Niu, X., Shan, S., Han, H., Chen, X.: Rhythmnet: end-to-end heart rate estimation from face via spatial-temporal representation. IEEE Trans. Image Process. **29**, 2409–2423 (2019)

30. Niu, X., Yu, Z., Han, H., Li, X., Shan, S., Zhao, G.: Video-based remote physiological measurement via cross-verified feature disentangling. In: Vedaldi, A., Bischof, H., Brox, T., Frahm, J.-M. (eds.) ECCV 2020. LNCS, vol. 12347, pp. 295–310. Springer, Cham (2020). https://doi.org/10.1007/978-3-030-58536-5_18

31. Nowara, E.M., Sabharwal, A., Veeraraghavan, A.: Ppgsecure: biometric presentation attack detection using photopletysmograms. In: 2017 12th IEEE International Conference on Automatic Face & Gesture Recognition (FG 2017), pp. 56–62. IEEE (2017)

32. Poh, M.Z., McDuff, D.J., Picard, R.W.: Advancements in noncontact, multiparameter physiological measurements using a webcam. IEEE Trans. Biomed. Eng. **58**(1), 7–11 (2010)

33. Ramachandra, R., Busch, C.: Presentation attack detection methods for face recognition systems: a comprehensive survey. ACM Comput. Surv. (CSUR) **50**(1), 1–37 (2017)

34. Rouast, P.V., Adam, M.T., Chiong, R., Cornforth, D., Lux, E.: Remote heart rate measurement using low-cost rgb face video: a technical literature review. Front. Comp. Sci. **12**(5), 858–872 (2018)

35. Roy, K., et al.: Bi-fpnfas: Bi-directional feature pyramid network for pixel-wise face anti-spoofing by leveraging fourier spectra. Sensors **21**(8), 2799 (2021)

36. Suh, K.H., Lee, E.C.: Face liveness detection for face recognition based on cardiac features of skin color image. In: First International Workshop on Pattern Recognition, vol. 10011, pp. 62–66. SPIE (2016)

37. Verkruysse, W., Svaasand, L.O., Nelson, J.S.: Remote plethysmographic imaging using ambient light. Opt. Express **16**(26), 21434–21445 (2008)

38. Wang, W., Den Brinker, A.C., Stuijk, S., De Haan, G.: Algorithmic principles of remote ppg. IEEE Trans. Biomed. Eng. **64**(7), 1479–1491 (2016)

39. Yu, Z., Li, X., Wang, P., Zhao, G.: Transrppg: remote photoplethysmography transformer for 3d mask face presentation attack detection. IEEE Signal Process. Lett. **28**, 1290–1294 (2021)

40. Yu, Z., Shen, Y., Shi, J., Zhao, H., Torr, P.H., Zhao, G.: Physformer: facial video-based physiological measurement with temporal difference transformer. In: Proceedings of the IEEE/CVF Conference on Computer Vision and Pattern Recognition, pp. 4186–4196 (2022)
41. Yu, Z., et al.: Searching central difference convolutional networks for face anti-spoofing. In: Proceedings of the IEEE/CVF Conference on Computer Vision and Pattern Recognition, pp. 5295–5305 (2020)
42. Zhang, K., Zhang, Z., Li, Z., Qiao, Y.: Joint face detection and alignment using multitask cascaded convolutional networks. IEEE Signal Process. Lett. **23**(10), 1499–1503 (2016)

MTFL: Multi-task Federated Learning for Classification of Healthcare X-Ray Images

Priyush Kumar, Indrajeet Kumar Sinha$^{(\boxtimes)}$, and Krishna Pratap Singh

Machine Learning and Optimization Lab, Department of Information Technology,
Indian Institute of Information Technology Allahabad,
Prayagraj, Uttar Pradesh, India
pcl2016004@iiita.ac.in

Abstract. Deep learning models have achieved state-of-the-art in many challenging domains, whereas it is a data-hungry method. Collecting sensitive and labelled medical data sets is challenging and costly. Recently, federated learning has been used to train a model without sharing the data at a central place for a single task. We propose a novel Multi-task federated learning (MTFL) approach to utilize the data sets of various similar kinds of tasks. We used two binary class X-ray data sets: Pneumonia disease classification and TB disease classification. We compared MTFL with federated learning for a single task and CNN with data in one place. Results show that MTFL has achieved better specificity and accuracy than other models.

Keywords: Federated Learning · Chest X-ray · Multi-Tasking · Pneumonia · TB · CNN · X-ray image classification · Federated Averaging

1 Introduction

Deep Learning (DL) models have already proven their worth in terms of better accuracy. They are now being utilised for various tasks such as image classification, object identification, and segmentation. DL approaches have also demonstrated the ability for recognition and segmentation in medical image processing [6,11]. However, prompted by privacy concerns, the lack of publicly available data sets has stagnated the progress and deployment in data-sensitive domains like medical. Collecting data from various sources is a big challenge and a bottleneck in advancing AI-based techniques.

Federated Learning [1,23] has emerged as a solution to learn a global model without sharing datasets from clients to a commonplace, and hence it preserves possible data leaks. Recent developments on Federated learning [15] focus on learning a common task using the client (say local) datasets. However, sometimes data sets for a task at various locations are very few, but a similar kind of another dataset

D. Gupta et al. (Eds.): CVIP 2022, CCIS 1777, pp. 572–585, 2023.
https://doi.org/10.1007/978-3-031-31417-9_43

may be available. Multi-task learning [18] is an important paradigm of learning in which different but similar tasks have been learned with a common parameter. In this setting, datasets of other one complement each other. However, no work has been done to deploy multi-task learning in the Federated learning setting.

Multi-task federated training is a novel approach in which a deep learning model, CNN, is obtained at the global server after aggregating local learning from the client's side. We considered the case that each client has data related to one task or other. After that, a common network is learned for all tasks together. We have proposed novel strategies for parameter sharing for multi-task. To demonstrate the working and evaluate the performance of the proposed model, we have taken two different datasets with a binary classification problem. We considered them two different tasks: one is to detect Pneumonia, and another is to detect Tuberculosis. In standard machine learning or deep learning training methods, we train a single model and fine-tune it until performance generalises for good predictions. But in our proposed method, we are developing a global multi-tasking model after aggregating local model parameters with different tasks which can classify or detect both types of disease, i.e., Pneumonia and Tuberculosis. Our main contributions to this paper are:

1. A novel multi-task federated learning is proposed where the model is developed using two binary class image datasets in a federated setting.
2. The proposed model is evaluated using metrics specificity and accuracy on chest X-ray and TB datasets.
3. Comparative analysis is done on CNN, FL and MTFL models.

Further, this paper follows as Sect. 2 gives a brief view of classification models on thorax image datasets, multi-task learning and federated learning, as well as state-of-the-art progress on these. Section 3 presents the proposed work on multi-task federated learning. Section 4 has the experimental setups and requirements. Section 5 presents the experimental results, and Sect. 6 concludes the observations.

2   Literature Survey

Deep learning has been extensively used in healthcare image datasets for classification problems [11]. Many works have been done for the deep learning-based solution to detect diseases such as Pneumonia, Tuberculosis from chest x-rays images and lung cancer from CT scan images. Hua et al. [7] proposed a CNN and a deep belief network for classifying lung nodules in CT scan images to detect lung cancer. In paper [14], S.I. Nafisah and G. Muhammad use advanced deep learning (DL) models to detect Tuberculosis from chest radiography images. They experimented on different deep learning models and obtained 99.1% accuracy from EfficientNetB3 (one of the CNN models). Lakhani et al. [10] proposed a deep CNN model to detect pulmonary TB from chest X-ray images using transfer learning models for the classification. Singh et al. [19] uses deep features to detect and categorise Osteoarthritis disease in the knee using medical radiographs. While Islam et al. [8] give comparative analyses for tuberculosis detection on chest x-rays using deep convolutional neural networks.

Many pioneering works have also been established to detect lung diseases using chest X-ray images. P. Rajpurkar et al. [16] have proven that ChexNet model performs better in terms of AUROC score than many other previous works for classifying different lung diseases. Similarly, Pulkit et al. performed a multi-label classifier using cascading convolutional networks for thoracic diseases [9]. Guan et al. [5] proposed attention-guided CNN for thorax disease Classification from chest X-ray images. They experiment with ResNet-50 and DenseNet-121 models and achieve an average AUC of 0.871, which is state-of-the-art.

A promising way of learning called Multi-task learning (MTL)[2] improves learning performance for multiple similar tasks. It leverages useful information among tasks, improving the generalization performance of all tasks. In [24] Yu Zhang and Qiang Yang have mentioned MTL's modelling, applications, and theoretical analyses. Trevor et al. [20] give the objective for MTL by discussing which tasks should be learned together.

Furthermore, Federated Learning, an idea introduced in 2016 by Google AI [12]. Over time Federated Learning (FL) process became mature and popular for decentralized data. The use of FL in the healthcare domain has recently grown well. Jie Xu et al. [22] have reviewed FL technologies in healthcare informatics. Rieke et al. [17] state how the FL setting can benefit Machine Learning in the healthcare sector and highlight the challenges. Beguier et al. [3] gave a model to predict breast cancer disease from genomic data in FL settings. Brisimi et al. [4] gave a model to classify the need for hospitalization in cardiac events using the FL framework.

By mentioning the gaps in the approaches mentioned so far, we aim to have a learning model without concern about all data in one place and with better generalization performance. We proposed our work to classify multi-task (TB and Pneumonia disease) using the CNN model in a federated structure. This work extends previous works as classification problems on X-ray image data by performing two binary problem learning in a distinct federated setting.

3   Methodology

Let d_k be the dataset at k^{th} client for $t_k{}^{th}$ task. Also, assume that all t_k tasks are similar to each other and data sets are distributed to various clients/location. Objective is to develop a learning model using d_k data sets without sharing to a single point.

3.1   Multi-task Learning

The main goal of the multi-task learning [2] approach is to develop a generalized model for different related tasks that performs better. Figure 1 describes a general setting for multi-task learning. Multi-task learning aims to improve generalization by jointly exploiting relationships between multiple tasks. The classical setting of multi-task learning considers m different tasks with their task-specific data, learned jointly through the following objective:

$$= \min_{W} \frac{1}{t_k} \sum_{t_k=1}^{t_k} \frac{1}{n_k} \sum_{k=1}^{n_k} f_{t_k}(W, d_k) \qquad (1)$$

Here, W is the model that is learning t_k tasks for their specific data $\{d_1, d_2, ..., d_k\}$, $f_{t_k}(.)$ is the loss for $t_k{}^{th}$ task.

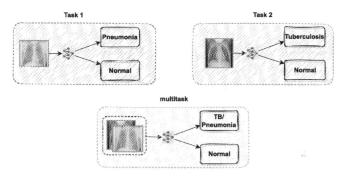

Fig. 1. Overview of tasks formation: Task 1 has classification problem of Pneumonia disease, Task 2 for Tuberculosis disease and Task 3 have both classification problems Pneumonia as well as Tuberculosis disease.

3.2   Federated Learning

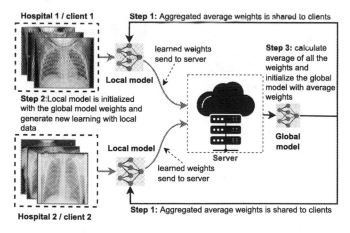

Fig. 2. Overview of federated learning architecture: server broadcasts its weight to all clients for initialization. After doing this, local models are trained on their local data. After training, local model weight is transferred to the server, where selective model weight is aggregated to update the server's weight. The process goes on till desired performance on the global model.

Federated learning [12] is multi-round collaborative learning without sharing local data. This learning gives advantages on data with the distributed user, where each user with some data wants to collaborate to train a learning model jointly. Without getting all data at one location for learning, the model is deployed to local users and learned parameters are shared only to the global server. The setting of Federated learning considers k different nodes with their local data is described in Fig. 2, learned collaboratively through the following objective function:

$$= \min_{W_G} \frac{1}{k} \sum_{k=1}^{k} \frac{n_k}{n} f_k(W_G, d_k) \qquad (2)$$

Here, k is the number of nodes participating in training, and W_G is the weight of the global model. $f_k(.)$ represents the loss of global model on the local data stored on k^{th} device represented by distribution d_k. The dataset size for k^{th} device is n_i, and for all participating devices is the sum n.

3.3   Multi-task Federated Learning

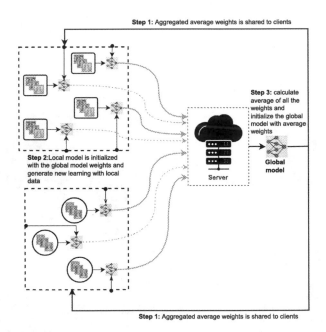

Fig. 3. Multi-task federated learning: the global model is developed using two binary class problems in a federated setting.

We have proposed a new Multi-task federated learning for various tasks and datasets located at n different clients. Multi-task federated learning aims to learn multiple tasks simultaneously in a collaborative manner. This work has provisioned the setting for multi-task Federated learning considering $t_k = 2$

different tasks distributed over n number of nodes, and each node has its task-specific data, learned collaboratively by solving the following objective function:

$$= \min_{W_G} \frac{1}{t_k} \sum_{t_k=1}^{t_k} \frac{n_{k_{t_k}}}{n_{t_k}} \sum_{k=1}^{k} f_{k_{t_k}}(W_G, d_{k_{t_k}}) \tag{3}$$

Here, W_G is the model that is learning t_k tasks for their specific data $\{d_1, d_2, ..., d_k\}$, $f_{k_{t_k}}(.)$ is the loss of kth client for $t_k{}^{th}$ task. k^{th} client for $t_k{}^{th}$ task having dataset of size $n_{k_{t_k}}$, and n_{t_k} is the sum of dataset size for all participating devices.

In our proposed method (Fig. 3), there are two models: The global and the local models. The local model architecture is similar to the global model. So each client will have the same model that the server has. The only difference is that they got trained separately on their data and then learned parameters shared to the server for aggregation. Then, global model weights are updated on aggregated weight.

Initially, the global model is initialized, and these initialized weights are shared with all the clients. Afterwards, the client initializes their model with the server's weights and stars training model using local datasets. Clients send back their weights to the server. The server selects k clients for aggregation of their weights and, after aggregation, broadcasts the updated weights to clients for the next round. In MTFL, active clients for both datasets follow the same procedure. To show the difference, we have shown clients of one dataset with orange and clients of another with green. Step-wise working of federated learning and Multi-Task Federated learning is given in Algorithm 1 and Algorithm 2, respectively.

Algorithm 1. Federated_Learning

Input: Server's initialization parameter: $\omega_G^{(0)}$, $d_1, d_2, ..., d_k$
Output: Optimized Server's parameter: $\omega_G^{(\tau)^*}$
1: Server determines the number of active clients k.
2: **for** each Communication round $\tau \in 1, 2..., T$ **do**
3:    **Select** clients κ from S
4:    **Send** $\omega_G^{(\tau-1)}$ to all clients
      Clients executes:
5:    **for** k^{th} client from k, where $k \in 1, 2....k$ **do**
6:       $\omega_k^{(\tau)} \leftarrow Local\_training(d_k, \omega_G^{(\tau-1)})$
7:       **Send** $\omega_k^{(\tau)}$ to **central Server**
8:    **end for**
      Server Executes Aggregation:
      //Server aggregate weights received from active clients.
9:    $\omega_G^{(\tau)} \leftarrow \frac{1}{k}(\sum_1^k \frac{n_k}{n}\omega_k^{(\tau)})$
10:   Server broadcasts $\omega_G^{(\tau)}$ parameters to all active clients.
11: **end for**

Algorithm 2. Multi-Task Federated_Learning

S_{pneu} is the set of clients among which Pneumonia dataset is distributed.
S_{tb} is the set of clients among which TB dataset is distributed
$k_{pneu} \subset S_{pneu}$
$k_{tb} \subset S_{tb}$

Input: Server's initialization parameter: $\omega_G^{(0)}$,
 Local Datasets for both task: $d_{1_{tb}}, d_{2_{tb}}, ..., d_{k_{tb}}$ and $d_{1_{pneu}}, d_{2_{pneu}}, ..., d_{k_{pneu}}$
Output: Optimized Server's parameter: $\omega_G^{(\tau)^*}$
 1: Initialization: global model $\omega_G^{(0)}$ at server.
 2: **for** each Communication round $\tau \in 1, 2..., T$ **do**
 3: **Send** $\omega_G^{(\tau-1)}$ to clients k_{pneu} and k_{tb}
 4: **Client** κ_{pneu} **executes:**
 5: $\omega_{k_{pneu}}^{(\tau)} \leftarrow Local\_training(k_{pneu}, \omega_G^{(\tau-1)})$
 6: **Send** $\omega_{k_{pneu}}^{(\tau)}$ to **central Server**
 7: **Client** k_{tb} **executes:**
 8: $\omega_{k_{tb}}^{(\tau)} \leftarrow Local\_training(k_{tb}, \omega_G^{(\tau-1)})$
 9: **Send** $\omega_{k_{tb}}^{(\tau)}$ to **central Server**
10: **Aggregation:**
   //Server aggregate weights received from active clients.
11: $\omega_G^{(\tau)} \leftarrow \frac{1}{N}(\sum_{k_{pneu}} \frac{n_{k_{pneu}}}{n_{pneu}} \omega_{k_{pneu}}^{(\tau)} + \sum_{k_{tb}} \frac{n_{k_{tb}}}{n_{tb}} \omega_{k_{tb}}^{(\tau)})$
12: Server broadcasts $\omega_G^{(\tau)}$ parameters to all active clients.
13: **end for**

The active clients participating in local training in a particular communication round are shown in bold lines communicating with the server. They are sharing learned weights with the server. Inactive clients shown in the dotted line do not share any parameters in that round. Figure 3 represent the training process of a particular communication round. As we can see, active clients of both datasets share the learned weights with the server. Then the server aggregates all received weights and will update the global model. Servers aggregated weight will be shared with all the clients for the next communication round, and further training will continue.

4   Experimental Setup

4.1   Dataset

In our experiments, we have used two datasets, one is **chest X-ray** [13], and the other is **TB chest X-ray** [21]. Both datasets are available publicly on Kaggle. Chest X-ray dataset consists of $5,856$ x-ray images in 2 classes, with $3,875$ images of Pneumonia class and $1,341$ of normal class. TB chest X-ray dataset consists of $4,200$ images of 2 classes, with 700 of TB class and 3500 images of normal class. We trained the centralized CNN model on Pneumonia and TB datasets separately. In which 20% of the data is randomly separated for testing,

20% data for validation and the remaining data for model training. For FL and MTFL, datasets are first partitioned into a training set (80%) and a validation set (20%). Afterwards, the training set is split into ten local datasets for local training, and the validation set is common. Figure 4 shows the visualizations for random samples of both datasets.

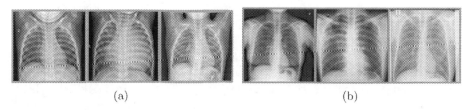

(a)   (b)

Fig. 4. Some random samples of images taken from (a) Pneumonia X-ray dataset (b) TB X-ray dataset.

4.2   Data Augmentation

Data augmentation is a technique that helps generate artificial data from existing datasets. The chest x-ray dataset used in our experiment is skewed to one class as 3,875 x-ray images belong to pneumonia and 1341 x-ray images belong to another class(normal). But we needed a balanced dataset for better performance of our models. The augmented images are the transformed versions of the existing images,i.e. re-scaling, zooming in-out or rotating the existing image to some predefined limit.

4.3   Global/Local Model

This work has used a CNN model consisting of an input layer, two alternating Conv2D layers, followed by a batch normalization layer. An activation function and max-pooling layer, one flatten layer and two dense layers. The activation function used is Relu, and the optimizer used is Adam. Both the global(sever) and local(client) model have the same architecture.

4.4   Construction of the Clients

Clients are the end devices which has their data. Generally, the model training in federated learning follows communication between clients and the server. Here, we are performing a simulation on this setting. We created multiple clients locally by creating local folders and distributing the dataset among those folders uniformly with the same proportion of data. The client will consider one folder as the data owner. This way, we have created ten clients of both dataset separately. In our case, no data overlapping is permitted.

4.5   Model Setting

We have demonstrated three models on two datasets and performed five experiments as discussed below:

- The first and second experiment is standard centralized training of our CNN model, where all the data is gathered, and the complete training process is carried out at the central server in one go. We have used the same CNN model architecture for both datasets. We trained it separately and recorded the result for further analysis.
- The third and fourth experiment is federated learning architecture for a single task. First, we distributed the dataset to ten clients. In training, we initialize the global model first, and then its weights are shared among all the clients for the local initialization. Then, local training is performed on local data and at the end of each communication round, aggregation of local learned weights is done to update global model weights. In this federated architecture, we trained separate CNN models for both datasets and recorded the results for further analysis.
- The fifth experiment is our proposed method, i.e. Multitasking federated learning. It is federated learning architecture for multiple tasks. In our case, one of the tasks is to detect Pneumonia and another task is to detect Tuberculosis. We have created ten separate clients for both datasets (i.e. chest X-ray and TB dataset).

We trained FL and MTFL models for thirty communication rounds while clients trained for five epochs. In each communication round, we randomly pick three clients among ten available clients for local training. In comparison, the CNN model used in centralized training is trained for 30 epochs.

4.6   Implementation Framework

Our experiment performed on a computer with GPU NVIDIA GEFORCE RTX 2060, a processing unit as Intel® Core™ i7 with six 2.60GHz cores and 16GBs of RAM. The experiments are implemented on Python 3.6 using deep learning libraries like Keras with Tensorflow 2.7.0, OpenCV, and Scikit-Learn. Jupyter notebook is used for editing and running implementation work.

4.7   Performance Measures

To examine and compare the model's performance we used precision, recall, F1-score, specificity, and accuracy as performance evaluation indicators.

Following are the Formula to calculate all the performance measure mentioned above are:

$$Precision = \frac{TP}{TP + FP} \tag{4}$$

$$Recall = \frac{TP}{TP + FN} \tag{5}$$

$$F1\ Score = 2 * \frac{Precision * Recall}{Precision + Recall} \tag{6}$$

$$Specificity = \frac{TN}{(TN + FP)} \tag{7}$$

$$Accuracy = \frac{TP + TN}{TP + FP + TN + FN} \tag{8}$$

where, TP-True positive, TN-True negative, FP-False positive, and FN-False negative.

5   Results and Discussion

This section presents the results and discussion of the multi-task federated learning model with Pneumonia and TB datasets. The proposed model is compared with a centralized CNN and Federated learning model.

5.1   Results on Chestx-Ray Dataset

We carried out three experiments a.) CNN with all Chestx-ray data at a single point, b.) FL with Chestx-ray data distributed at various clients, and c.) proposed MTFL with Chestx-ray and TB data sets distributed at various clients. A centralized CNN experiment is the baseline for other experiments. Training and validation accuracy of the three experiments given in Fig. 5. It shows that the CNN achieves accuracy quickly and also it is stable. However, MTFL and FL converge slowly and fluctuate too. Training and validation loss for each epoch is given in Fig. 6. CNN is stable after ten epochs, and FL becomes stable after 25. However, MTFL is still fluctuating but achieving accuracy. The reason behind this fluctuation is that our proposed multi-task model is trying to compensate for the training loss of both tasks simultaneously and updating weights so that loss on both datasets is minimized. This improvement can be observed more clearer with each communication round.

Relative performance on chest x-ray dataset with accuracy, precision, recall, F1-score and Specificity is given in Table 1. CNN performs better than the other two in terms of F1-score. However, the Specificity of CNN is 0.7649, which is very low compared to the other two. Specificity tells how our model performs on a healthy person to predict it as not having a disease. It improves in FL to 0.8247, But with the proposed MTFL, it increases to 0.9230, which shows that the multiple-task federated learning has supported to learning model in reducing the False-Positive ratio and is a very important issue in Health data. We may infer that multi-tasking has supported each other to classify with better F1-score and specificity.

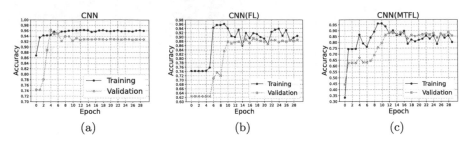

(a)   (b)   (c)

Fig. 5. Training and Validation accuracy of (a) CNN model (b) Federated global model (C) MTFL global model on chestx-ray dataset.

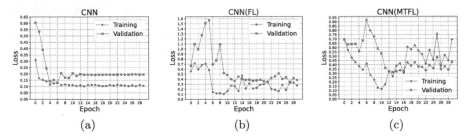

(a)   (b)   (c)

Fig. 6. Training and Validation loss of (a) CNN model (b) Federated client-1 CNN model (C) MTFL client-1 model on Pneumonia dataset.

Table 1. Comparative Analysis on Pneumonia dataset.

Model	Accuracy	Precision	Recall	F1 score	Specificity
CNN	0.8846	0.8714	0.9564	0.9119	0.7649
FL	0.8801	0.8977	0.9230	0.9102	0.8247
MTFL	0.8557	0.9464	0.8153	0.8760	0.9230

5.2   Results on Tuberculosis (TB) Dataset

Training and validation accuracy of the three experiments (a) CNN (b) FL, and (c) MTFL on TB dataset shown in Fig. 7. The performance of FL is similar to MTFL, which is better than CNN. We additionally observe that the MTFL needs a little more epoch for better accuracy.

We also compared the local training and validation loss for the three experiments, and the results are shown in Fig. 8. The performance of FL is similar to MTFL. The local training losses of (a) CNN decrease faster and are more stable in comparison to (b) FL and (c) MTFL. We also observe that our proposed model's training loss fluctuates dramatically due to multi-tasking but converges to better accuracy. Fluctuations in loss during training were observed because our proposed multi-task model tries to learn simultaneously. Both task losses try to compensate by updating weights to minimise the loss on both datasets. This improvement can be observed more clearer with each communication round.

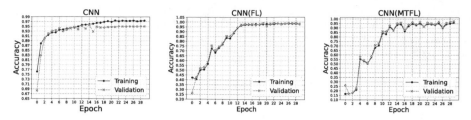

Fig. 7. Training and Validation accuracy of (a) CNN model (b) Federated global model (C) MTFL global model on TB dataset.

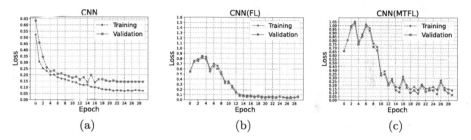

Fig. 8. Training and Validation loss of (a) CNN model (b) Federated client-1 CNN model (C) MTFL client-1 model on TB dataset.

Table 2. Comparative Analysis on TB dataset.

Model	Accuracy	Precision	Recall	F1 score	Specificity
CNN	0.9511	0.7796	0.9857	0.8706	0.9442
FL	0.9809	0.9843	0.9000	0.9402	0.9971
MTFL	0.9773	0.9352	0.9285	0.9318	0.9871

Relative performance in terms of accuracy, precision, recall, F1 score and specificity for all the three models on the TB dataset is given in Table 2. It shows the accuracy of FL is 0.9809 and is better than MTFL with 0.9773 and CNN with 0.9511. It means the distribution of data has contributed to better accuracy. Regarding the F1-score, FL 0.9402 and MTFL 0.9318 are better than CNN 0.8706. Also, the specificity of MTFL 0.9871 and FL 0.9971 is better than CNN 0.9442.

Further MTFL recall is better than the other two models. Therefore, we may infer that multi-task learning is helping to reduce the False rate (i.e. False-Positive, False-Negative). It may be that another similar dataset is helping to get the better feature for true recognition.

5.3 Discussion

During the testing with both datasets, MTFL learned model could reduce the False-Positive ratio, which may increase the model's acceptability. Table 1 and

2 shows that for MTFL training, TB data has supported to increase in the precision for pneumonia data testing (0.9464). However, pneumonia data has supported to increase in the recall for the TB data testing (0.9285). We may see that two datasets complement each other for decreasing a single MTFL fairer than a single task model. Moreover, MTFL can achieve accuracy with the same communication round as FL. Also, with the federated setting, data is at the local level only; hence leak of personal information is minimized. Though in this study, our inference is based on two tasks only, for more generalized acceptability of MTFL, a test with more than two tasks is needed.

6   Conclusion

This paper proposes a novel multi-task federated learning (MTFL) in which the model training on two binary class image datasets is performed in a federated setting. MTFL was applied on two different tasks to detect Pneumonia and Tuberculosis disease. Results show that MTFL achieves better specificity than a single model and federated learning. Our proposed model help in reducing false-positive recognition with better accuracy and without sharing data in a single point.

References

1. Abdulrahman, S., Tout, H., Ould-Slimane, H., Mourad, A., Talhi, C., Guizani, M.: A survey on federated learning: the journey from centralized to distributed on-site learning and beyond. IEEE Internet Things J. **8**(7), 5476–5497 (2021). https://doi.org/10.1109/JIOT.2020.3030072
2. Argyriou, A., Evgeniou, T., Pontil, M.: Multi-task feature learning. In: Advances in Neural Information Processing Systems, vol. 19 (2006)
3. Beguier, C., Terrail, J.O.d., Meah, I., Andreux, M., Tramel, E.W.: Differentially private federated learning for cancer prediction. arXiv preprint arXiv:2101.02997 (2021)
4. Brisimi, T.S., Chen, R., Mela, T., Olshevsky, A., Paschalidis, I.C., Shi, W.: Federated learning of predictive models from federated electronic health records. Int. J. Med. Inform. **112**, 59–67 (2018)
5. Guan, Q., Huang, Y., Zhong, Z., Zheng, Z., Zheng, L., Yang, Y.: Diagnose like a radiologist: attention guided convolutional neural network for thorax disease classification. arXiv preprint arXiv:1801.09927 (2018)
6. Hesamian, M.H., Jia, W., He, X., Kennedy, P.: Deep learning techniques for medical image segmentation: achievements and challenges. J. Digit. Imaging **32**(4), 582–596 (2019)
7. Hua, K.L., Hsu, C.H., Hidayati, S.C., Cheng, W.H., Chen, Y.J.: Computer-aided classification of lung nodules on computed tomography images via deep learning technique. OncoTargets Therapy **8** (2015)
8. Islam, M.T., Aowal, M.A., Minhaz, A.T., Ashraf, K.: Abnormality detection and localization in chest x-rays using deep convolutional neural networks. arXiv preprint arXiv:1705.09850 (2017)

9. Kumar, P., Grewal, M., Srivastava, M.M.: Boosted cascaded convnets for multilabel classification of thoracic diseases in chest radiographs. In: Campilho, A., Karray, F., ter Haar Romeny, B. (eds.) ICIAR 2018. LNCS, vol. 10882, pp. 546–552. Springer, Cham (2018). https://doi.org/10.1007/978-3-319-93000-8_62

10. Lakhani, P., Sundaram, B.: Deep learning at chest radiography: automated classification of pulmonary tuberculosis by using convolutional neural networks. Radiology **284**(2), 574–582 (2017)

11. Maier, A., Syben, C., Lasser, T., Riess, C.: A gentle introduction to deep learning in medical image processing. Z. Med. Phys. **29**(2), 86–101 (2019)

12. McMahan, B., Moore, E., Ramage, D., Hampson, S., Arcas, B.A.: Communication-efficient learning of deep networks from decentralized data. In: Artificial intelligence and statistics, pp. 1273–1282. PMLR (2017)

13. Mooney, P.: Chest x-ray images (pneumonia) (2021). https://www.kaggle.com/datasets/paultimothymooney/chest-xray-pneumonia

14. Nafisah, S.I., Muhammad, G.: Tuberculosis detection in chest radiograph using convolutional neural network architecture and explainable artificial intelligence. Neural Comput. Appl. 1–21 (2022)

15. Pfitzner, B., Steckhan, N., Arnrich, B.: Federated learning in a medical context: a systematic literature review. ACM Trans. Internet Technol. (TOIT) **21**(2), 1–31 (2021)

16. Rajpurkar, P., et al.: Chexnet: radiologist-level pneumonia detection on chest x-rays with deep learning. arXiv preprint arXiv:1711.05225 (2017)

17. Rieke, N., et al.: The future of digital health with federated learning. NPJ Digit. Med. **3**(1), 1–7 (2020)

18. Ruder, S.: An overview of multi-task learning in deep neural networks. arXiv preprint arXiv:1706.05098 (2017)

19. Singh, P.P., Prasad, S., Chaudhary, A.K., Patel, C.K., Debnath, M.: Classification of effusion and cartilage erosion affects in osteoarthritis knee MRI images using deep learning model. In: Nain, N., Vipparthi, S.K., Raman, B. (eds.) CVIP 2019. CCIS, vol. 1148, pp. 373–383. Springer, Singapore (2020). https://doi.org/10.1007/978-981-15-4018-9_34

20. Standley, T., Zamir, A.R., Chen, D., Guibas, L., Malik, J., Savarese, S.: Which tasks should be learned together in multi-task learning? (2019). https://doi.org/10.48550/ARXIV.1905.07553, https://arxiv.org/abs/1905.07553

21. Tawsifur Rahman, Muhammad Chowdhury, A.K.: Tuberculosis (tb) chest x-ray database (2021). https://www.kaggle.com/datasets/tawsifurrahman/tuberculosis-tb-chest-xray-dataset

22. Xu, J., Glicksberg, B.S., Su, C., Walker, P., Bian, J., Wang, F.: Federated learning for healthcare informatics. J. Healthc. Inform. Res. **5**(1), 1–19 (2021)

23. Zhang, C., Xie, Y., Bai, H., Yu, B., Li, W., Gao, Y.: A survey on federated learning. Knowl.-Based Syst. **216**, 106775 (2021). https://doi.org/10.1016/j.knosys.2021.106775, https://www.sciencedirect.com/science/article/pii/S0950705121000381

24. Zhang, Y., Yang, Q.: A survey on multi-task learning. IEEE Trans. Knowl. Data Eng. 1 (2021). https://doi.org/10.1109/TKDE.2021.3070203

Speech-Based Automatic Prediction of Interview Traits

Deepak Kumar$^{(\boxtimes)}$ and Balasubramanian Raman

Computer Science and Engineering Department, Indian Institute of Technology,
Roorkee, India
{d_kumar,bala}@cs.iitr.ac.in

Abstract. In this paper, we have proposed a novel deep-learning-based approach to predict the job interview traits termed hirability traits by extracting the speech features from a job interview audio-visual. We utilize a segmentation-based system due to each candidate's varying length of input audio. Using speech features, we employ: 1) Long short-term memory(LSTM) trained with low-level features, 2) Mel-Spectrogram based Convolutional Neural Networks (CNNs), and 3) The fusion of both, namely the CNN-LSTM model, to see the performance. We perform experiments on the MIT Interview dataset containing 138 mock-interview videos. To the best of our knowledge, we are the first to employ speech-only input-based deep learning models to automatically predict a candidate's overall performance and corresponding traits. We have evaluated our approach for continuous prediction (Regression) and note that: a) The fusion model (CNN-LSTM) is performing best among all three by preserving both temporal and spatial context of data, b) Segment length is affecting the performance as more size holds more comprehensive behavioral data, and c)Segment length of 1-minute is more suitable for our framework. Our proposed model can achieve 95.7% accuracy in the overall rating of the candidate. Other traits are also responding with good accuracy of prediction, including Excited: 95% and NotStressed: 94.8% prediction.

Keywords: Hirability Traits · Behavioral Analysis · Speech · Deep Learning Models · Mel-Spectrogram

1 Introduction

The human voice is an indicator of one's personality and even the human emotional state, as vocal characteristics are stable over time. Speech is a natural and effective way of communication among people [29]. Previously, the main focus of speech input was either speech recognition or speaker recognition [23], but now it has much more to do. Speech helps understand the human personality in different scenarios, including the first impression, job interview traits prediction [6,17] and emotion recognition [27].

Supported by the Ministry of Human Resource Development(MHRD) INDIA with reference grant number: OH-3123200428.

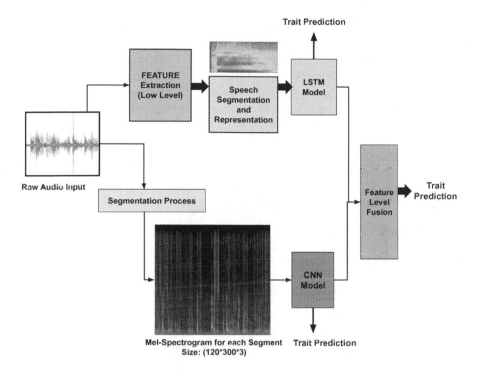

Fig. 1. Overview of proposed framework.

Prosody relates to the variations of tone that accompany speech [19] and includes such as applicant pauses [3], speaking time [5], speech fluency [3,14], pitch (voice fundamental frequency) [3,4], Amplitude Variability and Voice Breaks [3]. These characteristics are shown to affect interview ratings. All speaking activity cues are based on speaker segmentation. Many statistics are computed for speech energy, pitch, and voiced rate, including the mean, standard deviation, minimum, maximum, entropy, median, and quartiles [11,19] for the prediction of human traits. One interesting finding is that successful managers have certain psychological characteristics that could be inferred from speech input only [25].

People thinking about the personality of others is first and foremost influenced by their appearance, but it does not always result in the correct first impression [21]. Here comes speech, prosodic features, communication style, language, and even speech content, which changes the perception of one's personality. Images taken of the same person in different moods have changed personality impressions [28], so it is not helpful to always rely on only visual appearance. Job performance is highly correlated with personality traits [12] as these traits define human nature for long periods and reflect during the interaction process (in the interview).

In life and career, Job interviews play an important role. In the natural selection process, recognizing a candidate's hirability traits has to deal with many challenges compared to acted scenarios due to interaction, level of confidence, speaking style, and even level of comfort. Investigation and automatic prediction of Human traits, including personality traits, and job interview traits, is an active research area. Both verbal and non-verbal cues play an important role in human behavior analysis during job interviews. A common perception regarding job interviews is that the content of the interviewee's answers is the most crucial determinant for success [17]. The mental state and personality of one are reflected by the style of speaking, prosody, and language features [9].

In this work, we attempt to give an automatic prediction of job performance using speech features only and try to answer the following research questions:

1. Is only speech feature sufficient for the automatic prediction of job interview traits?
2. Is preserving the temporal context during the communication process help in effective prediction?
3. Does the fusion of low-level speech features and Visual features (Mel Spectrogram) support the performance improvement?

To answer these research questions we have designed a framework for effective prediction of continuous values of each trait. The proposed architecture is shown in Fig. 1, which automatically extracts the speech features and quantifies the six hirability characteristics, including Overall (Overall performance rating) Recommend Hiring (likelihood of candidate to be hired), Excited (level of Excitement), Friendly (level of friendliness), Not Stressed (Candidate was stressed or not), and Not Awkward (candidate behaving awkward or not) which we find more correlated with speech features. Our system can predict the six traits in terms of accuracy and correlation, where overall ratings have correlation value as 0.88 and prediction accuracy of 96%. By the experimental results, it is clearly shown that speech features are very effective in predicting interview traits which also mirrors the finding in [18].

Speech, besides being a powerful feature for the prediction of hirability traits, significantly less work has been done in this area. Our contributions include:

1. Only speech-based interview trait prediction by preserving the temporal context of the interaction.
2. Speech-visual (Mel-Spectrogram) based prediction of hirability traits and comparison with the other approaches.

To the best of our knowledge, this is the first work that employs deep learning models to learn candidates' speech features to predict the hirability traits.

We organized the remaining sections of the paper as follows: Sect. 2 briefly describes the Literature review, Sect. 3 describes the Proposed methodology, including feature extraction module, and Sect. 4 is about Experimental settings, including the dataset, ablation study and so on, Sect. 5 is about Results and discussion including Comparison with SOTA and the paper is then concluded in Sect. 6.

2   Literature Review

This section focuses on the works proposed in job interview performance estimation. Video Resumes [8,10,20,24] where candidates record a video explaining about themselves becoming more popular as prior screening, and human traits are examined to further recommendation of the candidate. But, this process lacks the interaction which happens in interview settings.

Based on job interview traits, many studies have examined the correlation between personality and Interview traits [15,16] and conclude that job performance is highly impacted by personality traits, also known as OCEAN (openness, conscientiousness, extraversion, agreeableness, and neuroticism) traits [2]. A few studies examine the automatic prediction of job interview traits, including the work by Madan et al. [11], which uses elementary head motion and facial action units to predict the hirability traits and also enables the explanations behind the results. A framework based on the multimodal features with their combinations is proposed by Naim et al. [18], which concludes that the prosodic features are significant during the interview process. Yagmur et al. [7] also provide an explainable regression-based framework for a recommendation of candidates during job interviews based on personality traits by using multimodal features as individuals and with their fusion. Parsons and Liden [22] observe that speech patterns could explain a remarkable variance in the candidate selection decision. In recent work, Adiani et al. [1] considered eye-gaze as one of the hirablity traits and worked on a webcam-based eye tracking algorithm to check the suitability for virtual job interview simulation platforms.

3   Proposed Methodology

3.1   Feature Extraction

Audio-Features: The interviewer and Interviewee are both involved in the interview process. Our primary focus is on analyzing the traits of interviewees for the hiring purpose. The MIT dataset annotates each interviewee segment's start and end timing. We have extracted the prosodic features in combination with Interspeech 2009 emotion challenge [26] based features, namely Voice Probability, MFCCs (Mel-frequency cepstral coefficients), ZCR (Zero-Crossing Rate), Fundamental Frequency, and root-mean-square (RMS). A total of 24-dimensional feature vectors have been formed. To extract these features, we have used librosa [13] python module with its default window length and stride. A speech feature vector is formed in an overlapping manner with 2-sec data having an overlap of 1 s.

Mel-Spectrogram: We have also used Mel-Spectrograms along with low-level hand-crafted features. Mel-Spectrograms (Spectrograms with Mel Scale as its y-axis.) are generated from the raw input audio with the help of librosa python library for audio processing [13]. For our settings, We compute a Fast Fourier

Transform (FFT) for each window of size 2048 with hop-length 512. The frequency spectrum is separated into 128 evenly spaced frequencies (number of Mel bands). We reshape the spectrograms to size (120*300*3) to be input into the CNN model.

3.2   Methodology

The CNN-LSTM Fusion architecture shown in Fig. 2 represents the main framework of our proposed model. This model performs the feature fusion of low-level voice features and spectrogram-based features, containing two modules: Left CNN and Right LSTM. The Left CNN model has three convolution layers with 16, 32, and 16 filters with max-pooling after each layer, followed by a flattened layer. A dense layer with 20 neurons is applied to have a 20-D feature vector from the CNN model. As the right input, one hidden LSTM layer with 20 neurons is used for low-level features and thus resulting in a 20-D feature vector. These 20-D features from each side input are concatenated and followed by one dense layer with 20 neurons. In the end, a dense layer with one neuron is added, followed by a linear layer for continuous value prediction of each trait. The complete model is trained with Adam Optimizer and MAE as a loss function.

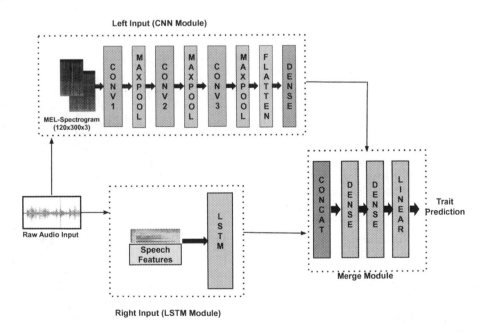

Fig. 2. Proposed fusion architecture takes left input from the CNN module and right from the LSTM module. CONV stands for the Convolution layer, CONCAT for the Concatenation layer, and LSTM for the hidden layer.

The proposed approach takes the data's spatial and temporal context for the prediction process. Learning sequences in segmented speech features makes the model teaching effective. On the other hand, spectrogram-based features help to understand the emphasized area of each corresponding audio segment visual, thus assisting the deep model in generating a practical part set for further concatenation. These merged inputs have Spatio-temporal properties, resulting in good accuracy and PCC.

4   Experiments and Results

4.1   Dataset

For the experimentation part, we have used the MIT (Massachusetts Institute of Technology) Interview dataset [18], which contains 138 mock-interview videos(audio-video recording) of students from MIT. A total of 69 participants participated in the process and gave mock interviews before and after the intervention. The entire duration is approximately 10.5 h, with an average length of 4.5 min. Interviews are recorded in a well-organized setup.

4.2   Experimental Settings

Label Type: We have modeled hirability traits as continuous variables for our experiments, and the results are presented in Table 1. The dataset contains only 138 videos, and the results are reported over ten-fold cross-validation repeated five times in (mean ± standard deviation) format. Validation split is used as 10 % of training data.

Audio Segments: The MIT dataset has varying audio lengths, so small segments are extracted from each data sample. The number of segments depends on the audio length and segment size. The label of the corresponding audio is repeated over each segment.

4.3   Performance Metrics

We work on continuous value prediction of job interview traits (regression) and report the test accuracy defined as 1-MAE (Mean Absolute Error) taken in [7] along with test PCC (Pearson correlation coefficient). Accuracy is calculated against the ground truth and predicted labels, while PCC reports the correlation between test labels and predicted test labels. A Zero value of PCC means no correlation, and one means fully correlated.

4.4   Models

SVR (Support Vector Regression): SVR is a supervised machine learning model that works on the concept of Support Vector Machines (SVMs) by finding the best fit line or hyperplane containing the maximum number of points and is used to predict the continuous values termed regression.

Random Forest (RF) Regression: It is also a supervised learning algorithm based on ensemble learning by combining the predictions of different machine learning algorithms so that prediction is more accurate as compared to a single model.

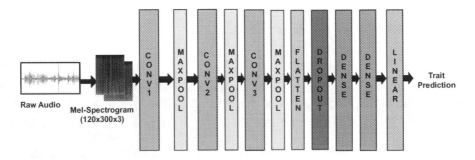

Fig. 3. Proposed CNN regression architecture. Model is trained with Mel-Spectrograms generated from the raw audio signals. CONV stands for Convolution layer.

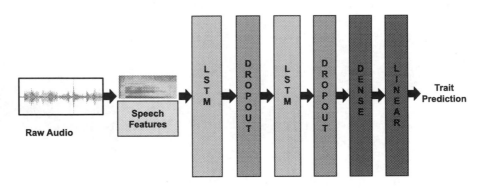

Fig. 4. Proposed LSTM architecture trained on low-level descriptors of speech signals. LSTM stands for LSTM hidden layer.

CNN Model: Convolutional Neural Networks have proven their efficiency in image Classification/Regression by extracting the features fast and accurately. For our model, we have trained CNN with Mel-Spectrograms of size (120*300*3) generated from raw audio inputs. We use three convolution layers with 16, 32, and 64 filters, respectively, and a max-pooling layer follows each convolution layer. At the end of the last max-pooling layer, a flattened layer is added following one dropout (0.5) layer and two dense layers with 256 and 1 neurons, respectively. In the end, a linear layer is added to predict the continuous value of each trait. The model is trained with tanh activation, Adam optimizer with a default learning rate of 0.01, and MAE loss function. Complete architecture is shown in Fig. 3.

LSTM Model: Long-short-term memory works on sequences and preserves the temporal context of the input data. We have trained LSTM with the speech features by extracting the low-level descriptor of the raw audio. Our LSTM model contains two hidden layers of 20 and 10 neurons, respectively, with activation function tanh. A dropout of 0.2 is applied after each hidden layer to avoid overfitting. The model is trained with Adam optimizer (LR = 0.01) and MAE loss function. The architecture of the model is shown in Fig. 4.

4.5   Ablation Study

We have also performed an ablation study to determine the proposed architecture and segment size. As the dataset contains only 138 videos with varying lengths, different segment sizes are formed from the main video, including the span of 15, 30, and 60 s. Results are computed for each span over each trait. For reference, Fig. 5 shows the different impacts of segment lengths for the trait "Overall," and the same trend follows for other labels. The 15-sec segment is giving reasonably good results proving that small behavioral slices can also help in hirability trait prediction. In contrast, more precise prediction is achieved with 1-min data (considering more comprehensive behavioral data). We have also performed experiments with hyper-parameters for different models to decide on the final working architecture. By the ablation study, it is concluded that segment size 60 is more suitable for further processing.

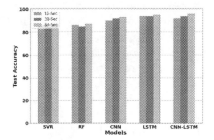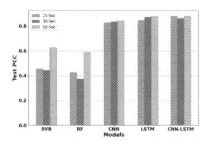

Fig. 5. Bar plots used for ablation study. Test Accuracy (left) and Test PCC (right) is plotted for different segment lengths for all used models.

5   Results and Discussion

5.1   Comparison with the State-of-the-Art (SOTA) Approaches

As per the literature review, we have found only one work that employs one of the speech-only-based features for predicting hirability traits on the MIT dataset. The approach [18] achieves a correlation of approximately Overall: 0.58 and Excited:0.76, while our presented method results in Overall:0.88 and Excited:0.93. And similar performance improvement patterns are accomplished for other traits as well. The comparison confirms the proposed approach's applicability to this problem.

5.2   Discussion

All the following findings are based on Table 1, which shows the regression results on the MIT dataset with different models:

Table 1. Regression results for all three deep learning models along with two basic ML models. Here, Ov:Overall, RH:RecommendHiring, Ex:Excited, Fr:Friendly, St:Not Stressed and Aw:Not Awkward.

Label	SVR		RF		CNN		LSTM		CNN-LSTM	
	Accuracy	PCC	Accuracy	PCC	Accuracy	PCC	Accuracy	PCC	Accuracy	PCC
Ov	0.87±0.01	0.63±0.07	0.87±0.01	0.59±0.09	0.93±0.02	0.84±0.07	0.95±0.02	0.88±0.09	0.96±0.02	0.88±0.08
RH	0.86±0.01	0.63±0.07	0.87±0.02	0.58±0.1	0.92±0.04	0.82±0.14	0.95±0.02	0.87±0.11	0.94±0.03	0.88±0.13
Ex	0.87±0.01	0.73±0.06	0.87±0.03	0.74±0.07	0.94±0.04	0.92±0.05	0.96±0.02	0.93±0.05	0.95±0.02	0.93±0.08
Fr	0.87±0.02	0.73±0.07	0.87±0.04	0.74±0.07	0.89±0.17	0.87±0.18	0.96±0.02	0.91±0.04	0.95±0.03	0.93±0.1
St	0.87±0.03	0.73±0.08	0.87±0.05	0.59±0.09	0.92±0.06	0.90±0.1	0.95±0.02	0.90±0.08	0.95±0.03	0.91±0.13
Aw	0.87±0.04	0.73±0.09	0.87±0.06	0.59±0.09	0.92±0.07	0.86±0.15	0.95±0.02	0.84±0.1	0.95±0.02	0.90±0.1

- Along with deep learning models, we have also trained two basic machine learning models: SVR and RF. Despite not learning any temporal dynamics of data, these models perform well.
- The segmentation process has provided a good amount of data samples for CNN training. The results of CNN are improving over the results from the basic machine learning models.
- By learning and preserving the temporal context of the data, LSTMs are giving a good performance with an average accuracy of 95%. The performance of LSTM is slightly better than CNN, which shows the capability of LSTM learning with a sufficient amount of data samples, while we still can say that CNN needs much more samples for results improvement.
- Results are much comparable with all three deep learning models, but our fusion model, which preserves both the temporal and spatial context of data, performs best. It provides average accuracy of 95% and a PCC of 0.93 for the trait Excited. And the same trend follows for other traits as well.
- The Performance of all three deep learning models shows the efficacy of human speech input for predicting hirability traits.
- Speech features are best performing for the trait Excited with all three experimental settings, showing that Excited people have much more to do with prosodic features.

Ultimately, it is concluded that human speech is capable enough to predict hirability traits.

6   Conclusion and Future Work

This work shows that hirability traits can be identified effectively by human speech only. The proposed approach has a novel contribution toward automatically predicting a candidate's traits during interview settings. Our model obtained significant results on the MIT dataset. This work extracts human speech features at low-level (Descriptors) and high-level (Mel-spectrograms) using different audio length segments. These segment length helps to understand the small and long human behavioral patterns. In future work, we aim to test the proposed model on different datasets containing more samples and will also incorporate other features, including facial features, EEG signals, etc.

References

1. Adiani, D., et al.: Evaluation of webcam-based eye tracking for a job interview training platform: Preliminary results. In: Degen, H., Ntoa, S. (eds.) Artificial Intelligence in HCI. HCII 2022. LNCS, vol. 13336, pp. 337–352. Springer, Cham (2022). https://doi.org/10.1007/978-3-031-05643-7_22
2. Costa, P.T., McCrae, R.R.: Neo personality inventory-revised (NEO PI-R). Psychological Assessment Resources Odessa, FL (1992)
3. DeGroot, T., Gooty, J.: Can nonverbal cues be used to make meaningful personality attributions in employment interviews? J. Bus. Psychol. **24**(2), 179–192 (2009)
4. Favre, S., Salamin, H., Dines, J., Vinciarelli, A.: Role recognition in multiparty recordings using social affiliation networks and discrete distributions. In: Proceedings of the 10th International Conference on Multimodal Interfaces, pp. 29–36 (2008)
5. Gifford, R., Ng, C.F., Wilkinson, M.: Nonverbal cues in the employment interview: Links between applicant qualities and interviewer judgments. J. Appl. Psychol. **70**(4), 729 (1985)
6. Gilpin, L.H., Olson, D.M., Alrashed, T.: Perception of speaker personality traits using speech signals. In: Extended Abstracts of the 2018 CHI Conference on Human Factors in Computing Systems, pp. 1–6 (2018)
7. Güçlütürk, Y., et al.: Multimodal first impression analysis with deep residual networks. IEEE Trans. Affect. Comput. **9**(3), 316–329 (2017)
8. Hiemstra, A.: Fairness in paper and video resume screening (2013)
9. Kapoor, A., Picard, R.W.: Multimodal affect recognition in learning environments. In: Proceedings of the 13th Annual ACM International Conference on Multimedia, pp. 677–682 (2005)
10. Kemp, K.J., Bobbitt, L.M., Beauchamp, M.B., Peyton, E.A.: Using one-minute video résumés as a screening tool for sales applicants. J. Market. Develop. Competit. **7**(1), 84–92 (2013)
11. Madan, S., Gahalawat, M., Guha, T., Subramanian, R.: Head matters: explainable human-centered trait prediction from head motion dynamics. In: Proceedings of the 2021 International Conference on Multimodal Interaction, pp. 435–443 (2021)
12. Mairesse, F., Walker, M.A., Mehl, M.R., Moore, R.K.: Using linguistic cues for the automatic recognition of personality in conversation and text. J. Artif. Intell. Res. **30**, 457–500 (2007)
13. McFee, B., et al.: librosa: audio and music signal analysis in python. In: Proceedings of the 14th Python in Science Conference, vol. 8, pp. 18–25. CiteSeer (2015)

14. McGovern, T.V.: The making of a job interviewee: the effect of nonverbal behavior on an interviewer's evaluations during a selection interview. Southern Illinois University at Carbondale (1976)

15. Mount, M.K., Barrick, M.R., Stewart, G.L.: Five-factor model of personality and performance in jobs involving interpersonal interactions. Hum. Perform. **11**(2–3), 145–165 (1998)

16. Moy, J.W., Lam, K.F.: Selection criteria and the impact of personality on getting hired. Personnel Review (2004)

17. Naim, I., Tanveer, M.I., Gildea, D., Hoque, M.E.: Automated prediction and analysis of job interview performance: the role of what you say and how you say it. In: 2015 11th IEEE International Conference and Workshops on Automatic Face and Gesture Recognition (FG), vol. 1, pp. 1–6. IEEE (2015)

18. Naim, I., Tanveer, M.I., Gildea, D., Hoque, M.E.: Automated analysis and prediction of job interview performance. IEEE Trans. Affect. Comput. **9**(2), 191–204 (2016)

19. Nguyen, L.S., Gatica-Perez, D.: I would hire you in a minute: Thin slices of nonverbal behavior in job interviews. In: Proceedings of the 2015 ACM on International Conference on Multimodal Interaction, pp. 51–58 (2015)

20. Nguyen, L.S., Gatica-Perez, D.: Hirability in the wild: analysis of online conversational video resumes. IEEE Trans. Multimedia **18**(7), 1422–1437 (2016)

21. Olivola, C.Y., Todorov, A.: Fooled by first impressions? reexamining the diagnostic value of appearance-based inferences. J. Exp. Soc. Psychol. **46**(2), 315–324 (2010)

22. Park, S., Gratch, J., Morency, L.P.: I already know your answer: using nonverbal behaviors to predict immediate outcomes in a dyadic negotiation. In: Proceedings of the 14th ACM International Conference on Multimodal Interaction, pp. 19–22 (2012)

23. Peacocke, R.D., Graf, D.H.: An introduction to speech and speaker recognition. In: Readings in Human-Computer Interaction, pp. 546–553. Elsevier (1995)

24. Rolls, J.A., Strenkowski, M.: Video technology: Resumes of the future (1993)

25. Rousey, C.L., Morrison, D., Deacon, D.: Choosing successful management. Consulting Psychol. J. Pract. Res. **47**(2), 108 (1995)

26. Schuller, B., Steidl, S., Batliner, A.: The interspeech 2009 emotion challenge (2009)

27. Shirian, A., Guha, T.: Compact graph architecture for speech emotion recognition. In: ICASSP 2021–2021 IEEE International Conference on Acoustics, Speech and Signal Processing (ICASSP), pp. 6284–6288. IEEE (2021)

28. Todorov, A., Porter, J.M.: Misleading first impressions: Different for different facial images of the same person. Psychol. Sci. **25**(7), 1404–1417 (2014)

29. Tsai, L.L.: Why college students prefer typing over speech input: the dual perspective. IEEE Access **9**, 119845–119856 (2021)

Pneumonia Detection Using Deep Learning Based Feature Extraction and Machine Learning

B. H. Shekar, Shazia Mannan$^{(\boxtimes)}$, and Habtu Hailu

Department of Computer Science, Mangalore University, Mangalgangothri,
Mangalore 574199, Karnataka, India
smannan81@gmail.com

Abstract. Pneumonia is a potentially fatal disease that accounts for huge loss of life worldwide, especially in paediatric cases. It can be caused by viral, bacterial, fungal or Covid-19 infection. In the case of Covid-19 Pneumonia, the disease progresses very swiftly if proper medical care is not provided for the patients. This work focuses on providing a model that can accurately detect Pneumonia from among various other pulmonary diseases. The proposed model uses CNN-based feature extractor along with machine learning classifiers: Random Forest (RF), Support Vector Machine (SVM) and Logistic Regression (LR). We have used five different datasets to overcome the concerns raised about generalization of the model in some of the previous works. Our proposed model gives encouraging results and shows marked improvement in classifying pneumonia.

Keywords: Feature extraction · Machine Learning classifiers · Densenet169 · Pneumonia · Covid-19

1 Introduction

Pulmonary diseases such as Pneumonia, Tuberculosis, Lung Cancer, COPD and such are also known as lung or respiratory diseases, which are caused when the respiratory tract and/or other parts of the lungs are afflicted by the disease-causing virus or bacteria [1]. Air cells known as alveoli make up our lungs. During pneumonia, these air cells become saturated with pus and fluid, causing breathing to become laboured and difficult, resulting in a lack of oxygen intake [2]. The most common symptoms that manifest during pneumonia are dyspnea, fever, myalgia, cough and cold. Pneumonia can affect one or both the lungs and can be caused due to bacterial, viral or fungal invasion and growth in the body [3]. Pneumonia is the primary cause of cessation of life in paediatric cases worldwide. According to the World Health Organisation (WHO), this infectious disease proved fatal for 740180 pre-schoolers in 2019 and also a large number of adults. It accounted for 14% of all deaths of toddlers and pre- school children.

B. H. Shekar and H. Hailu—Contributing authors.

© The Author(s), under exclusive license to Springer Nature Switzerland AG 2023
D. Gupta et al. (Eds.): CVIP 2022, CCIS 1777, pp. 597–609, 2023.
https://doi.org/10.1007/978-3-031-31417-9_45

Nosocomial Pneumonia, as the name indicates, is a healthcare-associated illness that was not present at the time of hospitalisation and manifests clinically after 48 h or longer of hospitalisation. Pneumonia that originated in normal environment other than a hospital is known as Community or commonly Acquired Pneumonia (CAP), and is a frequent cause of malaise and loss of life [4]. Common disease-producing pathogens which can lead to CAP are streptococcus pneumoniae, haemophilus influenzae and moraxella catarrhalis. The underlying cause of Pneumonia determines the severity of the disease. Pneumonia caused due to virus is milder and its symptoms appear gradually, whereas in the case of bacterial pneumonia the symptoms may appear gradually or even suddenly and its severity is more [5]. This type of Pneumonia may affect multiple lobes of the lungs leading to hospitalisation. Fungal Pneumonia is another type of Pneumonia which usually affects people having weak immune system. Another type to be added to this list is Covid-19 Pneumonia which results when the virus attacks the lungs of an infected person. Covid-19 Pneumonia can be fatal and needs immediate medical attention. It can cause scarring and long term effects on the functioning of the lungs even after recovery has been made.

Pneumonia can be life-endangering if it is not acted upon immediately and therefore the early and accurate diagnosis of Pneumonia is vital. Doctors recommend physical examination, checking up medical history along with a battery of medical tests which may include sputum or blood checks, Chest X-Rays(CXR), CT-scans or MRI to diagnose Pneumonia. Out of these CXRs are the cheapest and most routine way of detecting Pneumonia. CT-scans are also recommended for classifying Pneumonia, especially at an early stage since it provides a detailed report of the patient's condition. There is a shortage of medical professionals, more so in economically developing nations and rural areas, leading to delays in the diagnosis and thereby leading to increase in death rate [6]. Another factor affecting the accurate diagnosis of Pneumonia is its similarity to other ailments which have indistinguishable features like opacity, cavity or plural effusion [7]. Since X-ray images are hazy, they are often mis-classified by the radiologists leading to wrong treatment and consequent deterioration in the patient's condition. Considerable inconsistencies in the decisions made by radiologists in Pneumonia detection have been reported. Consequently, there is a pressing want for Computer-Aided Detection (CAD) tools that can be utilised for automated illness identification to assist radiologists in the rapid discovery of different forms of Pneumonia after image capture. Several medical problems, such as the categorization and detection of lung illnesses, the detection of skin cancer, the detection of brain tumours, the detection of breast cancer, and so on, have been solved with the help of solutions based on technologies developed with Artificial Intelligence(AI) [8–10].

In context of Pulmonary disease classification and detection, CheXneXt model given by [11] outperforms most of the other models for pneumonia detection. This deep learning model has 121 layers for accurately classifying Pneumonia by localizing the affected areas with the help of heat maps. Several models have been developed to help in classifying Pneumonia using CXRs. In many models handcrafted feature extraction methods are used followed by machine learning algorithms for classification. Some other models make use of various deep learning techniques for extracting features as well as for classifying data into appropriate classes or sets.

After going through the literature of previously done works, we can say that there is still scope for improvement in the accuracy rate for automatic detection of Pneumonia. In this work we propose a model based on a combination of CNN and machine learning algorithms. The CNN-based model, Densenet169 is being used only as a feature extractor and is not doing any classification since the last layers have been removed. A CNN can also be used as a feature extracting model if we use it along with the transfer learning method. Once the features have been extracted they are fed to the classifiers for accurately classifying each image to its correct class or category.

The paper is structured as follows: Sect. 2 contains the previous works done in this field. The methodology employed and the proposed architecture for the model is described in Sect. 3. Section 4 details the experimental setup, results achieved and the comparative analysis with existing SOTA works. The paper is concluded in Sect. 5.

2   Related Works

Li et al. [12] developed a modified CNN architecture consisting of a single convolutional layer that learnt DCT like features from the training set and produced good classification results. To overcome the problem of overfitting, they used methods such as input distortion and intense dropout on the publicly available ILD database.

Chowdhury et al. [13] improved upon existing methods for identifying pneumonia in digital CXR films with the help of a deep learning method pre-trained on the ImageNet dataset. The approach of transfer learning was used in order to validate the performance of a substantial number of deep CNNs which have been already trained on another set of data for the purpose of image enhancement. They trained the model in two different scenarios, with and without image augmentation, on two different datasets. The first contained normal and Covid-19 Pneumonia, and the second one contained regular, viral, and Covid-19 Pneumonia.

A Deep Learning approach for analyzing Pneumonia and cancer of the lungs was provided by [14]. They proposed two distinct DL techniques for evaluating lung samples. The first DL approach, called a Modified AlexNet (MAN), divides CXR films into subclasses: normal and pneumonia. The categorization in the MAN is done with a SVM, and the results are compared using Softmax. The second DL study uses a combination of handcrafted and trained features in Alexnet to enhance lung cancer classification accuracy.

Yadav et al. [15] investigated a CNN-based method that includes a SVM, transfer learning, and capsule network training techniques for diagnosing Pneumonia. They implement VGG16 and InceptionV3 algorithms for transfer learning. A small chest X-ray dataset [16] has been utilized for the training and evaluation of their method.

Abiyev et al. [17] proposed two CNN models which were trained using separate datasets. With [16] dataset, which only comprised of CXRs showing pneumonia infection and those showing no infections, the first model was trained for binary classification. Based on the Covid-19 radiography dataset, which comprised of chest X-ray images, the second model used transfer learning to build on the information learnt in the first experiment and worked on multi-class classifications for Covid-19, pneumonia, and normal images. On the test data, the model performed well in terms of most evaluation metrics.

A CAD method based on unsupervised pulmonary opacity detection method was proposed by [18] that could automatically evaluate CT scans to identify Covid-19 from community or commonly acquired pneumonia. The experimental result indicated that the proposed method had promising potential on Covid-19 and viral Pneumonia differential diagnosis from CT images.

A DL approach suggested by [19] evaluates several deep learning architectures such as VGG19-CNN, ResNet152V2, ResNet152V2 + Gated Recurrent Unit (GRU), and ResNet152V2 + Bidirectional GRU (Bi-GRU) for accurately classifying data into three sets: Covid-19, Pneumonia, and Lung Cancer, using a mixture of CXR and CT images. The VGG19 + CNN model presents the best outcome according to the results of the experiments.

Gaur et al. [20] proposed a model composed of EffcientNetB0, VGG16, and InceptionV3 while using transfer learning to correctly identify Covid-19 from CXRs while discriminating between normal and infected X-rays.

Rahman et al. [21] made progress in accurate detection of Pneumonia by using a number of CNN models: SqueezeNet, DenseNet201, ResNet18 and Alexnet on Kaggle Chest X-ray Pneumonia dataset which consists of a total of 5247 images representing three classes, Pneumococcal Pneumonia, Bronchial Pneumonia, and normal chest x-rays images. Three experiments were carried out for classifying (i) normal vs. Pneumonia images which attained an accuracy of 98%, (ii) bacterial vs. viral Pneumonia images which secured accuracy rate of 95% and (iii) normal, bacterial, and viral Pneumonia which achieved 93.3%. The transfer learning approach was employed by them in this work.

Four variant models; ResNet152V2, CNN, MobileNetV2, and a Long Short-Term Memory were developed by [22]. The results indicated that the proposed model had an improved accuracy of 99.22% and the ResNet152V2 models achieved the optimal results as compared to other models.

The work done till date has produced encouraging results but can be improved further. The purpose of this work is to gain better accuracy results as compared to previous work, by making use of various combinations of CNN-based algorithms for feature extraction and traditional Machine Learning(ML) models as classifiers.

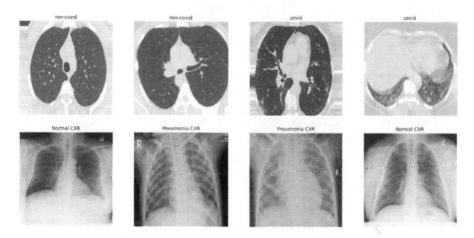

Fig. 1. Sample images from CT-Scan and X-ray.

3   Methodology

In this work the methodology employed consists of the following steps: i) Data Pre-processing, ii) Feature extraction using Densenet169 and iii) Classification using various Machine Learning methods such as Random Forest(RF), Support Vector Machine(SVM) and Logistic Regression(LR). The results obtained have been listed in Sect. 4.

3.1   The Proposed Architecture

Chest diseases are one of the primary cause of demise and illness worldwide. According to the WHO, around 1.5 crore adults as well as children are affected by them annually and this figure is expected to go up by 10% every year. Our paper focuses mainly on various types of Pneumonia and what could be done for its accurate and timely diagnosis. The study uses CXR and CT scan images for detecting Pneumonia- viral or Covid-19 related, in patients.

3.1.1   Pre-processing
In the pre-processing stage, the images have been resized to a standard format of 224*224*3 and the data has been normalized i.e. all the pixels making up the image have been rescaled between 0 & 1. For data augmentation, various approaches such as rotation, scaling, horizontal flipping and horizontal & vertical shifting have been utilised. The images are then randomly divided into two parts: training and testing in a ratio of 80% and 20%.

3.1.2   Feature Extraction Using DenseNet169
Densenet169 has been employed in this experiment as a feature-extractor model for obtaining features from images stored in the above mentioned datasets by

using transfer learning. In the DenseNet169 architecture, each layer has a direct connection to all remaining layers in the network. If the architecture has 'n' number of layers then there are n(n+1)/2 connecting lines between the layers. The layers contained within a block allow others to access and use the features extracted by them. Therefore DenseNet169 needs less number of parameters leading to a compact performance which produces better results as compared to other standard architectures. The output obtained after passing the input images to the Densenet169 model through all the layers of the model except the last layer, is then taken as input to the classifier being used. The resultant features are fed to different ML classifiers namely RF, SVM and LR for classification (Fig. 2).

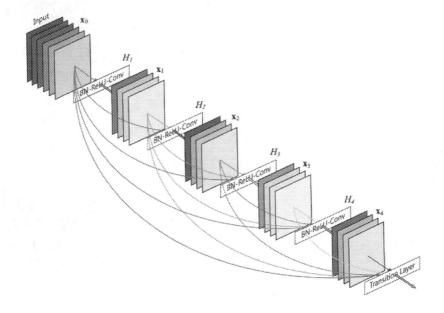

Fig. 2. 5-Layer Dense block sample.

3.1.3   Classification

The classification techniques entail foretelling a particular result based on a given set of inputs. The technique employs a training set comprising of a collection of features to forecast the final result. We have used conventional machine learning methods such as SVM, LR and RF to accurately group the extracted features into appropriate classes.

Support Vector Machine is a ML algorithm which can be used for classifying data into various sets. It follows supervised form of learning and can be used for regression as well. This method, developed by Vapnik, tries to divide the total space into fixed sets or categories to which we can simply add new data as and when it is made available. SVM works on labelled data.

The **Random Forest** algorithm is a supervised classification technique given by Breimann in 2001. It is utilises a large number of self-learning decision trees. For each individual decision tree, the RF first generates a random sample of the training dataset. The attributes are then randomly selected at each node to establish the optimum rule for separating the data and, eventually, selecting a class label. The basic premise underpinning the random forest technique is the training stage's generation of numerous "simple" decision trees and the classification stage's majority vote (mode) across them.

Logistic Regression which is a form of supervised learning tries to find out how several autonomous factors and a specific reliant variable are related to one another. It also calculates the chances of a particular case occurring by placing the data according to the logistic curve. Logistic regression can be classified into two kinds: binary logistic regression and multinomial logistic regression. Binary form of regression works when the dependent variable branches and the autonomous variables are extended or specific. Multinomial, as the name denotes, is used when we are working with more than two sets of dependent variables.

4   Experimental Setup, Results and Comparative Analysis

All the models have been executed on a computer with Intel(R) Core(TM) i5-1035G1 with 1.00 GHz–3.6 GHz CPU having 16 GB RAM on a 64-bit Windows 10 operating system. The proposed model was trained and tested in Python using the Keras package with Tensorflow. From the datasets being used, 80% of the images were taken for training whereas the remaining 20% were employed for testing purpose. All the three classifiers were used in combination with the feature extractor model. The model was executed using five different datasets mentioned in Table 1. A total of 3*5 = 15 experiments were carried out for Pneumonia classification.

Table 1. Datasets used in the experiment.

Name of Dataset	Classes	No. of Images	Image modality
Covid-19 and Common Pneumonia Dataset [DS1]	Pneumonia	328	CT Scan
	Covid-19	722	
SARS-Cov-2 Ct-scan Dataset [DS2]	Covid-19	1252	CT Scan
	Non-Covid	1230	
Mendeley's Covid Pneumonia Dataset [DS3]	Normal	2103	CT Scan
	Pneumonia	2105	
	Covid-19	1680	
Covid-Pneumonia-Normal-chest-x-raypa Dataset [DS4]	Normal	1525	X-ray
	Pneumonia	1525	
	Covid-19	1525	
Covid-19 Radiography Dataset [DS5]	Normal	1341	X-ray
	Pneumonia	1345	
	Covid-19	1143	

4.1   Dataset

To classify pneumonia we have utilised five separate datasets to show for the generalization of our proposed model. Since Covid-19 is an ongoing pandemic, it had no dataset before 2020. Datasets were created as and when data was made available and are still being continuously updated. This work makes use of five publicly available datasets listed below:

1. **Covid-19 and Common Pneumonia Dataset (DS1):** The dataset contains 1048 CT scan images belonging to 328 CAP and 722 covid classes. The CAP scans include images collected from patients who have viral, bacterial, fungal as well as mycoplasma Pneumonia. [23]
2. **SARS-Cov-2 Dataset (DS2):** Sars-Cov-2 dataset, available on link: https://www.kaggle.com/plameneduardo/sarscov2-ctscan-dataset, comprises of 2482 CT scans where 1230 belong to non-covid-19 patients and 1252 belong to positively tested Covid-19 patients.
3. **Mendeley's Covid Pneumonia Dataset (DS3):** This dataset is available at Kaggle link: https://www.kaggle.com/datasets/anaselmasry/ct-images-for-covid-normal-pneumonia-mendeley. It contains 5888 CT scan images belonging to three classes - Covid-19, Pneumonia and Normal. Normal i.e. having no abnormality and Pneumonia classes have 2103 and 2105 images respectively. The remaining 1680 images belong to Covid-19 patients.
4. **Covid-Pneumonia-Normal-chest-x-raypa Dataset (DS4):** This chest X-ray dataset is available on the Kaggle repository: https://www.kaggle.com/ amanullahasraf/covid19-pneumonia-normal-chestxray-pa-dataset. It comprises of 4575 images belonging to three different classes namely Covid-19, Pneumonia and Normal. Each class contains 1525 xray images.
5. **Covid-19 Radiography Dataset (DS5):** The dataset contains 1143 Covid-19 positive images, 1341 normal images and 1345 viral Pneumonia images. It can be accessed from the link: https://www.kaggle.com/datasets/ tawsifurrahman/covid19-radiography-database/versions/2. The dataset is being continuously updated.

4.2   Evaluation Metrics

The final output obtained from the said experiments have been very optimistic. Confusion matrix along with accuracy, precision, recall and F1-score have been used to evaluate the results. The confusion matrix gives an concise and pictoral representation of results along with stating the number of True Positives(TP), True Negatives(TN), False Positive(FP) and False Negative(FN). All evaluation metrics are arrived at by using the Eqs. 1, 2, 3 and 4.

$$Accuracy = \frac{(TP + TN)}{(TP + TN + FP + FN)} \tag{1}$$

$$Recall = \frac{TP}{(TP + FN)} \tag{2}$$

$$Precision = \frac{TP}{(TP + FP)} \tag{3}$$

$$F1 - Score = 2\frac{(Precision * Recall)}{(Precision + Recall)} \tag{4}$$

4.3   Results

After feeding the resultant features obtained from the Densenet169 model as input to each of the machine learning classifiers, encouraging results were obtained. The final outcome achieved thereafter have been listed in the Table 2.

With all the datasets used, the proposed model gave the good results for the Densenet169+SVM and Densenet169+LR combination. Here, SVM has been used with linear kernel and the value for n_estimator has been fixed at 50 after analysis. Densenet169+RF has produced less accuracy as compared to other extractor-classifier models for DS2, DS4 and DS5 in the experiments conducted though it is above 90%. As can be seen from Table 2, the best results were obtained when the model was run on DS1 with 100%, 100% and 100% accuracy for RF, SVM and LR classifiers respectively. The model accuracy for DS2 was 98.39% for SVM and 97.98% for LR. RF classifier gave an accuracy rate of 91.34%. Models using DS1 and DS3 have an accuracy of 100% for each of the classifiers. For DS5 the proposed model has attained 97.12%, 98.56% & 98.43% in multi-class classification.

Table 2. Results obtained for each combination of Densenet169+classifier and the dataset used.

Dataset	Classifier	Accuracy	Precision	Recall	F1-Score
Covid-19 and Common Pneumonia [DS1]	Random Forest	100	100	99	99
	SVM	100	100	100	100
	Logistic Regression	100	100	100	100
SARS-Cov-2 Ct-scan [DS2]	Random Forest	91.35	91.35	91.35	91.35
	SVM	98.39	98.40	98.39	98.39
	Logistic Regression	97.98	98.00	97.80	97.99
Mendeley's Covid Pneumonia [DS3]	Random Forest	100	100	100	100
	SVM	100	100	100	100
	Logistic Regression	100	100	100	100
Covid-Pneumonia-Normal-chest x-raypa [DS4] (3 Classes)	Random Forest	92.35	92.77	92.41	92.36
	SVM	94.54	94.85	94.58	94.52
	Logistic Regression	94.64	94.62	94.62	94.60
Covid-19 Radiography [DS5] (3 Classes)	Random Forest	97.13	97.24	97.16	97.19
	SVM	98.56	98.61	98.58	98.59
	Logistic Regression	98.43	98.47	98.45	98.46

In this section we compare our model's best results with other works that have used the same datasets as has been used in this work. Table 3 lists all the works using same datasets as in our experiment. As evident from Table 3 that our work has improved accuracy than most of the listed works (Figs. 3, 4, 5, 6 and 7).

Table 3. Performance comparison with existing works using same datasets.

Dataset	Work	Method	Accuracy
Covid & Common Pneumonia	Yan et al. [23]	MSCNN	97.7
	Han et al. [24]	Semi-Supervised	97.32
	Proposed Work	**Densenet169+ML Classifiers**	**100.00**
SARS-Cov-2 Ct-scan	Panwar et al. [25]	VGG-19 +Grad-CAM	95.61
	Silva et al. [26]	Voting based Deep learning	98.99
	Proposed Work	**Densenet169+ML Classifiers**	**98.39**
Covid-Pneumonia-Normal-chest-x-raypa	Haghanifar et al. [27]	CheXNet+Transfer learning	99.04
	Islam et al. [28]	CNN + LSTM	99.40
	Proposed Work	**Densenet169+ML Classifiers**	**94.64**
Covid-19 Radiography	Chowdhary et al. [13]	CNN	99.7
	Gaur et al. [20]	VGG16, InceptionV3 & EfficientNetB0	92.93
	Abiyev et al. [17]	CNN	98.3
	Proposed work	**Densenet169+ML Classifiers**	**98.56**

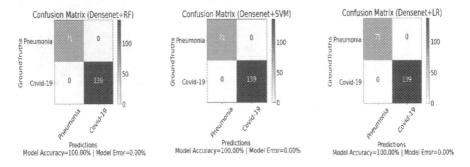

Fig. 3. Confusion Matrix for Covid-19 and Common Pneumonia Dataset having 2 classes.

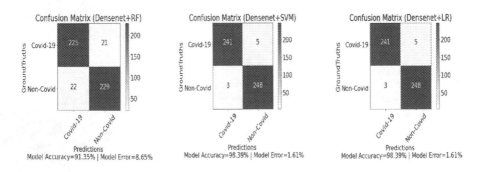

Fig. 4. Confusion Matrix for SARS-Cov-2 Ct-scan Dataset having 2 classes.

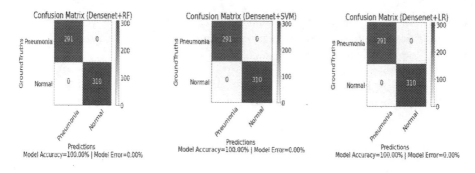

Fig. 5. Confusion Matrix for Mendeley's Covid Pneumonia Dataset having 2 classes.

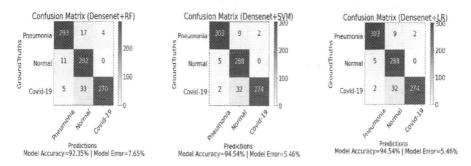

Fig. 6. Confusion Matrix for Covid-Pneumonia-Normal-chest-x-raypa Dataset having 3 classes.

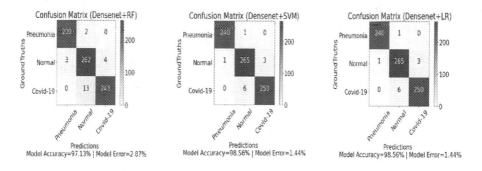

Fig. 7. Confusion Matrix for Covid-19 Radiography Dataset having 3 classes.

5   Conclusion

Pneumonia is a pulmonary disease that can turn deadly if timely medical intervention is not made available. It is one of the leading causes of deaths worldwide. The previous works have focused on various ML and DL methods for detecting various kinds of diseases. Nowadays, researchers are inclined towards using the DL methods more as they are producing promising results. Our proposed model evaluates various Densenet169 and classifier (SVM,RF and LR) combinations for classifying Pneumonia correctly from similar diseases. We got an accuracy of 100% for combinations of Densenet169+ML Classifiers while using DS1 & DS3. The combinations Densenet+SVM and Densenet+LR obtained 98.56% & 98.43% for DS5 and 98.39% & 97.98% for DS2. Therefore, we can say that our model is capable of accurately detecting Pneumonia from CXR and CT-Scan images.

References

1. Cruz, A.A.: Global surveillance, prevention and control of chronic respiratory diseases: a comprehensive approach. World Health Organization, Geneva (2007)
2. Wardlaw, T.M., Johansson, E.W., Hodge, M.J.: Pneumonia: the forgotten killer of children. UNICEF, New York (2006)
3. Gilani, Z., et al.: A literature review and survey of childhood pneumonia etiology studies: 2000–2010. Clin. Infect. Diseases **54**(suppl_2), 102–108 (2012)
4. Wunderink, R.G., Waterer, G.: Advances in the causes and management of community acquired pneumonia in adults. BMJ **358**, j2471 (2017)
5. Cunha, B.A., Brusch, J.L., et al.: Hospital-acquired pneumonia (nosocomial pneumonia) and ventilator-associated pneumonia. Drugs and Diseases (2018)
6. Aydogdu, M., Ozyilmaz, E., Aksoy, H., Gursel, G., Ekim, N.: Mortality prediction in community-acquired pneumonia requiring mechanical ventilation; values of pneumonia and intensive care unit severity scores. Tuberk. Toraks **58**(1), 25–34 (2010)
7. Stephen, O., Sain, M., Maduh, U.J., Jeong, D.-U.: An efficient deep learning approach to pneumonia classification in healthcare. J. Healthcare Eng. **2019**, 4180949 (2019)
8. Chowdhury, M.E., et al.: Wearable real-time heart attack detection and warning system to reduce road accidents. Sensors **19**(12), 2780 (2019)
9. Kallianos, K., et al.: How far have we come? artificial intelligence for chest radiograph interpretation. Clin. Radiol. **74**(5), 338–345 (2019)
10. Tahir, A.M., et al.: A systematic approach to the design and characterization of a smart insole for detecting vertical ground reaction force (vgrf) in gait analysis. Sensors **20**(4), 957 (2020)
11. Rajpurkar, P., et al.: Deep learning for chest radiograph diagnosis: A retrospective comparison of the chexnext algorithm to practicing radiologists. PLoS Med. **15**(11), 1002686 (2018)
12. Li, Q., bauthorCai, W., Wang, X., Zhou, Y., Feng, D.D., Chen, M.: Medical image classification with convolutional neural network. In: 2014 13th International Conference on Control Automation Robotics & Vision (ICARCV), pp. 844–848. IEEE (2014)
13. Chowdhury, M.E., et al.: Can AI help in screening viral and COVID-19 pneumonia? IEEE Access **8**, 132665–132676 (2020)
14. Bhandary, A., et al.: Deep-learning framework to detect lung abnormality-a study with chest x-ray and lung CT scan images. Pattern Recogn. Lett. **129**, 271–278 (2020)
15. Yadav, S.S., Jadhav, S.M.: Deep convolutional neural network based medical image classification for disease diagnosis. J. Big Data **6**(1), 1–18 (2019). https://doi.org/10.1186/s40537-019-0276-2

16. Kermany, D.S., et al.: Identifying medical diagnoses and treatable diseases by image-based deep learning. Cell **172**(5), 1122–1131 (2018)
17. Abiyev, R.H., Ismail, A.: Covid-19 and pneumonia diagnosis in x-ray images using convolutional neural networks. Mathematical Problems in Engineering 2021 (2021)
18. Xu, R., et al.: Unsupervised detection of pulmonary opacities for computer-aided diagnosis of covid-19 on CT images. In: 2020 25th International Conference on Pattern Recognition (ICPR), pp. 9007–9014. IEEE (2021)
19. Ibrahim, D.M., Elshennawy, N.M., Sarhan, A.M.: Deep-chest: Multi-classification deep learning model for diagnosing COVID-19, pneumonia, and lung cancer chest diseases. Comput. Biol. Med. **132**, 104348 (2021)
20. Gaur, L., Bhatia, U., Jhanjhi, N., Muhammad, G., Masud, M.: Medical image-based detection of covid-19 using deep convolution neural networks. Multimedia syst. **2021**, 1–10 (2021)
21. Rahman, T., et al.: Transfer learning with deep convolutional neural network (CNN) for pneumonia detection using chest x-ray. Appl. Sci. **10**(9), 3233 (2020)
22. Elshennawy, N.M., Ibrahim, D.M.: Deep-pneumonia framework using deep learning models based on chest x-ray images. Diagnostics **10**(9), 649 (2020)
23. Yan, T., Wong, P.K., Ren, H., Wang, H., Wang, J., Li, Y.: Automatic distinction between COVID-19 and common pneumonia using multi-scale convolutional neural network on chest CT scans. Chaos Solitons Fract. **140**, 110153 (2020)
24. Han, C.H., Kim, M., Kwak, J.T.: Semi-supervised learning for an improved diagnosis of COVID-19 in CT images. PLoS ONE **16**(4), 0249450 (2021)
25. Panwar, H., Gupta, P., Siddiqui, M.K., Morales-Menendez, R., Bhardwaj, P., Singh, V.: A deep learning and grad-cam based color visualization approach for fast detection of COVID-19 cases using chest x-ray and ct-scan images. Chaos Solitons Fract. **140**, 110190 (2020)
26. Silva, P., et al.: COVID-19 detection in CT images with deep learning: a voting-based scheme and cross-datasets analysis. Inf. Med. Unlocked **20**, 100427 (2020)
27. Haghanifar, A., Majdabadi, M.M., Choi, Y., Deivalakshmi, S., Ko, S.: COVID-CXNet: Detecting COVID-19 in frontal chest x-ray images using deep learning. Multimedia Tools Appl. **81**, 1–31 (2022)
28. Islam, M.Z., Islam, M.M., Asraf, A.: A combined deep CNN-LSTM network for the detection of novel coronavirus (COVID-19) using x-ray images. Inf. Med. Unlocked **20**, 100412 (2020)

Classification of Synthetic Aperture Radar Images Using a Modified DenseNet Model

Alicia Passah[(✉)] and Debdatta Kandar

Department of Information Technology, North-Eastern Hill University,
Shillong 793022, Meghalaya, India
`{alicia,dkandar}@nehu.ac.in`

Abstract. The popularity of deep learning has grown significantly among various researchers worldwide. Different deep learning models have been adopted in multiple applications wherein appreciable results are witnessed. However, several new models are yet to be explored for SAR image classification. Classification of SAR images are still suffering from issues such as misclassification or faulty predictions due to unreadable quality of images acquired by SAR systems, resulting in erroneous outcomes. This work focuses on applying one of the recent deep learning models called DenseNet to SAR image classification. Based on the study and experimental analysis carried in this work, a modified version of DenseNet called DenseNet179 is proposed in this work, by incorporating two types of dense blocks in the architecture of the model: one with the usual convolution, while the second with the depthwise convolution. The model is implemented and tested using the MSTAR benchmark acquired by the X-band SAR sensor. Results show that the incorporation of depthwise convolutions enables advanced feature learning of the model, with not as many parameters compared to all the DenseNet variants. The accuracy achieved on the new model is 93.9% which is higher than any of the variants of DenseNet implemented in this work for SAR image classification and outperforms various existing methods such as ATR-CNN and CDSPP.

Keywords: Deep Learning · DenseNet · Image Processing · SAR Images · Target Classification

1 Introduction

Synthetic Aperture Radar (SAR) is a radar popularly known for its self- illuminating nature. It is usually attached to a platform in motion and disburses electromagnetic waves to the earth's surface to record the echoing signals. The most important characteristic of a SAR radar is that it can work as a radar with a larger antenna, though the antenna used is smaller in size. This is because the path of the flight it travels determines the antenna size. Hence, a synthetically larger antenna could generate higher resolution image signals. This makes SAR

D. Gupta et al. (Eds.): CVIP 2022, CCIS 1777, pp. 610–622, 2023.
https://doi.org/10.1007/978-3-031-31417-9_46

images useful for a wide range of applications, including monitoring oil leakages in oceans, detecting illegal movement of carriers in ports, and even in military activities. Most of the applications involved categorising the images or targets precisely, and this process is called classification. Classifying SAR images manually is tedious, especially because SAR images are highly contaminated with grainy features called speckle noise. The images are therefore not predictable even by humans. Various algorithms from the statistical approach to the machine learning approaches have been developed to classify SAR images [3,5,21,23]. However, incorrect predictions or misclassification is an issue of concern. Since false predictions are not affordable in real SAR systems, therefore the classification of SAR images is still an open area of research. With the popularity of deep learning, researchers have started incorporating deep learning-based approaches in various fields, from diagnosing diseases, and fake news analysis, to detection of plant disease, and even in SAR image analysis [14,17,20,22]. However, new models are yet to be explored in SAR image classification. Hence, this motivates us to implement and analyse one of the deep learning models named DenseNet [10] on SAR image classification. The major contribution of the paper are as follows.

i. Four variants of DenseNets have been implemented and analysed for classifying SAR images.
ii. A modified DenseNet model has also been proposed in this work for SAR image classification.
iii. An analysis of the proposed model using normal as well as depthwise convolutions have also been carried out to prove the performance of the proposed model.
iv. Results have also been highlighted and compared with few existing methods.

The rest of the paper is set up as follows. Section 2 discusses the related background of this work. The implementation of the different DenseNet variants along with the results are discussed in Sect. 3. Section 4 discusses the proposed work, results, and the overall performance followed by a conclusion in Sect. 5.

2   Background

In this section, we present the related works that include the existing literature on SAR image classification using deep learning and a brief discussion on one of the deep learning models named DenseNet along with its different variants.

2.1   Existing Deep Learning Based Works on SAR Image Classification

Numerous works have been projected in the literature concerning several issues related to SAR image classification, such as limited labelled data, imprecise sealand masking, false alarms, classifying mixed size targets, and misclassification of targets or scenes in images [15]. The work by C. Bentes et al. [2] designed a deep learning model for classifying oceanographic targets with less labelled data.

The model is made up of a denoising auto-encoder and several convolutional layers. Focusing on the issue of limited SAR datasets causing severe overfitting, the model proposed by S. Chen et al. [5] comprised of only convolutional layers with no fully connected layers for classifying targets from the Moving Stationary Target Acquisition and Recognition (MSTAR) benchmark [12,16]. The model is, however, not adaptable to noisy images. A different work by C. Bentes et al. [3] proposed a model that learns from multiple resolution inputs to achieve better feature representations for the classification of MSTAR targets. The model is made up of only four convolutional layers and a dense layer. In the work proposed by C. Wang et al. [21], a model is designed for classifying different categories of sea and sea-ice. The model is comprised of the traditional convolutional architecture with only three convolution layers and two fully connected layers. Mis-classification and false alarms exist in the results of this work. Another work by R. Shang et al., MNet [18], aims to classify MSTAR targets using convolutional layers and a memory to store the learned data in order to process the subsequent unlabeled data. The architecture used in MNet is also comprised of only five convolutional layers. The aforementioned works show that only the traditional convolutional networks are adopted for various images, scenes or target classification. It may also be mentioned that these works face issues like misclassification and detection of false alarms. Therefore, evaluating the performance of SAR image classification using recent deep learning models such as DenseNet will help give insight into how classification of SAR images performs using the four variants of DenseNet. A modified DenseNet model have also been proposed and implemented in this work that has further helped improve classification performance compared to the original variants.

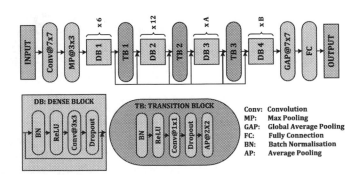

Fig. 1. Architecture of the DenseNet model

2.2 DenseNet Model and Its Variants

This sub-section explains a summary of the DenseNet model and its different variants, namely the DenseNet121, DenseNet169, DenseNet201, and DenseNet264.

DenseNet. The DenseNet [10] is a deep learning model made up of several convolutional layers. As the name suggests, DenseNet has dense connections in its architecture, meaning that every layer has a direct connection to every other layer in the network. This way, each layer shares knowledge about the information received from preceding layers with its subsequent layers. Like ResNet [8], the DenseNet was developed to solve the vanishing gradient issue caused by deeper layers. The DenseNet is known for its high computational efficiency due to the concatenation concept it follows in every connection it has with other layers. The DenseNet model is bagged with several advantages. The model has better generalisation capability as gradients are easily propagated due to independent connections to earlier layers. It also has less trainable parameters and low computational complexity. The features learned by the DenseNet model are more diversified due to the dense connections between every layer. The DenseNet model is made up of several dense blocks and transition layers. The overall architecture, along with the configuration of the dense blocks and transition blocks, is shown in Fig. 1.

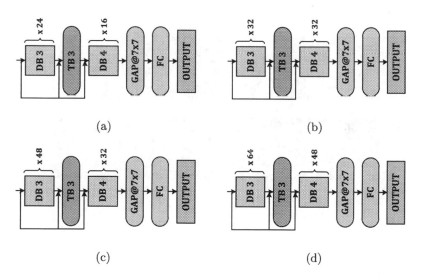

Fig. 2. The latter layers of: (a) DenseNet121, (b) DenseNet169, (c) DenseNet201, and (d) DenseNet264

Variants of DenseNet. There are different versions of DenseNet, with each version differing slightly in the depth and configuration of the layers. The first variant of DenseNet, named DenseNet121, has a total of 121 layers comprising 120 convolutional layers and 1 fully connected layer. The architecture used in DenseNet121 follows the same pattern shown in Fig. 1, except that it differs in the end layers and is shown in Fig. 2 (a). The DenseNet121 achieved a top-1 accuracy of 75.0% on the ImageNet Large Scale Visual Recognition Challenge (ILSVRC). The second variant of DenseNet, named DenseNet169, is a deeper version of DenseNet, having 169 layers with 168 convolutional layers and 1 fully connected layer. The architecture of DenseNet169 model also follows the pattern shown in Fig. 1, with latter layers shown in Fig. 2 (b). The DenseNet169 attained a top-1 accuracy of 76.2% on the ImageNet challenge. Another variant of Densenet called DenseNet201 is a far deeper model with a total of 201 layers comprising 200 convolutional layers and 1 fully connected layer. The end layers of the DenseNet201 are shown in Fig. 2 (c). The DenseNet201 achieved an accuracy of 77.3% on the top-1 level of the ImageNet challenge. The final variant of DenseNet is the DenseNet264 model. The model consists of 263 convolutional layers and 1 fully connected layer. Following the architecture shown in Fig. 1, the model's end layers are replaced by the model shown in Fig. 2 (d). The difference between all the variants of DenseNet lies only in the last two dense blocks with different numbers of convolutional layers. In the next section, the implementation that has been carried out for the classification of SAR images using the different variants of DenseNet along with their results are discussed.

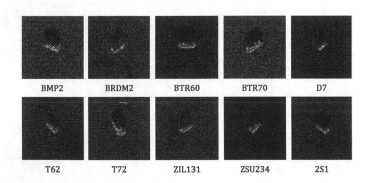

Fig. 3. Sample MSTAR images

3   Experimental Evaluation of the Different DenseNet Variants

3.1   Implementation

For our experiments, we have programmed all the variants of the DenseNet model using the Google collaboratory notebook. For the datasets, we have used the freely available MSTAR benchmark created by Sandia National Laboratory in collaboration with Defense Advanced Research Projects Agency (DARPA) cite [7] and Air Force Research Laboratory (AFRL) [1]. The data was collected using SAR sensor with X-band and consisted of military targets with ten different classes, which include four types of armoured personnel carriers: BMP-2, BRDM2, BTR60, BTR70; two kinds of tanks: T62 and T72; two types of trucks: ZIL131 and ZSU234; a bulldozer: D7; and a rocket launcher: 2S1. Sample images are shown in Fig. 3. A total of 4972 images are used in our experiments, where, 2747 are used for training the model, while the remaining 2225 are used for testing. We have also augmented the data during the experiments by applying a 40 degrees rotation range. Furthermore, the images are shifted horizontally and vertically by 0.2% and zoomed by a factor of 0.2. Augmentation helps generate a larger dataset for training deep learning models, allowing better generalisation of the model. The values of the hyper-parameters adopted at the time of model training are shown in Table 1. We have used the Adaptive Moment (Adam) [11] as optimizer with a learning rate of 1×10^{-4}. The models are trained for about 20 epochs. The results and observations obtained from our experiments on the four DenseNet variants are discussed in the following subsection.

Table 1. Hyperparameters used for training the deep learning models

Hyperparameters	Values
Optimizer	Adam
Learning rate	1×10^{-4}
Epoch	10
Batch size	20
Dropout	0.5

3.2 Results and Observations

The different variants of DenseNet react differently to the classification of SAR images. Our experimental results show that the DenseNet169 works best on SAR image classification by attaining an accuracy of 91.2% on the test data with a considerable number of parameters compared to DenseNet201 and DenseNet264. The DenseNet121 model also performed well with just 6.9 million parameters achieving an accuracy of 80% on the test data. However, when the model is further deepened, as in the case of DenseNet201 and DenseNet264, the classification performance on the MSTAR images dropped. Hence, from the results of our experiments on the DenseNet variants, we observe that the SAR image classification accuracy after a certain threshold on the number of layers, becomes inversely proportional to the depth of the network. Classification results of each DenseNet variant implemented on SAR data are shown in Table 2. We have also presented the confusion matrix of each case in Fig. 4. The number of parameters involved in each model is also highlighted in Table 2, wherein it is observed that the outperforming version of DenseNet is however, computationally expensive in nature.

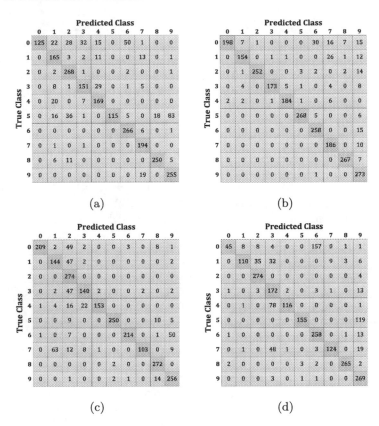

Fig. 4. The Confusion matrices depicting the class predictions of the four Densenet variants. (a) DenseNet121, (b) DenseNet169, (c) DenseNet201, (d) DenseNet264. (0-9 represents the ten classes; 0: 2S1, 1: BMP-2, 2: BRDM2, 3: BTR60, 4: BTR70, 5: D7, 6: T62, 7: T72, 8: ZIL131, 9: ZSU234).

4   Proposed Work

As observed from the results of the previous implementation on the different DenseNet variants for SAR image classification, the outperforming model attains an accuracy of 91.2%. However, the number parameters engaged are 12.5% million. Therefore, achieving better accuracy with relatively less number of parameters is challenging. We have therefore proposed a modified version of DenseNet that relatively has lesser parameters than DenseNet169 (the outperforming model), obtaining an improved classification accuracy. The architecture of the proposed model is shown in Fig. 5. The model follows the pattern of the original DenseNet model, except that it has two types of dense blocks. The first dense block is made up of only normal convolutions, while the second dense block is made up of both normal and depthwise convolutions. Hence the proposed architecture has a depthwise layer at every dense block, summing to a total of 58 depthwise layers. Therefore, the overall network consists of about

Table 2. Classification results of the different DenseNet models

Models	DenseNet121	DenseNet169	DenseNet201	DenseNet264
No. of Parameters	7.0 m	12.5 m	18.1 m	30.6 m
Accuracy	80.7%	91.2%	83.5%	75.4%

179 convolutional layers. hence we termed our proposed model as DenseNet179. It may be mentioned that the level of computation is much lower in a depthwise convolution than in a normal convolution. This is because each channel is convolved using respective filters unlike in normal convolution, where a single filter convolves the entire image depth. Therefore, we have incorporated depthwise convolution in the proposed DenseNet179. The detailed discussion on the experiments and results of the proposed DenseNet179 model are presented in the following subsections.

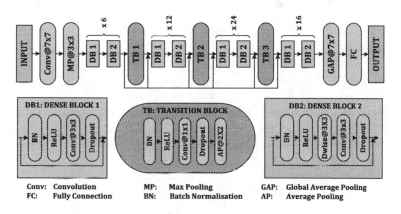

Fig. 5. Architecture of the Proposed DenseNet179 model

4.1 Implementation, Results and Discussions

The proposed model has been implemented and tested on the MSTAR benchmark using Google colaboratory notebook. The hyperparameters shown in Table 1 has been adopted for training the model. It is worth mentioning that the approach incorporated in the proposed DenseNet179 model has also been tested and evaluated in all the deeper variants of DenseNet in order to check their individual performances. A summary of the results of the proposed approach when applied to deeper variants of DenseNet are highlighted in Table 3. From the results, we realised that the deeper variants of DenseNet does not converge well when depthwise layers are added. This is because the models are already deep and further increasing the depth of the network results in saturation of the model, especially when there is not enough data. However, the proposed model has just the right number of layers to incorporate the desirable number of depthwise layers so as to achieve the considerable results.

Table 3. Performance of the deeper variants of DenseNet with depthwise layers

Models + Depthwise layers	No. of Parameters	Accuracy
DenseNet169	12.60 million	83.3%
DenseNet201	18.20 million	71.91%
DenseNet264	30.90 million	71.46%

The classification results attained by the proposed DenseNet179 model compared to all the four variants of DenseNet namely DenseNet121, DenseNet169, DenseNet201, and DenseNet264 are presented in Table 4. The proposed model attained a classification accuracy of 93.7% and outperforms all the other four DenseNet variants. This show that the use of depthwise convolution has helped in better discrimination of features because the depth of the network is also given emphasis during training, and relevant features are rarely interchanged between channels within the network thereby retaining their identity. The number of parameters involved in the proposed model is also at par with that of the DenseNet121 model. It is therefore realised that even with up to 179 total convolutions, the number of parameters is equivalent to that of only 121 convolutions. The confusion matrix associated with the results of the proposed model is presented in Fig. 6. In the proposed model, the number of layers have actually been increased but due to the use of depth wise convolution in place of the normal convolution, the computational complexity in terms of parameters, is controlled. To justify this, we have also implemented the model having the same number of layers as the proposed DenseNet179, but using the normal convolution layers. The performance of the two models is highlighted in Table 5. The performance of the proposed work have also been compared with several existing methods that use the same benchmark for classification of SAR images, and is highlighted in Table 6. It is observed that the proposed method with depthwise layers performed considerably well as compared to several other methods. The graphical representation of the classification accuracy comparing various methods have also been highlighted in Fig. 7.

Table 4. Results comparison of the proposed model and the different DenseNet variants

Models	No. of Parameters	Accuracy
DenseNet121	7.00 million	80.7%
DenseNet169	12.50 million	91.2%
DenseNet201	18.10 million	83.5%
DenseNet264	30.60 million	75.4%
Proposed Model	**7.04** million	**93.7%**

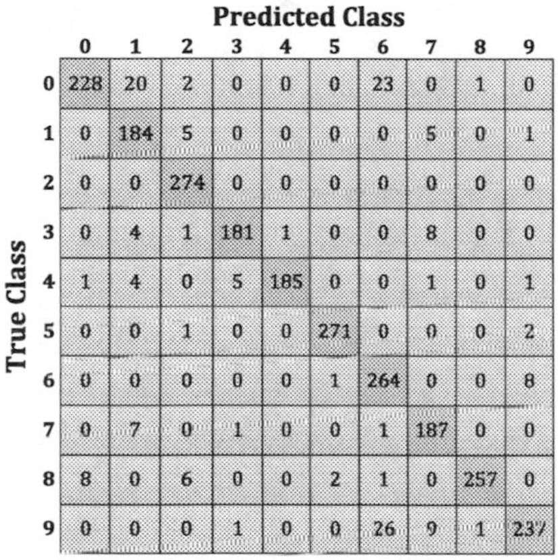

Predicted Class

True Class	0	1	2	3	4	5	6	7	8	9
0	228	20	2	0	0	0	23	0	1	0
1	0	184	5	0	0	0	0	5	0	1
2	0	0	274	0	0	0	0	0	0	0
3	0	4	1	181	1	0	0	8	0	0
4	1	4	0	5	185	0	0	1	0	1
5	0	0	1	0	0	271	0	0	0	2
6	0	0	0	0	0	1	264	0	0	8
7	0	7	0	1	0	0	1	187	0	0
8	8	0	6	0	0	2	1	0	257	0
9	0	0	0	1	0	0	26	9	1	237

Fig. 6. Confusion matrix depicting the class predictions of the proposed DenseNet179 model

Table 5. Performance comparison of the proposed model when using normal convolutions versus when using depthwise convolutions

Proposed Model:	No. of conv. layers	No. of Parameters	Accuracy
With normal convolutions	179	7.51 million	89.9%
With depthwise convolutions	179	7.04 million	93.7%

Table 6. Comparison of the proposed work with various existing methods that use the same dataset

Model	Accuracy
SVM [9]	85.88%
ATR-CNN [4]	90.00%
CNN-AD [6]	89.00%
EMACH [19]	88.00%
CDSPP [13]	91.00%
Proposed model	93.70%

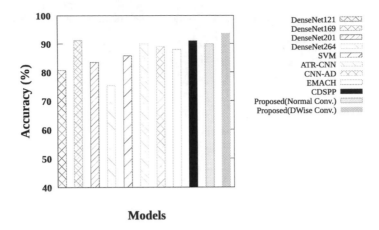

Fig. 7. Graphical comparisons of the results obtained by the different methods on SAR image classification

5   Conclusion

One of the prominent deep learning models named DenseNet has been implemented in this work focusing on the analysis of its different versions on SAR image classification using the MSTAR benchmark. A modified DenseNet model has also been proposed in this work that aims at improving the performance accuracy with complexity better than the original variants. Comparisons of the proposed model with several other works have also been done. It is observed from this work that the depthwise convolutions used in the proposed model helps in better feature learning with fewer number of parameters compared to the model with normal convolutions, even though the number of layers are the same. As future work, the proposed model can be optimized and tuned such that parameters will further be reduced while further increasing the overall classification accuracy. Other new models such as NasNet and EfficientNet can also be studied to classify SAR images.

References

1. AFRL: The Air Force Research Laboratory. https://www.afrl.af.mil/ (2022). Accessed 25 Jan 2022
2. Bentes, C., Velotto, D., Lehner, S.: Target classification in oceanographic sar images with deep neural networks: architecture and initial results. In: 2015 IEEE International Geoscience and Remote Sensing Symposium (IGARSS), pp. 3703–3706 (2015)
3. Bentes, C., Velotto, D., Tings, B.: Ship classification in TerrasSAR-X images with convolutional neural networks. IEEE J. Oceanic Eng. **43**(1), 258–266 (2018)
4. Chen, S., Wang, H.: Sar target recognition based on deep learning. In: 2014 International Conference on Data Science and Advanced Analytics (DSAA), pp. 541–547 (2014)

5. Chen, S., Wang, H., Xu, F., Jin, Y.: Target classification using the deep convolutional networks for SAR images. IEEE Trans. Geosci. Remote Sens. **54**(8), 4806–4817 (2016)

6. Cui, Z., Tang, C., Cao, Z., Dang, S.: Sar unlabeled target recognition based on updating CNN with assistant decision. IEEE Geosci. Remote Sens. Lett. **15**(10), 1585–1589 (2018)

7. DARPA: Defense Advanced Research Projects Agency. https://www.darpa.mil/ (2022). Accessed 25 Jan 2022

8. He, K., Zhang, X., Ren, S., Sun, J.: Deep residual learning for image recognition. In: Proceedings of the IEEE Conference on Computer Vision and Pattern Recognition, pp. 770–778 (2016)

9. Hearst, M.A., Dumais, S.T., Osuna, E., Platt, J., Scholkopf, B.: Support vector machines. IEEE Intell. Syst. Appl. **13**(4), 18–28 (1998)

10. Huang, G., Liu, Z., Van Der Maaten, L., Weinberger, K.Q.: Densely connected convolutional networks. In: 2017 IEEE Conference on Computer Vision and Pattern Recognition (CVPR), pp. 2261–2269 (2017)

11. Kingma, D.P., Ba, J.: Adam: a method for stochastic optimization. arXiv preprint arXiv:1412.6980, pp. 1–15 (2014)

12. Air Force Research Laboratory: MSTAR Public Targets (2021). https://www.sdms.afrl.af.mil/index.php?collection=mstar. Accessed 22 May 2020

13. Liu, M., Chen, S., Wu, J., Lu, F., Wang, J., Yang, T.: Configuration recognition via class-dependent structure preserving projections with application to targets in SAR images. IEEE J. Select. Top. Appl. Earth Observ. Remote Sens. **11**(6), 2134–2146 (2018). https://doi.org/10.1109/JSTARS.2018.2830103

14. Luo, X., Li, J., Chen, M., Yang, X., Li, X.: Ophthalmic disease detection via deep learning with a novel mixture loss function. IEEE J. Biomed. Health Inform. **25**(9), 3332–3339 (2021)

15. Passah, A., Sur, S.N., Paul, B., Kandar, D.: Sar image classification: a comprehensive study and analysis. IEEE Access **10**, 20385–20399 (2022)

16. Ross, T.D., Worrell, S.W., Velten, V.J., Mossing, J.C., Bryant, M.L.: Standard SAR ATR evaluation experiments using the MSTAR public release data set. In: Zelnio, E.G. (ed.) Algorithms for Synthetic Aperture Radar Imagery V, vol. 3370, pp. 566–573. International Society for Optics and Photonics (1998)

17. Saleh, H., Alharbi, A., Alsamhi, S.H.: OPCNN-FAKE: optimized convolutional neural network for fake news detection. IEEE Access **9**, 129471–129489 (2021)

18. Shang, R., Wang, J., Jiao, L., Stolkin, R., Hou, B., Li, Y.: SAR targets classification based on deep memory convolution neural networks and transfer parameters. IEEE J. Select. Top. Appl. Earth Observ. Remote Sens. **11**(8), 2834–2846 (2018)

19. Singh, R., Kumar, B.V.: Performance of the extended maximum average correlation height (emach) filter and the polynomial distance classifier correlation filter (pdccf) for multiclass SAR detection and classification. In: Algorithms for Synthetic Aperture Radar Imagery IX. vol. 4727, pp. 265–276. International Society for Optics and Photonics (2002)

20. Tetila, E.C., et al.: Automatic recognition of soybean leaf diseases using UAV images and deep convolutional neural networks. IEEE Geosci. Remote Sens. Lett. **17**(5), 903–907 (2020)

21. Wang, C., Zhang, H., Wang, Y., Zhang, B.: Sea ice classification with convolutional neural networks using sentinel-1 scansar images. In: IGARSS 2018–2018 IEEE International Geoscience and Remote Sensing Symposium, pp. 7125–7128 (2018)

22. Yu, H., et al.: Corn leaf diseases diagnosis based on k-means clustering and deep learning. IEEE Access **9**, 143824–143835 (2021)
23. Zhang, A., Yang, X., Fang, S., Ai, J.: Region level SAR image classification using deep features and spatial constraints. ISPRS J. Photogramm. Remote. Sens. **163**, 36–48 (2020)

Combining Non-local Sparse and Residual Channel Attentions for Single Image Super-resolution Across Modalities

Manali Bhavsar and Srimanta Mandal[(✉)] [iD]

Dhirubhai Ambani Institute of Information and Communication Technology,
Gandhinagar, Gujarat, India
{202011022,srimanta_mandal}@daiict.ac.in

Abstract. Single image super-resolution (SISR) is an ill-posed problem
that aims to generate a high-resolution (HR) image from a single low-
resolution (LR) image. The main objective of super-resolution is to add
relevant high-frequency detail to complement the available low-frequency
information. Classical techniques such as non-local similarity and sparse
representations have shown promising results in the SISR task. Nowadays, deep learning techniques such as convolutional neural networks
(CNN) can extract deep features to improve the SISR results. However, CNN does not explicitly consider similar information in the image.
Hence, we employ the non-local sparse attention (NLSA) module in the
CNN framework such that it can explore the non-local similarity within
an image. We consider sparsity in the non-local operation by focusing
on a particular group named attention bin among many groups of features. NLSA is intended to retain the long-range of non-local operation
modeling capacity while benefiting from the efficiency and robustness
of sparse representation. However, NLSA focuses on similarity in spatial dimension by neglecting any channel-wise significance. Hence, we
try to rescale the channel-specific features adaptively while taking into
account channel interdependence by using residual channel attention. We
combine the advantages of non-local sparse attention (NLSA) and residual channel attention to produce competitive results in different image
modalities such as optical color images, depth maps, and X-Ray without
re-training.

Keywords: Single Image Super Resolution · Deep Learning
Techniques · Channel Attention · Non-local Sparse Attention

1 Introduction

Single Image Super-Resolution (SISR) aims to produce a high resolution (HR)
image from a given low resolution (LR) image. Since multiple HR images can
generate the same LR image, SR reconstruction is an ill-posed problem. Hence,
choosing a particular solution among the many possibilities requires some regularization techniques. If multiple LR images of the same scene are available, the

D. Gupta et al. (Eds.): CVIP 2022, CCIS 1777, pp. 623–637, 2023.
https://doi.org/10.1007/978-3-031-31417-9_47

shift among the images can be used to regularize the problem in deriving an HR image. This kind of methods broadly lie in the category of multiple image super-resolution (MISR) [5,6,12,22]. The requirement of multiple sub-pixel shifted images become the bottleneck for this kind of method. Hence, the focus is shifted towards a group of techniques known as single image super-resolution (SISR).

In SISR, classical techniques such as non-local similarity and sparse representations are quite popular techniques [17,18]. Non-local similarity explores the recurrent pattern globally within an image. The method basically performs a linear combination of similar patches across the entire image to produce HR patch [17,21]. The sparse-representation based techniques use dictionaries to produce HR image patches. The dictionaries are either learned from HR-LR image pairs or are built using pre-defined transformations such as DCT, DWT, etc. [7,18,26,28]. Recent developments and advancements in deep architectures have demonstrated state-of-the-art outcomes in SR problems across several image datasets [25]. SRCNN [3], the first deep learning architecture for SR is developed based on convolutional neural network (CNN). Later on, the basic architecture is improved in several works for SR [4,9,10,23].

Most CNN-based methods do not consider similar information across images. Further, the significance of sparse representation is seldom considered in the SR task. Here, our goal is to combine the advantages of classical methods, such as non-local and sparse representation, with deep learning techniques. To retain the global modeling ability of the non-local similarity with efficiency and robustness, we try to impose sparse representation with non-local attention. Non-local sparse attention mechanism considers similar patterns across the image spatially. However, spatial attention often neglects the contributions of individual channels. Thus, we further incorporate residual channel attention blocks, where the channel attention (CA) mechanism adaptively re-scales channel-wise features. This CA mechanism enables our network to focus more on relevant channel-wise features while improving discriminative learning performance. Indicatively, we try to embed the non-local sparse attention and residual channel attention in a CNN framework to super-resolve a single image. Further, we demonstrate the ability of our network to super-resolve different image modalities such as color images, depth maps, and X-ray images. The salient point is that our network can produce very good results even without re-training it on other image modalities.

1.1   Contribution

The key contributions can be summarized as follows:

- We propose a deep architecture that contains non-local sparse attention and residual channel attention for single image super-resolution.
- Non-local sparse attention block enables the network to explore non-local spatial similarity in an image using sparse representation.
- Residual channel attention blocks assign different weights to each of the channels according to their importance.
- The proposed architecture is evaluated qualitatively and quantitatively on different image modalities without retraining individually.

The rest of the paper is organized as follows. Section 2 highlights a few existing deep learning architectures for the SISR task. Section 3 discusses the proposed method based on non-local sparse attention and channel attention. In Sect. 4, we discuss and compare the experimental results of our method. Section 5 concludes the paper.

2   Related Works

An overview of classical super-resolution methods can be found in [22]. Many recent works use deep CNNs to address the SISR issue due to their excellent feature representation capabilities. Super Resolution using Convolutional Neural Network(SRCNN) [3] works based on a simple three-layer network, where the LR image is first upscaled by the desired factor with the help of the bi-cubic interpolation method. The initial up-scaled image is then fed to the network for feature extraction by convolution and non-linear mapping. Finally, the extracted feature is used to reconstruct the HR image. Very Deep SR (VDSR) [9] increases the depth of the network by assembling more convolution layers with the residual practice. VDSR assembles hierarchical features using dense residual connections. Attention mechanisms in deep neural networks help focus on important data while suppressing the effect of less significant data.

The non-local sparse attention network (NLSN) [21] considers non-local information. The non-local operation looks globally for comparable patterns and aggregates those connected features selectively to improve the representation. Although non-local attention is perspective and appealing in fusing characteristics, using it in the SISR job will raise several overlooked issues: i) The deeper layers tend to produce feature with global receptive field. Hence, the mutual correlation across deep features may be inaccurately calculated. ii) Calculating feature similarity across every pixel location is essential for global non-local attention. As a result, we get quadratic computational cost to image size. One option for addressing the above-mentioned issues is to confine the searching range of non-local operation inside a local neighborhood. However, it lowers commuting costs by missing out on a lot of global data.

Combining the sparsity phenomenon along with non-local operation will reduce the computational complexity of non-local from quadratic to the asymptotic linear with respect to the spatial dimension [21]. Searching for similarities inside a narrower content correlated bins will also direct the module's attention to more insightful and related locations. So, non-local sparse attention (NLSA) maintains the conventional non-local operation's global modeling capability while benefiting from the resilience and efficiency of its sparse representation. However, NLSA neglects channel-wise significance.

The Residual Channel Attention Network (RCAN) [29] contains a residual in residual (RIR) module that comprises residual groups connected by long skip connection for constructing a very deep network. Each residual group consists of several residual channel attention blocks (RCAB) with a short skip connection. RCAB enables the network to concentrate more on informative channels, but spatial similarity gets neglected.

3   Proposed Architecture

The proposed architecture can be observed in Fig. 1, which consists of two main modules: i) Non-local sparse attention (NLSA) and ii) Residual channel attention (RCA). NLSA is used to embrace long-range features by minimizing the complexity. RCA is embedded in residual groups through residual channel attention blocks to incorporate channel-wise significance.

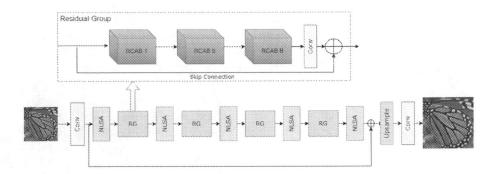

Fig. 1. Proposed Method Architecture

3.1   Non Local Sparse Attention Module

We first discuss non-local attention, followed by sparse representation of attention.

Non Local Attention. Non-local attention looks for spatial similarity across a given feature. Consider, the input feature $X \in R^{h \times w \times c}$, which is reshaped as $X \in R^{n \times c}$ where $n = hw$. The output of non-local attentions $y_i \in R^c$ is generated as:

$$y_i = \sum_{j=1}^{n} \frac{f(x_i, x_j)}{\sum_{\hat{j}=1}^{n} f(x_i, x_{\hat{j}})} g(x_j). \tag{1}$$

Here, $x_i, x_j, x_{\hat{j}}$ represents pixel-wise feature at respective location that is $i, j, \hat{j}$ on X. Here f computes mutual-similarity, and g represents the function for feature transformation, which can be computed as follows.

$$f(x_i, x_j) = e^{\theta(x_i)^T \phi(x_j)} = e^{(W_\theta x_i)^T W_\phi x_j}$$

$$g(x_j) = W_g x_j$$

Here, W_θ, W_ϕ, W_g are weight matrices, which means θ and ϕ are learned linear projections.

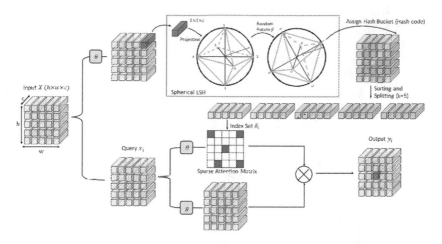

Fig. 2. Non-Local Sparse Attention [21]

Non-local Attention with Sparsity Constraint. Non-local attention comes with the limitations of the searching range. Hence, we apply sparsity constraint on non-local attention. The Eq. (1) can also be seen as $y_i = D\alpha_i$, which is sparse representation of y_i with D representing $[g(x_1), ..., g(x_n)] \in R^{c \times n}$ and α_i representing $[f(x_i, x_1), ..., f(x_i, x_n)] \in R^n$. According to Eq. (1), sparsity constraint on non-local attention can be employed by constraining the number of non-zeros of α to a minimum number k. From the above discussion, the general version of non-local attention with sparsity constraint may emerge as follows.

$$y_i = \sum_{j \in \delta_i} \frac{f(x_i, x_j)}{\sum_{\hat{j} \in \delta_i} f(x_i, x_{\hat{j}})} g(x_j) \tag{2}$$

$$y_i = D\alpha_i \quad s.t. \ ||\alpha_i||_0 \leq k \tag{3}$$

Non zero element indices of α_i is represented by δ_i, i.e., $\delta_i = \{j | \alpha_i[j] \neq 0\}$, $\alpha_i[j]$ is j^{th} element in α_i. This δ_i indicates the pixel location's group where the query should attend. The δ_i contains the identified locations from which we can calculate non-local attention; these groups are known as attention bins.

Target attention should be sparse and should contain the most significant elements. We can use Locality Sensitive Hashing (LSH) to create the desirable attention bin, which includes global and correlating components as well as the query element. If nearby elements are more likely than distant ones to share the same hash code, the hashing scheme is said to be locality sensitive. One type of LSH intended for angular distance is the spherical LSH. Intuitively, we can imagine it as the random rotation of a cross-polytope encircled by a hypersphere (see the first branch of Fig. 2). The hash function selects the nearest polytope vertex by projecting a tensor onto a hypersphere and represents it as a hash code. The smaller angular distance between two vectors is the deciding factor for assigning the same hash bin, which is the defined attention bin.

To obtain h hash bins, we must first take the projection of the targeted tensor onto one hypersphere and then randomly rotate that with a matrix $M \in R^{c \times h}$, a sample random rotation matrix with independent and identically distributed Gaussian entries $\hat{x} = M(\frac{x}{||x||_2})$. The hash bin is determined as $hb(x) = argmax_i(\hat{x})$. In this way, every element is associated with a hash bin. Thus, the entire space can be splitted into several bins of similar elements. $\delta_i = \{j | hb(x_j) = hb(x_i)\}$ can index the attention bin of x_i.

After determining δ_i for the target location i, the NLSA can be simply acquired from Eq. 2. Furthermore, as illustrated in Fig. 2, NLSA assigns each one of the pixel-wise features in X to a bin with a similar hash code depending on its content relevance, and only the elements of the related bin contribute to the output.

3.2   Residual Channel Attention Module

Residual channel attention is incorporated into the network through residual groups (RG). RG consists of multiple Residual Channel Attention Blocks (RCAB). The architecture of Residual Channel Attention Block is shown in Fig. 3.

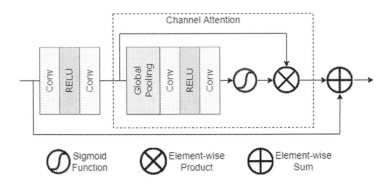

Fig. 3. Residual Channel Attention Block

RCAB contains residual blocks along with channel attention blocks. The channel attention processes the input data to produce a feature with weights highlighting channel-wise important features. Here, using global average pooling, we convert the channel-wise global spatial features into a channel descriptor. Further, short skip connections in the Residual group enable a smoother information flow from the input to the output. Additionally, it assists in addressing the over-fitting issue, which is often encountered by deep-learning models due to lesser data.

3.3 Loss Function

We use L_1 reconstruction loss to train the network. Given a training set $\{I_{LR}^i, I_{HR}^i\}_{i=1}^N$, which contains N LR inputs and their HR counterparts. The goal of the model is to minimize the L_1 loss function.

$$L(\Theta) = \frac{1}{N} \sum_{i=1}^{N} ||H_{model}(I_{LR}^i) - I_{HR}^i||_1 \tag{4}$$

Here H_{model} represents the output from the proposed model.

4 Experimental Results

4.1 Training and Implementation Details

For training, we set the number of bins to 144. In the network, we use five non-local sparse attention blocks and 4 Residual Groups, which contain 8 RCABs each. We use random cropped patches of size 48×48 for training. To optimize the model, we are using ADAM optimizer [11] with the parameters $\beta_1 = 0.9$, $\beta_2 = 0.99$ and $\epsilon = 10^{-8}$. This architecture is implemented using PyTorch and trained on Tesla T4 GPU.

We trained our network on DIV2K [25] image dataset, consisting 800 training images. In testing, we used the most popular benchmark test dataset for image super-resolution task namely, Set5 [1], Set14 [27], Urban100 [8]. B100 [19], and Manga109 [20].

4.2 Results and Comparison

In order to assess how effective our network is, we compare the result of the suggested network with those from state-of-the-art methods: SRCNN [3], VDSR [9], EDSR [14], NLRN [15], RNAN [30], SRFBN [13], RDN [31]. The quantitative results can be seen in Table 1 in terms of PSNR and SSIM values. The PSNR and SSIM values are imported from the respective literature.

We can notice in Table 1 that our method gives better results than the most of the existing methods like SRCNN [3], VDSR [9], EDSR [14], NLRN [15], RNAN [30], SRFBN [13], and RDN [31] for scale 2 for most of the datasets. For scale factor 3, our results are better as compared to SRCNN [3], VDSR [9], EDSR [14], NLRN [15] and RNAN [30]. For scale factor 4, our model is able to generate competitive results as compared to state-of-the-art approaches. Note that RNAN incorporates non-local information in the residual framework. NLRN also considers non-local information in a recurrent neural network. However, the results of our method are better than both of them for most of the cases. This also highlights the significance of considering spatial similarity as well as channel-wise significance.

Table 1. Quantitative Results (Scale 2, 3, and 4)

Method	Scale	Set5		Set14		B100		Urban100		Manga109	
		PSNR	SSIM	PSNR	SSIM	PSNR	SSIM	PSNR	SSIM	PSNR	SSIM
Bicubic	×2	33.66	0.9299	30.24	0.8688	29.56	0.8431	26.88	0.8403	30.80	0.9339
SRCNN [3]	×2	36.66	0.9542	32.45	0.9067	31.36	0.8879	29.50	0.8946	35.60	0.9663
VDSR [9]	×2	37.53	0.9590	33.05	0.9130	31.90	0.8960	30.77	0.9140	37.22	0.9750
EDSR [14]	×2	38.11	0.9602	33.92	0.9195	32.32	0.9013	32.93	0.9351	39.10	0.9773
NLRN [15]	×2	38.00	0.9603	33.46	0.9159	32.19	0.8992	31.81	0.9249	-	-
RNAN [30]	×2	38.17	0.9611	33.87	0.9207	32.32	0.9014	32.73	0.9340	39.23	0.9785
SRFBN [13]	×2	38.11	0.9609	33.82	0.9196	32.29	0.9010	32.62	0.9328	39.08	0.9779
RDN [31]	×2	38.24	0.9614	34.01	0.9212	32.34	0.9017	32.89	0.9353	39.18	0.9780
Our Method	×2	38.25	0.9613	33.91	0.9204	32.29	0.9008	32.74	0.9338	39.32	0.9784
Bicubic	×3	30.39	0.8682	27.55	0.7742	27.21	0.7385	24.46	0.7349	26.95	0.8556
SRCNN [3]	×3	32.75	0.9090	29.30	0.8215	28.41	0.7863	26.24	0.7989	30.48	0.9117
VDSR [9]	×3	33.67	0.9210	29.78	0.8320	28.83	0.7990	27.14	0.8290	32.01	0.9340
EDSR [14]	×3	34.65	0.9280	30.52	0.8462	29.25	0.8093	28.80	0.8653	34.17	0.9476
NLRN [15]	×3	34.27	0.9266	30.16	0.8374	29.06	0.8026	27.93	0.8453	-	-
RNAN [30]	×3	34.66	0.9290	30.52	0.8462	29.26	0.8090	28.75	0.8646	34.25	0.9483
SRFBN [13]	×3	34.70	0.9292	30.51	0.8461	29.24	0.8084	28.73	0.8641	34.18	0.9481
RDN [31]	×3	34.71	0.9296	30.57	0.8468	29.26	0.8093	28.80	0.8653	34.13	0.9484
Our Method	×3	34.67	0.9290	30.49	0.8439	29.19	0.8067	28.60	0.8601	34.23	0.9480
Bicubic	×4	28.42	0.8104	26.00	0.7027	25.96	0.6675	23.14	0.6577	24.89	0.7866
SRCNN [3]	×4	30.48	0.8628	27.50	0.7513	26.90	0.7101	24.52	0.7221	27.58	0.8555
VDSR [9]	×4	31.35	0.8830	28.02	0.7680	27.29	0.0726	25.18	0.7540	28.83	0.8870
EDSR [14]	×4	32.46	0.8968	28.80	0.7876	27.71	0.7420	26.64	0.8033	31.02	0.9148
NLRN [15]	×4	31.92	0.8916	28.36	0.7745	27.48	0.7306	25.79	0.7729	-	-
RNAN [30]	×4	32.49	0.8982	28.83	0.7878	27.72	0.7421	26.61	0.8023	31.09	0.9149
SRFBN [13]	×4	32.47	0.8983	28.81	0.7868	27.72	0.7409	26.60	0.8015	31.15	0.9160
RDN [31]	×4	32.47	0.8990	28.81	0.7871	27.72	0.7419	26.61	0.8028	31.00	0.9151
Our Method	×4	32.43	0.8973	28.73	0.7853	27.63	0.7372	26.39	0.7927	30.94	0.9125

The qualitative results are shown in Figs. 4, 5, 6 and 7, where we have compared our results with Bicubic interpolation, and two of the best performing methods RCAN [29] and NLSN [21]. Figure 4 shows the scale 2 results of the butterfly image of Set5. We can observe the edges of the cropped portion of an image. The edges of the bicubic interpolated image are smeared. One can observe that there are some artifacts near the edges of RCAN's result. The result of our method is very close to that of NLSN [21]. However, for scale factor 3, one can observe that the results of RCAN and NLSN are somewhat blurred, whereas the result of our architecture has sharper edges. In scale 4, Figs. 6 and 7 shows the qualitative results from Urban100 dataset's img_002.png and img_093.png. For both the figures, one can observe that the results of the proposed method are better as compared to the compared methods.

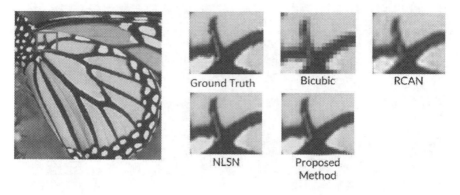

Fig. 4. Qualitative Results for Scale 2 (Set5: Butterfly.png)

Fig. 5. Qualitative Results for Scale 3 (Set14: comic.png)

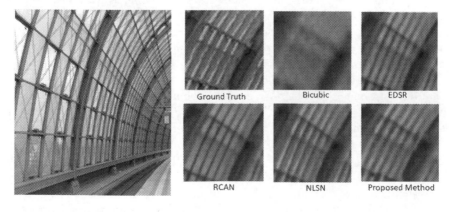

Fig. 6. Qualitative Results for Scale 4 (Urban100: img_002.png)

Fig. 7. Qualitative Results for Scale 4 (Urban100: img_093.png)

5   Results on Other Image Modalities

5.1   Depth Map

When comprehending a scene, people are able to capture the depth information necessary to produce stereo perception in addition to the scene's appearance (such as colour and texture). Numerous research areas that depend on high-quality depth data, such as autonomous navigation and 3D reconstruction, can be facilitated by a better understanding of the scene. Portable consumer-grade depth cameras, like Microsoft Kinect and Lidar, have become increasingly common and offer great convenience for quickly determining the depth of a scene. The resolution of a depth map, even when compared with a high-resolution colour image, is typically constrained due to the imaging limitations of depth cameras. Depth map super-resolution (SR) technique has drawn increasing attention as a potential solution to the urgent need for high-quality depth maps in applications [16]. Thus, in our work, we consider super-resolving depth maps for scale factor 4. Note that our network has not been trained with depth maps. We use the same training parameters as have been learned in the case of color images. The visual results can be observed in Figs. 8, 9. One can observe that sharpness of the edges of our results is better than that of Bi-cubic interpolated results.

The results are further evaluated quantitatively using Root Mean Squared Error(RMSE) values in Table 2. We use Middlebury dataset's Art, Books, Laundry, Reindeer and Teddy images. The individual RMSE vales are the average of both (left and right) depth maps associated to a scene present in that set.

5.2   Medical Images

We also make use of the computed tomography (CT) and chest X-ray images from the COVID-19 image dataset [2]. Electromagnetic waves are a category of radiation that includes X-rays. Images of the inside of your body are produced

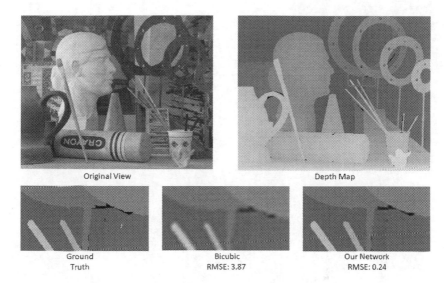

Fig. 8. Qualitative results of our network for scale 4 on MiddaleBury 2005 Art image [24]

Fig. 9. Qualitative results of our network for scale 4 on MiddaleBury 2005 Laundry image [24]

by X-ray imaging. The images show various body parts in various black and white shades. This is as a result of the different ways that various tissues absorb radiation. Bones appear white because calcium in them absorbs the most x-rays. Fat and other soft tissues have a grey appearance due to less absorption. Lungs appear black because air absorbs the least. The dataset is updated frequently,

Table 2. Quantitative results of depth map SR for scale 4 upsampling on Middlebury dataset in terms of RMSE values

Data	Bicubic	Our Network
Art	3.87	0.24
Books	1.61	0.26
Laundry	2.41	0.20
Reindeer	2.81	0.19
Teddy	2.86	0.29

and it's important to note that each image's resolution varies. The results of our network on some images of COVID-19 image dataset [2] are given in the Figs. 10 and 11. The quantitative results of these 4 images' average in PSNR are given in the Table 3.

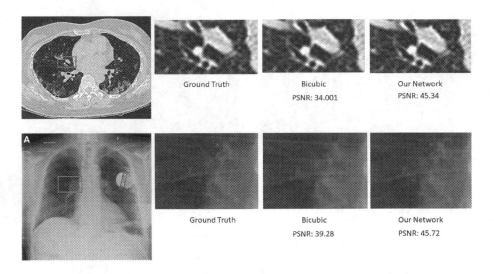

Fig. 10. Qualitative results of our network for scale 2

Table 3. Quantitative results for scale 2 in terms of PSNR

Data	Bicubic	Our Network
COVID-19	36.67	43.62

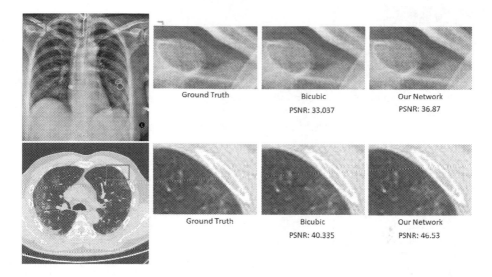

Fig. 11. Qualitative results of our network for scale 2

6   Conclusion

In the proposed method, for single image super-resolution, we have used non-local sparse attention that simultaneously adopts the advantages of sparse representations and non-local similarity.. Furthermore, to improve the ability of the network, we suggest a channel attention mechanism to adaptively rescale channel-wise features by taking into account inter-dependencies among channels. The combination of non-local sparse attention and channel attention utilizes both spatial similarity and channel-wise significance. Our proposed method produces super-resolved results that are comparable with state-of-the-art architectures in terms of qualitative and quantitative evaluation. The salient feature of our network is its ability to super-resolve images of different modalities without re-training.

References

1. Bevilacqua, M., Roumy, A., Guillemot, C., Alberi-Morel, M.L.: Low-complexity single-image super-resolution based on nonnegative neighbor embedding (2012)
2. Cohen, J.P., Morrison, P., Dao, L.: COVID-19 image data collection. arXiv 2003.11597 (2020). https://github.com/ieee8023/covid-chestxray-dataset
3. Dong, C., Loy, C.C., He, K., Tang, X.: Image super-resolution using deep convolutional networks. IEEE Trans. Pattern Anal. Mach. Intell. **38**(2), 295–307 (2015)
4. Dong, C., Loy, C.C., Tang, X.: Accelerating the super-resolution convolutional neural network. In: Leibe, B., Matas, J., Sebe, N., Welling, M. (eds.) ECCV 2016. LNCS, vol. 9906, pp. 391–407. Springer, Cham (2016). https://doi.org/10.1007/978-3-319-46475-6_25

5. Farsiu, S., Robinson, D., Elad, M., Milanfar, P.: Advances and challenges in super-resolution. Int. J. Imaging Syst. Technol. **14**(2), 47–57 (2004)
6. Farsiu, S., Robinson, M.D., Elad, M., Milanfar, P.: Fast and robust multiframe super resolution. IEEE Trans. Image Process. **13**(10), 1327–1344 (2004)
7. Glasner, D., Bagon, S., Irani, M.: Super-resolution from a single image. In: 2009 IEEE 12th International Conference on Computer Vision, pp. 349–356. IEEE (2009)
8. Huang, J.B., Singh, A., Ahuja, N.: Single image super-resolution from transformed self-exemplars. In: Proceedings of the IEEE Conference on Computer Vision and Pattern Recognition, pp. 5197–5206 (2015)
9. Kim, J., Lee, J.K., Lee, K.M.: Accurate image super-resolution using very deep convolutional networks. In: Proceedings of the IEEE Conference on Computer Vision and Pattern Recognition (CVPR) (2016)
10. Kim, J., Lee, J.K., Lee, K.M.: Deeply-recursive convolutional network for image super-resolution. In: Proceedings of the IEEE Conference on Computer Vision and Pattern Recognition, pp. 1637–1645 (2016)
11. Kingma, D.P., Ba, J.: Adam: A method for stochastic optimization. arXiv preprint arXiv:1412.6980 (2014)
12. Li, X., Hu, Y., Gao, X., Tao, D., Ning, B.: A multi-frame image super-resolution method. Signal Process. **90**(2), 405–414 (2010)
13. Li, Z., Yang, J., Liu, Z., Yang, X., Jeon, G., Wu, W.: Feedback network for image super-resolution. In: Proceedings of the IEEE/CVF Conference on Computer Vision and Pattern Recognition, pp. 3867–3876 (2019)
14. Lim, B., Son, S., Kim, H., Nah, S., Lee, K.M.: Enhanced deep residual networks for single image super-resolution. CoRR abs/1707.02921 (2017), https://arxiv.org/1707.02921
15. Liu, D., Wen, B., Fan, Y., Loy, C.C., Huang, T.S.: Non-local recurrent network for image restoration. Advances in Neural Information Processing Systems 31 (2018)
16. Mandal, S., Bhavsar, A., Sao, A.K.: Depth map restoration from undersampled data. IEEE Trans. Image Process. **26**(1), 119–134 (2017). https://doi.org/10.1109/TIP.2016.2621410
17. Mandal, S., Bhavsar, A., Sao, A.K.: Noise adaptive super-resolution from single image via non-local mean and sparse representation. Signal Process. **132**, 134–149 (2017). https://doi.org/10.1016/j.sigpro.2016.09.017
18. Mandal, S., Sao, A.K.: Employing structural and statistical information to learn dictionary(s) for single image super-resolution in sparse domain. Signal Process. Image Commun. **48**, 63–80 (2016). https://doi.org/10.1016/j.image.2016.08.006
19. Martin, D., Fowlkes, C., Tal, D., Malik, J.: A database of human segmented natural images and its application to evaluating segmentation algorithms and measuring ecological statistics. In: Proceedings Eighth IEEE International Conference on Computer Vision, ICCV 2001, vol. 2, pp. 416–423. IEEE (2001)
20. Matsui, Y., et al.: Sketch-based manga retrieval using manga109 dataset. Multimedia Tools Appl. **76**(20), 21811–21838 (2017)
21. Mei, Y., Fan, Y., Zhou, Y.: Image super-resolution with non-local sparse attention. In: Proceedings of the IEEE/CVF Conference on Computer Vision and Pattern Recognition, pp. 3517–3526 (2021)
22. Park, S.C., Park, M.K., Kang, M.G.: Super-resolution image reconstruction: a technical overview. IEEE Signal Process. Mag. **20**(3), 21–36 (2003)
23. Purohit, K., Mandal, S., Rajagopalan, A.: Mixed-dense connection networks for image and video super-resolution. Neurocomputing **398**, 360–376 (2020). https://doi.org/10.1016/j.neucom.2019.02.069

24. Scharstein, D., Pal, C.: Learning conditional random fields for stereo. In: 2007 IEEE Conference on Computer Vision and Pattern Recognition, pp. 1–8. IEEE (2007)

25. Timofte, R., Agustsson, E., Van Gool, L., Yang, M.H., Zhang, L.: NTIRE 2017 challenge on single image super-resolution: Methods and results. In: Proceedings of the IEEE Conference on Computer Vision and Pattern Recognition (CVPR) Workshops (2017)

26. Yang, J., Wright, J., Huang, T.S., Ma, Y.: Image super-resolution via sparse representation. IEEE Trans. Image Process. **19**(11), 2861–2873 (2010)

27. Zeyde, R., Elad, M., Protter, M.: On single image scale-up using sparse-representations. In: Boissonnat, J.-D., et al. (eds.) Curves and Surfaces 2010. LNCS, vol. 6920, pp. 711–730. Springer, Heidelberg (2012). https://doi.org/10.1007/978-3-642-27413-8_47

28. Zhang, L., Zuo, W.: Image restoration: From sparse and low-rank priors to deep priors [lecture notes]. IEEE Signal Process. Mag. **34**(5), 172–179 (2017)

29. Zhang, Y., Li, K., Li, K., Wang, L., Zhong, B., Fu, Y.: Image super-resolution using very deep residual channel attention networks. In: Ferrari, V., Hebert, M., Sminchisescu, C., Weiss, Y. (eds.) ECCV 2018. LNCS, vol. 11211, pp. 294–310. Springer, Cham (2018). https://doi.org/10.1007/978-3-030-01234-2_18

30. Zhang, Y., Li, K., Li, K., Zhong, B., Fu, Y.: Residual non-local attention networks for image restoration. arXiv preprint arXiv:1903.10082 (2019)

31. Zhang, Y., Tian, Y., Kong, Y., Zhong, B., Fu, Y.: Residual dense network for image super-resolution. In: Proceedings of the IEEE Conference on Computer Vision and Pattern Recognition, pp. 2472–2481 (2018)

An End-to-End Fast No-Reference Video Quality Predictor with Spatiotemporal Feature Fusion

Anish Kumar Vishwakarma[✉] and Kishor M. Bhurchandi

Vivesvaraya National Institute of Technology, Nagpur, India
anishvishwakarma@students.vnit.ac.in, bhurchandikm@vnit.ac.in

Abstract. This work proposes a reliable and efficient end-to-end No-Reference Video Quality Assessment (NR-VQA) model that fuses deep spatial and temporal features. Since both spatial (semantic) and temporal (motion) features have a significant impact on video quality, we have developed an effective and fast predictor of video quality by combining both. ResNet-50, a well-known pre-trained image classification model, is employed to extract semantic features from video frames, whereas I3D, a well-known pre-trained action recognition model, is used to compute spatiotemporal features from short video clips. Further, extracted features are passed through a regressor head that consists of a Gated Recurrent Unit (GRU) followed by a Fully Connected (FC) layer. Four popular and widely used authentic distortion databases LIVE-VQC, KoNViD-1k, LIVE-Qualcomm, and CVD2014, are utilized for validating the performance. The proposed model demonstrates competitive results with a considerably decreased computation complexity.

Keywords: video quality predictor · Deep spatiotemporal features · convolutional neural network · GRU

1 Introduction

Because of the rapid evolution of communication and multimedia technologies as well as the widespread access to the fast internet, video consumption has increased dramatically in recent years. Numerous social media websites and streaming video services allow users to rapidly upload and view videos. Due to the limited availability of communication resources, maintaining the quality of video services is crucial by optimizing resource utilization. Video Quality Assessment (VQA) models play a crucial role in this context. Depending on the accessibility of reference videos, VQA techniques are typically categorized as no-reference (NR), reduced-reference (RR), and full-reference (FR). FR and RR utilize full and partial access to reference videos, respectively. However, original videos are rarely available. Since reference videos are unavailable, NR techniques are suitable for the vast majority of practical applications. NR approaches are more complex as compared to FR and RR models in the absence of source videos.

This section provides a brief summary of the reported blind VQA frameworks. Using two-dimensional DCT of video frame differences and motion coherency,

© The Author(s), under exclusive license to Springer Nature Switzerland AG 2023
D. Gupta et al. (Eds.): CVIP 2022, CCIS 1777, pp. 638–645, 2023.
https://doi.org/10.1007/978-3-031-31417-9_48

the first blind VQA model with universal applicability was developed [14]. Motion coherency calculation, however, renders the method computationally intensive. Li et al. [10] extracted a wide range of spatiotemporal attributes from the 3-dimensional DCT of the 3D video blocks and applied them to a support vector regression with a linear kernel. Mittal et al. [12] designed a fully blind VQA model totally void of subjective scores, but the model's performance was pretty poor. Recent research has focused primarily on the creation of VQA frameworks for user-generated content (UGC). UGC videos are recorded by both professionals and non-professionals. Moreover, user-generated videos contain distortions due to inappropriate shooting environment, immature photographer, camera shake, in/out of focus, under/overexposure, etc. These authentic distortions make evaluation of the quality of user-generated videos significantly more complicated.

Korohonen [7] proposed an efficient and robust blind VQA model by extracting 75 different spatial and frequency domain features. This model extracts low-complexity features from each video frame, while only a few video frames were chosen for high-complexity features. The method is among the most effective VQA models for natural distortions. VIDEVAL [15] made use of features extracted from a number of leading IQA/VQA models. Very few extracted features were ultimately chosen for quality estimation. The model delivers exceptional performance. Dendi et al. [3] presented an NR-VQA method that uses Gabor filter bank and the three-dimensional mean subtracted contrast normalized (3D MSCN) coefficients of 3D video cubes. The performance of the model is average, and its computational load is extremely high. Based on the statistics of 3D-DWT of local video cubes, Vishwakarma and Bhurchandi [17] developed an effective and resilient blind VQA model. On synthetic distortion databases, the model performed wonderfully, whereas, on authentic distortion databases, its performance was average.

In addition to the blind VQA models based on hand-crafted features, the literature contains VQA models that were developed using CNN. However, designing a CNN-based VQA model is very challenging due to the unavailability of large video databases. Due to limited data size, CNN-based VQA models are very prone to overfitting. Also, tuning of a large number of trainable parameters is very cumbersome. CNN-based VQA models typically utilize prominent pre-trained CNN models to address these issues. Li et al. [9] developed an efficient model for evaluating video quality by combining a pre-trained ImageNet feature with a gated current unit (GRU). RAPIQUE [16] combined natural scene statistics with the ResNet-50 model's pre-trained deep features. Recently, a blind VQA model was developed that used 3D CNN and long-term short-term memory (LSTM) [18]. The VSFA model [9] utilized a pre-trained CNN model as a feature extractor, and GRU is used as a sequence-to-sequence modeling of extracted features.

This paper presents an end-to-end blind fast VQA technique that utilizes both spatial and temporal features extracted through prominent pre-trained image recognition and action recognition models, respectively, to address the above-mentioned limitations.

The following are the major contributions of this paper:

(i) Considering the significance of spatiotemporal features for VQA, both spatial and temporal features are extracted using well-known image recognition and action recognition models that have been pre-trained.

(ii) Leveraging the prominent image recognition pre-trained ResNet-50 model, the proposed model extracts high-level semantic (spatial) features. A prevalent pre-trained I3D model is used to extract motion (temporal) features.

(iii) A regression head consisting of GRU followed by an FC layer is trained and evaluated on four authentic distortion databases using extracted features.

(iv) Validation is performed carrying extensive experiments, including a comparison of performance, time complexity analysis, and ablation studies.

The remaining sections of the paper are organized as follows: We discuss the proposed VQA model in Sect. 2. Section 3 describes the VQA databases and experimental settings followed by performance benchmarking. Finally, Sect. 4 presents conclusion.

2 Proposed VQA Model

This section provides a comprehensive overview of the proposed blind VQA model. Due to the fact that video is a series of images, spatial information alone is insufficient for assessing video quality; temporal information also plays an essential role. In addition, manually crafted spatial and temporal feature extractors cannot achieve real-time quality evaluation performance due to the use of complex transforms or other computationally heavy statistical methods. In light of these considerations, the proposed method makes use of prominent image recognition and action recognition CNN models for extracting temporal and spatial features. Figure 1 depicts the framework of the proposed model. The proposed method employs a well-known pretrained ResNet-50 [5] model for capturing semantic features at higher level from video frames. The ResNet-50 is a popular model for image recognition that was trained using the ImageNet database [4], which has over 14 million images with 1000 classes. In addition, we use a well-known pre-trained action recognition model, I3D [1], which was trained on the kinetics database [6] containing 400 human action classes and over 400 video clips per class. In the proposed model, I3D extracts key motion (temporal) features from small video segments or clips. In this paper, a group of eight consecutive video frames was considered a video segment.

The reason for considering pre-trained CNN models is that distortion degrades the visual quality, and a pre-trained ResNet-50 model can effectively extract salient high-level semantic features that represent visual distortions. Similarly, the I3D model can effectively extract motion features that are equally important as video is a sequence of images called frames. Additionally, because the available VQA databases are limited in size, the overfitting problem can be avoided by utilizing pre-trained CNN models. The disparity between the size of

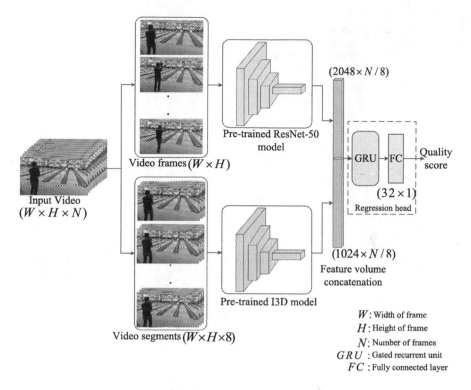

Fig. 1. The proposed VQA model.

the input of the pre-trained CNN model and the size of video frames is, nevertheless, a significant issue. Our primary objective is to extract spatial and temporal quality representing attributes utilizing pre-trained CNN models. We scaled down video frames to accommodate the input size of pre-trained CNN models. Further, features extracted through both pre-trained CNN models are concatenated and applied to the gated recurrent unit (GRU) [2] and output of GRU is further applied to fully connected layer that predict final quality score. GRU is a popular sequence to sequence modeling technique applied widely for natural language processing (NLP) tasks. However, video can also be considered as a sequence of video frames. In the proposed method, we employ GRU for learning the long-term dependencies of extracted features form the video clips.

3   Experiments

This section describes four widely used and publicly accessible VQA databases, followed by experimental settings and findings. Finally, the performance benchmarking of the proposed technique is presented.

3.1   VQA Databases

On four popular authentic distortion databases, the performance of the proposed method is evaluated. The comparison of the four VQA databases based on various parameters is shown in Table 1.

Table 1. Comparison of video quality databases.

Database parameters	KoNViD-1k [3]	LIVE-VQC [4]	LIVE-Qualcomm [5]	CVD2014 [6]
1. Number of Videos	1200	585	208	234
2. Video Resolution	540p	480p,720p,1080p,etc.	1080p	480p, 720p
3. Frame Rate (fr/sec)	24,25,30	20–30	30	9–30
4. Duration	8 s	10 s	15 s	11–28 s
5. No. of Cameras	>164	101	8	78
6. Subjective score methodology	Crowdsourcing	Crowdsourcing	Lab-based	Lab-based
7. Score Range	1–5	0–100	0–100	0–100

3.2   Experimental Settings and Performance Criteria

After the feature extraction stage, computed spatiotemporal features are passed through the regression head, which consists of a GRU and an FC layer. For training of the regression head, we experimented with various hyperparameter values. We choose a batch size of eight, a learning rate of 0.0001, the Adam optimizer, and a mean squared error loss function. To prevent the possibility of overfitting, we utilized early stopping. A maximum of 50 epochs were used to train the regression head. For performance analysis of the proposed method and other benchmark methods, four performance criteria were used: Pearson's linear correlation coefficient (PLCC), Spearman's rank-order correlation coefficient (SRCC), Kendall's rank-order correlation coefficient (KRCC), and root mean square error (RMSE). SRCC and KRCC reflect monotonicity, while PLCC and RMSE indicate prediction accuracy. Higher PLCC, SRCC, and KRCC, as well as a lower RMSE, are indicative of a better VQA performance.

3.3   Performance Analysis

Extensive experiments are conducted using eight benchmark methods: NIQE, BRISQUE, V-BLIINDS, VIIDEO, HIGRADE, NSTSS, VSFA, TLVQM, and the proposed method using four challenging authentic distortion databases. Each database is divided into 60% training, 20% validation, and 20% for testing. Subset of each database is mutually exclusive. We repeat the process for 10 times and reported median of the four performance criteria in Table 2. From Table 2, it is observed that for the KoNViD-1k database, the proposed method outperforms all the compared methods. For the CVD2014 database, the proposed method comes at second place, while for LIVE-VQC and LIVE-Qualcomm databases, the proposed method is in third position after TLVQM and VSFA. Both the

Table 2. Performance of the proposed method and existing NR-VQA techniques on the KoNViD-1k, LIVE-VQC, CVD2014, and LIVE-Qualcomm databases. Numbers in bold indicate top performance.

Database	Metric	NIQE [13]	BRISQUE [11]	V-BLIINDS [14]	VIIDEO [12]	HIGRADE [8]	NSTSS [3]	VSFA [9]	TLVQM [7]	Proposed
KoNViD-1k	SRCC ↑	0.541	0.676	0.703	0.298	0.723	0.653	0.772	**0.775**	**0.776**
	PLCC ↑	0.553	0.668	0.682	0.300	0.716	0.641	**0.775**	0.768	**0.788**
	KRCC ↑	0.379	0.476	0.518	0.207	0.532	0.455	0.562	**0.577**	0.590
	RMSE ↓	0.536	0.481	0.459	0.610	0.439	0.503	**0.409**	0.410	**0.401**
LIVE-VQC	SRCC ↑	0.595	0.611	**0.718**	0.049	0.581	0.626	0.697	**0.797**	0.653
	PLCC ↑	0.628	0.630	0.725	0.066	0.583	0.625	**0.742**	**0.798**	0.717
	KRCC ↑	0.383	0.416	0.507	-0.033	0.412	0.443	**0.510**	**0.608**	0.462
	RMSE ↓	14.021	13.104	11.765	17.019	14.165	13.013	**11.285**	**10.145**	11.915
CVD2014	SRCC ↑	0.580	0.630	0.700	-0.111	0.647	0.614	**0.821**	0.693	**0.819**
	PLCC ↑	0.610	0.640	0.710	0.059	0.689	0.652	**0.845**	0.715	**0.818**
	KRCC ↑	0.358	0.518	0.562	-0.077	0.473	0.435	**0.675**	0.504	**0.641**
	RMSE ↓	17.168	15.197	14.292	29.259	8.800	15.212	**11.328**	15.255	**13.869**
LIVE-Qualcomm	SRCC ↑	0.545	0.558	0.617	-0.141	0.673	0.589	**0.737**	**0.780**	0.697
	PLCC ↑	0.580	0.578	0.665	0.098	0.706	0.628	**0.732**	**0.810**	0.715
	KRCC ↑	0.328	0.365	0.405	-0.082	0.502	0.413	**0.552**	**0.586**	0.517
	RMSE ↓	10.858	10.731	10.760	12.308	15.467	10.554	**8.863**	7.271	8.927

LIVE-VQC and LIVE-Qualcomm databases consist of videos with very high resolution, such as 1920 × 1080. Prior to applying input to the pre-trained models, video frames must be resized (224 × 224 ×3) to match the input size of the pre-trained CNN networks. Due to this resizing operation, pre-trained CNN models may not extract sufficient spatial and temporal information from high-resolution video frames, such as those in the LIVE-VQC and LIVE-Qualcomm databases.

Further, importance of both the spatial and temporal features is demonstrated using ablation study. Table 3 shows the ablation study results on the KoNViD-1k and LIVE-VQC databases. It is observed that combination of spatial and temporal features significantly improve the overall performance. Also, it is evident from Table 3 that both spatial and temporal information are equally important for the VQA task. We also provide time requirements for the proposed model and other benchmark techniques. We used a Dell desktop computer with an Intel Core i7-4770 processor, 3.4 GHz, and 32 GB of RAM for time computation. It is observed from Table 4 that the proposed method is significantly faster than the other benchmark models.

Table 3. Ablation study results on the KoNViD-1k and LIVE-VQC databases.

Pre-trained model		KoNViD-1k				LIVE-VQC			
ResNet-50	I3D	SRCC	PLCC	KRCC	RMSE	SRCC	PLCC	KRCC	RMSE
✓		0.752	0.769	0.559	0.439	0.633	0.685	0.448	12.995
	✓	0.693	0.714	0.508	0.469	0.628	0.675	0.446	13.183
✓	✓	0.776	0.788	0.590	0.401	0.653	0.717	0.462	11.915

Table 4. The average computation time per frame with a resolution of 1920 × 1080 in the LIVE-VQC database, measured in seconds.

Model	NIQE [13]	BRISQUE [11]	VIIDEO [12]	V-BLLINDS [14]	TLVQM [7]	NSTSS [3]	Proposed
Time	0.951	0.396	2.882	8.429	1.097	6.618	**0.041**

4   Conclusion

In this paper, we presented a reliable and rapid end-to-end blind VQA model. The proposed model employs prominent pre-trained CNN models: ResNet-50 (image recognition) and I3D (action recognition) to design an efficient blind VQA model that avoids overfitting. The image and action recognition networks take due care of spatiotemporal features. The integration and successful application of spatial (high-level semantic features) and temporal (motion) features is found effective for an efficient NR-VQA model. Also, long-term dependencies are modeled using a sequence-to-sequence GRU model and is also found to significantly contribute to NR-VQA. Performance comparison, ablation study, and computation time comparison demonstrate the effectiveness of the proposed VQA model compared to state-of-the-art. Varying resolution, frame rates, and recording devices impact video quality estimates. Future extensions of the proposed work include a technique for avoiding the resizing of video frames to enhance the performance on high-resolution video databases, such as the LIVE-VQC and LIVE-Qualcomm databases.

References

1. Carreira, J., Zisserman, A.: Quo Vadis, action recognition? A new model and the kinetics dataset. In: Proceedings of the IEEE Conference on Computer Vision and Pattern Recognition, pp. 6299–6308 (2017)
2. Cho, K., Van Merriënboer, B., Bahdanau, D., Bengio, Y.: On the properties of neural machine translation: encoder-decoder approaches. arXiv preprint arXiv:1409.1259 (2014)
3. Dendi, S.V.R., Channappayya, S.S.: No-reference video quality assessment using natural spatiotemporal scene statistics. IEEE Trans. Image Process. **29**, 5612–5624 (2020)
4. Deng, J., Dong, W., Socher, R., Li, L.J., Li, K., Fei-Fei, L.: Imagenet: a large-scale hierarchical image database. In: 2009 IEEE Conference on Computer Vision and Pattern Recognition, pp. 248–255. IEEE (2009)
5. He, K., Zhang, X., Ren, S., Sun, J.: Deep residual learning for image recognition. In: Proceedings of the IEEE Conference on Computer Vision and Pattern Recognition, pp. 770–778 (2016)
6. Kay, W., et al.: The kinetics human action video dataset. arXiv preprint arXiv:1705.06950 (2017)
7. Korhonen, J.: Two-level approach for no-reference consumer video quality assessment. IEEE Trans. Image Process. **28**(12), 5923–5938 (2019)

8. Kundu, D., Ghadiyaram, D., Bovik, A.C., Evans, B.L.: No-reference quality assessment of tone-mapped HDR pictures. IEEE Trans. Image Process. **26**(6), 2957–2971 (2017)

9. Li, D., Jiang, T., Jiang, M.: Quality assessment of in-the-wild videos. In: Proceedings of the 27th ACM International Conference on Multimedia, pp. 2351–2359 (2019)

10. Li, X., Guo, Q., Lu, X.: Spatiotemporal statistics for video quality assessment. IEEE Trans. Image Process. **25**(7), 3329–3342 (2016)

11. Mittal, A., Moorthy, A.K., Bovik, A.C.: No-reference image quality assessment in the spatial domain. IEEE Trans. Image Process. **21**(12), 4695–4708 (2012)

12. Mittal, A., Saad, M.A., Bovik, A.C.: A completely blind video integrity oracle. IEEE Trans. Image Process. **25**(1), 289–300 (2015)

13. Mittal, A., Soundararajan, R., Bovik, A.C.: Making a "completely blind" image quality analyzer. IEEE Sig. Process. Lett. **20**(3), 209–212 (2012)

14. Saad, M.A., Bovik, A.C., Charrier, C.: Blind prediction of natural video quality. IEEE Trans. Image Process. **23**(3), 1352–1365 (2014)

15. Tu, Z., Wang, Y., Birkbeck, N., Adsumilli, B., Bovik, A.C.: UGC-VQA: benchmarking blind video quality assessment for user generated content. IEEE Trans. Image Process. **30**, 4449–4464 (2021)

16. Tu, Z., Yu, X., Wang, Y., Birkbeck, N., Adsumilli, B., Bovik, A.C.: Rapique: rapid and accurate video quality prediction of user generated content. IEEE Open J. Sig. Process. **2**, 425–440 (2021)

17. Vishwakarma, A.K., Bhurchandi, K.M.: 3D-DWT cross-band statistics and features for no-reference video quality assessment (NR-VQA). Optik, 167774 (2021)

18. You, J., Korhonen, J.: Deep neural networks for no-reference video quality assessment. In: 2019 IEEE International Conference on Image Processing (ICIP), pp. 2349–2353. IEEE (2019)

Low-Intensity Human Activity Recognition Framework Using Audio Data in an Outdoor Environment

Priyankar Choudhary[(✉)], Pratibha Kumari, Neeraj Goel, and Mukesh Saini

Indian Institute of Technology Ropar, Rupnagar, India
{2017csz0011,2017csz0006,neeraj,mukesh}@iitrpr.ac.in

Abstract. Audio-based activity recognition is an essential task in a wide range of human-centric applications. However, most of the work predominantly focuses on event detection, machine sound classification, road surveillance, scene classification, etc. There has been negligible attention to the recognition of low-intensity human activities for outdoor scenarios. This paper proposes a deep learning-based framework for recognizing different low-intensity human activities in a sparsely populated outdoor environment using audio. The proposed framework classifies 2.0 s long audio recordings into one of nine different activity classes. A variety of audio sounds in an outdoor environment makes it challenging to distinguish human activities from other background sounds. The proposed framework is an end-to-end architecture that employs a combination of mel-frequency cepstral coefficients and a 2D convolutional neural network to obtain a deep representation of activities and classify them. The extensive experimental analysis demonstrates that the proposed framework outperforms existing frameworks by 16.43% on the parameter F1-score. Additionally, we collected and provided an audio dataset for evaluation and benchmarking purposes to the research community.

Keywords: Device-free technique · Human activity recognition · Audio data · Convolution neural network

1 Introduction

Recognition of activities in a surrounding area is a critical area of research with applications in multiple domains, including healthcare, security, smart environments (city and home), and sports. Due to advances in microelectromechanical sensors, a target (human, animal, or vehicle) can be equipped with sensors to obtain different target specific information [25]. Such active sensing approaches, however, are only effective when the target actively and voluntarily supports the monitoring systems. Wildlife monitoring and intrusion detection are example applications where attaching a device to a target's body is challenging.

© The Author(s), under exclusive license to Springer Nature Switzerland AG 2023
D. Gupta et al. (Eds.): CVIP 2022, CCIS 1777, pp. 646–658, 2023.
https://doi.org/10.1007/978-3-031-31417-9_49

Consequently, other sensors such as seismic [19], audio [12], passive-infrared [24], and WiFi [6], etc., are currently being explored by researchers due to their device-free (passive) nature. An audio sensor is useful for device-free monitoring due to its low cost and ease of installation. Audio data has been mainly utilized for scene classification [18], machine sound classification [20], kitchen sound classification [22], abnormal activity classification [1], etc. There has been negligible attention on developing audio based human activity recognition framework for an outdoor environment.

This paper aims to utilize an audio sensor for recognition of human activities occurring along roadways and in sparsely populated outdoor scenarios, such as border areas. Unlike indoor sounds, outdoor sounds are unpredictable and are not muffled by walls. Outdoor audio recordings are inherently challenging to analyze, and noise can sneak in despite the best efforts. The set of human activities considered in this paper is (1) no activity (background noise), (2) running, (3) jogging, (4) walking, (5) jumping jacks, (6) jumping, (7) Hammer strike, (8) cycling, and (9) riding a bike. An example use case for the proposed system is intruder detection and activity recognition.

The primary contributions of our work are two-fold. (1) We exploit an end to end 2-Dimensional Convolutional Neural Network (2D CNN) based architecture to map the given audio data to the human activity class label. The proposed framework achieves better performance than state-of-the-art works. (2) We contribute a non-simulated audio dataset, collected in outdoor scenarios for human activity recognition [4].

The rest of the manuscript is organized as follows. Section 2 presents the related work. Dataset is described in Sect. 3. Section 4 discusses the proposed framework. The experimental setup, implementation details, and results are discussed in Sect. 5. Conclusions are summarized in Sect. 6.

2   Related Literature

Identification of audio sounds is also known as acoustic scene classification and comes under the field of computational auditory scene analysis [10]. The researchers in this field rely on different types of aural characteristics to differentiate the types of sound, i.e., music, speech, or environmental sounds. Music and speech signals generally follow some pattern, unlike environmental (indoor/outdoor) sounds. Construction sites, moving vehicles, machine operations, crowds, traffic, and loudspeakers are a few possible sound sources in an outdoor environment. Rashid et al. [20] used features from time, frequency, wavelet, and cepstral domain to achieve the representation of different sounds (nailing, hammering, sawing, drilling, no task). They achieved F1-score of 97% using the Support Vector Machine (SVM) classifier. Sherafat et al. [21] used Zero-Crossing Rate (ZCR), spectral flux, spectral roll-off, spectral centroid, entropy, root-mean-square, and energy to identify 5 different types of equipment (jackhammer, CAT259D, CAT308E, dozer 850K, and skyjack SJ6826) using an SVM classifier. Lee et al. [17] evaluated the accuracy of 9 different types of sounds (concrete breaking, ground excavating, bulldozer, piling, truck, grading, concrete mix, concrete grinding, drilling) generated from a construction site using 17 different classifiers. Their proposed approach used 14 different types of audio-based features and achieved an accuracy of 93.16%. Peltonen et al. [18] also performed the task of auditory scene recognition for a broader range of auditory environments (home and office environments, vehicles, and reverberant places) using different handcrafted features based K-Nearest Neighbour (KNN) classifier. The majority of research focuses on extracting handcrafted features and applying machine learning classifiers to recognize activities. Vafeiadis et al. [23] aimed to classify different kitchen sounds (mixer, dishwasher, utensils, and kitchen faucet) using different combinations of audio features using a gradient boosting classifier with an accuracy of 91.7%. Kraft et al. [15] extended their work to 21 different types of kitchen sounds. Chen et al. [3] classified different bathroom activities (washing hands, showering, urination, and brushing of teeth) using the Mel-frequency cepstral coefficients (MFCC) and Hidden Markov Model. The reported an accuracy above 84% for different sound classes. Doukas et al. [7] aimed to recognize falls based on movement and sound data, but this work requires attaching the device to the target body. Carletti et al. [1] proposed a Bag-of-Words based framework for the classification of glass breaks, screams, and gun-shots. Authors in [9] deployed the proposed framework for road surveillance to detect tire skidding, car crashes, etc., using audio data. Ekpezu et al. [8] used a CNN and a long-short Term Memory (LSTM) to classify different types of environmental sounds. Küçükbay et al. [16] aimed at classifying sounds of animals, humans, and vehicles using MFCC features based SVM classifier. Our work focuses on recognizing low sound intensive human activities using a CNN based architecture.

Fig. 1. Representative images from the three outdoor data collection areas

3   Dataset

The audio dataset was collected over 10 non-consecutive days for 9 predefined activity classes, viz., no activity (background noise), run, jog, walk, jumping jacks, jump, hammer strike on ground, cycling, and riding a bike. One Samsung Galaxy M31s smartphone was used to record the sounds of activities with a

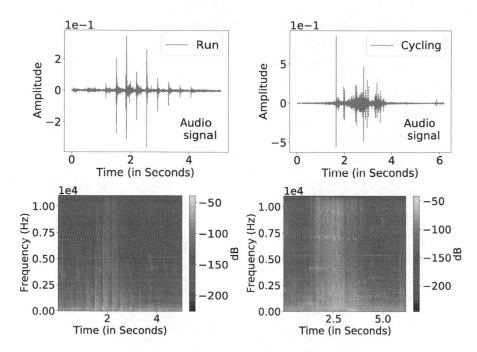

Fig. 2. Representative audio signals for running and cycling activities in time and frequency domain are shown in first and second rows, respectively

sampling rate 22050 Hz [13]. Figure 1 shows three different data collection locations. The white arrow on the ground indicates the path of the data collection. The location of the audio recorder is marked in blue-colored circle. Location-1 is a dry mud trail. An uneven grass surface characterizes Location-2. Location-3 is a hockey rink. Each data collection path is 10-21 m long and approximately 2 m wide. The audio recorder was positioned near the mid point of each data collection path.

A target goes to one of the ends (selected randomly) of the data collection path. The target initiates an activity at the selected end and completes it at the other end without stopping. Now, the target repeats the same process from the other end of the path, thus completing one round of the activity. The same process is not possible for the activities jump, jumping jacks, and hammerstrike. That is why these activities are performed at different distances from the mid-point of the path to introduce variations. An audio recorder could be positioned on either side of the road to introduce variation in sensor placement. Data collection timings were also changed to account for variations in background noise. Figure 2 illustrates the representative signals for activities running and cycling in both time and frequency domain. Different activities show different patterns in time as well as frequency domain. However, the frequency domain is less affected by noise as compared to the time domain [14]; therefore, frequency representation is used in further analysis.

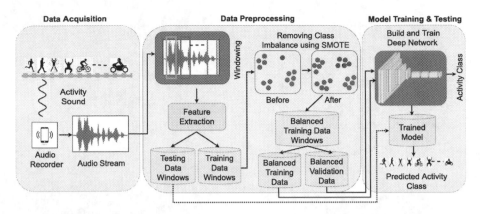

Fig. 3. Overview of the proposed human activity recognition framework

4   Methodology

The coarse-level flowchart of the proposed human activity recognition framework is shown in Fig. 3. Data acquisition, data preprocessing, and model training and testing are three major components of the proposed framework. In the data acquisition module, the sound of different human activities is recorded by an audio sensor, i.e., a mobile phone. The data preprocessing module arranges the incoming data stream in the form of small windows to represent an activity. On each window, we extract MFCC, a widely adopted frequency domain feature. After this, we split the windows into two partition as 'training data windows' and 'testing data windows'. Typically, real-world data faces the issue of class imbalance. Therefore, we remove class imbalance in 'training data windows' to avoid bias towards any class. Further, the balance training data windows are split into 'balanced validation data' and 'balanced training data'. Once data preprocessing is complete, the balanced training and validation data are used to train and fine-tune a deep model. Unbalanced testing data windows are fed to the trained deep model to predict activity class and hence computing the model efficacy. Now, we formulate the problem and then discuss all the steps involved in the proposed framework.

4.1   Problem Formulation

Without a loss of generality, we assume a 2D physical area of interest containing one audio recorder. The aim is to recognize human activity from a given online source of a continuous audio stream in an outdoor environment. $A_1, A_2, A_3, ... A_N$ are the N activity classes of interest in the predefined set S. The audio stream may also contain sounds that do not belong to S; these sounds are classified as no activity (background noise) and are assigned to class A_0.

4.2   Data Preprocessing

The major steps of data preprocessing include windowing, feature extraction, and resolving class imbalance.

- **Windowing:** Typically, classification is carried out on smaller windows to capture the non-stationary nature of audio scenes efficiently. Therefore, we accumulate audio samples up to ΔT seconds, resulting in a data window of length $\Delta T \times$ sampling rate. Each recording is split into overlapping windows with a length of ΔT seconds. A data window at any time t is denoted as W_t. Windowing process is performed on both training and testing data. A data window is regarded as one sample/instance.
- **Feature Extraction:** Outdoor sounds have a wide range of frequency contents. The MFCC feature has been widely used in audio scene classification for years. Windowing, applying the Discrete Fourier Transform (DFT), taking the log of the magnitude, warping the frequencies on a Mel scale, and then applying the inverse Discrete Cosine Transform (DCT) are steps involved for MFCC feature extraction. MFCC features are computed with a hop length of h, and k MFCC coefficients. Then an MFCC feature matrix with the size of $m \times n$ is obtained for each audio segment of ΔT seconds. We get the output of MFCC-based feature computation as a 2D matrix which is further used as an input for the proposed 2D-CNN based deep model.
- **Resolving Class Imbalance.** A class imbalance occurs when one targeted activity class has a disproportionately high number of samples compared to the other classes. Typically, all the machine/deep learning-based algorithms assume an approximately equal number of samples in each class; otherwise, the developed model tends to bias its prediction towards the class with majority of samples. We resolve the class imbalance using the Synthetic Minority Oversampling Technique (SMOTE), as proposed in [2]. Let us assume that the MFCC features at time t are represented as f_t. The class balancing process for f_t is performed as follows:
  1. Identify the minority class $A_i \in S$. Let $f_{t,A_i} \in A_i$. Compute the Euclidean distance between $f_{t,A_i} \in A_i$ and each $f_{t',A_i} \in A_i$, where $t \neq t'$, to identify the K-nearest neighbourhood of the sample under consideration (i.e., f_{t,A_i}).
  2. Identify the majority class $A_{bulk} \in S$ and compute its cardinality (i.e., N').
  3. Select R samples randomly from A_i. For each sample $f_{r,A_i} \in A_i$ ($r = 1, 2, 3, ..., R$) & $r \neq t$, repeat the following procedure till there are N' samples in minority class.

$$f'_{t,A_i} = f_{t,A_i} + \text{rand}(0,1) * |f_{t,A_i} - f_{r,A_i}| \tag{1}$$

  here, 'r' represents one specific timestamp and rand(0,1) represent a random number between 0 and 1. After resolving the class imbalance, we train a deep classifier to label an unknown activity instance.

Table 1. Parameters of proposed convolution neural network architecture (β indicates batch size)

Layer	Input Shape	Filters	Kernel size	Strides	Output shape
Conv1	$[\beta, 40, 502, 1]$	32	$(7, 7)$	$(1, 1)$	$[\beta, 40, 502, 32]$
Conv2	$[\beta, 40, 502, 32]$	32	$(7, 7)$	$(1, 1)$	$[\beta, 40, 502, 32]$
MP1	$[\beta, 40, 502, 32]$	–	$(2, 2)$	$(2, 2)$	$[\beta, 20, 251, 32]$
Conv3	$[\beta, 20, 251, 32]$	64	$(7, 7)$	$(1, 1)$	$[\beta, 20, 251, 64]$
MP2	$[\beta, 20, 251, 64]$	–	$(2, 2)$	$(2, 2)$	$[\beta, 10, 125, 64]$
Conv4	$[\beta, 10, 125, 64]$	128	$(7, 7)$	$(1, 1)$	$[\beta, 10, 125, 128]$
MP3	$[\beta, 10, 125, 128]$	–	$(4, 100)$	$(4, 100)$	$[\beta, 2, 1, 128]$
Flatten	$[\beta, 2, 1, 128]$	–	–	–	$[\beta, 256]$
FC1	$[\beta, 256]$	–	–	–	$[\beta, 128]$
FC2	$[\beta, 128]$	–	–	–	$[\beta, 32]$
FC3	$[\beta, 32]$	–	–	–	$[\beta, 9]$

4.3 Deep Model

The input to the proposed 2D CNN based model is MFCC features computed on ΔT seconds data windows. Specifically, f_t, a 2D matrix of size $m \times n$ is fed as the input to the network. Since the audio data stream is coming from an outdoor environment, various noises can affect it. This intrinsic challenge is well handled by mapping the handcrafted representation of signals into high-level representation using deep learning in literature. Therefore, we use a sequence of 2D convolutions and max pooling layers to extract the distinctive representation and then classification into 9 classes using a fully connected layer having 9 neurons and the softmax activation function.

The equation for getting the 9-class classification as a probabilistic map on input f_t can be written as follows:

$$\psi = \delta\left(FC_9\left(\Re\left(FC_{32} \odot FC_{128} \odot flatten\left(S_l(f_t)|_{l=1}^3\right)\right)\right)\right) \tag{2}$$

The $S_l(\cdot)$ represents a sequence of 2D convolution followed by max-pooling, and is computed using Eqs. 3 and 4. After this, the activation map is flattened into a one-dimensional vector using 'flatten'. Further, two fully connected layers with 128 and 32 neurons, namely FC_{128} and FC_{32}, are applied using $\odot$ operator. Here, $\odot$ represents cross-product between two hidden layers in a deep neural network. After that an activation function, namely rectified linear unit (ReLU), denoted by $\Re$ is applied. For getting the probability map for 9 class classification, a fully connected layer with 9 neurons as FC_9 with the softmax activation (δ) is added.

$$S_l(f_t) = \gamma_{0.20}\left(MP_{sz,sd}\left(\Re\left(K_{2^{8-l},cks,cs} \otimes S_{l+1}(f_t)\right)\right)\right) \tag{3}$$

$$S_4(f_t) = \Re\left(K_{32,cks,cs} \otimes f_t\right) \tag{4}$$

where $\otimes$ denote 2D convolution operation and $K_{x,cks,cs}$ is a convolutional kernel with parameters x, cks, and cs representing the number of kernels, kernel size, and kernel stride of the convolution kernels, respectively. We use $cks = (7{\times}7)$ and $cs =(1{\times}1)$. The $MP_{sz,sd}$ represents 2D max pooling operation with parameters sz and sd representing the pooling size and stride values, respectively. We keep $sz=\{2{\times}2,\ 2{\times}2,\ 2{\times}2,\ 4{\times}100\}$, and $sd=\{2{\times}2,\ 2{\times}2,\ 2{\times}2,\ 4{\times}100\}$ for $l \in \{4, 3, 2, 1\}$. $\gamma_{0.20}$ denotes a dropout layer with 20% dropout value. Table 1 summarizes the structure of the proposed network, and Fig. 4 shows the visualization of the network.

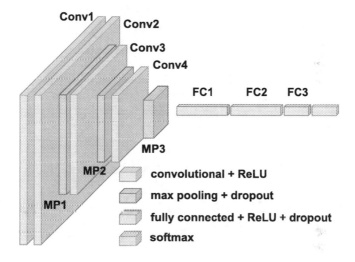

Fig. 4. Architecture of the proposed deep model (Conv: Convolution layer, FC: Fully connected layer, MP: Max-pooling layer)

5   Experiments and Result Analysis

5.1   Implementation Details

70 and 30% of data from each activity class are used for training and testing purposes, respectively. The validation set receives 10% of the training data, ensuring that the training and validation sets do not overlap. A lower data window is preferred in literature for acoustic scene classification [10]; therefore, a window length of 2.0 s with 50% overlap is considered in our work. The MFCC features were computed for 40 bands (k) with a hop-length of value 88 (h) on each W_t. The shape of the MFCC feature for one sample is 40×502 ($m \times n$). These MFCC values are fed as inputs to the deep model. Figure 5 depicts the training and validation loss over 50 epochs. Categorical-crossentropy and ReLU were used as loss and activation functions, respectively. The softmax activation

function was used at the last layer to obtain the class label. Adam was chosen as the optimizer with a learning rate of 0.00001. Further, we use F1-score to evaluate the efficacy of the proposed framework.

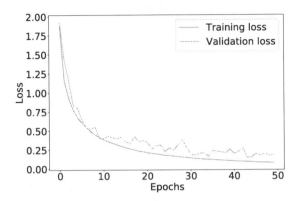

Fig. 5. Training and validation loss for the proposed deep model

Table 2. Comparison of existing works with proposed framework on parameter F1-score

Feature Type →	Handcrafted Features		Deep Features				
Activity Name ↓	Vafeiadis et al. [22]	Küçükbay et al. [16]	Ekpezu et al. CNN [8]	Ekpezu et al. LSTM [8]	VGGish [11] + ANN	OpenL3 [5] + ANN	Proposed
Noise	0.16	0.00	0.77	0.64	0.82	0.81	**0.90**
Run	0.03	0.00	0.51	0.50	0.50	0.65	**0.73**
Jog	0.00	0.00	0.52	0.38	0.53	0.64	**0.81**
Walk	0.00	0.00	0.64	0.74	0.63	0.64	**0.81**
Jumping Jacks	0.09	0.00	0.80	0.56	0.72	0.80	**0.91**
Jump	0.08	0.00	0.53	0.49	0.67	0.75	**0.93**
Hammer Strike	0.06	0.00	0.41	0.49	0.71	0.80	**0.87**
Bicycle	0.02	0.04	0.59	0.55	0.46	0.57	**0.73**
Bike	0.17	0.59	0.89	0.88	0.84	0.86	**0.93**
Mean	*0.07*	*0.16*	*0.63*	*0.58*	*0.65*	*0.63*	***0.85***

5.2 Comparison with Existing Works

We have compared the proposed framework with state-of-the-art deep learning and traditional handcrafted features based works, close to the task presented in this paper. The performance of the proposed framework is compared with two state-of-the-art transfer learning based methods, viz., VGGish [11] and OpenL3 [5]. Features extracted using transfer learning methods are further passed through an artificial neural network to obtain the class label of a given test sample. The artificial neural network has 3 layers with 50, 30, and 10 neurons in each layer. Adam was used as an optimizer with a learning rate of 0.00001. The network is trained for 1000 iterations.

In addition to the transfer-learning based methods, we also compare the proposed framework with the work of Ekpezu et al. [8], Küçükbay et al. [16], and Vafeiadis et al. [22]. Ekpezu et al. [8] provided two models viz., CNN and LSTM based for environmental sound classification. Küçükbay et al. [16] extracted MFCC features to classify sounds of animals, humans, and vehicles. Further, an SVM classifier (linear kernel) with a one-versus-all technique was used for the multiclass classification problem. In the work by Vafeiadis et al. [22], ZCR, MFCC, and discrete wavelet transform (Daubechies family with 3 levels, output shape training instances × 48315) are used to get a representation of an audio chunk. Further, PCA (number of principle components = 2000) is applied to reduce the feature dimension. Further, these features were fed as inputs to an SVM classifier with linear kernel to obtain the type of activity.

Table 2 compares the above-mentioned works using F1-score. Average F1-scores have been reported for each work to show the overall efficacy. We can see that the proposed framework outperforms other works for each activity class. We also observe that deep learning based works outperform the traditional hand-crafted feature based machine learning works. Class-wise best performance by other works is {0.82, 0.65, 0.64, 0.74, 0.80, 0.75, 0.80, 0.59, 0.89}, whereas the proposed framework achieves {0.90, 0.73, 0.81, 0.81, 0.91, 0.93, 0.87, 0.73, 0.93}. Thus, the proposed model shows an improvement of {9.75, 12.30, 26.56, 9.45, 13.75, 24.00, 8.75, 23.72, 4.49}% in F1-scores for the 9 classes. After analyzing the average performance across classes, i.e., mean F1-score values, we see that the proposed framework outperforms the best perming state-of-the-art work by 16.43%.

Predicted Label

	A_0	A_1	A_2	A_3	A_4	A_5	A_6	A_7	A_8
A_0	3101	125	64	102	9	5	9	129	42
A_1	45	269	13	0	0	0	1	1	0
A_2	49	11	305	0	0	0	1	0	0
A_3	18	0	0	258	0	1	0	1	0
A_4	11	0	1	0	125	1	0	0	0
A_5	9	0	0	1	1	138	3	0	0
A_6	4	0	0	0	2	1	73	0	0
A_7	50	0	0	1	0	0	0	250	0
A_8	26	0	1	0	0	0	0	0	455

(True Label)

Fig. 6. Confusion matrix for audio based human activity recognition. The activity classes are denoted as (A_0) background noise, (A_1) running, (A_2) jogging, (A_3) walking, (A_4) jumping jacks, (A_5) jump, (A_6) hammer strike on ground, (A_7) cycling, and (A_8) bike.

5.3   Analysis of Confusion Matrix

In Fig. 6, we show the confusion matrix to closely analyze the activity-wise performance of the proposed framework. Many instances of activity classes (A_1 to A_8) are classified as background noise (A_0). This indicates that noise is a critical issue in an outdoor environment. Similarly, many instances of background noise

(A_0) are classified as activities $(A_1$ to $A_8)$. The activity sounds can be drowned out when the background noise is too loud. Our main conclusion is that if we disregard the noise, the model can almost always classify any activity correctly. Running (A_1) and jogging (A_2) are very similar activities, so numerous instances of running and jogging are classified into each other. Even though jumping (A_5) and hammer strike on the ground (A_6) appear to be very similar, the proposed model produces few misclassifications for these classes. It signifies the discriminating ability of the proposed deep model. We also observe that cycling (A_7) and riding a bike (A_8) shows negligible misclassification except for the noise class (A_0).

6   Conclusion

In this paper, we presented a 2D CNN-based human activity recognition framework that exploits deep representation for activity recognition using audio data. We evaluated the proposed framework's efficacy against a variety of machine and transfer learning-based classifiers on a window of 2.0 s. We found that the proposed framework achieves the highest average F1-score of 85%. We also observe that deep learning based works perform better than machine learning based classifier. Additionally, we conclude that minimizing the effect of ambient noise is crucial for effective human activity recognition in outdoor environments.

References

1. Carletti, V., Foggia, P., Percannella, G., Saggese, A., Strisciuglio, N., Vento, M.: Audio surveillance using a bag of aural words classifier. In: 10th IEEE International Conference on Advanced Video and Signal Based Surveillance (AVSS), pp. 81–86. Krakow, Poland (2013)
2. Chawla, N.V., Bowyer, K.W., Hall, L.O., Kegelmeyer, W.P.: Smote: synthetic minority over-sampling technique. J. Artif. Intell. Res. **16**(1), 321–357 (2002)
3. Chen, J., Kam, A.H., Zhang, J., Liu, N., Shue, L.: Bathroom activity monitoring based on sound. In: Gellersen, H.-W., Want, R., Schmidt, A. (eds.) Pervasive 2005. LNCS, vol. 3468, pp. 47–61. Springer, Heidelberg (2005). https://doi.org/10.1007/11428572_4
4. Choudhary, P., Kumari, P.: An audio-seismic dataset for human activity recognition (2022). https://doi.org/10.21227/315c-zw20
5. Cramer, J., Wu, H.H., Salamon, J., Bello, J.P.: Look, listen, and learn more: design choices for deep audio embeddings. In: International Conference on Acoustics, Speech and Signal Processing (ICASSP), pp. 3852–3856. IEEE (2019)
6. Cui, W., Li, B., Zhang, L., Chen, Z.: Device-free single-user activity recognition using diversified deep ensemble learning. Appl. Soft Comput. **102**, 107066 (2021)
7. Doukas, C., Maglogiannis, I.: Advanced patient or elder fall detection based on movement and sound data. In: 2nd International Conference on Pervasive Computing Technologies for Healthcare, pp. 103–107. IEEE (2008)
8. Ekpezu, A.O., Wiafe, I., Katsriku, F., Yaokumah, W.: Using deep learning for acoustic event classification: the case of natural disasters. J. Acoust. Soc. Am. **149**(4), 2926–2935 (2021)

9. Foggia, P., Petkov, N., Saggese, A., Strisciuglio, N., Vento, M.: Audio surveillance of roads: A system for detecting anomalous sounds. IEEE Trans. Intell. Transp. Syst. **17**(1), 279–288 (2015)
10. Geiger, J.T., Schuller, B., Rigoll, G.: Large-scale audio feature extraction and SVM for acoustic scene classification. In: Workshop on Applications of Signal Processing to Audio and Acoustics, pp. 1–4. IEEE (2013)
11. Hershey, S., et al.: CNN architectures for large-scale audio classification. In: International Conference on Acoustics, Speech and Signal Processing (ICASSP), pp. 131–135. IEEE (2017)
12. Iravantchi, Y., Ahuja, K., Goel, M., Harrison, C., Sample, A.: PrivacyMic: utilizing inaudible frequencies for privacy preserving daily activity recognition. In: CHI Conference on Human Factors in Computing Systems, pp. 1–13. ACM (2021)
13. Jung, M., Chi, S.: Human activity classification based on sound recognition and residual convolutional neural network. Autom. Construct. **114**, 103177 (2020)
14. Khatun, A., Hossain, S., Sarowar, G.: A Fourier domain feature approach for human activity recognition & fall detection. arXiv preprint arXiv:2003.05209 (2020)
15. Kraft, F., Malkin, R., Schaaf, T., Waibel, A.: Temporal ICA for classification of acoustic events in a kitchen environment. In: Interspeech, Lisbon, Portugal, vol. 605. CiteSeer (2005)
16. Küçükbay, S.E., Sert, M., Yazici, A.: Use of acoustic and vibration sensor data to detect objects in surveillance wireless sensor networks. In: 21st International Conference on Control Systems and Computer Science (CSCS), pp. 207–212. IEEE, Bucharest, Romania (2017)
17. Lee, Y.C., Scarpiniti, M., Uncini, A.: Advanced sound classifiers and performance analyses for accurate audio-based construction project monitoring. J. Comput. Civ. Eng. **34**(5), 04020030 (2020)
18. Peltonen, V., Tuomi, J., Klapuri, A., Huopaniemi, J., Sorsa, T.: Computational auditory scene recognition. In: International Conference on Acoustics, Speech and Signal Processing (ICASSP). vol. 2, pp. II-1941. Orlando, FL, USA (2002)
19. Pucci, L., Testi, E., Favarelli, E., Giorgetti, A.: Human activities classification using biaxial seismic sensors. IEEE Sens. Lett. **4**(10), 1–4 (2020)
20. Rashid, K.M., Louis, J.: Activity identification in modular construction using audio signals and machine learning. Autom. Constr. **119**, 103361 (2020)
21. Sherafat, B., Rashidi, A., Lee, Y.C., Ahn, C.R.: Automated activity recognition of construction equipment using a data fusion approach. In: Computing in Civil Engineering 2019: Data, Sensing, and Analytics, pp. 1–8. ASCE (2019)
22. Vafeiadis, A., Votis, K., Giakoumis, D., Tzovaras, D., Chen, L., Hamzaoui, R.: Audio-based event recognition system for smart homes. In: IEEE SmartWorld, Ubiquitous Intelligence & Computing, Advanced & Trusted Computed, Scalable Computing & Communications, Cloud & Big Data Computing, Internet of People and Smart City Innovation, pp. 1–8. IEEE (2017)
23. Vafeiadis, A., Votis, K., Giakoumis, D., Tzovaras, D., Chen, L., Hamzaoui, R.: Audio content analysis for unobtrusive event detection in smart homes. Eng. Appl. Artif. Intell. **89**, 103226 (2020)

24. Yin, C., Chen, J., Miao, X., Jiang, H., Chen, D.: Device-free human activity recognition with low-resolution infrared array sensor using long short-term memory neural network. Sensors **21**(10), 3551 (2021)
25. Zhu, C., Sheng, W.: Wearable sensor-based hand gesture and daily activity recognition for robot-assisted living. IEEE Trans. Syst. Man Cybern. Syst. **41**(3), 569–573 (2011)

Detection of Narrow River Trails with the Presence of Highways from Landsat 8 OLI Images

Jit Mukherjee[✉][iD], Peeyush Gupta, Harshit Gautam,
and Renuka Chintalapati

Department of Computer Science and Engineering, Birla Institute of Technology,
Mesra, Ranchi 835215, India
jit.mukherjee@bitmesra.ac.in

Abstract. River is one of the most important land classes of our environment and civilization since the ancient times. Several factors including excessive river sedimentation, industrial waste, illegal mining, affect the river health to the extent of narrower river trails, change of courses, and different levels of water pollution. Hence, monitoring of river health has become a crucial issue, where remote sensing based observations are applied in recent times. There are several indexes to detect water bodies from multispectral images. However, detecting and isolating rivers, especially narrow rivers are found challenging. Further, higher degree of sinuosity triggers the change of river direction and narrowness of the river width. Due to this narrowness, a complete river trail appears as segments of disconnected trails. Additionally, the spectral properties of narrow river trails are found to be similar to different land classes, especially highways, when these indexes are used. In this work, we have proposed a novel technique to detect narrow river trails based on the spatial features and pixel associativity with the presence of highways without labelled dataset. The spatial texture of narrow river trails is assumed different from most of the other land classes detected in these water indexes. The roads, which are comprehensible from mid-resolution satellite images, are generally highways and have less sinuosity. These characteristics are considered here to separate narrow river trails from those land classes having near similar spectral characteristics. The proposed technique has precision, recall and accuracy of 84.52%, 71.51%, and 96.97%, respectively.

Keywords: River Trails · NDWI · Highways · Narrow Rivers · LANDSAT 8 · Hough Lines · Gabor Filter · Morphological Operations

1 Introduction

Water is a critical part of the environment. The planning, development, and management of water resources is important for maintaining the integrity of the ecosystem. It is crucial for climate changes, aquatic ecosystems, ecological

D. Gupta et al. (Eds.): CVIP 2022, CCIS 1777, pp. 659–673, 2023.
https://doi.org/10.1007/978-3-031-31417-9_50

processes, and the water cycle. However, increasing population and consequent increase in food requirements has lately put a lot of stress on allocation of water resources, and demands for a more holistic water management approach, especially in the sector of agriculture and irrigation. Adequate management is possible only with consistent and continuous monitoring of water resources, which involves detecting and inspecting the characteristics of different types of water bodies. Satellite imaging is one such cost-effective technology that could be used to inspect water resources with the help of reliable data sets. Among various water resources, rivers are one of the crucial aspects of our civilization. There are several factors, which impact river health directly. Hence, monitoring of river health and morphology have been discussed thoroughly in the literature. Multi-spectral images use different spectral indexes to study land classes. There are several indexes to detect water bodies from multispectral images. One of the widely used water indexes, Normalized Difference Water Index (NDWI) is defined to detect open water features using *Green* and Near Infra-red (*NIR*) bands [22]. However, *NDWI* has been found to be inefficient for a few land classes such as build up regions, roads, and shadows. Thus, an improvement over *NDWI* has been proposed using *Green* and short-wave infra-red (*SWIR-I*) bands named as Modified Normalized Difference Water Index (MNDWI). These indexes use manual threshold to detect water body regions by preserving the higher values. Hence, an automated technique has been proposed in [7] to detect water bodies without manual intervention. However, different land classes, mostly roads or highways, are falsely detected while using these indexes. Further, separation of rivers from such water bodies needs more experimentation and research.

1.1 Related Works

Fluvial remote sensing, on other hand, is one of the emerging areas of remote sensing [20]. As surface topography has significant effects on formation of river networks, digital terrain model (*DTM*) data has been used widely in the literature to detect river networks. *DTM* data has been found convenient to determine drainage networks in both globally and regionally [18,24]. However, *DTM* based river trail detection may suffer from faulty *DTM* processing using thresholds [15], limited spatial resolution [15], temporal topographic changes [25], crevasses, limited accuracies of *DTM* [12] and many more [14]. Thus, river trail detection using passive and active remote sensing is gaining attention due to such limitation of *DTM* data [2]. A supervised image classification technique has been applied on synthetic aperture radar (*SAR*) data to detect river drainage pattern and delineation of rivers in [10,13]. However, these works have not studied narrow river trail detection thoroughly. Further, in most of the cases *SAR* images are not acquired within regular time intervals and may suffer from speckle noises. The attention on river trail detection using multi-spectral images has been limited. In [30], Gabor filter is employed to detect rivers from Landsat images. It considers rivers as continuous but not as a series of disconnected curvilinear segments. Hence, it does not consider the additional complexity of narrow river trail detection and availability of highways in the surroundings. In such work, detection of river trails are addressed mostly by the determination of linear and curvilinear features, which itself is a well-studied image processing research problem. Curvilinear features are irregular and they can vary over time such as in a river trail. Further they can be discontinuous and their spatial contrast can vary significantly [31]. Detection of linear and curvilinear features from images have been studied by various features such as edges [3], gradient vector flow [28], learning based techniques [21], graph based techniques [5] and others. Each of these techniques has advantages in different scenarios. However, hough space based detection has been found to be effective in different applications to detect curvilinear structures in images [31]. There are several works for automated roads extraction from satellite images [26]. One of the major difficulties for road network extraction is their spectral similarities with other different land classes primarily the water bodies [26]. It has been further observed that narrow river trails have near similar spectral characteristics with highways.

1.2   Objectives and Contributions

As discussed, discussion on detection of narrow river trails using multispectral images has been limited in the literature. A few works detect rivers as continuous without considering the additional complexities of detecting narrow river trails, which may appear as isolated segments. Further, roads, and highways have similar spectral properties with narrow river trails. Hence, in this work, a novel technique has been proposed to detect narrow river trails with the presence of highways without any labelled dataset using multispectral images exclusively.

2   Methodology

The paper provides an amalgamation of different techniques consisting of spectral and spatial parameters as shown in Fig. 1. As shown in Fig. 1, the water index, *NDWI* is computed first from green and near infra-red bands. Further, the texture features are analysed using the Gabor filter over the *NDWI* image. The portions of straight lines detected by Hough lines are discarded further. Next, the isolated adjacent segments of river trails are joined using morphological operations. Further, the connected component analysis discards other regions than narrow river trails. Last, the final outcome is obtained by eroding the preserved connected components.

2.1   Spectral Index

A typical spectral index is defined as a simple or spectral ratio of two or more bands in a satellite image. A spectral ratio ($\phi(\lambda_1, \lambda_2)$) is shown in Eq. 1.

$$\phi(\lambda_1, \lambda_2) = \frac{\lambda_1 - \lambda_2}{\lambda_1 + \lambda_2} \tag{1}$$

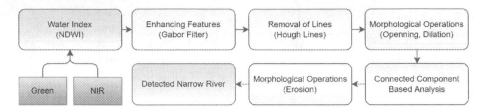

Fig. 1. The Proposed Methodology to Detect Narrow River Trails

Here, λ represents reflectance values of a spectral band. There are several spectral indexes to detect different land classes. Normalized Difference Water Index is proposed as a spectral index of green and near infra-red bands ($\frac{\lambda_{Green}-\lambda_{NIR}}{\lambda_{Green}+\lambda_{NIR}}$) in [22]. Higher values of *NDWI* preserve water bodies. However, it has been observed that *NDWI* is unproductive at suppressing the signal from different land classes such as highways, built-up surfaces [17]. Thus, a new index, Modi-fied Normalized Difference Water Index (MNDWI, $\frac{\lambda_{Green}-\lambda_{SWIR-I}}{\lambda_{Green}+\lambda_{SWIR-I}}$), is defined to differentiate constructed features from water and enhance open water body features [7,29]. Higher values of *MNDWI* preserves open water features. Due to fluctuating quality of water depending on the colour, composition, and depth of the water body under examination [8], in few cases *NDWI* provides superior outcome than *MNDWI* [1,17] and in other cases vice versa [6,11]. However, it has been observed that such water indexes can not separate narrow river trails from constructed features especially highways due to the less amount of open water content in narrow river trails as shown in Fig. 2. Further, other non water body regions also get falsely detected if the threshold is decreased to preserve narrow river trails as shown in Fig. 2. In this work, *NDWI* has been used for their wide applicability.

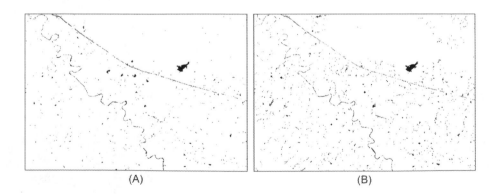

(A)   (B)

Fig. 2. Threshold applied to preserve higher values in (A) NDWI, (B) MNDWI

2.2   Enhancing Curvilinear Patterns

In this work, texture features of the water body index, i.e. *NDWI*, are considered to highlight the higher values. *NDWI* highlights a few locations which can be treated as noise. Hence, before applying texture features, the *NDWI* image is treated with Gaussian blur, where the image is convoluted with a Gaussian filter, to reduce noise to a certain degree. In *NDWI*, rivers, especially narrow rivers exhibit low spectral contrast with background and a few curvilinear features of a river are inseparable with the background [30]. Hence, Gabor filter [19] is applied to highlight the curvilinear patterns and contrast of a river detected by *NDWI*. Gabor filter has been found effective to enhance the contrast and curvilinear features in various applications such as blood vessels detection [16]. Gabor filter is a linear filter as shown in Eq. 2.

$$G(x, y; \Lambda, \theta, \psi, o, \gamma) = exp(-\frac{x'^2 + \gamma^2 y'^2}{2\sigma^2})exp(i(\frac{2\pi x'}{\Lambda} + \psi)) \tag{2}$$

Here, $x' =$ x cos θ+y sinθ and $y' = $ -x cos θ+y sin θ. Further, Λ represents the wavelength, σ depicts the scale of Gaussian envelope, ψ represents phase offset, γ specifies ellipticity of the Gabor function and θ is defined as the orientation of the Gabor kernel. In this work, a bank of Gabor filters with orientation θ uniformly distributed in the interval $[0, \pi]$, has been used to detect the features in different orientations. Given an *NDWI* image, the bank of Gabor filters is iteratively applied and local maxima is computed in each direction until a global maxima is found across all the filters. These enhances the curvilinear patterns and contrast of narrow rivers from *NDWI*, which are further studied.

2.3   Removal of Straight Lines

It has been observed that various features such as build up, shadow, roads are also enhanced along with water bodies when the bank of Gabor filter is applied. Most of the detected water bodies and these falsely detected regions are small with respect to a river trail. Hence, the length and size of a river trail can be a distinguishing factor. However, a long stretched road such as a highway can have similar or longer trails. As a typical highway has much lower sinuosity and bends compared to a narrow river, the linear structures over the outcome of Gabor filter are further considered. Thus, Hough line features are further studied to separate narrow river trails and highways [9]. First, boundaries are generated by applying Canny edge detection algorithm [4] to prevent detection of false lines and to give contrast between pixels to improve Hough line algorithm results. To discard any unwanted pixels which are not part of the edge, each pixel is checked if it is a local maximum in the direction of its gradient. It will be considered If the pixel is the local maximum, else it will be rejected [4].

A line can be represented in polar coordinates. All the lines passing through a pixel (x_0, y_0) can be represented as as shown in Eq. 3.

$$r = x_0 cos\theta + y_0 sin\theta \tag{3}$$

Such a point will result in a sinusoidal curve on the Hough space (θ, r) plane. Two points belong to the same line, if the curves of two different pixels intersect in Hough space (θ, r) [9]. By providing a minimum number of intersections, a line can be identified. A minimum length of line is also defined to remove falsely detected lines. By this process, the linear structures of the image are detected. These linear structures are mostly highways and rail lines. Such linear structures are removed to further process the rectified image.

2.4   Morphological Operations

Through the removal of linear structures, a segment of highways and rail lines are removed. However, a river can have a portion with linear structures. They are also removed by this procedure. Thus, the narrow river trail, which already appears as segments of river trails, becomes isolated with more segments. Hence, morphological operations are further applied. Previously, hough lines were applied over the edges detected by the Canny edge detector. Hence, the river trail has become a 2-tuple of trails along the edges, whereas the intermediate portion remains vacant. Hence, morphological closing is applied to fill in these gaps. Morphological closing is dilation followed by erosion operation. It is useful in closing holes inside the foreground objects. The closing of a set A by a structuring element B is shown in Eq. 4.

$$A.B = (A \oplus B) \ominus B \tag{4}$$

Here $\oplus$ and $\ominus$ are denoted for dilation and erosion operations respectively. In dilation, shapes contained in an image are expanded using a structuring element. The shapes are reduced by a structuring element in erosion. The intermediate portions of two edges are filled by this closing operation. However, different segments of the narrow river trail remain isolated. Hence, a morphological dilation operation is further applied. As morphological dilation expands the shapes, the isolated portions of the narrow river trail get connected.

2.5   Connected Component Analysis

The length and size of a complete river trail is bigger than most of the detected land classes. Therefore, a connected component based analysis is used to separate narrow river trails from other water bodies and falsely detected regions. In connected component based analysis, each connected component is assigned different labels such that they can be treated individually. For each connected component, if the size of the component is smaller than the half of width of the image, those connected components are discarded. Thus, the remaining connected components are considered as the dilated river trails. Further these images with dilated trails are eroded to get the actual shape of the narrow river trails. The similar structuring element is used for erosion, which is used for the morphological closing operations.

The proposed technique uses $NDWI$ and further studies it to detect the narrow river trail. Hence, the proposed technique can be used in any satellite modality which has $Green$ and NIR bands.

3   Data and Study Area

Damodar river has a tributary named Jamunia river. It flows through various districts in Jharkhand, India such as Hazaribagh, Giridih, Bokaro and Dhanbad. Jamunia river shows tortuous sinuosity. It runs near the grand trunk road which is one of the primary highways of India. Further, Gomoh railway station, which is at 23.8702° N, 86.1521° E is also close to selected region. It has been observed that railway tracks and highways have near similar spectral characteristics with narrow river trails. Hence, Jamunia river is chosen as the study area. The region of interest has diverse land classes such as narrow rivers, vegetation, crop lands, coal mining regions, urban land, highways, railway tracks and stations, bare lands, smaller hills, etc., In this work, Landsat 8 OLI/TIRS $L1$ data from path 140 and row 43 as per landsat reference system has been used. Landsat 8 provides eight multi-spectral bands $(0.43\,\mu m - 2.29\,\mu m)$, two thermal bands $(10.6\,\mu m - 12.51\,\mu m)$, one panchromatic band and a cirrus band. It has a temporal resolution of 16 days. The bands related to operational land imager (OLI) sensors of Landsat 8 have spatial resolution of 30 m except the panchromatic band. These images are corrected and ortho-rectified. $L1$ data provides top of atmosphere reflectance values. In this work, as multispectral images are prone to clouds, Landsat data with $< 10\%$ cloud cover are considered. High resolution Google Earth images are manually marked for ground truth generation.

4   Results and Discussion

In this work, Landsat 8 data from March, 2022 from Path 140, and Row 43 as per landsat reference system has been used. A region of interest having a national highway, a railway track, and the Jamunia river is cropped from the original image using $QGIS$. The results are obtained over this region of interest as shown in Fig. 3. The outcome of $NDWI$ over the region of interest is shown in Fig. 3 (A). As shown in Fig. 3 (A), the narrow trail can be visible and the river trail has multiple bends and curvilinear features. Further, in some portions, the contrast of these trails are lower than other water body regions. Additionally, the highway can be visible at the top of the Jamunia river and it has near similar spatial contrast with the narrow river trail. A few portions of railway track are also having higher values as shown in Fig. 3 (A). Different thresholds are applied to $NDWI$ and $MNDWI$ to detect the narrow river trail as shown in Fig. 2. It can be observed that narrow river trails can not be separated using thresholds. A higher threshold fails to detect significant portions of the narrow rivers. A lower threshold falsely detects different land classes which are not part of water bodies. Gabor filter is applied over this $NDWI$ image to enhance spatial contract and curvilinear features as shown in Fig. 3 (B). Before applying the Gabor filter, the image is treated with Gaussian blur, The parameters of the Gabor filter are empirically chosen as $\sigma = 1$, $\lambda = 3$ and a bank of 1024 filters is used. It can be observed that the comprehensibility of the narrow river trail has been increased and their curvilinear features are highlighted. However, as shown in Fig. 3 (B),

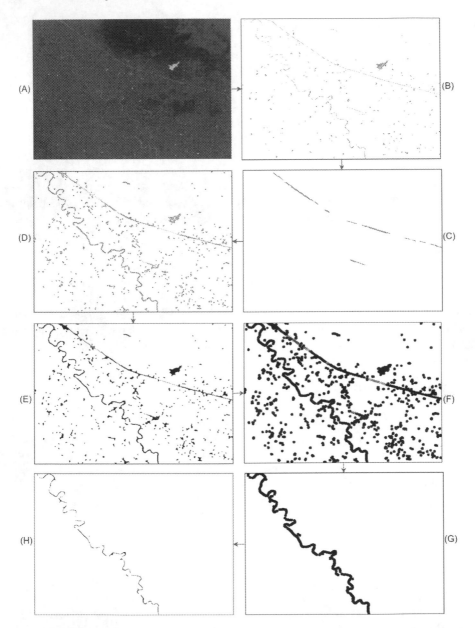

Fig. 3. Results: (A) Output of NDWI, (B) Gabor Filter applied on NDWI, (C) Detected lines using Hough Lines, (D) Removal of Lines, (E) Morphological Close to file holes, (F) Morphological Dilation to Connect Isolated Portions, (G) Connected Component Based Analysis, (H) Final Result - Detected Narrow River Trails.

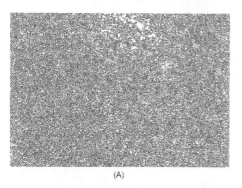
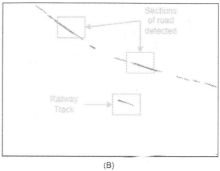

(A)   (B)

Fig. 4. Results: (A) Outcome without Gabor Filter, (B) Location of Falsely Detected Railway Tracks and Roads.

several other regions, mostly highways and railway tracks are falsely detected along with different water bodies including narrow river trails. To remove these falsely detected regions, hough lines are further studied. It is assumed that a typical narrow river trail has more bends than a highway and a railway track. A typical narrow river trail have higher degrees of sinuosity. There are several factors that create a higher degrees of sinuosity such as change of river direction, sedimentation on the river bank, and human intervention. Notwithstanding the fact that higher sinuosity adds more complexity to the problem of river trail detection as such narrow trails are difficult to detect from multi-spectral images, higher sinuosity can be used further to separate such falsely detected regions especially highways. A typical highway has much lower sinuosity and can have long stretches as straight lines, which a narrow river trail generally lacks. Smaller roads can have higher degrees of sinuosity and bends, especially which are inside a city. However, width of such typical roads are insignificant with respect to the spatial resolution of a multi-spectral image. The minimum length threshold for hough line is chosen empirically as 10. Thus, the linear potions of the images are detected as shown in Fig. 3 (C). These portions are removed from the obtained image after applying a bank of Gabor filters as shown in Fig. 3 (D). The location of roads and railway tracks, which are detected by hough lines are marked in Fig. 4 (B). *NDWI* has several small features which may get detected if Gaussian blur and Gabor filter is not applied. Figure 4 (A) shows the outcome after removal of linear features if Gabor filter and Gaussian blur are not applied. A narrow river can also have a few portions, where the trail follows a linear pattern. Hence, those linear portions can also be removed, which disconnects the river trail at multiple positions. A narrow river trail already appears as a segments of disconnected portions due to it's varying width, which may become insignificant to the spatial resolution of a satellite image. Hence, this removal of linear features introduce additional complexity. Therefore, the image is further treated with morphological operations to overcome this bottleneck. Furthermore, after applying Gabor filters the edges of the river trail are highlighted. However, the intermediate portions of the banks of rivers remain vacant. Hence, morphological opening is applied first to fill in these regions. In this work, a structuring element of the 9×9 kernel in the shape of eclipse is considered here empirically. As observed in Fig. 3 (E), the intermediate portions of the banks of the narrow river trail is filled up. However, different parts of the narrow river still remain disconnected. Hence, a morphological dilation is applied to connect these separated portions as shown in Fig. 3 (F). It also can be observed that the nearby lakes especially near the bend of the narrow river get falsely connected. As linear features are more prominent in roads and railway tracks than rivers, a connected component based analysis is studied to get the components with higher sizes. For connected components, the minimum number of pixels threshold is taken to be the half of the image width. The connected components which have higher size than the threshold are preserved (Fig. 3 (G)). As it is assumed here that the narrow river is one of the prominent land class of the image considered, the threshold value is kept as the half of the size of the image width. It needs further experimentation where the narrow river trail is a minor land class considering the size of a satellite image. It is treated as a future work. As observed in Fig. 3 (G) the proposed technique can separate other regions from the narrow river trail. However, it is the dilated version of the river trail. Hence, in the final step, a morphological erosion is applied with the same structuring element. The final outcome of the detect narrow trail is shown in Fig. 3 (H). It can be observed from Fig. 3 (A) and (H) that most of the narrow river trail portions are correctly detected by the proposed technique. A few water bodies which are close to the river trails are falsely detected. The proposed technique has been implemented using *Python* and *OpenCV*. It is an amalgamation of different techniques. The proposed technique can be implemented using *ArcGIS* or *QGIS*, if these techniques are available in such applications.

4.1   Validation

Ground truth regions are extracted from high resolution Google Earth images for validation. The region of interest has prominent land classes of bare lands, vegetation, lakes, and urban lands along with a narrow river trail, railway tracks and highway. Different samples of these land classes are extracted and their spectral responses are computed in different spectrum. In this work, *NDWI* and *MNDWI* are considered. Hence, reflectance values of these land classes in *Green*, *NIR*, and *SWIR-I* bands are studied for validation as shown in Fig. 5. As observed in Fig. 5, narrow rivers follow different patterns than other water bodies in near infra-red and short wave infra-red bands. These narrow trails have prominent river sandbanks. Further, their width may become so narrow considering the spatial resolution of a satellite image that the reflectance values of the surrounding regions are induced with their reflectance values as noise. These affect the reflectance values in the near infra-red and short wave infra-red bands for narrow trails. Thus, it may follow different patterns than a typical water body. However, it also can be observed from Fig. 5 that the reflectance pattern of a narrow trail follows near similar characteristics in roads and railway tracks.

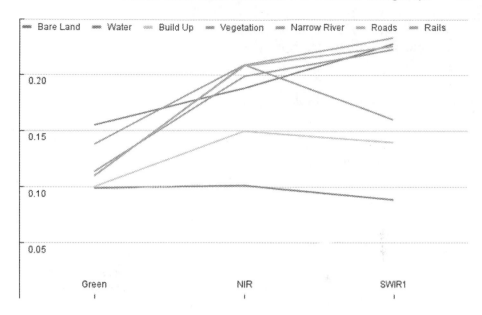

Fig. 5. Spectral Response of Different Land Classes in Green, NIR and SWIR-I bands (Color figure online)

It can be observed that the slope and change of values in near infra-red and short wave infra-red bands are near similar for roads and narrow river trails. Similar observations can be obtained for railway tracks and narrow river trails in green and short wave infra-red bands. However, near infra-red values of narrow river is found to be higher than railway tracks. Hence, it can be stated that narrow river bed follows different patterns than other land classes except roads. In some cases, it may follow similar characteristics with railway tracks. Hence, a hypothesis testing using t-test is studied further for validation. The null and alternative hypothesis are considered as $\mu_{NarrowRiver} = \mu_{Other}$, and $\mu_{NarrowRiver} \neq \mu_{Other}$, respectively where $\mu_{NarrowRiver}$ is considered as the mean of narrow river values and μ_{Other} is considered as the mean of roads or railways tracks. 100 random samples are taken from narrow river, highway and railway tracks to conduct the study. Table 1 shows the outcome of the t-test. As observed from Table 1, the null hypothesis can not be rejected for roads and narrow rivers as the p value is higher than 0.05 for both *NDWI* and *MNDWI*. Hence, *NDWI* and *MNDWI* can not significantly distinguish between roads and narrow rivers. Further, the null hypothesis can not be rejected for *MNDWI* in case of railway tracks and narrow rivers. However, the null hypothesis can be rejected for *NDWI* in case of railway tracks and narrow rivers. As *NDWI* is a spectral index of *Green* and *NIR* bands and railway track and narrow rivers follow different patterns in these bands as observed in Fig. 5. Hence, *NDWI* can distinguish railway tracks and narrow rivers. However, a portion of the railway track is falsely detected while detecting narrow rivers using *NDWI*. It is observed that the falsely detected portion is close to a railway junction whose spectral signature can be different than a railway track. Further experimentation in this regard is considered as a future work.

Table 1. T-test result for Narrow Rivers with Roads and Rail Tracks over NDWI and MNDWI.

Narrow River	Road			Rail Track		
	t_0	df	P Value	t_0	df	P Value
NDWI	0.192	198	0.848	2.26	198	0.0246
MNDWI	1.48	198	0.14	1.91	198	0.0575

Further, the ground truth images are used to compute the accuracy of the proposed technique. The proposed technique has precision, recall and accuracy of 84.52%, 71.51%, and 96.97%, respectively. A few lakes, especially oxbow lakes closer to the bend of the narrow trail are detected as narrow river trails by the proposed technique. The precision of the proposed algorithm can be improved if such lakes can be identified and separated. A few regions of river trail where contrast is very low in *NDWI* can not be detected by the proposed method. It affects the recall value of the proposed technique and is considered as one of the future directions. In the past, *DTM* and *SAR* images mostly used to detect drainage systems and river networks. *DTM* data has been found productive for the detection of river networks. However, it may suffer from several issues such as limited spatial resolution, temporal topographic changes, crevasses, limited accuracies of *DTM*, etc. [14]. Thus, passive and active remote sensing based techniques are given priority in the recent past. However, *SAR* images are not obtained in regular interval unlike Landsat images. Therefore, satellite modalities such as Landsat are more suitable for detection narrow river trails which can change its courses over time and prone to floods. Furthermore, *SAR* images require a series of processing and are affected by speckle noise. Multispectral images have been used in the past to detect river trails using Gabor filter [30]. However, it considers rivers as continuous but not as a series of disconnected curvilinear segments. Hence, it is incompatible for the detection narrow river trails. Further, it does not consider the near similar spectral properties of roads. The applicability of water body indexes using Landsat 8 images is studied in various works [6,23]. Most these techniques considers various classes of water bodies such as, lakes, rivers, lakes, dams, and others as a single class. A multi-modal supervised technique considering Landsat 7 and *GIS* data, have been studied for automated mapping of lakes through classification and texture analysis with overall accuracy of 94.88% [27]. In [1], rivers, lakes and different water bodies are identified using machine learning techniques where *j48* decision tree provides overall accuracy of 99.15%. However, they do not separate narrow river trails and do not consider the affect of roads in nearby regions. The proposed technique detects narrow river trails, which appears as disconnected segments with the presence of highways using Landsat images exclusively without any labelled dataset. However, the proposed technique is incompatible when the width of a narrow river trail is insignificant with respect to the spatial resolution of the satellite modality. Further, if two segments of a narrow river trail are very distant, the proposed technique may not provide adequate results. These are considered as some of the future directions of the work. In this work, the narrow river trail is considered to be at the salient regions of the image and prominent considering the image size. Further experimentation is needed to detect narrow rivers, which are at the non-salient regions and occupy a small segment of the image. It is considered as a future work. The proposed technique is an amalgamation of different methods. A few of them, e.g. gabor filter, have high time complexity. Real time detection of narrow river trails is considered as a future direction.

5   Conclusions

Detection of river trails has several applications on monitoring, river morphology, and flood prevention. A narrow river trail has near similar spectral characteristics with other land classes, primarily roads. Further, it is difficult to detect narrow river trail using conventional water index as their values are significantly different from a typical water body in a mid resolution multispectral image. Further, a narrow river trail appears as segments of disconnected portions, which creates additional research problems. In the past, DTM and SAR images were mostly used to detect river networks. Through experimentation to detect narrow rivers using multispectral images is yet to be obtained. Hence, in this work, a novel technique is proposed to detect narrow river trails using multispectral images with the presence of highways without any labelled dataset. The proposed technique assumes that a narrow river trail has higher degrees of sinuosity than roads. It uses a bank of Gabor filters to enhance the curvilinear features of a river and further separates them from roads through linear features. Further these disconnected trails are adjoined using morphological operations. Thereafter, using connected component analysis, narrow river trails are detected with precision, recall and accuracy of 84.52%, 71.51%, and 96.97%, respectively. Jamunia river of Jharkhand, India is chosen as the region of interest. Further experimentation to check seasonal invariability and applicability to different climatic regions is considered as a future work.

References

1. Acharya, T.D., Lee, D.H., Yang, I.T., Lee, J.K.: Identification of water bodies in a Landsat 8 OLI image using a j48 decision tree. Sensors **16**(7), 1075 (2016)
2. Benstead, J.P., Leigh, D.S.: An expanded role for river networks. Nat. Geosci. **5**(10), 678–679 (2012)
3. Berlemont, S., Olivo-Marin, J.C.: Combining local filtering and multiscale analysis for edge, ridge, and curvilinear objects detection. IEEE Trans. Image Process. **19**(1), 74–84 (2009)

4. Canny, J.: A computational approach to edge detection. IEEE Trans. Pattern Anal. Mach. Intell. PAMI-**8**(6), 679–698 (1986). https://doi.org/10.1109/TPAMI.1986. 4767851
5. De, J., et al.: A graph-theoretical approach for tracing filamentary structures in neuronal and retinal images. IEEE Trans. Med. Imaging **35**(1), 257–272 (2015)
6. Du, Z., et al.: Analysis of Landsat-8 OLI imagery for land surface water mapping. Remote Sens. Lett. **5**(7), 672–681 (2014)
7. Feyisa, G.L., Meilby, H., Fensholt, R., Proud, S.R.: Automated water extraction index: a new technique for surface water mapping using Landsat imagery. Remote Sens. Environ. **140**, 23–35 (2014)
8. Fisher, A., Flood, N., Danaher, T.: Comparing Landsat water index methods for automated water classification in eastern Australia. Remote Sens. Environ. **175**, 167–182 (2016)
9. Gao, R., Bischof, W.F.: Detection of linear structures in remote-sensed images. In: Kamel, M., Campilho, A. (eds.) ICIAR 2009. LNCS, vol. 5627, pp. 896–905. Springer, Heidelberg (2009). https://doi.org/10.1007/978-3-642-02611-9_88
10. Güneralp, İ, Filippi, A.M., Hales, B.U.: River-flow boundary delineation from digital aerial photography and ancillary images using support vector machines. GIScience Remote Sens. **50**(1), 1–25 (2013)
11. Ji, L., Zhang, L., Wylie, B.: Analysis of dynamic thresholds for the normalized difference water index. Photogramm. Eng. Remote. Sens. **75**(11), 1307–1317 (2009)
12. Kenward, T., Lettenmaier, D.P., Wood, E.F., Fielding, E.: Effects of digital elevation model accuracy on hydrologic predictions. Remote Sens. Environ. **74**(3), 432–444 (2000)
13. Klemenjak, S., Waske, B., Valero, S., Chanussot, J.: Automatic detection of rivers in high-resolution SAR data. IEEE J. Select. Top. Appl. Earth Observ. Remote Sens. **5**(5), 1364–1372 (2012)
14. Li, J., Wong, D.W.: Effects of dem sources on hydrologic applications. Comput. Environ. Urban Syst. **34**(3), 251–261 (2010)
15. Li, S., MacMillan, R., Lobb, D.A., McConkey, B.G., Moulin, A., Fraser, W.R.: Lidar dem error analyses and topographic depression identification in a hummocky landscape in the prairie region of Canada. Geomorphology **129**(3–4), 263–275 (2011)
16. Liu, J.L., Feng, D.Z.: Two-dimensional multi-pixel anisotropic gaussian filter for edge-line segment (els) detection. Image Vis. Comput. **32**(1), 37–53 (2014)
17. Liu, Z., Yao, Z., Wang, R.: Assessing methods of identifying open water bodies using Landsat 8 OLI imagery. Environ. Earth Sci. **75**(10), 1–13 (2016). https://doi.org/10.1007/s12665-016-5686-2
18. Liu, Z., Khan, U., Sharma, A.: A new method for verification of delineated channel networks. Water Resour. Res. **50**(3), 2164–2175 (2014)
19. Manthalkar, R., Biswas, P.K., Chatterji, B.N.: Rotation invariant texture classification using even symmetric Gabor filters. Pattern Recogn. Lett. **24**(12), 2061–2068 (2003)
20. Marcus, W.A., Fonstad, M.A.: Remote sensing of rivers: the emergence of a subdiscipline in the river sciences. Earth Surf. Proc. Land. **35**(15), 1867–1872 (2010)
21. Marín, D., Aquino, A., Gegúndez-Arias, M.E., Bravo, J.M.: A new supervised method for blood vessel segmentation in retinal images by using gray-level and moment invariants-based features. IEEE Trans. Med. Imaging **30**(1), 146–158 (2010)
22. McFeeters, S.K.: The use of the normalized difference water index (NDWI) in the delineation of open water features. Int. J. Remote Sens. **17**(7), 1425–1432 (1996)

23. Özelkan, E.: Water body detection analysis using NDWI indices derived from Landsat-8 OLI. Pol. J. Environ. Stud. **29**(2), 1759–1769 (2020)
24. Pavelsky, T.M., et al.: Assessing the potential global extent of Swot river discharge observations. J. Hydrol. **519**, 1516–1525 (2014)
25. Rinne, E., et al.: On the recent elevation changes at the Flade Isblink ice cap, northern greenland. J. Geophys. Res. Earth Surf. **116**(F3), 9 (2011)
26. Shahi, K., Shafri, H.Z., Taherzadeh, E., Mansor, S., Muniandy, R.: A novel spectral index to automatically extract road networks from worldview-2 satellite imagery. Egypt. J. Remote Sens. Space Sci. **18**(1), 27–33 (2015)
27. Verpoorter, C., Kutser, T., Tranvik, L.: Automated mapping of water bodies using Landsat multispectral data. Limnol. Oceanogr. Methods **10**(12), 1037–1050 (2012)
28. Van de Weijer, J., Van Vliet, L.J., Verbeek, P.W., van Ginkel, R.: Curvature estimation in oriented patterns using curvilinear models applied to gradient vector fields. IEEE Trans. Pattern Anal. Mach. Intell. **23**(9), 1035–1042 (2001)
29. Xu, H.: Modification of normalised difference water index (ndwi) to enhance open water features in remotely sensed imagery. Int. J. Remote Sens. **27**(14), 3025–3033 (2006)
30. Yang, K., Li, M., Liu, Y., Cheng, L., Huang, Q., Chen, Y.: River detection in remotely sensed imagery using Gabor filtering and path opening. Remote Sensing **7**(7), 8779–8802 (2015)
31. Zhang, H., Yang, Y., Shen, H.: Detection of curvilinear structure in images by a multi-centered Hough forest method. IEEE Access **6**, 22684–22694 (2018)

Unsupervised Image to Image Translation for Multiple Retinal Pathology Synthesis in Optical Coherence Tomography Scans

Hemanth Pasupuleti[1]($\boxtimes$), Abhishek R. Kothari[2], and G. N. Girish[1]

[1] Computer Science and Engineering Group, Indian Institute of Information Technology,
Sri City, India
satyasaihemanth.p@gmail.com
[2] Pink City Eye and Retina Center, Jaipur, India

Abstract. Image to Image Translation (I2I) is a challenging computer vision problem used in numerous domains for multiple tasks. Recently, ophthalmology became one of the major fields where the application of I2I is increasing rapidly. One such application is the generation of synthetic retinal optical coherence tomographic (OCT) scans. Existing I2I methods require training of multiple models to translate images from normal scans to a specific pathology: limiting the use of these models due to their complexity. To address this issue, we propose an unsupervised multi-domain I2I network with pre-trained style encoder that translates retinal OCT images in one domain to multiple domains. We assume that the image splits into domain-invariant content and domain-specific style codes, and pre-train these style codes. The performed experiments show that the proposed model outperforms state-of-the-art models like MUNIT and CycleGAN by synthesizing diverse pathological scans with lower FID scores (108.30-Kermany dataset; 60-TaeKeun datset) and higher LPIPS scores (0.146-Kermany dataset; 0.171-TaeKeun dataset).

Keywords: Image Synthesis · Optical Coherence Tomography · Generative Adversarial Networks · Image to Image Translation

1 Introduction

The human eye is one of the vital and complex organs which provides the ability to see and perceive the surrounding world. When the light enters the pupil and strikes the retina, it is converted into nerve signals that are processed by the brain. Due to the aging population and increase in the prevalence of diabetes, diseases like age-related macular degeneration (AMD) and Diabetic Macular Edema (DME) became reasons for the majority of vision loss [4, 22].

Optical Coherence Tomography (OCT) is a leading non-invasive imaging technique utilized to acquire cross-sectional retinal imaging in ophthalmology [14]. It helps ophthalmologists to diagnose diseases, monitor their progress, and navigate during surgery. Thus, playing a vital role in the treatment of retinal diseases. Several deep learning

© The Author(s), under exclusive license to Springer Nature Switzerland AG 2023
D. Gupta et al. (Eds.): CVIP 2022, CCIS 1777, pp. 674–685, 2023.
https://doi.org/10.1007/978-3-031-31417-9_51

methods were employed to automate this process and tackle various image analysis tasks like detection and segmentation in OCT imaging [9,10,21,30]. However, to achieve these tasks, a large dataset is usually required.

Traditional image augmentation methods like image shifting, rotation, scaling, and deformation are used widely in medical imaging but limit the diversity of the features obtained from the augmented images [10]. Goodfellow *et al.* proposed Generative Adversarial Networks (GANs) [11] that led to the emergence of using synthetically generated data for improving the performance of various medical image analysis tasks with deep learning [7,12].

This paper proposes a Generative Adversarial Network (GAN) model to generate images of the desired pathology from normal OCT B-scan images. Proposed model is evaluated with a comparison to other existing models by generating both prevalent and rare diseases.

2   Related Work

The advent of GANs led to their application in various fields like image generation [29], super-resolution [1], image inpainting [3,38], etc. They usually contain two networks: a generator that learns to generate images and a discriminator that distinguishes between the generated fake image and real image. Conditional GAN (cGAN) [27] is a variant of GAN where the class knowledge is provided into the network to impose control on the generated image. Image to Image Translation (I2I) falls into one of the cGAN applications where the model learns mapping to translate input images between different domains. Initially, researchers used input-output pair images to achieve the I2I task between two domains [16]. However, obtaining these paired images is often difficult for many tasks and CycleGAN [41] alleviates this problem by using unpaired images. CycleGAN displayed that it can produce high-quality images but it lacks in the diversity that is addressed by MUNIT [15].

Recently, Zheng *et al.* assessed the quality of high-resolution retinal OCT images generated by GANs [40]. The generated images were evaluated by two ophthalmologists, it was determined that synthetic retinal OCT scans aid in training and educational activities, and can also serve as data augmentation to enhance the existing dataset for building machine learning models. Xiao *et al.* [35] proposed an open set recognition system by using synthetic OCT images. These generated images are considered to be of unknown class and thus making the classifier able to detect rare or unknown diseases. Furthermore, Yoo *et al.* was conducted a study by focusing on the role of GAN-generated images in improving the accuracy of classifiers for detecting rare diseases [37]. They trained 5 CycleGAN models where each CycleGAN model translates from a normal retinal OCT image to one rare disease. The translated images were then evaluated by experts and also experimental results showed that these synthetic images help increase the accuracy of the classifier.

In all of these works, even though GANs have shown promising results they lack control between different classes since the models that were used only translate between two domains. Due to this, if we want to translate normal images into pathological images then we have to train an individual model for each pathology thus limiting the application of GANs in retinal imaging as it requires a lot of time. Models like

StarGANv2 [2] learn a many-to-many mapping between multiple domains which is not necessary since we only have to translate from a normal image to multiple pathological images. Hence, in this work, we propose a model that can generate multiple pathological images from normal images. Inspired by StarGANv2, we adapt the one generator and one discriminator policy while training the model in an unpaired fashion like MUNIT, without showing the real pathological images to the generator.

3   Methodology

In this section, we discuss the proposed method to generate multi-domain retinal OCT images.

3.1   Framework

Consider we have images that are normal without any pathology in the domain X and all the target pathological images of different classes be $Y_1, Y_2, Y_3, ..., Y_n$ (where n represents the class). Our goal is to learn the mapping $X \rightarrow \{Y_n \mid n > 0\}$ to generate the target image. Figure 1 represents the proposed architecture for unsupervised multi-domain I2I translation of OCT images.

Style Encoder Pre-training: Gram matrices have been introduced to represent the stylistic features of a reference image in neural style transfer [8]. Many models use learned style encoding that is similar to the style encoding obtained from gram matrices to enforce condition on generated image [15, 18]. The main problem with this approach is that they depend on the target dataset and don't capture styles that are not well represented. Recently, Meshry *et al.* [26] showed that style encoder pre-training mitigates this issue due to a more robust latent space representation and produces expressive results. While Meshry *et al.* [26] used triplet loss to train the network by selecting triplets using style distance metric, there has been a series of work exploring different triplet mining techniques and losses [31, 36].

The style encoder pre-training helps us to gain control over the pathologies especially in retinal OCT imaging where the diseases may have overlapping characteristics. It also enables us to generate various retinal OCT images with desired characteristics. In this work, we proceed to train the style encoder by using Easy Positive Hard Negative triplet mining proposed by Xuan *et al.* [36] with an aim to train the style embedding network such that the output embeddings of similar classes are close together.

Style Encoder: Given an input image x, our style encoder E, produces the style embeddings $s = E(x)$ that are lower-dimensional projections of Gram matrices.

Generator: Providing an image x, our generator G generates the output image $G(x, s)$ translating input to the target domain. Here, s is the style code of the target domain that is obtained from the pre-trained style encoder E. We feed the style information into the generator by using Adaptive Instance Normalization (AdaIN) [18].

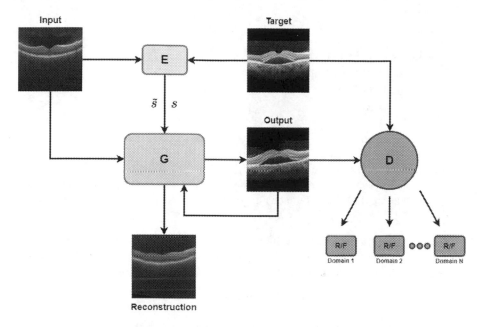

Fig. 1. Proposed Framework. The network architecture mainly consists of 3 parts: **(a)** Pretrained Style Encoder: We have one style encoder E that extracts the style codes of respective domains. These codes are then used for reference-guided synthesis. Here $s, \tilde{s}$ represent the corresponding style codes for target and input images. **(b)** Generator: We also use only one generator G that translates the input image into multiple target domains by utilizing the style code. **(c)** Discriminator: The discriminator D captures the relation between the real and fake images. It has multiple branches with outputs specific to the input domain that can be selected while training.

Training: There are two stages of training in the proposed approach:

- **Stage 1:** For all the classes present in a given dataset, cluster the style embeddings produced by the style encoder E.
- **Stage 2:** After successful training of Stage 1, we freeze the weights of E and train the generator G. The style encoder E delivers the target domain information into the generator which translates the input image.

Discriminator: Recently relativistic discriminators [17] have proved their ability to produce high quality images in various domains [5,23,33]. We adopt this relative discriminator with the multi-task discriminator [24] to design a relativistic multi-task discriminator. Given an image z and label $\hat{z}$, the discriminator D outputs multiple branches with each branch representing an individual label. For each branch, the outputs range from 0 to 1 representing fake and real images. The discriminator only targets to optimize the branch corresponding to the given label establishing an intraclass relationship. To further make the training more stable, we employ spectral normalization [28] and R1 regularization [25].

3.2   Losses

Adversarial Loss: There are a variety of losses with their functionality proposed for GANs. To avoid bad basins that result in the mode collapse we use Relative pairing hinge loss [32] for stable training and faster convergence.

$$L_D^{adv} = \mathbb{E}_{x,y}\left[max(0, 1 + (D_{\widehat{y}}(G(x,s)) - D_{\widehat{y}}(y)))\right] \tag{1}$$

$$L_G^{adv} = \mathbb{E}_{x,y}\left[max(0, 1 + (D_{\widehat{y}}(y) - D_{\widehat{y}}(G(x,s))))\right] \tag{2}$$

where $\widehat{y}$ is the corresponding class label for the target domain y and $D_{\widehat{y}}(.)$ denotes the output of the discriminator for the target class label $\widehat{y}$. The $s = E(y)$ is the style embedding generated for the reference image y.

Cycle Consistency Loss: To make sure that the model is preserving the source characteristics, we use cycle consistency loss. After generating image $G(x,s)$ from image x we again try to reconstruct the input image. Cycle consistency loss [2] is defined as,

$$L_{cyc} = \mathbb{E}_x[\|\ x - G(G(x,s), \widetilde{s})\ \|_1] \tag{3}$$

where s is the target domain style code and $\widetilde{s} = E(x)$ the style embedding for the input image x.

Style Consistency Loss: To ensure the reference and generated images have closely aligned style characteristics, we employ a style consistency loss to enforce style characteristics by reconstructing the style.

$$L_{sty} = \mathbb{E}_x\left[\|\ s - E(G(x,s))\ \|_1\right] \tag{4}$$

where $E(G(x,s))$ is the reconstructed style code from the output image $G(x,s)$ for input x and target style code s. When compared to other models [2, 15], the main difference here is that we only have one style encoder $E(.)$ with a single branch that enforces the Generator to bring style characteristics while reducing the need for itself to be trained.

Total Loss: The final total loss for generator that has to be minimized can be expressed as:

$$L_{totalG} = L_G^{adv} + \lambda_{cyc}L_{cyc} + \lambda_{sty}L_{sty} \tag{5}$$

where $\lambda_{cyc}, \lambda_{sty}$ are hyperparameters and are equal to 1.
The final total loss for discriminator that has to be minimized is given as:

$$L_{totalD} = L_D^{adv} + \frac{\gamma}{2}E_y[\|\nabla D_{\widehat{y}}(y)\|^2], \tag{6}$$

where γ is a hyperparameter set to 1.

4 Experiments and Results

In this section, the dataset preparation is described, and we analyze the performance of our model with standard baselines CycleGAN [41] and MUNIT [15]. All the comparative experiments were conducted using the provided author implementations.

4.1 Dataset Description

We use two publicly available datasets provided by *Kermany*[1] and *TaeKeun*[2] to conduct the experiments in this work to evaluate the proposed method. *Kermany*'s dataset consists of 4 prevalent classes of retinal OCT images: Normal, Drusen [22], DME [4], Chorodial Neovascularization(CNV) [6]. *TaeKeun*'s dataset has 5 diseases that are considered to be rare: central serous chorioretinopathy (CSC), macular hole (MH), retinitis pigmentosa (RP), macular telangiectasia (Mactel) and Stargardt disease. We aim to study the performance of various models given the limited amount of available data.

While *Kermany*'s dataset is a large scale dataset consisting of 27110 normal, 37455 CNV, 11598 DME, and 8866 drusen retinal images, *TaeKeun*'s dataset is collected from google with only 30 CSC, 30 MH, 24 Mactel, 19 RP, and 16 Stargardt disease images. For each class, we sample 1000 train images and 100 test images from the *Kermany*'s dataset. For *TaeKeun*'s dataset we randomly augment the images by shifting from −5% to +5%, rotating between −15° and +15°, scaling up to 20%, altering brightness between −10% and +10%, and elastic transformation [37]. We generated 400 images for training and 80 test images for each class. The normal images were utilized in the same ratio taken from *Kermany's* images for training the *TaeKeun's* dataset as well

4.2 Experimental Setup and Results

All of the experiments are done by implementing the models in Keras library on a single 12GB Nvidia Tesla K80 GPU with 64GB RAM and Intel Xeon E5-2670 processor. We train the models at 128×128 resolution with batch size 8 and learning rate 0.0001 for 100 epochs using Adam optimizer [19]. For CycleGAN and MUNIT we train multiple models for each normal and disease pair since they can translate between two domains only. To assess style-based translation fairly between MUNIT and our model we evaluate reference-based translation only.

Qualitative Evaluation: Figures 2 and 3 compares the generated images by the three models for the considered two datasets. We can observe that in Fig. 2 both CycleGAN and our model generate good quality images for CSC, MH, Mactel, RP and Strgardt pathology while MUNIT is still learning on *TaeKeun* dataset. The style encoder in the MUNIT needs to be trained along with the generator model which makes the training complex and slow, which is overcome by our pre-trained style encoder thus making

---

[1] https://data.mendeley.com/datasets/rscbjbr9sj/3.
[2] https://data.mendeley.com/datasets/btv6yrdbmv/2.

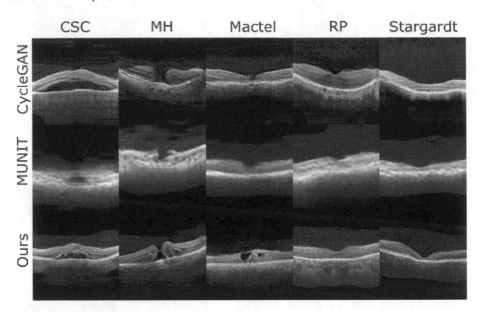

Fig. 2. Qualitative comparison of the models on the *TaeKeun* dataset. Each row corresponds to different models and the columns represent the generated target pathology. For MUNIT and our model, we generate using reference images.

Table 1. Quantitative comparison of the models with reference-guided synthesis for MUNIT and our model.

	Dataset			
Model	**TaeKeun**		**Kermany**	
	FID ↓	*LPIPS* ↑	*FID* ↓	*LPIPS* ↑
CycleGAN [41]	160.72	–	94.19	–
MUNIT [15]	182.71	0.077	89.18	0.020
Ours	108.30	0.171	60.8	0.147
Ground Truth	35.94	–	52.31	–

Table 2. Comparison of the number of Giga Multiply-accumulate operations (GMACs) and parameters required for generator to convert one image from one domain to another at 128×128 resolution.

Model	Resolution	Parameters	GMACs
CycleGAN [41]	128×128	11.38 M	14.22
MUNIT [15]	128×128	30.05 M	19.35
Ours	128×128	34.01 M	32.09

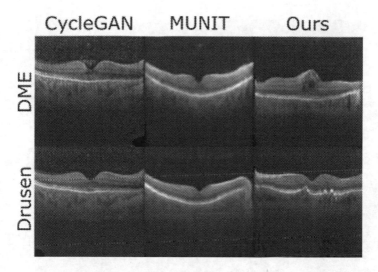

Fig. 3. Qualitative comparison of the models on the *Kermany* dataset. Columns and rows represent the model and its generated pathology.

the convergence faster. And in Fig. 3 for *Kermany* dataset, our pre-trained style encoder shows its ability to capture representations that are not prevalent and generate pathologies in case of DME and Drusen (refer column 3 of Fig. 3), where both CycleGAN and MUNIT fail to do so. Figure 4 shows the generation of pathological images for various input and reference images. We can see that the proposed model generates the reference pathology while preserving the content characteristics of the input image.

Quantitative Evaluation: The quality of the generated images are evaluated by comparing their similarity with real images (ground truth) using Fréchet Inception Distance (FID). We calculate the FID [13] score by calculating Fréchet distance between two multivariate gaussian distributions as,

$$d_f^2 \left(\mathcal{N}(\mu_r, C_r), \mathcal{N}(\mu_g, C_g) \right) = \| \mu_r - \mu_g \|^2 + tr(C_r + C_g - 2 \times \sqrt{C_r * C_g}) \quad (7)$$

where d_f^2 is FID score and μ_r, C_r and μ_g, C_g represent the mean and covariances of the activations of real and generated images that are fed into an Inception model trained on ImageNet dataset [34], lower the FID indicated better the quality of the generated images.

To evaluate the diversity of the images generated, we calculate the average Learned Perceptual Image Patch Similarity (LPIPS) [39] distance of randomly generated images. Given the reference and generated images, the LPIPS distance is the scaled l_2 distance of the normalized activations from deep feature extractor AlexNet which is trained on ImageNet [20].

We generate 10 pathological images from each normal retinal image for individual classes and calculate the metrics. Table 1 shows the obtained metrics for all the models. Since CycleGAN is limited in diversity we don't calculate LPIPS scores for it. We can

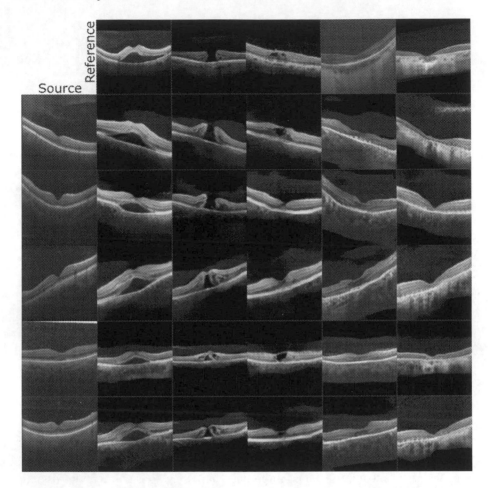

Fig. 4. Reference based synthesis on *TaeKeun* dataset. The first column presents the normal images that are given to our model as the source images while the first row corresponds to various pathologies that are provided as reference images. All the other images are outputs generated by our model translating from normal B-scan to pathological B-scan. Images in each row represent generated outputs for the same source image with different styles or domains. It can be noted that the source domain characteristics are well preserved while translating into the target domain.

observe that for *Kermany's* dataset both the CycleGAN and MUNIT fail to generate pathologies. Our model surpasses the performance of both of the models by generating higher quality images (with lower FID compared to CycleGAN and MUNIT) while also showing good diversity (higher LPIPS score). Table 2 shows computation complexity of proposed model with CycleGAN and MUNIT, the proposed model can achieve one-many domain translation i.e. $X \rightarrow \{Y_n \mid n > 0\}$ in 32.09 GMACs per 128×128 image, whereas the other two models can only translate between two domains i.e. $X \rightarrow \{Y_1\}$ at 14.22 and 19.35 GMACs per image, and note that our model need to be trained at once irrespective of the number of domains.

5 Conclusion and Future Work

In this work, a generative adversarial network model to generate synthetic pathological retinal OCT data was proposed. The proposed GAN model presents a pre-training style encoder which results in obtaining a robust style code that helps to achieve better results. We also introduced a new discriminator by combining multi-task discriminator and relative discriminator. The model is then evaluated on two distinct datasets and the results show that it can generate good quality images for several retinal diseases (such as DME, MH, RP and Stargardt) even with limited data and outperformed state-of-the-art models. Although our model achieves good results, it mainly depends on the style encoder pre-training. We have observed that bad pre-training may not cluster the style embeddings appropriately which in turn affects the discriminator and lose its ability to distinguish between different classes. This results in degradation of generated images and uncontrolled disease synthesis while drastically affecting the training of the model. In future work, different pre-training methods for style encoder and the maximum number of domains that the model can translate robustly need to be explored.

References

1. Bulat, A., Yang, J., Tzimiropoulos, G.: To learn image super-resolution, use a GAN to learn how to do image degradation first. In: Ferrari, V., Hebert, M., Sminchisescu, C., Weiss, Y. (eds.) ECCV 2018. LNCS, vol. 11210, pp. 187–202. Springer, Cham (2018). https://doi.org/10.1007/978-3-030-01231-1_12
2. Choi, Y., Uh, Y., Yoo, J., Ha, J.W.: StarGAN v2: diverse image synthesis for multiple domains. In: 2020 IEEE/CVF Conference on Computer Vision and Pattern Recognition (CVPR), pp. 8185–8194 (2020)
3. Demir, U., Unal, G.: Patch-based image inpainting with generative adversarial networks. arXiv e-prints arXiv:1803.07422 (2018)
4. Ding, J., Wong, T.Y.: Current epidemiology of diabetic retinopathy and diabetic macular edema. Curr. Diab. Rep. 12(4), 346–354 (2012)
5. Du, W., Chen, H., Yang, H., Zhang, Y.: Disentangled generative adversarial network for low-dose CT. EURASIP J. Adv. Sig. Process. 2021(1), 1–16 (2021). https://doi.org/10.1186/s13634-021-00749-z
6. Faridi, A., et al.: Sensitivity and specificity of oct angiography to detect choroidal neovascularization. Ophthalmol. Retina 1(4), 294–303 (2017)
7. Frid-Adar, M., Diamant, I., Klang, E., Amitai, M., Goldberger, J., Greenspan, H.: Gan-based synthetic medical image augmentation for increased CNN performance in liver lesion classification. Neurocomputing 321, 321–331 (2018)
8. Gatys, L.A., Ecker, A.S., Bethge, M.: A neural algorithm of artistic style. arXiv e-prints arXiv:1508.06576 (2015)
9. Girish, G., Saikumar, B., Roychowdhury, S., Kothari, A.R., Rajan, J.: Depthwise separable convolutional neural network model for intra-retinal cyst segmentation. In: 2019 41st Annual International Conference of the IEEE Engineering in Medicine and Biology Society (EMBC), pp. 2027–2031. IEEE (2019)
10. Girish, G., Thakur, B., Chowdhury, S.R., Kothari, A.R., Rajan, J.: Segmentation of intra-retinal cysts from optical coherence tomography images using a fully convolutional neural network model. IEEE J. Biomed. Health Inform. 23(1), 296–304 (2018)

11. Goodfellow, I., et al.: Generative adversarial nets. In: Ghahramani, Z., Welling, M., Cortes, C., Lawrence, N., Weinberger, K.Q. (eds.) Advances in Neural Information Processing Systems, vol. 27. Curran Associates, Inc. (2014)

12. Han, C., et al.: GAN-based synthetic brain MR image generation. In: 2018 IEEE 15th International Symposium on Biomedical Imaging (ISBI 2018), pp. 734–738 (2018)

13. Heusel, M., Ramsauer, H., Unterthiner, T., Nessler, B., Hochreiter, S.: GANs trained by a two time-scale update rule converge to a local Nash equilibrium. In: Guyon, I., et al. (eds.) Advances in Neural Information Processing Systems, vol. 30. Curran Associates, Inc. (2017)

14. Huang, D., et al.: Optical coherence tomography. Science **254**(5035), 1178–1181 (1991)

15. Huang, X., Liu, M.-Y., Belongie, S., Kautz, J.: Multimodal unsupervised image-to-image translation. In: Ferrari, V., Hebert, M., Sminchisescu, C., Weiss, Y. (eds.) ECCV 2018. LNCS, vol. 11207, pp. 179–196. Springer, Cham (2018). https://doi.org/10.1007/978-3-030-01219-9_11

16. Isola, P., Zhu, J.Y., Zhou, T., Efros, A.A.: Image-to-image translation with conditional adversarial networks. In: 2017 IEEE Conference on Computer Vision and Pattern Recognition (CVPR), pp. 5967–5976 (2017)

17. Jolicoeur-Martineau, A.: The relativistic discriminator: a key element missing from standard GAN. arXiv e-prints arXiv:1807.00734 (2018)

18. Karras, T., Laine, S., Aila, T.: A style-based generator architecture for generative adversarial networks. In: 2019 IEEE/CVF Conference on Computer Vision and Pattern Recognition (CVPR), pp. 4396–4405 (2019)

19. Kingma, D.P., Ba, J.: Adam: A Method for Stochastic Optimization. arXiv e-prints arXiv:1412.6980 (2014)

20. Krizhevsky, A., Sutskever, I., Hinton, G.E.: ImageNet classification with deep convolutional neural networks. Commun. ACM **60**(6), 84–90 (2017)

21. Li, Q., et al.: DeepRetina: layer segmentation of retina in OCT images using deep learning. Transl. Vis. Sci. Technol. **9**(2), 61 (2020)

22. Lim, L.S., Mitchell, P., Seddon, J.M., Holz, F.G., Wong, T.Y.: Age-related macular degeneration. Lancet **379**(9827), 1728–1738 (2012)

23. Liu, H., Jiang, B., Xiao, Y., Yang, C.: Coherent semantic attention for image inpainting. In: Proceedings of the IEEE/CVF International Conference on Computer Vision (ICCV) (2019)

24. Liu, M.Y., et al.: Few-shot unsupervised image-to-image translation. In: 2019 IEEE/CVF International Conference on Computer Vision (ICCV), pp. 10550–10559 (2019)

25. Mescheder, L., Geiger, A., Nowozin, S.: Which training methods for GANs do actually converge? arXiv e-prints arXiv:1801.04406 (2018)

26. Meshry, M., Ren, Y., Davis, L.S., Shrivastava, A.: Step: Style-based encoder pre-training for multi-modal image synthesis. In: 2021 IEEE/CVF Conference on Computer Vision and Pattern Recognition (CVPR), pp. 3711–3720 (2021)

27. Mirza, M., Osindero, S.: Conditional generative adversarial nets. arXiv e-prints arXiv:1411.1784 (2014)

28. Miyato, T., Kataoka, T., Koyama, M., Yoshida, Y.: Spectral normalization for generative adversarial networks. arXiv e-prints arXiv:1802.05957 (2018)

29. Radford, A., Metz, L., Chintala, S.: Unsupervised representation learning with deep convolutional generative adversarial networks. arXiv e-prints arXiv:1511.06434 (2015)

30. Schlegl, T., et al.: Fully automated detection and quantification of macular fluid in OCT using deep learning. Ophthalmology **125**(4), 549–558 (2018)

31. Schroff, F., Kalenichenko, D., Philbin, J.: FaceNet: a unified embedding for face recognition and clustering. In: 2015 IEEE Conference on Computer Vision and Pattern Recognition (CVPR), pp. 815–823 (2015)

32. Sun, R., Fang, T., Schwing, A.: Towards a better global loss landscape of gans. In: Larochelle, H., Ranzato, M., Hadsell, R., Balcan, M.F., Lin, H. (eds.) Advances in Neural Information Processing Systems, vol. 33, pp. 10186–10198. Curran Associates, Inc. (2020)
33. Wang, X., et al.: ESRGAN: enhanced super-resolution generative adversarial networks. In: Leal-Taixé, L., Roth, S. (eds.) ECCV 2018. LNCS, vol. 11133, pp. 63–79. Springer, Cham (2019). https://doi.org/10.1007/978-3-030-11021-5_5
34. Xia, X., Xu, C., Nan, B.: Inception-v3 for flower classification. In: 2017 2nd international conference on image, vision and computing (ICIVC), pp. 783–787. IEEE (2017)
35. Xiao, Y., et al.: Open-set oct image recognition with synthetic learning. In: 2020 IEEE 17th International Symposium on Biomedical Imaging (ISBI), pp. 1788–1792 (2020)
36. Xuan, H., Stylianou, A., Pless, R.: Improved embeddings with easy positive triplet mining. In: 2020 IEEE Winter Conference on Applications of Computer Vision (WACV), pp. 2463–2471 (2020)
37. Yoo, T.K., Choi, J.Y., Kim, H.K.: Feasibility study to improve deep learning in OCT diagnosis of rare retinal diseases with few-shot classification. Med. Biol. Eng. Comput. 59(2), 401–415 (2021)
38. Yu, J., Lin, Z., Yang, J., Shen, X., Lu, X., Huang, T.S.: Generative image inpainting with contextual attention. In: Proceedings of the IEEE Conference on Computer Vision and Pattern Recognition (CVPR) (2018)
39. Zhang, R., Isola, P., Efros, A.A., Shechtman, E., Wang, O.: The unreasonable effectiveness of deep features as a perceptual metric. In: 2018 IEEE/CVF Conference on Computer Vision and Pattern Recognition, pp. 586–595 (2018)
40. Zheng, C., et al.: Assessment of generative adversarial networks model for synthetic optical coherence tomography images of retinal disorders. Transl. Vis. Sci. Technol. 9(2), 29 (2020)
41. Zhu, J.Y., Park, T., Isola, P., Efros, A.A.: Unpaired image-to-image translation using cycle-consistent adversarial networks. In: 2017 IEEE International Conference on Computer Vision (ICCV), pp. 2242–2251 (2017)

Combining Deep-Learned and Hand-Crafted Features for Segmentation, Classification and Counting of Colon Nuclei in H&E Stained Histology Images

Pranay Dumbhare$^{(\boxtimes)}$, Yash Dubey, Vedant Phuse, Ankush Jamthikar, Himanshu Padole, and Deep Gupta$^{(\boxtimes)}$ 🆔

Department of Electronics and Communication Engineering, Visvesvaraya National Institute of Technology, Nagpur 440010, India chaitanydumbhare21@gmail.com, deepgupta@ece.vnit.ac.in

Abstract. Colon nuclei detection within Haematoxylin & Eosin (H&E) stained histology images is important to mitigate abnormalities or diseases like colon cancer in its early stages. Therefore, the objective of the proposed work is to perform the colon nuclei segmentation, classification, and counting of the nuclei or cellular composition. This paper presents a hybrid deep learning model that combines deep-learned features obtained from the ResNet50-based model with the handcrafted features. The proposed work uses the horizontal and vertical net (HoVer-Net) as baseline model presented by the CoNIC2022 challenge team and modified it to incorporate handcrafted features obtained using two feature descriptors such as local binary patterns and the histogram of oriented gradients. The proposed model is trained and validated using the CoNIC2022 dataset. The proposed model shows a significant improvement over the baseline HoVer-Net model in segmentation and classification as well as nuclei counting tasks. The proposed work demonstrates the usefulness of combining deep features with the handcrafted features in the colon nuclei identification task.

Keywords: Colon nuclei segmentation · HoVer-Net · Deep learning · Local binary pattern · Histogram of oriented gradients

1 Introduction

The manual assessment of Haematoxylin and Eosin (H&E) stained histology slides suffers from intra- or inter-observer variability [1]. To overcome these challenges in the visual assessment of tissues, there is a growing interest in digital pathology [2], which uses a class of histology images that are used to generate the whole slide images (WSI). Each WSI contains several nuclei of cells of different types, which can be analyzed to predict the clinical outcomes and grade the type of diseases, such as cancer [3]. Efficient segmentation and detection of nuclei cell types can provide important diagnostic information about the tissues

D. Gupta et al. (Eds.): CVIP 2022, CCIS 1777, pp. 686–698, 2023.
https://doi.org/10.1007/978-3-031-31417-9_52

that contribute to disease growth. This was the idea behind the CoNIC2022 challenge [4], which specifically required segmenting and classifying the colon nuclei as well as finding the cellular composition by counting the different types of nuclei present in the cells. Nuclei segmentation is a challenging task because of the heterogeneous nuclear shapes, sizes, structures, as well as overlapping nuclei clusters.

Similar to nuclei segmentation, nuclei classification is also an important task that can classify different types of cells. Currently, the colon cancer diagnosis is based on the human examination of relevant histopathological images by trained pathologists. This process is time-consuming and associated with intra-or inter-observer variability [5].

Artificial intelligence (AI) is gaining popularity in almost every domain and has greatly contributed to the field of healthcare including computational pathology. In recent years, several automated AI-based systems have been proposed for nuclei detection tasks. Hamad et al. [6] proposed a convolution neural network (CNN)-based system for colon nuclei classification using H&E stained histology images. Another study used the spatially constrained CNN that predicts the probability of any pixel being the centre of the nucleus [7]. Hofener et al. [8] proposed a deep learning-based approach to predict the proximity map of histological image pixels with the centre of nuclei. Most recently, Graham et al. [9] proposed a deep learning-based model called horizontal and vertical net (HoVer-Net) to simultaneously segment and classify nuclear occurrences in histology images. The HoVer-Net model is based on the prediction of horizontal and vertical distances between nuclear pixels and their centre of mass, which are further used to separate the grouped nuclei. The nuclear type is then determined for each segmented instance using a specialized up-sampling branch.

Motivated by this automatic segmentation, classification, and nuclei composition characteristics, we propose a modified architecture of the baseline HoVer-Net model by fusing the deep-learned features and handcrafted features. Although the deep learning-based model is self-sufficient to extract features from images (so-called deep features), recent studies have shown an improvement in the segmentation and classification tasks by using the predefined texture-based handcrafted features [10]. Therefore, we hypothesized that combining handcrafted features with deep features may result in an improvement in nuclei segmentation and classification tasks.

2   Methodology

2.1   Data Pre-processing and Augmentation

In the proposed work, the dataset provided by CoNIC2022 challenge is considered [4]. The CoNIC dataset is comprised of 4981 patches of size $256 \times 256 \times 3$ RGB extracted from the Lizard dataset [11], which contains the image sections from the colon tissues. Each RGB image patch is associated with an instance segmentation map and a classification map, as shown in Fig. 1. The instance segmentation map holds values ranging between 0 (background) and N (number

Raw Image   Instance Map   Classification Map

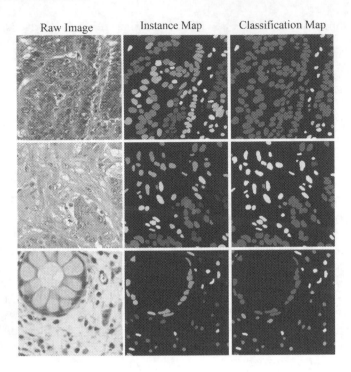

Fig. 1. Sample input images with the corresponding segmentation and classification maps

of nuclei) that label each nucleus. Similarly, the classification map holds values ranging between 0 (background) and C (number of classes) that provides the class for each pixel within the patch. In total there are six nuclei classes such as neutrophil, epithelial, lymphocyte, plasma, eosinophil, and connective tissue. These six nuclei classes and the background are used in the classification task. The size of the instance segmentation/classification map is $4981 \times 256 \times 256 \times 2$, with the first channel being the instance segmentation map and the second channel being the classification map. Both RGB images and the segmentation/classification maps are provided in the form of a .npy files and augmentation is done further using Gaussian blur [12] and median blur [13] operations. In a Gaussian blur, an input image is convolved with a Gaussian low-pass filter and generates the generic blurry image. In a median blur, the central element of the filter area in the image is replaced by the median value of surrounding pixels. Besides these operations, augmentation is also performed by perturbing the hue, saturation, contrast, and brightness of the input images. All these operations are performed on the training dataset so that the model has enough variety of data for training, and the features can be identified by the model with relatively higher ease.

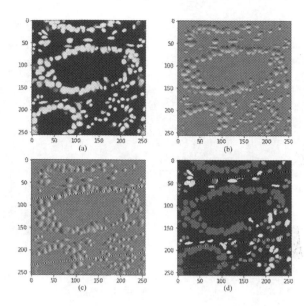

Fig. 2. The sample outputs from the three decoder branches of baseline HoVer-Net model. (a) Nuclei pixel map from the NP branch, (b and c) horizontal and vertical distance maps from the HoVer branch, and (d) nuclei classification map from the NC branch

2.2 HoVer-Net Baseline Model

The proposed study modifies the architecture of the baseline HoVer-Net model [9] for colon nuclei segmentation, classification, and counting tasks. The baseline HoVer-Net model was primarily designed for colon nuclei segmentation and showed better performance compared to the state-of-the-art studies [9]. To perform simultaneous segmentation and classification, HoVer-Net model takes advantage of the information encoded within both the vertical and horizontal distances of nuclear pixels to their centre of mass which are useful to separate the overlapping nuclei instances in the segmentation task. Then for each segmented instance, HoVer-Net model predicts the type of nucleus using a set of decoder branches. The better performance for the HoVer-Net model is attributed to the presence of three decoders such as such nuclear pixel (NP) branch, the HoVer branch (HV), and the nuclear classification branch (NC). The NP branch detects nuclei (Fig. 2 (a)), the HV branch predicts the horizontal and vertical distances of nuclear pixels to the centre of mass (Fig. 2 (b and c)), and the NC branch classifies the different types of nuclei (Fig. 2 (d)). The sample outputs of these three decoder branches are shown in Fig. 2.

2.3 Proposed Model

This section deals with the proposed model which fuses two unique types of texture-based features with deep-learned image representations. The modified

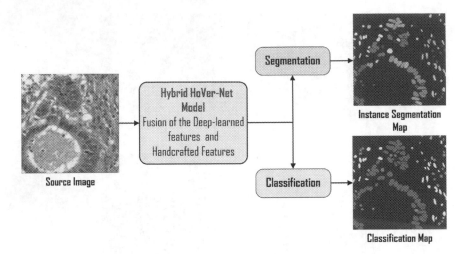

Fig. 3. The block diagram of the proposed hybrid deep learning model that demonstrates the working of the model on each individual image on the dataset

architecture is named as hybrid HoVer-Net model. The extracted features from the conventional feature descriptors, when used on their own are known to reflect on very limited aspects, as mentioned by Nguyen et al. [14], and hence are not able to do much. On another end, convolutional neural network-based models also provide good results with approx. 90% accuracy. However, as per results reported in Dalal et al. [15], Aziz et al. [16] and Song et al. [17], we observed that the accuracy can be increased to 94–99% by fusing the handcrafted features with machine learning models.

The proposed model works as described in the block diagram shown in Fig. 3. It takes the H&E stained cell patch as an image input and then performs segmentation as well as classification to provide the corresponding maps, i.e. the Instance Segmentation Map and Classification Map. Figure 4 shows the architecture of the proposed model, which has two parts (a) encoder and (b) decoder. The encoder hosts the pre-activated residual network with 50 layers (ResNet50) and the decoder contains three different parallel layered architectures for accurate segmentation and classification of the nuclei pixels. ResNet50 is popular architecture and has shown excellent performance in several computer vision applications. Therefore, it is adopted in the encoder for feature extraction. The ResNet50-based encoder provides the image representations of size $2048 \times 32 \times 32$. These image representations extracted by the encoder are also called deep features.

In the proposed model, a branch parallel to the ResNet50-based encoder is also added to obtain the handcrafted features from two popular predefined feature descriptors viz. local binary patterns (LBP) [18] and the histogram of oriented gradients (HoG) [15]. The choice of these feature descriptors in colon nuclei identification is motivated by their efficacy in different applications e.g.

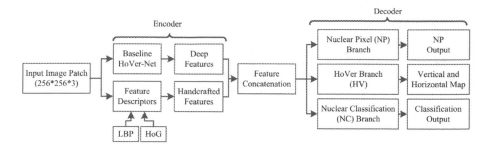

Fig. 4. The global view of the proposed hybrid deep learning model

Song et al. [17] for lung lesion detection and Aziz et al. [16] for mitotic nuclei. Multiple experimental results obtained by Li Song et al. [17] for lung lesion detection, and by Aziz Et Al [16] for mitotic nuclei, corroborate the fusion of HoG and LBP features with features extracted by machine/deep learning techniques.

In the decoder, the nuclear pixel (NP) branch predicts whether a pixel belongs to the nucleus or background. The HoVer branch predicts the horizontal and vertical distances of nuclear pixels to their centres of mass. Finally, the nuclear classification (NC) branch predicts the type of nucleus for each pixel and thus facilitates cellular composition by counting the nuclei. The proposed model is trained for 10 epochs over 3963 images and was then validated on the remaining 1018 images as provided in the CoNIC2022 challenge dataset.

2.4   Handcrafted Feature Descriptors

As mentioned above, two popular feature descriptors, two popular feature descriptors i.e. LBP and HoG are used in the proposed hybrid HoVer-Net model to generate handcrafted feature representations to reflect the sharp edges as in H&E staining technique is utilized in histopathological images to enhance the contrast in samples and this sharp contrast gives rise to the sharp edges. LBP is a simple yet very efficient texture descriptor, which considers a binary pattern from the surrounding pixels to decide the centre pixel intensity [18]. In the proposed hybrid HoVer-Net model, LBP feature map of dimensions 1×1024 is obtained. To match the dimension of the deep features (i.e. $2048 \times 32 \times 32$), LBP feature map of size 1×1024 is converted into the size $1 \times 32 \times 32$, giving a single feature map of dimension 32×32. on another end, HoG focuses on the structures or the shapes of objects in the input image. HoG can provide the edge directions as well. This is done by extracting the gradient and orientation (magnitude and direction) of the edges. The steps involved in HoG feature extraction are:

1. Pre-processing and reshaping the input image to size 64×128.
2. Calculating gradients (direction x and y) for a particular pixel.
3. Calculating the magnitude and orientation of gradients.
4. Creating histogram using gradients and orientation.
5. Normalizing the gradients.

6. Calculating the features for the complete image.

In the proposed model, HoG descriptor provides 33 feature maps of dimensions 32×32. These 33 feature maps from HoG and one feature map from LBP descriptor are then concatenated with deep features (2048) making the final 2082 feature maps each of dimension 32×32. These feature maps are then fed to the three decoder architectures of the proposed hybrid HoVer-Net model. The number of channels have been modified from 2048 to 2082 to improve the performance of segmentation, classification and counting of nuclei in histology images.

The other candidates such as GLCM [19], DWT [20], BRIEF [21], and ORB [22] were also considered for handcrafted feature extraction. The features were extracted using the above-listed feature extractors as well. However, the extracted features like ORB and BRIEF were not giving us the promising results as expected, thus not considered in the proposed study.

3   Experimental Details

3.1   Implementation and Parameter Settings

In the proposed model the HoG feature descriptor provides 33 feature maps of dimensions 32×32. For LBP the radius was set to 8 and the number of data points were set to 1022. To concatenate the handcrafted features with the deep features the dimensions of the output channels were changed from 2048 to 2082. The learning rate for the ADAM optimizer used here was 0.0001, and the batch size used for the training and validation of the model was 6.

3.2   Quantitative Performance Metrics

1. PQ and mPQ^+: Panoptic Quality (PQ) is used to assess the performance of nuclear instance segmentation. It is defined as:

$$PQ = DQ \times SQ \tag{1}$$

where DQ and SQ refer to detection quality and segmentation quality, respectively, which are given by,

$$DQ = \frac{|TP|}{|TP| + \frac{1}{2}|FP| + \frac{1}{2}|FN|} \tag{2}$$

where TP denotes true positive, FP denotes false positive, and FN denotes false negative.

$$SQ = \frac{\sum_{(x,y) \in TP} IoU(x,y)}{|TP|} \tag{3}$$

where x denotes a ground truth segment, y denotes a prediction segment and IoU denotes intersection over union that is formulated as,

$$IoU = \frac{TP}{TP + FP + FN} \tag{4}$$

For $IoU(x, y) > 0.5$, each (x, y) pair is uniquely matched over the entire set of prediction and ground truth segments [23]. This unique matching generates matched pairs (TP), unmatched ground truth segments (FN), and unmatched predicted segments (FP) for a particular type t. Hence we define multi-class PQ (mPQ^+), which takes the average of PQ over all classes T:

$$mPQ^+ = \frac{1}{T} \sum_t PQ_t \tag{5}$$

2. R^2: R^2 is a goodness-of-fit metric that measures the relationship strength between model's prediction $(\hat{y}_i)$ and ground truth (y_i) on the scale of 0 to 1. The closer the value of R^2 to 1, better is the model fitted. It is also called the coefficient of determination.

$$R^2 = 1 - \frac{\sum (y_i - \hat{y}_i)^2}{\sum (y_i - \bar{y})^2} \tag{6}$$

where $\bar{y}$ is the mean of predicted counts.

3. *Mean Squared Error* (MSE) : It is the average of the squares of the the differences between the actual values and the predicted values by a model.

$$MSE = \frac{1}{D} \sum_{i=1}^{D} (x_i - y_i)^2 \tag{7}$$

where D is the number of terms, and x_i and y_i are the actual values and the predicted values respectively.

4. *Dice Score*: Dice Score is a measure of accuracy. It is used to evaluate the performance of segmentation models. It is a measure of how similar the objects are to each other.[24].

$$Dice = \frac{2 \times TP}{(TP + FP) + (TP + FN)} \tag{8}$$

Dice score lies between 0.00 to 1.00, with higher dice score indicating the better model prediction. Dice score greater than 0.8 is generally considered to be a good score.

4   Results and Discussion

The proposed hybrid deep learning model performs segmentation, classification, and the counting of nuclei from histology images by fusing the deep features with handcrafted features. Table 1 compares the proposed model with the original baseline HoVer-Net model for 10 epochs and shows a consistent improvement

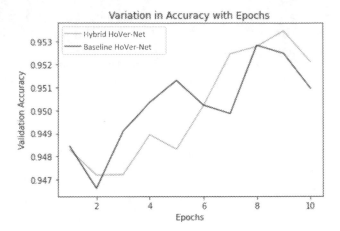

Fig. 5. Validation accuracy vs. the number of epochs for proposed and baseline model.

Table 1. Comparison between the proposed hybrid deep learning model and the baseline HoVer-Net model

Sr. No.	Validation Metric	Original HoVer-Net (B)	Modified HoVer-Net (C)	% Improvement = [(C-B)*100]/B
1	PQ	0.596	0.606	1.711
2	mPQ^+	0.437	0.444	1.596
3	R^2	0.714	0.775	8.536

by the proposed model in terms of PQ, mPQ^+, and R^2 metrics. On training for 10 epochs, the proposed model demonstrates an improvement of 1.71% (0.606 vs. 0.595) and 1.59% (0.4435 vs. 0.4365) in PQ and mPQ^+, respectively, over the baseline HoVer-Net model. The nuclei cellular composition predicted using the proposed hybrid model and the baseline model is also compared using the multi-class coefficient of determination (R^2). The proposed model demonstrated an improvement of 8.5% in R^2 value over the baseline model (0.775355 vs. 0.714375). Table 2 also compares the proposed model and the baseline model during the training and validation phases. Rows 1, 2, and 3 in Table 2 show the comparison between the two models based on mean squared error, accuracy, and the dice score. From the results given in Tables 1 and 2, the overall trend shows that the proposed model provides significantly better results for segmentation and classification compared to the baseline model. Note that both the proposed and baseline models are trained and evaluated for the same number of epochs. Although the overall training loss for both the models is comparable, the proposed model showed a significant improvement in the quantitative metrics such as validation accuracy and mean square error.

Figure 5 shows the variation in validation accuracy vs. epochs from the proposed hybrid HoVer-Net and baseline HoVer-Net model for 10 epochs. From Fig. 5, it is observed that the accuracy of the proposed hybrid HoVer-Net model is increased after the 6th epoch as compared to the baseline HoVer-Net.

Table 2. Performance metrics during the inference phases for the proposed and baseline HoVer-Net model

Sr. No.	Metric	Original HoVer-Net (B)	Modified HoVer-Net (C)	% Improvement = [(C-B)*100]/B
1	Mean Squared Error Loss	0.041	0.039	−4.473
2	Accuracy	0.951	0.952	0.151
3	Dice Score	0.836	0.842	0.741

Furthermore, a detailed comparative analysis was done among the performance of the proposed hybrid HoVer-Net model and other state-of-art literature as Naylor et al. (2018) [25], Saha et al. (2018) [26], Raza et al. (2018) [27], Dang et al. (2019) [28] and Graham et al. (2019) [9] using eight attributes and shown in Table 3. The majority of the available studies use the ResNet50-based model in their algorithms for image segmentation and classification. The proposed study uses a large number of images from the Lizard database provided by the CoNIC2022 challenge. Note that the proposed study extends the baseline HoVer-Net model by fusing the deep features with handcrafted features extracted using LBP and HoG which can combine both the sets of diverse features for colon nuclei segmentation, classification, and counting the number of cells in histology images. Moreover, Fig. 6 shows a few samples of source images out of the complete dataset and their corresponding predicted images from the proposed hybrid HoVer-Net model. From Fig. 6, it has been observed that the predicted images are compared with those with the ground truth images.

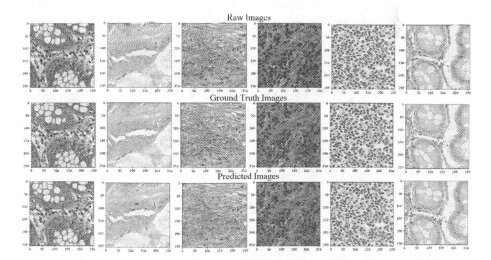

Fig. 6. The above figure shows six random image samples, taken from the dataset of H&E Stained Slides, as provided in the CoNIC Dataset. For each of the six images, the image in the first row is the raw image, which is to be segmented. The image in the second row is the ground truth showing the segments. The third row shows the predicted output for the respective images.

Table 3. Comparing the proposed with the state-of-the-art models

Sr. No.	Studies (Year)	Methods	Dataset	# Images	Handcrafted Features	Evaluation
1	Saha et al. (2018)	Her2Net	HER2 Image Database	158	No	Precision = 96.64%, Recall = 96.79%, F1-score = 96.71%, Accuracy = 98.33%
2	Naylor et al. (2018)	Regression task of Distance Map	Curie Institute and IIT Guwahati	80	No	F1 Score = 0.789, AJI score = 0.559, $Dice$ = 0.775, PQ = 0.432
3	Raza et al. (2018)	Micro-Net	Multiplexed Fluorescence Imaging Data, CPM and GLaS	229	No	$Dice$ = 0.792, AJI = 0.615, PQ = 0.542
4	Dang et al. (2019)	Modified Res-Net 50	NA	32	No	Dice Score average = 0.777-0.783
5	Graham et al. (2019)	HoVer-Net	CoN-SeP	41	No	$Dice$ = 0.853, PQ = 0.547
6	Proposed	Hybrid HoVer-Net	Lizard	4981	Yes	PQ = 0.606, mPQ^+ = 0.444, R^2 = 0.775

AJI: Aggregated Jaccard Index, PQ: Panoptic Quality, mPQ^+: multi-class Panoptic Quality, NPV: Negative Predicted Value

All of the above-given models are used for Segmentation and Classification, but only the HoVer-Net and Hybrid HoVer-Net models perform cellular composition.

5   Conclusion

This paper presents a hybrid deep learning model by combining deep-learned and handcrafted features obtained from the feature descriptors such as local binary patterns and the histogram of oriented gradients. The proposed hybrid model has demonstrated a significant improvement in multi-class panoptic quality and multi-class panoptic quality metrics, which are the key metrics used for segmentation and classification tasks. The proposed study also shows the importance of texture-based feature descriptors in addition to the deep-learned features for colon nuclei segmentation, classification, and cell counting in H&E stained histology images. Though the proposed hybrid HoVer-Net model shows a significantly better performance compared to the baseline model, this still suffers from the noise sensitivity and higher computational time as LBP and HOG are considered as handcrafted feature extractors in the proposed model. Therefore, further studies will be done by integrating the other features and aligning with the histology images to provide more positive results.

References

1. Tosta, T.A.A., de Faria, P.R., Neves, L.A., do Nascimento, M.Z.: Computational normalization of H&E-stained histological images: progress, challenges and future potential. Artif. Intell. Med. **95**, 118–132 (2019)
2. Campanella, G., et al.: Clinical-grade computational pathology using weakly supervised deep learning on whole slide images. Nat. Med. **25**(8), 1301–1309 (2019)
3. Duran-Lopez, L., Dominguez-Morales, J.P., Conde-Martin, A.F., Vicente-Diaz, S., Linares-Barranco, A.: Prometeo: a CNN-based computer-aided diagnosis system for WSI prostate cancer detection. IEEE Access **8**, 128:613–128:628 (2020)
4. Graham, S., et al.: Conic: colon nuclei identification and counting challenge 2022. arXiv Preprint arXiv:2111.14485 (2021)
5. Liu, W., Wang, H., Du, J., Jing, C.: Raman microspectroscopy of nucleus and cytoplasm for human colon cancer diagnosis. Biosens. Bioelectron. **97**, 70–74 (2017)
6. Hamad, A., Bunyak, F., Ersoy, I.: Nucleus classification in colon cancer H&E images using deep learning. Microsc. Microanal. **23**(S1), 1376–1377 (2017)

7. Sirinukunwattana, K., Raza, S.E.A., Tsang, Y.-W., Snead, D.R., Cree, I.A., Rajpoot, N.M.: Locality sensitive deep learning for detection and classification of nuclei in routine colon cancer histology images. IEEE Trans. Med. Imaging **35**(5), 1196–1206 (2016)

8. Höfener, H., Homeyer, A., Weiss, N., Molin, J., Lundström, C.F., Hahn, H.K.: Deep learning nuclei detection: a simple approach can deliver state-of-the-art results. Comput. Med. Imaging Graph. **70**, 43–52 (2018)

9. Graham, S., et al.: Hover-net: simultaneous segmentation and classification of nuclei in multi-tissue histology images. Med. Image Anal. **58**, 101563 (2019)

10. Khan, H., Shah, P.M., Shah, M.A., ul Islam, S., Rodrigues, J.J.: Cascading hand-crafted features and convolutional neural network for IoT-enabled brain tumor segmentation. Comput. Commun. **153**, 196–207 (2020)

11. Graham, S., et al.: Lizard: a large-scale dataset for colonic nuclear instance segmentation and classification. In: Proceedings of the IEEE/CVF International Conference on Computer Vision, pp. 684–693 (2021)

12. Gedraite, E.S., Hadad, M.: Investigation on the effect of a gaussian blur in image filtering and segmentation. In: Proceedings ELMAR-2011, pp. 393–396. IEEE (2011)

13. Lee, S.-H., Kwon, S.: Median blur filter speed optimization for binary image. Welcome Remarks, p. 70 (2018)

14. Nguyen, D.T., Pham, T.D., Baek, N.R., Park, K.R.: Combining deep and hand-crafted image features for presentation attack detection in face recognition systems using visible-light camera sensors. Sensors **18**(3), 699 (2018)

15. Dalal, N., Triggs, B.: Histograms of oriented gradients for human detection. In: 2005 IEEE Computer Society Conference on Computer Vision and Pattern Recognition (CVPR'05), vol. 1, pp. 886–893 (2005)

16. Aziz, A., Sohail, A., Fahad, L., Burhan, M., Wahab, N., Khan, A.: Channel boosted convolutional neural network for classification of mitotic nuclei using histopathological images. In: 2020 17th International Bhurban Conference on Applied Sciences and Technology (IBCAST), pp. 277–284. IEEE (2020)

17. Song, L., Liu, X., Ma, L., Zhou, C., Zhao, X., Zhao, Y.: Using hog-LBP features and MMP learning to recognize imaging signs of lung lesions. In: 25th IEEE International Symposium on Computer-Based Medical Systems (CBMS), pp. 1–4. IEEE (2012)

18. Ojala, T., Pietikainen, M., Maenpaa, T.: Multiresolution gray-scale and rotation invariant texture classification with local binary patterns. IEEE Trans. Pattern Anal. Mach. Intell. **24**(7), 971–987 (2002)

19. Marceau, D.J., Howarth, P.J., Dubois, J.-M.M., Gratton, D.J., et al.: Evaluation of the grey-level co-occurrence matrix method for land-cover classification using spot imagery. IEEE Trans. Geosci. Remote Sens. **28**(4), 513–519 (1990)

20. Bruce, L.M., Koger, C.H., Li, J.: Dimensionality reduction of hyperspectral data using discrete wavelet transform feature extraction. IEEE Trans. Geosci. Remote Sens. **40**(10), 2331–2338 (2002)

21. Calonder, M., Lepetit, V., Strecha, C., Fua, P.: BRIEF: binary robust independent elementary features. In: Daniilidis, K., Maragos, P., Paragios, N. (eds.) ECCV 2010. LNCS, vol. 6314, pp. 778–792. Springer, Heidelberg (2010). https://doi.org/10.1007/978-3-642-15561-1_56

22. Rublee, E., Rabaud, V., Konolige, K., Bradski, G.: Orb: an efficient alternative to sift or surf. In: International Conference on Computer Vision, pp. 2564–2571. IEEE (2011)

23. Kirillov, A., He, K., Girshick, R., Rother, C., Dollár, P.: Panoptic segmentation. In: Proceedings of the IEEE/CVF Conference on Computer Vision and Pattern Recognition, pp. 9404–9413 (2019)
24. Piramanayagam, S., Saber, E., Schwartzkopf, W., Koehler, F.W.: Supervised classification of multisensor remotely sensed images using a deep learning framework. Remote Sensing **10**(9), 1429 (2018)
25. Naylor, P., Laé, M., Reyal, F., Walter, T.: Segmentation of nuclei in histopathology images by deep regression of the distance map. IEEE Trans. Med. Imaging, **38**(2), 448–459 (2018)
26. Saha, M., Chakraborty, C.: Her2Net: a deep framework for semantic segmentation and classification of cell membranes and nuclei in breast cancer evaluation. IEEE Trans. Image Process. **27**(5), 2189–2200 (2018)
27. Raza, S.E.A., et al.: Micro-net: a unified model for segmentation of various objects in microscopy images. Med. Image Anal. **52**, 160–173 (2019)
28. Vu, Q.D., et al.: Methods for segmentation and classification of digital microscopy tissue images. Front. Bioeng. Biotechnol. 53 (2019)

Multiple Object Tracking Based on Temporal Local Slice Representation of Sub-regions

Sripranav Mannepalli$^{(\boxtimes)}$ ⬤, Ravi Venkata Sai Maheswara Reddy Satti⬤, Rohit Shakya⬤, and Kalidas Yeturu⬤

Indian Institute of Technology Tirupati, Tirupati, India
{cs18b036,ykalidas}@iittp.ac.in
https://www.iittp.ac.in/

Abstract. Multiple object tracking (MOT) involves consistent labeling of objects in a given scene. A scene consists of multiple frames and within each frame rectangular subregions are specified as objects of interest. The task is to label the same object across frames with same identifier. However challenges in this setting involve, change in posture of the object, mild background change in the object region, occlusion, lighting changes, speed of movement and other such critical parameters. MOT is important because of its various applications in mobile robots, autonomous driving, and video surveillance analysis. There a number of neural network based methods which add modules based on property of interest such as a sub-network for velocity, a network for physical motion characteristics and networks based on pixel and edge information characteristics. However they have difficulty dealing with long duration occlusions as well as generalization issues due to millions of parameters and implicit overfitting. We present a new idea called, *Temporal Local Slicing (TLS)* that obtains local information across frames for a given subregion in the object vectorization step. The vectorization involves histogram of pixel intensities for red, blue and green channels of the sub region. We have performed a total of five experiments and observed the effectiveness of TLS and also a new idea of *Gossip vectorization* in Multiple object tracking. The object recognition accuracy of TLS vectors is 99.5% and mAP score of 99.1% on train and test partition of a video scene. However the MOT specific scores have been MOTA 56%, IDF1 72%, Recall 56.7%, Precision 98.5% and LOCA 91.9%. These are non-trivial scores indicating potential value in the idea of *TLS* vectorization.

Keywords: object tracking · temporal local slice · gossip vectorization

1 Introduction

We present herewith a new idea of *temporal local slices* for vector representation of objects in an image and using that representation for *tracking across frames*.

Supplementary Information The online version contains supplementary material available at https://doi.org/10.1007/978-3-031-31417-9_53.

The labelled data of object identifiers is used to build a classifier and upon an incoming object, its correct label is predicted. The introduced ideas handle long duration occlusions in MOT domain as well as bring in new way of feeding in temporal information.

Multiple object tracking (MOT) is the task of determining the trajectories of all object instances in a video. It is a fundamental problem in computer vision, with applications such as autonomous driving, human computer interaction [4], virtual reality [7], biology, and visual surveillance [22]. Video tracking, in particular, is supporting new research in transportation engineering, such as the study of the behaviour and safety of all road users, including vehicles, cyclists, and pedestrians, whether motorised or non-motorized. Without needing to wait for an accident to occur, new techniques are being developed to undertake road safety diagnosis based on observation of road user interactions. Automatically tracking the objects in a video can aid in the analysis of enormous amounts of data with much higher accuracy without the need for user intervention. This resulted in breakthroughs that could only be made by mining massive amounts of observational data. Despite its importance, it remains a difficult undertaking and an uncharted field in the context of deep learning. Tracking-by-detection has become the dominant paradigm among state-of-the-art technologies in MOT in recent years. Given an input video, MOT's duty is essentially divided into locating objects, keeping their identities, and generating their separate paths [9]. Multiple object tracking, in contrast to Single Object Tracking (SOT) [20], which largely focuses on building sophisticated appearance models and/or motion models to deal with challenging elements such as scale changes, out-of-plane rotations, and lighting fluctuations, involves the solution of two additional tasks: calculating the number of objects, which typically fluctuates over time, and storing their identities.

Because of its academic and commercial possibilities, multiple object tracking (MOT) has gotten a lot of attention. Despite the fact that various ways have been presented to address this issue, it remains difficult due to issues such as sudden appearance changes and significant object occlusions. Some of the existing works are listed below. These include, the works based on Centroid based ID assignments, Kalman Filters, Dynamic programming, Linear programming and various Graph based approaches.

Centroid-Based ID Assignment: Centroid-based tracking [12] is an easy to understand, yet highly effective tracking algorithm. Centroid based tracking is a combination of multiple-step processes, and it involves simple math for calculating the distance between all pairs of centroids. IDs can be assigned to bounding-box centroids in their most basic form. This is accomplished by computing the centroids of each bounding box in the frame. In the following frame,the new centroids are examined and IDs are assigned to them based on their distance from previous centroids. The underlying assumption is that centroids only change a small amount from one frame to the next. As long as the centroids are spread apart from each other, this simple strategy works fine. However, as the number of objects to track increase, using this method might not be a good idea and this method may be confused in the assignment of IDs. This approach also fails when there are occlusions among multiple moving objects. In the cases of occlusions and hidden movements it may assign different ID to objects.

Kalman Filtering: The *Kalman Filter* is an algorithm, that can be used in practically any engineering problem that includes prediction in a temporal or time series sense, be it computer vision, guidance, navigation, or even economics. The basic idea behind a Kalman filter is to minimise mistakes while coming up with a best guess of object's present state based on existing detections and prior predictions. The Kalman filter is most effective for linear systems with Gaussian processes.

Kalman Filtering [10] is an improvement over previously discussed centroid-based tracking. In this model, velocity and position of an object is used to anticipate the objects next position. Gaussians are examined for this task. When it receives a new reading, it can allocate the measurement to its prediction and update itself using probability. It consumes a small memory and operates quiet fast. In many cases, it can outperforms the traditional centroid-based tracking since it uses both the position and velocity of the object. This overcomes many drawbacks the centroid based ID assignment has. However, this algorithm also fails to perform when there are occlusions among multiple moving objects. This algorithm also fails to perform in nonlinear tracking scenarios.

Unscented Kalman Filtering: In [23] an improvement over kalman filtering is presented. Unscented Kalman filtering (UKF) technique is used for reliable object detection and tracking, taking into account the ambiguity produced by occlusion among many moving objects. The problem of non-linear tracking which limits the traditional Kalman filtering can be solved in UKF, by using unscented transformation. It also estimates each object's velocity information to aid the object detection process, effectively delineating several moving occlusion objects.

Deep Sort Algorithm: Deep Sort [21] is the most popular and extensively used object tracking approach, and it is a very effective object tracking algorithm since it employs deep learning principles. A visual awareness of the bounding box, which is what we humans utilise almost every time in tracking and detection of objects, is one crucial component lacking from all of the preceding algorithms. Person's appearance as well as their distance and velocity are tracked. By computing the deep visual features of each bounding box and integrating this deep feature similarity into tracking method deep sort increases the reliable of tracking.

Dynamic Programming: Multiple object tracking makes extensive use of dynamic programming (DP). The Viterbi algorithm [6] can be expanded to optimise many tracks at the same time using a single chain. Extended DP has a computational cost of $O(mk^2n)$, where k denotes the number of observations at each stage, n the number of objects, and m the sequence length. As a result, extended DP is difficult to apply to large-scale challenges. An efficient approximate dynamic programming scheme [2] has been studied to find a single object's path with heuristics used to determine the sequence of path assignments in a multiple-camera setting. While basic algorithms like best-track-first assignment work well for multiple camera tracking, they don't always work when objects have complex mutual occlusion patterns, particularly in single camera applications.

Linear Programming: Linear programming (LP) is another popular approach that can be used for more efficient search in object tracking. A constant velocity assumption [1] is made in this model. Optimizing object tracks using 0–1 Integer Programming [13] has been studied for radar data association. Other approximation methods for solving similar integer LP formulations as [13] are studied in [14], which turn out to be quite similar to the sequential DP method [2].

K-shortest Paths Optimization: K-Shortest Paths Optimization is an interesting approach, [3], which improves the existing dynamic approach by reformulating it as a constrained flow optimization to get a convex problem. They use the k-shortest routes algorithm to solve it because of its unique structure. The basis of this approach is to find of global minima in the convex problem. This approach employs a simpler version of the linear programming techniques.

Graph-Based Approach: Graph-based approach [17] is based on deep learning to extract features and hand-crafted bipartite graph or network flow optimization. Multiple object tracking is viewed as a graph partitioning challenge in these approaches. They create a graph of all detections from all object detectors and try to segment it into trajectories. Local cues like point tracks and speed, global cues like appearance, and intermediate cues like trajectory straightness are all taken into account when determining how similar two detections are. These several clues are combined to make the method resistant to detection errors (missing or extra detections). They then create a Conditional Random Field and optimise it by combining message sending and move-making algorithms in an effective way.

We present here a new idea of *temporal local slicing (TLS)* for vectorization of subregions which are used for prediction of object labels. The vectors are used in clustering as well to bring in robustness to longer duration occlusions. A similar idea of long term video scene vectorization based on presence of tracking objects across frames has been discussed in our earlier work [16]. In this work the scene vectors are used for retrieval of similar scenes as well as anomaly detection. However the local vector representation of sub-regions did not consider temporal information across frames.

2   Methods and Materials

2.1   Problem Statements

- State space inconsistency - the number of possible target (state space) trajectories over time, which can increase or decrease at any time, and how to keep each object's trajectory despite occlusion.

– Occlusion - objects in the camera's frame of view disappearing and reappearing makes data association harder.
– When people are dressed identically, such as in the case of sports, similar traits can lead to ID switching.
– Multiple objects with minor visual appearance differences can lead to the assignment of same IDs.
– Camera perspective and focal depth - depending on the viewing angle of the camera and its distance from object, it is possible to recognise the same object as different objects in different scenarios.
– Other issues include track initialization and termination, object fragmentation, and so on.
– While some algorithms produce good results, they have an $O(n^2)$ time complexity, which means they require a long time to perform.

Our main proposed ideas of *temporal local slice* and *gossip vector* based vectorization of sub-region of an image in the context of a video scene is presented. An overview of the steps involved is presented in Fig. 1.

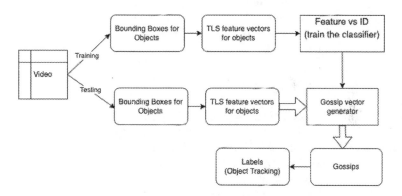

Fig. 1. An overview of our algorithm

2.2   Dataset

MOT Challenge [5]: Object detection, pedestrian detection, 3D reconstruction, optical flow, single-object short-term tracking, and stereo estimation are among the tasks covered by the Multiple object tracking benchmark. We used the MOT20-01 and MOT20-02 datasets for this experiment. The "MOT20-01" sequence is shot in a packed railway station indoors. It is quite a challenging scene and comes at a 25-frames-per-second video at 1080p resolution. Its duration is 17 s, it has 26647 number of boxes, and its ground truth for the tracks in this video is 90. The "MOT20-02" sequence is shot in a packed railway station indoors. It is quite a challenging scene and comes at a 25-frames-per-second video at 1080p resolution. Its duration is 111s, it has 202215 number of boxes, and its ground truth for the tracks in this video is 296.

All these images were in JPEG and named sequentially to a 6-digit file name (e.g. 000001.jpg). Detection and ground truth files are simple comma-separated value (CSV) files. Each line represents one object instance and contains 9 values. An example of this is given below.

1, −1, 794.2, 47.5, 71.2, 174.8, 0, −1, −1;

The first number indicates in which frame the object appears, while the second number identifies that object as belonging to a trajectory by assigning a unique ID (set to -1 in a detection file, as no ID is assigned yet). Each object can be assigned to only one trajectory. The next four numbers indicate the position of the bounding box of the pedestrian in 2D image coordinates. The position is indicated by the top-left corner as well as width and height of the bounding box.

2.3   Verification of Prediction

The followed the metrics provided by MOT challenge official website to verify the correctness of our predictions. We have observed non-trivial scores in a subset of the metrics used in standard practice in MOT area. All of these metrics have been explained in great detail in this paper [11].

2.4   Experimental Setup

The dataset used for classification are MOT20-01 and MOT20-02 [5]. The dataset is split into two partitions - 70% training set and 30% test data. For the purposes of classification of vectors, we have used random forest classifier with default parameters as in sklearn [15] and used grid search with cross validation for model selection.

The first step in MOT is object vectorization. We have essentially carried out two types of representations - (i) position free vectorization and (ii) adjustable level of temporal characteristics. The object region itself comes from third party object detectors such as Yolo [19].

2.5   Details of Technical Implementation

2.5.1   Vectorization Based on Temporal Local Slice (TLS)

We introduce a concept of TLS in which, a vector representation of a bounding box is obtained based on a cropped subregion of information from preceding image frames. The parameter TLS is hyper-parameter which can be adjusted by a user before vectorization. For instance, $TLS = 30$ means, a number of 30 frames are considered (including the present frame). In all these *temporal* frames, *a subregion is cut-through* to result in a *slice* and hence the abbreviation *TLS*. The RGB histogram values for these subregions is considered vector representation. In our experiments we have used $TLS = 15$ as default configuration, which corresponds to half a second of scene in that region in a *30 FPS* capture set up. An illustration of the procedure is presented in Fig. 2.

As further illustration, consider a person walking. A TLS setting (> 1) would appear as if the person is entering the bounding box and maturing to the central position in that small interval of time *and* within that small subregion. The details of the algorithm is presented in Algorithm 1.

2.5.2   *Gossip* Vectorization

We also introduce a concept of *gossip* in the vectorization of objects in video scenes. This is based on a vector representation of *similarities* between a given local subregion to *known subregions*. An illustration of the steps in gossip vectorization is presented in Fig. 3. The idea stems from the concept of *committee of experts* in the domain of *ensemble learning* which itself originates from the principle of *weighted voting*.

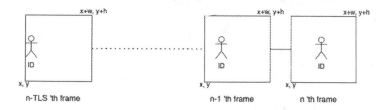

Fig. 2. TLS (Temporal Local Slicing)

Algorithm 1. TLS Method: find FeatureVector

1: Let $L = (x, y, h, w)$ denote Co-ordinates of the bounding-box in the current frame.
2: $K \leftarrow$ TLS number
3: $n \leftarrow 1$
4: $c \leftarrow$ current frame number
5: featureVector = RGB histogram at L in the current frame
6: **while** $n \leq K$ **do**
7:     $hist \leftarrow$ RGB histogram at L in frame[c-n]
8:     featureVector $\leftarrow \dfrac{hist + n \times featureVector}{n+1}$
9:     $n \leftarrow n + 1$

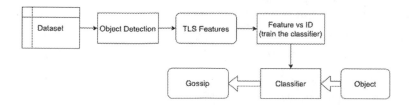

Fig. 3. Implementation of Gossip Vectorization

In this setting, an ANN is built based on the training data having identifiers (or *IDs*) of person objects. **The person objects need not even occur in the test data.** A multi-class classifier (ANN) is built whose *number of classes is equal to number of person identifiers.*

Given a query subregion or patch, the output of the ANN is an array of probability scores corresponding to each person class. The sum of probability scores would add up to 1. *The vector of probability scores itself is the vector representation.* The whole process can be visualized as a process of gossip arriving at similarities to known objects.

Gossip Vector Distance: The gossip vector is not regular feature vector. It is an array or probability scores which would sum up to 1. In order to compute distance between two gossip vectors, Kullback-Leibler divergence [8] measure is used. The steps are presented herewith.

- Let P, Q be two gossip vectors
- The ith element of a vector P, is denoted by $P[i]$
- $KL(P||Q) = \sum_{i=1} P[i] \times \log \frac{P[i]}{Q[i]}$
- In order to bring in similarity into picture, we have used symmetric KL divergence as measure $d(P, Q)$
- $d(P, Q) = \frac{KL(P||Q) + KL(Q||P)}{2}$

2.5.3   Clustering of Subregion Vectors

The clusters of sub-region specific vectors would result in *occlusion time free tracking.* However the object context needs to be maintained as reflected in the vector representation. In this set, DBSCAN algorithm [15,18] has been used for clustering.

2.5.4   High Throughput Distance Matrix Clustering

It has been noted that in case of *gossip vectors* and millions of such points, all pair distance calculation based on KL divergence has immense time complexity. The KL divergence step requires computation of natural logarithm computation and element-wise multiplications in matrix representation in a repeated fashion. In order to speed up computation, element-wise logarithm can be pre-computed. Matrix operations between $P, log(P), Q, log(Q)$ elements using *precomputed* components has drastically reduced time complexity. Details of the algorithm is presented in Supplementary material (Algorithm 5.1).

2.6   Experimental Set up

We have carried out a number of experiments as tabulated in Table 1 in order to deduce inferences on quality of vectorization and ability to perform tracking.

Table 1. Experiments and reference pseudocodes. The reference codes are pointing to supplementary material.

Experiment identifier	Purpose	Reference pseudocode
E1	Sanity test of RGB histogram vectorization	Sect. 5.2.1 (Algorithm 4)
E2	Sanity test of TLS vectorization for classification	Sect. 5.2.2 (Algorithm 5
E3	Sanity test of TLS features for clustering	Sect. 5.2.3 (Algorithm 6)
E4	Sanity test of gossip vector for clustering	Sect. 5.2.4 (Algorithm 7)
E5	Classification approach involving Gossip vectors made using TLS feature	Sect. 2.8 (Algorithm 2)

2.7 Flow Diagrams

The flow charts for the experiment 5 are presented. First, the TLS vectors for each bounding box in the ground-truth file are obtained. In the second step a classifier is built using ANN with softmax as an activation function. This is the training phase (Fig. 4). In the test phase, the TLS vectors of the bounding boxes in the detection file are presented to the model. The model then generated a vector of probabilities for its match against the trained classes of identifiers (*the gossip vector*). This is the testing phase (Fig. 5).

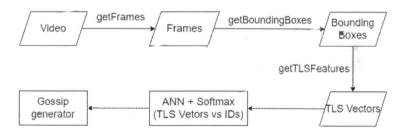

Fig. 4. Training in experiment 5

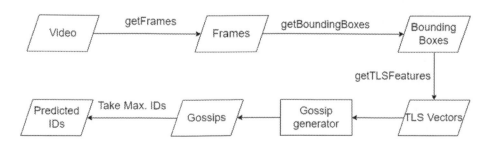

Fig. 5. Testing in experiment 5

2.8   Details of the Final Experiment

We have performed a total of 5 experiments on TLS and Gossip Vectorizations. This is the fifth and final experiment which shows that maximum probability item in the gossip vector captures the object-id. We have used ANNs to generate the gossips. The index of the maximum element in the gossip vector is the prediction ID.
The details of this experiment is given below.

– **Aim:** To show that maximum probability item in the gossip vector captures the object-id.
– **Expected outcome:** To have high accuracy when trained on Ground Truth file and tested on detection file.
– **Observed Outcome:**
  • Hypothesis PASSED
  • We have obtained good mot scores on the training data set.
– **Methodology:** The pseudo-code of the algorithm followed is given below. (Algorithm 2)
– **Conclusion:**
  • From this experiment, we conclude that the Classification of the proposed TLS-RGB Histograms gives good results.
– **Algorithm:**

Algorithm 2. A classification approach involving Gossip vectors made using TLS feature for detection files, training on ground truth files

---

1: R = Set of all bounding boxes (ground truth rectangles) in each frame   ▷ Each line in Ground Truth file has (frame-id, object-id, xl, yl, w, h) in each frame.
2: S = Set of all bounding boxes (detection rectangles) in each frame. ▷ Each line in detection file has (frame-id, -1, xl, yl, w, h) $Dataset$ = TLS feature vector(R)   ▷ Preparation of Dataset
3: $X = Dataset$
4: Y = The IDs of dataset X.
5: X' = TLS feature vector(S)   ▷ Building the Classifier
6: C = ANN+Softmax.   ▷ We used softmax as the activation function for the ANNs. The output in this case is the probability of different IDs, which we call the Gossip vector.
7: C.fit(X, Y)
8: $Gossips$ = C.predict(X')
9: $l = Gossips$.size()
10: n = 0
11: $predict$ = [ ]   ▷ List
12: **while** n < l **do**
13:     $predict$+=numpy.argmax($Gossips$[n])
14:     n+=1   ▷ Report the metrics specified in MOT website.

If there are two or more objects in a single frame with same predicted Id, then the object with maximum gossip vector value gets the preference.

3   Results and Discussion

Inferences from the 5 experiments carried out are presented. The algorithms followed in each of these experiments is given in pseudo-code format in the Sect. 5.2. The metrics used for the evaluation of these experiments is given in this paper [11]. Summary of observations is presented herewith.

- For Experiment 1 (Sect. 5.2.1), the RGB histogram vectorization has reported high accuracy and mAP scores in a multi class classification setting for label prediction (Table 2).
- For Experiment 2 (Sect. 5.2.2) (similar to experiment 1), however for *TLS vectorization* observed similar results (Table 2)
- For Experiment 3 (Sect. 5.2.3), the clustering of *TLS vectors* has produced non-trivial V-score metric (Table 3) with respect to ground truth labels.
- For Experiment 4 (Sect. 5.2.4) (similar to experiment 3), however for *gossip vectors* observed similar results (Table 3)
- For Experiment 5 (Sect. 2.8), 9 MOT metrics have been evaluated (Table 4) where high scores have been observed for precision and *LocA*, however recall has been low (Table 4)

Table 2. Evaluation Metrics and their values for Experiment 1 and 2

Experiment	Dataset	Accuracy	mAP Score	Precision	Recall
E-1	MOT20-01	0.97	0.96	0.97	0.95
E-1	MOT20-02	0.96	0.97	0.96	0.97
E-2	MOT20-01	0.99	0.99	0.99	0.99
E-2	MOT20-02	0.98	0.98	0.98	0.97

Table 3. Evaluation Metrics and their values for Experiment 3 and 4

Experiment	Dataset	Homogeneity Score	Completeness Score	V Measure Score
E-3	MOT20-01	0.594	0.759	0.666
E-3	MOT20-02	0.513	0.665	0.543
E-4	MOT20-01	0.638	0.730	0.681
E-4	MOT20-02	0.531	0.595	0.556

Table 4. Evaluation Metrics and their values for Experiment 5

Dataset	MOTA	IDF1	MT	ML	FP	FN	Rcll	Prcn	LocA
MOT20-01	56.069	72.029	20	11	178	8586	56.789	98.447	91.92
MOT20-02	49.497	65.101	68	34	421	72532	53.127	93.507	92.249

More details about experimental records are presented in the supplementary Sect. 5.2.

4   Conclusions and Future Directions

We report here a new way of addressing occlusion duration related challenge in the context of multi object tracking. The state of the algorithms build more and more complex neural networks adding modules for each concept of interest and attempting to learn millions of parameters from few video scenes. However we propose a different simplifying way to leverage temporal information in a video scene simultaneously incorporating positional information. This new idea we call *temporal local slice* (TLS) which has demonstrated high quality vectorization of objects. We also introduce another vectorization called *gossip vectorization* based on multi object similarity to training set of objects. This representation also resulted in non-trivial recognition accuracies. We present through a number of experiments on usefulness of TLS vectorization with respect to standard MOT evaluation metrics.

The knowledgebase of TLS vectors simplifies information to be learned from millions of images. When augmented with object detection neural networks, novel object detection algorithms can be developed based on kernel filter design and initialization. The overall methodology introduces simplifying ideas with potential value addition and future research directions.

References

1. Michael, B.D., Fabian, R., Bastian, L., Esther, K.M., Luc, V.G.: Robust tracking-by-detection using a detector confidence particle filter. In: 2009 IEEE 12th International Conference on Computer Vision, May 2010. https://doi.org/10.1109/ICCV.2009.5459278
2. Jerome, B., Francois, F., Pascal, F.: Robust people tracking with global trajectory optimization. In: 2006 IEEE Computer Society Conference on Computer Vision and Pattern Recognition (CVPR'06), June 2006. https://doi.org/10.1109/CVPR.2006.258
3. Jerome, B., Francois, F., Pascal, F.: Multiple object tracking using k-shortest paths optimization. IEEE Trans. Pattern Anal. Mach. Intell. 1806–1819 (2011). https://doi.org/10.1109/TPAMI.2011.21
4. Joshua, C., Matthew, S., Goldgof, D.B., Deborah, S.B., Rangachar, K.: Understanding transit scenes: a survey on human behavior-recognition algorithms. IEEE Trans. Intell. Transport. Syst. 206–224 (2010). https://doi.org/10.1109/TITS.2009.2030963
5. Patrick, D., et al.: Mot20: a benchmark for multi object tracking in crowded scenes (2020). https://arxiv.org/abs/2003.09003
6. Forney, G.D.: The Viterbi algorithm. Proc. IEEE **61**(3), 268–278 (1973). https://doi.org/10.1109/PROC.1973.9030
7. Uchiyama, H., Marchand, E.: Object detection and pose tracking for augmented reality: recent approaches, November 2012. https://hal.inria.fr/hal-00751704/
8. Kullback, S., Leibler, R.A.: On information and sufficiency. Ann. Math. Stat. **22**(1), 79 – 86 (1951). https://doi.org/10.1214/aoms/1177729694
9. Wenhan, L., Junliang, X., Anton, M., Xiaoqin, Z., Wei, L., Tae-Kyun, K.: Multiple object tracking: a literature review. Artif. Intell. ELSEVIER 293(103448) (2020). https://doi.org/10.1016/j.artint.2020.103448

10. Xin, L., Kejun, W., Wei, W., Yang, L.: A multiple object tracking method using Kalman filter. In: 2010 IEEE International Conference on Information and Automation, pp. 1862–1866 (2010). https://doi.org/10.1109/ICINFA.2010. 5512258
11. Luiten, J., et al.: HOTA: a higher order metric for evaluating multi-object tracking. Int. J. Comput. Vision, 1–31 (2020). https://doi.org/10.1007/s11263-020-01375-2
12. Hilda, M.F., Adriane, E.S.: Looking at the center of the targets helps multiple object tracking. J. Vision **10** (2010). https://doi.org/10.1167/10.4.19
13. Morefield, C.L.: Application of 0-1 integer programming to multitarget tracking problems. IEEE Trans. Autom. Control **AC-22**(3), 302–312 (1977). https:// ieeexplore.ieee.org/stamp/stamp.jsp?arnumber=1101500
14. Storms, P., Spieksma, F.: An LP-based algorithm for the data association problem in multitarget tracking. In: Proceedings of the Third International Conference on Information Fusion (2000). https://doi.org/10.1109/IFIC.2000.862699
15. Pedregosa, F., et al.: Scikit-learn: machine learning in Python. J. Mach. Learn. Res. **12**, 2825–2830 (2011)
16. Prashanth, K., Kalidas, Y., Jay, R.B.K., Sai, A.P.K., Aakash, D.: An algorithm for semantic vectorization of video scenes - applications to retrieval and anomaly detection. In: International Conference on Computer Vision and Image Processing (CVIP) 2020, vol. 1378, pp. 369–381 (2020). https://doi.org/10.1007/978-981-16-1103-2_31
17. Kumar, R., Guillaume, C., Monique, T.: Multiple object tracking by efficient graph partitioning. In: Brown, M.S., Cham, T.-J., Matsushita, Y. (eds.) ACCV - 12th Asian Conference on Computer Vision, November 2014, Singapore, Singapore. ffhal-01061450f (2014). https://hal.inria.fr/hal-01061450
18. Nadia, R., Imas, S.S.: Determination of optimal epsilon (EPS) value on DBScan algorithm to clustering data on peatland hotspots in Sumatra. IOP Conf. Ser. Earth Environ. Sci. https://iopscience.iop.org/article/10.1088/1755-1315/31/1/ 012012/pdf
19. Redmon, J., Divvala, S., Girshick, R., Farhadi, A.: You only look once: unified, real-time object detection. In: 2016 IEEE Conference on Computer Vision and Pattern Recognition (CVPR), pp. 779–788 (2016). https://doi.org/10.1109/CVPR.2016.91
20. Hu, W., Li, X., Luo, W., Zhang, X., Maybank, S., Zhang, Z.: Single and multiple object tracking using log-Euclidean Riemannian subspace and block-division appearance model. IEEE Trans. Pattern Anal. Mach. Intell. (2012). https://doi. org/10.1109/TPAMI.2012.42
21. Nicolai, W., Alex, B., Dietrich, P.: Simple online and realtime tracking with a deep association metric (2017). https://arxiv.org/abs/1703.07402
22. Xiaogang, W.: Intelligent multi-camera video surveillance: a review. Pattern Recogn. Lett. ELSEVIER, 3–19 (2012). https://doi.org/10.1016/j.patrec.2012.07. 005, https://www.sciencedirect.com/science/article/pii/S016786551200219X
23. Chen, X., Wang, X., Xuan, J.: Tracking multiple moving objects using unscented Kalman filtering techniques. In: International Conference on Engineering and Applied Science (ICEAS 2012), March 2012. https://arxiv.org/abs/1802.01235

An Ensemble Approach for Moving Vehicle Detection and Tracking by Using Ni Vision Module

Pankaj Pratap Singh[1]($\boxtimes$) (iD), Preeti Ramchiary[1], Jahirul Islam Bora[1], Rakesh Bhuyan[1], and Shitala Prasad[2] (iD)

[1] Department of Computer Science and Engineering, Central Institute of Technology Kokrajhar, Kokrajhar, Assam, India
pankajp.singh@cit.ac.in
[2] Institute for Infocomm Research, A*Star, Singapore, Singapore

Abstract. In the recent years, surveillance systems and video monitoring have been largely used for the management of traffic. Acquired images and video clips from the road traffic can be utilized in the Lab VIEW program environment. LabVIEW Vision Assistant is focusing on to discover the moving vehicles. This approach finds a formation of resemblance in the frames for vehicle and non-vehicle objects, while the vehicles tracking progress through image sequences. For improving the adaptive background mixture model, there is indeed of background subtraction method. In addition, it constructs the system more precisely with rapid learning also. Therefore, its performance shows the adaptability on the occurrence of any real time videos. This evolve system robustly detect the vehicles on resolving the background objects which help to track the vehicles effectively. The various types of attributes related to moving vehicles are extracted which are used in feature extraction techniques for tracking the vehicles. The extracted features utilize in the module of LabVIEW environment and Vision Assistant module works mainly in the detection of moving vehicles objects. This proposed work can help in reducing the cost of traffic monitoring systems and real automation of traffic observation systems.

Keywords: Vehicle Detection · Mean Shift Algorithm · LabView · Vision Development Module · Object Tracking

1 Introduction

Due to the rapidly increasing moving vehicles are raising issues of congestion and eventually on the environment also. It is indeed a better traffic monitoring system for the abovementioned challenging task by using image processing and computer vision approaches [2]. There has been a lot of work done previously in this domain of different types of object detection & tracking. In the 1980s, Lipton et al. [4] did a project to differentiate moving objects as humans or animals. A vision-based algorithm was developed and used for detection and classification of vehicles in monocular image sequences of

D. Gupta et al. (Eds.): CVIP 2022, CCIS 1777, pp. 712–721, 2023.
https://doi.org/10.1007/978-3-031-31417-9_54

traffic scenes recorded by a stationary camera [5]. This processing was happened in three levels such as raw image, region level and vehicle level. Also, a background subtraction and modeling technique which could predict the moving speed of an object using uncalibrated cameras. But this approach is not very successful in obtaining speed due to moving cameras and other issues. It was carried out by Dailey et al. [6]. Cheng et al. [1] used an image segmentation based method to achieve moving vehicle detection, but the major drawback was that it was computationally costly and hence took a lot of time for real time tracking process [4, 14]. In 2014, researchers presented an image segmentation and feature extraction technique using LabView for the same. Beymer et. al. [3] worked on addressing the real time system which could measure the traffic parameters. It uses an image processing method along with the occlusion reasoning that helps the traffic congested areas for tracking vehicles [2, 13].

Later, some more work has been carried out in this field and speed detection using Background subtraction and frame difference technique have been used [7]. The Lab view software is used for numerous purposes such as computations, machine vision and many more. Block representation is the simplest method in image processing instead of doing complicated programming. Using the Labview, Edge detection, histogram, object detection and pattern matching can also do in easy manner. In the Lab view environment, Vision assistant is an effective tool and can help in processing of image easily [9–11]. In 2013, various kind of information is extracted with the help of a hybrid approach by Singh and Garg [12].

After analyzing the NI vision module and also related image acquisition system, it can be certainly utilized for computer vision related applications. This is the key reason to generate an inquisitive interest in this area, Since, there has been a rapid increase in CCTV cameras in National and State Highways and can be used for traffic monitoring. An event of interest (e.g. an accident), it helps to monitor them but becomes difficult as the number of camera's increases. The large amount of data which is generated and can't be reviewed manually as it becomes impractical many times. Some of the areas for analyzing video, there is a need of only small amounts of computation method or almost no human input which can be called a good solution [1]. To detect and take out a lot of functional information on traffic such as vehicle number, type & speed can also make this process effective. After detecting the vehicles in video frames, the extracted image features are needed for further processing. These features can be called as actual properties of the image. Raw features of the vehicles are such as brightness, texture, edges, etc. Lots of CCTV cameras are installed in traffic sites but their monitoring is a major issue and also quite inefficient this process in manual manner. Extracting different attributes like color, size, type poses is also another challenge. Sometimes, it is also difficult to identify two or more vehicles which are in very close vicinity and distinguishing between vehicles behind one another is a problem. In low light areas and differences in contrast during the day can lead to poor image and poor detection of our target i.e. vehicle.

2   A Designed Framework for Ensemble Approach for Moving Vehicle Detection and Tracking

The proposed framework explains ensemble approach to achieve our goal of detecting and tracking moving vehicles. This is achieved using NI LabView and its Vision Development Module which contains the Vision Assistant (see Fig. 1). LabView is a resourceful graphical programming environment which helps to provide much more features. Initially, the open source based OpenCV libraries also utilizes for object detection and tracking, and integrated it with LabView for achieving the final result. Background subtraction method in OpenCV is used to differentiate the vehicles from the background objects. In this framework, LabView and Vision Assistant are used for finding the features. We carried out the motive by using Image Segmentation techniques, Feature Extraction. Color Plane extraction is used for conversion of color images into binary images. It gives better differentiation of foreground and background objects.

2.1   Automatic Vehicle Detection Using Vision Assistant and Tracker Module

Vehicle detection system is the system that allows tracking and monitoring of vehicles and this could be achieved by acquiring data from video clips and further processing them. Using Lab VIEW for the same reduces a lot of time and effort which could be utilized in improving and increasing the efficiency of the model.

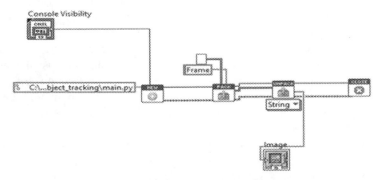

Fig. 1. Process block diagram of NI Vision Assistant module

The vehicle identification system can be implemented in the following steps:

- Image Acquisition and NI Smart camera capture the traffic video clips.
- Acquired video clips then accessed in the Lab VIEW environment, resulting in the image frames.
- Foreground object (vehicle) detection in Lab VIEW eliminates the background from the input frames of the video.
- For detection of the in motion vehicle at a certain meantime can capture the difference among the frames.

- Using historical masking, elements already in frame are ignored, where the stationary elements are being preserved.
- Vision Assistant (VA) in Lab VIEW mainly focuses on bringing out the real characteristics or attributes of the vehicles.
- After this, an abounding box is created around the object for reference.
- Using a tracker from an open CV, every detected object is set up to be tracked.
- Tracker ID of objects is updated constantly and ID is shown above the bounding box.

This model is set up in such a way that the moving vehicle objects are first detected using background subtraction and then a tracker is used to identify and constantly track the vehicles. The tracker gives a specific identifier to the objects and that ID is shown over the bounding boxes. This model is based on LabVIEW environment as it also keep a seamless interactive possibility with MyRio; one of the development boards by National Instruments. This gives us an advantage over the first created model which is implemented in Python and OpenCV. This standalone device can monitor and manage traffic individually. LabVIEW also has cloud based access which helps to store, manage and process the obtained or collected data in a centralized manner.

2.2 Automatic Vehicle Detection Using Labview Based Vision Assistant

There is a need of feature to track objects which can be visually distinctive from its background and it can be generated by using color plane extraction module. In this manner, a clear identification of objects is possible and also the continuous tracking of it. The main purpose of this tracking process is to track the objects such as a car, a person or etc. As much as better separation between the background and foreground objects, the accurate detection can be achieved. The used algorithm for the object tracking is the shape shift algorithm in place of using a traditional mean shift algorithm. Figure 4 shows the steps of LabView Vision Assistant for detection of vehicle objects.

Color Pattern Matching. As we mentioned above, the limitation in using object tracking module is that a clear differentiation of background and foreground is required for better tracking. But in case there is low light and a black car or object has to be tracked. It would be a nightmare for the previous tool to track it down. So for such situations we can input a certain range of color pixels that could be identified and tracked by the system. This can be achieved by using the color pattern matching function [8]. It has some controls which can be tweaked over to get better precision. The object gets tracked even in poor conditions as against the object tracking module.

Color Plane Extraction. Sometimes the acquired video clip is not very much readable. In such a scenario it becomes difficult for the system to track down the required object. In such a case we can use color plane extraction where the defined color of the required object is extracted from the pane. This makes the object white in color and separates it from the background. And thus a proper tracking is carried out.

Pattern Matching. There is also a feature to do a shape or pattern matching to attain object tracking. This module is a bit harder to conquer as in a video an object in a different direction could result in formation of different shapes or patterns. We are working this as if we can add three to four modules together in our system, we can achieve better results. Currently we have been able to test the above module to track an object in live video as well as pre-recorded videos. We would say that the system is pretty much able to do its job and a lot more is possible in this aspect in terms of refinement and accuracy.

Traditional Mean-Shift Algorithm. The mean shift algorithm is a machine learning algorithm which is a type of clustering algorithm. It is mostly used in image processing and computer vision. It assigns the data points continuously by shifting the points towards the highest density point in the area or the mode. This algorithm can track objects in real-time. The more there is distinction between background and the object, the better the output of it. It always tends to find a densely filled area of data or pixels in case of image as shown in Fig. 2. The object is surrounded by a bounding box to show the region of interest. This means that the object is to be known and defined initially. This method works only if there is a distinct color difference between foreground and background. Also, when tracking an object, how far or near the object is to the camera, the bounding box size remains same.

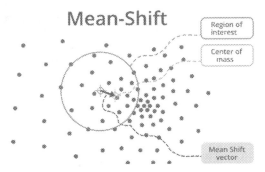

Fig. 2. Mean shift representation

Feature Extraction. We have also worked upon extracting object features to better identify and track the object. This approach is based on converting the image to binary so as to get better separation of background and foreground objects. Then a Threshold filter is used to particularly define the color range of our ROI that is the object. Now we get a pure blacked out image showing just the highlighted pixels of color range that we chose earlier. To more refine the system, we use advanced morphological filters to filter out small particles (see Fig. 3). Then we can get a precisely defined structure of our object i.e. the vehicle. In case of Mean Shift algorithm, some problems occur due to poor contrast or video footage, but the combination of mean shift and feature extraction techniques could provide result better as the improved model.

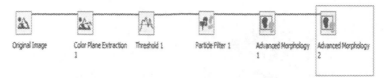

Fig. 3. LabView Vision Assistant script file preview

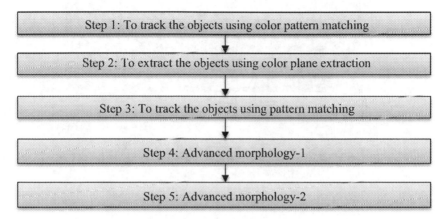

Fig. 4. A detailed step LabView Vision Assistant for detection of vehicle objects

3 Result and Discussion

Various types of moving vehicle videos in traffic are collected in the database [15]. In this proposed ensemble approach, NI Labview environment exploits for the vehicle detection and tracking as shown in Fig. 5. The objects are checked individually within the region of interest. A mask is applied for differentiating between the background and foreground using background subtraction method. The abovesaid challenge is resolved in LabVIEW environment by using the Python Integration Toolkit for simplified resolution. The extraction method is used from the Open CV library.

In the results, NI Vision Assistant is used to acquire and process the video clips as shown in Fig. 5. The frames of video clips are used to make precise adaptation of tracking the vehicle objects. Figures 6(a) and 6(b) show the moving vehicle detection and tracking using Color Pattern Matching in Vision Assistant, and shape adaptive mean shift algorithm respectively. Figure 6(b) results shows that it gives better results as compared to traditional mean shift algorithms. Color pattern matching based results extracts precisely an object of interest which is effective due the better utilization of color values. The results show the effectiveness of the proposed ensemble approach in the Figs. 5 and 6.

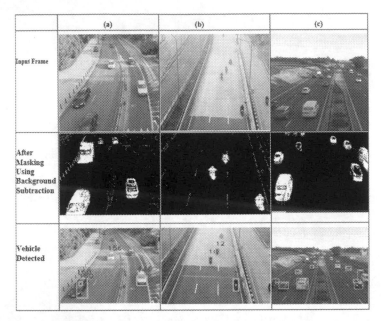

Fig. 5. Moving vehicle detected using an ensemble approach

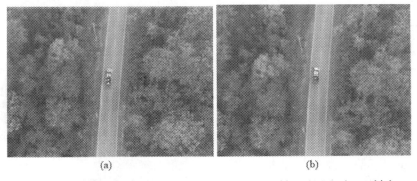

Fig. 6. (a) Moving vehicle tracking using Color Pattern Matching (b) Moving vehicle tracking using Adapted Shape Mean-Shift Algorithm

Figures 7(a) and 7(b) show the detection of moving vehicle in pre-recorded session and live video session respectively. Table 1 shows the different evaluation parameters of the detected vehicles using the extraction methods from the OpenCV library. Table 2 shows the different evaluation parameters of the detected vehicles using the vision assistant based ensemble approach. A comparison has been done to analyze the results.

(a)   (b)

Fig. 7. Vehicle detection in (a) pre-recorded session and (b) live video session

Table 1. Different evaluation parameters of the detected object outcomes using OpenCV

	Detected objects image results		
	Figure 5(a)	Figure 5(b)	Figure 5(c)
False Positive Rate (FPR)	0.25	0.087	0.095
False Alarm Rate (FAR)	0.46	0.34	0.39
Detection Rate	0.70	0.62	0.65
Accuracy	0.81	0.85	0.83
Precision	0.59	0.65	0.66
Intersection over Union (IoU)	0.65	0.62	0.7

Table 2. Different evaluation parameters of the detected object outcomes in Vision Assistant

	Detected objects image results		
	Pre-Recorded Video (Fig. 7)	Live Video Feed (Fig. 7)	Drone Shot Figure 6(b)
False Positive Rate (FPR)	0.012	0.053	0.003
False Alarm Rate (FAR)	0.28	0.4	0
Detection Rate	0.9	0.79	0.96
Accuracy	0.89	0.82	0.94
Precision	0.78	0.71	0.85
Intersection over Union (IoU)	0.87	0.7	0.95

4   Conclusion and Future Scope

In this ensemble approach the role of LabView along with Vision Assistant is more effective in case of graphical programming environment based model. Both methods are used for detecting moving vehicles. The ensemble approach based on the LabView and Vision Assistant model is providing better accuracy. The number of false positive detection is less though LABVIEW environment as compared to OpenCV environment based detection method. In the OpenCV system, there are some hits and misses that we are to face which reduces the precision. In OpenCV, most of the parameters are fixed, so as we cannot make many changes; it tends to work differently in different datasets.

In the Vision Development module, there are lots of customization options and can set the parameters and values as per the application requirement. This provides better detection and tracking efficiency. There has been an improvement in the Intersection over Union or IoU values. In our observation, the bounding boxes are more precisely created in the LabView and Vision assistant model. The setup and use of the Labview model is also easier than setting up the python and OpenCV environment. A much tech savvy mindset is needed to set up the OpenCV environment based detection and tracking. The used approach initially was a creative one in terms of the rich LABVIEW modules collection. It was also nice to see the result with the drone shots, as it may also open another way of dimension of vehicle detection.

References

1. Cheng, H., Shaw, B., Palen, J., Lin, B., Chen, B., Wang, Z.: Development and field test of a laser-based nonintrusive detection system for identification of vehicles on the highway. IEEE Trans. Intell. Transp. Syst. **6**(2), 147–155 (2005)
2. Cucchiara, R., Piccardi, M., Mello, P.: Image analysis and rule-based reasoning for a traffic monitoring system. IEEE Trans. Intell. Transp. Syst. **1**(2), 119–130 (2000)
3. Beymer, D., McLauchlan, P., Coifman, B., Malik, J.: A real-time computer vision system for measuring traffic parameters. In: Proceedings of IEEE Conference on Computer Vision and Pattern Recognition, pp. 495–501. San Juan, PR, USA (1977)
4. Lipton, A.J., Fujiyoshi, H., Patil, R.S.: Moving target classification and tracking from real-time video. In: IEEE Workshop on Application of Computer Vision, pp. 8–14. Princeton, NJ, USA (1998)
5. Gupte, S., Masoud, O., Martin, R.F.K., Papanikolopoulos, N.P.: Detection and classification of vehicles. IEEE Trans. Intell. Transp. Syst. **3**(1), 37–47 (2002)
6. Dailey, D., Cathey, F., Pumrin, S.: An algorithm to estimate mean traffic speed using uncalibrated cameras. IEEE Trans. Intell. Transp. Syst. **1**(2), 98–107 (2000)
7. Toufiq, P., Egammal, A., Mittal, A.: A framework for feature selection for background subtraction. In: IEEE Computer Society Conference on Computer Vision and Pattern Recognition, pp. 1916–1923. New York, NY, USA (2006)
8. Fu, K.S., Rosenfeld, A.: Pattern recognition and image processing. IEEE Trans. Comput. **25**(12), 1336–1346 (1976)
9. Ravi Kumar, A.V., Nataraj, K.R.: Result analysis of Labview and Matlab in application of image detection. Int. J. Comput. Appl. **48**(9), 6–10 (2012)
10. Panayi, G.C., Bovik, A.C., Rajashekar, U.: Image processing for everyone. In: 1st Signal Processing Education Workshop, Hunt, TX (2000)
11. Gururaj, M.S., Ramesh, M.H., Arvind, J.A.: A review on image tracking technique in Labview. Int. J. Sci. Dev. Res. **1**(6), 90–92 (2016)
12. Singh, P.P., Garg, R.D.: A hybrid approach for information extraction from high resolution satellite imagery. Int. J. Image Graph. **13**(2), 1340007(1–16) (2013)
13. Chanda, B., Majumder, D.: Digital Image Processing and Analysis, 488 p. PHI Learning Pub. (2003)

14. Comaniciu, D., Ramesh, V., Meer, P.: Real time tracking of non-rigid objects using mean-shift. In: Proceedings of International Conference on Computer Vision and Pattern Recognition, pp. 673–678. IEEE, Hilton Head, SC, USA (2000)
15. Videos of Moving vehicle traffic in highway Database. https://mega.nz/folder/yx8XHKiZ# Zpmy5ez2VgmSLbUaFvrSWA. Accessed Feb–June 2022

Leaf Spot Disease Severity Measurement in Terminalia Arjuna Using Optimized Superpixels

Sourav Samanta, Sanjoy Pratihar$^{(\boxtimes)}$, and Sanjay Chatterji

Computer Science and Engineering, Indian Institute of Information Technology,
Kalyani 741235, India
sanjoy@iiitkalyani.ac.in

Abstract. Early diagnosis of plant leaf disease, i.e., detection in the initial development stage, is a promising area of research focusing on smart agriculture involving computer vision. Automatic detection can significantly minimize human labor employment due to regular supervision. Terminalia Arjuna is a multi-purpose tree primarily found on the Indian subcontinent. The various chemical compounds of the Arjuna leaf are frequently used in medicine. Also, Terminalia Arjuna leaf is utilized in sericulture as a food source for moths. Leaf spot disease of Arjuna is common, and it is necessary to initiate treatment as soon as the disease appears on the leaves to prevent further spread on other leaves and other trees. This study used a multi-objective optimized simple linear iterative clustering (SLIC) algorithm to precisely locate leaf spots in affected areas. The entire leaf surface is segmented into two types of superpixels, healthy and unhealthy. The color moment features have been extracted for classification. The classification accuracy of two types of superpixels using four well-known classifiers has been reported, and SVM achieved the highest classification accuracy at 99.60%. Based on the categorized superpixels, the severity score of the leaf spot disease has been computed for various sample leaves. The experimental findings demonstrate the applicability and robustness of the proposed method.

Keywords: Smart sericulture · Terminalia Arjuna leaf · Early detection of leaf spot · Multi-objective cuckoo search · Simple Linear Iterative Clustering (SLIC)

1 Introduction

Computer vision-based early disease identification of plant leaves has emerged as an exciting and potentially fruitful research topic. In agriculture, the costs associated with human labor may be reduced if diseases can be detected automatically. This is also a step in the direction of farming that is based on the *Internet of Things (IoT)*, which is needed for Agriculture 4.0. Terminalia Arjuna [1] is most popularly referred to as *Arjuna* in India. It is a long evergreen tree that may grow to a height of between 20 and 30 m and belongs to the family Combretaceae. Although the Arjuna tree is most commonly found in India, it is also found in

D. Gupta et al. (Eds.): CVIP 2022, CCIS 1777, pp. 722–735, 2023.
https://doi.org/10.1007/978-3-031-31417-9_55

Myanmar, Pakistan, Sri Lanka, and a few other Asian countries [2]. Terminalia Arjuna is a multi-functional tree that has wide application in medicine [3], sericulture [4], and other ecological [5] uses. Many ancient Indian medicinal texts, including the Charaka Samhita, Sushruta Samhita, and Ashtanga Hridayam mentioned it as an ayurvedic remedy [1]. The study by Jain et al. [6] reviewed its various phytochemical and pharmacological aspects. They discussed the ethnic uses of various parts of the Arjuna tree. Its bark can treat heart diseases, ulcers, and snake bites. Fruit is utilized as a tonic and decongestant. The leaf is used to treat earaches. According to Ahmad et al. [7], the anticarcinogenic and antimutagenic properties of extracts of Arjuna have been investigated. These properties can prevent environmental carcinogenicity. Kaur et al. [8] studied the antimutagenic impact of benzene, chloroform, acetone, and methanol fractions from Terminalia Arjuna. Leaf of Terminalia Arjuna is the food of tropical Tasar silkworm *Antheraea mylitta Drury.* Abraham et al. [9] examined the induction of biomolecules in mature leaves of Arjuna subjected to the feeding of the silkworm. Mushke et al. [4] studied tissue regeneration methodologies, advances, and genetic transformation enhancements of Terminalia Arjuna as a host plant of the silkworm. Interesting research done by Sunil et al. [5] has explained that Terminalia Arjuna may serve as a keystone species in riparian habitats of South India because of its biological diversity. As a result of the prior conversation, the significance of Terminalia Arjuna has been abundantly evident. It, like other plants, is susceptible to plant diseases such as leaf spots, leaf curl, powdery mildew, and black nodal girdling disease [10].

In this study, the parameters of simple linear iterative clustering (SLIC) were optimized using a multi-objective cuckoo search to segment the leaf spot area on an arjuna leaf accurately. In addition, supervised machine learning is used to identify the category of superpixels, and disease severity has also been measured. The key mentions about the contributions of the paper are as given below:

1. Early and precise detection of leaf spot on Arjuna leaf using optimized SLIC algorithm.
2. Use of the optimized parameters (of the SLIC algorithm) tuned using multi-objective Cuckoo search for automated segmentation of the superpixels.
3. Roundness and standard deviation of the color components are used as the two objective functions to apply multi-objective optimization.
4. Minimal use of color momentum features for the classification of the super-pixels for disease severity measurement.

This paper is organized as follows: Sect. 1 discusses the importance of Terminalia Arjuna from various perspectives, along with a summary of the contributions made in this work. Section 2 discusses on recently published works on plant leaf disease detection techniques. Section 3 presents the theories and techniques used for the work. The proposed method has been explained in Sect. 4. The results are discussed in Sect. 5, and finally, Sect. 6 presents the conclusion and the future scopes of the work.

Table 1. A comparative study of the recent works.

Method	Name of the plant (leaf)	Performance
Sengar et al. [11]	Cherry	99.00%
Singh [12]	Sunflower	98.00%
Zhu et al. [13]	Grape	91.00%
Mukhopadhyay et al. [14]	Tea	83.00%
Chouhan et al. [15]	Pongamia Pinnata	96.07%
Pandey et al. [16]	Vigna mungo	95.69%
Sharma et al. [17]	Potato	92.90%
Proposed Method	Terminalia Arjuna	99.60%

2 Related Works

In recent years, different methods have been proposed to segment the lesion area of the plant leaf. Sengar et al. [11] introduced an adaptive pixel intensity-based thresholding method to identify the lesion area of powdery mildew disease of cherry leaves and obtained 99.0% accuracy. Singh [12] introduced particle-swarm optimization (PSO) based segmentation method to find out the lesion area along with texture feature extraction of six categories of sunflower disease. Then extracted texture features were used to train the classifier, and the minimum distance classifier obtained an average classification rate of 98%. Zhu et al. [13] proposed a disease detection method for five types of diseases of grape leaves. This method has used the back-propagation neural network (BPNN) for the recognition of grape diseases and shows an average accuracy of 91.0%. Pandey et al. [16] presents an automatic and non-destructive method for detecting three categories of Vigna mungo leaf. It utilized the feature extraction in the spatial domain and predicated the healthiness of the leaf with an accuracy of 95.69% by support vector machine (SVM). Zhang et al. [18] introduced segmentation of plant disease leaf using simple linear iterative clustering (SLIC). The use of superpixel increased the convergence speed of the Expectation The maximization (EM) algorithm and the results have shown that the method segmented the diseased area more precisely than other approaches. Another SLIC-based work proposed by Zhang et al. [19] to detect cucumber diseases. This hybrid method combines SLIC, expectation maximization (EM) algorithm, and the logarithmic frequency pyramid of orientation gradient histograms (PHOG). Finally, SVM has been used to classify different cucumber diseases and achieved good classification results. Khan et al. [20] proposed a further SLIC-based approach to segment diseased leaf areas that suffer from uneven illumination and complex natural environment challenges. In their process, the input image is first color-balanced before superpixels are generated by SLIC. Then, an empirically derived threshold is applied to the HOG and color channels of the superpixel in order to identify the targeted leaf area from the surrounding context. The lesion area of the leaf image is then segmented using K-means clustering. Chouhan et al. [15]

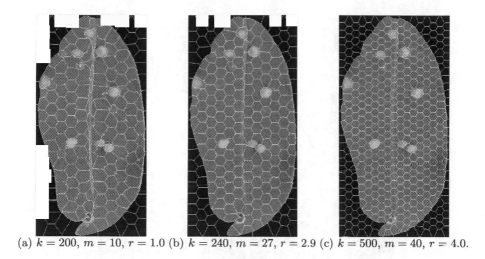

(a) $k = 200$, $m = 10$, $r = 1.0$ (b) $k = 240$, $m = 27$, $r = 2.9$ (c) $k = 500$, $m = 40$, $r = 4.0$.

Fig. 1. SLIC output under different parameter settings.

presented a hybrid technique that combines adaptive linear neuron (ADALINE) with SLIC-based clustering for disease area segmentation of Jatropha Curcas and Pongamia Pinnata leaf. Finally, Random Forest obtained an average accuracy of 90.95% and 96.07% for the categorization of health and disease status of Jatropha Curcas and Pongamia Pinnata leaf, respectively. Mukhopadhyay et al. [14] proposed non-dominated sorting genetic algorithm (NSGA-II) based multi-objective optimization segmentation of diseased tea leaves. They applied principal component analysis(PCA) for feature selection and multi-class SVM to classify the five tea leaf diseases. The method multi-class SVM obtained an average accuracy of 83%. A comparative study of the recent works on disease area detection is presented in Table 1. It demonstrates that the performance of the proposed method is comparable to that of the other methods.

3   Materials and Methods

Leaf spot is a common disease in Tasar food plants caused by fungal, bacterial, or viral infection [10]. The disease appears on any part of the leaf as circular or irregular patches. Copper brown spots appear on an infected leaf, usually 2-8 mm in diameter. This disease is seen all over India from July to November when there is a lot of humidity and high temperatures. Leaf spots weaken the plant, and the leaf yield is decreased by 8-12% due to ordinary leaf spot severity. In the dataset [21] used by us, circular leaf spots of varying stages in Arjuna leaves have been observed.

3.1   Simple Linear Iterative Clustering (SLIC)

The SLIC algorithm is a superpixel generation method proposed by Achanta et al. [22]. It segments the image into a different small clusters based on the

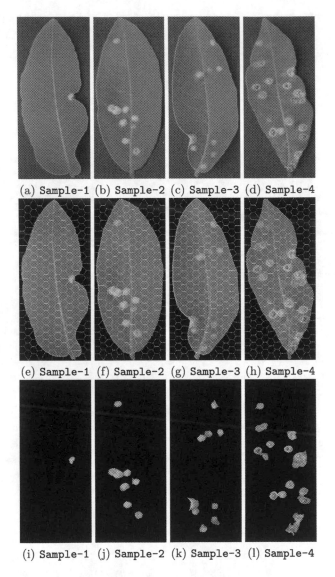

(a) Sample-1 (b) Sample-2 (c) Sample-3 (d) Sample-4

(e) Sample-1 (f) Sample-2 (g) Sample-3 (h) Sample-4

(i) Sample-1 (j) Sample-2 (k) Sample-3 (l) Sample-4

Fig. 2. (a)-(d): Sample Arjuna leaves; (e)-(h): MOCS optimized SLIC output; (i)-(l): Leaf spot superpixels.

similarity of LAB color and spatial distance. Because of the quick processing time, uniform superpixel block size, and regular contour, it is frequently employed in color image processing applications like optical remote sensing, natural scene, and other image segmentation tasks. The three parameters k, m, and r control the superpixel quality. In this work, the multi-objective Cuckoo search method has optimized the three parameters to generate the superpixels for early detection of circular leaf spots.

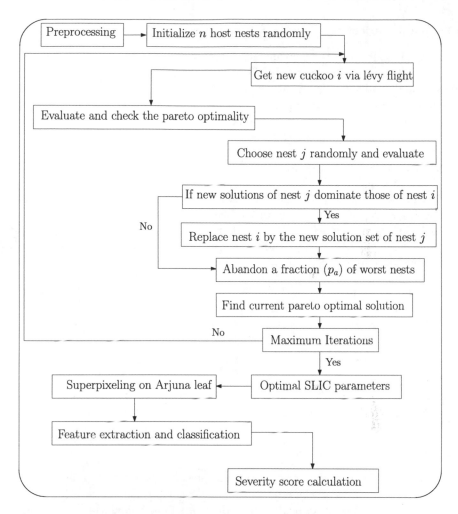

Fig. 3. Flow diagram of the proposed method.

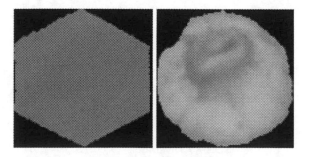

Fig. 4. Samples: healthy superpixel and non-healthy superpixel.

3.2   Multi-objective Cuckoo Search

The use of multi-objective optimization (MOO) has become the standard for solving real-world multiple criteria decision-making problem [23]. In most cases, the optimal trade-offs between the various criteria used in MOO models are stated as a series of Pareto optima. Finding the optimal Pareto solution from this collection for actual use is a difficult problem. Adopting the parasitic activity of Cuckoo brood and the lévy flying behavior of birds, the multi-objective Cuckoo search algorithm (MOCS) has been proposed by Yang and Deb [24]. The rules of the Cuckoo search algorithm [25] have been modified as follows.

- Each cuckoo deposits K eggs at a time into a nest that is selected at random. The egg e_k represents the solution of the k-th objective.
- Each nest is abandoned with probability p_a, and a new nest with K eggs is constructed based on egg similarities or differences. Diversification may be achieved by mixing at random.

In MOCS, the new solution, i.e., s_i^{t+1} generated by applying the lévy flight on old solution s_i^t as shown in Eq. 1. Here, $\alpha > 0$ defines the step size, which should be based on the problem scale and β defines the suggested lévy range, i.e., $(0 < \beta \leq 2)$.

$$s_i^{t+1} = s_i^t + \alpha \oplus L\acute{e}vy\,(\beta) \tag{1}$$

In recent years the MOCS has been applied in many optimization problems including design [24], dimensionality reduction [26], gene selection [27], etc.

3.3   Objective Functions

Objective 1. The first objective function is the sum of the standard deviation(σ) of each color component of the superpixels and denoted by Eq. 2. The minimization of this objective function indicates the reduction of color deviation in the super-pixel.

$$Objective - 1 = \sum_{i=1}^{k}\sum_{c=1}^{3}\sigma_c^k \tag{2}$$

Objective 2. The concept of sphericity in computational geometry is studied by Mitchell & Soga (2005) [28] and Rodriguez et al. (2012) [29]. Their study suggested that the perimeter sphericity of an object is defined by Eq. 3, where P_c is the perimeter of a circle having the same projected area as the object; P_s is the object's perimeter. Here the multi-objective optimization problem is formulated as a min-min problem, hence the Objective 2 has been defined in Eq. 4.

In the initial stage, the leaf spots in Terminalia Arjuna are mostly spherical in shape. As we aim at early detection of the leaf spots, the measurement of sphericity is taken as one of the objective functions.

$$S_p = \frac{P_c}{P_s} \qquad (3)$$

$$Objective-2 = \sum_{i=1}^{k} 1 - s_p^k, \qquad (4)$$

where k denotes the total number of superpixels.

3.4   Color Moment Features

The color information of an image can be viewed as a color probability distribution of the image. The histogram represents the discrete probability distribution. The color histogram of an image is as color features of the image. Moments provide a distinctive characterization of a probability distribution based on probability theory. Moments may therefore be used to characterize the color distribution of a picture if we understand it as a probability distribution. The color features include four moments: mean(μ), standard deviation(σ), skewness(s), and kurtosis(κ) (shown in Eqs. 5–8). The color momentum-based features have been used widely in the domain of image retrieval [30,31]. In this work, color moment features are extracted from the superpixels for the categorization of the superpixels into *healthy* and *non-healthy* superpixels.

$$\mu = \frac{\sum_{i,j} I_{i,j}}{n} \qquad (5)$$

$$\sigma = \sqrt{\frac{\sum_{i,j} (I_{i,j} - \mu)}{n}} \qquad (6)$$

$$s = \frac{\sum_{i,j} (I_{i,j} - \mu)^3}{n\sigma^3} \qquad (7)$$

$$\kappa = \frac{\sum_{i,j} (I_{i,j} - \mu)^4}{(n-1)\sigma^4} \qquad (8)$$

3.5   Dataset

The Terminalia Arjuna images were captured in a closed environment from March to May 2019 by the Madhav Institute of Technology and Science, India. The acquisition process was wi-fi enabled, and all the images were captured using a Nikon D5300 camera [21]. The images of leaves affected by circular leaf spots are considered from the dataset for this experiment.

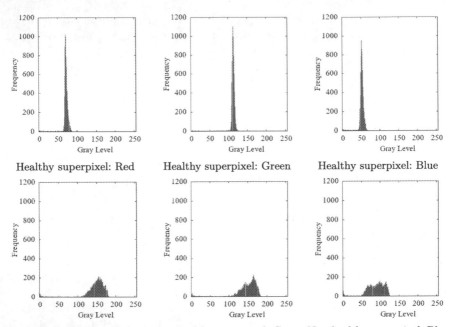

Healthy superpixel: Red   Healthy superpixel: Green   Healthy superpixel: Blue

Non-healthy superpixel: Red Non-healthy superpixel: Green Non-healthy superpixel: Blue

Fig. 5. Histogram of three color components of healthy and non-healthy superpixels.

4   Proposed Method

The flow of the proposed work is shown in Fig. 3. It has three distinct phases. The
Arjuna leaves are preprocessed in the initial phase to extract the leaf part from
the background by the thresholding method. In the second step, the parameters
of the SLIC algorithm are optimized by MOCS, which aims to minimize the standard deviation of each superpixel's color information and maximize the superpixel's circularity. Hence, a given range randomly generates the three parameters
to prepare the initial cuckoo nest. The initial nests are evaluated by two objective functions and ranked. Then the new nests are generated based on the best
cuckoo via lévy flight. An old solution of net i is replaced by a new solution set
of j when a new solution of nest j dominates those of nest i. After that few solutions are removed randomly from the worst set of the nest. Now, Pareto optimal
solutions are generated by evaluating each new nest for both objective functions.
These steps of the MOCS are continued until the maximum number of iterations
is reached. Finally, the Pareto optimal solutions are reported. This final Pareto
solution contains the optimized parameters of SLIC. In the third phase, SLIC
with optimum parameter settings is applied to the Arjuna leaf image to segment
it into superpixels. These superpixels are grouped into two categories: healthy
and non-healthy superpixels. The healthy superpixels are located in a whole-
some region of the leaf, whereas the non-healthy superpixels represent circular
leaf spots. The four color features are extracted from each color component of the

superpixels. Moreover, the feature vector of size 12 is extracted. Feature vectors are extracted from the superpixels of each category to train the classifiers. The leaf spot disease severity is determined in the final phase based on the classified superpixels (once each superpixel is categorized). The total number of healthy superpixels and non-healthy superpixels are denoted by h and nh, respectively, and are counted excluding the background superpixels (black superpixels) and tiny superpixels (smaller white segments on the leaves). Finally, the severity score is measured using Eq. 4.

$$\zeta = \frac{nh}{h + nh} \times 100\% \qquad (9)$$

5   Results and Analysis

Table 2. Color momentum feature values for two different super pixel types.

Sample	Channel	Color momentum features			
		Mean (μ)	STD (σ)	Skewness (s)	Kurtosis (κ)
Healthy	Red	52.3353	32.2455	-0.9648	1.9924
	Green	81.9848	50.364	-0.9844	2.0007
	Blue	37.8664	23.4455	-0.934	1.9783
Non-healthy	Red	112.2839	67.0173	-0.968	2.1208
	Green	113.201	67.6342	-0.9507	2.1137
	Blue	67.2733	42.5862	-0.64	1.9100

Experimental outcomes have been discussed in this section. The effects of the multi-objective optimization on the SLIC algorithm have been shown in Fig. 1. Figure 1(a)-(c) are the output of the SLIC under the lower and upper limits of the parameter settings. The output of SLIC under the optimized parameters has been shown in Fig. 1(b). It is evident from the visual analysis that the lower limit values of the parameters produce superpixels with irregular shapes and that the spots are not properly segmented, whereas the higher limit values produce superpixels with regular shapes, and the majority of superpixels representing the individual leaf spots are further segmented. Figure 1(b) superpixels are well shaped to segment the circular leaf spot. Although a small number of superpixels contain a small additional area in addition to the spot area. Figure 6 illustrates the Pareto front generated by a multi-objective cuckoo search for four different leaf samples. Both objective functions are minimized in this work. This one solution from the Pareto front has been employed in the SLIC algorithm to segment the leaf spot of the Arjuna leaf into superpixels, and it can depict the lesion area with superpixels accurately. Figure 2(a)-(d) exhibit four original circular

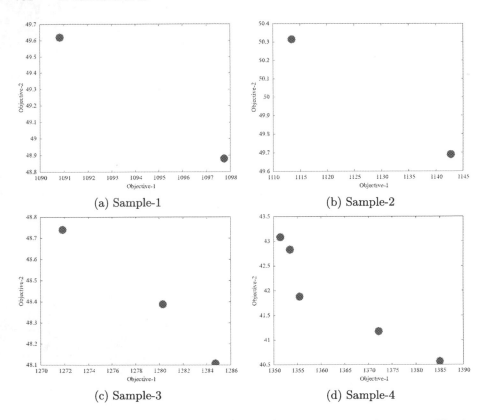

Fig. 6. Pareto solutions for different samples (X-axis: Objective function-1, Y-axis: Objective function-2).

leaf spot-affected Arjuna leaf images with varying degrees of disease at an early stage. MOCS optimized SLIC outcomes have been shown in Fig. 2(e)-(h). The two types of superpixels are shown in Fig. 4. The histogram plot of color components of each category of superpixels is displayed in Fig. 5. Histogram analysis proves that the two types of superpixels have noticeably distinct patterns of color distribution. The four color moments features with respect to each color component for both the samples shown in Fig. 4 are displayed in Table 2. Four different classification methods are used by us, namely, *decision tree (DT)*, *K-nearest neighbor (K-NN)*, *multi-layer perceptron (MLP)*, and *support vector machine (SVM)*. The detection accuracies by the four classifiers on our test dataset are shown in Fig. 7. The performances of the four classifiers are comparable, and SVM shows an accuracy of 99.6%. The spot detection accuracies using SVM are reported as 99.8%, 97.8%, 97.8%, and 94.9% for the sample images `Sample 1`, `Sample 2`, `Sample 3`, and `Sample 4` (as shown in Fig. 2) respectively. Finally, the severity scores of different Arjuna leaves are reported along with sample images in Fig. 8.

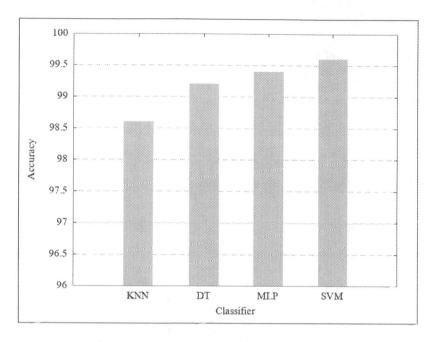

Fig. 7. Classification accuracy of healthy and non-healthy superpixel detection.

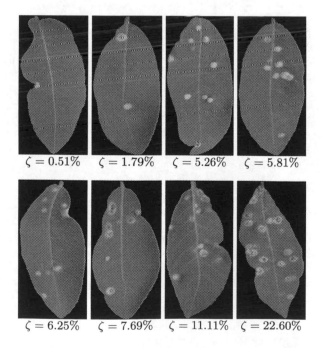

$\zeta = 0.51\%$ $\zeta = 1.79\%$ $\zeta = 5.26\%$ $\zeta = 5.81\%$

$\zeta = 6.25\%$ $\zeta = 7.69\%$ $\zeta = 11.11\%$ $\zeta = 22.60\%$

Fig. 8. Severity score with respect to various Arjuna leaf samples.

6   Conclusion

In this work, three parameters of the SLIC algorithm for precise detection of leaf spots on Arjuna leaves were optimized using a multi-objective Cuckoo search. The optimization considers the color components' standard deviation and the roundness of superpixels as objective functions. The severity score of the leaf spot disease is also determined based on the classified superpixels. The results suggest that the proposed method performs well in detecting the leaf spot severity in the early stage. This work can be further extended to work with categorization into more severity stages. Additionally, other objective functions can be considered to address the different shapes of leaf spots, even for other crop plants.

References

1. Dwivedi, S., Chopra, D.: Revisiting Terminalia arjuna – an ancient cardiovascular drug. J. Tradit. Complement. Med. **4**(4), 224–231 (2014)
2. Das, G., et al.: Plants of the genus terminalia: an insight on its biological potentials, pre-clinical and clinical studies. Front. Pharmacol. **11**, 561248 (2020)
3. Amalraj, A., Gopi, S.: Medicinal properties of terminalia arjuna (Roxb.) wight & arn.: a review. J. Tradit. Complement. Med. **7**(1), 65–78 (2017)
4. Mushke, R., Yarra, R., Kokkirala, V.R., Abbagani, S.: Cell, tissue culture, and gene transfer techniques for Tasar (wild) sericulture plants—introspect and prospect. J. Sustain. For. **33**(2), 173–183 (2014)
5. Sunil, C., Somashekar, R., Nagaraja, B.: Influence of Terminalia arjuna on the riparian landscapes of the river Cauvery of south India. Landsc. Res. **44**(8), 982–996 (2019)
6. Jain, S., Yadav, P.P., Gill, V., Vasudeva, N., Singla, N.: Terminalia arjuna a sacred medicinal plant: phytochemical and pharmacological profile. Phytochem. Rev. **8**(2), 491–502 (2009)
7. Ahmad, M.S., Ahmad, S., Gautam, B., Arshad, M., Afzal, M.: Terminalia arjuna, a herbal remedy against environmental carcinogenicity: An in vitro and in vivo study. Egypt. J. Med. Human Genetics **15**(1), 61–67 (2014)
8. Kaur, K., Arora, S., Kumar, S., Nagpal, A.: Antimutagenic activities of acetone and methanol fractions of Terminalia arjuna. Food Chem. Toxicol. **40**(10), 1475–1482 (2002)
9. Abraham, G., Thomas, G., Babu, C.: Induction of biomolecules in mature leaves of Terminalia arjuna due to feeding of Antheraea Mylitta Drury. Sci. World J. **4**, 887–891 (2004)
10. Diseases and pests of tropical Tasar food plants. https://silks.csb.gov.in/jhansi/diseases-and-pests-of-food-plants/. Accessed 20 June 2022
11. Sengar, N., Dutta, M.K., Travieso, C.M.: Computer vision based technique for identification and quantification of powdery mildew disease in cherry leaves. Computing **100**(11), 1189–1201 (2018). https://doi.org/10.1007/s00607-018-0638-1
12. Singh, V.: Sunflower leaf diseases detection using image segmentation based on particle swarm optimization. Artif. Intell. Agricul. **3**, 62–68 (2019)
13. Zhu, J., Wu, A., Wang, X., Zhang, H.: Identification of grape diseases using image analysis and BP neural networks. Multimedia Tools Appl. **11**, 14539–14551 (2019). https://doi.org/10.1007/s11042-018-7092-0

14. Mukhopadhyay, S., Paul, M., Pal, R., De, D.: Tea leaf disease detection using multi-objective image segmentation. Multimedia Tools Appl. **80**(1), 753–771 (2020). https://doi.org/10.1007/s11042-020-09567-1
15. Chouhan, S.S., Singh, U.P., Sharma, U., Jain, S.: Leaf disease segmentation and classification of jatropha curcas l. and pongamia pinnata l. biofuel plants using computer vision based approaches. Measurement **171** , 108796 (2021)
16. Pandey, C., Baghel, N., Dutta, M.K., Srivastava, A., Choudhary, N.: Machine learning approach for automatic diagnosis of chlorosis in Vigna mungo leaves. Multimedia Tools Appl. **80**(9), 13407–13427 (2021)
17. Sharma, S., Anand, V., Singh, S.: Classification of diseased potato leaves using machine learning. In: 2021 10th IEEE International Conference on Communication Systems and Network Technologies (CSNT), pp. 554–559 (2021)
18. Zhang, S., You, Z., Wu, X.: Plant disease leaf image segmentation based on Superpixel clustering and EM algorithm. Neural Comput. Appl. **31**(2), 1225–1232 (2017). https://doi.org/10.1007/s00521-017-3067-8
19. Zhang, S., Zhu, Y., You, Z., Wu, X.: Fusion of superpixel, expectation maximization and PHOG for recognizing cucumber diseases. Comput. Electron. Agric. **140**, 338–347 (2017)
20. Khan, S., Narvekar, M.: Novel fusion of color balancing and superpixel based approach for detection of tomato plant diseases in natural complex environment. J. King Saud Univ. - Comput. Inf. Sci. **34**, 3506–3516 (2020)
21. Chouhan, S.S., Singh, U.P., Kaul, A., Jain, S.: A data repository of leaf images: practice towards plant conservation with plant pathology. In: 2019 4th International Conference on Information Systems and Computer Networks (ISCON), pp. 700–707 (2019)
22. Achanta, R., Shaji, A., Smith, K., Lucchi, A., Fua, P., Süsstrunk, S.: SLIC superpixels compared to state-of-the-art superpixel methods. IEEE Trans. Pattern Anal. Mach. Intell. **34**(11), 2274–2282 (2012)
23. Limleamthong, P., Guillén-Gosálbez, G.: Combined use of bilevel programming and multi-objective optimization for rigorous analysis of pareto fronts in sustainability studies: application to the redesign of the UK electricity mix. Comput. Aided Chem. Eng. **43**, 1099–1104 (2018)
24. Yang, X.S., Deb, S.: Multiobjective cuckoo search for design optimization. Comput. Oper. Res. **40**(6), 1616–1624 (2013)
25. Yang, X.S., Deb, S.: Cuckoo search via levy flights (2009)
26. Yamany, W., El-Bendary, N., Hassanien, A.E., Emary, E.: Multi-objective cuckoo search optimization for dimensionality reduction. Procedia Comput. Sci. **96**, 207–215 (2016)
27. Othman, M.S., Kumaran, S.R., Yusuf, L.M.: Gene selection using hybrid multi-objective cuckoo search algorithm with evolutionary operators for cancer microarray data. IEEE Access **8**, 186348–186361 (2020)
28. Mitchell, J., Soga: Fundamentals of soil behavior. Wiley (2005)
29. Rodríguez, J.M., Johansson, J., Edeskär, T.: Particle shape determination by two-dimensional image analysis in geotechnical engineering (2012)
30. Maheshwary, P., Srivastav, N.: Retrieving similar image using color moment feature detector and k-means clustering of remote sensing images. In: 2008 International Conference on Computer and Electrical Engineering, pp. 821–824 (2008)
31. Huang, Z.C., Chan, P.P.K., Ng, W.W.Y., Yeung, D.S.: Content-based image retrieval using color moment and Gabor texture feature. In: 2010 International Conference on Machine Learning and Cybernetics, pp. 719–724 (2010)

Author Index

Printed in the United States
by Baker & Taylor Publisher Services